FUNDAMENTALS OF DATA STRUCTURES IN C++

FUNDAMENTALS OF DATA STRUCTURES IN C++

Ellis Horowitz
University of Southern California

Sartaj Sahni
University of Florida

Dinesh Mehta
University of Tennessee

COMPUTER SCIENCE PRESS
An imprint of W. H. Freeman and Company
New York

Library of Congress Cataloging-in-Publication Data

Horowitz, Ellis.
    Fundamentals of data structures in C++ / Ellis Horowitz, Sartaj Sahni, Dinesh Mehta.
      p. cm.
    Includes index.
    ISBN 0-7167-8292-8 (hardcover)
    1. C++ (Computer program language) 2. Data structures (Computer science) I. Sahni,
Sartaj. II. Mehta, Dinesh. III. Title.
QA76.73.C153H667 1995
005.7'3—dc20   94-48034
                                                         CIP

Cover illustration by Richard Elmer

Printed in the United States of America

Computer Science Press

An imprint of W. H. Freeman and Company
41 Madison Avenue, New York, NY 10010
20 Beaumont Street, Oxford OX1 2NQ England

Third printing 1997, RRD

To Ira, my son and my friend;
sharing your life has been a wonderful gift;
we teach each other new things every day.

– Ellis Horowitz

To my children,
    Agam, Neha, and Param

– Sartaj Sahni

To my parents, Prabha and Prakash Mehta;
to whom I owe everything

– Dinesh Mehta

CONTENTS

PREFACE

Why *Fundamentals of Data Structures in C++*? There are several answers. The first, and most important, is that instructors are moving to C++ as the language of choice to teach data structures. This is not surprising as C++'s ability to describe a hierarchy of abstract data types (classes) makes it an ideal language for expressing data structure representation and manipulation. The language includes features that support all of the important aspects of object-oriented programming including: information hiding, data abstraction and inheritance.

C++ Compilers and Features Used: We have chosen to present our programs using the proposed ANSI C++ standard. This is most easily accessible in the book: *The Annotated C++ Reference Manual* by Ellis and Stroustrop. All programs in this text have been compiled and tested. We have exercised the programs on an Intel/386 under DOS/Windows 3.1 using the Borland C/C++ 3.1 compiler. We have also compiled the programs using the GNU C++ compiler on a SUN Sparcstation under SUNOS 4.x. The C++ language is still evolving, and features such as templates and nested classes, not available a few years ago, are now available. Our experience has been that many commercial C++ compilers (especially older versions) do not properly support some of these newer features. Therefore, in this text, we minimize the use of nested classes, as this does not adversely affect the quality of our programs. However, we do use templates to enhance the reusability of our programs. In case your compiler does not support templates (or does support templates, but doesn't do so correctly), it is easy to modify the code by deleting/modifying template-related statements.

C++ Tutorials: This text assumes that the reader is familiar with C, but not necessarily with C++. We have provided C++ tutorials in the first four chapters to outline the relevant features of the language. Section 1.4 describes features of C++ not related to classes or inheritance that differ from C. Section 2.1 describes the C++ class. Section 3.1 describes template functions and classes, while Section 3.4 describes simple inheritance and uses it to relate two data structures. Section 4.11 elaborates on dynamic types and virtual functions.

Object-Oriented Programming: Rather than simply using C++ as a vehicle for programming the data structures of this text, we have also viewed it as our responsibility to use C++ features in a manner consistent with the principles of good object-oriented programming, and to explain why the language has been used in a certain way. For example, in Chapter 4, we describe the design process for the linked list data structure, and show how it can be made reusable with the addition of an iterator class and by the use of templates. The design process is emphasized because the concepts apply to any structure that uses nodes and pointers.

The concepts of data abstraction and information hiding are emphasized throughout the text and are integrated with the description of each data structure. One of the harder decisions we had to make was regarding the use of inheritance in the implementation of the data structures. A presentation that simultaneously teaches a data structure and shows how that data structure can be related to other data structures through inheritance could complicate the discussion for a student unfamiliar with, both, the data structure and the object-oriented paradigm. On the other hand, a text on data structures in C++ would be incomplete if it did not demonstrate the power of the object-oriented paradigm by using inheritance. We resolve this by first presenting the material on individual data structures without complicating it with a discussion of how the data structure would be incorporated into an object-oriented system. Next, after a set of data structures has been presented, we describe in a separate section (or explore in an exercise) how the data structures might be implemented in an object-oriented framework. This gives the instructor a choice of whether or not to use inheritance, based on the familiarity of students in the class with the object-oriented paradigm.

Finally, dynamic typing in C++ makes it possible to define a node pointer that can be used to point to different node structures. This was not possible in languages such as Pascal and C. Section 4.12 on heterogeneous lists exploits this feature.

For those instructors who have used *Fundamentals of Data Structures in C*, or *Fundamentals of Data Structures in Pascal*, you will find that this book retains the in-depth discussion of the algorithms and computing time analyses. In addition we have attempted to preserve the chapter organization and the presentation style of the earlier books, whenever desirable.

Readers are welcome to send suggestions for improvement of the book by sending electronic mail to us at *dmehta@utsi.edu*. A current list of the errata will be available via gopher from *gopher.utsi.edu* under the UTSI Computer Science academic degree program. This may also be obtained by sending us email.

USING THIS TEXT FOR A COURSE

For the instructor who intends to use this book and is teaching on a semester basis we present the following two possibilities, a medium pace and a rigorous pace. The medium pace is recommended when the course is for begining computer science majors, possibly their second or third course of the curriculum. Most people, including the authors, have taught according to the medium pace. The outline below corresponds to the curriculum recommended by the ACM, in particular course C2, (Curriculum '78, CACM 3/79, and CACM 8/85).

SEMESTER SCHEDULE - MEDIUM PACE

Week	Subject	Reading Assignment
1	Intro. to C++ and Algorithms	Chapter 1
2	C++ and Arrays	Chapter 2
3	Arrays (strings)	First program due
4	Stacks and Queues	Chapter 3
5	Linked Lists (singly and doubly linked)	Chapter 4
6	Linked Lists	Second program due
7	Trees (basic facts, binary trees)	Chapter 5
8	Trees (search, heap)	
9	Mid Term	
10	Graphs (basic facts, representations)	Chapter 6
11	Graphs (shortest paths, spanning trees, topological sorting)	Third program due
12	Internal Sorting (insertion, quick, and merge)	Chapter 7
13	Internal Sorting (heap, radix)	Fourth program due
14	Hashing	Chapter 8
15	Heap Structures (Selected Topics)	Chapter 9
16	Search Structures (Selected Topics)	Chapter 10

We recommend that several programming assignments be given, spaced somewhat evenly thoughout the semester. The aim of the first program is primarily to get the students familiar with the computing environment. The second program should emphasize list structures, as discussed in Chapter 4. There are several suggestions for projects at the end of the exercises of Chapter 4. One topic we have chosen to skip is external sorting. This leaves time to cover one of the most important of techniques, hashing. This topic is used in several courses later on in the curriculum, so it is important to cover it this semester. The instructor will likely not have time to cover the material in the Search Structures chapter. Perhaps one or two topics can be selectively chosen.

The more rigorous pace would be appropriate when the book is used for a first year graduate course, or for an advanced undergraduate course. Our suggested outline follows.

SEMESTER SCHEDULE - RIGOROUS PACE

Week	Subject	Reading Assignment
1	Intro. to C++ and Algorithms	Chapter 1
2	C++ and Arrays	Chapter 2
3	Stacks and Queues	Chapter 3
		First program due
4	Linked Lists	Chapter 4
5	Trees	Chapter 5
6	Trees continued	Second program due
7	Mid Term	
8	Graphs	Chapter 6
9	Graphs continued	Third program due
10	Internal Sorting	Chapter 7
11	External Sorting	Chapter 7
12	Hashing	Chapter 8
13	Heap Structures	Chapter 9
		Fourth program due
14	Heap Structures	Chapter 9
15	Search Structures	Chapter 10
16	Search Structures	Chapter 10

The programming assignments and midterm exam are paced exactly as in the medium case. However, the lectures proceed at a faster rate. For the rigorous pace, two weeks are allotted for Chapters 9 and 10. This allows the coverage of only a few topics selected from each chapter.

Finally we present a curriculum for an advanced Data Structures course. This presupposes that the student has already encountered the basic material, in particular the material on lists, trees, and graphs. Four weeks on advanced data structures gives the instructor enough time to cover all of the relevant topics in depth.

SEMESTER SCHEDULE - ADVANCED DATA STRUCTURES COURSE

Week	Subject	Reading Assignment
1	Review of Material on C++ and Algorithms	Chapters 1-2
2	Review of Basic List structures	Chapters 3-4
3	Review of Trees	Chapter 5

4	Review of Graphs	Chapter 6
5	Review of Internal Sorting	Chapter 7
		First program due
6	External Sorting	Chapter 7
7	External Sorting (continued)	
8	Hashing	Chapter 8
		Second program due
9	Heap Structures (min-max heaps, deaps, leftist trees)	Chapter 9
10		Mid Term
11	Heaps Structures (Fibonacci heaps)	Chapter 9
12	Search Structures (Optimal binary search trees)	Chapter 10
13	Search Structures (AVL trees, 2-3 trees, 2-3-4 trees)	Third program due
14	Search Structures (Red-black trees, splay trees, digital trees)	
15	Search Structures (B-trees, tries)	Fourth program due
16	Search Structures	

For schools on the quarter system, the following two quarter sequence is possible. It assumes prior exposure to algorithm analysis and elementary data structures at the level obtained from an advanced programming course.

QUARTER 1

Week	Subject	Reading Assignment
1	Review of algorithms and arrays	Chapters 1-2
2	Stacks and Queues	Chapter 3
3	Linked Lists (stacks, queues, polynomials)	Chapter 4
4	Linked Lists	
5	Trees (traversal, set representation)	Chapter 5
		First program due
6	Trees (heaps, search)	
		Mid Term
7	Graphs (traversal, components)	Chapter 6
8	Graphs (minimum spanning trees)	
9	Graphs (shortest paths)	Second program due
10	Graphs (activity networks)	

QUARTER 2

Week	Subject	Reading Assignment
1	Internal Sorting (insertion, quick,	Chapter 7
		bound, $O(1)$ space merging, merge sort)
2	Sorting (heap, radix, list, table)	
3	External Sorting	Chapter 7
4	Hashing	Chapter 8
5	Mid Term	First program due
6	Heap Structures (deaps,	Chapter 9
		Min-Max heaps, Leftist trees)
7	Heap Structures (Fibonacci Heaps)	
8	Search Structures (AVL trees,	Chapter 10
	2-3 trees, 2-3-4 trees)	
9	Search Structures (Red-black trees,	Second program due
	splay trees, digital trees)	
10	Search Structures (B-Trees, tries)	

ACKNOWLEDGEMENTS

We would like to thank the people who have assisted us in preparing this book. Thanks go to students of the *Advanced Data Structures* course at the University of Tennessee Space Institute and the University of Tennessee, Knoxville, for identifying errors in the manuscript; we especially thank George Blust and Anjanjyoti Das for their comments. We also thank Ketan Doshi (Remedy Corporation), Derek Ealy, Professor Mario Lopez (University of Denver), Sudhir Shetty (Arrowsmith Technologies, Inc.), and Rose Tsang (University of Minnesota) for debugging the manuscript and making a number of useful suggestions. We also thank Ying Shu (University of Southern California) for testing the programs on the GNU C++ compiler. Special thanks go to Barbara and Art Friedman, our first publishers who nurtured the book through its early years. Thanks also to the staff at W.H. Freeman for their support and encouragement. We especially wish to thank Associate Managing editior, Penny Hull. Her enthusiasm really helped the project along.

Ellis Horowitz
Sartaj Sahni
Dinesh Mehta
November 1994

CHAPTER 1

BASIC CONCEPTS

1.1 OVERVIEW: SYSTEM LIFE CYCLE

We assume that our readers have a strong background in structured programming, typically attained through the completion of an elementary programming course. Such an
initial course usually emphasizes mastering the syntax of a programming language (its
grammar rules) and applying this language to the solution of several relatively small
problems. These problems are frequently chosen so that they use a particular language
construct. For example, the programming problem might require the use of arrays or
while loops.

  In this text we want to move beyond these rudiments by providing the tools and
techniques necessary to design and implement large-scale computer systems. We believe that a solid foundation in data abstraction and encapsulation, algorithm
specification, and performance analysis and measurement provides the necessary methodology. In this chapter, we will discuss each of these areas in detail. We will also briefly
discuss recursive programming because many of you probably have only a fleeting ac-
quaintance with this important technique. However, before we begin, we want to place
these tools in a context that views programming as more than writing code. Good programmers regard large-scale computer programs as systems that contain many complex
interacting parts. As systems, these programs undergo a development process called the
system life cycle. This cycle consists of requirements, analysis, design, coding, and
verification phases. Although we will consider them separately, these phases are highly

1

interrelated and follow only a very crude sequential time frame. The References and Selected Readings section lists several sources on the system life cycle and its various phases that will provide you with additional information.

(1) Requirements. All large programming projects begin with a set of specifications that define the purpose of the project. These requirements describe the information that we, the programmers, are given (input) and the results that we must produce (output). Frequently the initial specifications are defined vaguely, and we must develop rigorous input and output descriptions that include all cases.

(2) Analysis. After we have delineated carefully the system's requirements, the analysis phase begins in earnest. In this phase, we begin to break the problem down into manageable pieces. There are two approaches to analysis: bottom-up and top-down. The bottom-up approach is an older, unstructured strategy that places an early emphasis on the coding fine points. Since the programmer does not have a master plan for the project, the resulting program frequently has many loosely connected, error-ridden segments. Bottom-up analysis is akin to constructing a building by first designing specific aspects of the building such as walls, a roof, plumbing, and heating, and then trying to put these together to construct the building. The specific purpose to which the building will be put is not considered in this approach. Although few of us would want to live in a home constructed using this technique, many programmers, particularly beginning ones, believe that they can create good, error-free programs without prior planning.

In contrast, the top-down approach begins by developing a high-level plan for dividing the program into manageable segments. This plan is subsequently refined to take into account low-level details. This technique generates diagrams that are used to design the system. Frequently, several alternate solutions to the programming problem are developed and compared during this phase. The top-down approach has been the preferred approach for developing complex software systems.

(3) Design. This phase continues the work done in the analysis phase. The designer approaches the system from the perspectives of the data objects that the program needs and the operations performed on them. The first perspective leads to the creation of abstract data types, whereas the second requires the specification of algorithms and a consideration of algorithm design strategies. For example, suppose that we are designing a scheduling system for a university. Typical data objects might include students, courses, and professors. Typical operations might include inserting, removing, and searching within each object or between them. That is, we might want to add a course to the list of university courses or search for the courses taught by a specific professor.

Since the abstract data types and the algorithm specifications are language-independent, we postpone implementation decisions. Although we must specify the information required for each data object, we ignore coding details. For example, we might decide that the student data object should include name, social security number, major, and phone number. However, we would not yet pick a specific implementation for the list of students. As we will see in later chapters, there are several possibilities, including arrays, linked lists, or trees. By deferring implementation issues as long as possible, we not only create a system that could be written in several programming languages, but we also have time to pick the most efficient implementations within our chosen language.

(4) Refinement and coding. In this phase, we choose representations for our data objects and write algorithms for each operation on them. The order in which we do this is crucial because a data object's representation can determine the efficiency of the algorithms related to it. Typically this means that we should write the algorithms that are independent of the data objects first.

Frequently at this point we realize that we could have created a much better system. Perhaps we have spoken with a friend who has worked on a similar project, or we realize that one of our alternate designs is superior. If our original design is good, it can absorb changes easily. In fact, this is a reason for avoiding an early commitment to coding details. If we must scrap our work entirely, we can take comfort in the fact that we will be able to write the new system more quickly and with fewer errors. A delightful book that discusses this "second system" phenomenon is Frederick Brooks's *The Mythical Man-Month*, cited in the "References and Selected Readings" section.

(5) Verification. This phase consists of developing correctness proofs for the program, testing the program with a variety of input data, and removing errors. Each of these areas has been researched extensively, and a complete discussion is beyond the scope of this text. However, we summarize briefly the important aspects of each area.

Correctness proofs: Programs can be proven correct using the same techniques that abound in mathematics. Unfortunately, these proofs are very time-consuming and difficult to develop for large projects. Frequently, scheduling constraints prevent the development of a complete set of proofs for a large system. However, selecting algorithms that have been proven correct can reduce the number of errors. In this text, we will provide you with an arsenal of algorithms, some of which have been proven correct using formal techniques, that you may apply to many programming problems.

Testing: Since our algorithms need not be written in a specific programming language, we can construct our correctness proofs before and during the coding phase. Testing, however, requires the working code and sets of test data. This data should be developed carefully so that it includes all possible scenarios. Frequently, beginning programmers assume that if their program ran without producing a syntax error, it must be correct. Little thought is given to the input data, and usually only one set of data is used. Good test data should verify that every piece of code runs correctly. For example, if our program contains a **switch** statement, our test data should be chosen so that we can check each **case** within the **switch** statement.

Initial system tests focus on verifying that a program runs correctly. Although this is a crucial concern, a program's running time is also important. An error-free program that runs slowly is of little value. Theoretical estimates of running time exist for many algorithms. We will derive these estimates as we introduce new algorithms. In addition, we may want to gather performance estimates for portions of our code. Constructing these timing tests is also a topic that we pursue later in this chapter.

Error removal: If done properly, the correctness proofs and system tests will indicate erroneous code. The ease with which we can remove these errors depends on the design and coding decisions made earlier. A large undocumented program written in "spaghetti" code is a programmer's nightmare. When debugging such programs, each corrected error possibly generates several new errors. On the other hand, debugging a well-documented program that is divided into autonomous units that interact through parameters is far easier, especially if each unit is tested separately and then integrated into the system.

1.2   OBJECT-ORIENTED DESIGN

Object-oriented design represents a fundamental change from the structured programming design method. The two approaches are similar in that both believe that the way to develop a complex system is by using the philosophy of divide-and-conquer; that is, break up a complex software design project into a number of simpler subprojects, and then tackle these subprojects individually. The two approaches disagree on *how* a project should be decomposed.

1.2.1   Algorithmic Decomposition Versus Object-Oriented Decomposition

Traditional programming techniques have used algorithmic decomposition. Algorithmic or functional decomposition views software as a *process*. It decomposes the software into modules that represent *steps* of the process. These modules are implemented by language constructs such as procedures in Pascal, subprograms in Fortran, and functions in C. The data structures required to implement the program are a secondary concern, which is addressed after the project has been decomposed into functional modules.

Object-oriented decomposition views software as a set of well-defined *objects* that model entities in the application domain. These objects interact with each other to form a software system. Functional decomposition is addressed after the system has been decomposed into objects.

The principal advantage of object-oriented decomposition is that it encourages the reuse of software. This results in flexible software systems that can evolve as system requirements change. It allows a programmer to use object-oriented programming languages effectively. Object-oriented decomposition is also more intuitive than algorithm-oriented decomposition because objects naturally model entities in the application domain.

1.2.2   Fundamental Definitions and Concepts of Object-Oriented Programming

Before proceeding, we provide definitions of basic terminology used in the object-oriented paradigm. Our definitions are adapted from *Object- Oriented Design with Applications*, by Grady Booch.

Definition: An *object* is an entity that performs computations and has a local state. It may therefore be viewed as a combination of data and procedural elements. (The original definition is due to Stefik and Bobrow; see the "References and Selected Readings" section.)

Definition: *Object-oriented programming* is a method of implementation in which

(1)   Objects are the fundamental building blocks.

(2)   Each object is an instance of some type (or class).

(3)   Classes are related to each other by inheritance relationships. (Programming methods that do not use inheritance are not considered to be object-oriented.)

Definition: A language is said to be an *object-oriented* language if

(1)   It supports objects.

(2)   It requires objects to belong to a class.

(3)   It supports inheritance.
(The original definition is due to Cardelli and Wagner; see the "References and Seleted Readings" section.)

A language that supports the first two features but does not support inheritance, is an *object-based language*.

1.2.3   Evolution of Programming Languages and History of C++

Higher order programming languages may be classified into four generations.

(1)   First Generation Languages: An example of this is FORTRAN. The salient feature of these languages is their ability to evaluate mathematical expressions.

(2)   Second Generation Languages: Examples of these include Pascal and C. The emphasis of these languages is on effectively expressing algorithms.

(3)   Third Generation Languages: An example of this is Modula, which introduced the concept of abstract data types.

(4)   Fourth Generation Languages (Object-Oriented languages): Examples include Smalltalk, Objective C, and C++. These languages emphasize the expression of the relationship between abstract data types through the use of inheritance.

C++ was designed by Bjarne Stroustrup of AT&T Bell Laboratories in the early 1980s. It was designed to incorporate the object-oriented paradigm into the C programming language. C is widely-used in industry because it is:

(1)   Efficient: it has a number of low-level features, which utilize hardware better than other languages.

(2)   Flexible: it can be used to solve problems in most application areas.

(3)   Available: compilers for C are readily available for most computers.

Other influences on the design of C++ were Simula67 and Algol68.

There are a number of features of C++ that improve on C, but do not implement data abstraction or inheritance. These are discussed later in this chapter. The C++ class, which implements data abstraction, is discussed in Chapter 2. C++ functions and classes can be made more powerful by augmenting them with *templates*. Templates are discussed in Chapter 3. Simple inheritance in C++ is also discussed in Chapter 3. Advanced concepts on inheritance and polymorphism are discussed in Chapter 4.

1.3   DATA ABSTRACTION AND ENCAPSULATION

The notions of abstraction and encapsulation are commonly used in human-machine interaction and are widely prevalent in the technology-oriented world we live in. Consider, for example, the video cassette recorder (VCR), which is an integral part of many households today. We make two observations about how VCRs are packaged and used.

(1) All our interactions with a VCR are made through buttons on the control panel such as PLAY, FFW (fast forward), REW (rewind), REC (record), etc. The VCR is packaged so that we cannot directly interact with the circuitry inside. So, the *internal representation* of the VCR is *hidden* from the user. This is the principle of *encapsulation*.

(2) The instruction manual that accompanies the VCR tells us *what* the VCR is supposed to do if we press a particular button. It does not tell us *how* it is implemented inside the VCR; it does not, for example, explain the sequence of electronic and mechanical events that result when the REW button is pressed. So, the instruction manual makes a clear distinction between *what* the VCR does and *how* it does it. This distinction is the principle of *abstraction*.

These same principles may be applied to the packaging or organizing of data in a computer program, resulting in the concepts of data encapsulation and data abstraction, which are defined below.

Definition: *Data Encapsulation* or *Information Hiding* is the concealing of the implementation details of a data object from the outside world.

Definition: *Data Abstraction* is the separation between the *specification* of a data object and its *implementation*.

We will see later that these concepts are of great importance in software development because they result in better quality programs and more efficient programming techniques. These, in turn, reduce the number of person-hours required to develop a software system, and hence reduce the total cost of the final software product.

First, however, we shall explore the fundamental data types of C++. These include **char**, **int**, **float**, and **double**. Some of these data types may be modified by keywords **short**, **long**, **signed**, and **unsigned**. The modifiers **short** and **long** specify the amount of storage allocated to the fundamental type they modify. The modifiers **signed** and **unsigned** specify whether the most significant bit in the binary representation of an integer represents a sign bit or not. C++ also supports types derived from the fundamental data types listed above. These include pointer and reference types. Ultimately, the real world abstractions we wish to deal with must be represented in terms of these data types. In addition to these types, C++ helps us by providing three mechanisms for grouping data together. These are the array, the struct, and the class. *Arrays* are collections of elements of the same basic data type; *structs* and *classes* are collections of elements whose data types need not be the same.

All programming languages provide at least a minimal set of predefined data types, plus the ability to construct new, or *user-defined* types.

Definition: A *data type* is a collection of *objects* and a set of *operations* that act on those objects. □

Whether your program is dealing with predefined data types or user-defined data types, these two aspects must be considered: objects and operations. For example, the data type **int** consists of the objects $\{0, +1, -1, +2, -2, \cdots , \text{MAXINT}, \text{MININT}\}$, where MAXINT and MININT are the largest and smallest integers that can be represented by an **int** on your machine. The operations on integers are many and would certainly include the arithmetic operators $+$, $-$, $*$, and $/$. There is also testing for equality/inequality and the operation that assigns an integer to a variable.

Definition: An *abstract data type (ADT)* is a data type that is organized in such a way that the specification of the objects and the specification of the operations on the objects is separated from the representation of the objects and the implementation of the operations. □

Throughout this text, we will emphasize the distinction between specification and implementation. To help us do this, we will typically begin with an ADT definition of the object that we intend to study. This will permit the reader to grasp the essential elements of the object, without having the discussion complicated by the representation of the objects or by the actual implementation of the operations. Once the ADT definition is fully explained, we will move on to discussions of representation and implementation. These are quite important in the study of data structures. To help us accomplish this goal, we introduce a notation for expressing an ADT. This notation is independent of the syntax of the C++ language. Later we shall see how the syntax of the C++ class can be used to express an ADT.

Example 1.1 [*Abstract data type* *NaturalNumber*]: As this is the first example of an ADT, we will spend some time explaining the notation. ADT 1.1 contains the ADT definition of *NaturalNumber*. The definition begins with the name of the abstract data type. There are two main sections in the definition: the objects and the functions. The objects are defined in terms of the integers, but we make no explicit reference to their representation. The function definitions are a bit more complicated. First, the definitions use the symbols x and y to denote two elements of the set *NaturalNumber*, whereas TRUE and FALSE are elements of the set of *Boolean* values. In addition, the definition makes use of functions that are defined on the set of integers, namely, plus, minus, equal, and less than. This is an indication that in order to define one data type, we may need to use operations from another data type. For each function, we place the result type to the left of the function name and a definition of the function to the right. The symbols "::=" should be read as "is defined as."

The first function, *Zero*, has no arguments and returns the natural number zero. The function *Successor(x)* returns the next natural number in sequence. Notice that if there is no next number in sequence, that is, if the value of x is already MAXINT, then we define the action of *Successor* to return MAXINT. Some programmers might prefer that in such a case *Successor* return an error flag. This is also perfectly permissible. Other functions are *Add* and *Subtract*. They might also return an error condition, although here we decided to return an element of the set *NaturalNumber*. □

Next, we see how the principles of data abstraction and data encapsulation help us to efficiently develop well-designed programs.

(1) Simplification of software development: The chief advantage of data abstraction is that it facilitates the decomposition of the complex task of developing a software system into a number of simpler subtasks. Consider the following scenario: A problem has been assigned to a single programmer or to a team of programmers. Suppose that a top-down review of the problem results in a decision that three data types A, B, and C will be used along with some additional code (which we will call *glue*) to facilitate interactions among the three data types. Assume, also, that the specifications of each data type are provided at the outset; i.e., the operations that each data type must support are completely specified.

ADT *NaturalNumber* is

   objects: An ordered subrange of the integers starting at zero and ending at the maximum integer (MAXINT) on the computer.

   functions:

      for all $x, y \in$ *NaturalNumber*; TRUE, FALSE $\in$ *Boolean*

      and where $+, -, <, ==$, and $=$ are the usual integer operations

Zero( ) : *NaturalNumber*	::=	0
IsZero(x) : *Boolean*	::=	**if** $(x == 0)$ *IsZero* = **true**
		else *IsZero* = **false**
Add(x, y) : *NaturalNumber*	::=	**if** $(x + y <= \text{MAXINT})$ *Add* = $x + y$
		else *Add* = MAXINT
Equal(x, y) : *Boolean*	::=	**if** $(x == y)$ *Equal* = TRUE
		else *Equal* = FALSE
Successor(x) : *NaturalNumber*	::=	**if** $(x == \text{MAXINT})$ *Successor* = x
		else *Successor* = $x + 1$
Subtract(x, y) : *NaturalNumber*	::=	**if** $(x < y)$ *Subtract* = 0
		else *Subtract* = $x - y$

end *NaturalNumber*

ADT 1.1: Abstract data type *NaturalNumber*

(a) Scenario 1 - A team of four programmers: the subtasks may be allotted to members of a team of four programmers as follows. A programmer is assigned to each of the three data types. Each programmer's job is to implement his/her data type according to the specifications agreed upon earlier. The fourth programmer implements the glue, assuming that the data types are, in fact, implemented according to the specifications. No programmer needs to know *how* the other programmers implement their portion of the code. Consequently, each programmer can focus exclusively on his/her portion of the code without worrying about what the other programmers are doing and how that might affect what he/she is doing.

(b) Scenario 2 - A single programmer: here data abstraction helps reduce the number of things the programmer has to keep in mind at any time. In the example, the programmer would implement each data type one by one according to the specifications. When the programmer implements data type *A*, he/she can do so without worrying about data types *B* and *C* and the glue. After the individual data types are implemented, the programmer can turn his/her attention to the glue. At this point, the programmer is no longer concerned with the implementations of the three data types, but rather with how to use operations on them to achieve the desired goal.

(2) Testing and Debugging: Breaking down a complex task into a number of easier sub-tasks also simplifies testing and debugging. In the above example, each data type can be tested and debugged separately. After each data type is tested and debugged, the entire program can be tested. If a bug is detected at this stage, it is unlikely that there is a bug in the data structures *A*, *B*, and *C* (represented by the shaded boxes of Figure 1.1(a)) because they have already been tested. So, the bug will most likely be in the glue represented by the unshaded portions of Figure 1.1(a). Compare this with the amount of code to be searched if we had *not* used data abstraction (represented by the unshaded portions Figure 1.1(b)). It is easy to see that employing data abstraction in software development leads to more efficient testing and debugging.

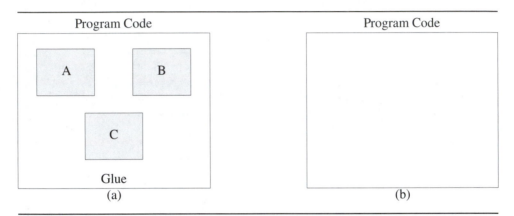

Figure 1.1: Unshaded areas represent code that has to be searched for bugs: (a) data abstraction is used (b) data abstraction is not used.

(3) Reusability: Data abstraction and encapsulation typically give rise to data structures that are implemented as distinct entities of a software system. This makes it easier to extract the code for a data structure and its operations from a software system and use it in another software system, rather than if it were inextricably integrated with the original software system. We will later discuss other techniques in C++ that enhance the reusability of software.

(4) Modifications to the representation of a data type: a significant consequence of information-hiding is that the implementation of a data type is not visible to the rest of the program. Specifically, the rest of the program does not have direct access to the internal representation of the data type. It manipulates the data type solely through a suite of operations that the data type has made available to it. Thus, a change in the internal implementation of a data type will not affect the rest of the program as long as the data type continues to provide the same operations, and as long as these operations continue to do the same things. All that is required is a change in the implementation of the operations that directly access the internal implementation of the data type.

This is easier to appreciate if we examine the consequences of *not* employing data encapsulation. Consider a program that directly manipulates the internal representation of its data types. Suppose a change is made to the implementation of a data type. You, the programmer, are now confronted with the tasks of first examining the program code to locate instances where the program accesses the internal representation of the data type and then making the appropriate changes. This could be an extremely laborious task if the program accesses the internal representation of the data type many times.

EXERCISES

For each of these exercises, provide a definition of the abstract data type using the form illustrated in ADT 1.1.

1. Add the following operations to the *NaturalNumber* ADT: *Predecessor*, *Is-Greater*, *Multiply*, *Divide*.

2. Create an ADT, *Set*. Use the standard mathematical definition and include the following operations: *Create*, *Insert*, *Remove*, *IsIn*, *Union*, *Intersection*, *Difference*.

3. Create an ADT, *Bag*. In mathematics a *bag* is similar to a *set* except that a bag may contain duplicate elements. The minimal operations should include *Create*, *Insert*, *Remove*, and *IsIn*.

4. Create an ADT, *Boolean*. The minimal operations are *And*, *Or*, *Not*, *Xor* (exclusive or), *Equivalent*, and *Implies*.

1.4   BASICS OF C++

The expression "a better C" is often used to describe the C++ language, implying that:

(1)   C and C++ have a lot of features in common.

(2)   C++ has a number of features not associated with either data abstraction or inheritance that improve on C.

In this section we will review features of the C++ language and identify similarities and differences with C. Our presentation assumes that readers are familiar with the C language.

1.4.1   Program Organization in C++

As in C, a single C++ program is usually spread out over a number of files. Two kinds of files are used in C++: header files and source files. Header files have a .h suffix and are used to store declarations. Some header files (such as <iostream.h>) are system-defined. Others are user-defined. Source files are used to store C++ source code. The suffix used in source-file names depends on the compiler. We will use a .C suffix for source files. Header files are included in the appropriate files through the use of the #include preprocessor directive.

Before a C++ program can run, its source files must be individually compiled, linked, and loaded. Because a C++ program typically consists of many source and header files, it is possible that a header file gets included multiple times, giving rise to compilation errors. To ensure that a header file is never included twice, the contents of a header file are enclosed inside the following preprocessor directives.

```
#ifndef FILENAME_H
#define FILENAME_H
// insert contents of the header file here
    .

    .

    .
#endif
```

Another consequence of using multiple source files is that the process of typing compilation commands every time we modify and recompile a program becomes rather tedious. To avoid this, we suggest that you use the *make* facility in UNIX, or its equivalent, to maintain a C++ program. In addition to saving the effort of repeatedly typing compilation commands, *make* also saves time by not recompiling source files that are not affected by modifications made to other files.

1.4.2 Scope in C++

Another consequence of using many files in a single program is that questions arise about the visibility of a variable declared in one file and used in other files. In view of this, we take a brief look at program scope in C++. C++ program text can be classified into one of four scopes:

File scope: Declarations that are not contained in a function definition or in a class definition belongs to a file scope.

Function scope: Labels can be used anywhere within the function definition in which they are declared. Only labels have function scope. Since labels are only used as the targets of **go to** statements; and since we do not plan to use **go to** statements in our programs because it results in unstructured programs, we will not be concerned with this type of program scope.

Local scope: A name declared in a block belongs to a local scope consisting of that block. It can also be used by sub-blocks contained within the block in which it was declared.

Class scope: Declarations associated with a class definition belongs to a class scope. Each class represents a distinct class scope. We discuss classes in greater detail later in Chapter 2.

Each variable has a scope or a context. A variable is uniquely identified by its scope and its name. A variable is visible to a program only from within its scope. For example, a variable defined in a block can only be accessed from within the block. A variable defined at file scope (a global variable), however, can be accessed anywhere in the program. Some questions that arise as a result are

(1) What do we do if a local variable reuses a global variable name in a block; but, we want to access the global variable?
Solution: use the scope operator **::** to access the global variable.

(2) A global variable is defined in file1.C, but used in file2.C. How do we declare the global variable in file2.C? If we declare it, as we normally declare variables, in file2.C, the compiler tells us that it is multiply defined. If we don't declare it, the compiler tells us that it hasn't been defined!
Solution: use **extern** to declare the variable in file2.C.

(3) In our program, both file1.C and file2.C define a global variable with the same name; but the two global variables are meant to be different entities. How do I get the program to compile without changing the global variable name in one of the files.
Solution: use **static** to declare the variables in both files.

For further details, the reader is referred to one of the introductory texts on C++ listed in the references at the end of the chapter.

1.4.3 C++ Statements and Operators

C++ statements have the same syntax and semantics as C statements. C++ statements are briefly reviewed later in this chapter in in the context of performance analysis and evaluation.

C++ operators are identical to C operators with the exception of **new** and **delete**. We will study **new** and **delete** shortly when we discuss dynamic memory management in C++. Another difference is that C++ uses the shift left (<<) and shift right (>>) operators for input and output. We will also study these shortly when discussing input/output in C++. An important difference between C and C++ is that C++ allows *operator over-loading*; that is, an operator is allowed to have different functions depending on the types of the operands that it is being applied to, and furthermore, these functions can be defined by a programmer. We will discuss operator overloading in detail in Chapter 2.

1.4.4   Data Declarations in C++

A data declaration associates a data type with a name. We have already listed the fundamental types of data provided by C++ in Section 1.3 on Data Abstraction and Encapsulation. Now, we list the various options available for declaring data in C++ below. All of
these options are available in C with the exception of the reference type.

(1)   Constant values: these consist of literals such as 5, 'a', or 4.3.

(2)   Variables: these are instances of data types that can be modified during the course
of a program.

(3)   Constant variables: these are variables that cannot be assigned a value during their
lifetime. Because of this, they must be initialized; that is, their contents must be
fixed at the time they are declared. A constant type is declared by adding the keyword **const** to its declaration (e.g., **const int** MAX = 500 ;).

(4)   Enumeration types: This is an alternate mechanism for declaring a series of integer
constants. It can also be used to create a new data type by giving the enumeration
type a name:

enum *Boolean* { FALSE, TRUE };

FALSE and TRUE are integer constants of type *Boolean*. Their values are 0 and 1,
respectively, by default.

(5)   Pointers: these hold memory addresses of objects. For example,

int *i* = 25 ;
int **np* ;
np = &*i* ;

Here *np* is declared to be a pointer to an integer. Next, it is assigned the address of
integer variable *i*. So, *np* is now a pointer to the integer stored in variable *i* (in this
case 25).

(6)   Reference types: This is a feature of C++ that is not a feature of C. The reference
type is a mechanism to provide an alternate name for an object. A reference to an
object of type *T* is declared by appending an & to *T* (i.e., *T&*). For example,

int *i* = 5 ;
int& *j* = *i* ;
i = 7 ;
printf ("i= %d, j= %d", *i, j*) ;

In the example j is a reference type. It represents an alternate name for i. When i's value is changed, j's value also changes correspondingly. When the printf statement is executed, the final value of i and j is 7.

1.4.5   Comments in C++

Comments in C++ are specified in two ways:

(1)   Multiline comments: these are identical to comments in C. All text enclosed within the /* */ delimiters is ignored by the compiler.

(2)   Single line comments: these are unique to C++. All text after // on a line is ignored by the compiler.

The C++ single-line comment format overcomes the following disadavantage of the C multi-line comment: if one muli-line comment is nested inside another, the portion of the text between the terminating delimiters of the inner and outer comments is not ignored by the compiler. This could result in the inclusion of code into the program that the programmer believes was commented out.

1.4.6   Input/Output in C++

To perform I/O in C++, it is necessary to include the system-defined header file iostream.h. The keyword **cout** is used for output to the standard output device. The **cout** keyword and each entity being printed are separated from each other by the << operator. The entities being output are printed in left to right order on the standard output device.

```
#include <iostream.h>

main()
{
    int n = 50 ; float f = 20.3 ;
    cout << "n: " << n << endl ;
    cout << "f: " << f << endl ;
}
```

Program 1.1: Output in C++

Program 1.1 prints the following on the standard output device:

n: 50
f: 20.3

The **cin** keyword is used for input in C++. The operator >> is used to separate variables being input. Whitespace (i.e., the tab, newline, or blank characters) is used to separate items corresponding to different variables on the standard input device

---

```
#include <iostream.h>

 main()
{
   int a, b ;
   cin >> a >> b ;
}
```

Program 1.2: Input in C++

When Program 1.2 is executed, both of the following inputs on the standard input device result in variable *a* being set to 5 and *b* to 10:

Input1:
5 10 <Enter>

Input2:
5 <Enter>
10 <Enter>

     An advantage of I/O in C++ is that it is format-free; that is, the programmer is not required to use formatting symbols to specify the type and order of items being input/output. Another advantage is that, like other C++ operators, I/O operators can be overloaded.

     File I/O in C++ is performed by including the header file fstream.h as shown in Program 1.3. A filestream variable (*outFile*, in our example) is initialized with a string which represents the name of the file (here my.out) and a second argument which specifies the mode in which the file will be used (e.g., ios::out specifies that the file is to be used for output). If the file is not opened, *outFile* = 0. If *outFile* is successfully opened, it is used instead of **cout** to direct output to file my.out.

```
#include <iostream.h>
#include <fstream.h>

 main()
{
    ofstream outFile("my.out", ios::out);
    if (!outFile) {
        cerr << "cannot open my.out " << endl; // standard error device
        return;
    }
    int n = 50 ; float f = 20.3 ;
    outFile << "n: " << n << endl;
    outFile << "f: " << f << endl;
}
```

Program 1.3: File I/O in C++

1.4.7 Functions in C++

There are two kinds of functions in C++: regular functions and member functions. Member functions are functions that are associated with specific C++ classes. We postpone a detailed discussion of member functions to Chapter 2. The features of functions that we review here are common to both types of functions.

A function consists of a function name, a list of arguments or *signature* (input), a return type (output), and the body (code that implements a function). In Program 1.4, *max* is the function name, **int** a, **int** b is the list of arguments, **int** is the return type, and the statements between { and } form the body of the function.

```
int max (int a, int b)
{
    if (a > b) return a;
    else return b;
}
```

Program 1.4: An example of a function

All functions in C++ return a value. If a function is not meant to return anything, we use **void** to denote its return type. A value is returned from a function by using the **return** statement. The **return** statement must return a value that is of the same type as the function's return type or can be converted to the desired type. The function terminates when a **return** statement is encountered. A function is invoked by supplying the actual arguments (e.g., *max*(*x*, 100) returns the larger of *x* and 100).   called

1.4.8   Parameter Passing in C++

In C++, arguments are passed by *value*. This is the default parameter-passing mechanism. When an object is passed by value, it is *copied* into the function's local storage. The function accesses this local copy. Consequently, any change made to a parameter that is passed by value inside the function only changes its local copy. In other words, passing by value does not affect the actual arguments.

   An argument may also be passed by *reference*. To do this, one needs to explicitly declare it to be a reference type. This is done by appending an & to its type specifier. In Program 1.4, we can pass *a* by reference by declaring it as **int**& *a* in the function's argument list. When an object is passed by reference, only the address of its location is copied into the function's local store; the object itself is not copied into the function's local store. Thus, the function accesses the objects referred to by the address; i.e., the actual arguments.

   The advantage of passing by value is that variables that were supplied as actual arguments to the function are not inadvertently modified by it. The advantage of passing by reference is that the function executes faster if the object being passed requires more memory than its address. This is because the overhead of copying the actual argument into the function's local store is replaced by the overhead of copying its address. Note that pass-by-reference would be slower for an argument type such as **char** that occupies less memory than its address. Another reason for using reference parameters is if you *want* the function to modify the actual argument. This technique is used if a function is to return two or more items to the calling function. One of these items is returned by using the **return** statement. The others are returned through the use of reference arguments.

   One technique for retaining the advantages of both parameter-passing methods is to pass *constant references* such as **const** *T*& *a*, where *T* is the type of the argument. Any attempt to modify a **const** argument in the function body will result in a compile-time error. It is also helpful to use the **const** keyword to characterize an argument that is not modified in a function, because it conveys this information to a user of the function. For a more detailed discussion on parameter passing mechanisms and the circumstances in which they should be used, see the book *Effective C++*, by Brad Meyers, listed in the references at the end of the chapter.

   There is one exception to the rule that the default parameter passing mechanism in C++ is pass-by-value: array types are passed by reference; that is, the array is *not* copied into the function's local store. Therefore, any changes made to the array inside the function *are* reflected in the actual array. When a function is invoked with an array argument *a* (e.g., *f*(*a*)), a *pointer to the first element of a* (i.e., &*a* [0]) is actually being passed. This is the reason that, in function definitions, arrays are usually denoted by pointers to the appropriate type (e.g., *f*(**int** ∗*a*)). Because arrays are passed in this manner, the function does not know the size of the array. This is typically rectified by explicitly passing the size of the array as a separate parameter of the function.

1.4.9   Function Name Overloading in C++

Finally, we discuss *function name overloading* in C++. Function overloading means that there can be more than one function with the same name *as long as they have different signatures*. For example, C++ would allow all the following to coexist even though they have the same name *max*:

int *max*(**int**, **int**);
int *max*(**int**, **int**, **int**);
int *max*(**int**∗, **int**);
int *max*(**float**, **int**);
int *max*(**int**, **float**);

1.4.10   Inline Functions

An inline function is declared by adding the keyword **inline** to the function definition as follows:

inline int *sum*(**int** *a*, **int** *b*)
{
   return *a* + *b* ;
}

The **inline** keyword tells the compiler that any calls to *sum* must be replaced by the body of *sum*. This eliminates the overhead of performing a function call and copying arguments when the program is executing. So, the statement *i* = *sum* (*x*, 12)**;** is replaced by *i* = *x* + 12 **;**.

    The objective of the **inline** and **const** keywords is to eliminate the use of preprocessor directives such as #define, which have traditionally been used to perform macro substitution. Excessive use of preprocessor directives makes it difficult to use programming tools such as debuggers and profilers effectively.

1.4.11   Dynamic Memory Allocation in C++

Objects may be allocated from and released to the free store during runtime through the use of the **new** and **delete** operators. The **new** operator creates an object of the desired type and returns a pointer to the data type that follows it. If it is unable to create the desired object, it returns 0. An object created by **new** exists for the duration of the program unless it is explicitly deleted by applying the **delete** operator to a pointer to the object:

int *ip = **new int;**
if (ip == 0) **cerr** << "Memory not allocated" << endl ;
.
.

delete ip ;

Operators **new** and **delete** can also be used to create and delete an array of objects as follows:

int *jp = **new int**[10] ; // jp is an array of integers
if (jp == 0) **cerr** << "Memory not allocated" << endl ;
.
.

delete [ ] jp ; // delete the array jp

The subscript operator ([ ]) is used to inform the compiler that the object being created or deleted is an array.

1.5   ALGORITHM SPECIFICATION

1.5.1   Introduction

The concept of an algorithm is fundamental to computer science. Algorithms exist for many common problems, and designing efficient algorithms plays a crucial role in developing large-scale computer systems. Therefore, before we proceed further, we discuss this concept more fully. We begin with a definition.

Definition: An *algorithm* is a finite set of instructions that, if followed, accomplishes a particular task. In addition, all algorithms must satisfy the following criteria:

(1) **Input.** Zero or more quantities are externally supplied.

(2) **Output.** At least one quantity is produced.

(3) **Definiteness.** Each instruction is clear and unambiguous.

(4) **Finiteness.** If we trace out the instructions of an algorithm, then for all cases, the algorithm terminates after a finite number of steps.

(5) **Effectiveness.** Every instruction must be basic enough to be carried out, in principle, by a person using only pencil and paper. It is not enough that each operation be definite as in (3); it also must be feasible. □

In computational theory, one distinguishes between an algorithm and a program, the latter of which does not have to satisfy the fourth condition. For example, we can think of an operating system that continues in a ''wait'' loop until more jobs are entered. Such a program does not terminate unless the system crashes. Since our programs will always terminate, we will use the terms algorithm and program interchangeably in this text.

We can describe an algorithm in many ways. We can use a natural language like English, although if we select this option, we must make sure that the resulting instructions are definite. Graphic representations called flowcharts are another possibility, but they work well only if the algorithm is small and simple. In this text, we will present most of our algorithms in C++, occasionally resorting to a combination of English and C++ for our specifications. Two examples should help to illustrate the process of translating a problem into an algorithm.

Example 1.2 [*Selection sort*]: Suppose we must devise a program that sorts a collection of $n \geq 1$ integers. A simple solution is given by the following:

From those integers that are currently unsorted, find the smallest and place it next in the sorted list.

Although this statement adequately describes the sorting problem, it is not an algorithm because it leaves several unanswered questions. For example, it does not tell us where and how the integers are initially stored or where we should place the result. We assume that the integers are stored in an array, a, such that the ith integer is stored in $a[i-1]$, $1 \leq i \leq n$. Program 1.5 is our first attempt at deriving a solution. Notice that it is written partially in C++ and partially in English.

To turn Program 1.5 into a real C++ program, two clearly defined subtasks remain: finding the smallest integer and interchanging it with $a[i]$. We can solve the latter problem by using the code:

$$temp = a[i]; a[i] = a[j]; a[j] = temp;$$

The first subtask can be solved by assuming the minimum is $a[i]$, checking $a[i]$ with $a[i+1]$, $a[i+2]$, $\cdots$ and whenever a smaller element is found, regarding it as the new

---

```
for (int i = 0; i < n ; i++ ) {
    examine a [i] to a [n −1] and suppose the smallest integer is at a [j];
    interchange a [i] and a [j] ;
}
```

Program 1.5: Selection sort algorithm

minimum. Eventually $a[n-1]$ is compared to the current minimum, and we are done. Putting all these observations together, we get the function *sort* (Program 1.6).

```
1  void sort (int *a, const int n)
2  // sort the n integers a[0] to a[n−1] into nondecreasing order
3  {
4      for ( int i = 0; i < n ; i++ )
5      {
6          int j = i;
7          // find smallest integer in a[i] to a[n − 1]
8          for ( int k = i + 1 ; k < n ; k++ )
9              if (a[k] < a[j]) j = k ;
10         // interchange
11         int temp = a[i]; a[i] = a[j]; a[j] = temp;
12     }
13 }
```

Program 1.6: Selection sort

At this point, the obvious question to ask is: Does this function work correctly?

Theorem 1.1: $sort(a,n)$ correctly sorts a set of $n \geq 1$ integers; the result remains in $a[0] \cdots a[n-1]$ such that $a[0] \leq a[1] \leq \cdots \leq a[n-1]$.

Proof: We first note that for any i, say $i = q$, following the execution of lines 6-11, it is the case that $a[q] \leq a[r]$, $q < r \leq n-1$. Also observe that when i becomes greater than q, $a[0] \cdots a[q]$ is unchanged. Hence, following the last execution of these lines (i.e., $i = n-1$), we have $a[0] \leq a[1] \leq \cdots \leq a[n-1]$. □

We observe at this point that the upper limit of the **for** loop in line 4 can be changed to $n - 1$ without damaging the correctness of the algorithm.

Example 1.3 [*Binary search*]: Assume that we have $n \geq 1$ distinct integers that are already sorted and stored in the array $a[0] \cdots a[n-1]$. Our task is to determine if the integer x is present and if so to return j such that $x = a[j]$; otherwise return -1. By making use of the fact that the set is sorted, we conceive of the following efficient method:

Let *left* and *right*, respectively, denote the left and right ends of the list to be searched. Initially, *left* = 0 and *right* = $n-1$. Let *middle* = (*left* + *right*) / 2 be the middle position in the list. If we compare $a[middle]$ with x, we obtain one of three results:

(1)   **x < a[middle].** In this case, if x is present, it must be in the positions between 0 and *middle* $- 1$. Therefore, we set *right* to *middle* $- 1$.

(2)   **x == a[middle].** In this case, we return *middle*.

(3)   **x > a[middle].** In this case, if x is present, it must be in the positions between *middle* + 1 and $n-1$. So, we set *left* to *middle* + 1.

If x has not been found and there are still integers to check, we recalculate *middle* and continue the search. The algorithm contains two subtasks: (1) determining if there are any integers left to check and (2) comparing x to $a[middle]$.

At this point you might try the method out on some sample numbers. This method is referred to as *binary search*. Note how at each stage the number of elements in the remaining set is decreased by about one-half. Note also that at each stage, x is compared with $a[middle]$ and depending on whether $x > a[middle]$, $x < a[middle]$, or $x == a[middle]$, we do a different thing. To implement this in C++ we could use the **if-else** construct:

if $(x > a[middle]) \ldots$
else if $(x < a[middle]) \ldots$
        else $\ldots$

From this construct it is not readily apparent that we are considering the three cases that can result from the comparison between x and $a[i]$. To make the program more transparent, we introduce a compare function that has value >, <, or =, depending on the outcome of the comparison. This function is given in Program 1.7.

```
char compare (int x, int y)
{
    if (x > y) return '>';
    else if (x < y) return '<';
        else return '=';
} // end of compare
```

Program 1.7: Comparing two elements

We can now refine the description of binary search to get a pseudo-C++ function. The result is given in Program 1.8.

---

int *BinarySearch* (**int** *∗a,* **const int** *x,* **const int** *n*)
// Search the sorted array *a* [0], · · · *,a* [*n*−1] for *x*
{
    for(initialize *left* and *right*; while there are more elements;)
    {
      let *middle* be the middle element;
      switch (*compare* (*x,* a[*middle*])){
        case '>': set *left* to *middle* + 1; **break;**
        case '<': set *right* = *middle* −1; **break;**
        case '=': found *x*;
      } // end of **switch**
    } // end of **for**
    not found;
} // end of *BinarySearch*

Program 1.8: Algorithm for binary search

Another refinement yields the C++ function of Program 1.9.

```
 1 int BinarySearch (int ∗a, const int x, const int n)
 2 // Search the sorted array a [0], ..., a [n−1] for x
 3 {
 4      for (int left = 0, right = n − 1; left <= right;) { // while more elements
 5          int middle = (left + right)/2;
 6          switch (compare (x, a[middle])) {
 7              case '>': left = middle + 1; break; // x > a[middle]
 8              case '<': right = middle − 1; break; // x < a[middle]
 9              case '=': return middle; // x == a[middle]
10          } // end of switch
11      } // end of for
12      return −1; // not found
13 } // end of BinarySearch
```

Program 1.9: C++ function for binary search

To prove this program correct we make assertions about the relationship between variables before and after the **for** loop of lines 4-11. As we enter this loop and if *x* is present in *a*, the following holds:

$$left \leq right \ \&\& \ a[left] \leq x \leq a[right] \ \&\& \ SORTED(a, n)$$

Now, if control passes out of the **for** loop past line 11, then we know the condition of line 4 is false, so *left* > *right*. This, combined with the above assertion, implies that *x* is not present.

Unfortunately, a complete proof takes us beyond the scope of this text, but those who wish to pursue program-proving should consult the references at the end of this chapter. □

1.5.2 Recursive Algorithms

We have emphasized the need to structure a program to make it easier to achieve the goals of readability and correctness. One of the most useful syntactical features for accomplishing this is the function. A set of instructions that perform a logical operation, perhaps a very complex and long operation, can be grouped together as a function. The function name and its parameters are viewed as a new instruction that can be used in other programs. Given the input-output specifications of a function, we do not even have to know how the task is accomplished, only that it is available. This view of the function implies that it is invoked, executed and returns control to the appropriate place in the calling function. What this fails to stress is that functions may call themselves (*direct recursion*) before they are done or they may call other functions that again invoke the calling function (*indirect recursion*). These recursive mechanisms are extremely powerful, but even more importantly, often they can express an otherwise complex process very clearly. For these reasons we introduce recursion here. 归纳法

Recursion is similar to the method of induction which is often used to prove mathematical statements. In mathematical induction, a statement about integers (e.g., the sum of the first *n* positive integers is $n(n+1)/2$) is proved by showing that the statement can be proved for integer *k* if it is assumed to be true for integer *k* − 1. Similarly, in recursion, we write a function to produce an output (say *n*!) for some input (here, *n*) by assuming that the same function will compute the correct output for input *n* − 1. In mathematical induction, we need a basis which can be directly proved (that is, the proof for the basis does not make any assumptions). Similarly, a recursive function requires a terminating condition. When the input to the function satisfies this terminating condition, the function directly computes the output without calling itself.

What kinds of problems are best solved by recursion? Typically, beginning programmers view recursion as a somewhat mystical technique that is useful only for some very special class of problems (such as computing factorials or Ackermann's function). This is unfortunate because any program that can be written using assignment, the **if-else** statement, and the **while** statement can also be written using assignment, **if-else**, and recursion. Of course, this does not mean that the resulting program will necessarily be easier to understand. However, there are many instances when this will be the case. When is recursion an appropriate mechanism for algorithm exposition? One instance is when the problem itself is recursively defined. Factorial fits this category, as well as binomial coefficients where

$$\begin{bmatrix} n \\ m \end{bmatrix} = \frac{n!}{m!(n-m)!}$$

can be recursively computed by the formula

$$\begin{bmatrix} n \\ m \end{bmatrix} = \begin{bmatrix} n-1 \\ m \end{bmatrix} + \begin{bmatrix} n-1 \\ m-1 \end{bmatrix}$$

We use two examples to show you how to develop a recursive algorithm. In the first example, we take the binary search function that we created in Example 1.3 and transform it into a recursive function. In the second example, we generate all possible permutations of a list of characters. To understand a recursive function, you must

(1)   Formulate in your mind a statement of what it is that the function is supposed to do, for a given input.

(2)   Verify that the function does achieve its goal if the recursive invocations to itself do what they are supposed to.

(3)   Ensure that a finite number of recursive invocations of the function eventually lead to an invocation which satisfies the terminating condition (otherwise, the function will keep calling itself and not terminate!).

(4)   The function should perform the correct computations if the terminating condition is encountered.

Example 1.4 [*Recursive binary search*]: Program 1.9 gave the iterative version of binary search. In the recursive version we pass *left* and *right* as parameters (Program 1.10). The **for** loop of Program 1.9 has been replaced by recursive calls in Program 1.10. To invoke the recursive function, we use the statement

$$BinarySearch(a, x, 0, n-1);$$

You should verify that *BinarySearch* satisfies the four conditions stated above for recursive functions. Notice that both the iterative (Program 1.9) and recursive (Program 1.10) functions perform the same computation. □

Example 1.5 [*Permutation generator*]: Given a set of $n \geq 1$ elements, the problem is to print all possible permutations of this set. For example if the set is $\{a, b, c\}$, then the set of permutations is $\{(a, b, c), (a, c, b), (b, a, c), (b, c, a), (c, a, b), (c, b, a)\}$. It is easy to see that given n elements, there are $n!$ different permutations. A simple algorithm can be obtained by looking at the the case of four elements (a,b,c,d). The answer can be constructed by writing

```
int BinarySearch (int *a, const int x, const int left, const int right)
// Search the sorted array a[left], · · · , a[right] for x
{
   if (left <= right) {
      int middle = (left + right)/2;
      switch (compare (x, a[middle])) {
         case '>': return BinarySearch(a, x, middle + 1, right); // x > a[middle]
         case '<': return BinarySearch(a, x, left, middle − 1);  // x < a[middle]
         case '=': return middle; // x == a[middle]
      } // end of switch
   } // end of if
   return −1; // not found
} // end of BinarySearch
```

Program 1.10: Recursive implementation of binary search

(1) a followed by all permutations of (b,c,d)

(2) b followed by all permutations of (a,c,d)

(3) c followed by all permutations of (a,b,d)

(4) d followed by all permutations of (a,b,c)

The expression "followed by all permutations" is the clue to recursion. It implies that we can solve the problem for a set with n elements if we have an algorithm that works on $n-1$ elements. These observations lead to Program 1.11, which is invoked by $perm(a, 0, n)$.

Try this algorithm out on sets of length one, two, and three to ensure that you understand how it works. □

Another time when recursion is useful is when the data structure that the algorithm is to operate on is recursively defined. We shall see several important examples of such structures in this book.

EXERCISES

1. Horner's rule is a means for evaluating a polynomial $A(x) = a_n x^n + a_{n-1} x^{n-1} + \cdots + a_1 x + a_0$ at a point x_0 using a minimum number of multiplications. This rule is:

$$A(x) = (\cdots (a_n x_0 + a_{n-1}) x_0 + \cdots + a_1) x_0 + a_0$$

Write a C++ program to evaluate a polynomial using Horner's rule. Determine how many times each statement is executed.

```
void perm (char *a, const int k, const int n)  // n is the size of a
// Generate all the permutations of a [k ], · · · ,a [n−1].
{
    if (k == n − 1) {  // output permutation
        for (int i = 0; i < n; i++) cout << a[i] << " ";
        cout << endl;
    }
    else {  // a [k ], · · · ,a [n−1] has more than one permutation. Generate these recursively.
        for (i = k; i < n; i++) {
            // interchange a[k] and a[i]
            char temp = a [k ]; a [k ] = a [i ]; a [i ] = temp;
            perm(a, k +1, n); // all permutations of a [k +1], · · · ,a [n−1]
            // interchange a [k ] and a [i ] again, to return to the original configuration
            temp = a [k ]; a [k ] = a [i ]; a [i ] = temp;
        }
    } // end of else
} // end of perm
```

Program 1.11: Recursive permutation generator

2. Given n Boolean variables $x_1, \cdots, x_n$ we wish to print all possible combinations of truth values they can assume. For instance, if $n = 2$, there are four possibilities: true, true; true, false; false, true; false, false. Write a C++ program to accomplish this and do a frequency count.

3. Write a C++ program that prints out the integer values of x, y, and z in nondecreasing order. What is the computing time of your method?

4. Write a C++ function that searches an array $a [n]$ for the element x. If x occurs, then set j to its position in the array, else set j to −1. Try writing this without using the **goto** statement.

5. Trace the action of the code

$$i = 0; j = n − 1 ;$$
```
do {
    k = (i + j)/2;
    if (a [k ] <= x) i = k + 1;
    else j = k − 1; }
while (i <= j);
```

on the elements 2, 4, 6, 8, 10, 12, 14, 16, 18, and 20 searching for $x = 1$, 3, 13, or 21.

6. Take any version of binary search, express it using assignment, **if-else**, and **goto**, and then give an equivalent recursive program.

7. The factorial function $n!$ has value 1 when $n \leq 1$ and value $n*(n-1)!$ when $n > 1$. Write both a recursive and an iterative C++ function to compute $n!$.

8. The Fibonacci numbers are defined as: $f_0 = 0$, $f_1 = 1$, and $f_i = f_{i-1}+f_{i-2}$ for $i > 1$. Write both a recursive and an iterative C++ function to compute f_i.

9. Write a recursive function for computing the binomial coefficient $\begin{bmatrix} n \\ m \end{bmatrix}$ as defined in Section 1.5.2, where $\begin{bmatrix} n \\ 0 \end{bmatrix} = \begin{bmatrix} n \\ n \end{bmatrix} = 1$. Analyze the time and space requirements of your algorithm.

10. Write an iterative function to compute a binomial coefficient; then transform it into an equivalent recursive function.

11. Ackermann's function $A(m,n)$ is defined as follows:

$$A(m,n) = \begin{cases} n + 1 & \text{, if } m = 0 \\ A(m-1, 1) & \text{, if } n = 0 \\ A(m-1, A(m,n-1)) & \text{, otherwise} \end{cases}$$

This function is studied because it grows very fast for small values of m and n. Write a recursive function for computing this function. Then write a nonrecursive algorithm for computing Ackermann's function.

12. The *pigeonhole principle* states that if a function f has n distinct inputs but less than n distinct outputs, then there exist two inputs a and b such that $a \neq b$ and $f(a) = f(b)$. Write a program to find the values a and b for which the range values are equal. Assume that the inputs are $1, 2, \cdots, n$.

13. Given n, a positive integer, determine if n is the sum of all of its divisors — i.e., if n is the sum of all t such that $1 \leq t < n$, and t divides n.

14. Consider the function $F(x)$ defined by

$$\textbf{if } (x \text{ is even}) \ F = x/2;$$
$$\textbf{else } F = F(F(3x + 1));$$

Prove that $F(x)$ terminates for all integers x. (Hint: Consider integers of the form $(2i + 1)2^k - 1$ and use induction.)

15. If S is a set of n elements, the *powerset* of S is the set of all possible subsets of S. For example, if $S = (a,b,c)$, then *powerset* $(S) = \{(\ ), (a), (b), (c), (a,b), (a,c), (b,c), (a,b,c)\}$. Write a recursive function to compute *powerset* (S).

16. [***Towers of Hanoi***] There are three towers and sixty-four disks of different diameters placed on the first tower. The disks are in order of decreasing diameter as one scans up the tower. Monks were supposed to move the disks from tower 1 to tower 3 obeying the following rules: (a) only one disk can be moved at any time

and (b) no disk can be placed on top of a disk with smaller diameter. Write a recursive function that prints the sequence of moves that accomplish this task.

1.6   PERFORMANCE ANALYSIS AND MEASUREMENT

One goal of this book is to develop skills for making evaluative judgments about programs. There are many criteria upon which we can judge a program, for instance:

(1)   Does it do what we want it to do?

(2)   Does it work correctly according to the original specifications of the task?

(3)   Is there documentation that describes how to use it and how it works?

(4)   Are functions created in such a way that they perform logical subfunctions?

(5)   Is the code readable?

The above criteria are all vitally important when it comes to writing software, most especially for large systems. Though we will not be discussing how to reach these goals, we will try to achieve them throughout this book with the programs we write. Hopefully this more subtle approach will gradually infect your own program-writing habits so that you will automatically strive to achieve these goals.

There are other criteria for judging programs that have a more direct relationship to performance. These have to do with their computing time and storage requirements.

Definition: The *space complexity* of a program is the amount of memory it needs to run to completion. The *time complexity* of a program is the amount of computer time it needs to run to completion. □

Performance evaluation can be loosely divided into two major phases: (1) a priori estimates and (2) a posteriori testing. We refer to these as *performance analysis* and *performance measurement* respectively.

1.6.1   Performance Analysis

1.6.1.1   Space Complexity

Function   *abc*   (Program   1.12)   computes   the   expression $a+b+b*c+(a+b-c)/(a+b)+4.0$; function *sum* (Program 1.13) computes the sum $\sum_{i=0}^{n-1} a[i]$ iteratively, where the $a[i]$'s are of type **float**; and function *rsum* (Program 1.14) is a recursive program that computes $\sum_{i=0}^{n-1} a[i]$.

```
float abc(float a, float b, float c)
{
    return a +b +b *c +(a +b −c)/(a +b)+4.0;
} // end of abc
```

Program 1.12: Function to compute $a +b +b*c + (a +b −c)/(a +b)+4.0$

```
line float sum (float *a, const int n)
  1 {
  2       float s = 0;
  3       for (int i = 0; i < n; i++)
  4           s += a[i];
  5       return s;
  6 }
```

Program 1.13: Iterative function for sum

```
line    float rsum (float *a, const int n)
  1     {
  2        if (n <= 0) return 0;
  3        else return  (rsum (a, n−1) + a [n−1]);
  4     }
```

Program 1.14: Recursive function for sum

The space needed by each of these programs is seen to be the sum of the following components:

(1)   A fixed part that is independent of the characteristics (e.g., number, size) of the inputs and outputs. This part typically includes the instruction space (i.e., space for the code), space for simple variables and fixed-size component variables (also called *aggregate*), space for constants, etc.

(2)   A variable part that consists of the space needed by component variables whose size is dependent on the particular problem instance being solved, the space needed by referenced variables (to the extent that this depends on instance characteris-

tics), and the recursion stack space (insofar as this space depends on the instance characteristics).

The space requirement $S(P)$ of any program P may therefore be written as $S(P) = c + S_P$(instance characteristics) where c is a constant.

When analyzing the space complexity of a program, we shall concentrate solely on estimating S_P (instance characteristics). For any given problem, we shall need to first determine which instance characteristics to use to measure the space requirements. This is very problem-specific, and we shall resort to examples to illustrate the various possibilities. Generally speaking, our choices are limited to quantities related to the number and magnitude of the inputs to and outputs from the program. At times, more complex measures of the interrelationships among the data items are used.

Example 1.6: For Program 1.12, the problem instance is characterized by the specific values of a, b, and c. Making the assumption that one word is adequate to store the values of each of a, b, c, and the value returned by abc, we see that the space needed by function abc is independent of the instance characteristics. Consequently, S_P(instance characteristics) $= 0$. □

Example 1.7: The problem instances for Program 1.13 are characterized by n, the number of elements to be summed. Since n is passed by value, one word must be allocated for it. Since a is actually the address of the first element in $a[\,]$ (i.e. $a[0]$), the space needed by it is also one word. So, the space needed by the function is independent of n and $S_{sum}(n) = 0$. □

Example 1.8: Let us consider the function *rsum*. As in the case of *sum*, the instances are characterized by n. The recursion stack space includes space for the formal parameters, the local variables, and the return address. Since a is the address of $a[0]$, it requires only one word of memory on the stack. Assume that the return address requires only one word of memory. Each call to *rsum* requires at least 4 words (including space for the values of n, a, the returned value, and the return address). Since the depth of recursion is $n+1$, the recursion stack space needed is $4(n+1)$. For $n = 1000$, the recursion stack space is 4004. □

1.6.1.2 Time Complexity

The time, $T(P)$, taken by a program P is the sum of the compile time and the run (or execution) time. The compile time does not depend on the instance characteristics. Also, we may assume that a compiled program will be run several times without recompilation. Consequently, we shall concern ourselves with just the run time of a program. This run time is denoted by t_P (instance characteristics).

Because many of the factors t_P depends on are not known at the time a program is conceived, it is reasonable to attempt only to estimate t_P. If we knew the characteristics of the compiler to be used, we could proceed to determine the number of additions, subtractions, multiplications, divisions, compares, loads, stores, and so on that would be made by the code for P. So, we could obtain an expression for $t_P(n)$ of the form

$$t_P(n) = c_a ADD(n) + c_s SUB(n) + c_m MUL(n) + c_d DIV(n) + \cdots$$

where n denotes the instance characteristics, and c_a, c_s, c_m, c_d, etc., respectively, denote the time needed for an addition, subtraction, multiplication, division, etc., and *ADD, SUB, MUL, DIV*, etc., are functions whose value is the number of additions, subtractions, multiplications, divisions, etc., that will be performed when the code for P is used on an instance with characteristic n.

Obtaining such an exact formula is in itself an impossible task, since the time needed for an addition, subtraction, multiplication, etc., often depends on the actual numbers being added, subtracted, multiplied, etc. In reality then, the true value of $t_P(n)$ for any given n can be obtained only experimentally. The program is typed, compiled, and run on a particular machine. The execution time is physically clocked and $t_P(n)$ obtained. Even with this experimental approach, one could face difficulties. In a multiuser system, the execution time will depend on such factors as system load, the number of other programs running on the computer at the time program P is run, the characteristics of these other programs, and so on.

Given the minimal utility of determining the exact number of additions, subtractions, etc., that are needed to solve a problem instance with characteristics given by n, we might as well lump all the operations together (provided that the time required by each is relatively independent of the instance characteristics) and obtain a count for the total number of operations. We can go one step further and count only the number of program steps.

A *program step* is loosely defined as a syntactically or semantically meaningful segment of a program that has an execution time that is independent of the instance characteristics. For example, the entire statement

return $a + b + b * c + (a + b - c)/(a + b) + 4.0$**;**

of Program 1.12 could be regarded as a step since its execution time is independent of the instance characteristics (this statement is not strictly true, since the time for a multiply and divide will generally depend on the actual numbers involved in the operation).

The number of steps any program statement is to be assigned depends on the nature of that statement. The following discussion considers the various statement types that can appear in a C++ program and states the complexity of each in terms of the number of steps:

(1)   *Comments*. Comments are nonexecutable statements and have a step count of zero.

(2)   *Declarative statements*. This category includes all statements that define or characterize variables and constants (**int, long, short, char, float, double, const,**

enum, **signed**, **unsigned**, **static**, **extern**), all statements that enable users to define their own data types (**class**, **struct**, **union**, **template**), all statements that determine access (**private**, **public**, **protected**, **friend**), and all statements that characterize functions (**void**, **virtual**). These count as zero steps, since these are either nonexecutable or their cost may be lumped into the cost of invoking the function they are associated with.

(3) *Expressions and assignment statements*. Most expressions have a step count of one. The exceptions are expressions that contain function calls. In this case, we need to determine the cost of invoking the functions. This cost can be large if the functions employ many-element pass-by-value parameters because the values of all actual parameters need to be assigned to the formal parameters. This is discussed further under function and function invocation. When the expression contains functions, the step count is the sum of the step counts assignable to each function invocation.

The assignment statement <variable> = <expr> has a step count equal to that of <expr> unless the size of <variable> is a function of the instance characteristics. In this latter case, the step count is the size of <variable> plus the step count of <expr>. For example, the assignment *a* = *b*, where *a* and *b* are of type *ElementList*, has a step count equal to the size of *ElementList*.

(4) *Iteration statements*. This class of statements includes the **for**, **while**, and **do** statements. We shall consider the step counts only for the control part of these statements. These have the following form:

> **for** (<init-stmt>; <expr1>; <expr2>)
> **while** <expr> **do**
> **do** ...**while** <expr>

Each execution of the control part of a **while** and **do** statement will be given a step count equal to the number of step counts assignable to <expr>. The step count for each execution of the control part of a **for** statement is one, unless the counts attributable to <init-stmt>, <expr1>, or <expr2> are a function of the instance characteristics. In this latter case, the first execution of the control part of the **for** has a step count equal to the sum of the counts for <init-stmt> and <expr1>; subsequent executions of the **for** statement have a step count equal to the sum of the step counts for <expr1> and <expr2>.

(5) *Switch statement*. This statement consists of a header followed by one or more sets of condition-statement pairs. We shall once again consider the costs for the control part of the statement.

```
switch (<expr>) {
    case cond1: <statement1>
    case cond2: <statement2>
                .
                .
                .
    default: <statement>
}
```

The header **switch** (<expr>) is given a cost equal to that assignable to <expr>. The cost of each condition is its cost plus that of all preceding conditions.

(6)   *If-else statement*. The **if-else** statement consists of three parts:

$$\textbf{if } (<expr>) <statements1>;$$
$$\textbf{else } <statements2>;$$

Each part is assigned the number of steps corresponding to <expr>, <statements1>, and <statements2> respectively. Note that if the **else** clause is absent, then no cost is assigned to it. Step counts are computed for the **arithmetic-if** operation in a similar manner.

(7)   *function invocation*. All invocations of functions count as one step unless the invocation involves pass-by-value parameters whose size depends on the instance characteristics. In this latter case, the count is the sum of the sizes of these value parameters. If the function being invoked is recursive, then we must also consider the local variables in the function being invoked. The sizes of local variables that are characteristic-dependent need to be added to the step count.

(8)   *memory management statements*. These include **new** *object*, **delete** *object*, and **sizeof**(*object*). The step count associated with each is 1. The statements **new** and **delete** can potentially invoke the constructor and destructor for *object*, respectively. In this case, the step counts are computed in a similar manner to a function invocation.

(9)   *function statements*. These count as zero steps because their cost has already been assigned to the invoking statements.

(10) *Jump statements*. These include **continue**, **break**, **goto**, **return**, and **return** <expr>. Each has a step count of one, with the possible exception of **return** <expr>. This has a step count of 1 unless the step count attributable to <expr> is a function of instance characteristics. In this case, the step count is the cost of <expr>.

With the above assignment of step counts to statements, we can proceed to determine the number of steps needed by a program to solve a particular problem instance. We can go about this in one of two ways. In the first method, we introduce a new variable, *count*, into the program. This is a global variable with initial value 0. Statements to increment *count* by the appropriate amount are introduced into the program. This is done so that each time a statement in the original program is executed, *count* is incremented by the step count of that statement.

Example 1.9: When the statements to increment *count* are introduced into Program 1.13, the result is Program 1.15. The change in the value of *count* by the time this program terminates is the number of steps executed by Program 1.13.

   Since we are interested in determining only the change in the value of *count*, Program 1.15 may be simplified to Program 1.16. It should be easy to see that for every initial value of *count*, Program 1.15 and Program 1.16 compute the same final value for *count*. It is easy to see that in the **for** loop, the value of *count* will increase by a total of $2n$. If *count* is zero to start with, then it will be $2n + 3$ on termination. So, each invocation of *sum* (Program 1.13) executes a total of $2n + 3$ steps. □

```
float sum (float *a, const int n)
{
    float s = 0;
    count++; // count is global
    for (int i = 0; i < n; i++) {
        count++; // for for
        s += a[i];
        count++; // for assignment
    }
    count++; // for last time of for
    count++; // for return
    return s;
}
```

Program 1.15: Program 1.13 with count statements added

```
void sum (float *a, const int n)
{
    for (int  i = 0 ; i < n ; i++)
        count += 2;
    count += 3;
}
```

Program 1.16: Simplified version of Program 1.15

Example 1.10: When the statements to increment *count* are introduced into Program 1.14, Program 1.17 is obtained. Let $t_{rsum}(n)$ be the increase in the value of *count* when Program 1.17 terminates. We see that $t_{rsum}(0) = 2$. When $n > 0$, *count* increases by 2 plus whatever increase results from the invocation of *rsum* from within the **else** clause. From the definition of t_{rsum}, it follows that this additional increase is $t_{rsum}(n-1)$. So, if the value of *count* is zero initially, its value at the time of termination is $2+t_{rsum}(n-1)$, $n > 0$.

```
float rsum (float *a, const int n)
{
    count++; // for if conditional
    if (n <= 0) {
        count++; // for return
        return 0;
    }
    else {
        count++ ; // for return
        return (rsum(a, n − 1) + a [n − 1]);
    }
}
```

Program 1.17: Program 1.14 with count statements added

When analyzing a recursive program for its step count, we often obtain a recursive formula for the step count (i.e., say $t_{rsum}(n) = 2+t_{rsum}(n-1)$, $n > 0$ and $t_{rsum}(0) = 2$). These recursive formulas are referred to as *recurrence relations*. This recurrence may be solved by repeatedly substituting for t_{rsum} as below:

$$
\begin{aligned}
t_{rsum}(n) &= 2 + t_{rsum}(n-1) \\
&= 2 + 2 + t_{rsum}(n-2) \\
&= 2 \times 2 + t_{rsum}(n-2) \\
&\quad . \\
&\quad . \\
&= 2n + t_{rsum}(0) \\
&= 2n + 2
\end{aligned}
$$

So, the step count for function *rsum* (Program 1.14) is $2n +2$. $\square$

Comparing the step count of Program 1.13 to that of Program 1.14, we see that the count for Program 1.14 is less than that for Program 1.13. From this, we cannot conclude that Program 1.13 is slower than Program 1.14. This is so because a step does not correspond to a definite time unit. Each step of *rsum* may take more time than every step of *sum*. So, it might well be (and we expect) that *rsum* is slower than *sum*.

The step count is useful in that it tells us how the run time for a program changes with changes in the instance characteristics. From the step count for *sum*, we see that if n is doubled, the run time will also double (approximately); if n increases by a factor of 10, we expect the run time to increase by a factor of 10; and so on. So, we expect the run time to grow *linearly* in n. We say that *sum* is a linear program (the time complexity is linear in the instance characteristic n).

Example 1.11 [*Matrix addition*]: Program 1.18 is a program to add two $m \times n$ matrices a and b together. Introducing the *count*-incrementing statements leads to Program 1.19. Program 1.20 is a simplified version of Program 1.19 that computes the same value for *count*. Examining Program 1.20, we see that line 5 is executed n times for each value of i or a total of mn times; line 6 is executed m times; and line 8 is executed once. If *count* is zero to begin with, it will be $2mn + 2m + 1$ when Program 1.20 terminates.

From this analysis we see that if $m > n$, then it is better to interchange the two **for** statements in Program 1.18. If this is done, the step count becomes $2mn + 2n + 1$. Note that in this example the instance characteristics are given by m and n. □

---

line void *add (matrix a, matrix b, matrix c,* **int** *m,* **int** *n)*
```
1 {
2   for (int i = 0; i < m; i++)
3     for (int j = 0 ; j < n ; j++)
4       c [i ][j ] = a [i ][j ] + b [i ][j ];
5 }
```

Program 1.18: Matrix addition

The second method to determine the step count of a program is to build a table in which we list the total number of steps contributed by each statement. This figure is often arrived at by first determining the number of steps per execution of the statement and the total number of times (i.e., frequency) each statement is executed. By combining these two quantities, the total contribution of each statement is obtained. By adding up the contributions of all statements, the step count for the entire program is obtained.

There is an important difference between the step count of a statement and its steps per execution (s/e). The step count does not necessarily reflect the complexity of the statement. For example, the statement

$$x = sum(a, m);$$

has a step count of 1, while the total change in *count* resulting from the execution of this statement is actually 1 plus the change resulting from the invocation of *sum* (i.e., $2m + 3$).

```
void add (matrix a, matrix b, matrix c, int m, int n)
{
    for (int i = 0; i < m ; i++)
    {
        count++; // for for i
        for (int j = 0; j < n; j++)
        {
            count++; // for for j
            c [i ][j ] = a [i ][j ] + b [i ][j ];
            count++; // for assignment
        }
        count++; // for last time of for j
    }
    count++; // for last time of for i
}
```

Program 1.19: Matrix addition with counting statements

```
line  void add (matrix a, matrix b, matrix c, int m, int n)
 1    {
 2        for (int i = 0; i < m; i++)
 3        {
 4            for (int j = 0; j < n ; j++)
 5                count += 2;
 6            count += 2;
 7        }
 8        count++;
 9    }
```

Program 1.20: Simplified program with counting only

The steps per execution of the above statement is $1+2m+3 = 2m+4$. *The s/e of a statement is the amount by which count changes as a result of the execution of that statement.*

In Table 1.1, the number of steps per execution and the frequency of each of the statements in function *sum* (Program 1.13) have been listed. The total number of steps required by the program is determined to be $2n+3$. It is important to note that the frequency of line 3 is $n+1$ and not n. This is so because i has to be incremented to n before the **for** loop can terminate.

Table 1.2 gives the step count for function *rsum* (Program 1.14). Line 2(a) refers to the **if** conditional of line 2, and line 2(b) refers to the statement in the **if** clause. Notice

line	s/e	frequency	total steps
1	0	1	0
2	1	1	1
3	1	$n+1$	$n+1$
4	1	n	n
5	1	1	1
6	0	1	0
	Total number of steps		$2n+3$

Table 1.1: Step table for Program 1.13

that under the s/e (steps per execution) column, line 3 has been given a count of $1+t_{rsum}(n-1)$. This is the total cost of line 3 each time it is executed. It includes all the steps that get executed as a result of the invocation of *rsum* from line 3. The frequency and total steps columns have been split into two parts: one for the case $n = 0$ and the other for the case $n > 0$. This is necessary because the frequency (and hence total steps) for some statements is different for each of these cases.

line	s/e	frequency $n = 0$	frequency $n > 0$	total steps $n = 0$	total steps $n > 0$
1	0	1	1	0	0
2(a)	1	1	1	1	1
2(b)	1	1	0	1	0
3	$1+t_{rsum}(n-1)$	0	1	0	$1+t_{rsum}(n-1)$
4	0	1	1	0	0
	Total number of steps			2	$2+t_{rsum}(n-1)$

Table 1.2: Step table for Program 1.14

Table 1.3 corresponds to function *add* (Program 1.18). Once again, note that the frequency of line 2 is $m+1$ and not m. This is so as i needs to be incremented up to m before the loop can terminate. Similarly, the frequency for line 3 is $m(n+1)$. When you have obtained sufficient experience in computing step counts, you may avoid constructing the frequency table and obtain the step count as in the following example.

line	s/e	frequency	total steps
1	0	1	0
2	1	$m+1$	$m+1$
3	1	$m(n+1)$	$mn+m$
4	1	mn	mn
5	0	1	0
		Total number of steps	$2mn+2m+1$

Table 1.3: Step table for Program 1.18

Example 1.12 [*Fibonnaci numbers*]: The Fibonacci sequence of numbers starts as

$$0, 1, 1, 2, 3, 5, 8, 13, 21, 34, 55, \cdots$$

Each new term is obtained by taking the sum of the two previous terms. If we call the first term of the sequence F_0 then $F_0 = 0$, $F_1 = 1$, and in general

$$F_n = F_{n-1} + F_{n-2},\ n \geq 2.$$

The program *fibonacci* (Program 1.21) inputs any nonnegative integer n and prints the value F_n.

To analyze the time complexity of this program, we need to consider the two cases: (1) $n = 0$ or 1 and (2) $n > 1$. Line 4 will be regarded as two lines: 4(a), the conditional part, and 4(b), the **if** clause. When $n = 0$ or 1, lines 4(a) and 4(b), get executed once each. Since each line has an s/e of 1, the total step count for this case is 2. When $n > 1$, lines 4(a), 6, and 13 are each executed once. Line 7 gets executed n times, and lines 8-12 get executed $n-1$ times each (note that the last time line 7 is executed, i is incremented to $n + 1$ and the loop exited). Line 6 has an s/e of 2; the remaining lines that get executed have an s/e of 1. The total steps for the case $n > 1$ is therefore $4n + 1$. □

Summary

The time complexity of a program is given by the number of steps taken by the program to compute the function it was written for. The number of steps is itself a function of the instance characteristics. Although any specific instance may have several characteristics (e.g., the number of inputs, the number of outputs, the magnitudes of the inputs and outputs), the number of steps is computed as a function of some subset of these. Usually, we choose those characteristics that are of importance to us. For example, we might wish to know how the computing (or run) time (i.e., time complexity) increases as the number of inputs increase. In this case the number of steps will be computed as a function of the number of inputs alone. For a different program, we might be

---

```
 1   void fibonacci (int n)
 2   // compute the Fibonacci number Fn
 3   {
 4        if (n <= 1)  cout << n << endl; //F0 = 0 and F1 = 1
 5        else { // compute Fn
 6            int fn; int fnm 2 = 0; int  fnm 1 = 1;
 7            for (int i = 2; i <= n; i++)
 8            {
 9                fn = fnm 1 + fnm 2 ;
10                fnm 2 = fnm 1 ;
11                fnm 1 = fn ;
12            } // end of for
13            cout << fn << endl;
14        } // end of else
15   } // end of fibonacci
```

Program 1.21: Fibonacci numbers

interested in determining how the computing time increases as the magnitude of one of the inputs increases. In this case the number of steps will be computed as a function of the magnitude of this input alone. Thus, before the step count of a program can be determined, we need to know exactly which characteristics of the problem instance are to be used. These define the variables in the expression for the step count. In the case of *sum*, we chose to measure the time complexity as a function of the number, n, of elements being added. For function *add*, the choice of characteristics was the number, m, of rows and the number, n, of columns in the matrices being added.

Once the relevant characteristics $(n, m, p, q, r, \cdots)$ have been selected, we can define what a step is. A step is any computation unit that is independent of the characteristics $(n, m, p, q, r, \cdots)$. Thus, 10 additions can be one step; 100 multiplications can also be one step; but n additions cannot. Nor can $m/2$ additions, $p + q$ subtractions, and so on be counted as one step.

A systematic way to assign step counts was also discussed. Once this has been done, the time complexity (i.e., the total step count) of a program can be obtained using either of the two methods discussed.

The examples we have looked at so far were sufficiently simple that the time complexities were nice functions of fairly simple characteristics like the number of elements, and the number of rows and columns. For many programs, the time complexity is not dependent solely on the number of inputs or outputs or some other easily specified characteristic. Consider the function *BinarySearch* (Program 1.9). This function searches $a[0], \cdots, a[n-1]$ for x. A natural parameter with respect to which you might wish to determine the step count is the number, n, of elements to be searched. That is, we would like to know how the computing time changes as we change the number of elements n. The parameter n is inadequate. For the same n, the step count varies with the position of x in a. We can extricate ourselves from the difficulties resulting from situations wherein the chosen parameters are not adequate to determine the step count uniquely by defining three kinds of step counts: best-case, worst-case, and average.

The *best-case step count* is the minimum number of steps that can be executed for the given parameters. The *worst-case step count* is the maximum number of steps that can be executed for the given parameters. The *average step count* is the average number of steps executed on instances with the given parameters.

1.6.1.3 Asymptotic Notation (O, Ω, Θ)

Our motivation to determine step counts is to be able to compare the time complexities of two programs that compute the same function and also to predict the growth in run time as the instance characteristics change.

Determining the exact step count (either worst-case or average) of a program can prove to be an exceedingly difficult task. Expending immense effort to determine the step count exactly is not a very worthwhile endeavor, since the notion of a step is itself inexact. (Both the instructions $x = y$ and $x = y + z + (x/y) + (x*y*z-x/z)$ count as one step.) Because of the inexactness of what a step stands for, the exact step count is not very useful for comparative purposes. An exception to this is when the difference in the step counts of two programs is very large, as in $3n + 3$ versus $100n + 10$. We might feel quite safe in predicting that the program with step count $3n + 3$ will run in less time than the one with step count $100n + 10$. But even in this case, it is not necessary to know that the exact step count is $100n + 10$. Something like, ''it's about $80n$, or $85n$, or $75n$,'' is adequate to arrive at the same conclusion.

For most situations, it is adequate to be able to make a statement like $c_1 n^2 \leq t_P(n) \leq c_2 n^2$ or $t_Q(n,m) = c_1 n + c_2 m$ where c_1 and c_2 are nonnegative constants. This is so because if we have two programs with a complexity of $c_1 n^2 + c_2 n$ and $c_3 n$ respectively, then we know that the one with complexity $c_3 n$ will be faster than the one with complexity $c_1 n^2 + c_2 n$ for sufficiently large values of n. For small values of n, either program could be faster (depending on c_1, c_2, and c_3). If $c_1 = 1$, $c_2 = 2$, and $c_3 = 100$ then $c_1 n^2 + c_2 n \leq c_3 n$ for $n \leq 98$, and $c_1 n^2 + c_2 n > c_3 n$ for $n > 98$. If $c_1 = 1$, $c_2 = 2$, and $c_3 = 1000$, then $c_1 n^2 + c_2 n \leq c_3 n$ for $n \leq 998$.

No matter what the values of c_1, c_2, and c_3, there will be an n beyond which the program with complexity $c_3 n$ will be faster than the one with complexity $c_1 n^2 + c_2 n$. This value of n will be called the *break-even point*. If the break-even point is zero, then the program with complexity $c_3 n$ is always faster (or at least as fast). The exact break-even point cannot be determined analytically. The programs have to be run on a computer in order to determine the break-even point. To know that there is a break-even point, it is adequate to know that one program has complexity $c_1 n^2 + c_2 n$ and the other $c_3 n$ for some constants c_1, c_2, and c_3. There is little advantage in determining the exact values of c_1, c_2, and c_3.

With the previous discussion as motivation, we introduce some terminology that will enable us to make meaningful (but inexact) statements about the time and space complexities of a program. In the remainder of this chapter, the functions f and g are nonnegative functions.

Definition [*Big "oh"*]: $f(n) = O(g(n))$ (read as "f of n is big oh of g of n") iff (if and only if) there exist positive constants c and n_0 such that $f(n) \le cg(n)$ for all $n, n \ge n_0$. ☐

Example 1.13: $3n + 2 = O(n)$ as $3n + 2 \le 4n$ for all $n \ge 2$. $3n + 3 = O(n)$ as $3n + 3 \le 4n$ for all $n \ge 3$. $100n + 6 = O(n)$ as $100n + 6 \le 101n$ for $n \ge 10$. $10n^2 + 4n + 2 = O(n^2)$ as $10n^2 + 4n + 2 \le 11n^2$ for $n \ge 5$. $1000n^2 + 100n - 6 = O(n^2)$ as $1000n^2 + 100n - 6 \le 1001n^2$ for $n \ge 100$. $6*2^n + n^2 = O(2^n)$ as $6*2^n + n^2 \le 7*2^n$ for $n \ge 4$. $3n + 3 = O(n^2)$ as $3n + 3 \le 3n^2$ for $n \ge 2$. $10n^2 + 4n + 2 = O(n^4)$ as $10n^2 + 4n + 2 \le 10n^4$ for $n \ge 2$. $3n + 2 \ne O(1)$ as $3n + 2$ is not less than or equal to c for any constant c and all $n, n \ge n_0$. $10n^2 + 4n + 2 \ne O(n)$. ☐

We write $O(1)$ to mean a computing time that is a constant. $O(n)$ is called linear, $O(n^2)$ is called quadratic, $O(n^3)$ is called cubic, and $O(2^n)$ is called exponential. If an algorithm takes time $O(\log n)$, it is faster, for sufficiently large n, than if it had taken $O(n)$. Similarly, $O(n \log n)$ is better than $O(n^2)$ but not as good as $O(n)$. These seven computing times, $O(1)$, $O(\log n)$, $O(n)$, $O(n \log n)$, $O(n^2)$, $O(n^3)$, and $O(2^n)$ are the ones we will see most often in this book.

As illustrated by the previous example, the statement $f(n) = O(g(n))$ states only that $g(n)$ is an upper bound on the value of $f(n)$ for all $n, n \ge n_0$. It does not say anything about how good this bound is. Notice that $n = O(n^2)$, $n = O(n^{2.5})$, $n = O(n^3)$, $n = O(2^n)$, and so on. For the statement $f(n) = O(g(n))$ to be informative, $g(n)$ should be as small a function of n as one can come up with for which $f(n) = O(g(n))$. So, while we shall often say $3n + 3 = O(n)$, we shall almost never say $3n + 3 = O(n^2)$, even though this latter statement is correct.

From the definition of O, it should be clear that $f(n) = O(g(n))$ is not the same as $O(g(n)) = f(n)$. In fact, it is meaningless to say that $O(g(n)) = f(n)$. The use of the symbol "=" is unfortunate because this symbol commonly denotes the "equals" relation. Some of the confusion that results from the use of this symbol (which is standard terminology) can be avoided by reading the symbol "=" as "is" and not as "equals."

Theorem 1.2 obtains a very useful result concerning the order of $f(n)$ (i.e., the $g(n)$ in $f(n) = O(g(n))$) when $f(n)$ is a polynomial in n.

Theorem 1.2: If $f(n) = a_m n^m + \cdots + a_1 n + a_0$, then $f(n) = O(n^m)$.

Proof: $f(n) \le \sum_{i=0}^{m} |a_i| n^i$

$$\le n^m \sum_{0}^{m} |a_i| n^{i-m}$$

$$\leq n^m \sum_0^m |a_i|, \text{ for } n \geq 1$$

So, $f(n) = O(n^m)$. □

Definition: [Omega] $f(n) = \Omega(g(n))$ (read as "f of n is omega of g of n") iff there exist positive constants c and n_0 such that $f(n) \geq cg(n)$ for all n, $n \geq n_0$. □

Example 1.14: $3n + 2 = \Omega(n)$ as $3n + 2 \geq 3n$ for $n \geq 1$ (actually the inequality holds for $n \geq 0$, but the definition of Ω requires an $n_0 > 0$). $3n + 3 = \Omega(n)$ as $3n + 3 \geq 3n$ for $n \geq 1$. $100n + 6 = \Omega(n)$ as $100n + 6 \geq 100n$ for $n \geq 1$. $10n^2 + 4n + 2 = \Omega(n^2)$ as $10n^2 + 4n + 2 \geq n^2$ for $n \geq 1$. $6*2^n + n^2 = \Omega(2^n)$ as $6*2^n + n^2 \geq 2^n$ for $n \geq 1$. Observe also that $3n + 3 = \Omega(1)$; $10n^2 + 4n + 2 = \Omega(n)$; $10n^2 + 4n + 2 = \Omega(1)$; $6*2^n + n^2 = \Omega(n^{100})$; $6*2^n + n^2 = \Omega(n^{50.2})$; $6*2^n + n^2 = \Omega(n^2)$; $6*2^n + n^2 = \Omega(n)$; and $6*2^n + n^2 = \Omega(1)$. □

As in the case of the "big oh" notation, there are several functions $g(n)$ for which $f(n) = \Omega(g(n))$. The function $g(n)$ is only a lower bound on $f(n)$. For the statement $f(n) = \Omega(g(n))$ to be informative, $g(n)$ should be as large a function of n as possible for which the statement $f(n) = \Omega(g(n))$ is true. So, while we shall say that $3n + 3 = \Omega(n)$ and $6*2^n + n^2 = \Omega(2^n)$, we shall almost never say that $3n + 3 = \Omega(1)$ or $6*2^n + n^2 = \Omega(1)$, even though both of these statements are correct.

Theorem 1.3 is the analogue of Theorem 1.2 for the omega notation.

Theorem 1.3: If $f(n) = a_m n^m + \cdots + a_1 n + a_0$ and $a_m > 0$, then $f(n) = \Omega(n^m)$.

Proof: Left as an exercise. □

Definition: [Theta] $f(n) = \Theta(g(n))$ (read as "f of n is theta of g of n") iff there exist positive constants c_1, c_2, and n_0 such that $c_1 g(n) \leq f(n) \leq c_2 g(n)$ for all n, $n \geq n_0$. □

Example 1.15: $3n + 2 = \Theta(n)$ as $3n + 2 \geq 3n$ for all $n \geq 2$, and $3n + 2 \leq 4n$ for all $n \geq 2$, so $c_1 = 3$, $c_2 = 4$, and $n_0 = 2$. $3n + 3 = \Theta(n)$; $10n^2 + 4n + 2 = \Theta(n^2)$; $6*2^n + n^2 = \Theta(2^n)$; and $10*\log n + 4 = \Theta(\log n)$. $3n + 2 \neq \Theta(1)$; $3n + 3 \neq \Theta(n^2)$; $10n^2 + 4n + 2 \neq \Theta(n)$; $10n^2 + 4n + 2 \neq \Theta(1)$; $6*2^n + n^2 \neq \Theta(n^2)$; $6*2^n + n^2 \neq \Theta(n^{100})$; and $6*2^n + n^2 \neq \Theta(1)$. □

The theta notation is more precise than both the "big oh" and omega notations. $f(n) = \Theta(g(n))$ iff $g(n)$ is both an upper and lower bound on $f(n)$.

Notice that the coefficients in all of the $g(n)$'s used in the preceding three examples have been 1. This is in accordance with practice. We shall almost never find ourselves saying that $3n + 3 = O(3n)$, or that $10 = O(100)$, or that $10n^2 + 4n + 2 = \Omega(4n^2)$, or that $6*2^n + n^2 = \Omega(6*2^n)$, or that $6*2^n + n^2 = \Theta(4*2^n)$, even though each of these statements is true.

Theorem 1.4: If $f(n) = a_m n^m + \cdots + a_1 n + a_0$ and $a_m > 0$, then $f(n) = \Theta(n^m)$.

Proof: Left as an exercise. $\square$

Let us reexamine the time complexity analyses of the previous section. For function *sum* (Program 1.13) we had determined that $t_{sum}(n) = 2n + 3$. So, $t_{sum}(n) = \Theta(n)$. $t_{rsum}(n) = 2n + 2 = \Theta(n)$ and $t_{add}(m,n) = 2mn + 2n + 1 = \Theta(mn)$.

Although we might all see that the O, Ω, and Θ notations have been used correctly in the preceding paragraphs, we are still left with the question, Of what use are these notations if one has to first determine the step count exactly? The answer to this question is that the asymptotic complexity (i.e., the complexity in terms of O, Ω, and Θ) can be determined quite easily without determining the exact step count. This is usually done by first determining the asymptotic complexity of each statement (or group of statements) in the program and then adding up these complexities. Tables 1.4 through 1.6 do just this for *sum*, *rsum*, and *add* (Programs 1.13, 1.14, and 1.18).

Note that in the table for *add* (Table 1.6), lines 3 and 4 have been lumped together even though they have different frequencies. This lumping together of these two lines is possible because their frequencies are of the same order.

line(s)	s/e	frequency	total steps
1	0	–	$\Theta(0)$
2	1	1	$\Theta(1)$
3	1	$n+1$	$\Theta(n)$
4	1	n	$\Theta(n)$
5	1	1	$\Theta(1)$
6	0	–	$\Theta(0)$

$$t_{sum}(n) = \Theta(\max_{1 \le i \le 6}\{g_i(n)\}) = \Theta(n)$$

Table 1.4: Asymptotic complexity of *sum* (Program 1.13)

Although the analyses of Tables 1.4 through 1.6 are actually carried out in terms of step counts, it is correct to interpret $t_P(n) = \Theta(g(n))$, or $t_P(n) = O(g(n))$, or $t_P(n) = \Omega(g(n))$ as a statement about the computing time of program P. This is so because each step takes only $\Theta(1)$ time to execute.

After you have had some experience using the table method, you will be in a position to arrive at the asymptotic complexity of a program by taking a more global approach. We elaborate on this method in the following examples.

Example 1.16 [*Permutation generator*]: Consider function *perm* (Program 1.11). Assume that a is of size n. When $k = n-1$, we see that the time taken is $\Theta(n)$. When $k <$

line	s/e	frequency		total steps	
		$n = 0$	$n > 0$	$n = 0$	$n > 0$
1	0	−	−	0	$\Theta(0)$
2(a)	1	1	1	1	$\Theta(1)$
2(b)	1	1	0	1	$\Theta(0)$
3	$2 + t_{rsum}(n-1)$	0	1	0	$\Theta(2 + t_{rsum}(n-1))$
4	0	−	−	0	$\Theta(0)$
		$t_{rsum}(n) =$		2	$\Theta(2 + t_{rsum}(n-1))$

Table 1.5: Asymptotic complexity of *rsum* (Program 1.14)

line(s)	s/e	frequency	total steps
1	0	−	$\Theta(0)$
2	1	$\Theta(m)$	$\Theta(m)$
3,4	1	$\Theta(mn)$	$\Theta(mn)$
5	0	−	$\Theta(0)$
		$t_{add}(m,n) =$	$\Theta(mn)$

Table 1.6: Asymptotic complexity of *add* (Program 1.18)

$n-1$, the **else** clause is entered. At this time, the second **for** loop is entered $n - k$ times. Each iteration of this loop takes $\Theta(t_{perm}(k + 1, n - 1))$ time. So, $t_{perm}(k, n-1) = \Theta((n - k)(t_{perm}(k + 1, n - 1)))$ when $k < n - 1$. Using the substitution method, we obtain $t_{perm}(0, n - 1) = \Theta(n\,(n\,!)), n \geq 1$. □

Example 1.17 [*Binary search*]: Let us obtain the time complexity of function *BinarySearch* (Program 1.9). The instance characteristic that we shall use is the number n of elements in a. Each iteration of the **for** loop takes $\Theta(1)$ time. We can show that the **for** loop is iterated at most $\lceil \log_2(n +1) \rceil$ times (see the book by S. Sahni cited in the references). Since an asymptotic analysis is being performed, we do not need such an accurate count of the worst-case number of iterations. Each iteration except for the last results in a decrease in the size of the segment of a that has to be searched by a factor of about 2. So, this loop is iterated $\Theta(\log n)$ times in the worst-case. As each iteration takes $\Theta(1)$ time, the overall worst-case complexity of *BinarySearch* is $\Theta(\log n)$. Note that, if a was passed by value, the complexity of using *BinarySearch* would be more than this because it would take $\Omega(n)$ time just to invoke the function. □

Example 1.18 [*Magic square*]: Our final example is a problem from recreational mathematics. A magic square is an $n \times n$ matrix of the integers 1 to n^2 such that the sum of every row, column, and diagonal is the same. Figure 1.2 gives an example magic square for the case $n = 5$. In this example, the common sum is 65.

15	8	1	24	17
16	14	7	5	23
22	20	13	6	4
3	21	19	12	10
9	2	25	18	11

Figure 1.2: Example magic square

H. Coxeter has given the following simple rule for generating a magic square when n is odd:

Start with 1 in the middle of the top row; then go up and left, assigning numbers in increasing order to empty squares; if you fall off the square imagine the same square as tiling the plane and continue; if a square is occupied, move down instead and continue.

The magic square of Figure 1.2 was formed using this rule. Program 1.22 is the C++ program for creating an $n \times n$ magic square for the case when n is odd. This results from Coxeter's rule.

```
void magic (int n)
// create a magic square of size n, n is odd
{
    const int MaxSize = 51;// maximum square size
    int square[MaxSize][MaxSize], k, l ;

    // check correctness of n
    if ((n > (MaxSize)) || (n < 1)) {cerr << "Error!..n out of range" << endl; return;}
    else if (!(n%2)) {cerr << "Error!..n is even" << endl; return;}

    //n is odd. Coxeter's rule can be used
    for (int i = 0; i < n ; i++) // initialize square to 0
        for (int j = 0; j < n; j++)
            square[i][j] = 0;
    square[0][(n−1)/2] = 1;  // middle of first row

    // i and j are current position
    int key = 2; i = 0; int j = (n−1)/2;
    while (key <= n * n) {
    // move up and left
        if (i − 1 < 0) k = n − 1; else k = i − 1;
        if (j − 1 < 0) l = n − 1; else l = j − 1;
        if (square[k][l])  i = (i+1)%n; // square occupied, move down
        else { // square [k ][l ] is unoccupied
            i = k;
            j = l;
        }
        square[i][j] = key;
        key++;
    } // end of while

    // output the magic square
    cout << "magic square of size " << n << endl;
    for (i = 0; i < n ; i++) {
        for (j = 0; j < n; j++)
            cout << square[i][j] << " ";
        cout << endl;
    }
}
```

Program 1.22: Magic square

The magic square is represented using a two-dimensional array having n rows and n columns. For this application it is convenient to number the rows (and columns) from zero to $n - 1$ rather than from one to n. Thus, when the program "falls off the square," i and/or j are set back to zero or $n - 1$.

The **while** loop is governed by the variable *key*, which is an integer variable initialized to 2 and increased by one each time through the loop. Thus, each statement within the **while** loop will be executed no more than $n^2 - 1$ times, and the computing time for *magic* is $O(n^2)$. Since there are n^2 positions in which the algorithm must place a number, we see that $O(n^2)$ is the best bound an algorithm for the magic square problem can have. □

1.6.1.4 Practical Complexities

We have seen that the time complexity of a program is generally some function of the instance characteristics. This function is very useful in determining how the time requirements vary as the instance characteristics change. The complexity function may also be used to compare two programs P and Q that perform the same task. Assume that program P has complexity $\Theta(n)$ and program Q is of complexity $\Theta(n^2)$. We can assert that program P is faster than program Q for sufficiently large n. To see the validity of this assertion, observe that the actual computing time of P is bounded from above by cn for some constant c and for all n, $n \geq n_1$, whereas that of Q is bounded from below by dn^2 for some constant d and all n, $n \geq n_2$. Since $cn \leq dn^2$ for $n \geq c/d$, program P is faster than program Q whenever $n \geq \max\{n_1, n_2, c/d\}$.

You should always be cautiously aware of the presence of the phrase "sufficiently large" in the assertion of the preceding discussion. When deciding which of the two programs to use, we must know whether the n we are dealing with is, in fact, sufficiently large. If program P actually runs in $10^6 n$ milliseconds, whereas program Q runs in n^2 milliseconds, and if we always have $n \leq 10^6$, then, other factors being equal, program Q is the one to use.

To get a feel for how the various functions grow with n, you are advised to study Table 1.7 and Figure 1.3 very closely. It is evident from the table and the figure that the function 2^n grows very rapidly with n. In fact, if a program needs 2^n steps for execution, then when $n = 40$, the number of steps needed is approximately $1.1*10^{12}$. On a computer performing 1 billion steps per second, this would require about 18.3 minutes. If $n = 50$, the same program would run for about 13 days on this computer. When $n = 60$, about 310.56 years will be required to execute the program and when $n = 100$, about $4*10^{13}$ years will be needed. So, we may conclude that the utility of programs with exponential complexity is limited to small n (typically $n \leq 40$).

Programs that have a complexity that is a polynomial of high degree are also of limited utility. For example, if a program needs n^{10} steps, then using our 1-billion-steps-per-second computer, we will need 10 seconds when $n = 10$; 3,171 years when $n = 100$; and $3.17*10^{13}$ years when $n = 1000$. If the program's complexity had been n^3 steps

$\log n$	n	$n \log n$	n^2	n^3	2^n
0	1	0	1	1	2
1	2	2	4	8	4
2	4	8	16	64	16
3	8	24	64	512	256
4	16	64	256	4096	65,536
5	32	160	1024	32,768	4,294,967,296

Table 1.7: Function values

instead, then we would need 1 second when $n = 1000$; 110.67 minutes when $n = 10,000$; and 11.57 days when $n = 100,000$.

Table 1.8 gives the time needed by a 1-billion-steps-per-second computer to execute a program of complexity $f(n)$ instructions. You should note that currently only the fastest computers can execute about 1 billion instructions per second. From a practical standpoint, it is evident that for reasonably large n (say $n > 100$), only programs of small complexity (such as n, $n \log n$, n^2, n^3) are feasible. Further, this is the case even if one could build a computer capable of executing 10^{12} instructions per second. In this case, the computing times of Table 1.8 would decrease by a factor of 1000. Now, when $n = 100$ it would take 3.17 years to execute n^{10} instructions and $4*10^{10}$ years to execute 2^n instructions.

1.6.2 Performance Measurement

Performance measurement is concerned with obtaining the actual space and time requirements of a program. These quantities are dependent on the particular compiler and options used as well as on the specific computer on which the program is run. Unless otherwise stated, all performance values provided in this book are obtained using the Borland C++ compiler on an IBM-compatible notebook PC with an Intel '386 processor operating at 25 MHz. Default compiler options are used.

In keeping with the discussion of the preceding section, we shall not concern ourselves with the space and time needed for compilation. We justify this by the assumption that each program (after it has been fully debugged) will be compiled once and then executed several times. Certainly, the space and time needed for compilation are important during program testing, when more time is spent on this task than in actually running the compiled code.

We shall not explicitly consider measuring the run-time space requirements of a program. Rather, we shall focus on measuring the computing time of a program. To obtain the computing (or run) time of a program, we need a clocking function. We assume

Figure 1.3: Plot of function values

the existence of a function *time* (*hsec*) that returns in the variable *hsec* the current time in hundredths of a second.

Suppose we wish to measure the worst-case performance of the sequential search function (Program 1.23). Before we can do this, we need to: (1) decide on the values of *n* for which the times are to be obtained and (2) determine, for each of the above values of *n*, the data that exhibits the worst-case behavior.

The decision on which values of *n* to use is to be based on the amount of timing we wish to perform and also on what we expect to do with the times once they are obtained. Assume that for Program 1.23, our intent is simply to predict how long it will take, in the worst-case, to search for *x* given the size *n* of *a*. An asymptotic analysis reveals that this time is $\Theta(n)$. So, we expect a plot of the times to be a straight line. Theoretically, if we know the times for any two values of *n*, the straight line is determined, and we can obtain the time for all other values of *n* from this line. In practice, we need the times for more

Time for $f(n)$ instructions on a 10^9 instr/sec computer

n	n	$n\log_2 n$	n^2	n^3	n^4	n^{10}	2^n
10	.01μs	.03μs	.1μs	1μs	10μs	10s	1μs
20	.02μs	.09μs	.4μs	8μs	160μs	2.84h	1ms
30	.03μs	.15μs	.9μs	27μs	810μs	6.83d	1s
40	.04μs	.21μs	1.6μs	64μs	2.56ms	121d	18min
50	.05μs	.28μs	2.5μs	125μs	6.25ms	3.1y	13d
100	.10μs	.66μs	10μs	1ms	100ms	3171y	$4*10^{13}$ y
1,000	1μs	9.96μs	1ms	1s	16.67min	$3.17*10^{13}$ y	$32*10^{283}$ y
10,000	10μs	130.03μs	100ms	16.67min	115.7d	$3.17*10^{23}$ y	
100,000	100μs	1.66ms	10s	11.57d	3171y	$3.17*10^{33}$ y	
1,000,000	1ms	19.92ms	16.67min	31.71y	$3.17*10^7$ y	$3.17*10^{43}$ y	

Table 1.8: Times on a 1-billion-steps-per-second computer

```
line int seqsearch (int *a, const int n, const int x) // a [0], · · · ,a [n ]
 1   {
 2     int i = n; a [0] = x;
 3     while (a [i] != x)
 4       i--;
 5     return i;
 6   } // end of seqsearch
```

Program 1.23: Sequential search

than two values of n. This is so for the following reasons:

(1) Asymptotic analysis tells us the behavior only for "sufficiently large" values of n. For smaller values of n the run time may not follow the asymptotic curve. To determine the point beyond which the asymptotic curve is followed, we need to examine the times for several values of n.

(2) Even in the region where the asymptotic behavior is exhibited, the times may not lie exactly on the predicted curve (straight line in the case of Program 1.23) because of the effects of low-order terms that are discarded in the asymptotic analysis. For instance, a program with asymptotic complexity $\Theta(n)$ can have an actual complexity that is $c_1 n + c_2 \log n + c_3$, or for that matter any other function of n in which the highest-order term is $c_1 n$ for some constant, $c_1, c_1 > 0$.

It is reasonable to expect that the asymptotic behavior of Program 1.23 will begin for some n that is smaller than 100. So, for $n > 100$ we shall obtain the run time for just a few values. A reasonable choice is $n = 200, 300, 400, \cdots, 1000$. There is nothing magical about this choice of values. We can just as well use $n = 500, 1000, 1500, \cdots$, 10,000 or $n = 512, 1024, 2048, \cdots, 2^{15}$. It will cost us more in terms of computer time to use the latter choices, and we will probably not get any better information about the run time of Program 1.23 using these choices.

For n in the range [0, 100] we shall carry out a more refined measurement, since we are not quite sure where the asymptotic behavior begins. Of course, if our measurements show that the straight-line behavior does not begin in this range, we shall have to perform a more detailed measurement in the range [100, 200] and so on, until the onset of this behavior is detected. Times in the range [0, 100] will be obtained in steps of 10 beginning at $n = 0$.

It is easy to see that Program 1.23 exhibits its worst-case behavior when x is chosen such that it is not one of the $a [i]$'s. For definiteness, we shall set $a [i] = i, 1 \le i \le n$ and $x = 0$.

At this time, we envision using a program such as Program 1.24 to obtain the worst-case times.

```
void TimeSearch() {
   int a[1001], n[20];
   for (int j = 1; j <= 1000; j++) // initialize a
     a[j] = j;
   for (j = 0; j < 10; j++) {// values of n
     n[j] = 10 * j; n[j +10] = 100 * (j + 1);
   }
   cout << "  n   time" << endl;
   for(j = 0; j < 20; j++) { // obtain computing times
      long start, stop;
      time (start) ; // start timer
      int k = seqsearch(a, n[j], 0); // unsuccessful search
      time (stop) ; // stop timer
      long runTime = stop − start ;
      cout << "   " << n[j] << "   " << runTime << endl;
   }
   cout << "Times are in hundredths of a second." << endl ;
}
```

Program 1.24: Program to time Program 1.23

The output obtained from this program is summarized in Figure 1.4. All the times are zero, indicating that the precision of our clock is inadequate.

To time a short event, it is necessary to repeat it several times and divide the total time for the event by the number of repetitions.

Since our clock has an accuracy of about one-hundredth of a second, we should not attempt to time any single event that takes less than about 1 second. With an event time of at least 1 second, we can expect our observed times to be accurate to 1 percent.

The body of Program 1.24 needs to be changed to that of Program 1.25. In this program, $r[j]$ is the number of times the search is to be repeated when the number of elements in the array is $n[j]$. Notice that rearranging the timing statements as in Programs Program 1.26 or Program 1.27 does not produce the desired results. For instance, from the data of Figure 1.4, we expect that with the structure of Program 1.26, the value output will still be 0 because in each iteration of the **for** loop, 0 gets added to *total*. With the structure of Program 1.27, we expect the program never to exit the **for** loop. Yet another alternative is to move the first call to *time* out of the **for** loop of Program 1.27 and change the assignment to *total* within the **for** loop to

$$\textbf{long } total = stop - start;$$

This approach can be expected to yield satisfactory times. This approach cannot be used

n	time	n	time
0	0	100	0
10	0	200	0
20	0	300	0
30	0	400	0
40	0	500	0
50	0	600	0
60	0	700	0
70	0	800	0
80	0	900	0
90	0	1000	0

Times in hundredths of a second

Figure 1.4: Output from Program 1.24

when the timing function available gives us only the time since the last invocation of *time*. Another difficulty is that the measured time includes the time needed to read the clock. For small n, this time may be larger than the time to run *seqsearch*. This difficulty can be overcome by determining the time taken by the timing function and subtracting this time later. In further discussion, we shall use the explicit repetition factor technique.

The output from the timing program, Program 1.25, is given in Figure 1.5. The times for n in the range [0, 100] are plotted in Figure 1.6. The remaining values have not been plotted because this would lead to severe compression of the range [0, 100]. The linear dependence of the worst-case time on n is apparent from this graph.

The graph of Figure 1.6 can be used to predict the run time for other values of n. For example, we expect that when $n = 24$, the worst-case search time will be 0.0031 hundredths of a second. We can go one step further and get the equation of the straight line. The equation of this line is $t = c + mn$, where m is the slope and c the value for $n = 0$. From the graph, we see that $c = 0.0008$. Using the point $n = 60$ and $t = 0.0066$, we obtain $m = (t-c)/n = 0.0058/60 = 0.000096$. So, the line of Figure 1.6 has the equation $t = 0.0008 + 0.000096n$, where t is the time in hundredths of a second. From this, we expect that when $n = 1000$, the worst-case search time will be 0.0975 hsec, and when $n = 500$, it will be 0.0491 hsec. Compared with the actual observed times of Figure 1.5, we see that these figures are very accurate!

An alternate approach to obtain a good straight line for the data of Figure 1.5 is to obtain the straight line that is the least-squares approximation to the data. The result is $t = 0.00085454 + 0.00009564n$. When $n = 1000$ and 500, this equation yields $t = 0.0966$ and 0.0487.

Now, we are probably ready to pat ourselves on the back for a job well done. However, this action is somewhat premature, since our experiment is flawed. First, the

```
void TimeSearch() {
   int a[1001], n[20];
    const long r[20] = {300000, 300000, 200000, 200000, 100000, 100000,
   100000, 80000, 80000, 50000, 50000, 25000, 15000, 15000, 10000, 7500, 7000,
   6000, 5000, 5000};

   for (int j = 1; j <= 1000; j++) // initialize a
      a[j] = j;

   for (j = 0; j < 10; j++) {// values of n
      n[j] = 10 * j ; n[j+10] = 100 * (j+1);
   }

   cout << "  n   totalTime   runTime" << endl;

   for(j = 0; j < 20; j++) { // obtain computing times
      long start, stop ;
      time (start); // start timer
      for (long b = 1; b <= r[j]; b++)
          int k = seqsearch(a, n[j], 0); // unsuccessful search
      time (stop) ; // stop timer
      long totalTime = stop - start ;
      float runTime = (float) (totalTime)/(float)(r[j]) ;
      cout << "  " << n[j] << "  " << totalTime << "  " << runTime << endl;
   }
   cout << "Times are in hundredths of a second." << endl;
}
```

Program 1.25: Timing program

measured time includes the time taken by the repetition **for** loop. So, the times of Figure 1.5 are excessive. This can be corrected by determining the time for each iteration of this statement. A quick test run indicates that 300,000 executions take only 50 hundredths of a second. So, subtracting the time for the **for** $(b = 1; b <= r[j]; b++)$ statement reduces the reported times by only 0.000016. We can ignore this difference, since the use of a higher repetition factor could well result in measured times that are lower by about 0.000016 hsec per search.

```
long total = 0;
for (long b = 1; b <= r[j]; b++)
{
    time (start);
    k = seqsearch (a, n[j], 0);
    time(stop);
    total += stop − start;
}
float runTime = (float) (total) / (float) (r[j]);
```

Program 1.26: Improper timing construct

```
for(long total = 0, i = 0; total < DesiredTime; i++)
{
    time (start);
    k = seqsearch (a,n[j],0);
    time (stop);
    total += stop − start;
}
float runTime = (float) (total) / (float) (i);
```

Program 1.27: Another improper timing construct

Summary

To obtain the run time of a program, we need to plan the experiment. The following issues need to be addressed during the planning stage:

(1)   What is the accuracy of the clock? How accurate do our results have to be? Once the desired accuracy is known, we can determine the length of the shortest event that should be timed.

(2)   For each instance size, a repetition factor needs to be determined. This is to be chosen such that the event time is at least the minimum time that can be clocked with the desired accuracy.

(3)   Are we measuring worst-case or average performance? Suitable test data need to be generated.

(4)   What is the purpose of the experiment? Are the times being obtained for comparative purposes, or are they to be used to predict actual run times? If the latter is the case, then contributions to the run time from such sources as the repetition loop

n	total	runTime	n	total	runTime
0	241	0.0008	100	527	0.0105
10	533	0.0018	200	505	0.0202
20	582	0.0029	300	451	0.0301
30	736	0.0037	400	593	0.0395
40	467	0.0047	500	494	0.0494
50	565	0.0056	600	439	0.0585
60	659	0.0066	700	484	0.0691
70	604	0.0075	800	467	0.0778
80	681	0.0085	900	434	0.0868
90	472	0.0094	1000	484	0.0968

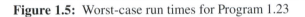

Times in hundredths of a second

Figure 1.5: Worst-case run times for Program 1.23

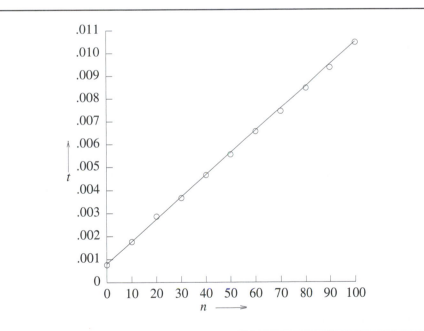

Figure 1.6: Plot of the data in Figure 1.5

and data generation need to be subtracted (in case they are included in the measured time). If the former is the case, then these times need not be subtracted (provided they are the same for all programs being compared).

(5)   In case the times are to be used to predict actual run times, then we need to fit a curve through the points. For this, the asymptotic complexity should be known. If the asymptotic complexity is linear, then a least-squares straight line can be fit; if it is quadratic, then a parabola is to be used (i.e., $t = a_0 + a_1 n + a_2 n^2$). If the complexity is $\Theta(n \log n)$, then a least-squares curve of the form $t = a_0 + a_1 n + a_2 n \log_2 n$ can be fit. When obtaining the least-squares approximation, one should discard data corresponding to "small" values of n, since the program does not exhibit its asymptotic behavior for these n.

1.6.3   Generating Test Data

Generating a data set that results in the worst-case performance of a program is not always easy. In some cases, it is necessary to use a computer program to generate the worst-case data. In other cases, even this is very difficult. In these cases, another approach to estimating worst-case performance is taken. For each set of values of the instance characteristics of interest, we generate a suitably large number of random test data. The run times for these test data are obtained. The maximum of these times is used as an estimate of the worst-case time for this set of values of the instance characteristics.

To measure average-case times, it is usually not possible to average over all possible instances of a given characteristic. Although it is possible to do this for sequential and binary search, it is not possible for a sort program. If we assume that all keys are distinct, then for any given n, $n!$ different permutations need to be used to obtain the average time. Obtaining average-case data is usually much harder than obtaining worst-case data. So, we often adopt the strategy outlined above and simply obtain an estimate of the average time.

Whether we are estimating worst-case or average time using random data, the number of instances that we can try is generally much smaller than the total number of such instances. Hence, it is desirable to analyze the algorithm being tested to determine classes of data that should be generated for the experiment. This is a very algorithm-specific task, and we shall not discuss it here.

EXERCISES

1.   Compare the two functions n^2 and $2^n/4$ for various values of n. Determine when the second becomes larger than the first.

2.   Prove by induction:

(a) $\displaystyle\sum_{1 \le i \le n} i = n(n+1)/2, \; n \ge 1$

(b) $\displaystyle\sum_{1 \le i \le n} i^2 = n(n+1)(2n+1)/6, \; n \ge 1$

(c) $\sum_{0 \le i \le n} x^i = (x^{n+1} - 1)/(x - 1), \ x \ne 1, \ n \ge 0$

3. Determine the frequency counts for all statements in the following two program segments:

```
1 for (i = 1; i <= n; i++)
2    for (j = 1; j <= i; j++)
3       for (k = 1; k <= j; k++)
4          x++;
```

```
1 i = 1;
2 while (i ≤ n)
3 {
4    x++;
5    i++;
6 }
```

(a)   (b)

4. (a) Introduce statements to increment *count* at all appropriate points in Program 1.28.

```
void d(ArrayElement *x, int n)
{
   int i = 1;
   do {
      x[i] += 2;
      i += 2;
   }
   while (i <= n);
   i = 1;
   while (i <= (n /2))
   {
      x[i] += x[i +1];
      i++;
   }
} // end of d
```

Program 1.28: Example program

(b) Simplify the resulting program by eliminating statements. The simplified program should compute the same value for *count* as computed by the program of (a).

(c) What is the exact value of *count* when the program terminates? You may assume that the initial value of *count* is 0.

(d) Obtain the step count for Program 1.28 using the frequency method. Clearly show the step count table.

5. Do Exercise 4 for function *transpose* (Program 1.29).

```
1  void transpose(matrix a; int n)
2  {
3    for (int i = 0; i < n−1; i++)
4      for (int j = i+1; j < n; j++)
5      {
6        MatrixElement t = a [i ][j ]; a [i ][j ] = a [j ][i ]; a [j ][i ] = t;
7      }
8  } // end of transpose
```

Program 1.29: Matrix transpose

6. Do Exercise 4 for Program 1.30. This program multiplies two $n \times n$ matrices a and b.

```
void mult( matrix a, matrix b, matrix c, int n)
{
  for (int i = 0; i < n ; i++)
    for (int j = 0; j < n ; j++)
    {
      c [i ][j ] = 0;
      for (int k = 0; k < n ; k++)
        c [i ][j ] += a [i ][k ] * b [k ][j ];
    }
} // end of mult
```

Program 1.30: Matrix multiplication

7. (a) Do Exercise 4 for Program 1.31. This program multiplies two matrices a and b where a is an $m \times n$ matrix and b is an $n \times p$ matrix.

   (b) Under what conditions will it be profitable to interchange the two outermost **for** loops?

8. Show that the following equalities are correct:

   (a) $5n^2 - 6n = \Theta(n^2)$

   (b) $n! = O(n^n)$

   (c) $2n^2 2^n + n\log n = \Theta(n^2 2^n)$

   (d) $\sum_{i=0}^{n} i^2 = \Theta(n^3)$

```
void prod(matrix a, matrix b, matrix c, int m, int n, int p)
{
   for (int i = 0; i < m ; i++)
      for (int j = 0; j < p ; j++)
      {
         c [i ][j ] = 0;
         for (int k = 0; k < n ; k++)
            c [i ][j ] += a [i ][k ] * b [k ][j ];
      }
} // end of prod
```

Program 1.31: Matrix multiplication

(e) $\sum_{i=0}^{n} i^3 = \Theta(n^4)$

(f) $n^{2^n} + 6*2^n = \Theta(2^{2^n})$

(g) $n^3 + 10^6 n^2 = \Theta(n^3)$

(h) $6n^3/(\log n + 1) = O(n^3)$

(i) $n^{1.001} + n\log n = \Theta(n^{1.001})$

(j) $n^{k+\varepsilon} + n^k \log n = \Theta(n^{k+\varepsilon})$ for all k and ε, $k \geq 0$, and $\varepsilon > 0$

(k) $10n^3 + 15n^4 + 100n^2 2^n = O(100n^2 2^n)$

(l) $33n^3 + 4n^2 = \Omega(n^2)$

(m) $33n^3 + 4n^2 = \Omega(n^3)$

9. Show that the following equalities are incorrect:

(a) $10n^2+9 = O(n)$

(b) $n^2 \log n = \Theta(n^2)$

(c) $n^2/\log n = \Theta(n^2)$

(d) $n^3 2^n + 6n^2 3^n = O(n^3 2^n)$

10. Obtain the average run time of function *BinarySearch* (Program 1.9). Do this for suitable values of n in the range $[0, 100]$. Your report must include a plan for the experiment as well as the measured times. These times are to be provided both in a table and as a graph.

11. Analyze the computing time of function *sort* (Program 1.6).

12. Obtain worst-case run times for function *sort* (Program 1.6). Do this for suitable values of n in the range [0, 100]. Your report must include a plan for the experiment as well as the measured times. These times are to be provided both in a table and as a graph.

13. Consider function *add* (Program 1.18).

    (a) Obtain run times for $n = 1, 10, 20, \cdots, 100$.

    (b) Plot the times obtained in part (a).

14. Do the previous exercise for matrix multiplication (Program 1.31).

15. A complex-valued matrix X is represented by a pair of matrices (A,B) where A and B contain real values. Write a program that computes the product of two complex-valued matrices (A,B) and (C,D), where $(A,B) * (C,D) = (A + iB) * (C + iD) = (AC - BD) + i(AD + BC)$. Determine the number of additions and multiplications if the matrices are all $n \times n$.

1.7 REFERENCES AND SELECTED READINGS

For a discussion of programming techniques and how to develop programs, see *The Science of Programming*, by D. Gries, Springer Verlag, New York, NY, 1981; *A Discipline of Programming*, by E. W. Dijkstra, Prentice-Hall, Englewood Cliffs, NJ, 1976; and *The Elements of Programming Style*, Second Edition, by B. W. Kernighan and P. J. Plauger, McGraw Hill, New York, NY, 1978.

A good discussion of tools and functions for developing very large software systems appears in the texts *Practical Strategies for Developing Very Large Software Systems*, by E. Horowitz, Addison-Wesley, Reading, MA, 1975, *The Mythical Man-Month*, by F. Brooks, Addison-Wesley, Reading, MA, 1979, and *Software engineering*, Third Edition, by I. Sommerville, Addison-Wesley, Wokingham, England, 1989.

For a further discussion of abstract data types see *Abstraction and Specification in Program Development*, by B. Liskov and J. Guttag, MIT Press, Cambridge, MA, 1988; *Algorithms and Data Structures*, by J. Kingston, Addison-Wesley, Reading, MA, 1990, and *Data Structures with Abstract Data Types and Pascal*, by D. Stubbs and N. Webre, Brooks/Cole Publishing Co., Monterey, CA, 1985.

Writing a correct version of binary search is discussed in the papers ''Programming pearls: Writing correct programs,'' by J. Bentley, *CACM*, 26, 1983, pp. 1040-1045; and ''Some lessons drawn from the history of the binary search algorithm,'' by R. Levisse, *The Computer Journal*, 26, 1983, pp. 154-163.

For a general discussion of permutation generation, see the paper ''Permutation generation methods,'' by R. Sedgewick, *Computer Surveys*, 9, 1977, pp. 137-164.

For a more detailed discussion of performance analysis and measurement, see *Software Development in Pascal*, Third Edition, by S. Sahni, NSPAN Printing and Publishing, Gainesville, FL, 1993.

For a discussion on the object-oriented paradigm, see *Object Oriented Design with Applications*, by Grady Booch; for a definition of objects, see the paper "Object-Oriented Programming: Themes and Variations, " by M. Stefik and D. Bobrow, *AI Magazine*, vol. 6(4), p. 41; for a definition of object-oriented languages, see the paper "On Understanding Types, Data Abstraction, and Polymorphism, " by L. Cardelli and P. Wegner, *ACM Computing Surveys*, vol 17 (4), p. 481.

For a detailed description of the C++ language, see *C++ Primer*, 2nd Edition, by Stanley B. Lippman, Addison-Wesley, Reading, MA, 1991; *The C++ Programming Language*, 2nd Edition, by Bjarne Stroustrup, Addison-Wesley, Reading, MA, 1991; and *The Annotated C++ Reference Manual*, by Margaret Ellis and Bjarne Stroustrup, Addison-Wesley, Reading, MA, 1990.

For advanced C++ programming techniques, see *Effective C++*, by Scott Meyers, Addison-Wesley, Reading, MA, 1992; *C++ Strategies and Tactics*, by Robert Murray, Addison-Wesley, Reading, MA, 1992; *Elements of C++ Programming Style*, by Tom Cargill, Addison-Wesley, Reading, MA, 1992; and *Advanced C++ Programming Styles and Idioms*, by James Coplien, Addison-Wesley, Reading, MA, 1992.

CHAPTER 2

ARRAYS

2.1 ABSTRACT DATA TYPES AND THE C++ CLASS

2.1.1 An Introduction to the C++ Class

Unlike Pascal and C, C++ provides an explicit mechanism, the *class*, to support the distinction between specification and implementation and to hide the implementation of an ADT from its users. However, it is the programmer's responsibility to use the class mechanism judiciously so that it does, in fact, represent an ADT. The C++ class consists of four components (Program 2.1):

(1) A class name: (e.g. *Rectangle*).

(2) Data members: the data that makes up the class (e.g. $x1$, $y1$, h, and w).

(3) Member functions: the set of operations that may be applied to the objects of a class (e.g. *GetHeight*(), *GetWidth*()).

(4) Levels of program access: these control the level of access to data members and member functions from program code that is outside the class. There are three levels of access to class members: public, protected, and private.

Any **public** data member (member function) can be accessed (invoked) from anywhere in the program. A **private** data member (member function) can only be accessed (invoked) from within its class or by a function or a class that is declared to be a **friend**. A **protected** data member (member function) can only be accessed (invoked) from within its class or from its subclasses or by a **friend**. We will discuss subclasses when we study inheritance in Chapter 3.

```
#ifndef RECTANGLE_H
#define RECTANGLE_H
// In the header file Rectangle.h
class Rectangle {
public:         //  the following members are public
   // The next four members are member functions
   Rectangle();      // constructor
   ~Rectangle();     // destructor
   int GetHeight();  // returns the height of the rectangle
   int GetWidth();   // returns the width of the rectangle
private:          // the following members are private
   // the following members are data members
   int x1, y1, h, w;
   // (x1, y1) are the coordinates of the bottom left corner of the rectangle
   // w is the width of the rectangle; h is the height of the rectangle
};
#endif
```

Program 2.1: Definition of the C++ class *Rectangle*

2.1.2   Data Abstraction and Encapsulation in C++

Data encapsulation is enforced in C++ by declaring all data members of a class to be **private** (or **protected**). External access to data members, if required, can be achieved by defining member functions that get and set data members. In Program 2.1, *GetHeight*() and *GetWidth*() are used to access the private data members *h* and *w*. Member functions that will be invoked externally are declared **public**; all others are declared **private** or **protected**.

Next, we discuss how the specification of the operations of a class is separated from their implementation in C++. The specification, which must be contained inside the public portion of the class definition of the ADT, consists of the names of every public member function, the type of its arguments, and the type of its result (This information about a function is known as its *function prototype*). There should also be a description of what the function does, which does not refer to the internal representation or implementation details. This requirement is quite important because it implies that an abstract data type is *implementation-independent*. This description may be achieved in C++ by using comments to describe what each member function does (like the VCR instruction manual mentioned in Chapter 1). Finally, the specification of an operation is physically separated from its implementation by placing it in an appropriately named header file (e.g. the contents of Program 2.1 are placed in *Rectangle.h*). The implementations of the functions are typically placed in a source file of the same name (e.g. the contents of Program 2.2 are placed in *Rectangle.C*). Note that C++ syntax does allow you to include the implementation of a member function inside its class definition. In this case, the function is treated as an *inline* function.

```
// In the source file Rectangle.C
#include "Rectangle.h"

// The prefix "Rectangle::" identifies GetHeight() and GetWidth() as member functions
// belonging to class Rectangle. It is required because the member functions
// are implemented outside their class definition

int Rectangle::GetHeight() { return h;}
int Rectangle::GetWidth() { return w;}
```

Program 2.2: Implementation of operations on *Rectangle*

2.1.3 Declaring Class Objects and Invoking Member Functions

Program 2.3 shows a fragment of code that illustrates how class objects are declared and how member functions that operate on these class objects are invoked. Class objects are declared and created in the same way that variables are declared or created. Members of an object are accessed or invoked by using the component selection operators, a dot (.) for direct component selection and an arrow (->), which we will write as →, for indirect component selection through a pointer.

2.1.4 Special Class Operations

Constructors and Destructors: The *constructor* and *destructor* are special member functions of a class. A constructor is a member function which initializes data members of an object. If a constructor is provided for a class, it is automatically executed when an object of that class is created. If a constructor is not defined for a class, memory is allo-

```
// In a source file main.C
#include <iostream.h>
#include "Rectangle.h"

main() {
    Rectangle r, s;     // r and s are objects of class Rectangle
    Rectangle *t = &s;  // t is a pointer to class object s
    .
    .
    .
    // use · to access members of class objects.
    // use → to access members of class objects through pointers.
    if (r.GetHeight () * r.GetWidth () > t →GetHeight () * t →GetWidth ())
        cout << " r ";
    else cout << " s ";
    cout << "has the greater area" << endl;
}
```

Program 2.3: A C++ code fragment demonstrating how *Rectangle* objects are declared and member functions invoked

cated for the data members of a class object, when it is created, but the data members are not initialized. The advantage of defining constructors for a class is that all class objects are well-defined as soon as they are created. This eliminates errors that result from accessing an undefined object. A destructor is a member function which deletes data members immediately before the object disappears. A constructor and destructor for **class** *Rectangle* are declared in Program 2.1.

A constructor must be declared as a public member function of its class; The name of a constructor must be identical to the name of the class to which it belongs; and a constructor must not specify a return type or return a value. Program 2.4 shows a constructor definition for **class** *Rectangle*.

```
Rectangle::Rectangle( int x, int y, int height, int width)
{
    x1 = x ; y1 = y ;
    h = height ; w = width ;
}
```

Program 2.4: Definition of a constructor for *Rectangle*

Constructors may be used to initialize *Rectangle* objects as follows:

Rectangle r (1, 3, 6, 6) ;
*Rectangle *s* = **new** *Rectangle* (0, 0, 3, 4) ;

These create *r*, a square of side 6 whose bottom left corner is at (1, 3); and *s*, a pointer to a *Rectangle* object of height 3 and width 4 whose bottom left corner is at the origin. Note that the declaration

Rectangle t ;

will result in a compile time error. The reason is that the compiler requires a *default constructor* (a constructor with no arguments) to initialize *t*. Had we not defined the constructor of Program 2.4, the compiler would have generated its own default constructor. However, since we have defined a constructor, it is our responsibility to provide a default constructor if we wish to use the above declaration. Program 2.5 shows a definition of the *Rectangle* constructor that also serves as a default constructor. This is achieved by providing a default value for each argument in the argument list. In this case, the default for each argument is the integer 0. If this constructor is used, the above declaration for object *t* will result in the creation of a *Rectangle* object, all of whose data members are initialized to 0.

Rectangle::*Rectangle*(**int** *x* = 0, **int** *y* = 0, **int** *height* = 0, **int** *width* = 0)
: *x*1 (*x*), *y*1 (*y*), *h* (*height*), *w* (*width*)
{ }

Program 2.5: Sophisticated definition of a constructor for *Rectangle*

The constructor of Program 2.5 also differs from that of Program 2.4 in another respect: its body is empty; the data members are initialized by using a member initialization list (consisting of a colon followed by a list of data members and the arguments to which they are to be initialized in parentheses). Program 2.4 first initializes the data members and then assigns arguments to them in two separate steps, while Program 2.5 directly initializes the data members to the corresponding arguments in a single step. Thus, the latter approach results in a more efficient constructor.

Destructors are automatically invoked when a class object goes out of scope or when a class object is deleted. Like a constructor, a destructor must be declared as a public member of its class; Its name must be identical to the name of its class prefixed with a tilde, ˜; a destructor must not specify a return type or return a value, and a destructor may not take arguments. If a destructor is not defined for a class, the deletion of an object of that class results in the freeing of memory associated with data members of the class. If a data member is a pointer to some other object, the space allocated to the pointer is returned, but the object that it was pointing to is not deleted. If we also wish to delete this object, we must define a destructor that explicitly does so.

Operator Overloading: Consider the operator == which is used to check for equality between two data items. The operator == may be used to check for equality between two **float** data items; it can also be used to check for equality between two **int** items. The hardware algorithms implementing operator == depend on the type of the operands being compared; that is, the algorithm for comparing two **float**s is different from the one used to compare two **int**s. This is an example of *operator overloading*. However, if we were to try to use operator == to check for equality between two *Rectangle* objects, the compiler would complain that operator == is not defined for *Rectangle* objects. C++ allows the programmer to overload operators for user-defined data types. This is done by providing a definition that implements the operator for the particular data type. This definition takes the form of a class member function or an ordinary function, depending on the operator. The function prototype used must adhere to the specifications for the particular operator. For details about the specifications for various operators, see one of the introductory texts listed at the end of this chapter.

Program 2.6 overloads operator == for **class** *Rectangle*. Our program uses the **this** pointer which we describe briefly: The C++ keyword **this**, when used inside a member function of a class, represents a pointer to the particular class object that invoked it. The class object, itself, is therefore represented by *this.

```
int Rectangle::operator== (const Rectangle& s)
{
    if (this == &s) return 1 ;
    if ((x1 == s.x1) && (y1 == s.y1) && (h == s.h) && (w == s.w) ) return 1 ;
    else return 0 ;
}
```

Program 2.6: Overloading **operator**== for **class** *Rectangle*

We can now use the operator == to determine whether two rectangles are identical. Our program first evaluates the expression "**this** == &*s*". This expression checks to see if the two rectangles being compared are the same object. This would happen in the following two cases:

if (*r* == *r*) · · ·

Rectangle& *u* = *r* ;
if (*r* == *u*) · · ·

In both cases, the expression "**this** == &*s*" evaluates to 1 because both operands represent the same object, and there is no need to compare the individual data members of the two rectangles. This is especially efficient if the class contains a large number of data members. If the expression evaluates to 0, then the two rectangles are not the same object, and the individual data members must be compared. Program 2.7 overloads operator << so that *Rectangle* objects can be output by using **cout**.

```
ostream& operator<< (ostream& os, Rectangle& r)
{
    os << "Position is: "<< r.x1 << " " ;
    os << r.y1 << endl ;
    os << "Height is: " << r.h << endl ;
    os << "Width is: " << r.w << endl ;
    return os ;
}
```

Program 2.7: Overloading **operator**<< for **class** *Rectangle*

Notice that **operator**<< accesses private data members of **class** *Rectangle*. Therefore, it must be made a **friend** of *Rectangle*. In general, we want to minimize the number of **friend** declarations in a class because a **friend** represents an exception to the data encapsulation principle. However, there are instances, such as this, when they are necessary. The statement:

cout << *r* ;

where *r* is defined as a square of side 6 with bottom left corner at (1, 3), will print the following:

Position is: 1 3
Height is: 6
Width is: 6

2.1.5   Miscellaneous Topics

In C++, a **struct** is identical to a **class**, except that the default level of access is public; that is, if the **struct** definition of a data type does not specify whether a given member (data or function) has **public**, **private**, or **protected** access, then the member has **public** access. In a class, the default is **private** access. Thus, the C++ **struct** is a generalization of the C **struct**.

A **union** is a structure that reserves storage for the largest of its data members so that only one of its data members can be stored, at any time. This is useful in applications where it is known that only one of many possible data items, each of a different type, needs to be stored in a structure; but there is no way to know what that data type is until runtime. The **struct** or **class** structures reserve memory for all their data members. Thus, using a **union** results in a more memory-efficient program, in these cases. We will use **union** in Chapter 4 on linked lists; we will also study a technique for improving on **union** by using inheritance.

A **static** class data member may be thought of as a global variable for its class. From the perspective of a class member function, a static data member is like any other data member. One difference is that each class object does not have its own exclusive copy. There is only one copy of a static data member and all class objects must share it. A second difference is that the declaration of a static data member in its class does not constitute a definition. Consequently, a definition of the data member is required somewhere else in the program. We will see an example of a static class member later in this chapter, when we implement the *Polynomial* data type.

2.1.6   ADTs and C++ classes

Example 2.1 [*Abstract data type NaturalNumber*]: ADT 1.2 contains the class definition of *NaturalNumber*. It is assumed that the *Boolean* type has already been defined elsewhere.

You will notice that the class definition of *NaturalNumber* in ADT 1.2 is very similar to the ADT definition of ADT 1.1. As a result, we will henceforth use the C++ class to define an ADT instead of the notation of ADT 1.1. Note that there is one significant aspect in which the format of ADT 1.1 differs from the C++ class: some operators in C++ such as **operator<<**, when overloaded for user-defined ADTs, do not exist as member functions of the corresponding class. Rather, these operators exist as ordinary C++ functions. Thus, these operations are declared outside the C++ class definition of the ADT even though they are actually part of the ADT.

---

class *NaturalNumber* {
// An ordered subrange of the integers starting at zero and ending at
// the maximum integer (MAXINT) on the computer
public:
  NaturalNumber Zero( );
  // returns 0

  Boolean IsZero( );
  // if *this is 0, return TRUE; otherwise, return FALSE

  NaturalNumber Add(*NaturalNumber y*);
  // return the smaller of *this + y and MAXINT;

  Boolean Equal(*NaturalNumber y*);
  // return TRUE if *this == y; otherwise return FALSE

  NaturalNumber Successor( );
  // if *this is MAXINT return MAXINT; otherwise return *this + 1

  NaturalNumber Subtract(*NaturalNumber y*);
  // if *this < y, return 0; otherwise return *this − y
};

ADT 1.2: Abstract data type *NaturalNumber*

EXERCISES

1. Overload **operator<** for **class** *Rectangle* such that $r < s$ if and only if the area of r is less than that of s.

2. Implement a class *Complex* which represents the Complex Number data type. Implement the following operations:

   (a) A constructor (including a default constructor which creates the complex number $0 + 0i$).

   (b) Overload **operator+** to add two complex numbers.

   (c) Overload **operator*** to multiply two complex numbers.

   (d) Overload << and >> to print and read complex numbers. To do this, you will need to decide what you want your input and output format to look like.

   Write a program according to the following specifications: use the constructor to define two complex numbers: $3 + 2i$ and $0 + 0i$. Input two complex numbers $5 + 3i$

and $0 + 0i$ using cin. Obtain the sum and product of all four complex numbers using operators $+$ and $*$, respectively. Print the results using cout.

3. Implement a **class** *Quadratic* that represents 2-degree polynomials i.e., polynomials of type ax^2+bx+c. Your class will require three data members corresponding to a, b, and c. Implement the following operations:

   (a) A constructor (including a default constructor which creates the 0 polynomial).

   (b) Overload **operator+** to add two polynomials of degree 2.

   (c) Overload $<<$ and $>>$ to print and read polynomials. To do this, you will need to decide what you want your input and output format to look like.

   (d) A function *eval* that computes the value of a polynomial for a given value of x.

   (e) A function that computes the two solutions of the equation $ax^2+bx+c = 0$. [**Hint**: use **class** *Complex* from the previous exercise.]

2.2 THE ARRAY AS AN ABSTRACT DATA TYPE

We begin our discussion by considering an array as an ADT. This is not the usual perspective, since many programmers view an array only as a consecutive set of memory locations. This is unfortunate because it clearly shows an emphasis on implementation issues. Although an array is usually implemented as a consecutive set of memory locations, this is not always the case. Intuitively, an array is a set of pairs, *<index, value>*, such that each index that is defined has a value associated with it. In mathematical terms, we call this a *correspondence* or a *mapping*. However, when considering an ADT, we are more concerned with the operations that can be performed on an array. Aside from creating a new array, most languages provide only two standard operations for arrays, one that retrieves a value and one that stores a value. ADT 2.1 shows a class definition of the array ADT.

The constructor *GeneralArray*(**int** *j*, *RangeList list*, **float** *initValue* = defaultValue) produces a new array of the appropriate size and type. All of the items are initially set to the floating point variable *initValue*. *Retrieve* accepts an *index* and returns the value associated with the index if the index is valid or an error if the index is invalid. *Store* accepts an *index*, and a value of type float, and replaces the *<index, oldvalue>* pair with the *<index, newvalue>* pair. The advantage of this ADT definition is that it clearly points out the fact that the array is a more general structure than ''a consecutive set of memory locations.''

GeneralArray is also more general than the C++ array as it is more flexible about the composition of the index set. The C++ array requires the index set to be a set of consecutive integers starting at 0. Also, C++ does not check an array index to ensure that it belongs to the range for which the array is defined. Because of these disadvantages, it is often beneficial to define a more general and robust array class. Some of the member functions required to implement such a class are examined in the exercises. A general ar-

---

class *GeneralArray* {
// **objects**: A set of pairs *<index, value>* where for each value of *index* in *IndexSet* there
// is a *value* of type **float** . *IndexSet* is a finite ordered set of one or more
// dimensions, for example, {0, $\cdots$, $n-1$} for one dimension,
// {(0, 0), (0, 1), (0, 2), (1, 0), (1, 1), (1, 2), (2, 0), (2, 1), (2, 2)} for two dimensions, etc.
public:
    GeneralArray(**int** *j*, *RangeList list*,**float** *initValue* = defaultValue)**;**
    // The constructor *GeneralArray* creates a *j* dimensional array of floats; the range
    // of the *k*th dimension is given by the *k*th element of *list*. For each index *i* in the
    // index set, insert *<i, initValue>* into the array.

    float *Retrieve*(*index i*)**;**
    // **if** (*i* is in the *index* set of the array) **return** the float associated with *i*
    // in the array; **else** signal an error.

    void *Store*(*index i*, **float** *x*);
    // **if** (*i* is in the index set of the array) delete any pair of the form *<i, y>* present
    // in the array and insert the new pair *<i, x>*; **else** signal an error.
}; // end of *GeneralArray*

ADT 2.1: Abstract data type *GeneralArray*

ray class would typically be internally implemented by using the C++ array. To do this, it is necessary to be able to map a position in the general array onto a position in the C++ array. This is discussed in Section 2.5.

    To simplify the discussion, we will hereafter use the C++ array. Therefore, before continuing, let us briefly review the C++ array. A C++ array *example* of **float**s with index set ranging from 0 to $n-1$ is defined by:
float *example*[*n*] **;**
    The *i*th element of *example* may be accessed in two ways: *example*[*i*] and *(example + i*). In the latter mechanism, the variable *example* is actually a pointer to the zeroth element of the array. The expression *example* + *i* is a pointer to the *i*th element of array *example*; it follows that *(example* + *i*) is the *i*th element of array *example*.

EXERCISES

1.   Implement a class *CppArray* which is identical to a one-dimensional C++ array (i.e., the index set is a set of consecutive integers starting at 0) except for the following:

    (i)   It performs range checking.

    (ii)   It allows one array to be assigned to another array through the use of the assignment operator (e.g., *cp*1 = *cp*2).

(iii)   It supports a function that returns the size of the array.

(iv)   It allows the reading or printing of arrays through the use of **cout** and **cin**.

To do this, you will have to define the following member functions on *CppArray*:

(a)   A constructor *CppArray* (**int** *size* = defaultSize, **float** *initvalue* = defaultValue). This creates an array of size *size* all of whose elements are initialized to *initvalue*.

(b)   A copy constructor *CppArray* (**const** *CppArray*& *cp2*). This creates an array identical to *cp2*. Copy constructors are used to initialize a class object with another class object as in the following:
CppArray a = b **;**

(c)   An assignment operator *CppArray*& **operator=** (**const** *CppArray*& *cp2*). This replaces the original array with *cp2*.

(d)   A destructor ˜*CppArray*().

(e)   The subscript operator **float**& **operator**[ ] (**int** *i*). This should be implemented so that it performs range-checking.

(f)   A member function **int** *GetSize*(). This returns the size of the array.

(g)   Implement functions to read and print the elements of a *CppArray* by overloading operators << and >>. These functions will have to be made **friend**s of *CppArray*.

2.3   THE POLYNOMIAL ABSTRACT DATA TYPE

Arrays are not only data structures in their own right; we can also use them to implement other abstract data types. For instance, let us consider one of the simplest and most common data structures: the *ordered,* or *linear*, *list*. We can find many examples of this data structure, including:

• Days of the week: (Sunday, Monday, Tuesday, Wednesday, Thursday, Friday, Saturday)

• Values in a deck of cards: (Ace, 2, 3, 4, 5, 6, 7, 8, 9, 10, Jack, Queen, King)

• Floors of a building: (basement, lobby, mezzanine, first, second)

• Years the United States fought in World War II: (1941, 1942, 1943, 1944, 1945)

• Years Switzerland fought in World War II: ( )

Notice that ''Years Switzerland fought in World War II'' is different because it contains no items. It is an example of an empty list, which we denote as ( ). The other lists all contain items that are written in the form $(a_0, a_1, \cdots, a_{n-1})$.

We can perform many operations on lists, including:

(1) Find the length, n, of the list.

(2) Read the list from left to right (or right to left).

(3) Retrieve the ith element, $0 \leq i < n$.

(4) Store a new value into the ith position, $0 \leq i < n$.

(5) Insert a new element at the position i, $0 \leq i < n$, causing elements numbered $i, i + 1, \cdots, n - 1$ to become numbered $i + 1, i + 2, \cdots, n$.

(6) Delete the element at position i, $0 \leq i < n$, causing elements numbered $i + 1, \cdots, n - 1$ to become numbered $i, i + 1, \cdots, n - 2$.

It is not always necessary to be able to perform all of these operations; many times a subset will suffice. In the study of data structures we are interested in ways of representing ordered lists so that these operations can be carried out efficiently.

Rather than state the formal specification of the ADT *ordered list*, we want to explore briefly its implementation. Perhaps the most common way to represent an ordered list is by an array where we associate the list element a_i with the array index i. We will refer to this as *sequential mapping* because, using the conventional array representation, we are storing a_i and a_{i+1} into consecutive locations i and $i + 1$ of the array. This gives us the ability to retrieve or modify the values of random elements in the list in a constant amount of time, essentially because a computer has random access to any word in its memory. We can access the list element values in either direction by changing the subscript values in a controlled way. Only operations (5) and (6) require real effort. Insertion and deletion using sequential allocation force us to move some of the remaining elements so that the sequential mapping is preserved in its proper form. It is precisely this overhead that leads us to consider nonsequential mappings of ordered lists in Chapter 4.

Let us jump right into a problem requiring ordered lists, which we will solve by using one-dimensional arrays. This problem has become the classical example for motivating the use of list-processing techniques, which we will see in later chapters. Therefore, it makes sense to look at the problem and see why arrays offer only a partially adequate solution. The problem calls for building an ADT for the representation and manipulation of symbolic polynomials. By "symbolic," we mean the list of coefficients and exponents that accompany a polynomial; e.g., two such polynomials are

$$A(x) = 3x^2 + 2x + 4 \text{ and } B(x) = x^4 + 10x^3 + 3x^2 + 1$$

The largest (or leading) exponent of a polynomial is called its *degree*. Coefficients that are zero are not displayed. The term with exponent equal to zero does not show the variable, since x raised to a power of zero is 1. There are standard mathematical definitions for the sum and product of polynomials. Assume that we have two polynomials, $A(x) = \sum a_i x^i$ and $B(x) = \sum b_i x^i$; then

$$A(x) + B(x) = \sum (a_i + b_i)x^i$$

$$A(x) \cdot B(x) = \sum (a_i \, x^i \cdot \sum (b_j \, x^j))$$

Similarly, we can define subtraction and division on polynomials, as well as many other operations.

We begin with an ADT definition of a polynomial. The particular operations in part are a reflection of what will be needed in our subsequent programs to manipulate polynomials. The definition is contained in ADT 2.2.

---

class *Polynomial* {
//**objects**: $p(x) = a_0 x^{e_0} + \cdots + a_n x^{e_n}$; a set of ordered pairs of $<e_i, a_i>$,
// where $a_i \in$ *Coefficient* and $e_i \in$ *Exponent*
// We assume that *Exponent* consists of integers ≥ 0
public:
  Polynomial();
  //return the polynomial $p(x) = 0$

  int operator!();
  //**if** *this is the zero polynomial, return 1; **else** return 0;

  Coefficient Coef(*Exponent e*);
  //return the coefficient of *e* in *this

  Exponent LeadExp();
  //return the largest exponent in *this

  Polynomial Add(*Polynomial poly*);
  // return the sum of the polynomials *this and *poly*

  Polynomial Mult(*Polynomial poly*);
  // return the product of the polynomials *this and *poly*

  float *Eval*(**float** *f*) ;
  // Evaluate the polynomial *this at *f* and return the result.
}; // end of *Polynomial*

ADT 2.2: Abstract data type *Polynomial*

2.3.1 Polynomial Representation

We are now ready to make some representation decisions. A very reasonable first decision would be to arrange unique exponents in decreasing order. This considerably simplifies many of the operations. We discuss three representations that are based on this principle:

Representation 1: One way to represent polynomials in C++ is to define the private data members of *Polynomial* as follows:

private:
    int *degree*; // *degree* ≤ MaxDegree
    float *coef* [MaxDegree + 1];

where MaxDegree is a constant representing the largest-degree polynomial that is to be represented. Now, if *a* is a *Polynomial* class object and $n \leq$ MaxDegree, then the polynomial $A(x)$ above would be represented as:

$a.degree = n$
$a.coef[i] = a_{n-i}, 0 \leq i \leq n$

Note that $a.coef[i]$ is the coefficient of x^{n-i} and the coefficients are stored in order of decreasing exponents. This representation leads to very simple algorithms for many of the operations on polynomials (addition, subtraction, evaluation, multiplication, etc.).

Representation 2: Representation 1 is, however, quite wasteful in its use of computer memory. For instance, if *a.degree* is much less than MaxDegree, then most of the positions in *a.coef* [0], $\cdots$, *a.coef* [*MaxDegree*] are unused. To avoid this waste, we define *coef* so that its size is *a.degree* + 1. This can be done by declaring the following private data members

private:
    int *degree*;
    float *∗coef*;

and adding the following constructor to *Polynomial*:

```
Polynomial::Polynomial(int d)
{
    degree = d;
    coef = new float [degree+1];
}
```

Representation 3: Although Representation 2 solves the problem mentioned earlier, it does not yield a desirable representation. To see this, let us consider polynomials that have many zero terms. Such polynomials are called *sparse*. For instance, the polynomial $x^{1000} + 1$ has two nonzero terms and 999 zero terms. Consequently, 999 of the entries in *coef* will be zero if Representation 2 is used.

Suppose we take the polynomial $A(x)$ defined above and keep only its nonzero coefficients. Then we will really have the polynomial

$$b_m x^{e_m} + b_{m-1} x^{e_{m-1}} + \cdots + b_0 x^{e_0}$$

where each b_i is a nonzero coefficient of A and the exponents e_i are decreasing $e_m > e_{m-1} > \cdots > e_0 \geq 0$. If all of A's coefficients are nonzero, then $m = n$, $e_i = i$, and $b_i = a_i$ for $0 \leq i \leq n$. Alternatively, if only a_n is nonzero, then $m = 0$, $b_0 = a_n$, and $e_0 = n$.

All our polynomials will be represented in a single array called *termArray*. Each element in *termArray* is of type *term*, which we define below. Since the single array *termArray* is to be shared by all *Polynomial* objects, we declare it as a static class data member of *Polynomial*.

class *Polynomial* ; // forward declaration

```
class term {
friend Polynomial;
private:
    float coef; //coefficient
    int exp; //exponent
};
```

The private data members of *Polynomial* are defined as follows:

```
private:
    static term termArray[MaxTerms];
    static int free ;
    int Start, Finish;
```

where MaxTerms is a constant. The required definitions of the static class members outside the class definition are:

term Polynomial::termArray[MaxTerms];
int *Polynomial::free* = 0; // location of next free location in *termArray*

Consider the two polynomials $A(x) = 2x^{1000} + 1$ and $B(x) = x^4 + 10x^3 + 3x^2 + 1$. These could be stored in the array *termArray* as shown in Figure 2.1. Note that *A.Start* and *B.Start* give the location of the first term of *A* and *B* respectively, whereas *A.Finish* and *B.Finish* give the location of the last term of *A* and *B*. The static class member *free* gives the location of the next free location in the array *termArray*. For our example, $A.Start = 0, A.Finish = 1, B.Start = 2, B.Finish = 5$, and $free = 6$.

	A.Start ↓	A.Finish ↓	B.Start ↓			B.Finish ↓	free ↓
coef	2	1	1	10	3	1	
exp	1000	0	4	3	2	0	
	0	1	2	3	4	5	6

Figure 2.1: Array representation of two polynomials

In general, any polynomial *A* that has *n* nonzero terms has *A.Start* and *A.Finish* such that $A.Finish = A.Start + n - 1$. If *A* has no nonzero terms (i.e., *A* is the zero polynomial), then $A.Finish = A.Start - 1$.

This representation scheme does not impose any limit on the number of polynomials that can be stored in *termArray*. The only limitation is that the total number of nonzero terms in all the polynomials together cannot exceed MaxTerms.

Before proceeding, we should compare our current representation with Representation 2. Representation 3 is definitely superior when many zero terms are present. $A(x) = 2x^{1000} + 1$ uses only 6 units of space (one for *A.Start*, one for *A.Finish*, two for the coefficients, and two for the exponents). However, when all terms are nonzero, as in $B(x)$ above, the Representation 3 uses about twice as much space as Representation 2. Unless we know beforehand that each of our polynomials has very few zero terms, Representation 3 is preferable.

2.3.2 Polynomial Addition

Let us now write a C++ function to add two polynomials, *A* and *B*, to obtain the sum $C = A + B$. It is assumed that Representation 3, above, is used to store *A* and *B*. Function *Add* (Program 2.8) adds $A(x)$ and $B(x)$ term by term to produce $C(x)$. The basic loop of this algorithm consists of merging the terms of the two polynomials, depending upon the result of comparing the exponents. The **switch** statement determines how the exponents are related and performs the proper action. Since the tests within the **switch** statement require two terms, if one polynomial runs out of terms, we must exit the loop. The remaining terms of the other polynomial can be copied directly in to the result. The terms of C are entered into the array *termArray* starting at the position *free* by calling function *NewTerm* (Program 2.9). In case there is not enough space in *termArray* to accommodate C, an error message is printed and the program terminates.

```
1  Polynomial Polynomial::Add(Polynomial B)
2  // return the sum of A (x) (in *this) and B (x)
3  {
4      Polynomial C ; int a = Start ; int b = B.Start ; C.Start = free ; float c ;
5      while ((a <= Finish) && (b <= B.Finish))
6        switch (compare (termArray [a ].exp, termArray [b ].exp)) {
7          case '=':
8                c = termArray [a ].coef + termArray [b ].coef;
9                if (c) NewTerm (c, termArray [a ].exp);
10               a++; b++;
11                break;
12          case '<':
13               NewTerm (termArray [b ].coef, termArray [b ].exp);
14               b++;
15                break;
16          case '>':
17               NewTerm (termArray [a ].coef, termArray [a ].exp);
18               a++;
19          } // end of switch and while
20      //add in remaining terms of A (x)
21      for (; a <= Finish ; a++)
22        NewTerm (termArray [a ].coef, termArray [a ].exp);
23      //add in remaining terms of B (x)
24      for (; b <= B.Finish; b++)
25        NewTerm (termArray [b ].coef, termArray [b ].exp);
26      C.Finish = free − 1;
27      return C;
28  } // end of Add
```

Program 2.8: Adding two polynomials

```
void Polynomial::NewTerm(float c, int e)
//Add a new term to C(x).
{
  if (free >= MaxTerms) {
        cerr << "Too many terms in polynomials" << endl;
        exit(1);
  }
  termArray[free].coef = c;
  termArray[free].exp = e;
  free++ ;
} // end of NewTerm
```

Program 2.9: Adding a new term

Analysis of *Add*: It is natural to carry out this analysis in terms of the number of nonzero terms in *A* and *B*. Let *m* and *n* be the number of nonzero terms in *A* and *B* respectively. The assignments of line 4 are made only once and hence contribute $O(1)$ to the overall computing time. If either $n = 0$ or $m = 0$, the **while** loop of line 5 is not executed.

In case neither *m* nor *n* equals zero, the **while** loop of line 5 is entered. Each iteration of the **while** loop requires $O(1)$ time. At each iteration, the value of *a* or *b* or both increases by 1. Since the iteration terminates when either *a* or *b* exceeds *A.Finish* or *B.Finish* respectively, the number of iterations is bounded by $m + n - 1$. This worst-case is achieved, for instance, when $A(x) = \sum_{i=0}^{n} x^{2i}$ and $B(x) = \sum_{i=0}^{n} x^{2i+1}$. Since none of the exponents are the same in *A* and *B*, $termArray[a].exp \neq termArray[b].exp$. Consequently, on each iteration the value of only one of *a* or *b* increases by 1. So, the worst-case for the **for** loops of lines 21 and 24 is bounded by $O(n + m)$, since the first cannot be iterated more than *m* times and the second more than *n*. Taking the sum of all of these steps, we obtain $O(n + m)$ as the asymptotic computing time of this algorithm. □

2.3.3 Disadvantages of Representing Polynomials by Arrays

As we create polynomials, *free* is continually incremented until it tries to exceed Max-Terms. When this happens must we quit? We must unless there are some polynomials that are no longer needed. There may be several such polynomials whose space can be reused. We could write a function that would compact the remaining polynomials, leaving a large, contiguous free space at one end. But this may require much data movement. Even worse, if we move a polynomial, we must change its start and end pointers. This demands a sophisticated compacting routine coupled with a disciplined use of names for polynomials.

An alternative solution is to use a single array of *terms* for each polynomial. The array is created dynamically by using **new**. This requires us to know the size of the polynomial prior to its creation. In operations such as addition, the only way to know the size of the resulting polynomial is to actually add the two original polynomials. Consequently, this approach requires us to run the addition algorithm twice: once to determine the number of terms in the resulting polynomial and once to actually perform the addition. This potentially slows down the program by a factor of 2. This approach is examined in the exercises.

In Chapter 4, we provide an elegant solution to these problems.

EXERCISES

1. Use the six operations defined in this section for an ordered list to arrive at an ADT specification for such a list.

2. If $A = (a_0, \cdots, a_{n-1})$ and $B = (b_0, \cdots, b_{m-1})$ are ordered lists, then $A < B$ if $a_i = b_i$ for $0 \le i < j$ and $a_j < b_j$, or, if $a_i = b_i$ for $0 \le i < n$ and $n < m$. Write a function that returns -1, 0, or $+1$, depending upon whether $A < B$, $A = B$, or $A > B$. Assume you can compare atoms a_i and b_j.

3. Assume that n lists, $n > 1$, are being represented sequentially in the one-dimensional array *space*[m]. Let *front*[i] be one less than the position of the first element in the ith list, and let *rear*[i] point to the last element in the ith list, $0 \le i < n$. Assume that $rear[i] \le front[i+1]$, $0 \le i < n$ and $front[n] = m - 1$. The functions to be performed on these lists are insertion and deletion.

    (a) Obtain suitable initial and boundary conditions for *front*[i] and *rear*[i].

    (b) Write a function *Insert*(**int** i, **int** j, **int** *item*) to insert *item* after the $(j-1)$'th element in list i. This function should fail to make an insertion only if there are already m elements in *space*.

4. Using the assumptions of the preceding exercise, write a function **int** *Delete*(**int** i, **int** j) that removes and returns the jth element of the ith list.

5. Write C++ functions to input and output polynomials represented as in this section. Your functions should overload the $<<$ and $>>$ operators.

6. Write a C++ function that multiplies two polynomials represented by the array *termArray*. What is the computing time of your function?

7. Write a C++ function that evaluates a polynomial at a value x_0 using the representation of the preceding exercise. Try to minimize the number of operations.

8. The polynomials $A(x) = x^{2n} + x^{2n-2} + \cdots + x^2 + x^0$ and $B(x) = x^{2n+1} + x^{2n-1} + \cdots + x^3 + x$ cause *Add* to work very hard. For these polynomials, determine the exact number of times each statement will be executed.

9. The declarations that follow give us an alternate representation of the polynomial ADT. The number of nonzero terms in the ith polynomial is given in *termArray* [i][0].*exp*. These terms are stored, in descending order of exponents, in

positions *termArray* [*i*][1], *termArray* [*i*][2], · · · . Write and test C++ functions to input, output, add, multiply, and evaluate polynomials represented in this way. Is this representation better or worse than the representation used in the text?

const int MaxTerms = 100; //max number of terms in a poly
const int MaxPolys = 20; //max number of polynomials

class *Polynomial* ; // forward declaration

class *term* {
friend *Polynomial*;
private:
   int *exp*;
   float *coef*;
};

private:
   static *term termArray*[MaxPolys][MaxTerms+1]; // in *Polynomial*

10. The declarations that follow give us the alternate representation of the polynomial ADT mentioned in Section 2.3.3. Each *Polynomial* object is represented by an array. This array is created dynamically once the number of terms in that polynomial are known. Write and test C++ functions to input, output, add, multiply, and evaluate polynomials represented in this way. Of these, functions that result in the creation of a new polynomial will have to first compute the number of terms required by the new polynomial and then actually populate its array with the appropriate terms. Is this representation better or worse than the representation used in the text?

class *Polynomial* ; // forward declaration

class *term* {
friend *Polynomial*;
private:
   int *exp*;
   float *coef*;
};

private:
   *term *termArray* ; // in *Polynomial*

2.4   SPARSE MATRICES

2.4.1   Introduction

A matrix is a mathematical object that arises in many physical problems. As computer scientists, we are interested in studying ways to represent matrices so that the operations to be performed on them can be carried out efficiently. A general matrix consists of m rows and n columns of numbers, as in Figure 2.2.

$$
\begin{array}{c}
\begin{array}{ccc}
\text{col 0} & \text{col 1} & \text{col 2}
\end{array} \\
\begin{array}{l}
\text{row 0} \\
\text{row 1} \\
\text{row 2} \\
\text{row 3} \\
\text{row 4}
\end{array}
\begin{bmatrix}
-27 & 3 & 4 \\
6 & 82 & -2 \\
109 & -64 & 11 \\
12 & 8 & 9 \\
48 & 27 & 47
\end{bmatrix}
\end{array}
$$

(a)

$$
\begin{array}{c}
\begin{array}{cccccc}
\text{col 0} & \text{col 1} & \text{col 2} & \text{col 3} & \text{col 4} & \text{col 5}
\end{array} \\
\begin{array}{l}
\text{row 0} \\
\text{row 1} \\
\text{row 2} \\
\text{row 3} \\
\text{row 4} \\
\text{row 5}
\end{array}
\begin{bmatrix}
15 & 0 & 0 & 22 & 0 & -15 \\
0 & 11 & 3 & 0 & 0 & 0 \\
0 & 0 & 0 & -6 & 0 & 0 \\
0 & 0 & 0 & 0 & 0 & 0 \\
91 & 0 & 0 & 0 & 0 & 0 \\
0 & 0 & 28 & 0 & 0 & 0
\end{bmatrix}
\end{array}
$$

(b)

Figure 2.2: Two matrices

The first matrix has five rows and three columns, the second six rows and six columns. In general, we write $m \times n$ (read ''m by n'') to designate a matrix with m rows and n columns. Such a matrix has mn elements. When m is equal to n, we call the matrix *square*.

It is very natural to store a matrix in a two-dimensional array, say $A[m][n]$. Then we can work with any element by writing $A[i][j]$, and this element can be found very quickly, as we will see in the next section. Now if we look at the second matrix of Figure 2.2, we see that it has many zero entries. Such a matrix is called *sparse*. There is no precise definition of when a matrix is sparse and when it is not, but it is a concept that we can all recognize intuitively. Above, only eight out of 36 possible elements are nonzero, and that is sparse! A sparse matrix requires us to consider an alternate form of representation. This comes about because in practice many of the matrices we want to deal with are large, e.g., 5000×5000, but at the same time they are sparse: say only 5000 out of 25 million possible elements are nonzero. On many computers today it would be impossible to store a full 5000×5000 matrix in the memory at once. Therefore, we seek an alternative representation for sparse matrices. The alternative representation should explicitly store only the nonzero elements.

Before developing a particular representation, we first must consider the operations that we want to perform on these matrices. A minimal set of operations includes matrix creation, transposition, addition, and multiplication. ADT 2.3 contains our specification of the matrix ADT.

---

class *SparseMatrix*
{
//**objects**: A set of triples, <*row, column, value*>, where *row* and *column* are integers and
//form a unique combination; *value* is also an integer.
public:
    SparseMatrix(**int** *MaxRow*, **int** *MaxCol*);
    // the constructor function creates a *SparseMatrix* that can hold up to *MaxItems* =
    // *MaxRow* × *MaxCol* and whose maximum row size is *MaxRow* and whose
    // maximum column size is *MaxCol*

    SparseMatrix Transpose();
    // returns the *SparseMatrix* obtained by interchanging the row and column value of
    // every triple in *this.

    SparseMatrix Add(*SparseMatrix b*);
    // **if** the dimensions of *a* (*this) and *b* are the same, then the matrix produced by adding
    // corresponding items, namely those with identical *row* and *column* values is returned
    // **else** error.

    SparseMatrix Multiply(*SparseMatrix b*);
    // **if** number of columns in *a* (*this) equals number of rows in *b* then the matrix *d*
    // produced by multiplying *a* by *b* according to the formula $d[i][j] =$
    // $\sum (a[i][k] \cdot b[k][j])$, where $d[i][j]$ is the (i, j)th element, is returned. *k* ranges from 0
    // to the number of columns in $a - 1$
    // **else** error
};

ADT 2.3: Abstract data type *SparseMatrix*

2.4.2 Sparse Matrix Representation

Before implementing any of these operations, we must establish the representation of the sparse matrix. By examining Figure 2.2, we know that we can characterize uniquely any element within a matrix by using the triple <*row, col, value* >. This means that we can use an array of triples to represent a sparse matrix. We require that these triples be stored by rows with the triples for the first row first, followed by those of the second row, and so on. We also require that all the triples for any row be stored so that the column indices are in ascending order. In addition, to ensure that the operations terminate, we must know the number of rows and columns and the number of nonzero elements in the matrix. Putting all this information together suggests that we define:

class *SparseMatrix* **;** // forward declaration

class *MatrixTerm* **{**
friend class *SparseMatrix*
private:
    int *row, col, value* **;**
};

and in **class** *SparseMatrix:*

private:
    int *Rows, Cols, Terms***;**
    MatrixTerm smArray[MaxTerms] **;**

where MaxTerms is a constant. Rows contains the number of rows; *Cols* contains the number of columns; and *Terms* contains the total number of nonzero entries. Figure 2.3(a) shows the representation of the matrix of Figure 2.2(b) using *smArray*. Positions 0 through 7 of *smArray* store the triples representing the nonzero entries. The row index is in the field *row*; the column index is in the field *col*; and the value is in the field *value*. The triples are ordered by row and within rows by columns.

2.4.3   Transposing a Matrix

Figure 2.3(b) shows the transpose of the matrix of Figure 2.3(a). To transpose a matrix, we must interchange the rows and columns. This means that if an element is at position $[i][j]$ in the original matrix, then it is at position $[j][i]$ in the transposed matrix. When $i = j$, the elements on the diagonal will remain unchanged. Since the original matrix is organized by rows, our first idea for a transpose algorithm might be the following:

for (each row i)
    take element $(i,j,value)$ and
    store it in $(j,i,value)$ of the transpose;

The difficulty is in not knowing where to put the element $(j,i,value)$ until all other elements that precede it have been processed. In Figure 2.3(a), for instance, we encounter

	row	col	value		row	col	value
smArray[0]	0	0	15	smArray[0]	0	0	15
[1]	0	3	22	[1]	0	4	91
[2]	0	5	-15	[2]	1	1	11
[3]	1	1	11	[3]	2	1	3
[4]	1	2	3	[4]	2	5	28
[5]	2	3	-6	[5]	3	0	22
[6]	4	0	91	[6]	3	2	-6
[7]	5	2	28	[7]	5	0	-15
	(a)				(b)		

Figure 2.3: Sparse matrix and its transpose stored as triples

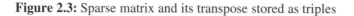

$(0, 0, 15)$ which becomes $(0, 0, 15)$
$(0, 3, 22)$ which becomes $(3, 0, 22)$
$(0, 5, -15)$ which becomes $(5, 0, -15)$
$(1, 1, 11)$ which becomes $(1, 1, 11)$

If we just place them consecutively, then we will need to insert many new triples, forcing us to move elements down very often. We can avoid this data movement by finding the elements in the order we want them, which would be

for (all elements in column j)
  place element (i, j, value) in position (j, i, value);

This says "find all elements in column 0 and store them in row 0, find all elements in column 1 and store them in row 1, etc." Since the rows are originally in order, this means that we will locate elements in the correct column order as well. The function *Transpose* (Program 2.10) computes and returns the transpose of A (*this).

It is not too difficult to see that the function is correct. The variable *CurrentB* always gives us the position in b where the next term in the transpose is to be inserted. The terms in $b.smArray$ are generated by rows. Since the rows of B are the columns of A, row c of B is obtained by collecting all the nonzero terms in column c of A. This is precisely what is being done in lines 11 to 19. On the first iteration of the **for** loop of lines 11 to 19, all terms from column 0 of A are collected, then all terms from column 1, and so on, until eventually all terms from the last column of A are collected.

Analysis of *Transpose*: Let *columns*, *rows*, and *terms* denote the number of columns, rows, and terms, respectively, in A. For each iteration of the loop of lines 11 to 19, the **if**

```
1   SparseMatrix SparseMatrix::Transpose( )
2   // return the transpose of a (*this)
3   {
4      SparseMatrix b ;
5      b.Rows = Cols ; // rows in b = columns in a
6      b.Cols = Rows ; // columns in b = rows in a
7      b.Terms = Terms ; // terms in b = terms in a
8      if (Terms > 0) // nonzero matrix
9      {
10        int CurrentB = 0 ;
11        for (int c = 0; c < Cols ; c++) // transpose by columns
12          for (int i = 0 ; i < Terms ; i++)
13          // find elements in column c
14            if (smArray [i].col == c) {
15               b.smArray [CurrentB].row = c;
16               b.smArray [CurrentB].col = smArray [i].row;
17               b.smArray [CurrentB].value = smArray [i].value;
18               CurrentB++;
19            }
20     } // end of if (Terms > 0)
21     return b;
22  } // end of transpose
```

Program 2.10: Transposing a matrix

clause of line 14 is tested *terms* times. Since the number of iterations of the loop of lines 11 to 19 is *columns*, the total time for line 14 is *terms · columns*. The assignments of lines 15, 16, and 17 take place exactly *terms* times, since there are only this many nonzero terms in the sparse matrix being generated. Lines 4-10 take a constant amount of time. The total time for the algorithm is therefore O(*terms · columns*). In addition to the space needed for *a* and *b*, the algorithm requires only a fixed amount of additional space, i.e., space for the variables *c*, *i*, and *CurrentB*. □

We now have a matrix transpose algorithm that we believe is correct and that has a computing time of O(*terms · columns*). This computing time is a little disturbing, since we know that in case the matrices had been represented as two-dimensional arrays, we could have obtained the transpose of a *rows × columns* matrix in time O(*rows · columns*). The algorithm for this has the simple form

```
for (int j = 0 ; j < columns ; j++)
  for (int i = 0 ; i < rows ; i++)
    B[j][i] = A[i][j];
```

The O($terms \cdot columns$) time for function $transpose$ becomes O($rows \cdot columns^2$) when $terms$ is of the order of $rows \cdot columns$. This is worse than the O($rows \cdot columns$) time using the simple form. Perhaps, in an effort to conserve space, we have traded away too much time. Actually, we can do much better by using a little more storage. We can, in fact, transpose a matrix represented as a sequence of triples in time O($terms + columns$). This algorithm, $FastTranspose$ (Program 2.11), proceeds by first determining the number of elements in each column of A. This gives us the number of elements in each row of B. From this information, the starting point in b of each of its rows is easily obtained. We can now move the elements of a one by one into their correct position in b.

The correctness of function $FastTranspose$ follows from the preceding discussion and the observation that the starting point, $RowStart[i]$, of row i, $i > 0$, of B is $RowStart[i-1] + RowSize[i-1]$, where $RowSize[i-1]$ is the number of elements in row $i-1$ of B. The computation of $RowSize$ and $RowStart$ is carried out in lines 11 to 15. In lines 16 to 23 the elements of a are examined one by one starting from the first and successively moving to the correct place in b. $RowStart[j]$ is maintained so that it is always the position in b where the next element in row j of B is to be inserted. If we try the algorithm on the sparse matrix of Figure 2.3, then after execution of the third **for** loop (line 15), the values of $RowSize$ and $RowStart$ are:

	[0]	[1]	[2]	[3]	[4]	[5]
RowSize =	3	2	1	0	1	1
RowStart =	0	3	5	6	6	7

There are four loops in $FastTranspose$, which are executed $columns$, $terms$, $columns - 1$, and $terms$ times respectively. Each iteration of the loops takes only a constant amount of time, so the asymptotic complexity is O($columns + terms$). The computing time of O($columns + terms$) becomes O($rows \cdot columns$) when $terms$ is of the order of $rows \cdot columns$. This is the same as when two-dimensional arrays were in use. However, the constant factor associated with $FastTranspose$ is larger than that for the array algorithm. When $terms$ is sufficiently small compared to its maximum of $rows \cdot columns$, $FastTranspose$ will be faster. Hence in this representation, we save both space and time! This was not true of $Transpose$, since $terms$ will almost always be greater than max$\{rows, columns\}$ and $columns \cdot terms$ will therefore always be at least $rows \cdot columns$. The constant factor associated with $Transpose$ is also larger than the one in the array algorithm. Finally, you should note that $FastTranspose$ requires more space than does $Transpose$. The space required by $FastTranspose$ can be reduced by utilizing the same space to represent the two arrays $RowSize$ and $RowStart$.

```
1   SparseMatrix SparseMatrix::FastTranspose()
2   //The transpose of a (*this) is placed in b and is found in O(terms +columns) time.
3   {
4       int *RowSize = new int[Cols];
5       int *RowStart = new int[Cols];
6       SparseMatrix b;
7       b.Rows = Cols ; b.Cols = Rows ; b.Terms = Terms;
8       if (Terms > 0) // nonzero matrix
9       {
10          // compute RowSize [i] = number of terms in row i of b
11          for (int i = 0 ; i < Cols ; i++) RowSize [i] = 0; // initialize
12          for (i = 0 ; i < Terms ; i++) RowSize[smArray[i].col]++ ;

13          //RowStart [i] = starting position of row i in b
14          RowStart[0] = 0 ;
15          for (i = 1 ; i < Cols ; i++) RowStart[i] = RowStart[i − 1] + RowSize[i − 1] ;

16          for (i = 0 ; i < Terms ; i++) // move from a to b
17          {
18              int j = RowStart[smArray[i].col];
19              b.smArray[j].row = smArray[i].col ;
20              b.smArray[j].col = smArray[i].row ;
21              b.smArray[j].value = smArray[i].value ;
22              RowStart[smArray[i].col]++ ;
23          } // end of for
24      } // end of if

25      delete [] RowSize ;
26      delete [] RowStart ;
27      return b ;
28  } // end of FastTranspose
```

Program 2.11: Transposing a matrix faster

2.4.4   Matrix Multiplication

Definition: Given A and B, where A is $m \times n$ and B is $n \times p$, the product matrix *Result* has dimension $m \times p$. Its $[i]$ $[j]$ element is

$$result_{ij} = \sum_{k=0}^{n-1} a_{ik}\, b_{kj}$$

for $0 \le i < m$ and $0 \le j < p.$ $\square$

The product of two sparse matrices may no longer be sparse, as Figure 2.4 shows.

$$\begin{bmatrix} 1 & 0 & 0 \\ 1 & 0 & 0 \\ 1 & 0 & 0 \end{bmatrix} \begin{bmatrix} 1 & 1 & 1 \\ 0 & 0 & 0 \\ 0 & 0 & 0 \end{bmatrix} = \begin{bmatrix} 1 & 1 & 1 \\ 1 & 1 & 1 \\ 1 & 1 & 1 \end{bmatrix}$$

Figure 2.4: Multiplication of two sparse matrices

We would like to multiply two sparse matrices A and B represented as ordered lists as in Figure 2.3. We need to compute the elements of *Result* by rows so that we can store them in their proper place without moving previously computed elements. To do this we pick a row of A and find all elements in column j of B for $j = 0, 1, \cdots, B.Col - 1$, where $B.Col$ is the number of columns in B. Normally, we would have to scan all of B to find all the elements in column j. However, we can avoid this by first computing the transpose of B. This puts all column elements in consecutive order. Once we have located the elements of row i of A and column j of B, we just do a merge operation similar to that used for polynomial addition in Section 2.3. An alternate approach is explored in the exercises.

Before we write a matrix multiplication function, it will be useful to define the function of Program 2.12, which stores a matrix term.

The function *Multiply* (Program 2.13) multiplies the matrices A and B to obtain the product matrix *Result* using the strategy outlined above. A, B, and *Result* are stored as sparse matrices in a, b, and *result* respectively. Function *Multiply* (which is invoked as *a.Multiply(b)*) makes use of variables *currRowIndex*, *currColIndex*, *currRowA*, *currColB*, and *currRowBegin*. The variable *currRowA* is the row of A that is currently being multiplied with the columns of B. *currRowBegin* is the position in a of the first element of row *currRowA*. *currColB* is the column of B that is currently being multiplied with row *currRowA* of A. *LastInResult* is the position occupied by the last element of *result*. *currRowIndex* and *currColIndex* are used to examine successive elements of row *currRowA* and column *currColB* of A and B, respectively. In addition to all this, line 17 of the algorithm introduces a dummy term into each of a and *bXpose*. This enables us to handle end conditions (i.e., computations involving the last row of A or last column of B) in an elegant way. This, however, requires that the number of terms in A and B be fewer than MaxTerms (lines 8 to 11), as otherwise we will not have the space for the dummy term. If matrices A and B are incompatible, or if there is no room in A or B for the dummy term, or if the number of terms in the product exceed *MaxTerms*, then *Multiply* calls the function *EmptyMatrix()*, which returns an empty sparse matrix with *Rows* = *Cols* = *Terms* = 0.

```
int SparseMatrix::StoreSum (int sum, int& LastInResult, int r, int c)
// If sum ≠ 0, then it along with its row and column position are stored as the
// (LastInResult+1)'st entry in result. LastInResult is incremented. 1 is returned to
// signal to the calling function that there is no memory available for the new term,
// and 0 otherwise.
{
   if (sum != 0) {
      if (LastInResult < MaxTerms - 1) {
         LastInResult++;
         smArray[LastInResult].row = r ;
         smArray[LastInResult].col = c ;
         smArray[LastInResult].value = sum;
         return 0;
      }
      else {
         cerr << "Number of terms in product exceeds MaxTerms" << endl ;
         return 1 ; //terminate program
      }
   }
   else return 0 ;
} // end of StoreSum
```

Program 2.12: Storing a matrix term

```
 1 SparseMatrix SparseMatrix::Multiply(SparseMatrix b)
 2 // Multiply two sparse matrices A (*this) and B producing Result.
 3 {
 4   if (Cols != b.Rows) {
 5      cout << "Incompatible matrices" << endl ;
 6      return EmptyMatrix() ;
 7   }
 8   if ((Terms == MaxTerms) || (b.Terms == MaxTerms)) {
 9      cout << "One additional space in a or b needed" << endl ;
10      return EmptyMatrix() ;
11   }
12   SparseMatrix bXpose = b.FastTranspose() ;
13   SparseMatrix result ;
14   int currRowIndex = 0, LastInResult = -1,
15         currRowBegin = 0, currRowA = smArray[0].row;
16   // set boundary conditions
17   smArray[Terms].row = Rows; bXpose.smArray[b.Terms].row = b.Cols;
```

```
18    bXpose.smArray[b.Terms].col = −1 ; int sum = 0;
19    while (currRowIndex < Terms) // generate row currRowA of result
20    {
21      int currColB = bXpose.smArray[0].row; int currColIndex = 0;
22      while (currColIndex <= b.Terms)
23      // multiply row currRowA of a by column currColB of b
24      {
25        if (smArray[currRowIndex].row != currRowA) // end of row currRowA
26        {
27          if (result.StoreSum(sum, LastInResult, currRowA, currColB))
28            return EmptyMatrix(); //error
29          else sum = 0 ; // reset sum
30          currRowIndex = currRowBegin;
31          // go to next column
32          while (bXpose.smArray[currColIndex].row == currColB) currColIndex++;
33          currColB = bXpose.smArray[currColIndex].row;
34        }
35        else if (bXpose.smArray[currColIndex].row != currColB)
36        // end of column currColB of b
37        {
38          if (result.StoreSum(sum, LastInResult, currRowA, currColB))
39            return EmptyMatrix(); // error
40          else sum = 0 ; // reset sum
41          // set to multiply row currRowA with next column
42          currRowIndex = currRowBegin;
43          currColB = bXpose.smArray[currColIndex].row;
44        }
45        else
46          switch (compare (smArray[currRowIndex].col,
47                  bXpose.smArray[currColIndex].col)) {
48          case '<':  // advance to next term in row.
49            currRowIndex++ ; break;
50          case '=':  // add to sum
51            sum += smArray[currRowIndex].value *
52                  bXpose.smArray[currColIndex].value;
53            currRowIndex++; currColIndex++; break;
54          case '>': // advance to next term in column currColB
55            currColIndex++;
56          } // end of switch
57      } // of while (currColIndex <= b.Terms)
58      while (smArray[currRowIndex].row == currRowA) // advance to next row
59        currRowIndex++;
60      currRowBegin = currRowIndex ; currRowA = smArray[currRowIndex].row;
61    } //end of while (currRowIndex < Terms)
```

62   *result.Rows = Rows*; *result.Cols = b.Cols* ; *result.Terms = LastInResult +* 1;
63   **return** *result*;
64 } // end of *Multiply*

Program 2.13: Multiplying sparse matrices

Analysis of *Multiply:* We leave the correctness proof of this algorithm as an exercise. Let us examine its computing time. In addition to the space needed for *a, b, result*, and some simple variables, space is also needed for the transpose matrix *bXpose*. Algorithm *FastTranspose* also needs some additional space. The exercises explore a strategy for *Multiply* that does not explicitly compute *bXpose*, and the only additional space needed is the same as that required by *FastTranspose*. Turning our attention to the computing time of *Multiply*, we see that lines 5 to 18 require only $O(B.Cols + B.Terms)$ time. The **while** loop of lines 19 to 61 is executed at most *A.Rows* times (once for each row of *A*). In each iteration of the **while** loop of lines 22 to 57, the value of *currRowIndex* or *currColIndex* or both increases by 1, or *currRowIndex* and *currColB* are reset. The maximum total increment in *currColIndex* over the whole loop is *B.Terms*. If t_r is the number of terms in row *r* of *A*, then the value of *currRowIndex* can increase at most t_r times before *currRowIndex* moves to the next row of *A*. When this happens, *currRowIndex* is reset to *currRowBegin* in line 30. At the same time *currColB* is advanced to the next column. Hence, this resetting can take place at most *B.Cols* times. The total maximum increment in *currRowIndex* is therefore $B.Cols \cdot t_r$. The maximum number of iterations of the **while** loop of lines 22 to 57 is therefore $B.Cols + B.Cols \cdot t_r + B.Terms$. The time for this loop while multiplying with row *r* of *A* is $O(B.Cols \cdot t_r + B.Terms)$. Lines 58 to 60 take only $O(t_r)$ time. Hence, the time for the outer **while** loop, lines 19 to 61, for the iteration with row *currRowA* of *A*, is $O(B.Cols \cdot t_r + B.Terms)$. The overall time for this loop is then $O(\Sigma_r(B.Cols \cdot t_r + B.Terms))$ = $O(B.Cols \cdot A.Terms + A.Rows \cdot B.Terms)$.

Once again, we may compare the computing time with the time to multiply matrices when arrays are used. The classical multiplication algorithm is:

```
for (int i = 0; i < A.Rows; i++)
  for (int j = 0; j <  B.Cols; j++)
  {
      sum = 0;
      for (int k = 0; k < A.Cols; k++)
          sum += a [i ][k] * b [k ][j];
      c [i ][j ] = sum;
  }
```

The time for this is $O(A.Rows \cdot A.Cols \cdot B.Cols)$. Since $A.Terms \le A.Rows \cdot A.Cols$ and $B.Terms \le A.Cols \cdot B.Rows$, the time for *Multiply* is at most $O(A.Rows \cdot A.Cols \cdot B.Cols)$. However, its constant factor is greater than that for matrix multiplication using arrays. In the worst case, when $A.Terms = A.Rows \cdot A.Cols$ or

B.Terms = *A.Cols · B.Rows*, *Multiply* will be slower by a constant factor. However, when *A.Terms* and *B.Terms* are sufficiently smaller than their maximum values, i.e., *A* and *B* are sparse, *Multiply* will outperform the above multiplication algorithm for arrays.

   The above analysis for *Multiply* is nontrivial. It introduces some new concepts in algorithm analysis and you should make sure you understand the analysis. □

2.4.5   Disadvantages of Representing Sparse Matrices by Arrays

This representation for sparse matrices permits one to perform operations such as addition, transpose, and multiplication efficiently. There are, however, other considerations that make this representation undesirable in certain applications. Since the number of terms in a sparse matrix is variable, we would like to represent all our sparse matrices in one array (as we did for polynomials in Section 2.3), rather than use a separate array for each matrix. This would enable us to make efficient utilization of space. However, when this is done, we run into difficulties in allocating space from this array to any individual matrix.

   An alternative solution is to use a single array for each sparse matrix. The array is created dynamically by using **new**. This approach requires us to compute the size of the sparse matrix prior to its creation. This approach is similar to that mentioned in Section 2.3.3 on polynomials and is further examined in the exercises.

   These difficulties are similar to those with the polynomial representation of the previous section and will become apparent when we study a similar representation for multiple stacks and queues in Section 3.7.

EXERCISES

1. How much time does it take to locate an arbitrary element $A[i][j]$ in the representation of this section and to change its value?

2. Analyze carefully the computing time and storage requirements of function *Fast-Transpose* (Program 2.11). What can you say about the existence of an even faster algorithm?

3. Write C++ functions to input and output a sparse matrix. These should be implemented by overloading the >> and << operators. You should design the input and output formats. However, the internal representation should be a one dimensional array of nonzero terms as used in this section. Analyze the computing time of your functions.

4. Rewrite function *FastTranspose* (Program 2.11) so that it uses only one array rather than the two arrays required to hold *RowSize* and *RowStart*.

5. Develop a correctness proof for function *Multiply* (Program 2.13).

6. Using the idea in *FastTranspose* of *A.Cols* row pointers, rewrite *Multiply* (Program 2.13) to multiply two sparse matrices *A* and *B* represented as in Section 2.4 without transposing *B*. What is the computing time of your algorithm?

7. A variation of the scheme discussed in this section for sparse matrix representation involves representing only the nonzero terms in a one-dimensional array v in the order described. In addition, a strip of $n \times m$ bits, $bits[n][m]$ is also kept. $bits[i][j] = 0$ if $A[i][j] = 0$, and $bits[i][j] = 1$ if $A[i][j] \neq 0$. The figure below illustrates the representation for the sparse matrix of Figure 2.2(b).

$$
\begin{bmatrix}
1 & 0 & 0 & 1 & 0 & 1 \\
0 & 1 & 1 & 0 & 0 & 0 \\
0 & 0 & 0 & 1 & 0 & 0 \\
0 & 0 & 0 & 0 & 0 & 0 \\
1 & 0 & 0 & 0 & 0 & 0 \\
0 & 0 & 1 & 0 & 0 & 0
\end{bmatrix}
\quad
\begin{bmatrix}
15 \\
22 \\
-15 \\
11 \\
3 \\
-6 \\
91 \\
28
\end{bmatrix}
$$

(a) On a computer with w bits per word, how much storage is needed to represent a sparse matrix $A_{n \times m}$ with t nonzero terms?

(b) Write an algorithm to add two sparse matrices A and C, represented as above, to obtain $D = A + C$. How much time does your algorithm take?

(c) Discuss the merits of this representation versus the representation of Section 2.4. Consider space and time requirements for such operations as random access, add, multiply, and transpose. Note that the random access time can be improved somewhat by keeping another array ra such that $ra[i] =$ number of nonzero terms in rows 0 through $i - 1$.

8. The declarations that follow give us an alternate representation of the sparse matrix ADT. Each *SparseMatrix* object is represented by an array. This array is created dynamically once the number of terms in that sparse matrix are known. Write and test C++ functions to input, output, add, multiply, and compute the transpose of sparse matrices represented in this way. Is this representation better or worse than the representation used in the text?

class *SparseMatrix* ; // forward declaration

class *MatrixTerm* {
friend *SparseMatrix*;
private:
   int *row, col, val* ;
};

   private:
      int *Rows, Cols, Terms* ;
      MatrixTerm *smArray* ; // in *SparseMatrix*

2.5   REPRESENTATION OF ARRAYS

Multidimensional arrays are usually implemented by storing the elements in a one-dimensional array. In this section, we develop a representation in which an arbitrary array element, say $A[i_1][i_2],...,[i_n]$, gets mapped onto a position in a one-dimensional C++ array so that it can be retrieved efficiently . This is necessary since programs using arrays may, in general, use array elements in a random order. In addition to being able to retrieve array elements easily, it is also necessary to be able to determine the amount of memory space to be reserved for a particular array. Assuming that each array element requires only one word of memory, the number of words needed is the number of elements in the array. If an array is declared $A[p_1 .. q_1][p_2 .. q_2], \cdots, [p_n .. q_n]$, where $p_i .. q_i$ is the range of index values in dimension i, then it is easy to see that the number of elements is

$$\prod_{i=1}^{n} (q_i - p_i + 1)$$

One of the common ways to represent an array is in *row major order* (see Exercise 4 at the end of this section for column major order). If we have the declaration

$$A[4..5][2..4][1..2][3..4]$$

then we have a total of $2*3*2*2 = 24$ elements. Using row major order, these elements will be stored as

$$A[4][2][1][3], A[4][2][1][4], A[4][2][2][3], A[4][2][2][4]$$

and continuing

$$A[4][3][1][3], A[4][3][1][4], A[4][3][2][3], A[4][3][2][4]$$

for three more sets of four until we get

$$A[5][4][1][3], A[5][4][1][4], A[5][4][2][3], A[5][4][2][4]$$

We see that the index at the right moves the fastest. In fact, if we view the indices as numbers, we see that they are, in some sense, increasing:

$$4213, 4214, \cdots, 5423, 5424$$

A synonym for row major order is *lexicographic order*.

The problem is how to translate from the name $A[i_1][i_2], ..., [i_n]$ to the correct location in the one-dimensional array. Suppose $A[4][2][1][3]$ is stored at position 0. Then

$A[4][2][1][4]$ will be at position 1 and $A[5][4][2][4]$ at position 23. These two addresses are easy to guess. In general, we can derive a formula for the address of any element. This formula makes use of only the starting address of the array plus the declared dimensions.

To simplify the discussion we shall assume that indices in dimension i run from 0 to $u_i - 1$ (that is, $p_i = 0$ and $q_i = u_i - 1$). The general case when p_i can be any integer is discussed in the exercises. Before obtaining a formula for the case of an n-dimensional array, let us look at the row major representation of one-, two-, and three-dimensional arrays. To begin with, if A is declared $A[u_1]$, then assuming one word per element, it may be represented in sequential memory as in Figure 2.5. If α is the address of $A[0]$, then the address of an arbitrary element $A[i]$ is just $\alpha + i$.

array element:	$A[0]$	$A[1]$	$A[2]$	$\cdots$	$A[i]$	$\cdots$	$A[u_1-1]$
address:	α	$\alpha+1$	$\alpha+2$	$\cdots$	$\alpha+i$	$\cdots$	$\alpha+u_1-1$

Figure 2.5: Sequential representation of $A[u_1]$

The two-dimensional array $A[u_1][u_2]$ may be interpreted as u_1 rows, $row_0, row_1, \cdots, row_{u_1-1}$, each row consisting of u_2 elements. In a row major representation, these rows would be represented in memory as in Figure 2.6.

Again, if α is the address of $A[0][0]$, then the address of $A[i][0]$ is $\alpha + i * u_2$, as there are i rows, each of size u_2, preceding the first element in the ith row. Knowing the address of $A[i][0]$, we can say that the address of $A[i][j]$ is then simply $\alpha + i * u_2 + j$.

Figure 2.7 shows the representation of the three-dimensional array $A[u_1][u_2][u_3]$. This array is interpreted as u_1 two-dimensional arrays of dimension $u_2 \times u_3$. To locate $A[i][j][k]$, we first obtain $\alpha + iu_2u_3$ as the address for $A[i][0][0]$ since there are i two-dimensional arrays of size $u_2 \times u_3$ preceding this element. From this and the formula for addressing a two-dimensional array, we obtain $\alpha + iu_2u_3 + ju_3 + k$ as the address of $A[i][j][k]$.

Generalizing on the preceding discussion, the addressing formula for any element $A[i_1][i_2], \cdots,[i_n]$ in an n-dimensional array declared as $A[u_1][u_2], \cdots, [u_n]$ may be easily obtained. If α is the address for $A[0][0] \cdots, [0]$ then $\alpha + i_1u_2u_3 \cdots u_n$ is the address for $A[i_1][0], \cdots, [0]$. The address for $A[i_1][i_2][0] \cdots, [0]$ is then $\alpha + i_1u_2u_3 \cdots u_n + i_2u_3u_4 \cdots u_n$.

Repeating in this way, the address for $A[i_1][i_2], \cdots, [i_n]$ is

Figure 2.6: Sequential representation of $A[u_1][u_2]$

$$
\begin{aligned}
\alpha &+ i_1 u_2 u_3 \cdots u_n \\
&+ i_2 u_3 u_4 \cdots u_n \\
&+ i_3 u_4 u_5 \cdots u_n \\
&\quad . \\
&\quad . \\
&\quad . \\
&+ i_{n-1} u_n \\
&+ i_n
\end{aligned}
$$

$$
= \alpha + \sum_{j=1}^{n} i_j a_j \text{ where }
\begin{cases}
a_j = \prod_{k=j+1}^{n} u_k & 1 \le j < n \\
a_n = 1
\end{cases}
$$

Note that a_j may be computed from a_{j+1}, $1 \le j < n$, using only one multiplication as $a_j = u_{j+1} a_{j+1}$. Thus, a compiler will initially take the declared bounds $u_1, \cdots, u_n$ and use them to compute the constants $a_1, \cdots, a_{n-1}$ using $n-2$ multiplications. The address of $A[i_1], \cdots, [i_n]$ can then be found using the formula, requiring $n-1$ more multiplications and n additions and n subtractions.

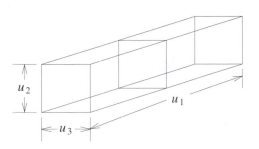

(a) 3-dimensional array $A[u_1][u_2][u_3]$ regarded as u_1 2-dimensional arrays

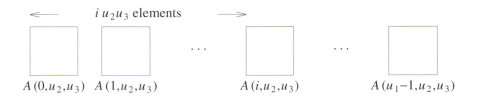

(b)   Sequential row major representation of a 3-dimensional array. Each 2-dimensional array is represented as in Figure 2.6

Figure 2.7: Sequential representation of $A[u_1][u_2][u_3]$

EXERCISES

1.   [**Programming Project**] Even though the multidimensional array is provided as a standard data object in C++, it is often useful to define your own class for multidimensional arrays. This gives a more robust class that:

(a)   Performs range checking.

(b)   Does not require the index set in each dimension to consist of consecutive integers starting at 0.

(c)   Allows array assignment.

(d)   Allows initialization of an array with another array.

(e)   Selects the range in each dimension of the array during runtime.

(f)   Allows dynamic modification of the range and size of the array.

(g)   Provides a mechanism to determine the size of an array.

Implement a class *mdArray* that stores floating point elements and provides the functionality specified above. You will need to define three pointer data members corresponding to one-dimensional arrays, which will be dynamically created: the array of elements, and arrays that store the lower and upper bounds of each dimension. In addition, you may require data members that store the number of dimensions and the total size of the array. The data members of your class must be initialized by a constructor that takes as input the number of dimensions and the range of each dimension. Also, provide operations to read/write array elements from/to a file.

2. How many values can be held by an array with dimensions $a[0..n]$, $b[-1..n][1..m]$, $c[-n..0][1..2]$?

3. Obtain an addressing formula for the element $A[i_1][i_2], \cdots, [i_n]$ in an array declared as $A[l_1..u_1][l_2..u_2], \cdots, [l_n..u_n]$. Assume a row major representation of the array with one word per element and α the address of $A[l_1][l_2], ..., [l_n]$.

4. Do the preceding exercise assuming a column major representation. In this, a two-dimensional array is stored sequentially by columns rather than by rows.

2.6   THE STRING ABSTRACT DATA TYPE

In this section, we turn our attention to a data type, the string, whose component elements are characters. As an ADT, we define a string to have the form $S = s_0, \cdots, s_{n-1}$, where s_i are characters taken from the character set of the programming language, and n is the length of the string. If $n = 0$, then S is an empty or null string.

There are several useful operations we could specify for strings. Some of these operations are similar to those required for other ADTs: creating a new empty string, reading a string or printing it out, appending two strings together (called *concatenation*), or copying a string. However, there are other operations that are unique to our new ADT, including comparing strings, inserting a substring into a string, removing a substring from a string, or finding a pattern in a string. We have listed the essential operations in ADT 2.4, which contains our specification of the string ADT.

C++ allows us to specify *string literal constants* by a sequence of characters enclosed in double quotation marks (e.g. "abc"). The string literal is internally represented as an array of **char**s. This array consists of the string characters followed by the null character which signals the end of the string. String literals may be assigned to variables of type **char**∗ (e.g., **char**∗ *str* = "abc";). Since the string is stored as an array, the *i*th character of string *str* is accessed by *str*[*i*]. Many C++ compilers also provide a string class in their class libraries. Such a class typically includes functions to copy and initialize strings, compare strings, delete and insert substrings and to convert numbers into strings and vice versa. In addition, functions to concatenate strings, return a substring, return the length of a string, and to search for a substring may be provided. In the remainder of this section, we shall examine the problem of string pattern matching. Some of the other string operations mentioned above are examined in the exercises.

---

class *String*
{
// **objects**: A finite ordered set of zero or more characters.
public:
    String(**char** **init*, **int** *m*);
    //Constructor that initializes ***this** to string *init* of length *m*

    int operator==(*String t*);
    // **if** (the string represented by ***this** equals *t*) **return** 1 (TRUE)
    // **else return** 0 (FALSE);

    int operator!();
    // **if** ***this** is empty **then return** 1 (TRUE); **else return** 0 (FALSE);

    int *Length*();
    // **return** the number of characters in ***this**

    String Concat(*String t*);
    // return a string whose elements are those of ***this** followed by those of *t*.

    String Substr(**int** *i*, **int** *j*);
    // return a string containing *j* characters of ***this** at positions $i, i+1, ..., i+j-1$
    // if these are valid positions of ***this**; otherwise, return the empty string.

    int *Find*(*String pat*);
    // return an index *i* such that *pat* matches the substring of ***this** that begins at position *i*.
    // Return -1 if *pat* is either empty or not a substring of ***this**
};

ADT 2.4: Abstract data type *String*

2.6.1   String Pattern Matching: A Simple Algorithm

Assume that we have two strings, *s* and *pat*, where *pat* is a pattern to be searched for in *s*. We will determine if *pat* is in *s* by using the function *Find.* The invocation *s.Find* (*pat*) returns an index *i* such that *pat* matches the substring of *s* that begins at position *i*. It returns -1 if and only if *pat* is either empty or is not a substring of *s*. Let us examine how a function *Find* may be implemented.

We assume that strings are represented by the private data member *str* of type **char***. As before, the first character is in position 0. The easiest but least efficient method is to sequentially consider each position of *s* and determine if it is the starting point of a match. Let *LengthP* and *LengthS* denote the lengths of the pattern *pat* and the string *s*, respectively. Positions of *s* to the right of position *LengthS* − *LengthP* need not be considered, as there are not enough characters to their right to complete a match with *pat*. Function *Find* (Program 2.14) implements this strategy. The complexity of this function is O(*LengthP* · *LengthS*).

```
int String::Find(String pat)
// i is set to −1 if pat does not occur in s (*this);
// otherwise i is set to point to the first position in *this, where pat begins.
{
    char *p = pat.str, *s = str ;
    int i = 0 ;  // i is starting point
    if (*p && *s)
        while (i <= Length() − pat.Length())
            if (*p++ == *s++) { //characters match, get next char in pat and s
                if (!*p) return i ; // match found
            }
            else { // no match
                i++ ; s = str + i ; p = pat.str ;
            }
    return −1 ; //pat is empty or does not occur in s
} // end of Find
```

Program 2.14: Exhaustive pattern matching

We can introduce heuristics into function *Find* that improve its performance on certain pairs of *s* and *pat*. For example, for each position *i* of *s* considered in function *Find*, we may check for a match of the last character of *pat* with the character at position $i + LengthP - 1$ of *s* before examining characters 0 through $LengthP - 2$ of *pat* for a match. The asymptotic complexity of the resulting pattern matching function is still O(*LengthP* · *LengthS*).

2.6.2 String Pattern Matching: The Knuth-Morris-Pratt Algorithm

Ideally, we would like an algorithm that works in O(*LengthP* + *LengthS*) time. This is optimal for this problem, as in the worst case it is necessary to look at all characters in the pattern and string at least once. We want to search the string for the pattern without moving backwards in the string. That is, if a mismatch occurs we want to use our knowledge of the characters in the pattern and the position in the pattern, where the mismatch occurred to determine where we should continue the search. Knuth, Morris, and Pratt have developed a pattern-matching algorithm that works in this way and has linear complexity. Using their example, suppose

$$pat = `a\,b\,c\,a\,b\,c\,a\,c\,a\,b"$$

Let $s = s_0 s_1 \cdots s_{m-1}$ be the string and assume that we are currently determining whether or not there is a match beginning at s_i. If $s_i \neq a$, then clearly we may proceed by comparing s_{i+1} and a. Similarly, if $s_i = a$ and $s_{i+1} \neq b$, then we may proceed by comparing s_{i+1} and a. If $s_i s_{i+1} = ab$ and $s_{i+2} \neq c$ then we have the situation

$$
\begin{array}{ccccccccccc}
s = & \text{`-} & a & b & ? & ? & ? & . & . & . & . & ?\text{'} \\
pat = & & \text{`}a & b & c & a & b & c & a & c & a & b\text{'}
\end{array}
$$

The ? implies that we do not know what the character in s is. The first ? in s represents s_{i+2}, where $s_{i+2} \neq c$. At this point we know that we may continue the search for a match by comparing the first character in pat with s_{i+2}. There is no need to compare this character of pat with s_{i+1}, since we already know that s_{i+1} is the same as the second character of pat, b, and so $s_{i+1} \neq a$. Let us try this again assuming a match of the first four characters in pat followed by a nonmatch, i.e., $s_{i+4} \neq b$. We now have the situation

$$
\begin{array}{ccccccccccc}
s = & \text{`-} & a & b & c & a & ? & ? & . & . & . & ?\text{'} \\
pat = & & \text{`}a & b & c & a & b & c & a & c & a & b\text{'}
\end{array}
$$

We observe that the search for a match can proceed by comparing s_{i+4} and the second character in pat, b. This is the first place a partial match can occur by sliding the pattern pat towards the right. Thus, by knowing the characters in the pattern and the position in the pattern where a mismatch occurs with a character in s, we can determine where in the pattern to continue the search for a match without moving backwards in s. To formalize this, we define a failure function for a pattern.

Definition: If $p = p_0 p_2 \cdots p_{n-1}$ is a pattern, then its *failure function, f,* is defined as

$$
f(j) = \begin{cases} \text{largest } k < j \text{ such that } p_0 p_1 \cdots p_k = p_{j-k} p_{j-k+1} \cdots p_j \text{ if such a } k \geq 0 \text{ exists} \\ -1 \qquad\qquad\qquad\qquad\qquad\qquad\qquad\qquad\qquad\qquad\qquad \text{otherwise.} \end{cases} \quad \square
$$

For the example pattern above, $pat = abcabcacab$, we have

j	0	1	2	3	4	5	6	7	8	9
pat	a	b	c	a	b	c	a	c	a	b
f	-1	-1	-1	0	1	2	3	-1	0	1

From the definition of the failure function, we arrive at the following rule for pattern matching: *If a partial match is found such that $s_{i-j} \cdots s_{i-1} = p_0 p_1 \cdots p_{j-1}$ and $s_i \neq p_j$ then matching may be resumed by comparing s_i and $p_{f(j-1)+1}$ if $j \neq 0$. If $j = 0$, then we may continue by comparing s_{i+1} and p_0.* This pattern-matching rule translates to function *FastFind* (Program 2.15). *FastFind* uses an array of **int**s, f, to represent the failure function. f is a private data member of *String*.

```
1 int String::FastFind(String pat)
2 {
3 // Determine if pat is a substring of s
4   int PosP = 0, PosS = 0 ;
5   int LengthP = pat.Length(), LengthS = Length();
6   while ((PosP < LengthP) && (PosS < LengthS))
7     if (pat.str[PosP] == str[PosS]) { // character match
8       PosP++ ; PosS++ ;
9     }
10    else
11        if (PosP == 0) PosS++;
12        else PosP = pat . f [PosP − 1] + 1 ;
13    if (PosP < LengthP) return −1;
14    else return PosS −LengthP;
15 } // end of FastFind
```

Program 2.15: Pattern-matching with a failure function

Analysis of *FastFind*: The correctness of *FastFind* follows from the definition of the failure function. To determine the computing time, we observe that lines 8 and 11 can be executed for a total of at most *LengthS* times, since in each iteration *PosS* is incremented by 1 but *PosS* is never decremented in the algorithm. As a result, *PosP* can move right on *pat* at most *LengthS* times (line 8). Since each execution of the **else** clause in line 12 moves *PosP* left on *pat*, it follows that this clause can be executed at most *LengthS* times, since otherwise *PosP* becomes less than 0. Consequently, the maximum number of iterations of the **while** loop is *LengthS*, and the computing time of *FastFind* is O(*LengthS*). □

From the analysis of *FastFind*, it follows that if we can compute the failure function in O(*LengthP*) time, then the entire pattern-matching process will have a computing time proportional to the sum of the lengths of the string and pattern. Fortunately, there is a fast way to compute the failure function. This is based upon the following restatement of the failure function:

$$f(j) = \begin{cases} -1 & \text{if } j = 0 \\ f^m(j - 1) + 1 & \text{where } m \text{ is the least integer } k \text{ for which } p_{f^k(j-1)+1} = p_j \\ -1 & \text{if there is no } k \text{ satisfying the above} \end{cases}$$

(Note that $f^1(j) = f(j)$ and $f^m(j) = f(f^{m-1}(j))$). This directly yields the function of Program 2.16 to compute f.

```
 1 void String::fail()
 2 // Compute the failure function for the pattern p (*this).
 3 {
 4   int LengthP = Length() ;
 5   f[0] = −1;
 6   for (int j = 1 ; j < LengthP ; j++)  // compute f [j]
 7   {
 8     int i = f [j−1] ;
 9     while ((*(str + j) != *(str+i+1)) && (i >= 0)) i = f [i];
10     if (*(str + j) == *(str + i + 1)) f [j] = i + 1 ;
11     else f [j] = −1;
12   }
13 } // end of fail
```

Program 2.16: Computing the failure function

Analysis of *fail*: In each iteration of the **while** loop the value of i decreases (by the definition of f). The variable i is reset at the beginning of each iteration of the **for** loop. However, it is either reset to −1 (when $j = 1$ or when the previous iteration went through line 11), or it is reset to a value 1 greater than its terminal value on the previous iteration (i.e., when the previous iteration went through line 10). Since only $LengthP - 1$ executions of line 8 are made, the value of i therefore has a total increment of at most $LengthP - 1$. Hence it cannot be decremented more than $LengthP - 1$ times. Consequently, the **while** loop is iterated at most $LengthP - 1$ times over the whole algorithm, and the computing time of *fail* is O($LengthP$). □

Note that when the failure function is not known in advance, pattern matching can be carried out in time O($LengthP + LengthS$) by first computing the failure function using function *fail* and then performing a pattern match using function *FastFind*.

EXERCISES

1. Write a function *String::frequency* that determines the frequency of occurrence of each of the distinct characters in the string. Test your function using suitable data.

2. Write a function, *String::Delete*, that accepts two integers, *start* and *length*. The function computes a new string that is equivalent to the original string, except that *length* characters beginning at *start* have been removed.

3. Write a function, *String::CharDelete*, that accepts a character *c*. The function returns the string with all occurrences of *c* removed.

4. Write a function to make an in-place replacement of a substring w of a string by the string x. Note that w may not be of the same size as x. What is the complexity of your function?

5. If $x = (x_0, ..., x_{m-1})$ and $y = (y_0, ..., y_{n-1})$ are strings, where x_i and y_i are letters of the alphabet, then x is less than y if $x_i = y_i$ for $0 \le i < j$ and $x_j < y_j$ or if $x_i = y_i$ for $0 \le i \le m$ and $m < n$. Write an algorithm that takes two strings x, y and returns either $-1, 0,$ or $+1$ if $x < y$, $x = y$, or $x > y$ respectively.

6. (a) Find a string and a pattern for which function *Find* (Program 2.14) takes times proportional to $LengthP \cdot LengthS$.

   (b) Do part (a) under the assumption that the function *Find* has been modified to check for a match with the last character of the pattern first (see text for an explanation of this heuristic).

7. Compute the failure function for each of the following patterns:

   (a) $a\,a\,a\,a\,b$;

   (b) $a\,b\,a\,b\,a\,a$; and

   (c) $a\,b\,a\,a\,b\,a\,a\,b\,b$.

8. Let $p_0 p_1 \ldots p_{n-1}$ be a pattern of length n. Let f be its failure function. Define $f^1(j) = f(j)$ and $f^m(j) = f(f^{m-1}(j))$, $0 \le j < n$ and $m > 1$. Show, using the definition of f, that

$$
f(j) = \begin{cases} -1 & \text{if } j = 0 \\ f^m(j-1)+1 & \text{where } m \text{ is the least integer } k \text{ for which } p_{f^k(j-1)+1} = p_j \\ -1 & \text{if there is no } k \text{ satisfying the above} \end{cases}
$$

9. The definition of the failure function may be strengthened to

$$
f(j) = \begin{cases} \text{largest } i < j \text{ such that } p_0 \cdots p_i = p_{j-i} \cdots p_j \text{ and } p_{i+1} \ne p_{j+1} \\ -1 \qquad \text{if there is no } i \ge 0 \text{ satisfying above} \end{cases}
$$

   (a) Obtain the new failure function for the pattern *pat* of the text.

   (b) Show that if this definition for f is used, then algorithm *FastFind* (Program 2.15) still works correctly.

   (c) Modify algorithm *fail* (Program 2.16) to compute f under this definition. Show that the computing time is still $O(m)$.

   (d) Are there any patterns for which the observed computing time of *FastFind* is more with the new definition of f than with the old one? Are there any for which it is less? Give examples.

2.7   REFERENCES AND SELECTED READINGS

The Knuth, Morris, Pratt pattern-matching algorithm can be found in ''Fast pattern matching in strings,'' *SIAM Journal on Computing*, 6:2, 1977, pp. 323-350.

2.8   ADDITIONAL EXERCISES

1. Given an array $a[n]$ produce the array $z[n]$ such that $z[0] = a[n-1]$, $z[1] = a[n-2]$, ..., $z[n-2] = a[1]$, $z[n-1] = a[0]$. Use a minimal amount of storage.

2. Let $L = (a_0, a_1, \cdots, a_{n-1})$ be a linear list represented in the array $M[n]$ using the following mapping: The ith element of L is stored in $M[i]$. Write an algorithm to make an in-place reversal of the order of elements in M. That is, the algorithm should transform M such that $M[i]$ contains the $(n-i-1)$th element of L. The only additional space available to your algorithm is that for simple variables. The input to the algorithm is M and n. How much time does your algorithm take to accomplish the reversal?

3. An $m \times n$ matrix is said to have a saddle point if some entry $a[i][j]$ is the smallest value in row i and the largest value in column j. Write a C++ function that determines the location of a saddle point if one exists. What is the computing time of your method?

4. When all the elements either above or below the main diagonal of a square matrix are zero, then the matrix is said to be triangular. Figure 2.8 shows a lower and an upper triangular matrix.

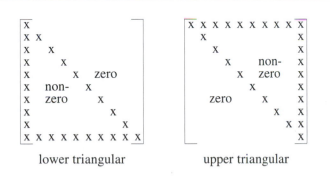

lower triangular   upper triangular

Figure 2.8: Lower and upper triangular matrices

In a lower triangular matrix, A, with n rows, the maximum number of nonzero terms in row i is $i+1$. Hence, the total number of nonzero terms is

$\sum_{i=0}^{n-1} (i + 1) = n (n + 1)/2$. For large n it would be worthwhile to save the space taken by the zero entries in the upper triangle. Obtain an addressing formula for elements a_{ij} in the lower triangle if this lower triangle is stored by rows in an array $B[n (n + 1)/2]$ with $A[0][0]$ being stored in $B[0]$. What is the relationship between i and j for elements in the zero part of A?

5. Let A and B be two lower triangular matrices, each with n rows. The total number of elements in the lower triangles is $n (n + 1)$. Devise a scheme to represent both the triangles in an array $c[n][n+1]$. [Hint: Represent the triangle of A as the lower triangle of c and the transpose of B as the upper triangle of c.] Write algorithms to determine the values of $A[i][j]$, $B[i][j]$, $0 \le i$, $j < n$, from the array c.

6. Another kind of sparse matrix that arises often in practice is the tridiagonal matrix. In this square matrix, all elements other than those on the major diagonal and on the diagonals immediately above and below this one are zero (Figure 2.9).

Figure 2.9: Tridiagonal matrix

If the elements in the band formed by these three diagonals are represented by rows in an array, b, with $A[0][0]$ being stored in $b[0]$, obtain an algorithm to determine the value of $A[i][j]$, $0 \le i$, $j < n$ from the array b.

7. A square band matrix $A_{n,a}$ is an $n \times n$ matrix in which all the nonzero terms lie in a band centered around the main diagonal. The band includes $a - 1$ diagonals below and above the main diagonal and also the main diagonal (Figure 2.10).

  (a) How many elements are there in the band of $A_{n,a}$?

  (b) What is the relationship between i and j for elements a_{ij} in the band of $A_{n,a}$?

  (c) Assume that the band of $A_{n,a}$ is stored sequentially in an array b by diagonals starting with the lowermost diagonal. Thus, $A_{4,3}$ above would have the following representation:

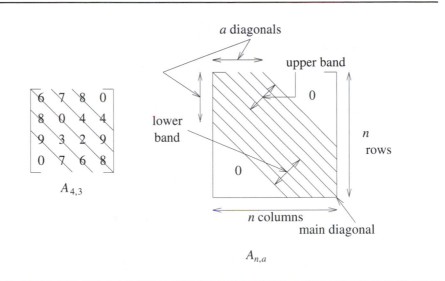

Figure 2.10: Square band matrix

b[0]	b[1]	b[2]	b[3]	b[4]	b[5]	b[6]	b[7]	b[8]	b[9]	b[10]	b[11]	b[12]	b[13]
9	7	8	3	6	6	0	2	8	7	4	9	8	4
a_{20}	a_{31}	a_{10}	a_{21}	a_{32}	a_{00}	a_{11}	a_{22}	a_{33}	a_{01}	a_{12}	a_{23}	a_{02}	a_{13}

Obtain an addressing formula for the location of an element a_{ij} in the lower band of $A_{n,a}$, e.g., $LOC(a_{20}) = 0$, $LOC(a_{31}) = 1$ in the example above.

8. A generalized band matrix $A_{n,a,b}$ is an $n \times n$ matrix A in which all the nonzero terms lie in a band made up of $a - 1$ diagonals below the main diagonal, the main diagonal, and $b - 1$ diagonals above the main diagonal (Figure 2.11).

   (a) How many elements are there in the band of $A_{n,a,b}$?

   (b) What is the relationship between i and j for elements a_{ij} in the band of $A_{n,a,b}$?

   (c) Obtain a sequential representation of the band of $A_{n,a,b}$ in the one-dimensional array c. For this representation, write a C++ function *value* (n,a,b,i,j,c) that determines the value of element a_{ij} in the matrix $A_{n,a,b}$. The band of $A_{n,a,b}$ is represented in the array c.

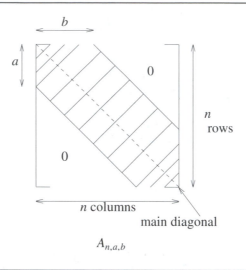

$A_{n,a,b}$

Figure 2.11: Generalized band matrix

9. [*Programming Project*] There are a number of problems, known collectively as "random walk" problems, that have been of longstanding interest to the mathematical community. All but the most simple of these are extremely difficult to solve and for the most part they remain largely unsolved. One such problem may be stated as

> A (drunken) cockroach is placed on a given square in the middle of a tile floor in a rectangular room of size $n \times m$ tiles. The bug wanders (possibly in search of an aspirin) randomly from tile to tile throughout the room. Assuming that he may move from his present tile to any of the eight tiles surrounding him (unless he is against a wall) *with equal probability*, how long will it take him to touch every tile on the floor at least once?

Hard as this problem may be to solve by probability theory techniques, it is easy to solve using the computer. The technique for doing so is called "simulation." This technique is widely used in industry to predict traffic flow, inventory control, and so forth. The problem may be simulated using the following method:

An $n \times m$ array *count* is used to represent the number of times our cockroach has reached each tile on the floor. All the cells of this array are initialized to zero. The position of the bug on the floor is represented by the coordinates $(ibug, jbug)$. The eight possible moves of the bug are represented by the tiles located at $(ibug + imove[k], jbug + jmove[k])$, where $0 \le k \le 7$ and

$$imove[0] = -1 \quad jmove[0] = 1$$
$$imove[1] = 0 \quad jmove[1] = 1$$
$$imove[2] = 1 \quad jmove[2] = 1$$
$$imove[3] = 1 \quad jmove[3] = 0$$
$$imove[4] = 1 \quad jmove[4] = -1$$
$$imove[5] = 0 \quad jmove[5] = -1$$
$$imove[6] = -1 \quad jmove[6] = -1$$
$$imove[7] = -1 \quad jmove[7] = 0$$

A *random walk* to one of the eight given squares is simulated by generating a random value for k lying between 0 and 7. Of course, the bug cannot move outside the room, so coordinates that lead up a wall must be ignored and a new random combination formed. Each time a square is entered, the count for that square is incremented so that a nonzero entry shows the number of times the bug has landed on that square so far. When every square has been entered at least once, the experiment is complete.

Write a program to perform the specified simulation experiment. Your program *MUST*:

(a) handle all values of n and m, $2 < n \le 40$, $2 \le m \le 20$

(b) perform the experiment for (1) $n = 15$, $m = 15$, starting point: (9,9) and (2) $n = 39$, $m = 19$, starting point: (0,0)

(c) have an iteration limit, that is, a maximum number of squares the bug may enter during the experiment (this avoids getting hung in an infinite loop); a maximum of 50,000 is appropriate for this exercise

(d) for each experiment, print (1) the total number of legal moves that the cockroach makes and (2) the final *count* array (this will show the density of the walk, that is, the number of times each tile on the floor was touched during the experiment).

(Have an aspirin.) This exercise was contributed by Steve Olson.

10. [*Programming Project*] Chess provides the setting for many fascinating diversions that are quite independent of the game itself. Many of these are based on the strange L-shaped move of the knight. A classical example is the problem of the knight's tour, which has captured the attention of mathematicians and puzzle enthusiasts since the beginning of the eighteenth century. Briefly stated, the problem is to move the knight, beginning from any given square on the chessboard, in such a manner that it travels successively to all 64 squares, touching each square once and only once. It is convenient to represent a solution by placing the numbers 1, 2, $\cdots$, 64 in the squares of the chessboard indicating the order in which the squares are reached. Note that it is not required that the knight be able to reach the initial position by one more move; if this is possible, the knight's tour

is called re-entrant. One of the more ingenious methods for solving the problem of the knight's tour was that given by J. C. Warnsdorff in 1823. His rule was that the knight must always be moved to one of the squares from which there are the fewest exits to squares not already traversed. Use Warnsdorff's rule to construct a particular solution to the problem by hand before reading any further.

The most important decisions to be made in solving a problem of this type are those concerning how the data is to be represented in the computer. Perhaps the most natural way to represent the chessboard is by an 8×8 array *board*, as shown in Figure 2.12. The eight possible moves of a knight on square (4,2) are also shown in this figure.

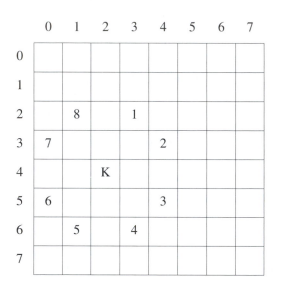

Figure 2.12: Legal moves for a knight

In general a knight at (i, j) may move to one of the squares $(i - 2, j + 1)$, $(i - 1, j + 2)$, $(i + 1, j + 2)$, $(i + 2, j + 1)$, $(i + 2, j - 1)$, $(i + 1, j - 2)$, $(i - 1, j - 2)$, $(i - 2, j - 1)$. Notice, however, that if (i, j) is located near one of the edges of the board, some of these possibilities could move the knight off the board, and, of course, this is not permitted. The eight possible knight moves may conveniently be represented by two arrays *ktmov1* and *ktmov2*:

ktmov1	ktmov2
−2	1
−1	2
1	2
2	1
2	−1
1	−2
−1	−2
−2	−1

Then a knight at (i,j) may move to $(i + ktmov1[k],j + ktmov2[k])$, where k is some value between 0 and 7, provided that the new square lies on the chessboard.

An algorithm to solve the knight's tour problem using Warnsdoff's rule is described below.

(a) *[**Initialize chessboard**]* For $0 \leq i,j \leq 7$, set *board* $[i][j]$ to 0.

(b) *[**Set starting position**]* Read and print i,j and then set *board*$[i][j]$ to 1.

(c) *[**Loop**]* For $2 \leq m \leq 64$, do steps (d) through (g).

(d) *[**Form set of possible next squares**]* Test each of the eight squares one knight's move away from (i,j) and form a list of the possibilities for the next square (*nexti* $[l]$,*nextj* $[l]$). Let *npos* be the number of possibilities. (That is, after performing this step we will have *nexti* $[l] = i + ktmov1[k]$ and *nextj* $[l]$ $= j + ktmov2[k]$, for certain values of k between 0 and 7. Some of the squares $(i + ktmov1[k], j + ktmov2[k])$ may be impossible for the next move either because they lie off the chessboard or because they have been previously occupied by the knight (i.e., they contain a nonzero number). In every case we will have $0 \leq npos \leq 8$.)

(e) *[**Test special cases**]* If *npos* $= 0$, the knight's tour has come to a premature end; report failure and then go to step (h). If *npos* $= 1$, there is only one possibility for the next move; set *min* $= 0$ and go right to step (g).

(f) *[**Find next square with minimum number of exits**]* For $1 \leq l \leq npos$ set *exits*$[l]$ to the number of exits from square (*nexti* $[l]$,*nextj* $[l]$). That is, for each of the values of l, examine each of the next squares (*nexti* $[l]$+*ktmov1*$[k]$, *nextj* $[l]$ + *ktmov2*$[k]$) to see if it is an exit from (*nexti* $[l]$,*nextj* $[l]$), and count the number of such exits in *exits* $[l]$. (Recall that a square is an exit if it lies on the chessboard and has not been previously occupied by the knight.) Finally, set *min* to the location of the minimum value of *exits*. (There may be more than one occurrence of the minimum value of *exits*. If this happens, it is convenient to let *min* denote the first such occurrence, although it is important to realize that by so doing we are not actually guaranteed finding a solution. Nevertheless, the chances of finding a complete knight's tour in this way are remarkably good, and that is sufficient for the purposes of this exercise.)

(g)   [***Move knight***] Set $i = nexti\,[min\,]$, $j = nextj\,[min\,]$, and $board[i\,][j\,] = m$. Thus, (i,j) denotes the new position of the knight, and $board[i\,][j\,]$ records the move in proper sequence.

(h)   [***Print***] Print out *board* showing the solution to the knight's tour and then terminate the algorithm.

The problem is to write a C++ program that corresponds to this algorithm. This exercise was contributed by Legenhausen and Rebman.

CHAPTER 3

STACKS AND QUEUES

3.1   Templates in C++

In this section, we will introduce the concept of templates. This is a mechanism provided by C++ to make classes and functions more reusable. We will discuss both template functions and template classes.

3.1.1   Templates Functions

Consider function *sort* of Program 1.3 which sorts an array of integers using the selection sort method. Suppose, we now wish to use selection sort to sort an array of floating point numbers. The code of Program 1.3 can be used to do this if the following changes are made:

1) In line 1, change **int** *∗a* to **float** *∗a*.
2) In line 2, replace ''integers'' with ''floats''.
3) In line 11, replace **int** with **float**.

From a practical standpoint, this can be achieved by using a screen editor to replicate the code for function *sort* and then making the changes listed above. This process would have to be repeated if we next wished to sort an array of, say, characters.

instant

Considerable software development time and memory can be saved if we use *templates* or *parameterized types*. A template may be viewed as a variable that can be instantiated to any data type, irrespective of whether this data type is a fundamental C++ type or a user-defined type. Function *sort* (Program 3.1) is defined using the parameterized type *KeyType*.

```
1 template <class KeyType>
2 void sort (KeyType *a, int n)
3 // sort the n KeyTypes a [0] to a [n − 1] into nondecreasing order
4 {
5      for ( int i = 0; i < n ; i++)
6      {
7           int j = i;
8           // find smallest KeyType in a [i ] to a [n − 1]
9           for ( int k = i+1 ; k < n; k++ )
10               if (a[k] < a[j]) { j = k;}
11          // interchange
12          KeyType temp = a[i]; a[i] = a[j]; a[j] = temp;
13     }
14 }
```

Program 3.1: Selection sort using templates

Function *sort* can now be used quite easily to sort an array of **int**s or **float**s as shown in Program 3.2. Function *sort* is instantiated to the type of the array argument that is supplied to it. For example, the first call to *sort* knows that it is to sort an array of floating point numbers because array *farray* is an array of floating point numbers.

```
float farray[100];
int intarray[250];
    .
    .
// assume that the arrays are initialized at this point
sort(farray, 100);
sort(intarray, 250);
```

Program 3.2: Code fragment illustrating template instantiation

Observe that *sort* uses the operator "<" to compare two *KeyType* objects in line 10, the operator "=" to assign one *KeyType* object to another in line 12, and the copy constructor which defines *temp* to be a variable of type *KeyType* and initializes it to a [i] in line 12.

The copy constructor is a special constructor which is invoked when an object is initialized with another object. An initialization may be distinguished from an assignment by the presence of a type specifier that specifies the type of the lhs (left hand side) object. The three operations <, =, and the copy constructor are automatically defined for **int** and **float**, but they are not pre-defined for user-defined data types. However, these operators may be overloaded by providing a function which implements a new meaning for the operators. An operator should be overloaded in a manner that is consistent with its usage. For example, function *sort* is based on the assumption that < is transitive. If operator < were overloaded for a data type so that it is not transitive, then *sort* will not work for that data type.

Suppose we want to use *sort* to sort an array of *Rectangle*s in nondecreasing order of their areas. We cannot instantiate *KeyType* to *Rectangle* as we did with **int** and **float** in Program 3.2 because operator "<" of line 10 is undefined for *Rectangle*. This can be easily remedied by overloading **operator<** so that it returns 1 if the first operand has less area than the second and 0, otherwise. If the assignment operator and copy constructor for a class are not defined by the user, the compiler creates its own default implementation for each. For both operations, this default implementation simply copies individual data members of the rhs object into the lhs object. This is sufficient for the *Rectangle* example, and so the user does not need to explicitly define the implementations of these operations.

3.1.2   Using Templates to Represent Container Classes

A *container class* is a class that represents a data structure that contains or stores a number of data objects. Objects can usually be added to or deleted from a container class. The array is an example of a container class as it is used to store a number of objects. We begin by introducing a container class that we will call *Bag*. Our specification for the **class** *Bag* is that it is a data structure into which objects can be inserted and from which objects can be deleted, like a bag of groceries. A bag can have multiple occurrences of the same element, but we do not care about the position of an element; nor do we care which element is removed when a delete operation is performed. We implement *Bag* by using a C++ array to hold its objects. Program 3.3 contains the class definition of a *Bag* of integers.

We implement insertion into the *Bag* by storing the element into the first available position in the array. Deletion is implemented by deleting the element in the middle position of the array, and then moving all elements to its right, one position to the left. Our implementation decisions for choosing the positions at which an element will be inserted or deleted were arbitrary. We could have just as easily decreed that elements should be inserted into the middle position and deleted from the last position of the array. In either case, our specification for the *Bag* data structure is satisfied. Program 3.4 contains our implementation of its operations.

---

class *Bag*
{
public:
  Bag (**int** *MaxSize* = DefaultSize) ; // constructor
  ~*Bag*() ; // destructor

  void *Add*(**int**) ; // insert an integer into bag
  int * *Delete*(**int**&) ; // delete an integer from bag

  Boolean IsFull() ; // return TRUE if the bag is full; FALSE otherwise
  Boolean IsEmpty() ; // return TRUE if the bag is empty; FALSE otherwise

private:
  void *Full*() ; // action when bag is full
  void *Empty*(); // action when bag is empty

  int *array* ;
  int *MaxSize* ; // size of array
  int *top* ; // highest position in array that contains an element
};

Program 3.3: Definition of **class** *Bag* containing integers

Most of the operations on *Bag* need no explanation. We have declared member functions *Full*(), *Empty*(), *IsFull*(), and *IsEmpty*() as **inline** because of their small size (each contains only two lines of code). This eliminates the overhead of performing a function call.

Notice that member function *Delete* returns a pointer to an integer rather than an integer. Suppose we define *Delete* so that it returns the integer that is deleted from the bag. What would the function return if the bag is empty? The function must return an integer. So we could designate an integer (e.g., −1) which could be returned to signal to the calling function that the bag is empty. Now, suppose that *Delete* returns −1. How does the calling function know whether the integer −1 was returned because it was deleted from the bag or because the bag was empty? In view of these difficulties, we define *Delete* to return a pointer to the deleted integer. If the bag is empty, the 0 pointer is returned. However, this raises another question: if a pointer to an integer is returned, where is the integer that the pointer points to? In the *Bag* example, the integer is physically present in *array*. So, we could conceivably return a pointer to the appropriate array element. In other container classes we will study, this is not possible because the element to be deleted no longer exists after *Delete* terminates. In these cases, it is necessary to copy the element to be deleted to some other location before it is deleted. This is

```
Bag::Bag (int MaxBagSize): MaxSize ( MaxBagSize ) {
   array = new int[MaxSize] ; top = −1 ;
}

Bag::˜Bag() { delete [ ] array ;}

inline Boolean Bag::IsFull() {
   if (top == MaxSize − 1) return TRUE ; else return FALSE ;
}

inline Boolean Bag::IsEmpty() {
   if (top == −1) return TRUE ; else return FALSE ;
}

inline void Bag::Full() {
   cerr << "Data structure is full" << endl ;
}

inline void Bag::Empty() {
   cerr << "Data structure is empty" << endl ;
}

void Bag::Add(int x) {
   if (IsFull()) Full() ; else array[++top] = x ;
}

int* Bag::Delete(int& x)
{
   if (IsEmpty()) { Empty() ; return 0 ; }
   int deletePos = top / 2 ; x = array[deletePos] ;
   for (int index = deletePos ; index < top ; index++)
      array[index] = array[index + 1] ; // compact upper half of array
   top −− ; return &x ;
}
```

Program 3.4: Implementation of operations on *Bag*

achieved by passing a reference parameter to the function. The element is copied into this reference parameter and a pointer to it is returned. The location corresponding to this reference parameter does not go out of scope on termination of *Delete*, and the pointer contains the address of a valid location. Even though the reference parameter is not required in *Bag* and the other representations of this chapter, we use it to be consistent with other implementations that will follow in later chapters.

As we have defined it, *Bag* can only be used to store integers. We would like to implement *Bag* using templates so that it can be used to store objects of any data type. Container classes are particularly suitable for implementation using *templates* because the algorithms for basic container class operations are usually independent of the type of objects that it contains. For example, the algorithm to insert an element into *Bag* does not depend on the type of its elements. Program 3.5 contains a template class definition for a *Bag* and Program 3.6 contains the implementation of some of its operations. These are obtained from Program 3.3 and Program 3.4, respectively, by prefixing the class definition of *Bag* and the definitions of all its member functions that are outside the class (in our example, all member functions are defined outside the class definition) with the statement:

template<class *Type*>

Next, **int** is replaced by *Type* when it refers to an object being stored in *Bag*. Finally, in all member functions headers, the instance of "*Bag*" that associates the function with **class** *Bag* is followed by <*Type*>. Notice, also, that the single input parameter to member function*Add* is made a constant reference. This is done because it is now possible that *Type* represents a large object, and considerable overhead may be incurred if it is passed by value. (It is assumed that *Type* will not be instantiated to a reference type such as **int**&; otherwise the expression *Type*& will become **int**&&, which is an error.)

The following two statements instantiate the template class *Bag* to **int** and *Rectangle*, respectively. So, *a* is a *Bag* of integers and *r* is a *Bag* of *Rectangle*s.

Bag<**int**> *a* ;
Bag<*Rectangle*> *r* ;

3.2   THE STACK ABSTRACT DATA TYPE

We shall now study two data types that are frequently used in computer science. These data types, the stack and the queue, are special cases of the more general data type *ordered list* that we discussed in Chapter 2. Recall that $A = a_0, a_1, \cdots, a_{n-1}$ is an ordered list of $n \geq 0$ elements. We refer to the a_i's as *atoms* or *elements* that are taken from some set. The null or empty list, denoted by ( ), has $n = 0$ elements. In this section we begin by defining the ADT *stack* and follow with its implementation. In Section 3.3 we look at the queue.

```
template <class Type>
class Bag
{
public:
    Bag (int MaxSize = DefaultSize) ; // constructor
    ~Bag() ; // destructor

    void Add(const Type&) ; // insert element into bag
    Type * Delete(Type&) ; // delete element from bag

    Boolean IsFull() ;  // return TRUE if the bag is full; FALSE otherwise
    Boolean IsEmpty() ; // return TRUE if the bag is empty; FALSE otherwise

private:
    void Full() ; //  action when bag is full
    void Empty(); // action when bag is empty

    Type *array ;
    int MaxSize ; // size of array
    int top ; // highest position in array that contains an element
};
```

Program 3.5: Definition of template **class** *Bag*

A *stack* is an ordered list in which insertions and deletions are made at one end called the *top*. Given a stack $S = (a_0, \cdots, a_{n-1})$, we say that a_0 is the bottom element, a_{n-1} is the top element, and a_i is on top of element a_{i-1}, $0 < i < n$. The restrictions on the stack imply that if we add the elements A, B, C, D, E to the stack, in that order, then E is the first element we delete from the stack. Figure 3.1 illustrates this sequence of operations. Since the last element inserted into a stack is the first element removed, a stack is also known as a *Last-In-First-Out (LIFO)* list.

Example 3.1 [*System stack*]: Before we discuss the stack ADT, we look at a special stack, called the system stack, that is used by a program at run time to process function calls. Whenever a function is invoked, the program creates a structure, referred to as an *activation record* or a *stack frame*, and places it on top of the system stack. Initially, the activation record for the invoked function contains only a pointer to the previous stack frame and a return address. The previous stack frame pointer points to the stack frame of the invoking function; the return address contains the location of the statement to be executed after the function terminates. Since only one function executes at any given time, the function whose stack frame is on top of the system stack is chosen. If this function

---

```
template <class Type>
Bag<Type>::Bag (int MaxBagSize): MaxSize ( MaxBagSize ) {
  array = new Type[MaxSize] ;
  top = -1 ;
}

template <class Type>
Bag<Type>::~Bag() {
  delete [ ] array ;
}

template <class Type>
void Bag<Type>::Add(const Type& x) {
  if (IsFull()) Full() ;
  else array[++top] = x ;
}

template <class Type>
Type* Bag<Type>::Delete(Type& x) {
  if (IsEmpty()) { Empty() ; return 0 ; }
  int deletePos = top / 2 ;
  x = array[deletePos] ;
  for (int index = deletePos ; index < top ; index++)
    array[index] = array[index + 1] ; // compact upper half of array
  top -- ;
  return &x ;
}
```

Program 3.6: Implementation of operations on *Bag*

invokes another function, the local variables and the parameters of the invoking function are added to its stack frame. A new stack frame is then created for the invoked function and placed on top of the system stack. When this function terminates, its stack frame is removed and the processing of the invoking function, which is again on top of the stack, continues. A simple example illustrates this process. (We refer the reader who wants a more detailed discussion of stack frames to Holub's book on compiler design cited in the References and Selected Readings section.)

Assume that we have a main function that invokes function $a1$. Figure 3.2(a) shows the system stack before $a1$ is invoked; Figure 3.2(b) shows the system stack after $a1$ has been invoked. Frame pointer *fp* is a pointer to the current stack frame. The system also maintains separately a stack pointer, *sp*, which we have not illustrated.

Figure 3.1: Inserting and deleting elements in a stack

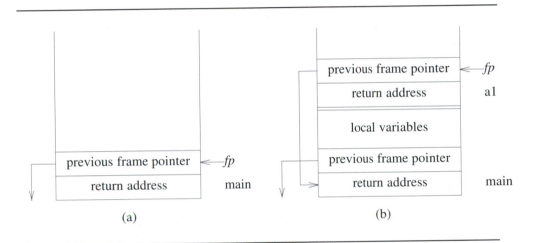

Figure 3.2: System stack after function call

Since all functions are stored similarly in the system stack, it makes no difference if the invoking function calls itself. That is, a recursive call requires no special strategy; the run-time program simply creates a new stack frame for each recursive call. However, recursion can consume a significant portion of the memory allocated to the system stack; it could consume the entire available memory. □

Our discussion of the system stack suggests a basic set of operations, including insert an item, delete an item, and check for stack full or empty. These are given in the ADT specification (ADT 3.1).

The easiest way to implement this ADT is by using a one-dimensional array, say *stack* [*MaxSize*], where *MaxSize* is the maximum number of entries. The first, or bottom,

---

```
template <class KeyType>
class Stack
{
// objects: A finite ordered list with zero or more elements.
public:
    Stack (int MaxStackSize = DefaultSize) ;
    // Create an empty stack whose maximum size is MaxStackSize

    Boolean IsFull() ;
    // if number of elements in the stack is equal to the maximum size of
    // the stack, return TRUE (1); otherwise, return FALSE (0)

    void Add (const KeyType& item ) ;
    // if IsFull(), then StackFull(); else insert item into the top of the stack.

    Boolean IsEmpty() ;
    // if number of elements in the stack is 0, return TRUE (1) else return FALSE (0).

    KeyType* Delete(KeyType&) ;
    // if IsEmpty(), then StackEmpty() and return 0;
    // else remove and return a pointer to the top element of the stack.
};
```

ADT 3.1: Abstract data type *Stack*

element of the stack is stored in *stack* [0], the second in *stack* [1], and the *i*th in *stack* [*i* −1]. Associated with the array is a variable, *top*, which points to the top element in the stack. Initially, *top* is set to −1 to denote an empty stack. This results in the following data member declarations and constructor definition of *Stack*:

```
private:
    int top ;
    KeyType *stack ;
    int MaxSize ;

template <class KeyType>
Stack<KeyType>::Stack (int MaxStackSize) : MaxSize (MaxStackSize)
{
    stack = new KeyType[MaxSize] ;
    top = −1 ;
}
```

The member functions *IsFull( )* and *IsEmpty( )* are implemented as follows:

```
template <class KeyType>
inline Boolean  Stack<KeyType>::IsFull()
{
   if (top == MaxSize −1) return TRUE ;
   else return FALSE ;
}
```

```
template <class KeyType>
inline Boolean  Stack<KeyType>::IsEmpty()
{
   if (top == −1) return TRUE ;
   else return FALSE ;
}
```

The *Add* and *Delete* operations use these functions as shown in Programs 3.7 and 3.8.

```
template <class KeyType>
void Stack<KeyType>::Add (const KeyType& x)
// add x to stack
{
   if (IsFull()) StackFull();
   else stack[++top] = x ;
}
```

Program 3.7: Adding to a stack

```
template <class KeyType>
KeyType* Stack<KeyType>::Delete (KeyType& x)
// Remove top element from stack.
{
   if (IsEmpty()) { StackEmpty(); return 0;}
   x = stack [top −−];
   return &x ;
}
```

Program 3.8: Deleting from a stack

The value returned by *Delete* is of type *KeyType**, rather than *KeyType* or *Key-Type&* to handle the case when the stack is empty. In this case, 0 is returned. Our reasons for passing a reference parameter to the function and returning a pointer are similar to those used in the *Bag* data structure defined in Section 3.1.2.

StackFull( ) and *StackEmpty*( ) are functions that we leave unspecified, since they will depend upon the particular application. Often when a stack becomes full, the *StackFull*( ) function will signal that more storage needs to be allocated and the program rerun. *StackEmpty*( ) is often a meaningful condition in the context of the application for which the stack is being used. In Sections 3.5 and 3.6, we will see important applications of stacks where *StackEmpty*( ) signals the end of processing.

EXERCISES

1. Write C++ code for the *StackFull*( ) function so that it dynamically creates an array *stack* of twice the size of the current array. The elements that were present in the original array should still occupy the first *MaxSize* positions.

2. Consider the railroad switching network given in Figure 3.3. Railroad cars numbered 1, 2, 3, . . ., n are initially in the top right track segment (in this order, left to right). Railroad cars can be moved into the vertical track segment one at a time from either of the horizontal segments and then moved from the vertical segment to any one of the horizontal segments. The vertical segment operates as a stack as new cars enter at the top and cars depart the vertical segment from the top. For instance, if $n = 3$, we could move car 1 into the vertical segment, move 2 in, move 3 in, and then take the cars out producing the new order 3, 2, 1. For $n = 3$ and 4 what are the possible permutations of the cars that can be obtained? Are any permutations not possible?

Figure 3.3: Railroad switching network

3.3   THE QUEUE ABSTRACT DATA TYPE

A *queue* is an ordered list in which all insertions take place at one end and all deletions take place at the opposite end. Given a queue $Q = (a_0, a_1, \cdots, a_{n-1})$, a_0 is the front element, a_{n-1} is the rear element, and a_i is behind a_{i-1}, $1 \leq i < n$. The restrictions on a queue imply that if we insert A, B, C, D, and E in that order, then A is the first element deleted from the queue. Figure 3.4 illustrates this sequence of events. Since the first element inserted into a queue is the first element removed, queues are also known as *First-In-First-Out (FIFO)* lists. The ADT specification of the queue appears in ADT 3.2.

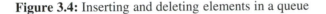

A	A B	A B C	A B C D	A B C D E	B C D E
↑	↑ ↑	↑ ↑	↑ ↑	↑ ↑	↑ ↑
f,r	f r	f r	f r	f r	f r
	add	add	add	add	delete

f = queue front   r = queue rear

Figure 3.4: Inserting and deleting elements in a queue

The representation of a queue in sequential locations is more difficult than that of the stack. The simplest scheme employs a one-dimensional array and two variables, *front* and *rear*. *front* is one less than the position of the first element in the queue, and *rear* is the position of the last element in the queue. This results in the following data member declarations and constructor definition of *Queue*:

private:
   int *front, rear* ;
   KeyType *queue ;
   int *MaxSize* ;

template <**class** *KeyType*>
Queue<*KeyType*>::*Queue* (**int** *MaxQueueSize*) : *MaxSize* (*MaxQueueSize*)
{
   queue = **new** *KeyType*[*MaxSize*] ;
   front = *rear* = −1 ;
}

The member functions *IsFull*( ) and *IsEmpty*( ) are implemented as follows:

---

template <**class** *KeyType*>
class *Queue*
{
// **objects**: A finite ordered list with zero or more elements.
public:
   Queue(**int** *MaxQueueSize* = DefaultSize) ;
   // Create an empty queue whose maximum size is *MaxQueueSize*

   Boolean IsFull( )**;**
   // if number of elements in the queue is equal to the maximum size of
   // the queue, return TRUE (1); otherwise, return FALSE (0)

   void *Add* (**const** *KeyType*& *item*) **;**
   // if *IsFull*( ), then *QueueFull*(); else insert *item* at rear of the queue.

   Boolean IsEmpty( ) **;**
   // if number of elements in the queue is equal to 0, return TRUE (1)
   // else return FALSE (0).

   KeyType∗ *Delete*(*KeyType*&) **;**
   // if *IsEmpty*(), then *QueueEmpty*() and return 0;
   // else remove the item at the front of the queue and return a pointer to it.
};

ADT 3.2: Abstract data type *Queue*

template <**class** *KeyType*>
inline *Boolean Queue*<*KeyType*>::*IsFull*()
{
   if (*rear* == *MaxSize* −1) **return** TRUE **;**
   else return FALSE **;**
}

template <**class** *KeyType*>
inline *Boolean Queue*<*KeyType*>::*IsEmpty*()
{
   if (*front* == *rear*) **return** TRUE **;**
   else return FALSE **;**
}

The above implementation of *IsFull*( ) does not correspond accurately to the specification provided in ADT 3.2, since it is possible that *rear* = *MaxSize* −1 and *front* > −1. In this case, the number of elements in the queue is less than *MaxSize*. We shall account for this discrepancy later. The *IsEmpty*( ) and *IsFull*( ) operations are used in the *Add* (Program 3.9) and *Delete* (Program 3.10) functions.

```
template <class KeyType>
void Queue<KeyType>::Add (const KeyType& x)
// add x to the queue
{
    if (IsFull()) QueueFull();
    else queue[++rear] = x ;
}
```

Program 3.9: Adding to a queue

```
template <class KeyType>
KeyType* Queue<KeyType>::Delete ()
// Remove front element from queue
{
    if (IsEmpty()) { QueueEmpty(); return 0;}
    x = queue[++front];
    return x ;
}
```

Program 3.10: Deleting from a queue

This sequential representation of a queue has pitfalls that are best illustrated by an example.

Example 3.2 [*Job scheduling*]: Queues are frequently used in computer programming, and a typical example is the creation of a job queue by an operating system. If the operating system does not use priorities, then the jobs are processed in the order they enter the system. Figure 3.5 illustrates how an operating system might process jobs if it used a sequential representation for its queue.

It should be obvious that as jobs enter and leave the system, the queue gradually shifts to the right. This means that eventually the rear index equals *MaxSize* − 1, suggesting that the queue is full. In this case, *QueueFull*( ) should move the entire queue to the left so that the first element is again at *queue* [0] and *front* is −1. It should also recalculate *rear* so that it is correctly positioned. Shifting an array is very time-consuming, particularly when there are many elements in it. In fact, *QueueFull*( ) has a worst-case complexity of O(*MaxSize*). □

front	rear	Q[0]	[1]	[2]	[3]	[4]	[5]	[6]	...	Comments
−1	−1		queue		empty					initial
−1	0	J1								Job 1 joins Q
−1	1	J1	J2							Job 2 joins Q
−1	2	J1	J2	J3						Job 3 joins Q
0	2		J2	J3						Job 1 leaves Q
0	3		J2	J3	J4					Job 4 joins Q
1	3			J3	J4					Job 2 leaves Q

Figure 3.5: Insertion and deletion from a queue

Let us look at an example (Figure 3.6) that shows what could happen, in the worst case, if each time a queue of size $MaxSize = n$ becomes full we choose to move the entire queue left so that it starts at $q[0]$. To begin, assume there are n elements J1, $\cdots$, Jn in the queue, and we next receive alternate requests to delete and add elements. Each time a new element is added, the entire queue of $n-1$ elements is moved left.

front	*rear*	q[0]	[1]	[2]	...	[n−1]	Next Operation
−1	n−1	J1	J2	J3	...	Jn	initial state
0	n−1		J2	J3	...	Jn	delete J1
−1	n−1	J2	J3	J4	...	Jn+1	add Jn+1
							(jobs J2 through
							Jn are moved)
0	n−1		J3	J4	...	Jn+1	delete J2
−1	n−1	J3	J4	J5	...	Jn+2	add Jn+2

Figure 3.6: Queue example

A more efficient queue representation is obtained by regarding the array *queue* [*MaxSize*] as circular. When *rear* == *MaxSize* − 1, the next element is entered at $q[0]$ in case that spot is free. Using the same conventions as before, *front* will always point one position counterclockwise from the first element in the queue. Again, *front* == *rear* if the queue is empty. Note, however, that *front* == *rear* is also true if the queue is full (i.e., if it contains *MaxSize* elements)! This poses a problem in the implementation of the *Add* and *Delete* functions because it is not possible to determine whether *front* == *rear* because the queue is full or because it is empty. To overcome this, we permit a maximum of *MaxSize* − 1 rather than *MaxSize* elements to be in the queue at any time.

Initially we have *front* == *rear* == 1. Figure 3.7 illustrates some of the possible configurations for a circular queue containing the four elements J1-J4. The assumption of circularity changes the *Add* and *Delete* functions slightly. To add an element, we first compute *newrear* to be one position clockwise from *rear*.

if (*rear* == *MaxSize* − 1) *newrear* = 0 ;
else *newrear* = *rear*+1 ;

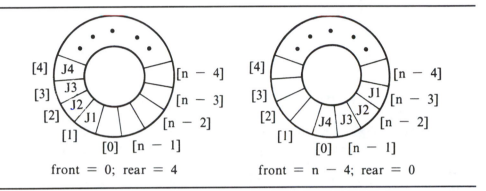

front = 0; rear = 4   front = n − 4; rear = 0

Figure 3.7: Circular queue of *MaxSize* = n elements and four jobs: J1, J2, J3, J4

template <**class** *KeyType*>
void *Queue*<*KeyType*>::*Add* (**const** *KeyType*& x)
// add x to the circular queue
{
    int *newrear* = (*rear* + 1) % *MaxSize* ;
    if (*front* == *newrear*) *QueueFull*();
    else *queue*[*rear* = *newrear*] = x ;
}

Program 3.11: Adding to a circular queue

Using the modulus operator, which computes remainders, this is equivalent to (*rear*+1) % MaxSize. If *newrear* is equal to *front*, then the queue is full. If not, we set *rear* equal to *newrear* and insert the new element there. Similarly, it will be necessary to move *front* one position clockwise each time a deletion is made. Again, using the modulus operator, this can be accomplished by *front* = (*front* + 1) % *MaxSize*. An examination of the algorithms (Programs 3.11 and 3.12) indicates that addition and deletion can now be carried out in a fixed amount of time or O(1).

```
template <class KeyType>
KeyType* Queue<KeyType>::Delete (KeyType& x)
// remove front element from queue
{
    if (front == rear) { QueueEmpty(); return 0;}
    front = (front + 1) % MaxSize;
    x = queue[front] ; return &x ;
}
```

Program 3.12: Deleting from a circular queue

One way to use all *MaxSize* positions would be to use an additional variable, *LastOp*, to record the last operation performed on the queue. This variable is initialized to "delete." Following each addition, it is set to "add" and following each deletion, it is set to "delete." Now when *front == rear*, we can determine whether the queue is empty or full by examining the value of *LastOp*. If *LastOp* is "add," then the queue is full. Otherwise, it is empty. The use of the variable *LastOp* as described above does, however, slow down the queue add and delete functions. Since the *Add* and *Delete* functions will be used many times in any problem involving queues, the loss of one queue position will be more than made up for by the reduction in computing time. Hence, we favor the implementations of Programs 3.11 and 3.12 over those that result from the use of the variable *LastOp*.

The functions *QueueFull* and *QueueEmpty* have been used without explanation, but they are similar to *StackFull* and *StackEmpty*. Their function will depend on the particular application.

EXERCISES

1. Write functions *Add* and *Delete* (Programs 3.11 and 3.12) using the variable *LastOp* as discussed in this section. The queue should now be able to hold up to *MaxSize* elements. The complexity of each of your functions should be $\Theta(1)$.

2. A double-ended queue (deque) is a linear list in which additions and deletions may be made at either end. Obtain a data representation mapping a deque into a one-dimensional array. Write algorithms to add and delete elements from either end of the deque.

3. A linear list is being maintained circularly in an array $c[n]$ with *front* and *rear* set up as for circular queues.

    (a) Obtain a formula in terms of *front*, *rear*, and *n* for the number of elements in the list.

    (b) Write an algorithm to delete the kth element in the list.

(c)   Write an algorithm to insert an element *y* immediately after the *k*th element.

What is the time complexity of your algorithms for (b) and (c)?

3.4   SUBTYPING AND INHERITANCE IN C++

Inheritance is used to express *subtype* relationships between ADTs. This is also referred to as the IS-A relationship. We say that a data object of Type *B* IS-A data object of Type *A* if *B* is more specialized than *A* or *A* is more general than *B*; that is, all *B*s are *A*s, but not all *A*s are *B*s; or the set of all objects of Type *B* is a subset of the set of all objects of Type *A*. For example, *Chair* IS-A *Furniture*, *Lion* IS-A *Mammal*, *Rectangle* IS-A *Polygon*.

Consider the relationship between *Bag* and *Stack*. A bag is simply a data structure into which elements can be inserted and from which elements can be deleted. A stack is also a data structure into which elements can be inserted and from which elements can be deleted. However, a stack is more specialized in that it requires that elements be deleted in last-in first-out order. So, a stack can be used instead of a bag, but a bag cannot be used for an application that requires a stack. So, *Stack* IS-A *Bag* or *Stack* is a subtype of *Bag*. The IS-A relationship is a fundamental, conceptual relationship between the specifications of two ADTs. The relationship is not affected by the implementation of either ADT. So, *Stack* IS-A *Bag* is true, even if their implementations are changed (as long as their ADT specifications are met).

C++ provides a mechanism to express the IS-A relationship called *public inheritance*. Program 3.13 shows how public inheritance is implemented in C++. The declaration ": **public** *Bag*" appended to class name "*Stack*" implies that *Stack* publicly inherits from *Bag*. Here, *Bag*, representing the more general ADT is called the *base class*, while *Stack*, representing the more specialized ADT is called the *derived class*. You will notice that some member functions are preceded by the keyword **virtual**. We will discuss this in the next chapter.

An important consequence of inheritance is that the derived class (*Stack*) inherits all the non-private members (data and functions) of the base class (*Bag*). This means that any members in *Bag* that are protected or public are also members of *Stack*. So *array*, *MaxSize*, and *top* are all data members of *Stack* even though they are not defined in the class definition of *Stack*. Similarly, *IsFull*, *IsEmpty*, *Full*, *Empty*, and *Add* are all member functions of *Stack* even though they are not defined in *Stack*.

Another important consequence of public inheritance is that inherited members have the same level of access in the derived class as they did in the base class. So all three data members and functions *Full* and *Empty* are protected members of *Stack*. Functions *IsFull*, *IsEmpty*, and *Add* are all public members of *Stack*.

The member functions inherited by *Stack* from *Bag* have the same prototypes. This is a reuse of the *interface* of a base class. Notice also that the only operation that has different implementations in *Bag* and *Stack* is *Delete*. The other operations all have

---

```
class Bag
{
public:
    Bag (int MaxSize = DefaultSize) ; // constructor
    virtual ~Bag() ; // destructor

    virtual void Add(int) ; // insert element into bag
    virtual int* Delete(int&) ; // delete element from bag

    virtual Boolean IsFull() ;  // return TRUE if the bag is full; FALSE otherwise
    virtual Boolean IsEmpty() ; // return TRUE if the bag is empty; FALSE otherwise
protected:
    virtual void Full() ; //  action when bag is full
    virtual void Empty() ; // action when bag is empty

    int *array ;
    int MaxSize ; // size of array
    int top ; // highest position in array that contains an element
};

class Stack : public Bag
{
public:
    Stack (int MaxSize = DefaultSize) ; // constructor
    ~Stack() ; // destructor
    int* Delete(int&) ; // delete element from stack
};
```

Program 3.13: Definition of *Bag* and *Stack*

identical implementations. C++ allows us to reuse the base-class implementation of an operation in a derived class. In the event that the implementation of a derived class operation must be different from the base class implementation, it is also possible to override the base class implementation. In our example, only *Delete* is reimplemented in the derived class. (The constructor and destructor cannot be inherited and therefore must also be redefined in the derived class.) The implementation of all *Bag* operations are assumed to be identical to those in Program 3.4. In Program 3.14, we show member functions of *Stack* that need to be reimplemented. The implementations of all other functions are inherited from *Bag* and hence do not have to be reimplemented.

Stack::*Stack* (**int** *MaxStackSize*) : *Bag*(*MaxStackSize*) { }
// Constructor for *Stack* calls constructor for *Bag*.

Stack::~*Stack*() { }
// Destructor for *Bag* is automatically called when *Stack*
// is destroyed. This ensures that *array* is deleted.

int∗ *Stack*::*Delete*(**int**& *x*)
{
   if (*IsEmpty*()) { *Empty*() ; **return** 0 ; }
   x = *array* [*top* −−] ;
   return &*x* ;
}

Program 3.14: Implementation of *Stack* operations

The following code fragment illustrates how inheritance works:

Bag b(3) ; // uses *Bag* constructor to create array of size 3
Stack s(3) ; // uses *Stack* constructor to create array of size 3

b . *Add*(1) ; *b* . *Add*(2) ; *b* . *Add*(3) ;
// use *Bag*::*Add*. *Bag*::*Add* calls functions *Bag*::*IsFull* and *Bag*::*Full*

s . *Add*(1) ; *s* . *Add*(2) ; *s* . *Add*(3) ;
// *Stack*::*Add* not defined, so use *Bag*::*Add*. *Bag*::*Add* calls *Bag*::*IsFull* and
// *Bag*::*Full* because these have not been redefined in *Stack*

int *x* ;
b.*Delete*(*x*) ; // uses *Bag*::*Delete*, which calls *Bag*::*IsEmpty* and *Bag*::*Empty*
s.*Delete*(*x*) ;
// uses *Stack*::*Delete*, which calls *Bag*::*IsEmpty* and *Bag*::*Empty* because these
// have not been redefined in *Stack*.

All operations on base class objects (such as *b* in the example) work in exactly the same way they would have, had there been no inheritance. Operations on derived class objects (such as *s* in the example) work differently: if an operation is defined in *Stack*, then that operation is used. If an operation is not defined in *Stack*, then the operation defined in the class that *Stack* inherits from (*Bag* in our example) is used. After executing the above code, *b* contains 1 and 3, while *s* contains 1 and 2.

The *Queue* ADT is also a subtype of *Bag*. It is more specialized than *Bag* because it requires that elements be deleted in first-in first-out order. Therefore, *Queue* can also be represented as a derived class of *Bag*. However, there is not as much similarity between the implementations of *Bag* and *Queue* as there was between *Bag* and *Stack*. Like *Bag* and *Stack*, *Queue* uses an array, but unlike them, it requires data members *front* and *rear*. The implementations of operations *IsFull*, *IsEmpty*, *Add*, and *Delete* are different from those of *Bag* and *Stack*. This means that a larger number of operations need to be redefined in *Queue* than were redefined in *Stack*. Even though there is not much reuse of implementation, there is still reuse of interfaces because the redefined functions of *Queue* have the same prototypes as the original functions in *Bag*. The exercises explore a full implementation of *Queue* as a derived class of *Bag*.

Before concluding, we note that there is another important consequence of public inheritance that we have not discussed in this section. This is known as *dynamic binding*. We will discuss dynamic binding in Chapter 4.

EXERCISES

1. Implement *Stack* as a publicly derived class of *Bag* using templates.
2. Implement *Queue* as a publicly derived class of *Bag* using templates.
3. For each of the following pairs state whether they are linked by the IS-A relationship. Justify your answer.
    (a) *Rectangle* and *Trapezium*.
    (b) *Rectangle* and *Circle*.
    (c) *Lion* and *Tiger*.
    (d) *Floppy Disk* and *Magnetic Tape*.
    (e) *Floppy Disk* and *Secondary Storage*.

3.5 A MAZING PROBLEM

The rat in a maze experiment is a classical one from experimental psychology. A rat (or mouse) is placed through the door of a large box without a top. Walls are set up so that movements in most directions are obstructed. The rat is carefully observed by several scientists as it makes its way through the maze until it eventually reaches the exit. There is only one way out, but at the end is a nice chunk of cheese. The idea is to run the experiment repeatedly until the rat will zip through the maze without taking a single false path. The trials yield its learning curve.

We can write a computer program for getting through a maze, and it will probably not be any smarter than the rat on its first try through. It may take many false paths before finding the right one. But the computer can remember the correct path far better than the rat. On its second try it should be able to go right to the end with no false paths taken, so there is no sense rerunning the program. Why don't you sit down and try to write this program yourself before you read on and look at our solution. Keep track of how many times you have to go back and correct something. This may give you an idea of your own learning curve as we rerun the experiment throughout the book.

Let us represent the maze by a two-dimensional array, $maze[i][j]$, where $1 \leq i \leq m$ and $1 \leq j \leq p$. A value of 1 implies a blocked path, and a 0 means one can walk right on through. We assume that the rat starts at $maze[1][1]$, and the exit is at $maze[m][p]$. An example is given in Figure 3.8.

0	1	0	0	0	1	1	0	0	0	1	1	1	1	1
1	0	0	0	1	1	0	1	1	1	0	0	1	1	1
0	1	1	0	0	0	0	1	1	1	1	0	0	1	1
1	1	0	1	1	1	1	0	1	1	0	1	1	0	0
1	1	0	1	0	0	1	0	1	1	1	1	1	1	1
0	0	1	1	0	1	1	1	0	1	0	0	1	0	1
0	0	1	1	0	1	1	1	0	1	0	0	1	0	1
0	1	1	1	1	0	0	1	1	1	1	1	1	1	1
0	0	1	1	0	1	1	0	1	1	1	1	1	0	1
1	1	0	0	0	1	1	0	1	1	0	0	0	0	0
0	0	1	1	1	1	1	0	0	0	1	1	1	1	0
0	1	0	0	1	1	1	1	1	0	1	1	1	1	0

entrance (top-left), exit (bottom-right)

Figure 3.8: An example maze (can you find a path?)

With the maze represented as a two-dimensional array, the location of the rat in the maze can at any time be described by the row, i, and the column, j, of its position. Now let us consider the possible moves the rat can make from a point $[i][j]$ in the maze. Figure 3.9 shows the possible moves from any point $[i][j]$. The position $[i][j]$ is marked by an X. If all the surrounding squares have a 0, then the rat can choose any of these eight squares as its next position. We call these eight directions by the names of the points on a compass: north, northeast, east, southeast, south, southwest, west, and northwest, or N, NE, E, SE, S, SW, W, and NW.

We must be careful here because not every position has eight neighbors. If $[i][j]$ is on a border where either $i = 1$ or m, or $j = 1$ or p, then less than eight, and possibly only three, neighbors exist. To avoid checking for border conditions, we surround the maze by a border of ones. The array will therefore be declared as $maze[m+2][p+2]$. Another device that will simplify the problem is to predefine the possible directions to move in a table, $move$, as in Figure 3.10. The data types needed are

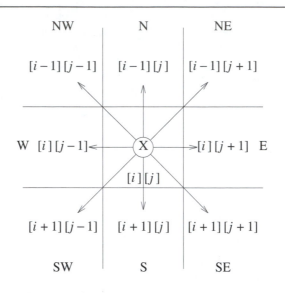

	NW	N	NE

Figure 3.9: Allowable moves

struct *offsets*
{
   int a, b ;
};

enum directions { N, NE, E, SE, S, SW, W, NW };
offsets move[8] ;

If we are at position $[i][j]$ in the maze and we wish to find the position $[g][h]$ that is southwest of us, then we set

$g = i + move[SW].a;$ $h = j + move[SW].b;$

For example, if we are at position [3][4], then the position to the southwest is given by [3 + 1 = 4] [4 + (−1) = 3].

As we move through the maze, we may have the chance to go in several directions. Not knowing which one to choose, we pick one but save our current position and the direction of the last move in a list. This way, if we have taken a false path, we can return and try another direction. With each new location we will examine the possibilities, starting from the north and looking clockwise. Finally, in order to prevent us from going down the same path twice, we use another array, *mark*[*m* + 2][*p* + 2], which is initially zero. *mark*[*i*][*j*] is set to 1 once we arrive at that position. We assume *maze*[*m*][*p*]

q	$move\,[q\,].a$	$move\,[q\,].b$
N	-1	0
NE	-1	1
E	0	1
SE	1	1
S	1	0
SW	1	-1
W	0	-1
NW	-1	-1

Figure 3.10: Table of moves

$= 0$, since otherwise there is no path to the exit. Program 3.15 is a first pass at an algorithm.

```
initialize stack to the maze entrance coordinates and direction east;
while (stack is not empty)
{
  (i,j,dir) = coordinates and direction deleted from top of stack ;
  while (there are more moves)
  {
    (g,h) = coordinates of next move ;
    if (( g == m ) && ( h == p )) success ;
    if ( (!maze [g ][h]) // legal move
              && (!mark [g ][h]) // haven't been here before
    {
          mark [g ][h] = 1 ;
          dir = next direction to try ;
          add (i,j,dir) to top of stack;
          i = g;  j = h;  dir = north;
    }
  }
}
cout << "no path found" << endl ;
```

Program 3.15: First pass at finding a path through a maze

This is not a C++ program, and yet it describes the essential processing without too much detail. The use of indentation for delineating important blocks of code plus the use of C++ reserved words make the looping and conditional tests transparent.

What remains to be pinned down? Using the three arrays *maze*, *mark*, and *move*, we need only specify how to represent the list of new triples. Since the algorithm calls for removing first the most recently entered triple, this list should be a stack. We can use the sequential representation we saw before. All we need to know now is a reasonable bound on the size of this stack. Since each position in the maze is visited at most once, at most *mp* elements can be placed into the stack. Thus, *mp* locations is a safe but somewhat conservative bound. The maze of Figure 3.11 has only one path from entrance to exit. It has $\lceil m/2 \rceil (p-2) + 2$ positions.

entrance

0	0	0	0	0	0	0	0	1
1	1	1	1	1	1	1	1	0
1	0	0	0	0	0	0	0	1
0	1	1	1	1	1	1	1	1
1	0	0	0	0	0	0	0	1
1	1	1	1	1	1	1	1	0
1	0	0	0	0	0	0	0	1
0	1	1	1	1	1	1	1	1
1	0	0	0	0	0	0	0	0

exit

Figure 3.11: A maze with a long path

Thus, *mp* is not too crude a bound. We are now ready to give a precise maze algorithm (Program 3.16).

The arrays *maze, mark,* and *move,* are assumed global to *path*. Further, *stack* is defined to be a stack of *items* where the struct *items* is defined as

struct *items* {
  int *x, y, dir* ;
};

Since *stack* is of size *mp*, the *StackFull* condition will never occur. The **operator<<** is overloaded for both *Stack* and *items* as shown in Program 3.17. We assume that **operator<<** has been given access to the private data members of *Stack* through the use of the **friend** declaration. Now, what can we say about the computing time of this function? It is interesting that even though the problem is easy to grasp, it is difficult to make any but the most trivial statement about the computing time. The reason for this is that the

```
void path(int m, int p)
// Output a path (if any) in the maze; maze[0][i] = maze [m +1][i] =
// maze [j][0] = maze [j ][p +1] = 1, 0 ≤ i ≤ p +1, 0 ≤ j ≤ m+1.
{
    // start at (1,1)
    mark[1][1] = 1 ;
    Stack<items> stack(m*p) ;
    items temp ;
    temp.x = 1 ; temp.y = 1 ; temp.dir = E ;
    stack.Add(temp) ;

    while (!stack.IsEmpty()) // stack not empty
    {
        temp = *stack.Delete (temp) ; // unstack
        int i = temp.x ; int j = temp.y ; int d = temp.dir ;
        while (d < 8) // move forward
        {
            int g = i + move[d].a ; int h = j + move[d].b ;
            if ((g == m) && (h == p)) { // reached exit
                // output path
                cout << stack ;
                cout << i << " " << j << endl ; // last two squares on the path
                cout << m << " " << p << endl ;
                return;
            }
            if ((!maze[g][h]) && (!mark[g][h])) { // new position
                mark[g][h] = 1 ;
                temp.x = i ;  temp.y = j ; temp.dir = d+1 ;
                stack.Add(temp) ; // stack it
                i = g ; j = h ; d = N ; // move to (g,h)
            }
            else d++ ; // try next direction
        }
    }
    cout << "no path in maze " << endl ;
}
```

Program 3.16: Finding a path through a maze

```
template <class KeyType>
ostream& operator<<(ostream& os, Stack<KeyType>& s)
{
    os << "top = " << s.top << endl ;
    for (int i = 0 ; i <= s.top ; i++)
        os << i << ":" << s.stack[i] << endl ;
    return os ;
}

ostream& operator<<(ostream& os, items& item)
{
    return os << item.x << "," << item.y << ","  << item.dir ;
}
```

Program 3.17: Overloading **operator**<<

number of iterations of the main **while** loop is entirely dependent upon the given maze. What we can say is that each new position $[i][j]$ that is visited gets marked, so paths are never taken twice. There are at most eight iterations of the inner **while** loop for each marked position. Each iteration of the inner **while** loop takes a fixed amount of time, O(1), and if the number of zeros in *maze* is z, then at most z positions can get marked. Since z is bounded above by mp, the computing time is O(mp). (In actual experiments, however, the rat may be inspired by the watching psychologists and the invigorating odor from the cheese at the exit. It might reach its goal by examining far fewer paths than those examined by algorithm *path*. This may happen despite the fact that the rat has no pencil and only a very limited mental stack. It is difficult to incorporate the effect of the cheese odor and the cheering of the psychologists into a computer algorithm.) Note that the array *mark* can be eliminated altogether and *maze*[g][h] changed to 1 instead of setting *mark*[g][h] to 1, but this will destroy the original maze.

EXERCISES

1. (a) Find a path through the maze of Figure 3.8.

   (b) Trace out the action of function *path* (Program 3.16) on the maze of Figure 3.8. Compare this to your own attempt in (a).

2. What is the maximum path length from start to finish for any maze of dimensions $m \times p$?

3.6 EVALUATION OF EXPRESSIONS

3.6.1 Expressions

When pioneering computer scientists conceived the idea of higher-level programming languages, they were faced with many hurdles. One of these was how to generate machine-language instructions to evaluate an arithmetic expression. An assignment statement such as

$$X = A/B - C + D * E - A * C$$

might have several meanings, and even if it were uniquely defined, say by a full use of parentheses, it still seemed a formidable task to generate a correct instruction sequence. Fortunately the solution we have today is both elegant and simple. Moreover, it is so simple that this aspect of compiler writing is really one of the more minor issues.

An expression is made up of operands, operators, and delimiters. The expression above has five operands: A, B, C, D, and E. Though these are all one-letter variables, operands can be any legal variable name or constant in our programming language. In any expression, the values that variables take must be consistent with the operations performed on them. These operations are described by the operators. In most programming languages there are several kinds of operators that correspond to the different kinds of data a variable can hold. First, there are the basic arithmetic operators: plus, minus, times, and divide ($+$, $-$, $*$, $/$). Other arithmetic operators include unary minus, and %. A second class is the relational operators: $<$, $<=$, $==$, $<>$, $>=$, and $>$. These are usually defined to work for arithmetic operands, but they can just as easily work for character string data. ('CAT' is less than 'DOG' since it precedes 'DOG' in alphabetical order.) The result of an expression that contains relational operators is one of two constants: **true** (1) or **false** (0). Such an expression is called boolean, named after the mathematician George Boole, the father of symbolic logic. There also may be logical operators such as &&, ||, and !.

The first problem with understanding the meaning of an expression is to decide in what order the operations are carried out. This means that every language must uniquely define such an order. For instance, if $A = 4$, $B = C = 2$, $D = E = 3$, then in the above equation we might want X to be assigned the value

$$((4/2) - 2) + (3 * 3) - (4 * 2)$$
$$= 0 + 9 - 8$$
$$= 1$$

However, the true intention of the programmer might have been to assign X the value

$$(4/(2 - 2 + 3)) * (3 - 4) * 2$$
$$= (4/3) * (-1) * 2$$
$$= -2.6666666$$

Of course, the programmer could specify the latter order of evaluation by using parentheses:

$$X = ((A/(B - C + D)) * (E - A) * C$$

To fix the order of evaluation, we assign to each operator a priority. Then within any pair of parentheses we understand that operators with the highest priority will be evaluated first. A set of sample priorities from C++ is given in Figure 3.12. The highest priority is 1.

---

priority	operator
1	unary minus, !
2	$*, /, \%$
3	$+, -$
4	$<, <=, >=, >$
5	$==, !=$
6	&&
7	$\|$

Figure 3.12: Priority of operators in C++

Unary minus and the logical **NOT** have top priority, followed by $*$, $/$, and $\%$. When we have an expression where two adjacent operators have the same priority, we need a rule to tell us which one to perform first. For example, do we want the value of $A/B*C$ to be understood as $(A/B) * C$ or $A/(B*C)$? Convince yourself that there will be a difference by trying $A = B = C = 2$. The C++ rule is that for all priorities, evaluation of operators of the same priority will proceed left to right. So, $A/B*C$ will be evaluated as $(A/B) * C$. Remember that by using parentheses we can override these rules, as expressions are always evaluated with the innermost parenthesized expression first.

Now that we have specified priorities and rules for breaking ties we know how $X = A/B - C + D*E - A*C$ will be evaluated, namely, as

$$X = (((A/B) - C) + (D * E)) - (A * C)$$

3.6.2   Postfix Notation

How can a compiler accept an expression and produce correct code? The answer is given by reworking the expression into a form we call *postfix notation*. If e is an expression with operators and operands, the conventional way of writing e is called *infix*, because the operators come *in*-between the operands. (Unary operators precede their operand.) The *postfix* form of an expression calls for each operator to appear *after* its operands. For example,

infix $A*B/C$ has postfix $AB*C/$

If we study the postfix form of $A*B/C$, we see that the multiplication comes immediately after its two operands A and B. Now imagine that $A*B$ is computed and stored in T. Then we have the division operator, $/$, coming immediately after its two operands T and C.

Let us look at our previous example

$$\text{infix:} \quad A/B - C + D*E - A*C$$

$$\text{postfix:} \quad AB/C - DE*+AC*-$$

and trace out the meaning of the postfix expression.

Suppose that every time we compute a value, we store it in the temporary location T_i, $i \geq 1$. If we read the postfix expression left to right, the first operation is division. The two operands that precede this are A and B. So, the result of A/B is stored in T_1, and the postfix expression is modified as in Figure 3.13. This figure also gives the remaining sequence of operations. The result is stored in T_6. Notice that if we had parenthesized the expression, this would change the postfix only if the order of normal evaluation were altered. Thus, $(A/B) - C + (D*E) - A*C$ will have the same postfix form as the previous expression without parentheses. But $(A/B) - (C+D)*(E-A)*C$ will have the postfix form $AB/CD + EA - *C*-$.

operation	postfix
$T_1 = A/B$	$T_1C-DE*+AC*-$
$T_2 = T_1-C$	$T_2DE*+AC*-$
$T_3 = D*E$	T_2T_3+AC*-
$T_4 = T_2+T_3$	T_4AC*-
$T_5 = A*C$	T_4T_5-
$T_6 = T_4-T_5$	T_6

Figure 3.13: Postfix evaluation

What are the virtues of postfix notation that enable easy evaluation of expressions? To begin with, the need for parentheses is eliminated. Second, the priority of the operators is no longer relevant. The expression may be evaluated by making a left to right scan, stacking operands, and evaluating operators using as operands the correct number from the stack and finally placing the result onto the stack (see Program 3.18). This evaluation process is much simpler than attempting direct evaluation from infix notation.

---

void *eval(expression e)*
// Evaluate the postfix expression *e*. It is assumed that the last token (a token
// is either an operator, operand, or '#') in *e* is '#.' A function *NextToken* is
// used to get the next token from *e*. The function uses the stack *stack*
{
   Stack<token> stack ; //initialize *stack*
   for (*token x = NextToken* (*e*) ; *x* != '#'; *x* = *NextToken* (*e*))
     if (*x* is an operand) *stack.Add(x)* // add to *stack*
     else { // operator
       remove the correct number of operands for operator *x* from *stack*; perform the
       operation *x* and store the result (if any) onto the stack;
     }
} // end of *eval*

Program 3.18: Evaluating postfix expressions

3.6.3   Infix to Postfix

To see how to devise an algorithm for translating from infix to postfix, note that the order of the operands in both forms is the same. In fact, it is simple to describe an algorithm for producing postfix from infix:

(1)   Fully parenthesize the expression.

(2)   Move all operators so that they replace their corresponding right parentheses.

(3)   Delete all parentheses.

For example, $A/B - C + D * E - A * C$, when fully parenthesized, yields

$$((((A / B) - C) + (D * E)) - (A * C))$$

The arcs join an operator and its corresponding right parenthesis. Steps 2 and 3 yield

$$AB/C - DE * + AC * -$$

Since the order of the operands is the same in infix and postfix, when we scan an expression for the first time, we can form the postfix by immediately passing any operands to the output. To handle the operators, we store them in a stack until it is time to pass them to the output.

For example, since we want $A + B * C$ to yield $ABC * +$, our algorithm should perform the following sequence of stacking (these stacks will grow to the right):

next token	stack	output
none	empty	none
A	empty	A
+	+	A
B	+	AB

At this point the algorithm must determine if $*$ gets placed on top of the stack or if the $+$ gets taken off. Since $*$ has higher priority, we should stack $*$, producing

*	+*	AB
C	+*	ABC

Now the input expression is exhausted, so we output all remaining operators in the stack to get

$$ABC * +$$

For another example, $A * (B + C) * D$ has the postfix form $ABC + * D *$, and so the algorithm should behave as

next token	stack	output
none	empty	none
A	empty	A
*	*	A
(	*(	A
B	*(	AB
+	*(+	AB
C	*(+	ABC

At this point we want to unstack down to the corresponding left parenthesis and then delete the left and right parentheses. This gives us

)	*	ABC +
*	*	ABC +*
D	*	ABC +* D
done	empty	ABC +* D *

These examples motivate a priority-based scheme for stacking and unstacking operators. The left parenthesis complicates things, since when it is not in the stack, it behaves as an operator with high priority, whereas once it gets in, it behaves as one with low priority (no operator other than the matching right parenthesis should cause it to get unstacked). We establish two priorities for operators: *isp* (in-stack priority) and *icp* (in-coming priority). The *isp* and *icp* of all operators in Figure 3.12 is the priority given in Figure 3.12. In addition, we assume that *isp*('(') returns 8, *icp*('(') returns 0, and *isp*('#') returns 8. These priorities result in the following rule: *Operators are taken out of the stack as long as their in-stack priority is numerically less than or equal to the in-coming priority of the new operator*. Our algorithm to transform from infix to postfix is given in Program 3.19.

```
void postfix (expression e)
// Output the postfix form of the infix expression e. NextToken
// and stack are as in function eval (Program 3.18). It is assumed that
// the last token in e is '#.' Also, '#' is used at the bottom of the stack
{
    Stack<token> stack; // initialize stack
    token y ;
    stack.Add('#');
    for (token x = NextToken(e) ; x != '#' ; x = NextToken(e))
    {
        if (x is an operand)  cout << x ;
        else if (x == ')')  // unstack until '('
            for (y = *stack.Delete (y); y != '('; y = *stack.Delete (y)) cout << y ;
        else { // x is an operator
            for (y = *stack.Delete (y); isp (y) <= icp (x); y = *stack.Delete (y)) cout << y ;
            stack.Add(y);   // restack the last y that was unstacked
            stack.Add(x);
        }
    }

    // end of expression; empty stack
    while (!stack.IsEmpty()) cout << *stack.Delete(y) ;
} // end of postfix
```

Program 3.19: Converting from infix to postfix form

Analysis of *postfix*: The algorithm makes only a left-to-right pass across the input. The time spent on each operand is O(1). Each operator is stacked and unstacked once. Hence, the time spent on each operator is also O(1). So, the complexity of function *postfix* is $\Theta(n)$, where n is the number of tokens in the expression. □

EXERCISES

1. Write the postfix form of the following expressions:

    (a) $A * B * C$

    (b) $-A + B - C + D$

    (c) $A * -B + C$

    (d) $(A + B) * D + E/(F + A * D) + C$

    (e) $A \&\& B \,||\, C \,||\, ! \, (E > F)$ (assuming C++ precedence)

    (f) $! \, (A \&\& ! \, ((B < C) \,||\, (C > D))) \,||\, (C < E)$

2. Use the priorities of Figure 3.12 together with those for '(' and '#' to answer the following:

    (a) In function *postfix* (Program 3.19), what is the maximum number of elements that can be on the stack at any time if the input expression e has n operators and delimiters?

    (b) What is the answer to (a) if e has n operators and the depth of nesting of parentheses is at most 6?

3. Another expression form that is easy to evaluate and is parenthesis-free is known as *prefix*. In this way of writing expressions, the operators precede their operands. For example:

infix	prefix
$A * B / C$	$/*ABC$
$A/B - C + D * E - A * C$	$- + - /ABC * DE * AC$
$A * (B + C)/D - G$	$-/* A + BCDG$

    Notice that the order of operands is not changed in going from infix to prefix.

    (a) What is the prefix form of the expressions in Exercise 1?

    (b) Write an algorithm to evaluate a prefix expression e. (Hint: Scan e right to left and assume that the leftmost token of e is '#.')

    (c) Write an algorithm to transform an infix expression e into its prefix equivalent. Assume that the input expression e begins with a '#' and that the prefix expression should begin with a '#.'

    What is the time complexity of your algorithms for (b) and (c)? How much space is needed by each of these algorithms?

4. Write an algorithm to transform from prefix to postfix. Carefully state any assumptions you make regarding the input. How much time and space does your algorithm take?

5.   Do the preceding exercise, but this time for a transformation from postfix to prefix.

6.   Write an algorithm to generate fully parenthesized infix expressions from their postfix form. What is the complexity (time and space) of your algorithm?

7.   Do the preceding exercise starting from prefix form.

3.7   MULTIPLE STACKS AND QUEUES

Until now we have been concerned only with the representations of a single stack or a single queue in the memory of a computer. For these two cases we have seen efficient sequential data representations. What happens when a data representation is needed for several stacks and queues? We limit ourselves to sequential mappings of these data objects into an array $M[m]$. If we have only two stacks to represent, then the solution is simple. We can use $M[0]$ for the bottommost element in stack 0 and $M[m-1]$ for the corresponding element in stack 1. Stack 0 can grow toward $M[m-1]$ and stack 1 toward $M[0]$. It is therefore possible to utilize efficiently all the available space. Can we do the same when more than two stacks are to be represented? The answer is no, because a one-dimensional array has only two fixed points, $M[0]$ and $M[m-1]$, and each stack requires a fixed point for its bottommost element. When more than two stacks, say n, are to be represented sequentially, we can initially divide the available memory $M[m]$ into n segments and allocate one of these segments to each of the n stacks. This initial division of $M[m]$ into segments may be done in proportion to expected sizes of the various stacks if these are known. In the absence of such information, $M[m]$ may be divided into equal segments. For each stack i we shall use $b[i]$ to represent a position one less than the position in M for the bottommost element of that stack. $t[i]$, $0 \le i \le n-1$ will point to the topmost element of stack i. We shall use the boundary condition $b[i] == t[i]$ iff the ith stack is empty. If we grow the ith stack in memory indices lower than the $(i+1)$th, then with roughly equal initial segments we have

$$b[i] = t[i] = \lfloor m/n \rfloor \ i - 1, \ 0 \le i < n$$

as the initial values of $b[i]$ and $t[i]$ (see Figure 3.14). Stack i, $0 \le i < n$, can grow from $b[i]+1$ up to $b[i+1]$ before it catches up with the $(i+1)$th stack. It is convenient both for the discussion and the algorithms to define $b[n] = m-1$. This scheme results in the *Add* and *Delete* algorithms of Programs 3.20 and 3.21. The algorithms assume that M is global (or a static class data member) and that *Add* and *Delete* are regular functions. The exercises examine an implementation where multiple stacks are stored in a single class, *MultipleStack*.

The algorithms to add and delete appear to be as simple as in the case of only one or two stacks. This is not really the case, since the *StackFull* condition in algorithm *Add* does not imply that all m locations of M are in use. In fact, there may be a lot of unused space between stacks j and $j+1$ for $0 \le j < n$ and $j \ne i$ (Figure 3.15). The function *StackFull(i)* should therefore determine whether there is any free space in M and shift stacks around so as to make some of this free space available to the ith stack.

Figure 3.14: Initial configuration for n stacks in $M[m]$. All stacks are empty and memory is divided into roughly equal segments

```
template <class Type>
void Add (const int i, const Type& x)
// Add x to the ith stack.
{
    if (t [i] == b [i +1]) StackFull (i) ;
    else M[++t[i]] = x ;
}
```

Program 3.20: Adding to the ith stack

```
template <class Type>
items* Delete (const int i, Type& x)
{
    if (t[i] == b[i]) { StackEmpty(i); return 0;}
    x = M [t [i ]--];
    return &x ;
}
```

Program 3.21: Deleting from the ith stack

Figure 3.15: Configuration when stack i meets with stack $i + 1$ but there is still free space elsewhere in M

Several strategies are possible for the design of algorithm *StackFull*. We shall discuss one strategy in the text and look at some others in the exercises. The primary objective of algorithm *StackFull* is to permit the adding of elements to stacks so long as there is some free space in M. One way to guarantee this is to design *StackFull* along the following lines:

(1) Determine the least, j, $i < j < n$, such that there is free space between stacks j and $j + 1$, i.e., $t[j] < b[j+1]$. If there is such a j, then move stacks $i + 1$, $i + 2$, ..., j one position to the right (treating $M[0]$ as leftmost and $M[m-1]$ as rightmost), thereby creating a space between stacks i and $i + 1$.

(2) If there is no j as in (1), then look to the left of stack i. Find the largest j such that $0 \leq j < i$ and there is space between stacks j and $j + 1$, i.e., $t[j] < b[j + 1]$. If there is such a j, then move stacks $j + 1$, $j + 2$, ..., i one space left, creating a free space between stacks i and $i + 1$.

(3) If there is no j satisfying either the conditions of (1) or (2), then all m spaces of M are utilized, and there is no free space.

The writing of algorithm *StackFull* using the above strategy is left as an exercise. It should be clear that the worst-case performance of this representation for the n stacks together with the above strategy for *StackFull* would be rather poor. In fact, in the worst case $O(m)$ time may be needed for each insertion (see Exercises). In the next chapter we shall see that if we do not limit ourselves to sequential mappings of data objects into arrays, then we can obtain a data representation for m stacks that has a much better worst-case performance than the representation described here. Sequential representations for n queues and other generalizations are discussed in the exercises.

EXERCISES

1. Two stacks are to be represented in an array $M[m]$ as described in this section. Write algorithms *Add* and *Delete* to add x and delete an element from stack i, $0 \le i \le 1$. Your algorithms should be able to add elements to the stacks so long as there are fewer than m elements in both stacks together and should run in $O(1)$ time.

2. Obtain a data representation mapping a stack s and a queue q into a single array $M[n]$. Write algorithms to add and delete elements from these two data objects. What can you say about the suitability of your data representation?

3. Implement a C++ template class *MultipleStack* using the data structures and algorithms described in this section. The array M should be declared as a static class data member and the operations *Add* and *Delete* implemented as member functions of *MultipleStack*.

4. Write a C++ function implementing the strategy for *StackFull(i)* outlined in this section.

5. For the *Add* and *Delete* algorithms (Programs 3.20 and 3.21) and the *StackFull(i)* algorithm of the preceding exercise, produce a sequence of adds and deletes that will require $O(m)$ time for each add. Use $n = 2$ and start from a configuration representing a full utilization of $M[m]$.

6. It has been empirically observed that most programs that get close to using all available space eventually run out of space. In light of this observation, it seems futile to move stacks around providing space for other stacks to grow in if there is only a limited amount of space that is free. Rewrite the algorithm of the preceding exercise so that the algorithm terminates if there are fewer than c free spaces. c is an empirically determined constant that is provided to the algorithm.

7. Another strategy for the *StackFull(i)* condition is to redistribute all the free space in proportion to the rate of growth of individual stacks since the last call to *StackFull*. This would require the use of another array, $lt[n]$, where $lt[j]$ is the value of $t[j]$ at the last call to *StackFull*. Then the amount by which each stack has grown since the last call is $t[j] - lt[j]$. The amount for stack i is actually $t[i] - lt[i] + 1$, since we are attempting to add another element to i.

    Write algorithm *StackFull(i)* to redistribute all the stacks so that the free space between stacks j and $j + 1$ is in proportion to the growth of stack j since the last call to *StackFull*. *Stackfull(i)* should assign at least one free location to stack i.

8. Design a data representation sequentially mapping n queues into an array $M[m]$. Represent each queue as a circular queue within M. Write functions *Add*, *Delete*, and *QueueFull* for this representation.

9. Design a data representation, sequentially mapping n data objects into an array $M[m]$. n_1 of these data objects are stacks, and the remaining $n_2 = n - n_1$ are queues. Write algorithms to add and delete elements from these objects. Use the

same *SpaceFull* algorithm for both types of data objects. This algorithm should provide space for the *i*th data object if there is some space not currently being used. Note that a circular queue with space for r elements can hold only $r - 1$ elements.

3.8   REFERENCES AND SELECTED READINGS

You will find an excellent discussion of the system stack and activation records in *Compiler Design in C*, by A. Holub, Prentice-Hall, Englewood Cliffs, NJ, 1990. The structure of our activation record (Figure 3.2) is based on Holub's discussion.

3.9   ADDITIONAL EXERCISES

1. [***Programming Project***] [Landweber] People have spent so much time playing card games of solitaire that the gambling casinos are now capitalizing on this human weakness. A form of solitaire is described below. Your assignment is to write a computer program to play the game, thus freeing hours of time for people to return to more useful endeavors.

    To begin the game, 28 cards are dealt into seven piles. The leftmost pile has one card, the next two cards, and so forth, up to seven cards in the rightmost pile. Only the uppermost card of each of the seven piles is turned face up. The cards are dealt left to right, one card to each pile, dealing to one less pile each time, and turning the first card in each round face up. On the topmost face-up card of each pile you may build in descending sequences red on black or black on red. For example, on the 9 of spades you may place either the 8 of diamonds or the 8 of hearts. All face-up cards on a pile are moved as a unit and may be placed on another pile according to the bottommost face-up card. For example, the 7 of clubs on the 8 of hearts may be moved as a unit onto the 9 of clubs or the 9 of spades.

    Whenever a face-down card is uncovered, it is turned face up. If one pile is removed completely, a face-up king may be moved from a pile (together with all cards above it) or the top of the waste pile (see below) into the vacated space. There are four output piles, one for each suit, and the object of the game is to get as many cards as possible into the output piles. Each time an ace appears at the top of a pile or the top of the stack, it is moved into the appropriate output pile. Cards are added to the output piles in sequence, the suit for each pile being determined by the ace on the bottom.

    From the rest of the deck, called the stock, cards are turned up one by one and placed face up on a waste pile. You may always play cards off the top of the waste pile, but only one at a time. Begin by moving a card from the stock to the top of the waste pile. If there is ever more than one possible play to be made, the following order must be observed:

(a) Move a card from the top of a playing pile or from the top of the waste pile to an output pile. If the waste pile becomes empty, move a card from the stock to the waste pile.

(b) Move a card from the top of the waste pile to the leftmost playing pile to which it can be moved. If the waste pile becomes empty, move a card from the stock to the waste pile.

(c) Find the leftmost playing pile that can be moved and place it on top of the leftmost playing pile to which it can be moved.

(d) Try (a), (b), and (c) in sequence, restarting with (a) whenever a move is made.

(e) If no move is made via (a) through (d), move a card from the stock to the waste pile and retry (a).

Only the topmost card of the playing piles or the waste pile may be played to an output pile. Once played on an output pile, a card may not be withdrawn to help elsewhere. The game is over when either all the cards have been played to the output, or the stock pile has been exhausted and no more cards can be moved.

When played for money, the player pays the house $52 at the beginning and wins $5 for every card played to the output piles. Write your program so that it will play several games and determine your net winnings. Use a random number generator to shuffle the deck. Output a complete record of two games in easily understood form. Include as output the number of games played and the net winnings (+ or −).

2. [*Programming Project*] [Landweber] We want to simulate an airport landing and takeoff pattern. The airport has three runways, runway 1, runway 2, and runway 3. There are four landing holding patterns, two for each of the first two runways. Arriving planes will enter one of the holding pattern queues, where the queues are to be as close in size as possible. When a plane enters a holding queue, it is assigned an integer *id* number and an integer giving the number of time units the plane can remain in the queue before it must land (because of low fuel level). There is also a queue for takeoffs for each of the three runways. Planes arriving in a takeoff queue are also assigned an integer *id*. The takeoff queues should be kept approximately the same size.

At each time, up to three planes may arrive at the landing queues and up to three planes may arrive at the takeoff queues. Each runway can handle one takeoff or landing at each time slot. Runway 3 is to be used for takeoffs except when a plane is low on fuel. At each time unit, planes in either landing queue whose air time has reached zero must be given priority over other landings and takeoffs. If only one plane is in this category, runway 3 is to be used. If more than one, then the other runways are also used (at each time, at most three planes can be serviced in this way).

Use successive even (odd) integers for *id*'s of planes arriving at takeoff (landing) queues. At each time unit assume that arriving planes are entered into queues before takeoffs or landings occur. Try to design your algorithm so that neither landing nor takeoff queues grow excessively. However, arriving planes must be placed at the ends of queues. Queues cannot be reordered.

The output should clearly indicate what occurs at each time unit. Periodically output (a) the contents of each queue; (b) the average takeoff waiting time; (c) the average landing waiting time; (d) the average flying time remaining on landing; and (e) the number of planes landing with no fuel reserve. (b) and (c) are for planes that have taken off or landed, respectively. The output should be self-explanatory and easy to understand (and uncluttered).

The input can be from a terminal, a file, or it can be generated by a random number generator. For each time unit the input consists of the number of planes arriving at take-off queues, the number of planes arriving at landing queues, and the remaining flying times for each plane arriving at a landing queue.

CHAPTER **4**

LINKED LISTS

4.1 SINGLY LINKED LISTS

In the previous chapters, we studied the representation of simple data structures using an array and a sequential mapping. These representations had the property that successive nodes of the data object were stored a fixed distance apart. Thus, (1) if the element a_{ij} of a table was stored at location L_{ij}, then $a_{i,j+1}$ was at the location $L_{ij} + c$ for some constant c; (2) if the ith node in a queue was at location L_i, then the $(i + 1)$th node was at location $(L_i + c) \% n$ for the circular representation; (3) if the topmost node of a stack was at location L_T, then the node beneath it was at location $L_T - c$, and so on. These sequential storage schemes proved adequate for the functions we wished to perform (accessing an arbitrary node in a table, insertion or deletion of nodes within a stack or queue). However, when a sequential mapping is used for ordered lists, operations such as insertion and deletion of arbitrary elements become expensive. For example, consider the following list of three-letter English words ending in AT:

(BAT, CAT, EAT, FAT, HAT, JAT, LAT, MAT, OAT, PAT, RAT, SAT, TAT, VAT, WAT)

To make this list complete we naturally want to add the word GAT, which means gun or revolver. If we are using an array to keep this list, then the insertion of GAT will require us to move elements already in the list either one location higher or lower. We must move either HAT, JAT, LAT, $\cdots$, WAT or BAT, CAT, EAT, and FAT. If we have to do many such insertions into the middle, neither alternative is attractive because of the amount of data movement. On the other hand, suppose we decide to remove the word LAT, which refers to the Latvian monetary unit. Then again, we have to move many elements so as to maintain the sequential representation of the list.

When our problem called for several ordered lists of varying sizes, sequential representation again proved to be inadequate. By storing each list in a different array of maximum size, storage may be wasted. If a list is to be stored in an array which is dynamically allocated, the size of the list, if unknown, must first be computed. By maintaining the lists in a single array a potentially large amount of data movement is needed. This was explicitly observed when we represented several stacks, queues, polynomials, and matrices. All these data objects are examples of ordered lists. Polynomials are ordered by exponent, whereas matrices are ordered by rows and columns. In this chapter we shall present an alternate representation for ordered lists that will reduce the time needed for arbitrary insertion and deletion.

An elegant solution to this problem of data movement in *sequential* representations is achieved by using *linked* representations. Unlike a sequential representation, in which successive items of a list are located a fixed distance apart, in a linked representation these items may be placed anywhere in memory. In other words, in a sequential representation the order of elements is the same as in the ordered list, whereas in a linked representation these two sequences need not be the same. To access elements in the list in the correct order, with each element we store the address or location of the next element in that list. Thus, associated with each data item in a linked representation is a pointer to the next item. This pointer is often referred to as a link. In general, a *node* is a collection of data, *data* 1, $\cdots$, *data n* and links *link* 1, $\cdots$, *link m*. Each item in a node is called a *field*. A field contains either a data item or a link.

Figure 4.1 shows how some of the nodes of the list we considered before may be represented in memory by using pointers. The elements of the list are stored in a one-dimensional array called *data*, but the elements no longer occur in sequential order, BAT before CAT before EAT, and so on. Instead we relax this restriction and allow them to appear anywhere in the array and in any order. To remind us of the real order, a second array, *link*, is added. The values in this array are pointers to elements in the *data* array. Since the list starts at *data*[8] = BAT, let us set a variable *first* = 8. *link*[8] has the value 3, which means it points to *data*[3], which contains CAT. The third element of the list is pointed at by *link*[3], which is EAT. By continuing in this way we can list all the words in the proper order. We recognize that we have come to the end when *link* has a value of zero. Some of the values of *data* and *link* (e.g., *data*[2], *link*[2], *data*[5], *link*[5]) are undefined. We shall ignore this for the moment.

It is customary to draw linked lists as an ordered sequence of nodes with links being represented by arrows, as in Figure 4.2. Notice that we do not explicitly put in the values of the pointers but simply draw arrows to indicate they are there. The arrows reinforce in our own mind the facts that (1) the nodes do not actually reside in sequential locations and (2) the locations of nodes may change on different runs. Therefore, when we write a program that works with lists, we do not look for a specific address except when we test for zero.

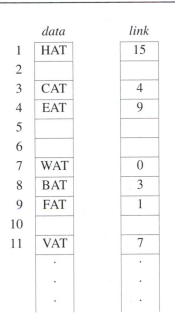

	data	link
1	HAT	15
2		
3	CAT	4
4	EAT	9
5		
6		
7	WAT	0
8	BAT	3
9	FAT	1
10		
11	VAT	7
·	·	·

Figure 4.1: Nonsequential list representation

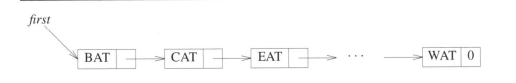

Figure 4.2: Usual way to draw a linked list

Let us now see why it is easier to make arbitrary insertions and deletions using a linked list rather than a sequential list. To insert the data item GAT between FAT and HAT, the following steps are adequate:

(1)   Get a node that is currently unused; let its address be x.

(2)   Set the *data* field of this node to GAT.

(3)   Set the *link* field of x to point to the node after FAT, which contains HAT.

(4)   Set the *link* field of the node containing FAT to x.

Figure 4.3(a) shows how the arrays *data* and *link* will be changed after we insert GAT. Figure 4.3(b) shows how we can draw the insertion using our arrow notation. The new arrows are dashed. The important thing to notice is that when we insert GAT, we do not have to move any elements that are already in the list. We have overcome the need to move data at the expense of the storage needed for the second field, *link*, but usually this penalty is not too severe.

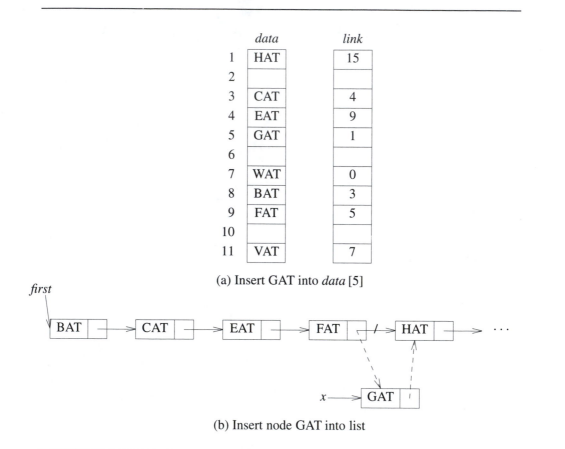

(a) Insert GAT into *data* [5]

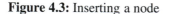

(b) Insert node GAT into list

Figure 4.3: Inserting a node

Now suppose we want to delete GAT from the list. All we need to do is find the element that immediately precedes GAT, which is FAT, and set *link*[9] to the position of HAT which is 1. Again, there is no need to move the data around. Even though the *link* data member of GAT still contains a pointer to HAT, GAT is no longer in the list (see Figure 4.4).

first

Figure 4.4: Delete GAT from list

4.2   REPRESENTING LISTS IN C++

In the following subsections, we will see how linked lists are implemented in C++.

4.2.1   Defining A List Node in C++

To define the structure of a node, we need to know the type of each of its fields. The *data* field in the example of the previous section is simply an array of characters, and the *link* field is a pointer to another node .

If the type of the node in our earlier example is denoted by *ThreeLetterNode*, then the data type *ThreeLetterNode* may be defined as a class as follows:

class *ThreeLetterNode* {
private:
      char *data*[3] ;
      *ThreeLetterNode *link* ;
};

More complicated list structures can also be defined. Example 4.1 defines two node structures that can be combined with each other to form a complex list structure.

Example 4.1: The class definitions

class *nodea* {
private:
      int *data*1 ;
      char *data*2 ;
      float *data*3 ;
      *nodea *linka* ;
      *nodeb *linkb* ;
};

```
class nodeb {
private:
     int data ;
     nodeb *link ;
};
```

defines *nodea* to consist of three data fields and two link fields, whereas nodes of type *nodeb* will consist of one data field and one link data field. Note that the *linkb* data member of nodes of type *nodea* must point to nodes of type *nodeb*. Figure 4.5 illustrates a possible configuration for *nodea* and *nodeb*. □

Figure 4.5: Illustration of the node structures *nodea* and *nodeb*

4.2.2   Designing a List in C++

We have seen how to represent a single node in C++. Next, we will design a C++ representation of the entire linked list data structure. The basic elements of our design are especially important because they apply not just to linked lists, but also to other linked data structures (such as trees) that we will study later. As is typical with any design process, we will explore different alternatives, some of which will turn out to be infeasible or undesirable.

Design Attempt 1: Let us consider an approach that has been used to represent lists in other programming languages. In this approach, the variable *first*, in the *ThreeLetter-Node* example, is considered to be a global variable and declared as

ThreeLetterNode *first* ;

The data members of the node pointed to by *first* may be referenced in the following way:

first→ *data*, *first*→ *link*

and the components of the *data* data member are referenced as

first→ *data* [0], *first*→ *data* [1], *first*→ *data* [2]

This is shown diagrammatically in Figure 4.6.

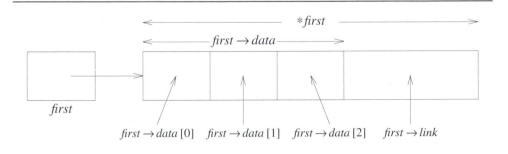

Figure 4.6: Referencing the data members of a node

There is, however, a flaw in our implementation of list nodes. Notice that the data members *data* and *link* of **class** *ThreeLetterNode* are declared as **private**. This is in keeping with the data encapsulation principles discussed in Chapter 1. The consequence of declaring *data* and *link* as **private** is that the expressions *first*→*link*, *first*→*data* [0], *first*→*data* [1], and *first*→*data* [2] will all result in compile-time errors because private data members cannot be accessed from outside the class!

Design Attempt 2: How do we overcome the drawback of our first attempt? Making the data members public would do the trick, but that violates data encapsulation. A solution might be to define public member functions *GetLink* (), *SetLink* (), *GetData* (), and *Set-Data* () on *ThreeLetterNode* which are used to indirectly access the data members. This is not a good solution, however, because it means that any function in the program can still access data members of *ThreeLetterNode* through these functions. The ideal solution would only grant those functions that perform list manipulation operations (like inserting a node into or deleting a node from a linked list) access to data members of *ThreeLetter-Node*. No other functions should have access to data members of *ThreeLetterNode*, irrespective of whether the access is direct or through public member functions.

Design Attempt 3: Let us try to tackle this data structure design problem from a different perspective: the data structure we are interested in implementing is a singly linked list (which is also called a *chain*) of three-letter words. This suggests that our program should contain a class corresponding to the entire list data structure. Let us call this class *ThreeLetterList*. This class should support member functions that carry out list manipulation operations. Thus, we will be using a composite of *two* classes, *ThreeLetterNode* and *ThreeLetterList*, to implement a singly linked list. The conceptual relationship between the two classes may be characterized by the following statement: a typical object of class *ThreeLetterList* consists of zero or more objects of class *ThreeLetterNode*; or, *ThreeLetterList* HAS-A *ThreeLetterNode*.

Definition: We say that a data object of Type *A* HAS-A data object of Type *B* if *A* conceptually contains *B* or *B* is a part of *A*. For example, *Computer* HAS-A *Processor*, *Book* HAS-A *Page*, etc. HAS-A relationships between ADTs are usually expressed by making the contained class a data member of the containing class. This is possible when the Type *A* object contains a fixed number of Type *B* objects. □

Figure 4.7 shows the *conceptual* relationship between the two classes.

ThreeLetterList

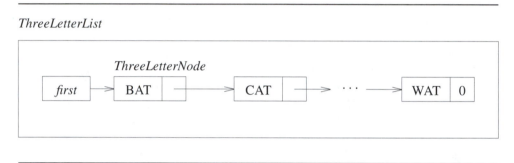

Figure 4.7: Conceptual relationship between *ThreeLetterList* and *ThreeLetterNode*

Figure 4.7 suggests that an object of class *ThreeLetterList physically* contains many objects of class *ThreeLetterNode*; that is objects of *ThreeLetterNode* are declared as data members of *ThreeLetterList*. But, the number of nodes in a linked list is not a constant; on the contrary, it varies with each insert or delete operation performed on the list. So, it is impossible to know in advance the number of *ThreeLetterNode*s to include in *ThreeLetterList*. For this reason, the *ThreeLetterList* class is defined so that it only contains the *access pointer*, *first*, which points to the first node in the list. Figure 4.8 shows the *actual* relationship between *ThreeLetterList* and *ThreeLetterNode* objects. It shows that *ThreeLetterNode* objects are not physically contained inside *ThreeLetterList*. The only data member contained in *ThreeLetterList* is the pointer *first*.

We are now finally ready to propose a solution to our dilemma of how to define **class** *ThreeLetterNode* so that only list manipulation operations have access to its data members. This is achieved by declaring *ThreeLetterList* to be a **friend** of *ThreeLetterNode*. Only member functions of *ThreeLetterList* and *ThreeLetterNode* can now access the private data members of *ThreeLetterNode*. The class definitions of *ThreeLetterList* and *ThreeLetterNode* are shown in Program 4.1.

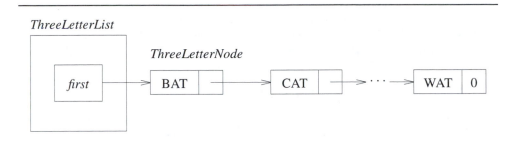

Figure 4.8: Actual relationship between *ThreeLetterList* and *ThreeLetterNode*

---

class *ThreeLetterList* **;** // forward declaration

class *ThreeLetterNode* {
friend class *ThreeLetterList* **;**
private:
    char *data* [3] **;**
    *ThreeLetterNode *link* **;**
};

class *ThreeLetterList* {
public:
    // List Manipulation operations

  .

  .

private:
    *ThreeLetterNode *first* **;**
};

Program 4.1: Composite classes

Nested Classes: An alternate method for representing a linked list in C++ is to use nested classes, where one class is defined inside the definition of another class. Here, class *ThreeLetterNode* is *defined* inside the private portion of the definition of class *ThreeLetterList*, as shown in Program 4.2. This ensures that *ThreeLetterNode* objects cannot be accessed outside class *ThreeLetterList*. Notice that the data members of *ThreeLetterNode* are public. This ensures that they can be accessed by member functions of *ThreeLetterList*. Using nested classes achieves the same effect as our previous approach which uses composite classes. We use the composite class approach in the rest of the text. One of our reasons for preferring composite classes over nested classes is that the node class can be used by two data structures. For example, the same node structure may need to be used in both a singly linked list and in a circular list. (We will see this later in the chapter.) In this situation it is more natural to use composite classes rather than nested classes.

```
class ThreeLetterList {
public:
     // List Manipulation operations
   .

   .
private:
   class ThreeLetterNode {  // nested class
   public:
      char data [3] ;
      ThreeLetterNode *link ;
   };
   ThreeLetterNode *first ;
};
```

Program 4.2: Nested classes

4.2.3   Pointer Manipulation in C++

Nodes of a predefined type may be created using the C++ command **new**. If f is of type *ThreeLetterNode** then following the call $f =$ **new** *ThreeLetterNode*, **f* denotes the node of type *ThreeLetterNode* that is created. Similarly, if y and z are of type nodea* and *nodeb**, respectively, (Example 4.1) then following the sequence of calls

$y =$ **new** *nodea* ;
$z =$ **new** *nodeb* ;

*y, and **z*, respectively, denote nodes of type *nodea*, and *nodeb* that are created. These nodes may be deleted in the following way:

delete f ; **delete** y ; **delete** z ;

C++ also allows pointer variables to be assigned the null pointer constant 0. This constant is used to denote a pointer data member that points to no node (e.g., the *link* data member in the last node of Figure 4.3(b)) or an empty list (as in *first* = 0). Addition of integers to pointer variables is permitted in C++ (but is generally only used in the context of arrays) . Thus, if x is a pointer variable, the expresssion $x + 1$ is valid, but may have no logical meaning. Two pointer variables of the same type may also be compared to see if both point to the same node. Thus, if x and y are pointer variables of the same type, then the expressions $x == y$, $x \mathrel{!=} y$, $x == 0$, $x \mathrel{!=} 0$ are all valid. The effect of the assignments $x = y$ and $*x = *y$ on the initial configuration of Figure 4.9(a) is given in Figure 4.9(b) and (c). Pointers can also be output in C++ using **cout**. This prints the location in memory that the pointer is addressing.

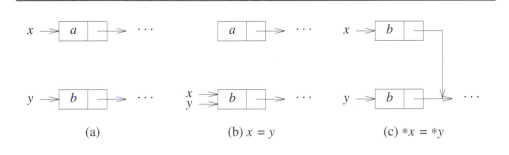

(a) (b) $x = y$ (c) $*x = *y$

Figure 4.9: Effect of pointer assignments

4.2.4 List Manipulation Operations

The pointer manipulation operations of the preceding section can be used to implement list operations. These must be declared as member functions of the list class so that they can access the fields of individual list nodes. In this section, we will look at some examples of list manipulation functions. All the examples of this section assume the existence of classes *ListNode* and *List*, where **class** *ListNode* is defined as:

```
class ListNode {
private:
    int data ;
    ListNode *link ;
};
```

The access pointer *first*, which points to the first node in the list, is assumed to be a private data member of *List*. It is also assumed that the member functions are declared in the appropriate class definitions. Other list manipulation operations are examined in the exercises.

Example 4.2: Function *List* ::*Create*2 (Program 4.3) creates a linked list with two nodes of type *ListNode*. The *data* field of the first node is set to 10 and that of the second to 20. Function *Create*2 uses the constructor for *ListNode* (*ListNode* ::*ListNode*) to initialize the fields of the two newly created nodes. The resulting list structure is shown in Figure 4.10. □

---

void *List* :: *Create2*()
{
    first = **new** *ListNode* (10) ; // create and initialize first node
    // create and initialize second node and place its address in *first* →*link*
    first →*link* = **new** *ListNode* (20) ;
}

ListNode ::*ListNode*(**int** *element* = 0) // 0 is the default argument
                                                 // in constructor for *ListNode*
{
    data = *element* ;
    link = 0 ; // null pointer constant
}

Program 4.3: Creating a two-node list

Figure 4.10: A two-node list

Example 4.3: Let *first* be a pointer to a linked list, as before. *first* == 0 if the list is empty (i.e., there are no nodes on the list). Let *x* be a pointer to some arbitrary node in the list. Program 4.4 inserts a node with *data* field 50 following the node pointed to by *x*. Once again, the default constructor for *ListNode* is used to initialize the fields of the new node. The resulting list structures for the two cases *first* == 0 and *first* != 0 are shown in Figure 4.11. □

Example 4.4: Let *first* and *x* be as in Example 4.3. Let *y* point to the node (if any) that precedes *x*, and let *y* == 0 if *x* == *first*. Function *List* ::*Delete* (Program 4.5) deletes node *x* from the list. □

```
void List ::Insert50(ListNode *x)
{
    ListNode *t = new ListNode (50) ; //create and initialize new node
    if (!first) // insert into empty list
    {
        first = t ;
        return; // exit List ::Insert 50
    }
    // insert after x
    t →link = x →link ;
    x →link = t ;
}
```

Program 4.4: Inserting a node

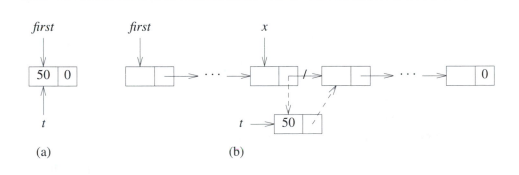

(a)   (b)

Figure 4.11: Inserting into an empty and nonempty list

EXERCISES

The following exercises are based on the definitions of Section 4.2.4. All algorithms are to be implemented as member functions of **class** *List* and are therefore assumed to have access to the data members of **class** *ListNode*.

1. Write an algorithm *length* to count the number of nodes in a singly linked list. The last node has *link* field 0. What is the time complexity of your algorithm?

2. Let *x* be a pointer to an arbitrary node in this list. Write an algorithm to delete this node from the list. If *x* == *first*, then *first* should be reset to point to the new first node in the list. What is the time complexity of your algorithm?

```
void List ::Delete(ListNode *x, ListNode *y)
{
    if (!y) first = first →link ;
    else y →link = x →link ;
    delete x ; // return the node
}
```

Program 4.5: Deleting a node

3. Write a function to delete every other node beginning with node *first* (i.e., the first, third, fifth, and so on nodes of the list are deleted). What is the time complexity of your algorithm?

4. Let $x = (x_1, x_2, \cdots, x_n)$ and $y = (y_1, y_2, \cdots, y_m)$ be two linked lists. Write an algorithm to merge the two lists together to obtain the linked list $z = (x_1, y_1, x_2, y_2, \cdots, x_m, y_m, x_{m+1}, \cdots, x_n)$ if $m \le n$ and $z = (x_1, y_1, x_2, y_2, \cdots, x_n, y_n, y_{n+1}, \cdots, y_m)$ if $m > n$. Following the merge, x and y should represent empty lists because each node initially in x or y is now in z. No additional nodes may be used. What is the time complexity of your algorithm?

5. Let $x = (x_1, x_2, \cdots, x_n)$ and $y = (y_1, y_2, \cdots, y_m)$ be two linked lists. Assume that in each linked list, the nodes are in nondecreasing order of their data-field values. Write an algorithm to merge the two lists to obtain a new linked list z in which the nodes are also in this order. Following the merge, x and y should represent empty lists because each node initially in x or y is now in z. No additional nodes may be used. What is the time complexity of your algorithm?

6. It is possible to traverse a singly linked list in both directions (i.e., left to right and a restricted right-to-left traversal) by reversing the links during the left-to-right traversal. A possible configuration for a list under this scheme is given in Figure 4.12. Assume that l and r are data members of *List*.

Figure 4.12: Possible configuration for a singly linked list traversed in both directions

The pointer r points to the node currently being examined and l to the node on its left. Note that all nodes to the left of r have their links reversed.

(a)   Write an algorithm to move pointer r, n nodes to the right from any given position (l,r). If n is greater than the number of nodes to the right, set r to 0 and l to the rightmost node in the list.

(b)   Write an algorithm to move r, n nodes to the left from any given position (l,r). If n is greater than the number of nodes to the left, set l to 0 and r to the leftmost node in the list.

4.3   A REUSABLE LINKED LIST CLASS

The cost of developing software systems is significant. A contributor is the large number of programmer-hours required to develop, test, and maintain software. Thus, there is a need for software development strategies that reduce the number of person-hours spent without sacrificing the quality of the software. One technique for this is software reuse. The basic principle of software reusability is that when we initially design and develop software, we must try and do so in a manner that makes it possible to reuse the software in the future. This typically requires a greater investment of time when the software is first developed but pays dividends in terms of time saved when the software is reused.

In this section, we will augment the list class of the previous section so that it becomes more reusable. If we are later required to develop software for an application that uses linked lists, we will be able to reuse our linked list class.

4.3.1   Implementing Linked Lists with Templates

We have already seen that the template mechanism can be used to make a container class more reusable. A linked list is clearly a container class, and is therefore a good candidate for implementation with templates. Program 4.6 contains the template definition of the linked list. Notice that *List<Type>* has been made a friend of *ListNode<Type>*. This means that the members of *ListNode*<**int**> can be accessed by members of *List*<**int**>, but not by members of, say, *List*<**float**>. Similarly, notice that *first* is declared to be a pointer to object *ListNode<Type>* in the class definition of *List<Type>*. This ensures that an object of type *List*<**int**>, say, only consists of nodes of type *ListNode*<**int**>.

An empty linked list of integers *intlist* would be defined as:

List<**int**> *intlist* ;

---

template <**class** *Type*> **class** *List* ; // forward declaration

template <**class** *Type*>
class *ListNode* {
friend class *List* <*Type* > ;
private:
    Type data ;
    ListNode *∗link* ;
};

template <**class** *Type*>
class *List* {
public:
    List () { *first* = 0 ;}; // constructor initializing *first* to 0
    // List manipulation operations
    .
    .
    .
private:
    ListNode <*Type* > *∗first* ;
};

Program 4.6: Template definition of linked lists

4.3.2   Linked Lists Iterators

An *iterator* is an object that is used to traverse all the elements of a container class. The following discussion motivates the need for iterators of a container class. Consider the following operations that one might wish to perform on a container class C, all of whose elements are integers:

(1)   Print all integers in C.

(2)   Obtain the maximum, minimum, mean, median, or mode of all integers in C.

(3)   Obtain the sum, product, or sum of squares of all integers in C.

(4)   Obtain all integers in C that satisfy some property P (for example, P could be *is a positive integer*, *is a square of an integer*, etc.).

(5)   Obtain the integer x from C such that, for some function f, $f(x)$ is maximum. □

Notice that the solutions to each of these problems require one to traverse all elements of the container class. The pseudo-code for these problems typically takes the following form:

initialization step ;
for each item in *C*
{
    current = current item of *C* ;
    body ;
}
postprocessing step ;

For example, to find the maximum of all elements in the container class, we would use the following pseudo-code:

---

1 **int** $x = -$ MAXINT ; // initialization statement
2 **for** each item in *C*
3 {
4   *current* = current item of *C* ;
5   x = max(*current*, x) ; // body
6 }
7 **return** x ; // postprocessing step

Program 4.7: Pseudo-code for computing maximum element

The C++ implementation of lines 2 and 4 depends on the container class being used. For an array *a* of size *n*, these are:

2 **for** (**int** $i = 0$; $i < n$; i++)
4 *current* = $a[i]$;

For the linked list of Program 4.6, these are:

2 **for** (*ListNode*<**int**> *ptr* = *first* ; *ptr* != 0 ; *ptr* = *ptr*→*link*)
4 *current* = *ptr*→*data* ;

All operations of the type discussed above have to be implemented as member functions of the particular container class. If the container class is the template list class defined earlier, all operations will be member functions of *List* <*Type* >. There are, however, some drawbacks to this approach:

(1) Since *List* <*Type* > is a template class, all of its operations should preferably be independent of the type of object to which *Type* is instantiated. However, many of the operations described above do not make sense in the context of certain object types. For example, computing the sum of all objects in a list does not make sense if the objects are of type *Rectangle*.

(2) The number of operations supported by *List <Type >* can become quite large, making the class definition rather unwieldy. A class definition should be as compact as possible so that it is easier for a class user to understand. Moreover, classes are often part of a class library designed by one programmer or programming team. It is not feasible for the class designer to predict all the operations required by a particular user of the class. If a user requires an operation that is not supported by the class, he or she would be forced to add that operation to the container class definition. This is not considered to be a good practice since the resulting class definition may not be consistent with the objectives with which the original class was designed.

(3) Even if it is acceptable for the user to add member functions to a class, he or she would have to learn how to traverse the container class, which would entail learning how the container class is implemented.

These arguments suggest that the iterative operations described above be moved outside the definition of *List <Type >*. This suggestion is further supported by the fact that none of these operations modify or update the contents of the linked list. However, each operation needs to access private data members of *List <Type >* and *ListNode <Type >*. Rather than making all these operations **friend**s of *List <Type >* and *ListNode <Type >* (which involves a modification of the class), we define a third class *ListIterator <Type >*, which handles the details of the linked list traversal and also retrieves elements stored in the list. Class *ListIterator<Type>* is defined as follows:

(1) *ListIterator<Type>* is declared as a **friend** of both *List<Type>* and *ListNode<Type>*.

(2) A *ListIterator<Type>* object is initialized with the name of a *List<Type>* object *l* with which it will be associated.

(3) The *ListIterator <Type >* object contains a private data member *current* of type *ListNode <Type > ***. At all times, *current* points to a node of list *l*.

(4) The *ListIterator <Type >* object defines public member functions *NotNull* () , *NextNotNull* (), *First* (), and *Next* () to perform various tests on and to retrieve elements of *l*.

Program 4.8 contains the updated implementation of the linked list, and Program 4.9 defines member functions on *ListIterator <Type >*. The operation to compute the sum of all elements in a linked list of integers may now be implemented using *ListIterator* as in Program 4.10. Notice that function *sum* does not require access to the private data members of *List <Type >* or *ListNode <Type >*.

The exercises examine why it is better to define a third class *ListIterator* than to augment the *List* class with the private variable *current* and the four public member functions.

```
enum Boolean { FALSE, TRUE};
template <class Type> class List ;
template <class Type> class ListIterator ;

template <class Type> class ListNode {
friend class List <Type > ; friend class ListIterator <Type > ;
private:
     Type data ;
     ListNode *link ;
};

template <class Type> class List {
friend class ListIterator <Type > ;
public:
     List () {first = 0 ;};
     // List manipulation operations

         .
         .
private:
     ListNode <Type > *first ;
};

template <class Type> class ListIterator {
public:
     ListIterator(const List <Type >& l): list (l), current (l.first) {};
     Boolean  NotNull () ;
     Boolean NextNotNull () ;
     Type* First () ;
     Type* Next () ;
private:
     const List <Type >& list ; // refers to an existing list
     ListNode <Type >* current ; // points to a node in list
};
```

Program 4.8: Template definition of linked lists

4.3.3   Linked List Operations

Perhaps the most important decision when designing a reusable class is choosing which operations to include. It is important to provide enough operations so that the class can be used in many applications. It is also important not to include too many operations be-

---

```
template <class Type> // check that the current element in list is non-null
Boolean ListIterator <Type >::NotNull () {
   if (current) return TRUE ;
   else return FALSE ;
}


template <class Type> // check that the next element in list is non-null
Boolean ListIterator <Type >::NextNotNull () {
   if (current && current →link) return TRUE ;
   else return FALSE ;
}


template <class Type> // return a pointer to the first element of list
Type* ListIterator <Type >::First () {
   if (list . first) return &list . first →data;
   else return 0 ;
}


template <class Type> // return a pointer to the next element of list
Type* ListIterator <Type >::Next () {
   if (current) {
     current = current →link ;
     if (current) return &current →data ;
   }
   else return 0;
}
```

Program 4.9: List iterator functions

cause this will make the class bulky. Examples of operations that would be included in most reusable classes are constructors (including default and copy constructors), a destructor, an assignment operator (**operator=**), the test-for-equality operator (**operator==**), and operators to input and output a class object (obtained by overloading **operator>>** and **operator<<**, respectively). Other operators may also be overloaded depending on the class. We will see how to implement the destructor for linked lists later in the chapter.

Some of the operations that should be provided in a linked list class would perform insertions to, deletions from, and other manipulations of the linked list. There could be a number of variations under each of these categories. For example, there could be an insertion operation that inserts an element into the front of a list and another that attaches an element to the end of a list, as in Program 4.11. In order to perform this opera-

```
int sum(const List<int>& l)
{
    ListIterator<int> li (l) ; // li is associated with list l
    if (!li.NotNull ()) return 0 ; // empty list, return 0
    int retvalue = *li.First () ; // get first element
    while (li.NextNotNull ())  // make sure that next element exists
        retvalue += *li.Next () ; // get it, add it to the current total
    return retvalue ;
}
```

Program 4.10: Using iterators to compute the sum of elements

tion efficiently, we assume the existence of a private data member *last* in **class** *List<Type>*, which points to the last node in the linked list.

```
template <class Type>
void List <Type >::Attach(Type k)
{
    ListNode <Type >*newnode = new ListNode <Type >(k) ;
    if (first == 0) first = last = newnode ;
    else {
        last →link = newnode ;
        last = newnode ;
    }
}
```

Program 4.11: Attaching a node to the end of a list

Another useful operation is one that inverts a chain (Program 4.12). This routine is especially interesting because it can be done '' in place'' if we make use of three pointers.

You should try out this algorithm on at least three examples, the empty list and lists of length 1 and 2, to convince yourself that you understand the mechanism. For a list of $m \geq 1$ nodes, the **while** loop is executed m times, so the computing time is linear or $O(m)$.

Another useful function is one that concatenates two chains (Program 4.13). The complexity of this algorithm is also linear in the length of the first chain.

```
template <class Type>
void List <Type >::Invert ()
// A chain x is inverted so that if x = (a₁, ···, aₙ),
// then, after execution, x = (aₙ, ···, a₁).
{
    ListNode <Type > *p = first, *q = 0 ;  // q trails p
    while (p) {
        ListNode <Type > *r = q ; q = p ;  // r trails q
        p = p →link ;  // p moves to next node
        q →link = r ;  // link q to preceding node
    }
    first = q ;
}
```

Program 4.12: Inverting a list

```
template <class Type>
void List <Type >::Concatenate (List <Type > b)
// this = (a₁, ···, aₘ) and b = (b₁, ···, bₘ), m, n ≥ 0,
// produces the new chain z = (a₁, ···, aₘ, b₁, ···, bₙ) in this .
{
    if (! first) { first = b.first ; return;}
    if (b.first) {
        for (ListNode <Type > *p = first ; p →link ; p = p →link) ;  // no body
        p →link = b.first ;
    }
}
```

Program 4.13: Concatenating two chains

4.3.4   Reusing a Class

Having designed and developed a reusable set of classes for linked lists, we should now try to reuse them in applications that require linked lists. In Section 4.6, we illustrate how **class** *Polynomial* can be implemented by reusing the linked list class.

Having said that, however, there are some scenarios where one should not attempt to reuse a class, but rather design a new one. We present two such scenarios below:

(1)   One of the disadvantages of reusing a class (say C_1) to implement another class (say C_2) is that, sometimes, this is less efficient than directly implementing class

C_2. If efficiency is of paramount importance, the latter approach is usually the better course of action. In Section 4.5, we will use linked lists to implement stacks and queues. Since each is an important data structure, which will itself be reused in other applications, we implement them directly to make them as efficient as possible.

(2)   Another scenario in which classes should not be reused is when the operations required by the application are complex and specialized, and therefore not offered by the class. In this situation, also, it is preferable to develop the application directly rather than to "force" the application to reuse an existing class. In Section 4.7, we will use linked lists to solve the problem of finding equivalence classes. The list operations required by our algorithm are specialized and not likely to be implemented in a reusable linked list class. Hence, we implement equivalence classes directly.

EXERCISES

The following exercises assume that linked lists are defined as in Program 4.8. All algorithms are to be implemented by employing *ListIterator* <*Type* > to traverse a list. Define your own operations on *ListIterator<Type>* if necessary.

1.   Write an algorithm to print all elements of a linked list by overloading operator<<.

2.   Write an algorithm to compute the minimum of all elements of a linked list.

3.   Let $x = (x_1, x_2, \cdots, x_n)$ be a linked list. Write an algorithm to compute the expression $\sum_{i=1}^{n-5}(x_i * x_{i+5})$. [**Hint**: use two iterators to simultaneously traverse x. Note that it is not possible for multiple iterators to be defined on the same list if the iterator operations are implemented as member functions of *List* <*Type* >.]

4.4   CIRCULAR LISTS

A *circular list* may be obtained by modifying the singly linked list (chain) so that the *link* field of the last node points to the first node in the list. Figure 4.13 shows how the chain of Figure 4.2 is modified to form a circular list.

This structure has some advantages over the chain (as we shall see later). The C++ implementation of circular lists is very similar to that for chains except for some minor differences: To check whether a pointer *current* points to the last node of a circular list, we check for (*current* →*link* == *first*) instead of (*current* →*link* == 0). Secondly, the algorithms for insertion into and deletion from a circular list must ensure that the *link* field of the last node points to the first node of the list upon completion.

Let us take a look at an operation on a circular list. Suppose we want to insert a new node at the front of the list of Figure 4.14. We have to change the *link* data member of the node containing x_3, which requires that we move down the entire length of *a* until we find the last node. It is more convenient if the access pointer of a circular list points to the last node rather than to the first (Figure 4.15).

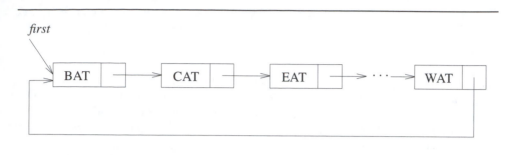

Figure 4.13: A circular list

Figure 4.14: Example of a circular list

Figure 4.15: Pointing to the last node of a circular list

Now we can write functions that insert a node at the front (Program 4.14) or at the rear of a circular list in a fixed amount of time. To insert x at the rear, one only needs to add the statement $last = x$ to the **else** clause of *InsertFront*. The code of Program 4.14 assumes the existence of a *ListNode* class identical to that used in the previous section and the existence of **class** *CircList* similar to that of **class** *List* of the previous section. It is assumed that *CircList* contains the private data member *last* that points to the last node on the circularly linked list. In some applications, using the structure of Figure 4.13 causes problems as the empty list has to be handled as a special case. To avoid such spe-

```
template <class Type>
void CircList ::InsertFront( ListNode <Type > *x)
// Insert the node pointed at by x at the "front" of the circular
// list this, where last points to the last node in the list.
{
    if (! last) { // empty list
        last = x ; x→link = x ;
    }
    else {
        x→link = last→link ; last→link = x ;
    }
}
```

Program 4.14: Inserting at the front

cial cases, we introduce a dummy head node into each circular list (i.e., each instance of a circular list will contain one additional node). Thus, the empty list will have the representation of Figure 4.16(a) and the list of Figure 4.13 will have the representation of Figure 4.16(b).

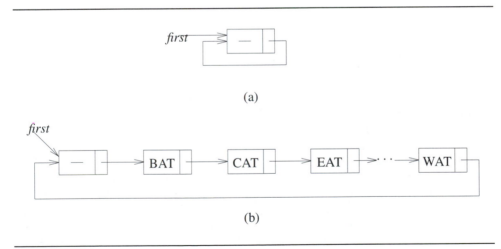

(a)

(b)

Figure 4.16: A circular list with a head node

EXERCISES

1. Do Exercise 1 of Section 4.2 for the case of circularly linked lists.

2. Do Exercise 2 of Section 4.2 for the case of circularly linked lists.

3. Do Exercise 3 of Section 4.2 for the case of circularly linked lists.

4. Do Exercise 4 of Section 4.2 for the case of circularly linked lists.

5. Do Exercise 5 of Section 4.2 for the case of circularly linked lists.

6. Do Exercise 6 of Section 4.2 for the case of circularly linked lists.

7. Write template class definitions for representing the circularly linked list. You will need to define three template classes *ListNode*, *CircList*, and *CircIterator*. Assume that **class** *CircList* contains a single private data member *last* that points to the last element in the circularly linked list. Implement the iterator member functions *First*(), *Next*(), *NotNull*(), and *NextNotNull*() so that they perform the identical functions as the corresponding operations for the singly linked list.

8. Repeat the previous exercise for the circularly linked list with a head node. This time, assume that **class** *CircList* contains a single private data member, *first*, that points to the head node.

9. Do Exercise 1 of Section 4.3 for the case of circularly linked lists.

10. Do Exercise 2 of Section 4.3 for the case of circularly linked lists.

11. Do Exercise 3 of Section 4.3 for the case of circularly linked lists.

4.5   LINKED STACKS AND QUEUES

We have already seen how to represent stacks and queues sequentially. Such a representation proves to be efficient if we have only one stack or one queue. However, when several stacks and queues coexist, there is no efficient way to represent them sequentially. In this section we present a good solution to this problem using linked lists. Figure 4.17 shows a linked stack and a linked queue.

Notice that the direction of links for both the stack and the queue is such that it facilitates insertion and deletion of nodes. In the case of Figure 4.17(a), you can easily add a node at the top or delete one from the top. In Figure 4.17(b), you can easily add a node at the rear, and both addition and deletion can be performed at the front, although for a queue we normally do not want to add nodes at the front. The integer Stack data structure is defined in Program 4.15. The integer Queue data structure is assumed to be defined similarly. Algorithms for insertion and deletion from stacks and queues are presented in Programs 4.16 - 4.19.

A collection of *m* stacks and *n* queues is obtained by the following:

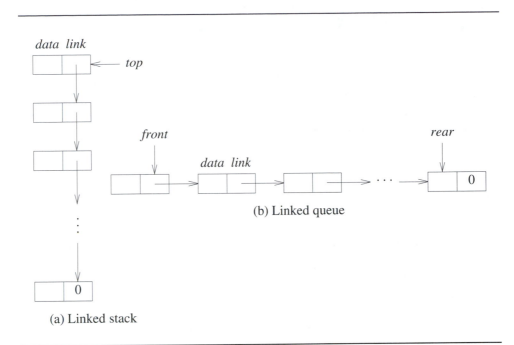

(b) Linked queue

(a) Linked stack

Figure 4.17: Linked stack and queue

Stack* stack = **new** *Stack* [*m*] ;
Queue* queue = **new** *Queue* [*n*] ;

The *Stack* constructor ensures that *top* is initialized to 0 for each stack. The condition *top* == 0 signals that the stack is empty. It is assumed that the *Queue* constructor initial-izes *front* to 0. The condition *front* == 0 signals that the queue is empty.

This solution to the *n*-stack, *m*-queue problem is both computationally and concep-tually simple. There is no need to shift stacks or queues around to make space. Compu-tation can proceed as long as there are free nodes. Although additional space is needed for the *link* field, the cost is no more than a factor of 2.

EXERCISES

1. Implement the stack data structure in C++ using templates.

2. Implement the queue data structure in C++ using templates.

3. Consider the hypothetical data object $X2$. $X2$ is a linear list with the restriction that although additions to the list may be made at either end, deletions can be made from one end only. Design a linked-list representation for $X2$. Write addi-

---

class *Stack* ; // forward declaration

class *StackNode* {
friend class *Stack* ;
private:
   int *data* ;
   StackNode *∗link* ;
   StackNode(**int** *d* = 0, *StackNode* *∗l* = 0) : *data*(*d*), *link*(*l*) { }; // constructor
};

class *Stack* {
public:
   Stack () { *top* =0 ;}; // constructor
   void *Add*(**const int**) ;
   int∗ *Delete*(**int**&) ;
private:
   StackNode *∗top* ;
   void *StackEmpty* () ;
};

Program 4.15: Stack class definition

---

void *Stack* ::*Add*(**const int** *y*) {
   top = **new** *StackNode*(*y*, *top*) ;
}

Program 4.16: Adding to a linked stack

tion and deletion algorithms for $X2$. Specify initial and boundary conditions for your representation.

4. Let p be a pointer to a circularly linked list. Show how this list may be used as a queue (i.e., write algorithms to add and delete elements). Specify the value for p when the queue is empty.

5. Implement the stack data structure using the reusable linked list class of Section 4.3.

6. Implement the queue data structure using the reusable linked list class of Section 4.3.

```
int * Stack ::Delete(int& retvalue)
// Delete top node from stack and return a pointer to its data
{
        if (top == 0) {StackEmpty () ; return 0 ;} // return null pointer constant
        StackNode *delnode = top ;
        retvalue = top →data ;  // get data field of top node
        top = top →link ; // remove top node
        delete delnode ;    // free the node
        return &retvalue ;   // return pointer to data
}
```

Program 4.17: Deleting from a linked stack

```
void Queue ::Add(const int y)
{
    if (front == 0) front = rear = new QueueNode(y, 0) ; // empty queue
    else rear = rear →link = new QueueNode(y, 0) ; // attach node and update rear
}
```

Program 4.18: Adding to a linked queue

```
int* Queue ::Delete(int& retvalue)
// delete the first node in queue and return a pointer to its data
{
        if (front == 0) {QueueEmpty () ; return 0 ;}
        QueueNode *x = front ;
        retvalue = front →data ; // get data
        front = x →link ;     // delete front node
        delete x ; // free the node
        return &retvalue ;
}
```

Program 4.19: Deleting from a linked queue

4.6 POLYNOMIALS

4.6.1 Polynomial Representation

Let us tackle a reasonable-sized problem using linked lists. This problem, the manipulation of symbolic polynomials, has become a classic example of the use of list processing. As in Chapter 2, we wish to be able to represent any number of different polynomials as long as their combined size does not exceed our block of memory. In general, we want to represent the polynomial $A(x) = a_m x^{e_m} + \cdots + a_1 x^{e_1}$, where the a_i are nonzero coefficients and the exponents e_i are nonnegative integers such that $e_m > e_{m-1} > \cdots > e_2 > e_1 \geq 0$. We will define a *Polynomial* class to implement polynomials. Since a polynomial is to be represented by a list, we have *Polynomial* IS-IMPLEMENTED-BY *List*.

Definition: We say that a data object of Type A IS-IMPLEMENTED-IN-TERMS-OF a data object of Type B if the Type B object is central to the implementation of the Type A object. This relationship is usually expressed by declaring the Type B object as a data member of the Type A object. $\square$

Thus, we will make the linked list object *poly* a data member of *Polynomial*. We will employ the linked list template classes developed in Program 4.8 to implement the linked list. Each *ListNode* will represent a term in the polynomial. To do this, the list template *Type* is instantiated to **struct** *Term*; where, *Term* consists of two data members *coef* and *exp*. We use **struct** rather than **class** to define *Term* to emphasize that the data members of *Term* are public. The data members of *Term* are made public so that any function that has access to a *Term* object also has access to its data members. This does not violate data encapsulation for *Polynomial* because the linked list and its contents, including all *Term* objects are all private and cannot be accessed. Assuming that the coefficients are integers, the required class declarations are developed in Program 4.20.

Even though polynodes contain two fields *data* and *link*, and *data* contains two fields *coef* and exp, we will draw polynodes as follows for simplicity.

For instance, the polynomials $a = 3x^{14} + 2x^8 + 1$ and $b = 8x^{14} - 3x^{10} + 10x^6$ would be stored as in Figure 4.18.

4.6.2 Adding Polynomials

To add two polynomials a and b, we use the list iterators *Aiter* and *Biter* to examine their terms starting at the nodes pointed to by *a.first* and *b.first*. Two variables p and q are used to move along the terms of a and b. If the exponents of two terms are equal, then the coefficients are added. A new term is created for the result if the sum of the

```
struct Term
// all members of Term are public by default
{
    int coef ; // coefficient
    int exp ;  // exponent
    void Init(int c, int e) { coef = c ; exp = e ;}};
};

class Polynomial
{
friend Polynomial operator+(const Polynomial&, const Polynomial&) ;
private:
    List <Term> poly ;
};
```

Program 4.20: Polynomial class definition

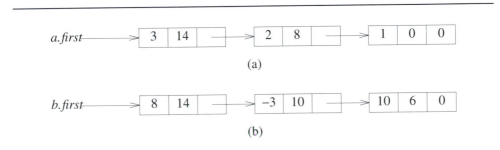

(a)

(b)

Figure 4.18: Polynomial representation of $3x^{14}+2x^8+1$ and $8x^{14}-3x^{10}+10x^6$

coefficients is not zero. If the exponent of the current term in *a* is less than the exponent of the current term in *b*, then a copy of the term in *b* is created and attached to the *Polynomial* object *c*. The variable *q* is advanced to the next term. Similar action is taken on *a* if $p \rightarrow exp > q \rightarrow exp$. Figure 4.19 illustrates this addition process on the polynomials *a* and *b* of the example of Figure 4.18.

Each time a new node is generated, its *coef* and *exp* data members are set and it is appended to the end of *c* by function *List::Attach* (Program 4.11) provided by **class** *List*. The complete addition algorithm is specified by the function **operator+()** (Program 4.21).

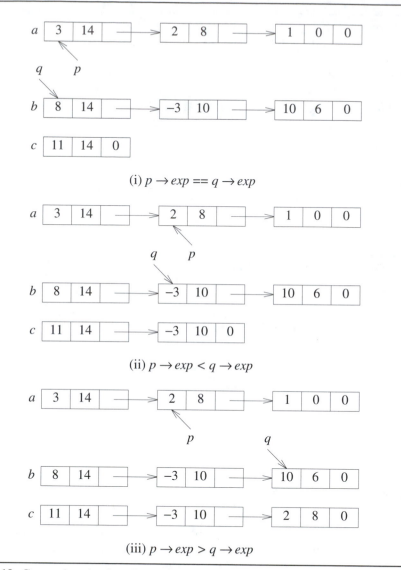

Figure 4.19: Generating the first three terms of $c = a + b$

This is our first complete example of the use of list processing, so it should be carefully studied. The basic algorithm is straightforward, using a merging process that streams along the two polynomials, either copying terms or adding them to the result. Thus, the main **while** loop of lines 7-22 has three cases depending upon whether the exponents of the terms are ==, <, or >.

```
1 Polynomial operator+(const Polynomial& a , const Polynomial& b) {
2 // Polynomials a and b are added and the sum returned
3      Term *p, *q, temp ;
4      ListIterator <Element > Aiter (a.poly) ; ListIterator <Element > Biter (b.poly) ;
5      Polynomial c ;
6      p = Aiter. First () ; q = Biter. First () ; // get first node in a and b
7      while (Aiter . NotNull () && Biter . NotNull ()) { // current node is not null
8          switch (compare(p →exp,q →exp )) {
9              case '=':
10                  int x = p →coef + q →coef ; temp . Init (x,q →exp) ;
11                  if (x) c . poly . Attach (temp) ;
12                  p = Aiter.Next () ; q = Biter.Next () ; // advance to next term
13                  break;
14              case '<':
15                  temp.Init(q →coef, q →exp) ; c.poly.Attach (temp) ;
16                  q = Biter.Next () ; // next term of b
17                  break;
18              case '>':
19                  temp . Init(p →coef, p →exp) ; c.poly.Attach (temp) ;
20                  p = Aiter . Next () ; // next term of a
21          }
22      }
23      while (Aiter.NotNull ()) {  // copy rest of a
24          temp.Init(p →coef, p →exp) ; c.poly.Attach (temp) ;
25          p = Aiter.Next () ;
26      }
27      while (Biter.NotNull ()) {  // copy rest of b
28          temp.Init(q →coef, q →exp) ; c.poly.Attach (temp) ;
29          q=Biter.Next () ;
30      }
31      return c ;
32 }
```

Program 4.21: Adding two polynomials

Analysis of *operator+():* The following operations contribute to the computing time:

(1)   coefficient additions

(2)   exponent comparisons

(3)   additions/deletions to available space

(4)   creation of new nodes for c

Let us assume that each of these four operations, if done once, takes a single unit of time. The total time taken by algorithm **operator+()** is then determined by the number of times these operations are performed. This number clearly depends on how many terms are present in the polynomials a and b. Assume that a and b have m and n terms, respectively:

$$a(x) = a_m x^{e_m} + \cdots + a_1 x^{e_1},\ b(x) = b_n x^{f_n} + \cdots + b_1 x^{f_1}$$

where

$$a_i, b_i \neq 0 \text{ and } e_m > \cdots > e_1 \geq 0, f_n > \ldots > f_1 \geq 0$$

Then clearly the number of coefficient additions can vary as

$$0 \leq \text{coefficient additions} \leq \min\{m,n\}$$

The lower bound is achieved when none of the exponents are equal; the upper bound is achieved when the exponents of one polynomial are a subset of the exponents of the other polynomial.

As for exponent comparisons, one comparison is made on each iteration of the first **while** loop. On each iteration either p or q or both move to the next term in their respective polynomials. Since the total number of terms is $m + n$, the number of iterations and hence the number of exponent comparisons is bounded by $m + n$. You can easily construct a case when $m + n - 1$ comparisons will be necessary — e.g., $m = n$ and

$$e_n > f_n > e_{n-1} > f_{n-1} > \cdots > e_2 > f_2 > e_1 > f_1$$

The maximum number of terms in c is $m + n$, so no more than $m + n$ new nodes are created. In summary, the maximum number of executions of any of the statements in **operator+()** is bounded above by $m + n$. Therefore, the computing time is $O(m + n)$. If the algorithm is implemented and run on a computer, the time taken will be $c_1 m + c_2 n + c_3$, where c_1, c_2, and c_3 are constants. Since any algorithm that adds two polynomials must look at each nonzero term at least once, algorithm **operator+()** is optimal to within a constant factor. □

4.6.3   Erasing Polynomials

The use of linked lists is well suited to polynomial operations. We can easily imagine writing a collection of functions for input, output, assignment, addition, subtraction, and multiplication of polynomials using linked lists as the means of representation. Consider a function that reads in polynomials $a(x)$, $b(x)$, and $c(x)$ and then computes and prints $d(x) = a(x) * b(x) + c(x)$:

```
void func ()
{
     Polynomial a, b, c, d, t ;
     cin >> a ; // read and create polynomials
     cin >> b ;
     cin >> c ;
     t = a * b ;
     d = t + c ;
     cout << d ;
}
```

What happens to these polynomials after function *func* has been exited? The answer is that the memory occupied by the class objects a, b, c, t, and d is returned once these objects go out of scope. Unfortunately, this means that only the *Polynomial* class objects and the *List* <*Term*> objects they physically contain are deleted. *ListNode* <*Term*> objects are not physically contained in *List* <*Term*> objects (and therefore not physically contained in *Polynomial* objects). So, these objects do not get automatically freed up by the system. Worse still, it is not possible to access these objects because all *first* data members were deleted when the function was exited. The memory they occupy is lost to the program as it is not returned to the system. Figure 4.20 illustrates the process. If function *func* is used many times in a program, it is possible that these lost nodes will eventually occupy all the memory causing the program to crash. To prevent this, we define a destructor to delete all objects that are conceptually part of a class but not physically part of it. The destructor is implemented in Program 4.22:

Now, when a *Polynomial* object goes out of scope, the system first checks to see if a destructor exists for that class. If so, the destructor is executed. We have not defined a destructor on *Polynomial*, so a destructor is not executed. Next, if the class object contains other class objects as data members, they are deleted. *Polynomial* contains a single data member *poly* of type *List*. Since a destructor is defined on *List*, it is executed on *poly*. Finally, the data members of *poly* (*poly . first* and *poly . last*) are deleted.

4.6.4   Circular List Representation of Polynomials

It is possible to free all the nodes in a list more efficiently by employing a circular list instead of a chain. Figure 4.21 shows the circular list representation of a polynomial.

We delete nodes that are no longer in use is so that these nodes may be reused later. This objective, together with an efficient erase algorithm for circular lists, may be met by maintaining our own list (as a chain) of nodes that have been ''deleted.'' When a new node is needed, we may examine this list. If this list is not empty, then one of the nodes on it may be made available for use. Only when this list is empty do we need to use command **new** to create a new node.

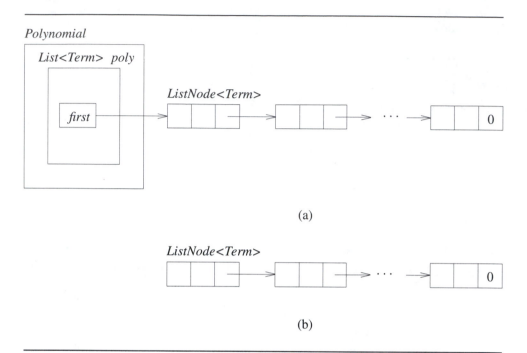

Polynomial

List<Term> poly

first

ListNode<Term>

0

(a)

ListNode<Term>

0

(b)

Figure 4.20: (a) and (b), respectively, show a polynomial object before and after it goes out of scope.

```
template <class Type>
List <Type >::~List ()
// Free all nodes in the chain
{
    ListNode <Type >* next ;
    for (; first ; first = next) {
        next = first →link ;
        delete first ;
    }
}
```

Program 4.22: Erasing a polynomial

Figure 4.21: Circular list representation of $3x^{14} + 2x^8 + 1$

Let *av* be a static class member of *CircList* <*Type* > of type *ListNode*<*Type*>* that points to our chain of nodes that have been "deleted." (We implement the chain directly rather than reusing our linked list class for efficiency reasons.) This list will henceforth be called the *available-space list* or *av list*. Initially, $av = 0$. Instead of using the commands **new** and **delete**, we shall now use the functions *CircList* ::*GetNode* (Program 4.23) and *CircList* ::*RetNode* (Program 4.24).

```
template <class Type>
ListNode <Type >* CircList ::GetNode()
// Provide a node for use.
{
    ListNode <Type >* x ;
    if (!av) x = new ListNode <Type > ;
    else { x = av ; av = av→link ; }
    return x ;
}
```

Program 4.23: Getting a node

As illustrated by function *CircList* <*Type* >::˜*CircList* (Program 4.25), a circular list may now be erased in a fixed amount of time independent of the number of nodes on the list. Figure 4.22 is a schematic showing the link changes involved in erasing a circular list.

A direct changeover to the structure of Figure 4.21, however, causes some problems during addition and other operations, as the zero polynomial has to be handled as a special case. To avoid such special cases you may introduce a head node into each polynomial (i.e., each polynomial, zero or nonzero, will contain one additional node). The *exp* and *coef* data members of this node will not be relevant. Thus, the zero polynomial will have the representation of Figure 4.23(a), and $a = 3x^{14} + 2x^8 + 1$ will have the representation of Figure 4.23(b).

For this circular list with head node representation, the test for *first* == 0 may be removed from ˜*CircList*(). The only changes to be made for algorithm **operator+**() (Pro-

```
template <class Type>
void CircList <Type >::RetNode(ListNode <Type >* x)
// Free the node pointed to by x.
{
    x→ link = av;
    av = x;
}
```

Program 4.24: Returning a node

```
template <class KeyType>
void CircList <Type >::~CircList ()
// Erase the circular list pointed by first.
{
    if (first) {
        ListNode* second = first→ link; // second node
        first→ link = av; // first node linked to av
        av = second; //second node of list becomes front of av list
        first = 0;
    }
}
```

Program 4.25: Erasing a circular list

gram 4.21) to work are in the implementation of the iterator functions *First* (), *Next* (), *NotNull* (), and *NextNotNull* () and in the implementation of *Attach* (the link field of the last node must point to the headnode).

A further simplification in the addition algorithm is possible if the *exp* field of the head node is set to -1. Now when all nodes of a have been examined, $p = a$ and $exp(p) = -1$. Since $-1 \leq exp(q)$, the remaining terms of b can be copied by further executions of the case statement. The same is true if all nodes of b are examined before those of a. This implies that there is no need for additional code to copy the remaining terms as in **operator+()**. The final algorithm takes the simple form given in Program 4.26.

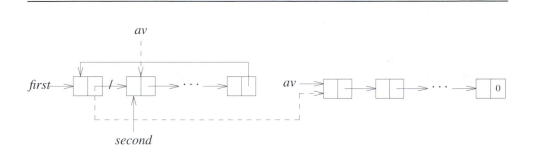

Figure 4.22: Dashes indicate changes involved in erasing a circular list

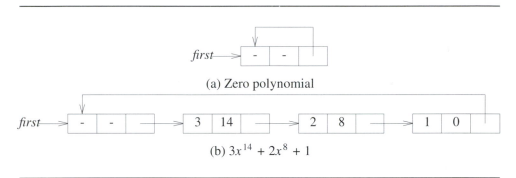

Figure 4.23: Example polynomials

4.6.5 Summary

Let us review what we have done so far. We have introduced the notions of a singly linked list (chain), and a singly linked circular list. Each node on one of these lists consists of exactly one link data member and some number of other data members. In all of our examples, all nodes on any given list had the same data members. The concept of a singly linked list does not require this property and in subsequent sections we shall see lists that violate it.

In dealing with polynomials, we found it convenient to use circular lists. This required us to introduce the notion of an available space list. Such a list consists of all nodes that have been used at least once and are currently not in use. By using the available-space list and the functions *GetNode*, *RetNode*, and *~CircList*, it became possible to erase circular lists in constant time and to reuse all nodes currently not in use. As

---

```
Polynomial operator+(const Polynomial& a, const Polynomial& b)
{
    Term *p, *q, temp;
    CircListIterator <Term > Aiter (a.poly) ; CircListIterator <Term > Biter (b.poly) ;
    Polynomial c; // assume the constructor creates a head node with exp = −1
    p = Aiter.First () ; q = Biter.First () ;
    while (1)
        switch (compare (p →exp,q →exp )) {
            case '=':
                if (p →exp == −1) return c ;
                else {
                    int sum = p →coef + q →coef ;
                    if (sum) {
                        temp.Init(sum, q →exp);
                        c.poly.Attach (temp) ;
                    }
                    p = Aiter.Next () ;
                    q = Biter.Next () ;
                }
                break;
            case '<':
                temp.Init(q →coef, q →exp);
                c.poly.Attach (temp) ;
                q = Biter.Next () ;
                break;
            case '>':
                temp.Init(p →coef, p →exp) ;
                c.poly.Attach (temp) ;
                p = Aiter.Next () ;
        } // end of switch and while
}
```

Program 4.26: Adding circularly represented polynomials

we continue, we shall see more problems that call for variations in node structure and list representation because of the operations we wish to perform.

EXERCISES

1. When a class object *CO* is passed by value, it is copied into the function's local store. The algorithm for copying the object is specified by the *copy constructor*. If the class definition of *CO* does not define the copy constructor, the default copy constructor is used. The default copy constructor only copies all the objects *physically* contained in *CO*. Define a copy constructor for a singly linked list that copies all the nodes of the list into the new list.

2. Write an algorithm to read in n pairs of coefficients and exponents, (c_i, e_i), $1 \le i \le n$, of a univariate polynomial and to convert the polynomial into the circularly linked list representation described in this section. Assume that $e_i > e_{i+1}$, $1 \le i < n$, and that $c_i \ne 0$, $1 \le i \le n$. Your algorithm should leave *first* pointing to the head node. Show that this operation can be performed in time $O(n)$.

3. Let a and b be two polynomials represented as circular lists with headnodes. Write an algorithm to compute the product polynomial $c = a*b$. Your algorithm should leave a and b unaltered. Show that if n and m are the number of terms in a and b, respectively, then this multiplication can be carried out in time $O(nm^2)$ or $O(mn^2)$. If a and b are dense, show that the multiplication takes $O(mn)$.

4. Write an algorithm, *Polynomial*::*Eval* (x), to evaluate the polynomial at the point x, where x is some real number. Assume that the polynomial is represented as a circularly linked list with a headnode.

5. [**Programming Project**] Design a linked allocation system to represent and manipulate univariate polynomials with integer coefficients (use circular linked lists with head nodes). Each term of the polynomial will be represented as a node. Thus, a node in this system will have three data members as below:

Exponent	Link
Coefficient	

    To erase polynomials efficiently, we need to use an available-space list and associated functions as described in Section 4.6. The external (i.e., for input or output) representation of a univariate polynomial will be assumed to be a sequence of integers of the form: n, c_1, e_1, c_2, e_2, c_3, e_3 . . . , c_n, e_n, where e_i represents an exponent and c_i a coefficient; n gives the number of terms in the polynomial. The exponents are in decreasing order — i.e., $e_1 > e_2 > \cdots > e_n$.

    Write and test the following functions:

    (a) *istream&* **operator>>**(*istream&* *is*, *Polynomial&* *x*): Read in an input polynomial and convert it to its circular list representation using a head node.

    (b) *ostream&* **operator<<**(*ostream&* *os*, *Polynomial&* *x*): Convert x from its linked list representation to its external representation and output it.

(c)   *Polynomial* ::*Polynomial*(**const** *Polynomial*& *a*) [Copy Constructor]: Initialize the polynomial *this to the polynomial *a*.

(d)   **const** *Polynomial*& *Polynomial*::**operator**=(**const** *Polynomial*& *a*) [Assignment Operator]: Assign polynomial *a* to *this.

(e)   *Polynomial*::˜*Polynomial* () [Destructor]: Return all nodes of the polynomial *this to the available-space list.

(f)   *Polynomial* **operator+** (**const** *Polynomial*& *a*, **const** *Polynomial*& *b*) [Addition]: Create and return the polynomial *a* + *b*. *a* and *b* are to be left unaltered.

(g)   *Polynomial* **operator−** (**const** *Polynomial*& *a*, **const** *Polynomial*& *b*) [Subtraction] : Create and return the polynomial *a* − *b*. *a* and *b* are to be left unaltered.

(h)   *Polynomial* **operator**∗(**const** *Polynomial*& *a*, **const** *Polynomial*& *b*) [Multiplication]: Create and return the polynomial *a* ∗ *b*. *a* and *b* are to be left unaltered.

(i)   **float** *Polynomial* ::*Evaluate*(**float** *x*): Evaluate the polynomial *this at *x* and return the result.

4.7   EQUIVALENCE CLASSES

Let us put together some of these ideas on linked and sequential representations to solve a problem that arises in the design and manufacture of very large-scale integrated (VLSI) circuits. One of the steps in the manufacture of a VLSI circuit involves exposing a silicon wafer using a series of masks. Each mask consists of several polygons. Polygons that overlap are electrically equivalent. Electrical equivalence specifies a relationship among mask polygons. This relation has several properties that it shares with other relations, such as the conventional mathematical equivalence. Suppose we denote an arbitrary relation by the symbol ≡, and suppose that

(1)   For any polygon *x*, $x \equiv x$ (e.g., *x* is electrically equivalent to itself). Thus, ≡ is *reflexive*.

(2)   For any two polygons *x* and *y*, if $x \equiv y$, then $y \equiv x$. Thus, the relation ≡ is *symmetric*.

(3)   For any three polygons *x*, *y*, and *z*, if $x \equiv y$ and $y \equiv z$, then $x \equiv z$ (e.g., if *x* and *y* are electrically equivalent and *y* and *z* are also, then so also are *x* and *z*). The relation ≡ is *transitive*.

Definition: A relation ≡ over a set *S*, is said to be an *equivalence relation* over *S* iff it is symmetric, reflexive, and transitive over *S*. □

Equivalence relations are numerous. For example, the "equal to" (=) relationship is an equivalence relation, since (1) $x = x$, (2) $x = y$ implies $y = x$, and (3) $x = y$ and $y = z$ implies $x = z$. One effect of an equivalence relation is to partition the set S into equivalence classes such that two members x and y of S are in the same equivalence class iff $x \equiv y$. For example, if we have 12 polygons numbered 0 through 11 and the following overlap pairs are defined:

$$0 \equiv 4, 3 \equiv 1, 6 \equiv 10, 8 \equiv 9, 7 \equiv 4, 6 \equiv 8, 3 \equiv 5, 2 \equiv 11, \text{ and } 11 \equiv 0$$

then, as a result of the reflexivity, symmetry, and transitivity of the relation $\equiv$, we get the following partitioning of the 12 polygons into three equivalence classes:

$$\{0, 2, 4, 7, 11\}; \{1, 3, 5\}; \{6, 8, 9, 10\}$$

These equivalence classes are important, as each such class defines a *signal net*. The signal nets can be used to verify the correctness of the masks.

The algorithm to determine equivalence classes works in essentially two phases. In the first phase the equivalence pairs (i,j) are read in and stored. In phase two we begin at 0 and find all pairs of the form $(0, j)$. The values 0 and j are in the same class. By transitivity, all pairs of the form (j, k) imply k is in the same class as 0. We continue in this way until the entire equivalence class containing 0 has been found, marked, and printed. Then we find an object not yet output. This is in a new equivalence class. The objects in this equivalence class are found as before and output.

```
void equivalence()
{
    initialize;
    while more pairs
    {
        read the next pair (i,j);
        process this pair;
    }
    initialize for output;
    for (each object not yet output)
        output the equivalence class that contains this object;
} // end of equivalence
```

Program 4.27: First pass at equivalence algorithm

The first design for this algorithm might be as in Program 4.27. Let m and n represent the number of related pairs and the number of objects, respectively. Now we need to determine which data structure should be used to hold these pairs. Easy random access would suggest a *Boolean* array, say $pairs[n][n]$. The element $pairs[i][j] = \text{TRUE}$ if and only if i and j are paired directly in the input. However, this could potentially be wasteful of space since very few of the array elements may be used. Any algorithm that uses this data structure would require $\Theta(n^2)$ time, just to initialize the array.

These considerations lead us to consider a linked list to represent each row. Each node on the list requires only a *data* and a *link* field. However, we still need random access to the *i*th row, so a one-dimensional array, *seq*[*n*], can be used as the head nodes of the *n* lists.

Looking at the second phase of the algorithm we need a mechanism that tells us whether or not object *i* is yet to be printed. A *Boolean* array, *out*[*n*], can be used for this. The next refinement of the algorithm (Program 4.28) follows.

```
void equivalence()
{
   read n; // read in number of objects
   initialize seq to 0 and out to FALSE;
   while more pairs // input pairs
   {
      read the next pair (i,j);
      put j on the seq [i] list;
      put i on the seq [j] list;
   }
   for (i = 0 ; i < n ; i++)
      if (out [i]  == FALSE) {
         out [i] = TRUE ;
         output the equivalence class that contains object i ;
      }
} // end of equivalence
```

Program 4.28: A more detailed version of equivalence algorithm

Let us simulate the algorithm, as we have it so far, on the previous data set. After the **while** loop is completed the lists will look as they do in Figure 4.24. For each relation $i \equiv j$, two nodes are used. *seq* [*i*] points to a list of nodes that contains every number directly equivalent to *i* by an input relation.

In phase two we can scan the *seq* array and start with the first, *i*, $0 \le i < n$ such that *out* [*i*] == FALSE. Each element in the list *seq* [*i*] is printed. To process the remaining lists which, by transitivity, belong in the same class as *i*, a stack of their nodes is created. This is accomplished by changing the *link* data members so they point in the reverse direction. The complete function is given in Program 4.29.

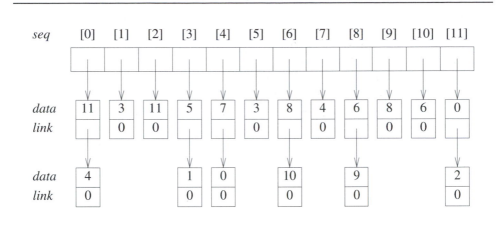

Figure 4.24: Lists after pairs have been input

enum *Boolean* { FALSE, TRUE };

class *ListNode* {
friend void *equivalence* () ;
private:
   int *data* ;
   ListNode ∗*link* ;
   ListNode(**int**) ;
};

typedef *ListNode* ∗*ListNodePtr* ;
// so we can create an array of pointers using **new**

ListNode ::*ListNode*(**int** *d*)
{
   data = *d* ;
   link = 0 ;
}

void *equivalence* ()
// Input the equivalence pairs and output the equivalence classes
{
   ifstream inFile("equiv.in", ios::in) ; // "equiv.in" is the input file

```
if(!inFile) {
  cerr << "Cannot open input file " << endl ;
  return;
}
int i, j, n ;
inFile >> n ;  // read number of objects
// initialize seq and out
ListNodePtr *seq = new ListNodePtr [n ] ;
Boolean *out = new Boolean [n ] ;
for (i = 0 ; i < n ; i++) {
  seq [i ] = 0 ;
  out [i ] = FALSE ;
}


// Phase 1: input equivalence pairs
inFile >> i >> j ;
while (inFile.good ()) {  // check end of file
  ListNode *x = new ListNode (j) ; x →link = seq [i ] ; seq [i ] = x ; // add j to seq [i ]
  ListNode *y = new ListNode (i) ; y →link = seq [j ] ; seq [j ] = y ; // add i to seq [j ]
  inFile  >> i >> j ;
}


// Phase 2: output equivalence classes
for (i = 0 ; i < n ; i++)
  if (out [i ] == FALSE) {  // needs to be output
    cout << endl << "A new class: " << i;
    out [i ] = TRUE  ;
    ListNode *x = seq [i ] ; ListNode *top = 0 ;  // init stack
    while (1) {  // find rest of class
        while (x) {  // process the list
            j = x →data ;
            if (out [j ] == FALSE) {
              cout << ", " << j ;
              out [j ] = TRUE ;
              ListNode *y = x →link ;
              x →link = top ;
              top = x ;
              x = y ;
            }
            else x = x →link ;
        } // end of while(x)
        if (!top) break ;
        else {
            x = seq [top →data ] ;
```

```
        top = top →link ; // unstack
      }
    } // end of while(1)
  } // end of if(out [i ] == FALSE)
  for (i = 0; i < n; i++)
    while (seq[i]) {
      ListNode *delnode = seq[i];
      seq[i] = delnode→link;
      delete delnode;
    }
  delete [ ] seq; delete [ ] out;
} // end of equivalence
```

Program 4.29: Algorithm to find equivalence classes

Analysis of *equivalence*: The initialization of *seq* and *out* takes O(n) time. The processing of each input pair in phase 1 takes a constant amount of time. Hence, the total
time for this phase is O($n + m$), where m is the number of input pairs. In phase 2 each
node is put onto the linked stack at most once. Since there are only 2m nodes and the **for**
loop is executed n times, the time for this phase is O($m + n$). Hence, the overall computing time is O($m + n$). Any algorithm that processes equivalence relations must look at
all m equivalence pairs and at all n polygons at least once. Thus, no algorithm can have
a computing time less than O($m + n$). This means that function *equivalence* is optimal
to within a constant factor. Unfortunately, the space required by the algorithm is also
O($m + n$). In Chapter 5 we shall see an O(n)-space solution to this problem.

4.8 SPARSE MATRICES

4.8.1 Sparse Matrix Representation

In Chapter 2, we saw that when matrices were sparse (i.e., many of the entries were
zero), then much space and computing time could be saved if only the nonzero terms
were retained explicitly. In the case where these nonzero terms did not form any ''nice''
pattern such as a triangle or a band, we devised a sequential scheme in which each
nonzero term was represented by a structure with three data members: row, column, and
value. These terms were organized sequentially. However, as matrix operations such as
addition, subtraction, and multiplication are performed, the number of nonzero terms in
matrices will vary. Matrices representing partial computations (as in the case of polynomials) will be created and will have to be destroyed later to make space for additional
matrices. Thus, sequential schemes for representing sparse matrices suffer from the same
inadequacies as similar schemes for polynomials. In this section we study a very general
linked-list scheme for sparse-matrix representation. As we have already seen, linked

schemes facilitate efficient representation of varying-size structures, and here, too, our scheme overcomes the aforementioned shortcomings of the sequential representation studied in Chapter 2.

In the data representation we use, each column of a sparse matrix is represented by a circularly linked list with a head node. In addition, each row is also a circularly linked list with a head node.

Each node is represented by the class *MatrixNode*. This class has a field called *head*, which is used to distinguish between head nodes and nodes representing nonzero matrix elements. Each head node has three additional fields: *down*, *right*, and *next*. The total number of head nodes is max {number of rows, number of columns}. The head node for row *i* is also the head node for column *i*. The *down* field of a head node is used to link into a column list; the *right* field is used to link into a row list. The *next* field links the head nodes together.

All other nodes have six fields: *head, row, col, down, right*, and *value* (Figure 4.25). The *down* field is used to link to the next nonzero term in the same column and the *right* field links to the next nonzero term in the same row. Thus, if $a_{ij} \neq 0$, then there is a node with *head* = FALSE, *value* = a_{ij}, *row* = *i*, and *col* = *j*. This node is linked into the circular linked lists for row *i* and column *j*. Hence, the node is simultaneously in two different lists.

down	*head*	*right*
next		

(a) head node

down	*head*	*row*	*col*	*right*
value				

(b) typical node

(c) set up for a_{ij}

Figure 4.25: Node structure for sparse matrices

As noted earlier, each head node is in three lists: a row list, a column list, and a list of head nodes. The list of head nodes itself has a head node that is identical to the nodes used to represent nonzero elements. The *row* and *col* fields of this node are used to store the matrix dimensions. The entire matrix is represented by class *Matrix* with the data member *headnode*, which points to this node.

The linked structure obtained for the 6×7 matrix, *A*, of Figure 4.26 is shown in Figure 4.27. Although Figure 4.27 does not show the values of the *head* fields, these values are readily determined from the node structure shown. For each nonzero term of *A*, we have one six-field node that is in exactly one column list and one row list. The head nodes are marked H0 to H6 and are drawn twice to simplify the figure. As seen in the figure, the *right* field of *headnode* is used to link into the list of head nodes. Notice that the whole matrix may be referenced through the head node, *headnode*, of the list of head nodes.

$$\begin{bmatrix} 0 & 0 & 11 & 0 & 0 & 13 & 0 \\ 12 & 0 & 0 & 0 & 0 & 0 & 14 \\ 0 & -4 & 0 & 0 & 0 & -8 & 0 \\ 0 & 0 & 0 & 0 & 0 & 0 & 0 \\ 0 & 0 & 0 & 0 & 0 & 0 & 0 \\ 0 & -9 & 0 & 0 & 0 & 0 & 0 \end{bmatrix}$$

Figure 4.26: 6×7 sparse matrix A

If we wish to represent an $n \times m$ sparse matrix with r nonzero terms, the number of nodes needed is $\max\{n,m\} + r + 1$. Although each node may require several words of memory, the total storage needed will be less than nm for sufficiently small r.

The required node structure may be defined in C++ using an anonymous **union** as in Program 4.30. Since all nodes contain fields *head*, *down* and *right*, these are declared outside the anonymous union. Head nodes also contain *next* while all other nodes contain *row*, *col*, and *value*. These fields are all incorporated into **struct** *Triple*. Space is allocated by the union declaration for the larger of fields *next* and *triple* (which is an object of type *Triple*). Because of this, fields *row*, *col*, and *value* are accessed indirectly through *triple*.:

4.8.2 Sparse Matrix Input

The first operation we shall consider is that of reading in a sparse matrix and obtaining its linked representation. We assume that the first input line consists of *s.row* (the number of rows), *s.col* (the number of columns), and *s.value* (the number of nonzero terms). The line is followed by *s.value* lines of input; each of these is a triple of the form (i, j, a_{ij}). These triples consist of the *row*, *col*, and *value* data members of the nonzero terms of the matrix. We also assume that these triples are ordered by rows and within rows by columns.

For example, the input for the 6×7 sparse matrix of Figure 4.26, which has seven nonzero terms, would take the following form: 6, 7, 7; 0, 2, 11; 0, 5, 13; 1, 0, 12; 1, 6, 14; 2, 1, −4; 2, 5, −8; 5, 1, −9. We shall not concern ourselves here with the actual format of this input on the input media (tape, disk, terminal, etc.) but shall assume that we have a mechanism to get the next triple (see Exercises for a possible input format). The function **operator>>** (Program 4.31) also makes use of an auxiliary array *head*, of size $max(s.row, s.col)$. *head*[i] is a pointer to the head node for column i and hence also for row i, permitting us efficient random access to columns while the input matrix is set up. Function **operator>>** proceeds first by setting up all the head nodes and then by setting up each row list, simultaneously building the column lists. The *next* data member of head node i is used initially to keep track of the last node in column i. Eventually, in line 30, the head nodes are linked together through this data member.

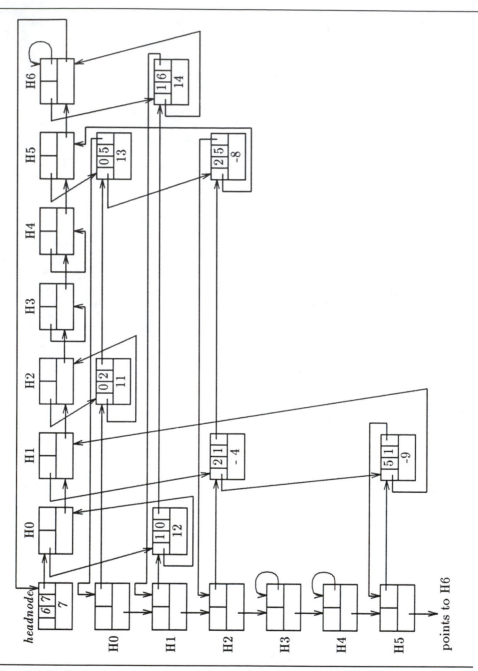

Figure 4.27: Linked representation of the sparse matrix *A* of Figure 4.26 (the *head* data member of a node is not shown)

```
enum Boolean { FALSE, TRUE };
struct Triple { int value, row, col ; };
class Matrix ; // forward declaration
class MatrixNode
{
friend class Matrix ;
friend istream& operator>>(istream&, Matrix&) ; // for reading in a matrix
private:
    MatrixNode *down , *right ;
    Boolean head ;
    union {   // anonymous union
            MatrixNode *next ;
            Triple triple ;
    };
    MatrixNode(Boolean, Triple *) ; // constructor
};

MatrixNode::MatrixNode(Boolean b, Triple * t) // constructor
{
    head = b ;
    if (b) { right = next = down = this;} // row/column head node
    else triple = *t ;  // head node for list of headnodes OR element node
}

typedef MatrixNode * MatrixNodePtr ; // to allow subsequent creation of array of pointers

class Matrix
{
friend istream& operator>>(istream&, Matrix&) ;
public:
    ~Matrix() ; // destructor
private:
    MatrixNode *headnode ;
};
```

Program 4.30: Class definition for sparse matrices

Analysis of *operator>>:* Since **new** works in a constant amount of time, all the head nodes may be set up in O(max{n,m}) time, where n is the number of rows and m the number of columns in the matrix being input. Each nonzero term can be set up in a constant amount of time because of the use of the variable *last* and a random access scheme for the bottommost node in each column list. Hence, the **for** loop of lines 16-27 can be

```
1 istream& operator>>(istream& is, Matrix& matrix)
2 // Read in a matrix and set up its linked representation.
3 // An auxiliary array head is used.
4 {
5   Triple  s ; int p ;
6   is >> s.row >> s.col >> s.value ;   // matrix dimensions
7   if (s.row > s.col) p = s.row ; else  p = s.col ;
8   // set up headnode for list of head nodes.
9   matrix.headnode = new MatrixNode(FALSE, &s) ;
10  if (p == 0) { matrix.headnode →right = matrix.headnode ; return is ;}
11  // at least one row or column
12  MatrixNodePtr *head = new MatrixNodePtr [p ] ;  // initialize head nodes
13  for (int i = 0 ; i < p ; i++)
14    head [i ] = new MatrixNode(TRUE, 0) ;
15  int CurrentRow = 0 ; MatrixNode *last = head [0] ; // last node in current row

16  for (i = 0 ; i < s.value ; i++)  // input triples
17  {
18    Triple t ;
19    is >> t.row >> t.col >> t.value ;
20    if (t.row > CurrentRow) { // close current row
21      last →right = head [CurrentRow ] ;
22      CurrentRow = t.row ;
23      last = head [CurrentRow ] ;
24    } // end of if
25    last = last →right = new MatrixNode(FALSE, &t) ;  // link new node into row list
26    head [t.col]→next = head [t.col]→next →down = last ; // link into column list
27  } // end of for

28  last →right = head [CurrentRow ] ; // close last row
29  for (i = 0 ; i < s.col ; i++) head [i ]→next →down = head [i ] ; // close all column lists
30  // link the head nodes together
31  for (i = 0 ; i < p − 1 ; i++) head [i ]→next = head [i +1] ;
32  head [p −1]→next = matrix.headnode ;
33  matrix.headnode →right =  head [0] ;
34  delete [ ] head;
35  return is ;
36 }
```

Program 4.31: Reading in a sparse matrix

carried out in O(r) time. The rest of the algorithm takes O(max{n,m}) time. The total time is therefore O(max{n,m} + r) = O($n + m + r$)). Note that this time is asymptotical-ly better than the input time of O(nm) for an $n \times m$ matrix using a two-dimensional array but slightly worse than the sequential sparse method of Section 2.3. □

4.8.3 Erasing a Sparse Matrix

All the nodes of a sparse matrix may be returned one at a time using **delete**. A faster way to return the nodes is to set up an available-space list as was done for polynomials. Assume that *av* points to the front of this list and that this list is linked through the data member *right*. Function *Matrix::˜Matrix* () (Program 4.32) solves our problem in an efficient way.

Matrix::˜Matrix ()
// Return all nodes to the *av* list. This list is a chain linked via the *right*
// field. *av* is a global variable of type *MatrixNode* ∗ and points to its first node.
{
    if (!*headnode*) **return;** // no nodes to dispose
    MatrixNode ∗*x* = *headnode* →*right* , ∗*y* ;
    headnode →*right* = *av* ; *av* = *headnode* ; // return *headnode*
    while (*x* != *headnode*) { // erase by rows
        y = *x* →*right* ;
        x →*right* = *av* ;
        av = *y* ;
        x = *x* →*next* ; // next row
    }
    headnode = 0 ;
}

Program 4.32: Erasing a sparse matrix

Analysis of ˜Matrix(): Since each node is in only one row list, it is sufficient to return all the row lists of the matrix *a*. Each row list is circularly linked through the data member *right*. Thus, nodes need not be returned one by one, as a circular list can be erased in a constant amount of time. The computing time for the algorithm is readily seen to be O($n + m$). Note that even if the available-space list had been linked through the data member *down*, erasing still could have been carried out in O($n + m$) time. □

    The subject of manipulating sparse matrix structures is studied further in the exer-cises. The representation studied here is rather general. For most applications this generality is not needed. A simpler representation resulting in simpler algorithms is discussed in the exercises.

EXERCISES

In Exercises 1 to 5, the sparse matrix representation described in this section is assumed.

1. Let a and b be two sparse matrices. Write an algorithm, **operator+**(a, b), to create the matrix $c = a + b$. Your algorithm should leave the matrices a and b unchanged and set up c as a new matrix in accordance with this data representation. Show that if a and b are $n \times m$ matrices with r_A and r_B nonzero terms, then this addition can be carried out in $O(n + m + r_A + r_B)$ time.

2. Let a and b be two sparse matrices. Write an algorithm, **operator***(a, b), to set up the structure for $c = a*b$. Show that if a is an $n \times m$ matrix with r_A nonzero terms and if b is an $m \times p$ matrix with r_B nonzero terms, then c can be computed in time $O(pr_A + nr_B)$. Can you think of a way to compute c in $O(\min\{pr_A, nr_B\})$?

3. Write an algorithm **operator<<( )** to write out the terms of a sparse matrix a as triples (i, j, a_{ij}). The terms are to be output by rows and within rows by columns. Show that this operation can be performed in time $O(n + r_A)$ if there are r_A nonzero terms in a and a is an $n \times m$ matrix.

4. Write an algorithm, *Transpose* (a), to compute the matrix $b = a^T$, the transpose of the sparse matrix a. What is the computing time of your algorithm?

5. Design an algorithm to implement the copy constructor for sparse matrices. What is the computing time of your algorithm?

6. A simpler and more efficient representation for sparse matrices can be obtained when one is limited to the operations of addition, subtraction, and multiplication. Now, nodes have the data members *down*, *right*, *row*, *col*, and *value*. Each nonzero term is represented by a node. These nodes are linked together to form two circular lists. The first list, the row list, is made up by linking nodes by rows and within rows by columns. The linking is done via the *right* data member. The second list, the column list, is made up by linking nodes via the *down* data member. In this list, nodes are linked by columns and within columns by rows. These two lists share a common head node. In addition, a node is added to contain the dimensions of the matrix. The matrix A of Figure 4.26 has the representation shown in Figure 4.28.

    Provide a C++ class definition for this representation.

7. For the representation of Exercise 6, write algorithms to

    (a)   read a matrix (**operator>>**)

    (b)   erase a matrix

    (c)   add two matrices (**operator+**)

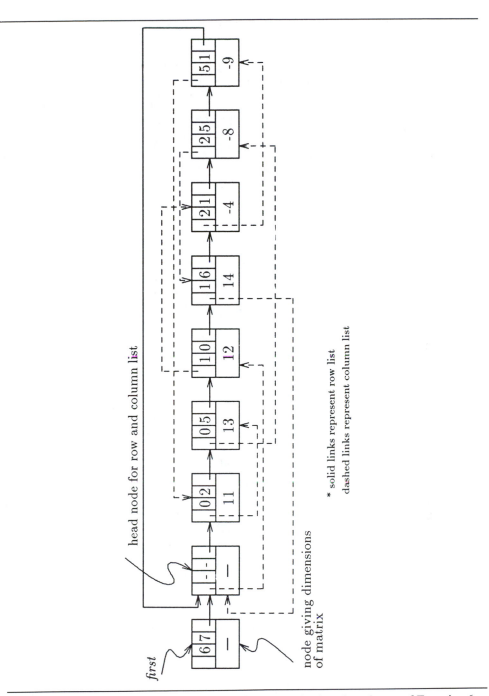

Figure 4.28: Representation of matrix *A* of Figure 4.26 using the scheme of Exercise 6

(d)   multiply two matrices (**operator***)

(e)   print out a matrix   (**operator<<**)

For each of these algorithms obtain computing times. How do these times compare with the corresponding times for the representation of this section?

8.   Compare the sparse representations of Exercise 6 and this section with respect to some other operations. For example, how much time is needed to output the entries in an arbitrary row or column?

9.   [*Programming Project*] In this project, we shall implement a complete linked-list system to perform arithmetic on sparse matrices using the representation of Section 4.8. First, design a convenient node structure assuming *value* is an integer.

Since we shall need to erase circular lists, we shall utilize the available-space list concept described in this section. So, we may begin by writing and testing the functions associated with this list. Next, write and test the following functions for matrix operations:

(a)   *istream*& **operator>>**(*istream*& *os*, *Matrix*& *m*):
 Read in the matrix and set it up according to the representation of this section. The first input line gives the matrix dimensions. The next several lines contain one triple, (row, column, value), each. The last triple ends the input file. These triples are in increasing order by rows. Within rows, the triples are in increasing order of columns. The data is to be read in one line at a time and converted to internal representation.

(b)   *ostream*& **operator<<**(*ostream*& *os*, **const** *Matrix*& *m*):
 Print out the terms of *m*. To do this, you will have to design a suitable output format. In any case, the output should be ordered by rows and within rows by columns.

(c)   *Matrix* ::*Matrix*(**const** *Matrix*& *a*) [Copy Constructor]: Initialize the sparse matrix ***this** to the sparse matrix *a*.

(d)   **const** *Matrix*& *Matrix*::**operator=**(**const** *Matrix*& *a*) [Assignment Operator]: Assign sparse matrix *a* to ***this**.

(e)   *Matrix*::~*Matrix* () [Destructor]: Return all nodes of the sparse matrix ***this** to the available-space list.

(f)   *Matrix* **operator+**(**const** *Matrix*& *a*, **const** *Matrix*& *b*): Create and return the sparse matrix $a + b$. *a* and *b* are to be left unaltered.

(g)   *Matrix* **operator−**(**const** *Matrix*& *a*, **const** *Matrix*& *b*) : Create and return the sparse matrix $a - b$. *a* and *b* are to be left unaltered.

(h)   *Matrix* **operator*** (**const** *Matrix*& *a*, **const** *Matrix*& *b*): Create the sparse matrix $c = a * b$. *a* and *b* are to be left unaltered.

(i)   *Matrix Matrix* ::*Transpose* (**const** *Matrix*& *a*) : Create the sparse matrix a^t. *a* is to be left unaltered.

10. [***Programming Project***] Do Exercise 9 using the representation of Exercise 6.

4.9   DOUBLY LINKED LISTS

So far we have been working chiefly with singly linked linear lists. For some problems these would be too restrictive. One difficulty with these lists is that if we are pointing to a specific node, say *p*, then we can easily move only in the direction of the links. The only way to find the node that precedes *p* is to start at the beginning of the list. The same problem arises when one wishes to delete an arbitrary node from a singly linked list. As can be seen from Example 4.4, easy deletion of an arbitrary node requires knowing the preceding node. If we have a problem in which moving in either direction is often necessary, then it is useful to have doubly linked lists. Each node now has two link data members, one linking in the forward direction and one in the backward direction.

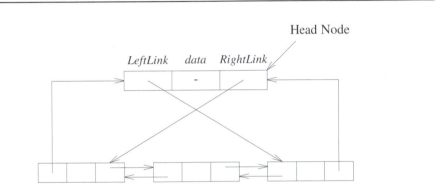

Figure 4.29: Doubly linked circular list with head node

A node in a doubly linked list has at least three fields — e.g., *data, llink* (left link), and *rlink* (right link). A doubly linked list may or may not be circular. A sample doubly linked circular list with three nodes is shown in Figure 4.29. Besides these three nodes, a special node called a head node has been added. As was true in the earlier sections, head nodes are convenient for the algorithms. The *data* field of the head node usually contains no information. Now suppose that *p* points to any node in a doubly linked list. In this case *p* == *p*→*llink*→*rlink* == *p*→*rlink*→*llink*. This formula reflects the essential virtue of this structure — namely, that one can go back and forth with equal ease. An empty list is not really empty, since it always has its head node and it appears as in Figure 4.30. Program 4.33 contains the class definition of a doubly linked list of integers. To work with these lists we must be able to insert and delete nodes. Function *DblList::Delete* (Program 4.34) deletes node *x* from the list. *x* now points to a node that

Figure 4.30: Empty doubly linked circular list with head node

class *DblList* ;

class *DblListNode* {
friend class *DblList* ;
private:
  int *data* ;
  DblListNode *llink*, *rlink* ;
};

class *DblList* {
public:
  // List manipulation operations
   .
   .
private:
  DblListNode *first* ; // points to head node
};

Program 4.33: Class definition of a doubly linked list

is no longer part of the list. Figure 4.31 shows how the method works on a doubly linked list with only a single node. Even though the *rlink* and *llink* data members of node *x* still point to the head node, this node has effectively been removed, as there is no way to access *x* through *first*. Insertion is only slightly more complex (see Program 4.35).

EXERCISES

1. Devise a representation for a list in which insertions and deletions can be made at either end. Such a structure is called a *deque*. Write a function for inserting at either end.

```
void DblList ::Delete(DblListNode *x)
{
    if (x == first) cerr << "Deletion of head node not permitted" << endl ;
    else {
        x →llink →rlink = x →rlink ;
        x →rlink →llink = x →llink ;
        delete x ;
    }
}
```

Program 4.34: Deletion from a doubly linked circular list

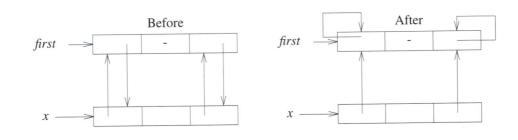

Figure 4.31: Deletion from a doubly linked circular list

```
void DblList ::Insert(DblListNode *p, DblListNode *x)
// insert node p to the right of node x
{
    p →llink = x ; p →rlink = x →rlink ;
    x →rlink →llink = p ; x →rlink = p ;
}
```

Program 4.35: Insertion into a doubly linked circular list

2. Consider the operation XOR (exclusive OR, also written as $\oplus$) defined as follows (for i, j binary):

$$i \oplus j = \begin{cases} 0 & \text{if } i \text{ and } j \text{ are identical} \\ 1 & \text{otherwise} \end{cases}$$

This definition differs from the usual OR of logic, which is defined as

$$i \text{ OR } j = \begin{cases} 0 & \text{if } i = j = 0 \\ 1 & \text{otherwise} \end{cases}$$

The definition can be extended to the case in which i and j are binary strings (i.e., take the XOR of corresponding bits of i and j). So, for example, if $i = 10110$ and $j = 01100$, then $i \text{ XOR } j = i \oplus j = 11010$. Note that

$$a \oplus (a \oplus b) = (a \oplus a) \oplus b = b$$

and

$$(a \oplus b) \oplus b = a \oplus (b \oplus b) = a$$

This notation gives us a space-saving device for storing the right and left links of a doubly linked list. The nodes will now have only two data members: *info* and *link*. If l is to the left of node x and r to its right, then $link(x) = l \oplus r$ (as in the case of the storage management algorithms, we assume that available memory is an array *memory* $[i]$, $1 \le i \le n$, and that the *link* data member just gives us the position of the next node in this array). For the leftmost node $l = 0$, and for the rightmost node $r = 0$. Let (l, r) be a doubly linked list so represented; l points to the leftmost node and r to the right most node in the list.

(a) Write an algorithm to traverse the doubly linked list (l, r) from left to right, listing the contents of the *info* data member of each node.

(b) Write an algorithm to traverse the list right to left, listing the contents of the *info* data member of each node.

3. [**Programming Project**]: Implement doubly linked circular lists with head nodes using three template classes (similar to our implementation of singly linked lists). In addition to the iterator member functions developed for chains, define an iterator member function that returns the previous list element.

4.10   GENERALIZED LISTS

4.10.1   Representation of Generalized Lists

In Chapter 2 a linear list was defined to be a finite sequence of $n \geq 0$ elements, $\alpha_0, \cdots, \alpha_{n-1}$, which we write as $A = (\alpha_0, \cdots, \alpha_{n-1})$. The elements of a linear list are restricted to atoms; thus, the only structural property a linear list has is that of position (i.e., α_i precedes α_{i+1}, $0 \leq i < n-1$). Relaxing this restriction on the elements of a list and permitting them to have a structure of their own leads to the notion of a generalized list. Now, the elements α_i, $0 \leq i \leq n-1$, may be either atoms or lists.

Definition: A *generalized list*, A, is a finite sequence of $n \geq 0$ elements, $\alpha_0, \cdots, \alpha_{n-1}$, where α_i is either an atom or a list. The elements α_i, $0 \leq i \leq n-1$, that are not atoms are said to be the *sublists* of A. □

The list A itself is written as $A = (\alpha_0, \cdots, \alpha_{n-1})$. A is the *name* of the list $(\alpha_0, \cdots, \alpha_{n-1})$, and n is the *length* of the list. By convention, all list names are represented by capital letters. Lowercase letters are used to represent atoms. If $n \geq 1$, then α_0 is the *head* of A, and $(\alpha_1, \cdots, \alpha_{n-1})$ is the *tail* of A.

This definition is our first example of a recursive *definition*, so study it carefully. The definition is recursive because within our description of a list, we use the notion of a list. This may appear to be circular, but it is not. It is a compact way of describing a potentially large and varied structure. We will see more such definitions later. Some examples of generalized lists are

(1) $D = (\,)$: the null, or empty, list; its length is zero.

(2) $A = (a, (b,c))$: a list of length two; its first element is the atom a, and its second element is the linear list (b,c).

(3) $B = (A, A, (\,))$: a list of length three whose first two elements are the list A, and the third element is the null list.

(4) $C = (a, C)$: a recursive list of length two; C corresponds to the infinite list $C = (a, (a, (a, \cdots)\,)$.

D is the empty list. For list A, we have $head(A) = \text{`}a\text{'}$ and $tail(A) = ((b,c))$; $tail\,(A)$ also has a head and tail, which are (b,c) and $(\,)$, respectively. Looking at list B, we see that $head(B) = A$ and $tail(B) = (A, (\,))$. Continuing, we have $head\,(tail\,(B)) = A$ and $tail\,(tail\,(B)) = ((\,))$, both of which are lists.

Two important consequences of our definition for a list are (1) lists may be shared by other lists as in example (3), where list A makes up two of the sublists of B; and (2) lists may be recursive as in example (4). The implications of these two consequences for the data structures needed to represent lists will become evident.

First, let us restrict ourselves to the situation in which the lists being represented are neither shared nor recursive. To see where this notion of a list may be useful, consider the problem of representing polynomials in several variables. For example,

$$P(x,y,z) = x^{10}y^3z^2 + 2x^8y^3z^2 + 3x^8y^2z^2 + x^4y^4z + 6x^3y^4z + 2yz$$

You can easily think of a sequential representation for P, say using a structure with four fields to represent a single array element: *coef, expx, expy*, and *expz*. But this would mean that polynomials in a different number of variables would need a different number of fields, adding another conceptual inelegance to other difficulties we have already seen with the sequential representation of polynomials. If we used linear lists, we might conceive a node of the form

coef	expx	expy
expz	link	

These nodes would have to vary in size depending on the number of variables, causing difficulties in storage management. The idea of using a general list structure with nodes of fixed size arises naturally if we consider rewriting $P(x,y,z)$ as

$$((x^{10} + 2x^8)y^3 + 3x^8y^2)z^2 + ((x^4 + 6x^3)y^4 + 2y)z$$

Every polynomial can be written in this fashion, factoring out a main variable z, followed by a second variable y, and so on. Looking carefully now at $P(x,y,z)$, we see that there are two terms in the variable z, Cz^2 and Dz, where C and D are polynomials themselves, but in the variables x and y. Looking more closely at $C(x,y)$, we see that it is of the form $Ey^3 + Fy^2$, where E and F are polynomials in x. Continuing in this way, we see that every polynomial consists of a variable plus coefficient-exponent pairs. Each coefficient is itself a polynomial (in one less variable) if we regard a single numerical coefficient as a polynomial in zero variables.

We see that every polynomial, regardless of the number of variables in it, can be represented using nodes of the type *PolyNode*, defined as

```
enum Triple { var, ptr, no };
class PolyNode
{
  PolyNode *link ;
  int exp ;
  Triple trio ;
  union {
    char vble ;
    PolyNode *dlink ;
    int coef ;
  };
};
```

In this representation, there are three types of nodes, depending on the value of *trio*. If *trio == var*, then the node is the head node for a list; in this case, the field *vble* is used to indicate the name of the variable on which that list is based and the *exp* field is set to 0. Note that the type of the data member *vble* can be changed to **int** if all variables are kept in a table and *vble* just gives the corresponding table index. If *trio* == *ptr*, then the coefficient is itself a list and is pointed by the field *dlink*. If *trio* == *no*, then the coefficient is an integer and is stored in the field *coef*. In both these cases, *exp* represents the exponent of the variable on which that list is based.

The polynomial $P = 3x^2y$ now takes the representation given in Figure 4.32. Here P points to a head node which indicates that the upper list is based on y. Hence the next term in the list refers to the term $y^1 = y$. The coefficient of this term is the polynomial represented by the lower list. This polynomial is $3x^2$. The polynomial $P(x,y,z)$ defined before has the list representation shown in Figure 4.33. For simplicity, the *trio* data member is omitted from Figure 4.33. The value of this data member for each node is self-evident.

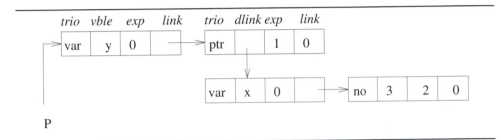

Figure 4.32: Representation of $3x^2y$

Every generalized list can be represented using the node structure

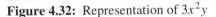

| tag = FALSE/TRUE | data/dlink | link |

This data structure may be defined in C++ as:

```
enum Boolean { FALSE, TRUE };
class GenList ; // forward declaration
class GenListNode {
friend class GenList ;
private:
   GenListNode *link ;
   Boolean tag ;
   union {
      char data ;
      GenListNode *dlink ;
   };
};
```

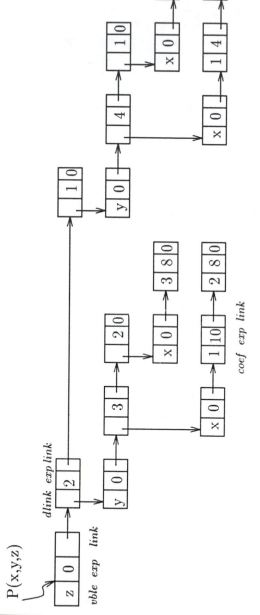

Figure 4.33: Representation of $P(x,y,z)$

```
class GenList {
public:
    // List manipulation operations
    .
private:
    GenListNode *first ;
};
```

where the type of the *data* field changes from one application to the next. The *data/dlink* data member holds an atom if *head (A)* is an atom and holds a pointer to the list representation of *head (A)* if *head (A)* is a list. (The exercises examine how a mulitvariate polynomial could be stored using this structure.) Using this node structure, the example lists (1) to (4) have the representation shown in Figure 4.34.

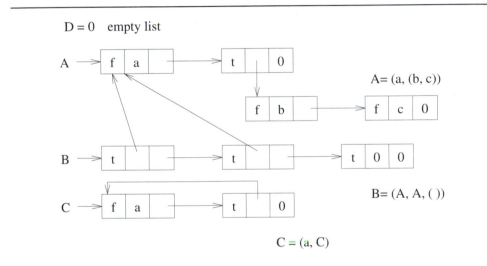

Figure 4.34: Representation of lists (1) to (4) (page 221; an *f* in the *tag* data member represents the value false, whereas a *t* represents the value true)

4.10.2   Recursive Algorithms for Lists

Now that we have seen a particular example where generalized lists are useful, let us return to their definition. When a data object is defined recursively, it is often easy to describe algorithms that work on these objects recursively. A recursive algorithm consists of two components - the recursive function itself (the *workhorse*) and a second function that invokes the recursive function at the top level (the *driver*). Therefore, when a recursive algorithm is used to implement a class operation, we are actually required to implement two class member functions. The driver is declared as a public member function while the workhorse is declared as a private member function.

4.10.2.1 Copying a List

To see how recursion is useful, let us write a function (Program 4.36) that produces an exact copy of a nonrecursive list l in which no sublists are shared. We will assume the nodes of l are of type *GenListNode* as defined earlier.

```
// Driver
void GenList ::Copy(const GenList& l)
{
    first = Copy (l.first) ;
}

// Workhorse
GenListNode* GenList ::Copy(GenListNode* p)
// Copy the nonrecursive list with no shared sublists pointed at by p
{
    GenListNode *q = 0 ;
    if (p) {
        q = new GenListNode ;
        q →tag = p →tag ;
        if (! p →tag) q →data = p →data ;
        else q →dlink = Copy (p →dlink) ;
        q →link = Copy (p →link) ;
    }
    return q ;
}
```

Program 4.36: Copying a list

Program 4.36 reflects exactly the definition of a list. We see immediately that *Copy* works correctly for an empty list. A simple proof using induction will verify the correctness of the entire function. Now let us consider the computing time of this algorithm. The empty list takes a constant amount of time. For the list $A = ((a,b),((c,d),e))$, which has the representation of Figure 4.35, p takes on the values given in Figure 4.36. The sequence of values should be read down the columns; b, r, s, t, u, v, w, and x are the addresses of the eight nodes of the list. From this example one should be able to see that nodes with tag = FALSE will be visited twice, whereas nodes with tag = TRUE will be visited three times. Thus, if a list has a total of m nodes, no more than $3m$ executions of any statement will occur. Hence, the algorithm is O(m), or linear, which is the best we can hope to achieve. Another factor of interest is the maximum depth of recursion or, equivalently, how many locations are needed for the recursion stack. Again, by carefully following the algorithm on the previous example, we see that the maximum depth is a combination of the lengths and depths of all sublists. However, a simple upper bound is m, the total number of nodes. Although this bound will be extremely large in many cases, it is achievable, for instance, if A = $((((a)))))$.

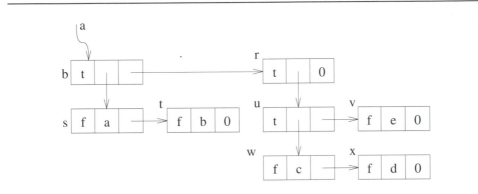

Figure 4.35: Linked representation for A

level of recursion	value of p	continuing level	p	continuing level	p
1	b	2	r	3	u
2	s	3	u	4	v
3	t	4	w	5	0
4	0	5	x	4	v
3	t	6	0	3	u
2	s	5	x	2	r
1	b	4	w	3	0
				2	r
				1	b

Figure 4.36 Values of parameters in execution of *GenList* ::*Copy* (A)

4.10.2.2 List Equality

Another useful function determines whether two lists are identical. To be identical, the lists must have the same structure and the same data in corresponding data members. Again, using the recursive definition of a list, we can write a short recursive function (Program 4.37) to accomplish this task.

```
// Driver - assumed to be a friend of GenList
int operator==(const GenList& l, const GenList& m)
// l and m are non-recursive lists.
// The function returns 1 if the two lists are identical and 0, otherwise.
{
   return equal (l.first,m.first) ;
}


// Workhorse - assumed to be a friend of GenListNode
int equal(GenListNode* s, GenListNode *t)
{
   int x ;
   if ((!s) && (!t)) return 1 ;
   if (s && t && (s →tag == t →tag))
   {
      if (! s →tag)
         if (s →data == t →data) x = 1 ; else x = 0 ;
      else x = equal(s →dlink, t →dlink) ;
      if (x) return  equal(s →link, t →link) ;
   }
   return 0 ;
}
```

Program 4.37: Determining if two lists are identical

Function **operator**== returns the value 1 or 0. Its computing time is clearly no more than linear when no sublists are shared, since it looks at each node of l and m no more than three times. For unequal lists the function terminates as soon as it discovers that the lists are not identical.

4.10.2.3   List Depth

Another handy operation on nonrecursive lists is the function that computes the depth of a list. The depth of the empty list is defined to be zero and, in general,

$$depth\ (s) = \begin{cases} 0 & \text{if } s \text{ is an atom} \\ 1 + \max\ \{depth\ (x_1),\ \cdots,\ depth\ (x_n)\} & \text{if } s \text{ is the list } (x_1,\ \cdots,\ x_n),\ n \geq 1 \end{cases}$$

Function *depth* (Program 4.38) is a very close transformation of the definition, which is itself recursive. By now you have seen several programs of this type, and you should be feeling more comfortable both reading and writing recursive algorithms.

```
// Driver
int GenList ::depth ()
// Compute the depth of a non-recursive list
{
    return depth (first) ;
}

// Workhorse
int GenList ::depth(GenListNode *s)
{
    if (!s) return 0 ;
    GenListNode *p = s ; int m = 0 ;
    while (p) {
        if (p →tag) {
            int n = depth (p →dlink) ;
            if (m < n) m = n ;
        }
        p = p →link ;
    }
    return m +1 ;
}
```

Program 4.38: Computing the depth of a list

4.10.3   Reference Counts, Shared and Recursive Lists

In this section we shall consider some of the problems that arise when lists are allowed to be shared by other lists and when recursive lists are permitted. Sharing of sublists can, in some situations, result in great savings in storage used, as identical sublists occupy the same space. To facilitate specifying shared sublists, we extend the definition of a list to allow for naming of sublists. A sublist appearing within a list definition may be named through the use of a list name preceding it. For example, in the list $A = (a, (b,c))$, the sublist (b,c) could be assigned the name Z by writing $A = (a,Z(b,c))$. In fact, to be consistent, we would then write $A(a,Z(b,c))$ which would define the list A as above.

Lists that are shared by other lists, such as list A of Figure 4.34, create problems when you wish to add or delete a node at the front. If the first node of A is deleted, it is necessary to change the pointers from list B to point to the second node. If a new node is added, pointers from B have to be changed to point to the new first node. However, we normally do not know all the points from which a particular list is being referenced. (Even if you did have this information, addition and deletion of nodes could require a large amount of time.) This problem is easily solved through the use of head nodes. If you expect to perform any additions and deletions at the front of lists, then the use of a head node with each list or named sublist will eliminate the need to retain a list of all pointers to any specific list. If each list is to have a head node, then lists (1) to (4) are represented as in Figure 4.37. The values in the *data/dlink* fields of the head nodes is the reference count of the corresponding list and are explained below. Even in situations in which you do not wish to add or delete nodes from lists dynamically, as in the case of multivariate polynomials, head nodes prove useful in determining when the nodes of a particular structure may be returned to the storage pool. For example, let t and u be program variables representing the two polynomials $(3x^4 + 5x^3 + 7x)y^3$ and $(3x^4 + 5x^3 + 7x)y^6 + (6x)y$ of Figure 4.38. If *~Polynomial*() is to erase a polynomial, then the invocation **delete** t should not return the nodes corresponding to the coefficient $3x^4 + 5x^3 + 7x$, since this sublist is also part of u.

Thus, whenever lists are being shared by other lists, we need a mechanism to help determine whether or not the list nodes may be physically returned to the available-space list. This mechanism is generally provided through the use of a reference count maintained in the head node of each list. Since the *data* field of the head nodes is free, the reference count is maintained in this field. (Alternatively, a third variant may be introduced, with *tag* having three possible values: 0, 1, and 2.) This reference count of a list is the number of pointers (either program variables or pointers from other lists) to that list. If the lists (1) to (4) of Figure 4.37 are accessible via the program variables x, y, z, and w, then the reference counts for the lists are

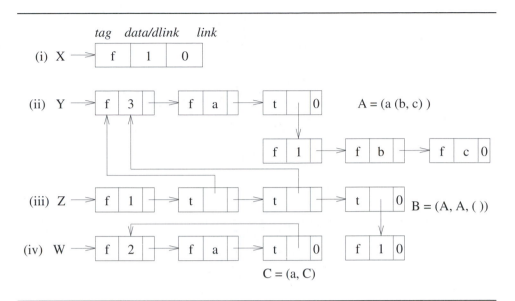

Figure 4.37: Structure with head nodes for lists (1) to (4)

(1) $ref(x) = 1$ accessible only via x

(2) $ref(y) = 3$ pointed to by y and two pointers from z

(3) $ref(z) = 1$ accessible only via z

(4) $ref(w) = 2$ accessible via w and one pointer from itself

Now a call to $t.\tilde{\ }GenList\,()$ (list erase) should result only in a decrementing by 1 of the reference counter of $t.first$. Only if the reference count becomes zero are the nodes of t to be physically returned to the available-space list. The same is to be done with the sublists of t.

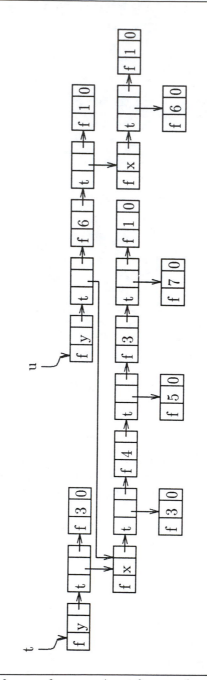

Figure 4.38: $t = (3x^4 + 5x^3 + 7x)y^3$, $u = (3x^4 + 5x^3 + 7x)y^6 + (6x)y$

Assume that **class** *GenList* is unchanged and **class** *GenListNode* is defined as

```
class GenListNode
{
friend class GenList ;
private:
   GenListNode *link ;
   int tag ; // 0 for data, 1 for dlink, 2 for ref
   union {
      char data ;
      GenListNode *dlink ;
      int ref ;
   };
};
```

A recursive algorithm to erase a list is given in Program 4.39. This proceeds by examining the top-level nodes of a list whose reference count has become zero. Any such sublists encountered are erased, and finally, the top-level nodes are linked into the available-space list.

A call to $y.\tilde{}GenList$ () now has only the effect of decreasing the reference count of y to 2. Such a call followed by a call to $z.\tilde{}GenList$ () results in

(1)   the reference count of z becomes zero

(2)   the next node is processed and $y.first \rightarrow ref$ reduces to 1

(3) $y.first \rightarrow ref$ becomes zero and the five nodes of list $A(a, (b,c))$ are returned to the available-space list

(4)   the top-level nodes of z are linked into the available-space list.

The use of head nodes with reference counts solves the problem of determining when nodes are to be physically freed in the case of shared sublists. However, for recursive lists, the reference count never becomes zero. $w.\tilde{}GenList$ () results in $w.first \rightarrow ref$ becoming one. The reference count does not become zero, even though this list is no longer accessible either through program variables or through other structures. The same is true in the case of indirect recursion (Figure 4.39). After calls to $r.\tilde{}GenList$ () and $s.\tilde{}GenList$ (), $r.first \rightarrow ref = 1$ and $s.first \rightarrow ref = 2$ but the structure consisting of r and s is no longer being used, so it should have been returned to the available-space list.

Unfortunately, there is no simple way to supplement the list structure of Figure 4.39 so as to be able to determine when recursive lists may be physically erased. It is no longer possible to return all free nodes to the available-space list when they become free. When recursive lists are being used, it is possible to run out of available space, even though not all nodes are in use.

```
// Driver
GenList::˜GenList ()
// Each head node has a reference count. We assume first ≠ 0.
{
    Delete (first) ;
    first = 0 ;
}
```

```
// Workhorse
void GenList ::Delete(GenListNode* x)
{
    x →ref −− ;  // decrement reference count of head node.
    if (!x →ref)
    {
        GenListNode *y = x ;  // y traverses top-level of x.
        while (y →link) { y = y →link ; if (y →tag == 1) Delete (y →dlink) ;}
        y →link = av ;   // attach top-level nodes to av list
        av = x ;
    }
}
```

Program 4.39: Erasing a list recursively

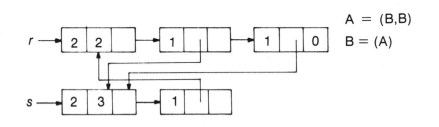

Figure 4.39: Indirect recursion of lists A and B pointed to by program variables r and s

EXERCISES

1. Express a multivariate polynomial by using the following node structure that can be used to represent any generalized list:

    | tag = FALSE/TRUE | data/dlink | link |

2. Why is it not possible to use the program of Program 4.36 to copy lists with shared sublists?

3. Implement generalized lists with reference counts using templates. Your implementation should support the copy constructor and destructor for this class.

4. Write a nonrecursive version of algorithm *GenList::~GenList* () (Program 4.39).

5. Write a nonrecursive version of algorithm **operator==** (Program 4.37).

6. Write a nonrecursive version of algorithm *GenList* ::*depth* (Program 4.38).

7. Write a function that inverts an arbitrary nonrecursive list *l* with no shared sublists, and and all of its sublists. For example, if $l = (a,(b,c))$, then inverse $(l) = ((c,b),a)$.

8. Devise a function that produces the list representation of an arbitrary list, given its linear form as a string of atoms, commas, blanks, and parentheses. For example, for the input $l = (a, (b,c))$, your function should produce the structure of Figure 4.40.

Figure 4.40: Structure for Exercise 8

9. One way to represent generalized lists is through the use of two data member nodes and a symbol table that contains all atoms and list names, together with pointers to these lists. Let the two fields of each node be named *alink* and *blink*. Then *blink* either points to the next node on the same level, if there is one, or it is 0. The *alink* points either to a node at a lower level or, in the case of an atom or list name, to the appropriate entry in the symbol table. For example, the list

$B(A, (D,E),(\;),B)$ would have the representation given in Figure 4.41. This figure assumes that all pointers are integer addresses.

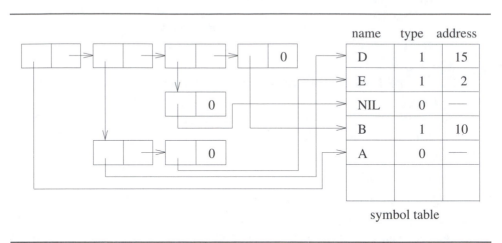

symbol table

Figure 4.41: Representation for Exercise 9

(The list names D and E were already in the table at the time the list B was input. A was not in the table and is assumed to be an atom.)

The symbol table retains a type bit for each entry. This bit is 1 if the entry is a list name and 0 for an atom. The NIL atom may be in the table, or *alink* can be set to 0 to represent the NIL atom. Write an algorithm **operator>>** to read in a list in parenthesis notation and to set up its linked representation as above, with x set to point to the first node in the list. Note that no head nodes are in use. You may need to use variant records or simulate pointers by integers (or both). The following subalgorithms may be used by **operator>>**:

(a)   **int** *get(a)* searches the symbol table for the name a. -1 is returned if a is not found in the table; otherwise, the position of a in the table is returned.

(b)   *put(a,t,p)* enters a into the table. p is the position at which a was entered. If a is already in the table, then the type and address data members of the old entry are changed. $t = 0$ to enter an atom or $t <> 0$ to enter a list with first node t. (Note: This permits definition of lists using indirect recursion.)

(c)   *NextToken* gets the next token in the input list. (A token may be a list name, atom, '(', ')' or ','. A '#' is returned if there are no more tokens.)

(d)   **new** *GenListNode* gets a node for use.

You may assume that the input list is syntactically correct. If a sublist is labeled, as in the list $C(D,E(F,G))$, the structure should be set up as in the case

$C(D, (F,G))$, and E should be entered into the symbol table as a list with the appropriate starting address.

10. [**Wilczynski**] Following the conventions of LISP, assume nodes with two data members: *HEAD* and *TAIL*. If $A = ((a(bc)))$, then $HEAD(A) = (a(bc))$, $TAIL(A)$ = NIL, $HEAD(HEAD(A)) = a$, and $TAIL(HEAD(A)) = ((bc))$. $CONS(A,B)$ gets a new node T, stores A in its *HEAD*, B in its *TAIL*, and returns T. B must always be a list. If $L = a$ and $M = (bc)$, then $CONS(L,M) = (abc)$ and $CONS(M,M) = ((bc)bc)$. Three other useful functions are: $ATOM(X)$ which is true if X is an atom else false, $NULL(X)$ which is true if X is NIL, else false, $EQUAL(X,Y)$ which is true if X and Y are the same atoms or equivalent lists, else false.

(a) Give a sequence of *HEAD* and *TAIL* operations for extracting a from the lists: $((cat))$, $((a))$, $((mart))$, and $(((cb))a)$.

(b) Write recursive functions for the standard LISP functions *COPY*, *REVERSE*, and *APPEND*.

(c) Implement this LISP subsystem. Store atoms in an array and write functions *MakeGenList* and *GenListPrint* for input and output of lists.

4.11   VIRTUAL FUNCTIONS AND DYNAMIC BINDING IN C++

We have already seen that public inheritance is used to express the IS-A relationship between ADTs. In this section, we will study another consequence of public inheritance called *dynamic types*. We will see how C++ *virtual functions* support dynamic types. These concepts are illustrated with an example in which a *Rectangle* class is publicly derived from a *Polygon* class (Program 4.40). We will discuss the details of this example later. For now, however, the reader should be satisfied that the *Rectangle* IS-A *Polygon* relationship does hold.

Dynamic Types and Public Inheritance: An important consequence of public inheritance is that a pointer to a derived class type is implicitly converted to a pointer to its base class; and a reference to a derived class type is implicitly converted to a reference to its base class. For example, a function whose formal parameter is a reference to *Polygon*, can take on an actual parameter that is a reference to *Rectangle*; or, a pointer to a *Polygon* type can be assigned the address of a *Rectangle* object. In the following example, the dynamic type of *s* becomes *Rectangle* since it is assigned the address of a rectangle:

Rectangle r; // instance of derived class
Polygon $*s = \&r$; // assign rectangle to polygon

This is a logical interpretation of the IS-A relationship — since *Rectangle* IS-A *Polygon*, it is reasonable to expect it to have all the attributes of *Polygon* and thus, to use it instead of *Polygon*.

```
class Polygon
{
public:
    int GetId(); // non-virtual member function
    virtual Boolean Concave(); // virtual member function
    virtual int Perimeter() = 0; // pure virtual member function
protected:
    int id;
};
```

```
class Rectangle : public Polygon // Rectangle publicly inherits from Polygon
{
public:
    Boolean Concave(); // redefined in Rectangle
    int Perimeter(); // defined in Rectangle
    // GetId() and id are inherited from Polygon
    // They, respectively, become public and protected members of Rectangle
private:
    // additional data members required to specialize Rectangle
    int x1, y1, h, w;
};
```

```
// GetId() must never be redefined in a derived class
int Polygon::GetId() {return id;}
```

```
// Default implementation of Concave() in Polygon. A polygon is
// concave if it is possible to construct a line joining two points in the polygon
// that does not entirely lie within the polygon.
Boolean Polygon::Concave() {return TRUE;}
```

```
// Rectangle must define Perimeter() because it is a pure virtual function.
int Rectangle::Perimeter() { return 2*(h + w );}
```

```
// The default implementation of Concave() does not apply to rectangles.
//  So, it has to be redefined.
Boolean Rectangle::Concave() { return FALSE;}
```

Program 4.40: Public inheritance

However, this raises the following question: suppose there is an ordinary class member function whose implementation for rectangles differs from its implementation for polygons. What would happen if we were to call this operation on object s in the above example? The answer is that the the implementation for polygons would be used because s is defined as a *Polygon* pointer. But, this is clearly incorrect since s actually points to a rectangle object. This situation is remedied in C++ which provides *virtual functions*. A virtual function is dynamically bound — that is, the operation corresponding to the dynamic type of the object that invoked it, is used. If a virtual function is invoked by s in the above example, it would use the rectangle implementation because the dynamic type of s is *Rectangle*. Next, we discuss the three types of member functions (non-virtual, virtual, and pure virtual) and the conditions in which each should be used:

(a) Virtual member functions. A member function of a base class is virtual if its prototype in its class definition is preceded by the keyword **virtual**. If a virtual function, whose implementation is redefined in a derived class, is invoked by a base class object, then the implementation corresponding to the current dynamic type of that base class object is used. For example, the code of Program 4.41 uses the implementation defined in class *Rectangle*. If the implementation of a virtual function is not redefined in the derived class, the implementation defined in *Polygon* is used. Virtual functions are therefore used to provide an interface and a default implementation for a function. In Program 4.40, *Concave* is declared as a **virtual** function. The default implementation returns TRUE which covers the case for concave polygons (i.e., it is possible to find two points on a polygon so that the line joining them does not lie entirely within the polygon). However, the rectangle is an exception to this — it is convex — so we reimplement *Concave* inside **class** *Rectangle*, so that it returns FALSE.

Rectangle r;
.
.
// assume r is initialized at this point
Polygon *$*s$ = &*r*;
$s \rightarrow$*Concave* () ; *// returns FALSE*

Program 4.41: Virtual member function operation

(b) Non-virtual member functions. These are not preceded by the **virtual** keyword in the base class. *GetId*() is a non-virtual member function in the example. Its purpose is to return *id*, an identification number associated with each polygon object. While non-virtual functions can be legally redefined in a derived class, it is considered to be bad programming practice to do so. To illustrate this point, let us assume that we have reimplemented function *GetId*() in *Rectangle*. Now there is an inconsistency in the actions of the two code fragments of Program 4.42, which one would expect to give the same outcome if *Rectangle* IS-A *Polygon*. In the first fragment, the implementation in the base class is used, while in the second, the implementation in the derived class is used!

So, we will use non-virtual functions in base classes only if they will not be redefined in a derived class. (If a function is to be redefined in a derived class, declare it as **virtual**.) Thus, a non-virtual member function is used to provide both its interface and its implementation to a derived class.

Rectangle r;

.

.

// assume *r* is initialized at this point
Polygon *s = &*r*;
s →*GetId* (); *//* uses the function implemented in *Polygon*
Rectangle *t = &*r*;
t →*GetId* (); *//* uses the function implemented in *Rectangle*

Program 4.42: Reimplementing a non-virtual function.

(c) Pure virtual functions. A virtual member function is said to be pure if it is not implemented by its class. It is assigned the value 0 to indicate that it is pure. If a base class contains one or more pure virtual functions, it is called an *abstract* class. Two consequences of using a pure virtual function are:

(i)   You are not allowed to create instances of the abstract base class. For example, the following is illegal:

   Polygon p; *//* illegal

   Note that it is legal to declare pointers to abstract classes:
   Polygon *q; *//* legal

(ii)   Pure virtual functions *must* be redefined in the derived class.

As with regular virtual functions, the code fragment of Program 4.43 uses the implementation of the derived class.

When should you use pure virtual functions? Consider a scenario where it is obvious that a base class must support a particular function. However, the implementation of the function requires additional information that only a derived class can provide. In this case, the function is declared as a pure virtual function. The responsibility for implementing the function is passed on to the derived class. Thus, a pure virtual function provides only its interface to a derived class. Consider the function *Perimeter()* used to com-

---

Rectangle r;

.

.

// assume r is initialized at this point
Polygon ∗s = &r;
s→Perimeter(); // returns perimeter of *r*

Program 4.43: Pure, virtual member function operation

pute the perimeter of a polygon in Program 4.40. Any polygon must have a perimeter, so it is reasonable to declare *Perimeter()* as a member function of *Polygon*. However, it is impossible to implement *Perimeter()* for *Polygon* without more information about the polygon. Hence, it is declared as a pure virtual function. The implementation of *Perimeter()* is left to classes that are derived from *Polygon* such as *Rectangle*.

In the next section, we discuss an application of dynamic types that allows us to create a heterogeneous list.

4.12   HETEROGENEOUS LISTS

A *heterogeneous* list is one that contains nodes of different types. In Sections 4.8 and 4.11, we have studied list structures that contain nodes of two or more different types. For example, in Section 4.8 on sparse matrices, we used two types of nodes: head nodes and element nodes (Figure 4.25). However, even though these nodes are conceptually different, their definitions were coalesced into a single class definition through the use of the **union** facility (Program 4.30). This is necessary because any pointer in the list structure may point to exactly one type of node. If each of the two node-types has its own distinct class definition, then it is not possible to define a pointer that can point to both node types. This is achieved by merging the two node types into one class definition.

A disadvantage of merging node types using **union** is that each node is allocated space for the largest node type. Program 4.44 defines a composite of classes that represent a chain of nodes such that each node contains either a character, an integer, or a floating point number.

Let $S(x)$ denote the space occupied by an object of type x. Then,

$$S(CombinedNode) = S(Data) + S(CombinedNode *)$$
$$= S(\textbf{int}) + \max(\ S(\textbf{char}),\ S(\textbf{int}),\ S(\textbf{float})\ ) + S(CombinedNode *)$$

Assuming that a **char** requires 1 byte, an **int** or a pointer requires 2 bytes, and a **float** requires 4 bytes, we have $S(CombinedNode) = 8$ bytes. If a *CombinedNode* object is being used to represent a character, only 5 of its 8 bytes are being utilized; or if it is being used to represent an integer, only 6 of its 8 bytes are being utilized. If the linked list contains an equal number of each type of object (i.e., one-third of all nodes contain characters,

---

struct *Data*
{
    int *id* ; // id = 0, 1, or 2 if the node contains a **char**, an **int**, or **float**, respectively
    union {
        int *i*;
        char *c*;
        float *f*;
    };
};

class *CombinedNode*
// use **union** to merge different node types into one class definition
{
friend class *List*;
friend class *ListIterator*;
private:
    Data data;
    *CombinedNode *link*;
};

class *List*
{
friend class *ListIterator*;
public:
  // List manipulation operations follow

  .
private:
    *CombinedNode *first*;
};

// **class** *ListIterator* is defined as in Section 4.3, except that the return types
// of *First* and *Next* are *Data*

Program 4.44: Using **union** to implement a list of mixed nodes

one-third integers and one-third floats), then the unused or excess space occupied by the list is approximately 20.83% of the total space.

    Program 4.45 implements heterogeneous lists by using public inheritance. This is done as follows:

(1) An abstract base class *Node* is defined. This class contains data members common to all node types to be used in the node structure. In our example, there is only one such

// **struct** *Data* is assumed to be defined as in Program 4.44

class *Node* {
friend class *List*;
friend class *ListIterator*;
protected:
    Node *link*;
    virtual *Data GetData*() = 0 ;
};

template<**class** *Type*>
class *DerivedNode*: **public** *Node* {
friend class *List*; **friend class** *ListIterator*;
public:
  DerivedNode(*Type item*) : *data* (*item*) { *link* = 0 ;};
private:
  Type data;
  Data GetData() ;
};

Data DerivedNode<**char**>::*GetData*()
{
  Data t; *t.id* = 0; *t.c* = *data*; **return** *t*;
}
// The implementations of *GetData*() for *DerivedNode*<**int**> and *DerivedNode*<**float**>
// are similar to that of *DerivedNode*<**char**>::*GetData*().

Program 4.45: Using public inheritance to implement a list of mixed nodes (continued on next page)

field: *link* of type *Node**. (Note that it is not necessary to have an *id* field to identify the type of data contained in the node. This does not result in further space savings, however, because the C++ compiler implicitly maintains a pointer in **class** *Node* which determines the dynamic type of the object.)

(**2**) A template class *DerivedNode*<*Type*> which is publicly derived from *Node* is defined. This class contains the additional field required to contain an object of type *Type* that will be stored in the node. Note that *DerivedNode*<*Type*> IS-A *Node* justifying our use of public inheritance.

(**3**) We define a single pure virtual function *GetData* on *Node* that retrieves and returns the data in the node. Since the type of the data depends on the type of the node, it is not

---

```
class List {
friend class ListIterator;
public:
//  List manipulation operations follow

 .

 .

private:
  Node *first;
};


class ListIterator {
public:
    ListIterator(const List& l): list (l), current (l.first) { };
    Data* First (); // minor change in homogeneous list implementation
    Data* Next (); // minor change in homogeneous list implementation
    Boolean NotNull (); // implemented as for homogeneous lists
    Boolean NextNotNull (); // implemented as for homogeneous lists
private:
    const List& list;
    Node* current;
    Data temp;
};

Data* ListIterator ::First () {
    if (list . first) {
        temp = list . first →GetData (); // use GetData to retrieve element
        return &temp;
    }
    return 0;
}
```

Program 4.45: Using public inheritance to implement a list of mixed nodes

possible to implement this operation in **class** *Node*, justifying our decision to make it a pure virtual function. Class *DerivedNode<Type>* contains a different implementation of *GetData* for each type that the template *Type* is expected to be instantiated to (in our case, **char**, **int**, and **float**). In each case, function *GetData* places the node element in the appropriate field of a *Data* object.

(4) Classes *List* and *ListIterator* are unchanged with the exception of the implementation of operations *First* and *Next*. These now use *GetData* to access the data. Notice that if *GetData* were to directly return the node element, rather than placing the element in a

Data object, then it is not possible to define *First* and *Next*, because their return types could vary from one invocation to the next.

The key point here is that because of dynamic typing through public inheritance, a pointer to *Node** (i.e., *link*) may be used to point to nodes of type *DerivedNode*<**char**>, *DerivedNode*<**int**>, and *DerivedNode*<**float**>. This eliminates the problem that necessitated the artificial union of the different node types. The technique presented here can also be applied to other linked structures, such as trees.

EXERCISES

1. Write C++ code to insert an integer at the beginning of the homogeneous list of Program 4.44. Repeat for the heterogeneous list of Program 4.45.

2. Using iterators, write C++ code for printing all elements in the heterogeneous list of Program 4.45.

3. Write an algorithm to obtain the sum of all the floating point numbers in the heterogeneous list of Program 4.45.

4. Reimplement the class definition for sparse matrices (Program 4.30) using heterogeneous lists.

5. Reimplement the algorithm for reading in a matrix and setting up the linked representation using the class definition of the previous exercise.

6. Write an algorithm to compute the memory requirements of the homogeneous list of Program 4.44. Repeat for the heterogeneous list of Program 4.45. Use the *sizeof* () function to determine the memory requirements of a node in your machine.

7. Implement heterogeneous linked stacks and queues so that these data structures can contain objects of type **char**, **int**, and **float**.

4.13 REFERENCES AND SELECTED READINGS

A more detailed discussion on list iterators may be found in "C++ Strategies and Tactics," Addison-Wesley, by Robert B. Murray. More list copying algorithms may be found in "Copying list structures using bounded workspace," by G. Lindstrom, *CACM*, 17:4, 1974, pp. 198-202; "A nonrecursive list moving algorithm," by E. Reingold, *CACM*, 16:5, 1973, pp. 305-307; and "Bounded workspace garbage collection in an address-order preserving list processing environment," by D. Fisher, *Information Processing Letters*, 3:1, 1974, pp. 29-32.

CHAPTER 5

TREES

5.1 INTRODUCTION

5.1.1 Terminology

In this chapter we shall study a very important data object, the tree. Intuitively, a tree structure means that the data are organized so that items of information are related by branches. One very common place where such a structure arises is in the investigation of genealogies. There are two types of genealogical charts that are used to present such data: the *pedigree* and the *lineal* chart. Figure 5.1 gives an example of each.

The pedigree chart of Figure 5.1(a) shows someone's ancestors, in this case those of Dusty, whose two parents are Honey Bear and Brandy. Brandy's parents are Coyote and Nugget, who are Dusty's grandparents on her father's side. The chart continues one more generation back to the great-grandparents. By the nature of things, we know that the pedigree chart is normally two-way branching, though this does not allow for inbreeding. When inbreeding occurs, we no longer have a tree structure unless we insist that each occurrence of breeding is separately listed. Inbreeding may occur frequently when describing family histories of flowers or animals.

The lineal chart of Figure 5.1(b), though it has nothing to do with people, is still a genealogy. It describes, in somewhat abbreviated form, the ancestry of the modern European languages. Thus, this is a chart of descendants rather than ancestors, and each

246

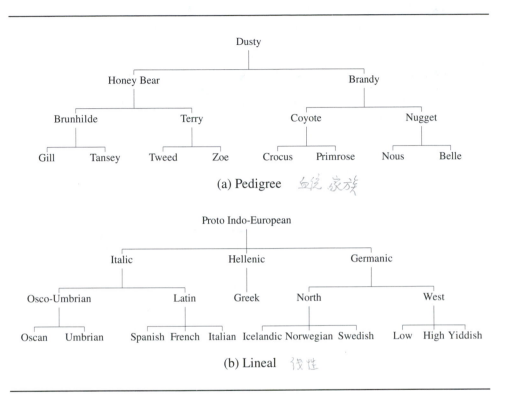

(a) Pedigree 血统 家族

(b) Lineal 後性

Figure 5.1: Two types of genealogical charts

item can produce several others. Latin, for instance, is the forebear of Spanish, French, and Italian. Proto Indo-European is a prehistoric language presumed to have existed in the fifth millenium B.C. This tree does not have the regular structure of the pedigree chart, but it is a tree structure nevertheless.

With these two examples as motivation, let us define formally what we mean by a tree.

Definition: A *tree* is a finite set of one or more nodes such that

(1)   There is a specially designated node called the *root*.

(2)   The remaining nodes are partitioned into $n \geq 0$ disjoint sets $T_1, \cdots, T_n$, where each of these sets is a tree. $T_1, \cdots, T_n$ are called the *subtrees* of the root. □

Notice that we have an instance of a recursive definition. If we return to Figure 5.1, we see that the roots of the trees are Dusty and Proto Indo-European. Tree (a) has two subtrees, whose roots are Honey Bear and Brandy; tree (b) has three subtrees, with roots Italic, Hellenic, and Germanic. The condition that $T_1, \cdots, T_n$ be disjoint sets prohibits subtrees from ever connecting together (i.e., there is no cross-breeding). It follows that every item in a tree is the root of some subtree of the whole. For instance, Osco-Umbrian is the root of a subtree of Italic, which itself has two subtrees with the roots Oscan and Umbrian. Umbrian is the root of a tree with no subtrees.

There are many terms that are often used when referring to trees. A *node* stands for the item of information plus the branches to other nodes. Consider the tree in Figure 5.2. This tree has 13 nodes, each item of data being a single letter for convenience. The root is *A*, and we will normally draw trees with the root at the top.

LEVEL

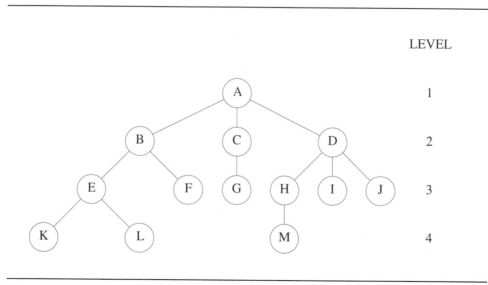

Figure 5.2: A sample tree

The number of subtrees of a node is called its *degree*. The degree of *A* is 3, of *C* is 1, and of *F* is zero. Nodes that have degree zero are called *leaf* or *terminal* nodes. {*K,L,F,G,M,I,J*} is the set of leaf nodes. Consequently, the other nodes are referred to as *nonterminals*. The roots of the subtrees of a node *X* are the *children* of *X*. *X* is the *parent* of its children. Thus, the children of *D* are *H*, *I*, and *J*; the parent of *D* is *A*. Children of the same parent are said to be *siblings*. *H*, *I*, and *J* are siblings. We can extend this terminology if we need to so that we can ask for the grandparent of *M*, which is *D*, and so on. The *degree of a tree* is the maximum of the degree of the nodes in the tree. The tree of Figure 5.2 has degree 3. The *ancestors* of a node are all the nodes along the path from the root to that node. The ancestors of *M* are *A*, *D*, and *H*.

The *level* of a node is defined by letting the root be at level one. If a node is at level *l*, then its children are at level *l* + 1. Figure 5.2 shows the levels of all nodes in that tree. The *height* or *depth* of a tree is defined to be the maximum level of any node in the tree. Thus, the depth of the tree in Figure 5.2 is 4.

5.1.2 Representation of Trees

5.1.2.1 List Representation

There are several ways to draw a tree besides the one presented in Figure 5.2. One useful way is as a list. The tree of Figure 5.2 could be written as the list

$$(A\,(B\,(E\,(K,L),F),C\,(G),D\,(H\,(M),I,J)))$$

The information in the root node comes first, followed by a list of the subtrees of that node. This way of drawing trees leads to a memory representation of trees that is the same as that used for generalized lists in Chapter 4. Figure 5.3 shows the resulting memory representation for the tree of Figure 5.2. If we use this representation, we can make use of many of the general functions that we originally wrote for handling lists.

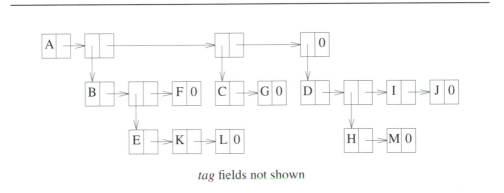

tag fields not shown

Figure 5.3: List representation of the tree of Figure 5.2

For several applications it is desirable to have a representation that is specialized to trees. One possibility is to represent each tree node by a memory node that has fields for the data and pointers to the tree node's children. Since the degree of each tree node may be different, we may be tempted to use memory nodes with a varying number of pointer fields. However, as it is often easier to write algorithms for a data representation when the node size is fixed, in practice one uses only nodes of a fixed size to represent tree nodes. For a tree of degree k, we could use the node structure of Figure 5.4. Each child field is used to point to a subtree. Lemma 5.1 shows that using this node structure is very wasteful of space.

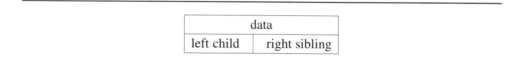

Figure 5.4: Possible node structure for a tree of degree k

Lemma 5.1: If T is a k-ary tree (i.e., a tree of degree k) with n nodes, each having a fixed size as in Figure 5.4, then $n(k-1)+1$ of the nk child fields are 0, $n \geq 1$.

Proof: Since each non-0 child field points to a node and there is exactly one pointer to each node other than the root, the number of non-0 child fields in an n-node tree is exactly $n-1$. The total number of child fields in a k-ary tree with n nodes is nk. Hence, the number of 0 fields is $nk - (n-1) = n(k-1)+1$. $\quad\square$

We shall develop two specialized fixed-node-size representations for trees. Both of these require exactly two link, or pointer, fields per node.

5.1.2.2 Left Child-Right Sibling Representation

Figure 5.5 shows the node structure used in the left child–right sibling representation.

data	
left child	right sibling

Figure 5.5: Left child-right sibling node structure

To convert the tree of Figure 5.2 into this representation, we first note that every node has at most one leftmost child and at most one closest right sibling. For example, in Figure 5.2, the leftmost child of A is B, and the leftmost child of D is H. Similarly, the closest right sibling of B is C, and the closest right sibling of H is I. Strictly speaking, since the order of children in a tree is not important, any of the children of a node could be the leftmost child, and any of its siblings could be the closest right sibling. For the sake of definiteness, we choose the nodes based on how the tree is drawn. The *left child* field of each node points to its leftmost child (if any), and the *right sibling* field points to its closest right sibling (if any). Figure 5.6 shows the tree of Figure 5.2 redrawn using the left child-right sibling representation.

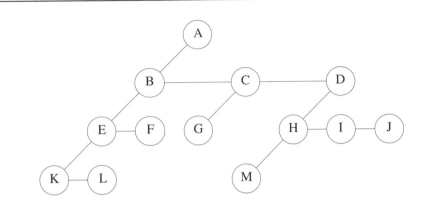

Figure 5.6: Left child-right sibling representation of tree of Figure 5.2

5.1.2.3   Representation as a Degree-Two Tree

To obtain the degree-two tree representation of a tree, we simply rotate the right-sibling pointers in a left child-right sibling tree clockwise by 45 degrees. This gives us the degree-two tree displayed in Figure 5.7. In the degree-two representation, we refer to the two children of a node as the left and right children. Notice that the right child of the root node of the tree is empty. This is always the case since the root of the tree we are transforming can never have a sibling. Figure 5.8 shows two additional examples of trees represented as left child-right sibling trees and as left child-right child (or degree-two) trees. Left child-right child trees are also known as *binary trees*.

EXERCISES

1. Write a function that reads in a tree represented as a list and creates its internal representation using nodes with three fields: *tag*, *data*, and *link*.

2. Write a function that reverses the process in Exercise 1 and takes a pointer to a tree and prints out its list representation.

3. [*Programming Project*] Write the C++ class definition for trees using the list representation described in this section. Write C++ functions that

    (a) [**operator>>()**]: accept a tree represented as a parenthesized list as input and create the generalized list representation of the tree (see Figure 5.3)

    (b) [copy constructor]: initialize a tree with another tree represented as a generalized list

Figure 5.7: Left child-right child tree representation of tree of Figure 5.2

   (c)   [**operator==()**]: test for equality between two trees represented as generalized lists

   (d)   [destructor]: erase a tree represented as a generalized list

   (e)   [**operator<<()**]: output a tree in its parenthesized list notation

Test the correctness of your functions using suitable test data.

5.2   BINARY TREES

5.2.1   The Abstract Data Type

We have seen that we can represent any tree as a binary tree. In fact, binary trees are an
important type of tree structure that occurs very often. Binary trees are characterized by
the fact that any node can have at most two branches (i.e., there is no node with degree
greater than two). For binary trees we distinguish between the subtree on the left and

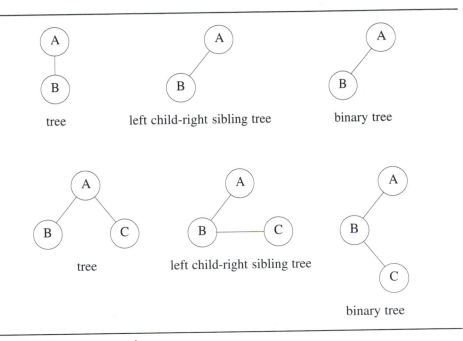

Figure 5.8: Tree representations

that on the right, whereas for trees the order of the subtrees is irrelevant. Also, a binary tree may have zero nodes. Thus, a binary tree is really a different object from a tree.

Definition: A *binary tree* is a finite set of nodes that either is empty or consists of a root and two disjoint binary trees called the *left subtree* and the *right subtree*. □

ADT 5.1 contains the specification for the binary tree ADT. This structure defines only a minimal set of operations on binary trees, which we use as a foundation on which to build additional operations.

Let us carefully review the distinctions between a binary tree and a tree. First, there is no tree having zero nodes, but there is an empty binary tree. Second, in a binary tree we distinguish between the order of the children; in a tree we do not. Thus, the two binary trees of Figure 5.9 are different, since the first binary tree has an empty right subtree, while the second has an empty left subtree. Viewed as trees, however, they are the same, despite the fact that they are drawn slightly differently.

Figure 5.10 shows two special kinds of binary trees. The first is a *skewed* tree, skewed to the left, and there is a corresponding tree that skews to the right. The tree of Figure 5.10(b) is called a *complete* binary tree. This kind of binary tree will be defined formally later. Notice that all terminal nodes are on adjacent levels. The terms that we *struct*

---

template <class *KeyType>* *no data member*
class *BinaryTree*
{
// **objects**: A finite set of nodes either empty or consisting of a
// root node, left *BinaryTree* and right *BinaryTree*.
public:
  BinaryTree ();
  // creates an empty binary tree

  Boolean IsEmpty ();
  // if the binary tree is empty, return TRUE (1); else return FALSE (0)

  BinaryTree(BinaryTree bt 1, *Element <KeyType > item, BinaryTree bt* 2);
  // creates a binary tree whose left subtree is *bt* 1, whose right subtree // is *bt* 2, and
  whose root node contains *item*

  BinaryTree Lchild ();
  // if *IsEmpty* (), return error; else return the left subtree of *∗**this**

  Element <KeyType > Data ();
  // if *IsEmpty* (), return error; else return the data in the root node of *∗**this**

  BinaryTree Rchild ();
  // if *IsEmpty* (), return error; else return the right subtree of *∗**this**
};

ADT 5.1: Abstract data type *BinaryTree*

Figure 5.9: Two different binary trees

introduced for trees such as degree, level, height, leaf, parent, and child all apply to binary trees in the natural way.

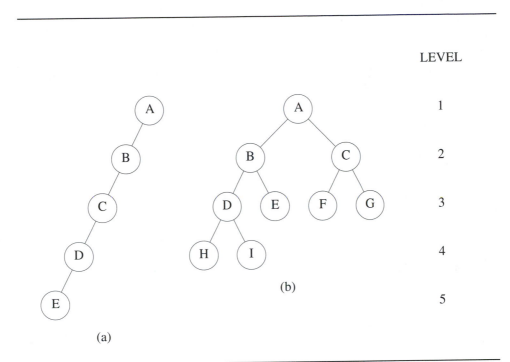

Figure 5.10: Skewed and complete binary trees

5.2.2   Properties of Binary Trees

Before examining data representations for binary trees, let us make some observations about such trees. In particular, we want to determine the maximum number of nodes in a binary tree of depth k and the relationship between the number of leaf nodes and the number of degree-two nodes in a binary tree.

Lemma 5.2 [*Maximum number of nodes*]:

(1)   The maximum number of nodes on level i of a binary tree is 2^{i-1}, $i \geq 1$.

(2)   The maximum number of nodes in a binary tree of depth k is $2^k - 1$, $k \geq 1$.

Proof:

(1) The proof is by induction on i.

Induction Base: The root is the only node on level $i = 1$. Hence, the maximum number of nodes on level $i = 1$ is $2^{i-1} = 2^0 = 1$.

Induction Hypothesis: Let i be an arbitrary positive integer greater than 1. Assume that the maximum number of nodes on level $i - 1$ is 2^{i-2}.

Induction Step: The maximum number of nodes on level $i - 1$ is 2^{i-2} by the induction hypothesis. Since each node in a binary tree has a maximum degree of 2, the maximum number of nodes on level i is two times the maximum number of nodes on level $i-1$, or 2^{i-1}.

(2) The maximum number of nodes in a binary tree of depth k is

$$\sum_{i=1}^{k} (\text{maximum number of nodes on level } i) = \sum_{i=1}^{k} 2^{i-1} = 2^k - 1 \quad \square$$

Lemma 5.3 [*Relation between number of leaf nodes and degree-2 nodes*]: For any nonempty binary tree, T, if n_0 is the number of leaf nodes and n_2 the number of nodes of degree 2, then $n_0 = n_2 + 1$.

Proof: Let n_1 be the number of nodes of degree one and n the total number of nodes. Since all nodes in T are at most of degree two, we have

$$n = n_0 + n_1 + n_2 \tag{5.1}$$

If we count the number of branches in a binary tree, we see that every node except the root has a branch leading into it. If B is the number of branches, then $n = B+1$. All branches stem from a node of degree one or two. Thus, $B = n_1 + 2n_2$. Hence, we obtain

$$n = B + 1 = n_1 + 2n_2 + 1 \tag{5.2}$$

Subtracting Eq. (5.2) from Eq. (5.1) and rearranging terms, we get

$$n_0 = n_2 + 1 \quad \square$$

In Figure 5.10(a), $n_0 = 1$ and $n_2 = 0$; in Figure 5.10(b), $n_0 = 5$ and $n_2 = 4$.

We are now ready to define full and complete binary trees.

Definition: A *full binary tree* of depth k is a binary tree of depth k having $2^k - 1$ nodes, $k \geq 0$. $\square$

By Lemma 5.2, $2^k - 1$ is the maximum number of nodes in a binary tree of depth k. Figure 5.11 shows a full binary tree of depth 4. Suppose we number the nodes in a full binary tree starting with the root on level 1, continuing with the nodes on level 2, and so on. Nodes on any level are numbered from left to right. This numbering scheme gives us the definition of a complete binary tree.

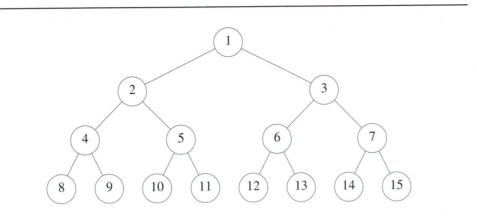

Figure 5.11: Full binary tree of depth 4 with sequential node numbers

Definition: A binary tree with n nodes and depth k is *complete* iff its nodes correspond to the nodes numbered from 1 to n in the full binary tree of depth k. $\square$

From Lemma 5.2, it follows that the height of a complete binary tree with n nodes is $\lceil \log_2(n + 1) \rceil$.

5.2.3   Binary Tree Representations

5.2.3.1   Array Representation

The numbering scheme used in Figure 5.11 suggests our first representation of a binary tree in memory. Since the nodes are numbered from 1 to n, we can use a one-dimensional array to store the nodes. (If the C++ array is used to represent the tree, the zero'th position is left empty.) Using Lemma 5.4 we can easily determine the locations of the parent, left child, and right child of any node, i, in the binary tree.

Lemma 5.4: If a complete binary tree with n nodes is represented sequentially, then for any node with index i, $1 \leq i \leq n$, we have

(1)   *parent* (*i*) is at ⌊ *i* / 2 ⌋ if *i* ≠ 1. If *i* = 1, *i* is at the root and has no parent.

(2)   *LeftChild* (*i*) is at 2*i* if 2*i* ≤ *n*. If 2*i* > *n*, then *i* has no left child.

(3)   *RightChild* (*i*) is at 2*i* + 1 if 2*i* + 1 ≤ *n*. If 2*i* + 1 > *n*, then *i* has no right child.

Proof: We prove (2). (3) is an immediate consequence of (2) and the numbering of nodes on the same level from left to right. (1) follows from (2) and (3). We prove (2) by induction on *i*. For *i* = 1, clearly the left child is at 2 unless 2 > *n*, in which case *i* has no left child. Now assume that for all *j*, 1 ≤ *j* ≤ *i*, *LeftChild* (*j*) is at 2*j*. Then the two nodes immediately preceding *LeftChild* (*i* +1) are the right and left children of *i*. The left child is at 2*i*. Hence, the left child of *i* + 1 is at 2*i* + 2 = 2(*i* + 1) unless 2(*i* + 1) > *n*, in which case *i* + 1 has no left child. □

This representation can clearly be used for all binary trees, though in most cases there will be a lot of unutilized space. Figure 5.12 shows the array representation for both trees of Figure 5.10. For complete binary trees such as the one in Figure 5.10(b), the representation is ideal, as no space is wasted. For the skewed tree of Figure 5.10(a), however, less than half the array is utilized. In the worst case a skewed tree of depth *k* will require $2^k - 1$ spaces. Of these, only *k* will be used.

5.2.3.2   Linked Representation

Although the array representation is good for complete binary trees, it is wasteful for many other binary trees. In addition, the representation suffers from the general inadequacies of sequential representations. Insertion and deletion of nodes from the middle of a tree require the movement of potentially many nodes to reflect the change in level number of these nodes. These problems can be overcome easily through the use of a linked representation. Each node has three fields, *LeftChild*, *data*, and *RightChild*. As with linked lists, we will use two classes to define a tree using a linked representation:

```
class Tree; // forward declaration
class TreeNode {
friend class Tree;
private:
    TreeNode *LeftChild;
    char data;
    TreeNode *RightChild;
};
```

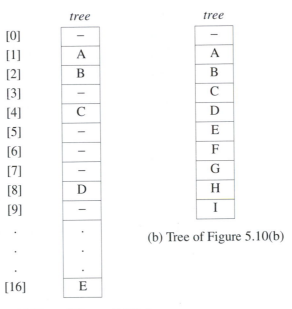

(b) Tree of Figure 5.10(b)

(a) Tree of Figure 5.10(a)

Figure 5.12: Array representation of the binary trees of Figure 5.10

```
class Tree {
public:
    // Tree operations
        .
private:
    TreeNode *root;
};
```

We shall draw a tree node using either of the representations of Figure 5.13.

Although with this node structure it is difficult to determine the parent of a node, we shall see that for most applications, this structure is adequate. If it is necessary to be able to determine the parent of random nodes, then a fourth field, *parent*, may be included in **class** *TreeNode*. The representation of the binary trees of Figure 5.10 using this node structure is given in Figure 5.14. The root of the tree is stored in the data member *root* of **class** *Tree*. This data member serves as the access pointer to the tree.

Figure 5.13: Node representations

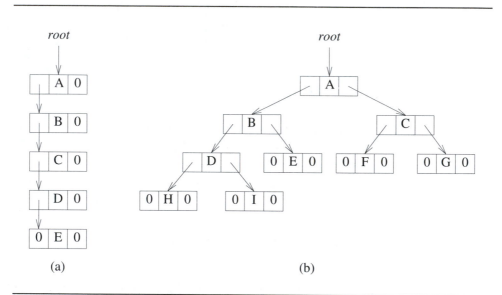

Figure 5.14: Linked representation for the binary trees of Figure 5.10

EXERCISES

1. For the binary tree of Figure 5.15, list the terminal nodes, the nonterminal nodes, and the level of each node.

2. What is the maximum number of nodes in a k-ary tree of height h? Prove your answer.

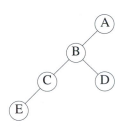

Figure 5.15: Binary tree for Exercise 1

3. Draw the internal memory representation of the binary tree of Figure 5.15 using (a) sequential and (b) linked representations.

4. Write the C++ class definition for trees in the linked representation using templates.

5. Write the C++ class definition for trees in the linked representation using *nested* classes.

5.3   BINARY TREE TRAVERSAL AND TREE ITERATORS

5.3.1   Introduction

There are many operations that we often want to perform on trees. One notion that arises frequently is the idea of traversing a tree or visiting each node in the tree exactly once. When a node is visited, some operation (such as outputting its *data* field) is performed on it. A full traversal produces a linear order for the nodes in a tree. This linear order, given by the order in which the nodes are visited, may be familiar and useful. When traversing a binary tree, we want to treat each node and its subtrees in the same fashion. If we let L, V, and R stand for moving left, visiting the node, and moving right when at a node, then there are six possible combinations of traversal: *LVR, LRV, VLR, VRL, RVL,* and *RLV*. If we adopt the convention that we traverse left before right, then only three traversals remain: *LVR, LRV,* and *VLR*. To these we assign the names *inorder, postorder,* and *preorder*, respectively, because of the position of the *V* with respect to the *L* and the *R*. For example, in postorder, we visit a node after we have traversed its left and right subtrees, whereas in preorder the visiting is done before the traversal of these subtrees.

There is a natural correspondence between these traversals and producing the infix, postfix, and prefix forms of an expression. Consider the binary tree of Figure 5.16. This tree contains an arithmetic expression with the binary operators add (+), multiply (*), and divide (/) and the variables A, B, C, D, and E. For each node that contains an operator, its left subtree gives the left operand and its right subtree the right operand. We will not worry for now how this binary tree was formed but assume that it is available. We use this tree to illustrate each of the traversals.

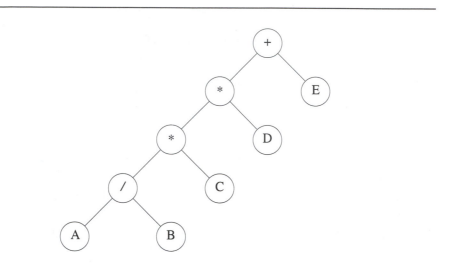

Figure 5.16: Binary tree with arithmetic expression

5.3.2 Inorder Traversal

Informally, *inorder traversal* calls for moving down the tree toward the left until you can go no farther. Then you "visit" the node, move one node to the right and continue. If you cannot move to the right, go back one more node. A precise way of describing this traversal is by using recursion as in Program 5.1.

This recursive function (workhorse) assumes that when a node is visited, we write out its *data* field (line 13). In other applications of inorder traversal, this line may be replaced by code to perform some other function on the node being visited. Recursion is an elegant device for describing this traversal. Figure 5.17 is a trace of how function *inorder*(*TreeNode* *) (Program 5.1) works on the tree of Figure 5.16. Read down the left column first and then the right one. Including the initial invocation, the function is invoked a total of 19 times. The elements get output in the following order:

$$A / B * C * D + E$$

which is the *in*fix form of the expression.

```
1 void Tree ::inorder ()
2 // Driver calls workhorse for traversal of entire tree. The driver is
3 // declared as a public member function of Tree.
4 {
5    inorder(root) ;
6 }


7 void Tree ::inorder(TreeNode *CurrentNode)
8 // Workhorse traverses the subtree rooted at CurrentNode (which is a pointer to a node
9 // in a binary tree). The workhorse is declared as a private member function of Tree.
10 {
11    if (CurrentNode) {
12      inorder(CurrentNode →LeftChild);
13      cout << CurrentNode →data;
14      inorder (CurrentNode →RightChild);
15    }
16 }
```

Program 5.1: Inorder traversal of a binary tree

5.3.3   Preorder Traversal

The C++ code for the second form of traversal, *preorder*, is given in Program 5.2. In words, we would say "visit a node, traverse left, and continue. When you cannot continue, move right and begin again or move back until you can move right and resume." The nodes of Figure 5.16 would be output in *pre*order as

$$+ * * / A B C D E$$

which we recognize as the *pre*fix form of the expression.

5.3.4   Postorder Traversal

The code for *postorder* traversal is given in Program 5.3. On the tree of Figure 5.16, this function produces the following output:

$$A B / C * D * E +$$

which is the *post*fix form of our expression.

Call of inorder	Value in CurrentNode	Action	Call of inorder	Value in CurrentNode	Action
Driver	+		10	C	
1	*		11	0	
2	*		10	C	cout << 'C'
3	/		12	0	
4	A		1	*	cout << '*'
5	0		13	D	
4	A	cout << 'A'	14	0	
6	0		13	D	cout << 'D'
3	/	cout << '/'	15	0	
7	B		Driver	+	cout << '+'
8	0		16	E	
7	B	cout << 'B'	17	0	
9	0		16	E	cout << 'E'
2	*	cout << '*'	18	0	

Figure 5.17: Trace of Program 5.1

```
1 void Tree ::preorder () {
2 // Driver calls workhorse for traversal of entire tree.  The driver is
3 // declared as a public member function of Tree.
4    preorder (root);
5 }
6 void Tree ::preorder(TreeNode *CurrentNode)
7 // Workhorse traverses the subtree rooted at CurrentNode (which is a pointer to a node
8 // in a binary tree). The workhorse is declared as a private member function of Tree.
9 {
10    if (CurrentNode) {
11       cout << CurrentNode →data;
12       preorder (CurrentNode →LeftChild);
13       preorder (CurrentNode →RightChild);
14    }
15 }
```

Program 5.2: Preorder traversal of a binary tree

```
 1 void Tree ::postorder () {
 2 // Driver calls workhorse for traversal of entire tree.  The driver is
 3 // declared as a public member function of Tree.
 4   postorder (root);
 5 }
 6 void Tree ::postorder(TreeNode *CurrentNode)
 7 // Workhorse traverses the subtree rooted at CurrentNode (which is a pointer to a node
 8 // in a binary tree). The workhorse is declared as a private member function of Tree.
 9 {
10   if (CurrentNode) {
11     postorder (CurrentNode →LeftChild );
12     postorder (CurrentNode →RightChild );
13     cout << CurrentNode →data;
14   }
15 }
```

Program 5.3: Postorder traversal of a binary tree

5.3.5 Iterative Inorder Traversal

Since the tree is a container class, we would like to implement a tree traversal algorithm by using iterators, as we did for linked lists. To do this, we first need to implement the tree traversal method without using recursion. Such a version for inorder traversal is given in Program 5.4. This program USES-A template *Stack* class similar to that of ADT 3.1.

Definition: We say that a data object of Type A USES-A data object of Type B if a Type A object uses a Type B object to perform a task. This relationship is typically expressed by employing the Type B object in a member function of Type A. The Type B object may be passed as an argument to the member function or used as a local variable in the function. The USES-A relationship is similar to the IS-IMPLEMENTED-IN-TERMS-OF relationship. The difference is that the degree to which the Type B object is used is less in the USES-A relationship. □

For our purposes, the template is instantiated to *TreeNode*∗. The program also assumes the existence of member functions *Add* and *Delete*, similar to those in Chapter 3 to add an element to a sequential stack and to delete an element from such a stack, respectively. The *Delete* operation returns a pointer to the deleted element. If the stack is empty, *Delete* returns 0.

Analysis of *NonrecInorder:* Let n be the number of nodes in the tree. If we consider the action of Program 5.4, we note that every node of the tree is placed on the stack once.

```
1 void Tree::NonrecInorder()
2 // nonrecursive inorder traversal using a stack
3 {
4    Stack<TreeNode*> s; // declare and initialize stack
5    TreeNode *CurrentNode = root;
6    while(1) {
7       while (CurrentNode) { // move down LeftChild fields
8          s.Add(CurrentNode); // add to stack
9          CurrentNode = CurrentNode →LeftChild;
10      }
11      if (! s.IsEmpty()) { // stack is not empty
12         CurrentNode = *s.Delete(CurrentNode); // delete from stack
13         cout << CurrentNode →data << endl;
14         CurrentNode = CurrentNode →RightChild;
15      }
16      else break;
17   }
18 }
```

Program 5.4: Nonrecursive inorder traversal

Thus, the statements on lines 8 to 9 and 12 to 14 are executed n times. Moreover, *CurrentNode* will equal 0 once for every 0 link in the tree, which is exactly

$$2n_0 + n_1 = n_0 + n_1 + n_2 + 1 = n + 1$$

Every step will be executed no more than some constant times n, so the time complexity is $O(n)$. The run time can be reduced by a constant factor by eliminating some of the unneccessary stacking (see Exercises). The space required for the stack is equal to the depth of the tree. This is at most n. □

We will now use function *Tree::NonrecInorder* to obtain an iterator for the inorder traversal of a tree. The key observation required to perform this transformation is that each iteration of the **while** loop of lines 6-17 in Program 5.4 yields the next element in the inorder traversal of the tree. We will begin by defining the **class** *InorderIterator*. This class is assumed to be declared as a **friend** of classes *TreeNode* and *Tree*. The data members required for this class include an object of type *Tree* which is used to represent the tree object with which the iterator will be associated. In addition, the two local variables *s* and *CurrentNode* required by Program 5.4 are included as data members of *InorderIterator*. The member function *Next* will be used to obtain the next inorder element in the tree. Program 5.5 contains the class definition of *InorderIterator*. The iterator class constructor initializes its *Tree* data member to the tree with which the iterator will be associated. The remainder of the constructor code performs any initializations performed in Program 5.4 prior to the execution of the **while** loop of line 6. Finally, the code implementing *Next()* is obtained by extracting lines 7-16 of Program 5.4 corresponding to a single iteration of the **while** loop. Instead of printing the element obtained, it is returned to the invoking function. The resulting code is in Program 5.6.

```
class InorderIterator {
public:
    char * Next ();
    InorderIterator(Tree tree) :t (tree ) { CurrentNode = t.root;}};
private:
    const Tree& t;
    Stack <TreeNode *> s;
    TreeNode *CurrentNode;
};
```

Program 5.5: Definition of inorder iterator class

```
char *InorderIterator ::Next ()
{
    while (CurrentNode) {
        s.Add (CurrentNode );
        CurrentNode = CurrentNode →LeftChild;
    }
    if (! s.IsEmpty ()) {
        CurrentNode = *s.Delete (CurrentNode );
        char& temp = CurrentNode →data;
        CurrentNode = CurrentNode →RightChild; // update CurrentNode
        return &temp;
    }
    else return 0; // tree has been traversed, no more elements
}
```

Program 5.6: Code for obtaining the next inorder element

5.3.6   Level-Order Traversal

Whether written iteratively or recursively, the inorder, preorder, and postorder traversals all require a stack. We now turn to a traversal that requires a queue. This traversal, called *level-order traversal*, visits the nodes using the ordering scheme suggested in Figure 5.11. Thus, we visit the root first, then the root's left child, followed by the root's right child. We continue in this manner, visiting the nodes at each new level from the leftmost node to the rightmost node.

The code for this traversal, given in Program 5.7 assumes the existence of a template *Queue* class similar to that of ADT 3.2. Further, we assume that the queue ADT is implemented using the circular queue of Section 3.3. For our purposes, the template is instantiated to *TreeNode**. The program also assumes the existence of member functions *Add* and *Delete*, similar to those in Chapter 3 to add an element to and to delete an element from a circular queue, respectively. The *Delete* operation returns a pointer to the deleted element. If the queue is empty, *Delete* returns 0.

```
void Tree ::LevelOrder ()
// Traverse the binary tree in level order
{
    Queue <TreeNode *>  q;
    TreeNode *CurrentNode = root;
    while (CurrentNode) {
        cout << CurrentNode →data << endl;
        if (CurrentNode →LeftChild) q.Add (CurrentNode →LeftChild);
        if (CurrentNode →RightChild) q.Add (CurrentNode →RightChild);
        CurrentNode = *q.Delete (CurrentNode );
    }
}
```

Program 5.7: Level-order traversal of a binary tree

We begin by adding the root to the queue. The traversal works by deleting the node at the front of the queue, writing out the node's *data* field, and adding the node's left and right children to the queue (unless they are 0). Since a node's children are at the next lower level, and we add the left child before the right child, the nodes are output using the ordering scheme found in Figure 5.11. The level-order traversal of the tree in Figure 5.16 is

$$+ * E * D / C A B$$

5.3.7   Traversal without a Stack

Before we leave the topic of tree traversal, we shall consider one final question. Is binary tree traversal possible without the use of extra space for a stack? (Note that a recursive tree traversal algorithm also implicitly uses a stack.) One simple solution is to add a *parent* field to each node. Then we can trace our way back up to any root and down again. Another solution, which requires two bits per node, represents binary trees as threaded binary trees. We study this in Section 5.5. If the allocation of this extra space is too costly, then we can use the *LeftChild* and *RightChild* fields to maintain the paths back to the root. The stack of addresses is stored in the leaf nodes. The exercises examine this algorithm more closely.

EXERCISES

1. Write out the inorder, preorder, postorder, and level-order traversals for the binary trees of Figure 5.10.

2. Do Exercise 1 for the binary tree of Figure 5.11.

3. Do Exercise 1 for the binary tree of Figure 5.15.

4. Implement an iterator class *LevelIterator* to traverse a binary tree in level order similar to the inorder iterator described in the text.

5. Write a nonrecursive version of function *preorder* (Program 5.2).

6. Use the results of the previous exercise to implement **class** *PreorderIterator* similar to the inorder iterator described in the text.

7. Write a nonrecursive version of function *postorder* (Program 5.3).

8. Use the results of the previous exercise to implement **class** *PostorderIterator* similar to the inorder iterator described in the text.

9. [**Programming Project**]: Write the C++ template class definition for binary trees. Next, define iterators for inorder, preorder, postorder, and level order traversals on binary trees. (At this point, your program will contain six class definitions). Finally, write a function that prints all tree elements in each of the four orders.

10. Rework *NonrecInorder* (Program 5.4) so that it is as fast as possible. (Hint: Minimize the stacking and the testing within the loop.)

11. Program 5.8 performs an inorder traversal without using threads, a stack, or a *parent* field. Verify that the algorithm is correct by running it on a variety of binary trees that cause every statement to execute at least once.

```
void Tree ::NoStackInorder ()
// Inorder traversal of binary tree using a fixed amount of additional storage
{
    if (!root) return; // empty binary tree
    TreeNode *top = 0, *LastRight = 0, *p, *q, *r, *r 1;
    p = q = root;
    while (1) {
        while (1) {
            if ((!p →LeftChild) && (!p →RightChild)) { // leaf node
                cout << p →data; break;
            }
            if (!p →LeftChild) { // visit p and move to p →RightChild
                cout << p →data;
                r = p →RightChild; p →RightChild = q;
                q = p; p = r;
            }
            else { // move to p →LeftChild
                r = p →LeftChild; p →LeftChild = q;
                q = p; p = r;
            }
        } // end of inner while
        // p is a leaf node, move upward to a node whose
        // right subtree has not yet been examined
        TreeNode *av = p;
        while (1) {
            if (p == root) return;
            if (!q →LeftChild) { // q is linked via RightChild
                r = q →RightChild; q →RightChild = p;
                p = q; q = r;
            }
            else if (!q →RightChild) { // q is linked via LeftChild
                r = q →LeftChild; q →LeftChild = p;
                p = q; q = r; cout << p →data;
            }
            else // check if p is a RightChild of q
                if (q == LastRight) {
                    r = top; LastRight = r →LeftChild;
                    top = r →RightChild; // unstack
                    r →LeftChild = r →RightChild = 0;
                    r = q →RightChild; q →RightChild = p;
                    p = q; q = r;
                }
                else { // p is LeftChild of q
```

```
          cout << q →data; // visit q
          av →LeftChild = LastRight; av →RightChild = top;
          top = av; LastRight = q;
          r = q →LeftChild; q →LeftChild = p; // restore link to p
          r1 = q →RightChild; q →RightChild = r;
          p = r1;
          break;
        }
    } // end of inner while loop
  } // end of outer while loop
}
```

Program 5.8: O(1) space inorder traversal

12. Write a nonrecursive version of function *postorder* (Program 5.3) using only a fixed amount of additional space. (Use the ideas of the previous exercise.)

13. Do the preceding exercise for the case of *preorder* (Program 5.2).

5.4   ADDITIONAL BINARY TREE OPERATIONS

5.4.1   Copying Binary Trees

Using the definition of a binary tree and the recursive version of the traversals, we can easily write other routines for working with binary trees. For instance, if we want to implement a copy constructor to initialize a binary tree with an exact copy of another binary tree, we can modify the postorder traversal algorithm only slightly to get Program 5.9.

5.4.2   Testing Equality

Another problem that is especially easy to solve using recursion is determining the equivalence of two binary trees. Binary trees are equivalent if they have the same topology and the information in corresponding nodes is identical. By the same topology we mean that every branch in one tree corresponds to a branch in the second in the same order and vice versa. The function **operator**==() calls the helper function *equal* (Program 5.10) which traverses the binary trees in preorder, though any order could be used.

```
// Copy constructor
Tree ::Tree(const Tree& s)  // driver
{
  root = copy (s.root);
}


TreeNode* Tree ::copy(TreeNode *orignode)  // Workhorse
// This function returns a pointer to an exact copy of the binary tree rooted at orignode.
{
  if (orignode) {
    TreeNode *temp = new TreeNode;
    temp →data = orignode →data;
    temp →LeftChild = copy (orignode →LeftChild );
    temp →RightChild = copy (orignode →RightChild );
    return temp;
  }
  else return 0;
}
```

Program 5.9: Copying a binary tree

5.4.3   The Satisfiability Problem

Consider the set of formulas we can construct by taking variables $x_1, x_2, x_3, \cdots$, and the operators $\wedge$ (**and**), $\vee$ (**or**), and $\neg$ (**not**). These variables can hold only one of two possible values, *true* or *false*. The set of expressions that can be formed using these variables and operators is defined by the following rules:

(1)   a variable is an expression

(2)   if x and y are expressions then $x \wedge y, x \vee y$, and $\neg x$ are expressions

(3)   parentheses can be used to alter the normal order of evaluation, which is **not** before **and** before **or**.

This set defines the formulas of the *propositional calculus* (other operations such as implication can be expressed using $\wedge$, $\vee$, and $\neg$). The expression

$$x_1 \vee (x_2 \wedge \neg x_3)$$

is a formula (read "x_1 or x_2 and not x_3"). If x_1 and x_3 are *false* and x_2 is *true*, then the value of this expression is

```
// Driver- assumed to be a friend of class Tree.
int operator==(const Tree& s, const Tree& t)
{
   return equal (s.root,t.root);
}
```

```
// Workhorse - assumed to be a friend of TreeNode.
int equal (TreeNode *a, TreeNode *b)
// This function returns 0 if the subtrees at a and b are not equivalent.
// Otherwise, it will return 1.
{
   if ((!a) && (!b)) return 1;  // both a and b are 0
   if (a && b   // both a and b are non-0
         && (a →data == b →data) // data is the same
         && equal (a →LeftChild,b →LeftChild ) // left subtrees are the same
         && equal (a →RightChild,b →RightChild )) // right subtrees are the same
            return 1;
   return 0;
}
```

Program 5.10: Binary tree equivalence

$$false \vee (true \wedge \neg false)$$
$$= false \vee true$$
$$= true$$

The *satisfiability problem* for formulas of propositional calculus asks if there is an assignment of values to the variables that causes the value of the expression to be true.

Again, let us assume that our formula is already in a binary tree, say

$$(x_1 \wedge \neg x_2) \vee (\neg x_1 \wedge x_3) \vee \neg x_3$$

in the tree of Figure 5.18. The inorder traversal of this tree is

$$x_1 \wedge \neg x_2 \vee \neg x_1 \wedge x_3 \vee \neg x_3$$

which is the infix form of the expression. The most obvious algorithm to determine satisfiability is to let (x_1, x_2, x_3) take on all possible combinations of *true* and *false* values and to check the formula for each combination. For n variables there are 2^n possible combinations of *true* $= t$ and *false* $= f$. For example, for $n = 3$, the eight combinations are: (t,t,t), (t,t,f), (t,f,t), (t,f,f), (f,t,t), (f,t,f), (f,f,t), (f,f,f). The algorithm will take $O(g\, 2^n)$, or exponential time, where g is the time to substitute values for $x_1, x_2,$ $\cdots, x_n$ and evaluate the expression.

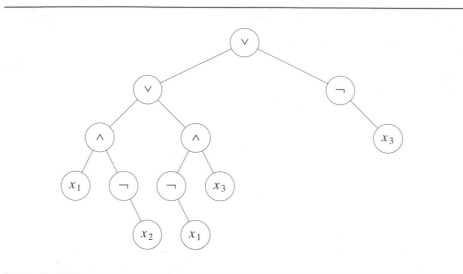

Figure 5.18: Propositional formula in a binary tree

To evaluate an expression we can traverse its tree in postorder, evaluating subtrees until the entire expression is reduced to a single value. This corresponds to the postfix evaluation of an arithmetic expression that we saw earlier. Viewing this from the perspective of the tree representation, for every node we reach, the values of its arguments (or children) have already been computed. So when we reach the $\vee$ node on level 2, the values of $x_1 \wedge \neg x_2$ and $\neg x_1 \wedge x_3$ will already be available to us, and we can apply the rule for **or**. Notice that a node containing $\neg$ has only a right branch, since **not** is a unary operator.

For the purposes of our evaluation algorithm, we assume each node has four fields:

LeftChild	data	value	RightChild

where *LeftChild*, *data*, and *RightChild* are as described earlier and *value* is of type *Boolean*. This node structure may be defined in C++ as

```
enum Boolean { FALSE, TRUE };
enum TypesOfData { LogicalNot, LogicalAnd, LogicalOr, LogicalTrue, LogicalFalse};

class SatTree; // forward declarartion

class SatNode {
friend class SatTree;
private:
   SatNode *LeftChild;
   TypesOfData data;
   Boolean value;
   SatNode *RightChild;
};


class SatTree {
public:
   void PostOrderEval ();
   void rootvalue () {cout << root →value;};
private:
   SatNode *root;
   void PostOrderEval (SatNode *);
};
```

Also we assume that for leaf nodes, $t\rightarrow data$ contains the current value (i.e., *LogicalTrue* or *LogicalFalse*) of the variable represented at the node. The first version of our algorithm for the satisfiability problem is Program 5.11. In this, n is the number of variables in the formula and *formula* is the binary tree that represents the formula.

```
for all 2ⁿ possible truth value combinations for the n variables
{
   generate the next combination;
   replace the variables by their values;
   evaluate the formula by traversing the tree it points to in postorder;
   if (formula.rootvalue ()) { cout << combination ; return; }
}
cout << ''no satisfiable combination'';
```

Program 5.11: First version of satisfiability algorithm

We can evaluate a formula using Program 5.12, which is a modified version of function *postorder* (Program 5.3).

```
void SatTree ::PostOrderEval () // Driver
{
   PostOrderEval (root);
}

void SatTree ::PostOrderEval (SatNode *s) // Workhorse
{
  if (s) {
    PostOrderEval (s →LeftChild);
    PostOrderEval (s →RightChild);
    switch (s →data) {
       case LogicalNot: s →value = ! s →RightChild →value; break;
       case LogicalAnd: s →value = s →LeftChild →value && s →RightChild →value;
                        break;
       case LogicalOr: s →value = s →LeftChild →value || s →RightChild →value;
                        break;
       case LogicalTrue: s →value = TRUE; break;
       case LogicalFalse: s →value = FALSE;
    }
  }
}
```

Program 5.12: Evaluating a formula

EXERCISES

1. Write a C++ function to count the number of leaf nodes in a binary tree, *T*. What is its computing time?

2. Write an algorithm, *SwapTree* (), that takes a binary tree and swaps the left and right children of every node. An example is given in Figure 5.19.

3. [*Programming Project*] Devise an external representation for the formulas in propositional calculus. Write a function that reads such a formula and creates its binary tree representation. What is the complexity of your function?

4. What is the computing time for *PostOrderEval* (Program 5.12)?

5. Write a recursive algorithm for erasing all nodes in a binary tree [Destructor].

6. Write a recursive algorithm for assigning one tree to another [**operator=**].

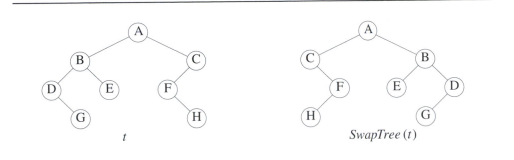

Figure 5.19: A *SwapTree* example

5.5   THREADED BINARY TREES

5.5.1   Threads

If we look carefully at the linked representation of any binary tree, we notice that there are more 0-links than actual pointers. As we saw before, there are $n + 1$ 0-links and $2n$ total links. A clever way to make use of these 0-links has been devised by A. J. Perlis and C. Thornton. Their idea is to replace the 0-links by pointers, called threads, to other nodes in the tree. These threads are constructed using the following rules:

(1)   A 0 *RightChild* field in node p is replaced by a pointer to the node that would be visited after p when traversing the tree in inorder. That is, it is replaced by the inorder successor of p.

(2)   A 0 *LeftChild* link at node p is replaced by a pointer to the node that immediately precedes node p in inorder (i.e., it is replaced by the inorder predecessor of p).

Figure 5.20 shows the binary tree of Figure 5.10(b) with its new threads drawn in as broken lines. This tree has 9 nodes and 10 0-links, which have been replaced by threads. If we traverse the tree in inorder, the nodes will be visited in the order $H, D, I, B, E, A, F, C, G$. For example, node E has a predecessor thread that points to B and a successor thread that points to A.

In the memory representation we must be able to distinguish between threads and normal pointers. This is done by adding two boolean fields, *LeftThread* and *RightThread*, to the record. If $t \rightarrow LeftThread ==$ TRUE, then $t \rightarrow LeftChild$ contains a thread; otherwise it contains a pointer to the left child. Similarly if $t \rightarrow RightThread ==$ TRUE, then $t \rightarrow RightChild$ contains a thread; otherwise it contains a pointer to the right child. This node structure is now given by the C++ class definition of Program 5.13.

In Figure 5.20 we see that two threads have been left dangling. One is the *LeftChild* of H and the other the *RightChild* of G. In order that we leave no loose

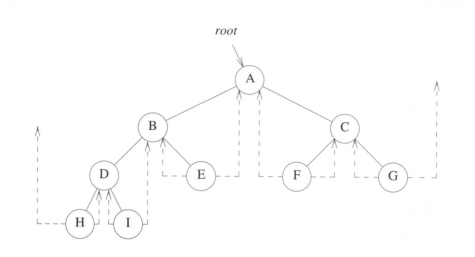

Figure 5.20: Threaded tree corresponding to Figure 5.10(b)

threads, we will assume a head node for all threaded binary trees. The original tree is the left subtree of the head node. An empty binary tree is represented by its head node as in Figure 5.21. The complete memory representation for the tree of Figure 5.20 is shown in Figure 5.22.

Figure 5.21: An empty threaded binary tree

5.5.2   Inorder Traversal of a Threaded Binary Tree

By using the threads, we can perform an inorder traversal without making use of a stack. Observe that for any node x in a binary tree, if $x \rightarrow RightThread$ == TRUE, then the inorder successor of x is $x \rightarrow RightChild$ by definition of threads. Otherwise the inorder

```
class ThreadedNode {
friend class ThreadedTree;
friend class ThreadedInorderIterator;
private:
    Boolean LeftThread;
    ThreadedNode *LeftChild;
    char data;
    ThreadedNode *RightChild;
    Boolean RightThread;
};

class ThreadedTree {
friend class ThreadedInorderIterator;
public:
    // Tree manipulation operations follow

        .
        .

private:
    ThreadedNode *root;
};

class ThreadedInorderIterator {
public:
    char *Next ();
    ThreadedInorderIterator(ThreadedTree tree): t(tree) { CurrentNode = t.root;}};
private:
    ThreadedTree t;
    ThreadedNode *CurrentNode;
};
```

Program 5.13: Class definition for threaded binary trees

successor of x is obtained by following a path of left-child links from the right child of x until a node with *LeftThread* == TRUE is reached. Function *Next* () (Program 5.14) finds and returns the inorder successor of node *CurrentNode* in a threaded binary tree.

The interesting thing to note about function *Next* () is that it is now possible to find the inorder successor of any arbitrary node in a threaded binary tree without using an additional stack. Since the tree is the left subtree of the head node and because of the choice of *RightThread* = FALSE for the head node, the inorder sequence of nodes in the original binary tree is obtained by function *Inorder*() (Program 5.15). The computing time of this function is readily seen to be O(n) for an n-node tree.

f = FALSE; t = TRUE

Figure 5.22: Memory representation of threaded tree

```
char* ThreadedInorderIterator::Next ()
// Find the inorder successor of CurrentNode in a threaded binary tree
{
    ThreadedNode *temp = CurrentNode →RightChild;
    if (! CurrentNode →RightThread)
        while (! temp →LeftThread) temp = temp →LeftChild;
    CurrentNode = temp;
    if (CurrentNode == t.root) return 0;
    else return &CurrentNode →data;
}
```

Program 5.14: Finding the inorder successor in a threaded binary tree

```
void ThreadedInorderIterator ::Inorder ()
{
    for (char *ch = Next (); ch; ch = Next ())
        cout << *ch << endl;
}
```

Program 5.15: Inorder traversal of threaded binary tree

We have seen how to use the threads of a threaded binary tree for inorder traversal. These threads also simplify the algorithms for preorder and postorder traversal.

5.5.3   Inserting a Node into a Threaded Binary Tree

We now examine how to make insertions into a threaded tree. This will give us a function for growing threaded trees. We shall study only the case of inserting r as the right child of a node s. The case of insertion of a left child is given as an exercise. The cases for insertion are

(1)   If s has an empty right subtree, then the insertion is simple and diagrammed in Figure 5.23(a).

(2)   If the right subtree of s is not empty, then this right subtree is made the right subtree of r after insertion. When this is done, r becomes the inorder predecessor of a node that has a *LeftThread* == TRUE field, and consequently there is a thread which has to be updated to point to r. The node containing this thread was previously the inorder successor of s. Figure 5.23(b) illustrates the insertion for this case.

In both cases s is the inorder predecessor of r. The details are given in function *InsertRight* (Program 5.16). It is assumed that function *InorderSucc*(r) returns the inorder successor of r, using an algorithm similar to that used in *Next* ().

EXERCISES

1.   Write an algorithm that inserts a new node l as the left child of node s in a threaded binary tree. The left subtree of s becomes the left subtree of l.

2.   Write a function to traverse a threaded binary tree in postorder. What are the time and space requirements of your function?

3.   Write an algorithm for traversing a threaded binary tree in preorder. What are the time and space requirements of your method?

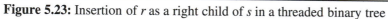

Figure 5.23: Insertion of *r* as a right child of *s* in a threaded binary tree

4. Consider threading a binary tree using preorder threads rather than inorder threads as in the text. Which of the traversals can be done without the use of a stack? For those that can be performed without a stack, write an algorithm and analyze its space complexity.

```
void ThreadedTree ::InsertRight(ThreadedNode *s, ThreadedNode *r)
// Insert r as the right child of s
{
    r→RightChild = s→RightChild;
    r→RightThread = s→RightThread;
    r→LeftChild = s;
    r→LeftThread = TRUE; // LeftChild is a thread
    s→RightChild = r; // attach r to s
    s→RightThread = FALSE;
    if (! r→RightThread) {
        ThreadedNode *temp = InorderSucc (r); // returns the inorder successor of r
        temp →LeftChild = r;
    }
}
```

Program 5.16: Inserting *r* as the right child of *s*

5. Consider threading a binary tree using postorder threads rather than inorder threads as in the text. Which of the traversals can be done without the use of a stack? For those that can be performed without a stack, write an algorithm and analyze its space complexity.

5.6   HEAPS

5.6.1   Priority Queues

Heaps are frequently used to implement *priority queues*. In this kind of queue, the element to be deleted is the one with highest (or lowest) priority. At any time, an element with arbitrary priority can be inserted into the queue. A data structure that supports these two operations is called a max (min) priority queue. In C++, we will represent the max (min) priority queue as an abstract class as follows:

```
template <class Type>
class MaxPQ {
public:
    virtual void Insert(const Element <Type >&) = 0;
    virtual Element <Type >* DeleteMax (Element <Type >&) = 0;
};
```

It is assumed that *Element<Type>* is a **struct** with a *key* data member in addition to other data members. We represent *MaxPQ* using pure virtual functions (and hence make it an abstract class) because it can be realized by a number of different data structures. Without knowing which data structure will be used, it is impossible to implement the *MaxPQ* operations. However, we know that any data structure D that implements a max priority queue must implement the operations *Insert* and *DeleteMax*. This is ensured by implementing D as a publicly derived class of *MaxPQ*.

Example 5.1: Suppose that we are selling the services of a machine. Each user pays a fixed amount per use. However, the time needed by each user is different. We wish to maximize the returns from this machine under the assumption that the machine is not to be kept idle unless no user is available. This can be done by maintaining a priority queue of all persons waiting to use the machine. Whenever the machine becomes available, the user with the smallest time requirement is selected. Hence, a min priority queue is required. When a new user requests the machine, his/her request is put into the priority queue.

If each user needs the same amount of time on the machine but people are willing to pay different amounts for the service, then a priority queue based on the amount of payment can be maintained. Whenever the machine becomes available, the user paying the most is selected. This requires a max priority queue. □

Example 5.2: Suppose that we are simulating a large factory. This factory has many machines and many jobs that require processing on some of the machines. An *event* is said to occur whenever a machine completes the processing of a job. When an event occurs, the job has to be moved to the queue for the next machine (if any) that it needs. If this queue is empty, the job can be assigned to the machine immediately. Also, a new job can be scheduled on the machine that has become idle (provided that its queue is not empty).

To determine the occurrence of events, a priority queue is used. This queue contains the finish time of all jobs that are presently being worked on. The next event occurs at the least time in the priority queue. So, a min priority queue can be used in this application. □

A max (min) heap may be used to implement a max (min) priority queue. Before defining a heap and developing functions to add to and delete from it, let us examine some other representations for a priority queue. We shall assume that each deletion removes the element with largest key value from the queue. The conclusions we draw are the same when the smallest element is to be deleted.

The simplest way to represent a priority queue is as an unordered linear list. Suppose that we have n elements in this queue. If the list is represented sequentially, additions are most easily performed at the end of this list. Hence, the insert time is $\Theta(1)$. A deletion requires a search for the element with largest key, followed by its deletion. Since it takes $\Theta(n)$ time to find the largest element in an n-element unordered list, the delete time is $\Theta(n)$. If a chain is used, additions can be performed at the front of the chain in $\Theta(1)$ time. Each deletion takes $\Theta(n)$ time. An alternative is to use an ordered linear list. The elements are in nondecreasing order if a sequential representation is used and in nonincreasing order if an ordered chain is used. The delete time for each representation is $\Theta(1)$ and the insert time $O(n)$. As we shall see shortly, when a max heap is used, both additions and deletions can be performed in $O(\log n)$ time.

5.6.2 Definition of a Max Heap

In Section 5.2.2, we defined a complete binary tree. In this section we present a special form of a complete binary tree that is useful in many applications.

Definition: A *max (min) tree* is a tree in which the key value in each node is no smaller (larger) than the key values in its children (if any). A *max heap* is a complete binary tree that is also a max tree. A *min heap* is a complete binary tree that is also a min tree. □

Some examples of max heaps and min heaps are shown in Figures 5.24 and 5.25, respectively.

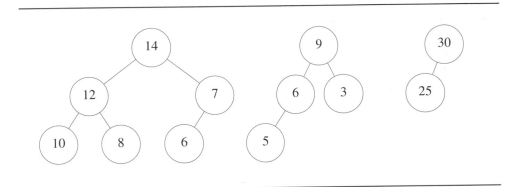

Figure 5.24: Max heaps

From the definitions, it follows that the key in the root of a min tree is the smallest key in the tree, whereas that in the root of a max tree is the largest. When viewed as an ADT, a max heap is very simple. The basic operations are

(1)   creation of an empty heap

(2)   insertion of a new element into the heap

(3)   deletion of the largest element from the heap

These operations are defined in ADT 5.2.

Since a max heap is a complete binary tree, we represent it using an array *heap*. Since the size of the array is not known in advance, *heap* is declared as a pointer to the element. The private data members of **class** *MaxHeap* are as follows:

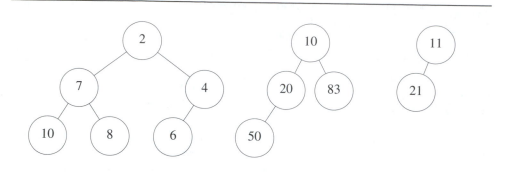

Figure 5.25: Min heaps

private:
    *Element<Type> *heap*;
    int *n*; // current size of max heap
    int *MaxSize*; // Maximum allowable size of heap

Program 5.17 defines the *MaxHeap* constructor.

MaxHeap::MaxHeap (**int** *sz = DefaultSize*)
{
    MaxSize = sz; *n = 0*;
    heap = **new** *Element <Type >*[*MaxSize +*1]; // *heap* [0] is not used
}

Program 5.17: Max heap constructor

5.6.3   Insertion into a Max Heap

A max heap with five elements is shown in Figure 5.26(a). When an element is added to this heap, the resulting six-element heap must have the structure shown in Figure 5.26(b), because a heap is a complete binary tree. If the element to be inserted has key value 1, it may be inserted as the left child of 2. If instead, the key value of the new element is 5, then this cannot be inserted as the left child of 2 (as otherwise, we will not have a max heap following the insertion). So, the 2 is moved down to its left child (Figure 5.26(c)), and we determine if placing the 5 at the old position of 2 results in a max heap. Since the parent element (20) is at least as large as the element being inserted (5),

---

template <**class** *KeyType*>
class *MaxHeap* : **public** *MaxPQ<KeyType>*
{
// **objects**: A complete binary tree of *n* > 0 elements organized so
// that the value in each node is at least as large as those in its children
public:
   MaxHeap(**int** *sz* = DefaultSize);
   // Create an empty heap that can hold a maximum of *sz* elements.

   Boolean IsFull ();
   // If number of elements in the heap is equal to the maximum size of the
   // heap, return TRUE (1); otherwise, return FALSE

   void *Insert(Element<KeyType> item)*;
   // If *IsFull* (), then error; else insert *item* into the heap.

   Boolean IsEmpty ()
   // If number of elements in heap is 0, return TRUE (1); else return FALSE (0)

   Element<KeyType>* Delete(KeyType& x);
   // If *IsEmpty* (), return 0; else remove an instance of the largest element
   // in the heap and save it in *x*. Return a pointer to *x*.
};

ADT 5.2: Abstract data type *MaxHeap*

it is all right to insert the new element at the position shown in the figure. Next, suppose that the new element has value 21 rather than 5. In this case, the 2 moves down to its left child as in Figure 5.26(c). The 21 cannot be inserted into the old position occupied by the 2, as the parent of this position is smaller than 21. Hence, the 20 is moved down to its right child and the 21 inserted into the root of the heap (Figure 5.26(d)).

To implement the insertion strategy just described, we need to go from an element to its parent. If a linked representation is used, an additional *parent* field is to be added to each node. However, since a heap is a complete binary tree, the formula-based representation can be used. Lemma 5.4 enables us to locate the parent of any element easily. Program 5.18 performs an insertion into a max heap.

Analysis of *Insert*: The insertion function begins at a leaf of a complete binary tree and moves up toward the root. At each node on this path, $O(1)$ amount of work is done. Since a complete binary tree with n elements has a height $\lceil \log_2(n+1) \rceil$, the **for** loop of the insertion function is iterated $O(\log n)$ times. Hence, the complexity of function *Insert* is $O(\log n)$. □

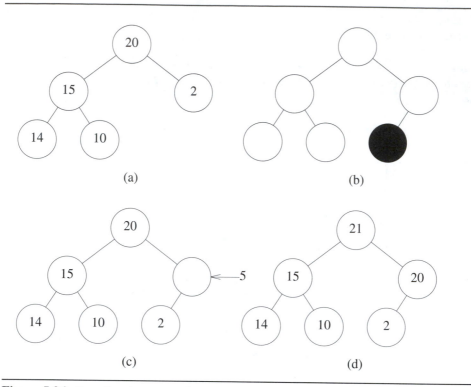

Figure 5.26: Insertion into a max heap

5.6.4   Deletion from a Max Heap

When an element is to be deleted from a max heap, it is taken from the root of the heap. For instance, a deletion from the heap of Figure 5.26(d) results in the removal of the element 21. Since the resulting heap has only five elements in it, the binary tree of Figure 5.26(d) needs to be restructured to correspond to a complete binary tree with five elements. To do this, we remove the element in position 6 (i.e., the element 2). Now we have the right structure (Figure 5.27(a)), but the root is vacant and the element 2 is not in the heap. If the 2 is inserted into the root, the resulting binary tree is not a max heap. The element at the root should be the largest from among the 2 and the elements in the left and right children of the root. This element is 20. It is moved into the root, thereby creating a vacancy in position 3. Since this position has no children, the 2 may be inserted here. The resulting heap is shown in Figure 5.26(a).

Now, suppose we wish to perform another deletion. The 20 is to be deleted. Following the deletion, the heap has the binary tree structure shown in Figure 5.27(b). To

```
template <class Type>
void MaxHeap<Type>::Insert(const Element <Type >& x)
// insert x into the max heap
{
  if (n == MaxSize) { HeapFull (); return;}
  n++;
  for (int i = n; 1;) {
    if (i == 1) break; // at root
    if (x.key <= heap [i /2].key) break;
    // move from parent to i
    heap [i] = heap [i /2];
    i /= 2;
  }
  heap [i] = x;
}
```

Program 5.18: Insertion into a max heap

      (a)   (b)   (c)

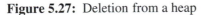

Figure 5.27: Deletion from a heap

get this structure, the 10 is removed from position 5. It cannot be inserted into the root, as it is not large enough. The 15 moves to the root, and we attempt to insert the 10 into position 2. This is, however, smaller than the 14 below it. So, the 14 is moved up and the 10 inserted into position 4. The resulting heap is shown in Figure 5.27(c).

Program 5.19 implements this strategy to delete from a heap.

```
template <class Type>
Element <Type >* MaxHeap <Type >::DeleteMax (Element <Type >& x)
// Delete from the max heap
{
  if (!n) { HeapEmpty (); return 0;}
  x = heap [1]; Element <Type > k = heap [n ]; n--;
  for (int i = 1, j = 2; j <= n; )
  {
    if (j < n) if (heap [j ].key < heap [j +1].key) j++;
    // j points to the larger child
    if (k.key >= heap [j ].key) break;
    heap [i ] = heap [j ];    // move child up
    i = j; j *= 2;   // move i and j down
  }
  heap [i ] = k;
  return &x;
}
```

Program 5.19: Deletion from a max heap

Analysis of _DeleteMax_: Since the height of a heap with n elements is $\lceil \log_2(n+1) \rceil$, the **for** loop of this function is iterated $O(\log n)$ times. Each iteration of this for loop takes $O(1)$ time. Hence, the complexity of function _DeleteMax_ is $O(\log n)$. $\square$

EXERCISES

1. Compare the run-time performance of max heaps with that of unordered and ordered linear lists as a representation for priority queues. For this comparison, program the max heap insertion and deletion algorithms, as well as algorithms to perform these tasks on unordered and ordered linear lists that are maintained as sequential lists in a one-dimensional array. Generate a random sequence of n values and insert these into the priority queue. Next, perform a random sequence of m inserts and deletes starting with the initial queue of n values. This sequence is to be generated so that the next operation in the sequence has an equal chance of being either an insert or a delete. Care should be taken so that the sequence does not cause the priority queue to become empty at any time. Measure the time taken for the sequence of m operations using both a max heap and an unordered list. Divide the total time by m and plot the times as a function of n. Do this for $n =$ 100, 500, 1000, 2000, 3000, and 4000. Set m to be 1000. Make some qualitative statements about the relative performance of the two representations for a priority queue.

2. Write an algorithm to insert into a min heap. Use the notation of Program 5.18. The complexity of your algorithm should be O(log n). Show that this is the case.

3. Write an algorithm to delete the smallest item from a min heap. Use the notation of Program 5.19. The complexity of your algorithm should be O(log n). Show that this is the case.

4. The worst-case number of comparisons performed during an insertion into a max heap can be reduced to O(loglog n) by performing a binary search on the path from the new leaf to the root. This does not affect the number of data moves though. Write an insertion algorithm that uses this strategy. Redo Exercise 1 using this insertion algorithm. Based on your experiments, what can you say about the value of this strategy over the one used in Program 5.18?

5.7   BINARY SEARCH TREES

5.7.1   Definition

Although a heap is well suited for applications that require priority queues, it is not suited for applications in which arbitrary elements are to be deleted from the element list. Deletion of an arbitrary element from an n-element heap takes O(n) time (it takes this much time just to locate the element to be deleted). This is no better than the time needed for arbitrary deletions from an unordered linear list.

A *binary search tree* has a better performance than any of the data structures studied so far when the functions to be performed are search, insert, and delete. In fact, with a binary search tree, these functions can be performed both by key value and by rank (i.e., find an element with key x; find the fifth smallest element; delete the element with key x; delete the fifth smallest element; insert an element and determine its rank; and so on).

Definition: A *binary search tree* is a binary tree. It may be empty. If it is not empty then it satisfies the following properties:

(1)   Every element has a key and no two elements have the same key (i.e., the keys are distinct).

(2)   The keys (if any) in the left subtree are smaller than the key in the root.

(3)   The keys (if any) in the right subtree are larger than the key in the root.

(4)   The left and right subtrees are also binary search trees. □

There is some redundancy in this definition. Properties (2), (3), and (4) together imply that the keys must be distinct. So, property (1) can be replaced by the property: The root has a key.

Some examples of binary trees in which the elements have distinct keys are shown in Figure 5.28. The tree of Figure 5.28(a) is not a binary search tree, despite the fact that it satisfies properties (1), (2), and (3). The right subtree fails to satisfy property (4). This subtree is not a binary search tree, as its right subtree has a key value (22) that is smaller than that in the subtree's root (25). The binary trees of Figures 5.28(b) and (c) are binary search trees.

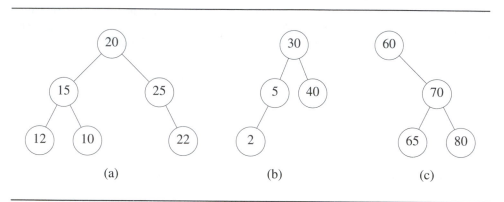

(a) (b) (c)

Figure 5.28: Binary trees

5.7.2   Searching a Binary Search Tree

Since the definition of a binary search tree is recursive, it is easiest to describe a recursive search method. Suppose we wish to search for an element with key x. We begin at the root. If the root is 0, then the search tree contains no elements and the search is unsuccessful. Otherwise, we compare x with the key in the root. If x equals this key, then the search terminates successfully. If x is less than the key in the root, then no element in the right subtree can have key value x, and only the left subtree is to be searched. If x is larger than the key in the root, only the right subtree needs to be searched. The subtrees may be searched recursively as in Program 5.20. This function assumes a linked representation for the search tree (which is assumed to be an object of **class** *BST*). Each node (*BstNode*) has the three fields: *LeftChild*, *RightChild*, and *data*. *data* is an object of **class** *Element<Type>* and has at least the field *key*, which is of type *Type*. The recursion of Program 5.20 is easily replaced by a **for** loop, as in Program 5.21.

If we wish to search by rank, each node should have an additional field *LeftSize*, which is one plus the number of elements in the left subtree of the node. For the search tree of Figure 5.28(b), the nodes with keys 2, 5, 30, and 40, respectively, have *LeftSize* equal to 1, 2, 3, and 1. Program 5.22 searches for the kth smallest element.

As can be seen, a binary search tree of height h can be searched by key as well as by rank in O(h) time.

```
template <class Type> //Driver
BstNode <Type >* BST <Type >::Search(const Element <Type >& x)
// Search the binary search tree (*this) for an element with key x.
// If such an element is found, return a pointer to the node that contains it.
{
   return Search(root, x);
}

template <class Type> // Workhorse
BstNode <Type >* BST <Type >::Search(BstNode <Type >* b, const Element <Type >& x)
{
   if (!b) return 0;
   if (x.key == b →data.key) return b;
   if (x.key < b →data.key) return Search (b →LeftChild,x);
   return Search (b →RightChild,x);
}
```

Program 5.20: Recursive search of a binary search tree

```
template <class Type>
BstNode <Type >* BST <Type >::IterSearch(const Element <Type >& x)
// Search the binary search tree for an element with key x
{
   for (BstNode <Type > *t = root;  t;)
   {
      if (x.key == t →data.key) return t;
      if (x.key < t →data.key) t = t →LeftChild;
      else t = t →RightChild;
   }
   return 0;
}
```

Program 5.21: Iterative search of a binary search tree

5.7.3   Insertion into a Binary Search Tree

To insert a new element x, we must first verify that its key is different from those of existing elements. To do this, a search is carried out. If the search is unsuccessful, then the

```
template <class Type>
BstNode <Type >* BST <Type >::Search(int k)
// Search the binary search tree for the kth smallest element
{
  BstNode<Type> *t = root;
  while (t)
  {
    if (k == t →LeftSize) return t;
    if (k < t →LeftSize) t = t →LeftChild;
    else {
      k −= LeftSize;
      t = t →RightChild;
    }
  }
  return 0;
}
```

Program 5.22: Searching a binary search tree by rank

element is inserted at the point the search terminated. For instance, to insert an element with key 80 into the tree of Figure 5.28(b), we first search for 80. This search terminates unsuccessfully, and the last node examined is the one with key 40. The new element is inserted as the right child of this node. The resulting search tree is shown in Figure 5.29(a). Figure 5.29(b) shows the result of inserting the key 35 into the search tree of Figure 5.29(a).

Program 5.23 implements the insert strategy just described. If a node has a *Left-Size* field, then this is to be updated too. Regardless, the insertion can be performed in $O(h)$ time, where h is the height of the search tree.

5.7.4 Deletion from a Binary Search Tree

Deletion of a leaf element is quite easy. For example, to delete 35 from the tree of Figure 5.29(b), the left-child field of its parent is set to 0 and the node disposed. This gives us the tree of Figure 5.29(a). To delete the 80 from this tree, the right-child field of 40 is set to 0, obtaining the tree of Figure 5.28(b), and the node containing 80 is disposed.

The deletion of a nonleaf element that has only one child is also easy. The node containing the element to be deleted is disposed, and the single-child takes the place of the disposed node. So, to delete the element 5 from the tree of Figure 5.29(a), we simply change the pointer from the parent node (i.e., the node containing 30) to the single-child node (i.e., the node containing 2).

(a)   (b)

Figure 5.29: Inserting into a binary search tree

When the element to be deleted is in a nonleaf node that has two children, the element is replaced by either the largest element in its left subtree or the smallest one in its right subtree. Then we proceed to delete this replacing element from the subtree from which it was taken. For instance, if we wish to delete the element with key 30 from the tree of Figure 5.29(b), then we replace it by either the largest element, 5, in its left subtree or the smallest element, 35, in its right subtree. Suppose we opt for the largest element in the left subtree. The 5 is moved into the root, and the tree of Figure 5.30(a) is obtained. Now we must delete the second 5. Since this node has only one child, the pointer from its parent is changed to point to this child. The tree of Figure 5.30(b) is obtained. One may verify that regardless of whether the replacing element is the largest in the left subtree or the smallest in the right subtree, it is originally in a node with a degree of at most one. So, deleting it from this node is quite easy. We leave the writing of the deletion function as an exercise. It should be evident that a deletion can be performed in $O(h)$ time if the search tree has a height of h.

5.7.5   Joining and Splitting Binary Trees

Although search, insert, and delete are the operations most frequently performed on a binary search tree, the following additional operations are useful in certain applications:

(a)   *C.ThreeWayJoin* (A,x,B): This creates a binary search tree C consisting of the elements initially in the binary search trees A and B, as well as the single element x. It is assumed that each element in A has a smaller key than $x.key$ and that each element in B has a larger key than $x.key$. The join operation may destroy both A and B.

(b)   *C.TwoWayJoin* (A,B): This joins the two binary search trees A and B to obtain a

---

```
template <class Type>
Boolean BST <Type >::Insert(const Element <Type >& x)
// Insert x into the binary search tree
{
    // Search for x.key, q is parent of p
    BstNode <Type > *p = root;  BstNode <Type > *q = 0;
    while (p) {
        q = p;
        if (x.key == p →data.key) return FALSE; // x.key is already in tree
        if (x.key < p →data.key) p = p →LeftChild;
        else p = p →RightChild;
    }

    // Perform insertion
    p = new BstNode <Type >;
    p →LeftChild = p →RightChild = 0; p →data = x;
    if (!root) root = p;
    else if (x.key < q →data.key) q →LeftChild = p;
      else q →RightChild = p;
    return TRUE;
}
```

Program 5.23: Insertion into a binary search tree

single binary search tree C that contains all the elements originally in A and B. It is assumed that all keys of A are smaller than all keys of B and that the join operation is to destroy both A and B.

(c) $A.Split(i,B,x,C)$: The binary search tree A is split into three parts: B is a binary search tree that contains all elements of A that have key less than i; if A contains an element with key i, then this element is copied into the reference parameter x, and a pointer to x returned (otherwise, 0 is returned to indicate that there is no element in A with key i); C is a binary search tree that contains all records of A that have key larger than i. The split operation may destroy A.

A three-way join operation is particularly easy to perform. We simply obtain a new node and set its data field to x, its left-child pointer to A, and its right-child pointer to B. This node is made the root of C. The time taken for this operation is O(1), and the height of the new tree C is max$\{height(A), height(B)\} + 1$.

Consider the two-way join operation. If either A or B is empty, the result is C. When neither is empty, we may first delete from A the record x with the largest key. Let the resulting binary search tree be A'. To complete the operation, we perform the three-

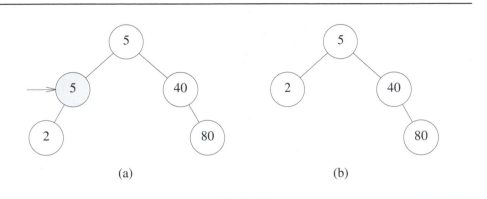

(a)   (b)

Figure 5.30: Deletion from a binary search tree

way join operation *C.ThreeWayJoin* (*A´,x,B*). The overall time required to perform the two-way join operation is O(*height* (*A*)), and the height of *C* is max{*height* (*A*), *height* (*B*)} + 1. The run time can be made O(min{*height* (*A*), *height* (*B*)}) if we retain with each tree its height. Then we delete the record with the largest key value from *A* if the height of *A* is no more than that of *B*; otherwise, we delete from *B* the record with the smallest key value. This is followed by a three-way join operation.

   To perform a split, we first note that splitting at the root (i.e., *i* = *A.root →data . key*) is particularly easy. In this case, *B* is the left subtree of *A*, *x* is the record in the root, and *C* is the right subtree of *A*. If *i* is smaller than the key at the root, then the root together with its right subtree is to be in *C*. When *i* is larger than the key at the root, the root together with its left subtree is to be in *B*. Using these observations, we can perform a split by moving down the search tree *A* searching for a record with key *i*. As we move down, we construct the two search trees *B* and *C*. The algorithm for this is given in Program 5.24. To simplify the code, we begin with two head nodes *Y* and *Z* for *B* and *C*, respectively. *B* is grown as the right subtree of *Y*; *C* is grown as the left subtree of *Z*. *L* (*R*) points to the node of *Y* (*Z*) at which further subtrees of *A* that are to be part of *B* (*C*) may be attached. Attaching a subtree to *B* (*C*) is done as the right (left) child of *L* (*R*).

Analysis of *Split:* The **while** loop maintains the invariant that all keys in the subtree with root *p* are larger than those in *Y* and smaller than those in *Z*. The correctness of the function is easy to establish, and its complexity is seen to be O(*height* (*A*)). One may verify that neither *B* nor *C* has a height larger than that of *A*. □

```
template <class Type> Element <Type >*
Element <Type >* BST <Type >::Split(Type i, BST <Type >& B, Element <Type > &x, BST <Type >& C)
// Split the binary search tree with respect to key i
{
    if (!root) {B.root = C.root = 0; return 0;} // empty tree
    // create head nodes for B and C
    BstNode <Type > *Y = new BstNode <Type >; BstNode <Type > *L = Y;
    BstNode <Type > *Z = new BstNode <Type >; BstNode <Type > *R = Z;
    BstNode <Type > *t = root;
    while (t)
        if (i == t →data.key) { // split at t
            L →RightChild = t →LeftChild;
            R →LeftChild = t →RightChild;
            x = t →data;
            B.root = Y →RightChild; delete Y;
            C.root = Z →LeftChild; delete Z;
            return &x;
        }
        else if (i < t →data.key) {
            R →LeftChild = t;
            R = t; t = t →LeftChild;
        }
        else {
            L →RightChild = t;
            L = t; t = t →RightChild;
        }
    // Set 0 pointers and delete head nodes
    L →RightChild = R →LeftChild = 0;
    B.root = Y →RightChild; delete Y;
    C.root = Z →LeftChild; delete Z;
    return 0;
}
```

Program 5.24 Splitting a binary search tree

5.7.6   Height of a Binary Search Tree

Unless care is taken, the height of a binary search tree with n elements can become as large as n. This is the case, for instance, when Program 5.23 is used to insert the keys [1, 2, 3, . . ., n], in this order, into an initially empty binary search tree. It can, however, be shown that when insertions and deletions are made at random using the functions given here, the height of the binary search tree is $O(\log n)$ on the average.

Search trees with a worst-case height of O(log n) are called *balanced search trees*. Balanced search trees that permit searches, inserts, and deletes to be performed in O(h) time exist. Most notable among these are AVL, 2-3, 2-3-4, red/black, and B trees. These are discussed in Chapter 10.

EXERCISES

1. Write a C++ function to delete an element X from a binary search tree. What is the time complexity of your algorithm?

2. Write a program to start with an initially empty binary search tree and make n random insertions. Use a uniform random number generator to obtain the values to be inserted. Measure the height of the resulting binary search tree and divide this height by $\log_2 n$. Do this for $n = 100, 500, 1000, 2000, 3000, \cdots, 10,000$. Plot the ratio *height* $/\log_2 n$ as a function of n. The ratio should be approximately constant (around 2). Verify that this is so.

3. Suppose that each node in a binary search tree also has the field *LeftSize* as described in the text. Write a function to insert an element x into such a binary search tree. The complexity of your algorithm should be O(h), where h is the height of the search tree. Show that this is the case.

4. Do Exercise 3, but this time write a function to delete the element with the kth smallest key in the binary search tree.

5. Write a C++ function that implements the three-way join operation in O(1) time.

6. Write a C++ function that implements the two-way join operation in O(*height* (A)) time, where A is one of the two trees being joined.

7. Any algorithm that merges together two sorted lists of size n and m, respectively, must make at least $n + m - 1$ comparisons in the worst case. What implications does this result have on the time complexity of any comparison-based algorithm that combines two binary search trees that have n and m elements, respectively?

8. In Chapter 7, we shall see that every comparison-based algorithm to sort n elements must make O($n \log n$) comparisons in the worst case. What implications does this result have on the complexity of initializing a binary search tree with n elements?

9. Notice that a binary search tree can be used to implement a priority queue.

    (a) Write a C++ class definition for a binary search tree. This class should be a publicly derived class of **class** *MaxPQ*.

    (b) Write a C++ function to delete the largest element in a binary search tree. Your function should have complexity O(h), where h is the height of the search tree. Since h is O($\log n$) on average, we can perform each of the priority queue operations in average time O($\log n$).

    (c) Compare the actual performance of heaps and binary search trees as data structures for priority queues. For this comparison, generate random sequences of insert and delete max operations and measure the total time taken for each sequence by each of these data structures.

5.8   SELECTION TREES

5.8.1   Introduction

Suppose we have k ordered sequences, called *runs*, that are to be merged into a single ordered sequence. Each run consists of some records and is in nondecreasing order of a designated field called the *key*. Let n be the number of records in all k runs together. The merging task can be accomplished by repeatedly outputting the record with the smallest key. The smallest has to be found from k possibilities, and it could be the leading record in any of the k runs. The most direct way to merge k runs is to make $k-1$ comparisons to determine the next record to output. For $k > 2$, we can achieve a reduction in the number of comparisons needed to find the next smallest element by using the data structure *selection tree*. There are two kinds of selection trees: *winner trees* and *loser trees*.

5.8.2   Winner Trees

A *winner tree* is a complete binary tree in which each node represents the smaller of its two children. Thus, the root node represents the smallest node in the tree. Figure 5.31 illustrates a winner tree for the case $k = 8$.

The construction of this winner tree may be compared to the playing of a tournament in which the winner is the record with the smaller key. Then, each nonleaf node in the tree represents the winner of a tournament, and the root node represents the overall winner, or the smallest key. Each leaf node represents the first record in the corresponding run. Since the records being merged are generally large, each node will contain only a pointer to the record it represents. Thus, the root node contains a pointer to the first record in run 4.

A winner tree may be represented using the sequential allocation scheme for binary trees that results from Lemma 5.4. The number above each node in Figure 5.31 is the address of the node in this sequential representation. The record pointed to by the root has the smallest key and so may be output. Now, the next record from run 4 enters the winner tree. It has a key value of 15. To restructure the tree, the tournament has to be replayed only along the path from node 11 to the root. Thus, the winner from nodes 10 and 11 is again node 11 ($15 < 20$). The winner from nodes 4 and 5 is node 4 ($9 < 15$). The winner from 2 and 3 is node 3 ($8 < 9$). The new tree is shown in Figure 5.32. The tournament is played between sibling nodes and the result put in the parent node. Lemma 5.4 may be used to compute the address of sibling and parent nodes efficiently. Each new comparison takes place at the next higher level in the tree.

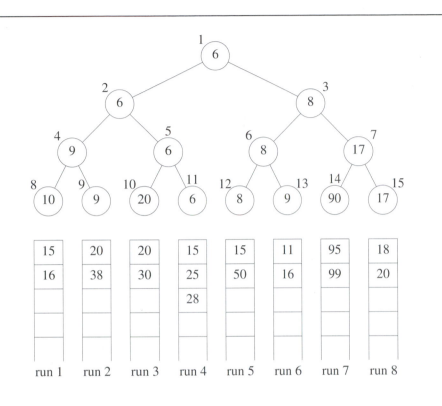

Figure 5.31: Winner tree for $k = 8$, showing the first three keys in each of the eight runs

Analysis of merging runs using winner trees: The number of levels in the tree is $\lceil \log_2(k + 1) \rceil$. So, the time to restructure the tree is $O(\log_2 k)$. The tree has to be restructured each time a record is merged into the output file. Hence, the time required to merge all n records is $O(n \log_2 k)$. The time required to set up the selection tree the first time is $O(k)$. Thus, the total time needed to merge the k runs is $O(n \log_2 k)$. $\square$

5.8.3 Loser Trees

After the record with the smallest key value is output, the winner tree of Figure 5.31 is to be restructured. Since the record with the smallest key value is in run 4, this restructuring involves inserting the next record from this run into the tree. The next record has key value 15. Tournaments are played between sibling nodes along the path from node 11 to the root. Since these sibling nodes represent the losers of tournaments played

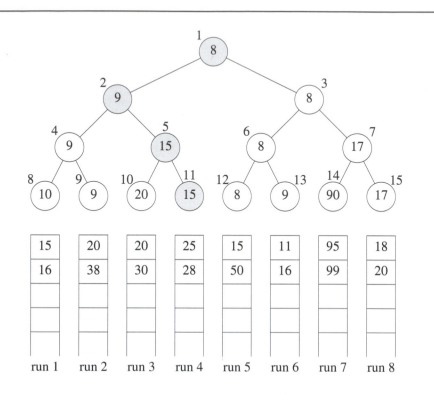

Figure 5.32: Winner tree of Figure 5.31 after one record has been output and the tree restructured (nodes that were changed are shaded)

earlier, we can simplify the restructuring process by placing in each nonleaf node a pointer to the record that loses the tournament rather than to the winner of the tournament. A selection tree in which each nonleaf node retains a pointer to the loser is called a *loser tree*. Figure 5.33 shows the loser tree that corresponds to the winner tree of Figure 5.31. For convenience, each node contains the key value of a record rather than a pointer to the record represented. The leaf nodes represent the first record in each run. An additional node, node 0, has been added to represent the overall winner of the tournament. Following the output of the overall winner, the tree is restructured by playing tournaments along the path from node 11 to node 1. The records with which these tournaments are to be played are readily available from the parent nodes. As a result, sibling nodes along the path from 11 to 1 are not accessed.

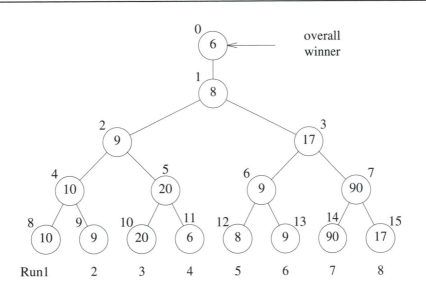

Figure 5.33: Loser tree corresponding to winner tree of Figure 5.31

EXERCISES

1. Write C++ class definitions for winner and loser trees.

2. Write a function to construct a winner tree for records R_i, $1 \leq i \leq k$, with key values K_i, $1 \leq i \leq k$. Let the tree nodes be T_i, $1 \leq i < k$, with T_i, $1 \leq i < k$, a pointer to the winner of a tournament. Assume that k is a power of 2. Show that this construction can be carried out in time $O(k)$.

3. Do Exercise 2 for the case when k is not restricted to being a power of 2.

4. Write a function to construct a loser tree for records R_i, $1 \leq i \leq k$, with key values K_i, $1 \leq i \leq k$. Let the tree nodes be T_i, $0 \leq i < k$, with T_i, $1 \leq i < k$, a pointer to the loser of a tournament and T_0 a pointer to the overall winner. Show that this construction can be carried out in time $O(k)$. Assume that k is a power of 2.

5. Do Exercise 4 for the case when k is not restricted to being a power of 2.

6. Write an algorithm, using a tree of losers, to carry out a k-way merge of k runs, $k \geq 2$. Use the data structures of Exercise 4 and assume the existence of a function to initialize the loser tree. This initialization function runs in linear time. Show that if there are n records in all k runs together, then the computing time is $O(n \log_2 k)$.

7. Do the previous exercise for the case in which a tree of winners is used. This time use the data structures of Exercise 2 and assume the existence of a linear-time procedure to initialize the winner tree.

8. Compare the performance of your algorithms for the preceding two exercises for the case $k = 8$. Generate eight runs of data, each having 100 records. Use a random number generator for this (the keys obtained from the random number generator will need to be sorted before the merge can begin). Measure the time taken to merge the eight runs using the two strategies. Approximately how much faster is the loser-tree scheme?

5.9 FORESTS

Definition: A *forest* is a set of $n \geq 0$ disjoint trees. □

A three-tree forest is shown in Figure 5.34. The concept of a forest is very close to that of a tree because if we remove the root of a tree, we obtain a forest. For example, removing the root of any binary tree produces a forest of two trees. In this section, we briefly consider several forest operations, including transforming a forest into a binary tree and forest traversals. In the next section, we use forests to represent disjoint sets.

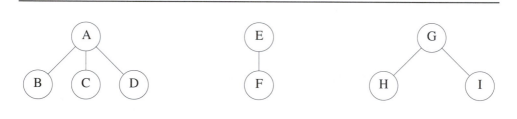

Figure 5.34: Three-tree forest

5.9.1 Transforming a Forest into a Binary Tree

To transform a forest into a single binary tree, we first obtain the binary tree representation of each of the trees in the forest and then link these binary trees together through the *RightChild* field of the root nodes. Using this transformation, the forest of Figure 5.34 becomes the binary tree of Figure 5.35.

We can define this transformation in a formal way as follows:

Definition: If $T_1, \cdots, T_n$ is a forest of trees, then the binary tree corresponding to this forest, denoted by $B(T_1, \cdots, T_n)$,

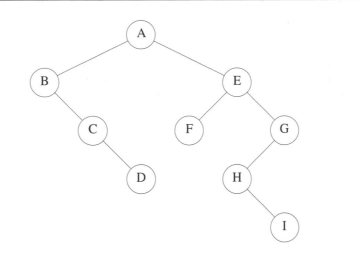

Figure 5.35: Binary tree representation of forest of Figure 5.34

(1) is empty if $n = 0$

(2) has root equal to root (T_1); has left subtree equal to $B(T_{11}, T_{12}, \cdots, T_{1m})$, where $T_{11}, \cdots, T_{1m}$ are the subtrees of root(T_1); and has right subtree $B(T_2, \cdots, T_n)$.
 □

5.9.2 Forest Traversals

Preorder and inorder traversals of the corresponding binary tree T of a forest F have a natural correspondence to traversals on F. Preorder traversal of T is equivalent to visiting the nodes of F in *forest preorder*, which is defined as follows:

(1) If F is empty then return.

(2) Visit the root of the first tree of F.

(3) Traverse the subtrees of the first tree in forest preorder.

(4) Traverse the remaining trees of F in forest preorder.

Inorder traversal of T is equivalent to visiting the nodes of F in *forest inorder*, which is defined as follows:

(1)   If *F* is empty then return.

(2)   Traverse the subtrees of the first tree in forest inorder.

(3)   Visit the root of the first tree.

(4)   Traverse the remaining trees in forest inorder.

The proofs that preorder and inorder traversals on the corresponding binary tree are the same as preorder and inorder traversals on the forest are left as exercises. There is no natural analog for postorder traversal of the corresponding binary tree of a forest. Nevertheless, we can define the *postorder traversal of a forest* as follows:

(1)   If *F* is empty then return.

(2)   Traverse the subtrees of the first tree of *F* in forest postorder.

(3)   Traverse the remaining trees of *F* in forest postorder.

(4)   Visit the root of the first tree of *F*.

In a *level-order traversal of a forest*, nodes are visited by level, beginning with the roots of each tree in the forest. Within each level, nodes are visited from left to right. One may verify that the level-order traversal of a forest and that of its associated binary tree do not necessarily yield the same result.

EXERCISES

1.   Write a C++ class definition for a forest of trees using templates.

2.   Define the inverse transformation of the one that creates the associated binary tree from a forest. Are these transformations unique?

3.   Prove that the preorder traversal of a forest and the preorder traversal of its associated binary tree give the same result.

4.   Prove that the inorder traversal of a forest and the inorder traversal of its associated binary tree give the same result.

5.   Prove that the postorder traversal of a forest and that of its corresponding binary tree do not necessarily yield the same result.

6.   Prove that the level-order traversal of a forest and that of its corresponding binary tree do not necessarily yield the same result.

7.   Write a nonrecursive function to traverse the associated binary tree of a forest in forest postorder. What are the time and space complexities of your function?

8.   Do the preceding exercise for the case of forest level-order traversal.

5.10   SET REPRESENTATION

5.10.1   Introduction

In this section we study the use of trees in the representation of sets. We shall assume that the elements of the sets are the numbers 0, 1, 2, 3, $\cdots$, $n-1$. These numbers might, in practice, be indices into a symbol table where the actual names of the elements are stored. We shall assume that the sets being represented are pairwise disjoint (i.e., if S_i and S_j, $i \neq j$, are two sets, then there is no element that is in both S_i and S_j). For example, when $n = 10$, the elements may be partitioned into three disjoint sets, $S_1 = \{0, 6, 7, 8\}$, $S_2 = \{1, 4, 9\}$, and $S_3 = \{2, 3, 5\}$. Figure 5.36 shows one possible representation for these sets. In this representation, each set is represented as a tree. Notice that for each set we have linked the nodes from the children to the parent, rather than our usual method of linking from the parent to the children. The reason for this change in linkage will become apparent when we discuss the implementation of set operations.

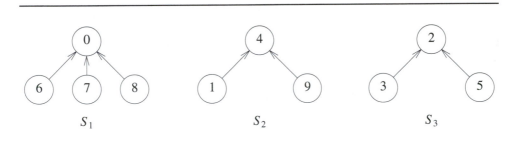

Figure 5.36: Possible tree representation of sets

The operations we wish to perform on these sets are:

(1)   *Disjoint set union*. If S_i and S_j are two disjoint sets, then their union $S_i \cup S_j = \{$all elements x such that x is in S_i or $S_j\}$. Thus, $S_1 \cup S_2 = \{0, 6, 7, 8, 1, 4, 9\}$. Since we have assumed that all sets are disjoint, we can assume that following the union of S_i and S_j, the sets S_i and S_j do not exist independently; that is, they are replaced by $S_i \cup S_j$ in the collection of sets.

(2)   *Find(i)*. Find the set containing element i. Thus, 3 is in set S_3, and 8 is in set S_1.

5.10.2   Union and Find Operations

Let us consider the union operation first. Suppose that we wish to obtain the union of S_1 and S_2 (see Figure 5.36). Since we have linked the nodes from children to parent, we simply make one of the trees a subtree of the other. $S_1 \cup S_2$ could then have one of the representations of Figure 5.37.

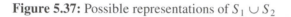

Figure 5.37: Possible representations of $S_1 \cup S_2$

To obtain the union of two sets, all that has to be done is to set the parent field of one of the roots to the other root. This can be accomplished easily if, with each set name, we keep a pointer to the root of the tree representing that set. If, in addition, each root has a pointer to the set name, then to determine which set an element is currently in, we follow parent links to the root of its tree and use the pointer to the set name. The data representation for S_1, S_2, and S_3 may then take the form shown in Figure 5.38.

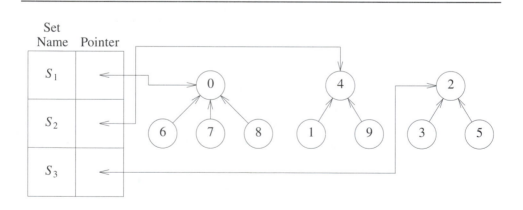

Figure 5.38: Data representation for S_1, S_2, and S_3

In presenting the union and find algorithms we shall ignore the actual set names and just identify sets by the roots of the trees representing them. This will simplify the discussion. The transition to set names is easy. If we determine that element i is in a tree

with root j, and j has a pointer to entry k in the set name table, then the set name is just
name[k]. If we wish to unite sets S_i and S_j, then we wish to unite the trees with roots
FindPointer(S_i) and *FindPointer*(S_j). Here *FindPointer* is a function that takes a set
name and determines the root of the tree that represents it. This is done by an examination of the [set name, pointer] table. As we shall see, in many applications the set name
is just the element at the root. The operation of *find*(i) now becomes: Determine the root
of the tree containing element i. The function *union*(i,j) requires two trees with roots i
and j to be joined. Another simplifying assumption we shall make is that the set elements are the numbers 0 through $n-1$.

Since the set elements are numbered 0 through $n-1$, we represent the tree nodes
using an array *parent*[*MaxElements*], where *MaxElements* is the maximum number of
elements. The ith element of this array represents the tree node that contains element i.
This array element gives the parent pointer of the corresponding tree node. Figure 5.39
shows this representation of the sets, S_1, S_2, and S_3 of Figure 5.36. Notice that root
nodes have a parent of -1.

i	[0]	[1]	[2]	[3]	[4]	[5]	[6]	[7]	[8]	[9]
parent	-1	4	-1	2	-1	2	0	0	0	4

Figure 5.39: Array representation of S_1, S_2, and S_3 of Figure 5.36

Program 5.25 contains the class definition and constructor for the data structure.

We can now implement *find*(i) by simply following the indices starting at i and continuing until we reach a node with parent value -1. For example, *find*(5) starts at 5 and then
moves to 5's parent, 2. Since *parent* [2] $= -1$, we have reached the root. The operation
union(i,j) is equally simple. We pass in two trees with roots i and j. Assuming that we
adopt the convention that the first tree becomes a subtree of the second, the statement
parent [i] $= j$ accomplishes the union. Program 5.26 implements the union and find
operations as just discussed.

Analysis of *SimpleUnion* and *SimpleFind*: Although these two algorithms are very
easy to state, their performance characteristics are not very good. For instance, if we
start off with n elements each in a set of its own (i.e., $S_i = \{i\}, 0 \leq i < n$), then the initial
configuration consists of a forest with n nodes, and *parent* [i] $= -1, 0 \leq i < n$. Now let us
process the following sequence of *union-find* operations:

$$union(0,1), \ union(1,2), \ union(2,3), \ union(3,4), \ \cdots, union(n-2,n-1)$$
$$find(0), find(1), \ \cdots, find(n-1)$$

This sequence results in the degenerate tree of Figure 5.40. Since the time taken for a
union is constant, the $n-1$ unions can be processed in time O(n). However, each find

---

```
class Sets {
public:
    // Set operations follow
    .
    .
    .
private:
    int *parent;
    int n; // number of set elements
};

Sets ::Sets(int sz = HeapSize)
{
    n = sz;
    parent = new int[sz ];
    for (int i = 0; i < n; i++) parent [i ] = −1;
}
```

Program 5.25: Class definition and constructor for *Sets*

```
void Sets ::SimpleUnion(int i, int j)
// Replace the disjoint sets with roots i and j, i != j with their union
{
    parent [i ] = j;
}

int Sets ::SimpleFind(int i)
// Find the root of the tree containing element i
{
    while (parent [i ] >= 0) i = parent [i ];
    return i;
}
```

Program 5.26: Simple algorithms for union and find

---

requires following a sequence of *parent* pointers from the element to be found to the root. Since the time required to process a find for an element at level i of a tree is $O(i)$, the total time needed to process the n finds is $O(\Sigma_{i=1}^{n} i) = O(n^2)$. $\square$

Figure 5.40: Degenerate tree

We can improve the performance of our union and find algorithms by avoiding the creation of degenerate trees. In order to accomplish this we shall make use of a weighting rule for $union(i,j)$.

Definition [*Weighting rule for union(i,j)*]: If the number of nodes in the tree with root i is less than the number in the tree with root j, then make j the parent of i; otherwise make i the parent of j. □

When we use the weighting rule to perform the sequence of set unions given before, we obtain the trees of Figure 5.41. In this figure, the unions have been modified so that the input parameter values correspond to the roots of the trees to be combined.

To implement the weighting rule, we need to know how many nodes there are in every tree. To do this easily, we maintain a *count* field in the root of every tree. If i is a root node, then $count[i]$ equals the number of nodes in that tree. Since all nodes other than the roots of trees have a non-negative number in the *parent* field, we can maintain the count in the *parent* field of the roots as a negative number. Initially, the *parent* field of all nodes contains -1. Using this convention, we obtain the union function of Program 5.27.

Analysis of *WeightedUnion* and *SimpleFind*: The time required to perform a union has increased somewhat but is still bounded by a constant (i.e., it is $O(1)$). The find algorithm remains unchanged. The maximum time to perform a find is determined by Lemma 5.5.

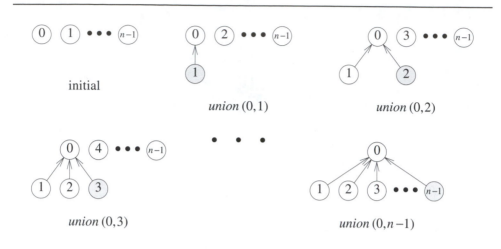

Figure 5.41: Trees obtained using the weighting rule

```
void Sets ::WeightedUnion(int i, int j)
// Union sets with roots i and j, i≠j, using the weighting rule.
// parent [i ] = −count [i ] and parent [j ] = −count [j ].
{
    int temp = parent [i ] + parent [j ];
    if (parent [i ] > parent [j ]) { // i has fewer nodes
        parent [i ] = j;
        parent [j ] = temp;
    }
    else { // j has fewer nodes (or i and j have the same number of nodes)
        parent [j ] = i;
        parent [i ] = temp;
    }
}
```

Program 5.27: Union algorithm with weighting rule

Lemma 5.5: Assume that we start with a forest of trees, each having one node. Let T be a tree with m nodes created as a result of a sequence of unions each performed using function *WeightedUnion*. The height of T is no greater than $\lfloor \log_2 m \rfloor + 1$.

Proof: The lemma is clearly true for $m = 1$. Assume it is true for all trees with i nodes, $i \leq m - 1$. We shall show that it is also true for $i = m$. Let T be a tree with m nodes created by function *WeightedUnion*. Consider the last union operation performed, $union(k,j)$. Let a be the number of nodes in tree j and $m - a$ the number in k. Without loss of generality we may assume $1 \leq a \leq m/2$. Then the height of T is either the same as that of k or is one more than that of j. If the former is the case, the height of T is $\leq \lfloor \log_2 (m - a) \rfloor + 1 \leq \lfloor \log_2 m \rfloor + 1$. If the latter is the case, the height of T is $\leq \lfloor \log_2 a \rfloor + 2 \leq \lfloor \log_2 m/2 \rfloor + 2 \leq \lfloor \log_2 m \rfloor + 1$. $\square$

Example 5.3 shows that the bound of Lemma 5.5 is achievable for some sequence of unions.

Example 5.3: Consider the behavior of function *WeightedUnion* on the following sequence of unions starting from the initial configuration $parent[i] = -count[i] = -1, 0 \leq i < n = 8$:

$$union(0,1), \quad union(2,3), \quad union(4,5), \quad union(6,7),$$
$$union(0,2), \quad union(4,6), \quad union(0,4)$$

The trees of Figure 5.42 are obtained. As is evident, the height of each tree with m nodes is $\lfloor \log_2 m \rfloor + 1$. $\square$

From Lemma 5.5, it follows that the time to process a find is $O(\log m)$ if there are m elements in a tree. If an intermixed sequence of $u - 1$ union and f find operations is to be processed, the time becomes $O(u + f \log u)$, as no tree has more than u nodes in it. Of course, we need $O(n)$ additional time to initialize the n-tree forest. $\square$

Surprisingly, further improvement is possible. This time the modification will be made in the find algorithm using the *collapsing rule*.

Definition [*Collapsing rule*]: If j is a node on the path from i to its root and $parent[i] \neq root(i)$, then set $parent[j]$ to $root(i)$. $\square$

Function *CollapsingFind* (Program 5.28) incorporates the collapsing rule.

Example 5.4: Consider the tree created by function *WeightedUnion* on the sequence of unions of Example 5.3. Now process the following eight finds:

$$find(7), find(7), \cdots, find(7)$$

If *SimpleFind* is used, each *find*(7) requires going up three parent link fields for a total of 24 moves to process all eight finds. When *CollapsingFind* is used, the first *find*(7) re-

(a) Initial height-1 trees

(b) Height-2 trees following *union* (0,1), (2,3), (4,5), and (6,7)

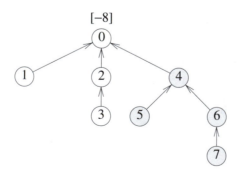

(c) Height-3 trees following *union* (0,2) and (4,6)

(d) Height-4 tree following *union* (0,4)

Figure 5.42: Trees achieving worst-case bound

```
int Sets ::CollapsingFind(int i)
// Find the root of the tree containing element i.
// Use the collapsing rule to collapse all nodes from i to the root
{
    for (int r = i; parent [r] >= 0; r = parent [r]); // find root
    while (i != r) {
        int s = parent [i];
        parent [i] = r;
        i = s;
    }
    return r;
}
```

Program 5.28: Find algorithm with collapsing rule

quires going up three links and then resetting two links. Note that even though only two parent links need to be reset, function *CollapsingFind* will actually reset three (the parent of 4 is reset to 0). Each of the remaining seven finds requires going up only one link field. The total cost is now only 13 moves. □

Analysis of *WeightedUnion* and *CollapsingFind*: Use of the collapsing rule roughly doubles the time for an individual find. However, it reduces the worst-case time over a sequence of finds. The worst-case complexity of processing a sequence of unions and finds using *WeightedUnion* and *CollapsingFind* is stated in Lemma 5.6. This lemma makes use of a function $\alpha(p,q)$ that is related to a functional inverse of Ackermann's function $A(i,j)$. These functions are defined as follows:

$$
\begin{aligned}
A(1,j) &= 2^j, & \text{for } j \geq 1 \\
A(i,1) &= A(i-1,2) & \text{for } i \geq 2 \\
A(i,j) &= A(i-1,A(i,j-1)) & \text{for } i,j \geq 2
\end{aligned}
$$

$$
\alpha(p,q) = \min\{z \geq 1 \mid A(z, \lfloor p/q \rfloor) > \log_2 q\}, \quad p \geq q \geq 1
$$

The function $A(i,j)$ is a very rapidly growing function. Consequently, α grows very slowly as p and q are increased. In fact, since $A(3,1) = 16$, $\alpha(p,q) \leq 3$ for $q < 2^{16} = 65,536$ and $p \geq q$. Since $A(4,1)$ is a very large number and in our application q will be the number, n, of set elements and p will be $n + f$ (f is the number of finds), $\alpha(p,q) \leq 4$ for all practical purposes. □

Lemma 5.6 [*Tarjan and Van Leeuwen*]: Assume that we start with a forest of trees, each having one node. Let $T(f,u)$ be the maximum time required to process any intermixed sequence of f finds and u unions. Assume that $u \geq n/2$. Then

$$k_1(n + f\,\alpha(f + n,n)) \le T(f,u) \le k_2(n + f\,\alpha(f + n,n))$$

for some positive constants k_1 and k_2. $\square$

The requirement that $u \ge n/2$ in Lemma 5.6, is really not significant, as when $u < n/2$, some elements are involved in no union operation. These elements remain in singleton sets throughout the sequence of union and find operations and can be eliminated from consideration, as find operations that involve these can be done in O(1) time each. Even though the function $\alpha(f,u)$ is a very slowly growing function, the complexity of our solution to the set representation problem is not linear in the number of unions and finds. The space requirements are one node for each element.

In the exercises, we explore alternatives to the weight rule and the collapsing rule that preserve the time bounds of Lemma 5.6.

5.10.3 Application to Equivalence Classes

Consider the equivalence pairs processing problem of Section 4.7. The equivalence classes to be generated may be regarded as sets. These sets are disjoint, as no polygon can be in two equivalence classes. Initially, all n polygons are in an equivalence class of their own; thus $parent[i] = -1, 0 \le i < n$. If an equivalence pair, $i \equiv j$, is to be processed, we must first determine the sets containing i and j. If these are different, then the two sets are to be replaced by their union. If the two sets are the same, then nothing is to be done, as the relation $i \equiv j$ is redundant; i and j are already in the same equivalence class. To process each equivalence pair we need to perform two finds and at most one union. Thus, if we have n polygons and m equivalence pairs, we need to spend O(n) time to set up the initial n-tree forest, and then we need to process $2m$ finds and at most min$\{n-1, m\}$ unions. (Note that after $n-1$ unions, all n polygons will be in the same equivalence class and no more unions can be performed.) If we use *WeightedUnion* and *CollapsingFind*, the total time to process the equivalence relations is O($n + m\alpha(2m, \min\{n-1, m\})$). Although this is slightly worse than the algorithm of Section 4.7, it needs less space and is on line. By "on line," we mean that as each equivalence is processed, we can tell which equivalence class each polygon is in.

Example 5.5: Consider the equivalence pairs example of Chapter 4. Initially, there are 12 trees, one for each variable. $parent[i] = -1, 0 \le i < 12$. The tree configuration following the processing of each equivalence pair is shown in Figure 5.43. Each tree represents an equivalence class. It is possible to determine if two elements are currently in the same equivalence class at each stage of the processing simply by making two finds. $\square$

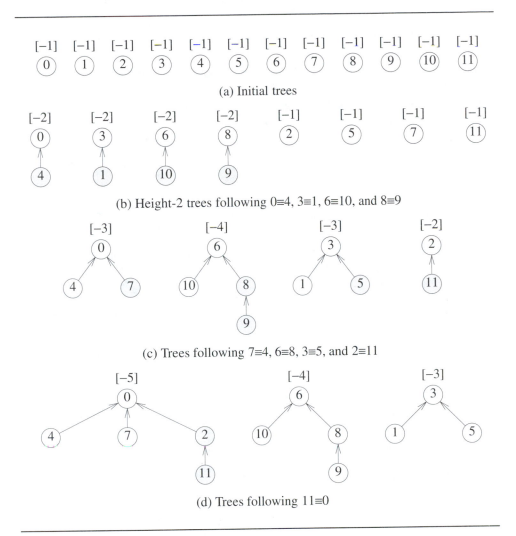

(a) Initial trees

(b) Height-2 trees following 0≡4, 3≡1, 6≡10, and 8≡9

(c) Trees following 7≡4, 6≡8, 3≡5, and 2≡11

(d) Trees following 11≡0

Figure 5.43: Trees for Example 5.5

EXERCISES

1. Suppose we start with n sets, each containing a distinct element.

    (a) Show that if u unions are performed, then no set contains more than $u + 1$ elements.

    (b) Show that at most $n - 1$ unions can be performed before the number of sets becomes 1.

(c) Show that if fewer than $\lceil n/2 \rceil$ unions are performed, then at least one set with a single element in it remains.

(d) Show that if u unions are performed, then at least $\max\{n - 2u, 0\}$ singleton sets remain.

2. Using the result of Example 5.5, draw the trees after processing the instruction *union*(11,9).

3. Experimentally compare the performance of *SimpleUnion* and *SimpleFind* (Program 5.26) with *WeightedUnion* (Program 5.27) and *CollapsingFind* (Program 5.28). For this, generate a random sequence of union and find operations.

4. (a) Write a function *HeightUnion* that uses the *height rule* for union operations instead of the weighting rule. This rule is defined below:

    Definition [*Height Rule*]: If the height of tree i is less than that of tree j, then make j the parent of i, otherwise make i the parent of j. □

    Your function must run in $O(1)$ time and should maintain the height of each tree as a negative number in the *parent* field of the root.

    (b) Show that the height bound of Lemma 5.5 applies to trees constructed using the height rule.

    (c) Give an example of a sequence of unions that start with singleton sets and create trees whose height equals the upper bound given in Lemma 5.5. Assume that each union is performed using the height rule.

    (d) Experiment with functions *WeightedUnion* (Program 5.27) and *HeightUnion* to determine which one produces better results when used in conjunction with function *CollapsingFind* (Program 5.28).

5. (a) Write a function *SplittingFind* that uses *path splitting* for the find operations instead of path collapsing. This is defined below:

    Definition [*Path Splitting*]: In path splitting, the parent pointer in each node (except the root and its child) on the path from i to the root is changed to point to the node's grandparent. □

    Note that when path splitting is used, a single pass from i to the root suffices. Tarjan and Van Leeuwen have shown that Lemma 5.6 holds when path splitting is used in conjunction with either the weight or height rule for unions.

    (b) Experiment with functions *CollapsingFind* (Program 5.28) and *SplittingFind* to determine which produces better results when used in conjunction with function *WeightedUnion* (Program 5.27).

6. (a) Write a function *HalvingFind* that uses *path halving* for the find operations instead of path collapsing. This is defined below:

    Definition [*Path Halving*]: In path halving, the parent pointer of every other node (except the root and its child) on the path from i to the root is changed to point to the node's grandparent. □

Note that path halving, like path splitting (Exercise 5) can be implemented with a single pass from i to the root. However, in path halving, only half as many pointers are changed as in path splitting. Tarjan and Van Leeuwen have shown that Lemma 5.6 holds when path halving is used in conjunction with either the weight or height rule for unions.

(b)   Experiment with functions *CollapsingFind* and *HalvingFind* to determine which one produces better results when used in conjunction with function *WeightedUnion*.

5.11   AN OBJECT-ORIENTED SYSTEM OF TREE DATA STRUCTURES

An object-oriented system is one in which various ADTs represented by classes are related to each other through public inheritance. While we have seen examples in which two ADTs are related to each other through inheritance, we have not studied a system consisting of a *large number* of interrelated ADTs. In this section, we attempt to illustrate how some of the tree data structures that we have studied in this chapter can be organized into an object-oriented system.

Figure 5.44 shows an inheritance graph that shows the relationships between a number of tree data structures.

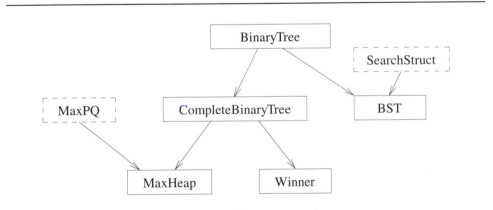

Figure 5.44: Inheritance graph showing the relationship between different ADTs.

Dashed boxes represent abstract base classes, while solid boxes represent classes that are not abstract base classes. An arrow drawn from one ADT to another implies that the second ADT is publicly derived from the first. Class *MaxPQ* is an abstract base class representing the max-priority queue ADT. Class *SearchStruct* is an abstract base class, which defines the standard search structure operations such as *Search*, *Insert*, and *Delete* as pure virtual functions. Class *BST* represents a binary search tree, which is a search structure, and is therefore derived from *SearchStruct*. Class *MaxHeap* is a max priority queue and is derived from *MaxPQ*. The pure virtual functions must be defined in the derived class ensuring that the abstract base class operations are implemented. Classes *CompleteBinaryTree* and *BST* both represent binary trees and are derived from class *BinaryTree*. Classes *WinnerTree* and *MaxHeap* are both complete binary trees and are derived from class *CompleteBinaryTree*. Notice that classes *MaxHeap* and *BST* are derived from two classes, thus inheriting members from each. This is known as *multiple inheritance*. Program 5.29 and Program 5.30 show the class definitions for the ADTs depicted in Figure 5.44.

Notice that class *BinaryTree* is implemented using nodes and pointers. The definition of the node class *BinaryTreeNode* is nested inside the definition of class *BinaryTree*. Meanwhile, class *CompleteBinaryTree* is implemented using arrays. Class *BST* inherits its representation from class *BinaryTree*, while classes *WinnerTree* and *MaxHeap* inherit their representations from class *CompleteBinaryTree*. For simplicity, we only consider the constructor and the inorder traversal operator. Observe that the constructors for *Max-Heap* and *WinnerTree* are implemented by invoking the constructor for *CompleteBinaryTree*.

Program 5.31 shows the implementations of the inorder traversal operations on classes *BinaryTree* and *CompleteBinaryTree*. The recursive inorder traversal is implemented using two functions: the driver and the workhorse. The driver and workhorse defined for class *BinaryTree* are inherited by class *BST*. These operations are redefined in class *CompleteBinaryTree*. The redefined operations are inherited by classes *MaxHeap* and *WinnerTree*. Note that the workhorse for class *CompleteBinaryTree* takes an integer argument, while the workhorse for *BinaryTree* takes a node-pointer argument. Even though the two have different signatures, the former *hides* the latter in class *CompleteBinaryTree*. This means that the workhorse of class *CompleteBinaryTree* cannot be invoked with a node-pointer argument.

EXERCISES

1. Enlarge the object-oriented system of this section by adding classes *MinPQ*, *MinHeap*, and *LoserTree*.

2. Modify the object-oriented system of this section by using inorder iterator classes to perform the inorder traversal.

3. Add a function *GetSize()* that returns the number of elements in a tree. This function must be defined for each tree ADT defined in the object-oriented system of this section.

```
enum Boolean {FALSE, TRUE};
const int DefaultSize = 20 ;

class MaxPQ {
public:
    virtual void Insert(const int) = 0; // pure virtual functions
    virtual int* DeleteMax(int&) = 0;
};

class SearchStruct {
public:
    virtual void Insert(const int) = 0; // pure virtual functions
    virtual int* Delete(int&) = 0;
    virtual Boolean Search(const int) = 0;
};

class BinaryTree {
public:
    virtual void inorder(); // driver
    BinaryTree() {root = 0;}; // constructor
protected:
    class BinaryTreeNode { // nested class
    public:
        BinaryTreeNode *LeftChild, *RightChild;
        int data;
    };
    BinaryTreeNode *root;
    virtual void inorder(BinaryTreeNode *);                    // workhorse
};
```

Program 5.29: Class definitions of base classes depicted in Figure 5.44

5.12 COUNTING BINARY TREES

As a conclusion to our chapter on trees, we consider three disparate problems that amazingly have the same solution. We wish to determine the number of distinct binary trees having n nodes, the number of distinct permutations of the numbers from 1 through n obtainable by a stack, and the number of distinct ways of multiplying $n + 1$ matrices. Let us begin with a quick look at these problems.

```
class CompleteBinaryTree : public BinaryTree {
public:
    virtual void inorder(); // driver
    CompleteBinaryTree(int sz = DefaultSize) : MaxSize(sz), n(0) {
        tree = new int[MaxSize + 1];
    };
protected:
    int *tree, MaxSize, n ;
    virtual void inorder(int); // hides BinaryTree::inorder(BinaryTreeNode *)
};


class MaxHeap : public MaxPQ, public CompleteBinaryTree {
// multiple inheritance
public:
    MaxHeap (int sz = DefaultSize) : CompleteBinaryTree(sz) {};
    virtual void Insert(const int);
    virtual int* DeleteMax(int&);
};


class WinnerTree : public CompleteBinaryTree {
public:
    WinnerTree (int sz = DefaultSize) : CompleteBinaryTree(sz) {};
};


class BST : public SearchStruct, public BinaryTree {
// multiple inheritance
public:
    BST( ) {root = 0 ;};
    virtual void Insert(const int);
    virtual int* Delete(int&);
    virtual Boolean Search(const int);
};
```

Program 5.30: Class definitions of derived ADTs depicted in Figure 5.44

5.12.1 Distinct Binary Trees

We know that if $n = 0$ or $n = 1$, there is only one binary tree. If $n = 2$, then there are two distinct trees (Figure 5.45), and if $n = 3$, there are five such trees (Figure 5.46). How many distinct trees are there with n nodes? Before deriving a solution, we will examine the two remaining problems. You might attempt to sketch out a solution of your own before reading further.

```
void BinaryTree::inorder() { inorder(root);}

void BinaryTree::inorder(BinaryTreeNode *CurrentNode) {
    if (CurrentNode) {
      inorder(CurrentNode→LeftChild);
      cout << CurrentNode→data;
      inorder(CurrentNode→RightChild);
    }
}

void CompleteBinaryTree::inorder() { inorder(1);}

void CompleteBinaryTree::inorder(int current) {
    if (current <= n) {
      inorder(2*current);
      cout << tree [current ];
      inorder(2*current+1);
    }
}
```

Program 5.31: Inorder traversal of *BinaryTree* and *CompleteBinaryTree*

and

Figure 5.45: Distinct binary trees with $n = 2$

5.12.2   Stack Permutations

In Section 5.3, we introduced preorder, inorder, and postorder traversals and indicated that each traversal requires a stack. Suppose we have the preorder sequence $A\ B\ C\ D\ E\ F$ $G\ H\ I$ and the inorder sequence $B\ C\ A\ E\ D\ G\ H\ F\ I$ of the same binary tree. Does such a pair of sequences uniquely define a binary tree? Put another way, can this pair of sequences come from more than one binary tree?

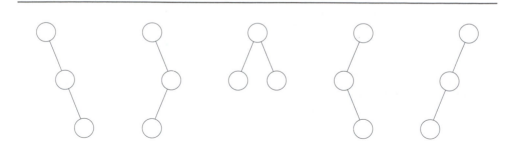

Figure 5.46: Distinct binary trees with $n = 3$

To construct the binary tree from these sequences, we look at the first letter in the preorder sequence, A. This letter must be the root of the tree by definition of the preorder traversal (VLR). We also know by definition of the inorder traversal (LVR) that all nodes preceding A in the inorder sequence ($B\ C$) are in the left subtree, and the remaining nodes ($E\ D\ G\ H\ F\ I$) are in the right subtree. Figure 5.47(a) is our first approximation to the correct tree.

Moving right in the preorder sequence, we find B as the next root. Since no node precedes B in the inorder sequence, B has an empty left subtree, which means that C is in its right subtree. Figure 5.47(b) is the next approximation. Continuing in this way, we arrive at the binary tree of Figure 5.48(a). By formalizing this argument (see the exercises), we can verify that every binary tree has a unique pair of preorder/inorder sequences.

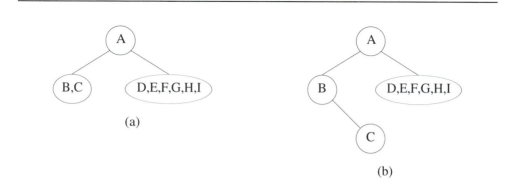

Figure 5.47: Constructing a binary tree from its inorder and preorder sequences

Let the nodes of an n-node binary tree be numbered from 1 through n. The inorder permutation defined by such a binary tree is the order in which its nodes are visited during an inorder traversal of the tree. A preorder permutation is similarly defined.

As an example, consider the binary tree of Figure 5.48(a) with the node numbering of Figure 5.48(b). Its preorder permutation is 1, 2, $\cdots$, 9, and its inorder permutation is 2, 3, 1, 5, 4, 7, 8, 6, 9.

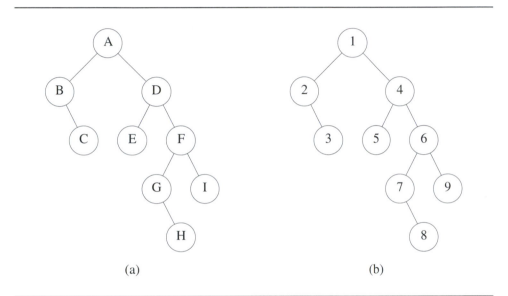

(a)   (b)

Figure 5.48: Binary tree constructed from its inorder and preorder sequences

If the nodes of the tree are numbered such that its preorder permutation is 1, 2, $\cdots$, n, then from our earlier discussion it follows that distinct binary trees define distinct inorder permutations. Thus, the number of distinct binary trees is equal to the number of distinct inorder permutations obtainable from binary trees having the preorder permutation, 1, 2, $\cdots$, n.

Using the concept of an inorder permutation, we can show that the number of distinct permutations obtainable by passing the numbers 1 through n through a stack and deleting in all possible ways is equal to the number of distinct binary trees with n nodes (see the exercises). If we start with the numbers 1, 2, and 3, then the possible permutations obtainable by a stack are

$$(1, 2, 3) \ (1, 3, 2) \ (2, 1, 3) \ (2, 3, 1) \ (3, 2, 1)$$

Obtaining (3, 1, 2) is impossible. Each of these five permutations corresponds to one of the five distinct binary trees with three nodes (Figure 5.49).

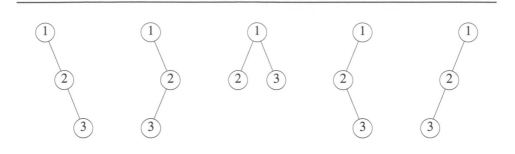

Figure 5.49: Binary trees corresponding to five permutations

5.12.3 Matrix Multiplication

Another problem that surprisingly has a connection with the previous two involves the product of n matrices. Suppose that we wish to compute the product of n matrices:

$$M_1 * M_2 * \cdots * M_n$$

Since matrix multiplication is associative, we can perform these multiplications in any order. We would like to know how many different ways we can perform these multiplications. For example, if $n = 3$, there are two possibilities:

$$(M_1 * M_2) * M_3$$
$$M_1 * (M_2 * M_3)$$

and if $n = 4$, there are five:

$$((M_1 * M_2) * M_3) * M_4$$
$$(M_1 * (M_2 * M_3)) * M_4$$
$$M_1 * ((M_2 * M_3) * M_4)$$
$$(M_1 * (M_2 * (M_3 * M_4)))$$
$$((M_1 * M_2) * (M_3 * M_4))$$

Let b_n be the number of different ways to compute the product of n matrices. Then $b_2 = 1$, $b_3 = 2$, and $b_4 = 5$. Let M_{ij}, $i \leq j$, be the product $M_i * M_{i+1} * \cdots * M_j$. The product we wish to compute is M_{1n}. We may compute M_{1n} by computing any one of the products $M_{1i} * M_{i+1,n}$, $1 \leq i \leq n$. The number of distinct ways to obtain M_{1i} and $M_{i+1,n}$ are b_i and b_{n-i}, respectively. Therefore, letting $b_1 = 1$, we have

$$b_n = \sum_{i=1}^{n-1} b_i \, b_{n-i}, n > 1$$

If we can determine the expression for b_n only in terms of n, then we have a solution to our problem.

Now instead let b_n be the number of distinct binary trees with n nodes. Again an expression for b_n in terms of n is what we want. Then we see that b_n is the sum of all the possible binary trees formed in the following way: a root and two subtrees with b_i and b_{n-i-1} nodes, for $0 \le i < n$ (Figure 5.50). This explanation says that

$$b_n = \sum_{i=0}^{n-1} b_i \, b_{n-i-1} \,, \; n \ge 1 \,, \text{ and } b_0 = 1 \tag{5.3}$$

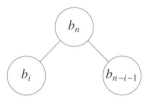

Figure 5.50: Decomposing b_n

This formula and the previous one are essentially the same. Therefore, the number of binary trees with n nodes, the number of permutations of 1 to n obtainable with a stack, and the number of ways to multiply $n + 1$ matrices are all equal.

5.12.4   Number of Distinct Binary Trees

To obtain the number of distinct binary trees with n nodes, we must solve the recurrence of Eq. (5.3). To begin we let

$$B(x) = \sum_{i \ge 0} b_i \, x^i \tag{5.4}$$

which is the generating function for the number of binary trees. Next observe that by the recurrence relation we get the identity

$$xB^2(x) = B(x) - 1$$

Using the formula to solve quadratics and the fact that $B(0) = b_0 = 1$ (Eq.(5.3)), we get

$$B(x) = \frac{1 - \sqrt{1-4x}}{2x}$$

We can use the binomial theorem to expand $(1 - 4x)^{1/2}$ to obtain

$$B(x) = \frac{1}{2x} \left[1 - \sum_{n \ge 0} \binom{1/2}{n} (-4x)^n \right] = \sum_{m \ge 0} \binom{1/2}{m+1} (-1)^m \, 2^{2m+1} \, x^m \tag{5.5}$$

Comparing Eqs. (5.4) and (5.5), we see that b_n, which is the coefficient of x^n in $B(x)$, is

$$\begin{bmatrix} 1/2 \\ n+1 \end{bmatrix} (-1)^n \, 2^{2n+1}$$

Some simplification yields the more compact form

$$b_n = \frac{1}{n+1} \begin{bmatrix} 2n \\ n \end{bmatrix}$$

which is approximately

$$b_n = O(4^n/n^{3/2})$$

EXERCISES

1. Prove that every binary tree is uniquely defined by its preorder and inorder sequences.

2. Do the inorder and postorder sequences of a binary tree uniquely define the binary tree? Prove your answer.

3. Do the inorder and preorder sequences of a binary tree uniquely define the binary tree? Prove your answer.

4. Do the inorder and level-order sequences of a binary tree uniquely define the binary tree? Prove your answer.

5. Write an algorithm to construct the binary tree with given preorder and inorder sequences.

6. Repeat Exercise 5 with the inorder and postorder sequences.

7. Prove that the number of distinct permutations of $1, 2, \cdots, n$ obtainable by a stack is equal to the number of distinct binary trees with n nodes. (Hint: Use the concept of an inorder permutation of a tree with preorder permutation $1, 2, \cdots, n$).

5.13 REFERENCES AND SELECTED READINGS

For other representations of trees, see *The Art of Computer Programming: Fundamental Algorithms*, Second Edition, by D. Knuth, Addison-Wesley, Reading, MA, 1973.

For the use of trees in generating optimal compiled code, see *Compilers: Principles, Techniques, and Tools*, by A. Aho, R. Sethi, and J. Ullman, Addison-Wesley, Reading, MA, 1986.

Tree traversal algorithms may be found in "Scanning list structures without stacks and tag bits," by G. Lindstrom, *Information Processing Letters*, 2:2, 1973, pp. 47-51, and "Simple algorithms for traversing a tree without an auxiliary stack," by B. Dwyer, *Information Processing Letters*, 2:5, 1973, pp. 143-145.

For more on data structures for the set representation problems see ''Worst case analysis of set union algorithms,'' by R. Tarjan and J. Van Leeuwen, *Journal of the ACM*, 31:2, 1984, pp. 245-281.

CHAPTER 6

GRAPHS

6.1 THE GRAPH ABSTRACT DATA TYPE

6.1.1 Introduction

The first recorded evidence of the use of graphs dates back to 1736, when Leonhard Euler used them to solve the now classical Königsberg bridge problem. In the town of Königsberg (now Kaliningrad) the river Pregel (Pregolya) flows around the island Kneiphof and then divides into two. There are, therefore, four land areas that have this river on its borders (see Figure 6.1(a)). These land areas are interconnected by seven bridges labeled $a-g$. The land areas themselves are labeled $A-D$. The Königsberg bridge problem is to determine whether, starting at one land area, it is possible to walk across all the bridges exactly once in returning to the starting land area. One possible walk is

- start from land area B
- walk across bridge a to island A
- take bridge e to area D
- take bridge g to C
- take bridge d to A

- take bridge *b* to *B*
- take bridge *f* to *D*

This walk does not go across all bridges exactly once, nor does it return to the starting land area *B*. Euler answered the Königsberg bridge problem in the negative: The people of Königsberg will not be able to walk across each bridge exactly once and return to the starting point. He solved the problem by representing the land areas as vertices and the bridges as edges in a graph (actually a multigraph) as in Figure 6.1(b). His solution is elegant and applies to all graphs. Defining the *degree* of a vertex to be the number of edges incident to it, Euler showed that there is a walk starting at any vertex, going through each edge exactly once and terminating at the start vertex iff the degree of each vertex is even. A walk that does this is called *Eulerian*. There is no Eulerian walk for the Königsberg bridge problem, as all four vertices are of odd degree.

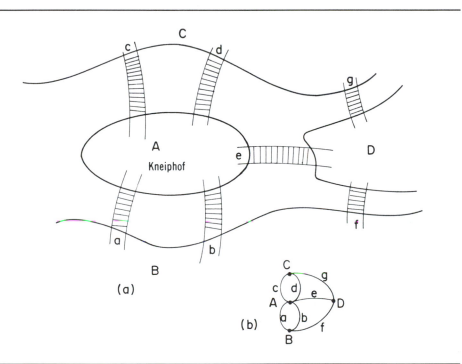

Figure 6.1: (a) Section of the river Pregel in Königsberg; (b) Euler's graph

Since this first application, graphs have been used in a wide variety of applications. Some of these applications are: analysis of electrical circuits, finding shortest routes, project planning, identification of chemical compounds, statistical mechanics, genetics, cybernetics, linguistics, social sciences, and so on. Indeed, it might well be said that of all mathematical structures, graphs are the most widely used.

6.1.2 Definitions

A graph, G, consists of two sets, V and E. V is a finite, nonempty set of *vertices*. E is a set of pairs of vertices; these pairs are called *edges*. $V(G)$ and $E(G)$ will represent the sets of vertices and edges, respectively, of graph G. We will also write $G = (V,E)$ to represent a graph. In an *undirected graph* the pair of vertices representing any edge is unordered. Thus, the pairs (u,v) and (v,u) represent the same edge. In a *directed graph* each edge is represented by a directed pair $<u,v>$; u is the *tail* and v the *head* of the edge. Therefore, $<v,u>$ and $<u,v>$ represent two different edges. Figure 6.2 shows three graphs: G_1, G_2, and G_3. The graphs G_1 and G_2 are undirected. G_3 is a directed graph.

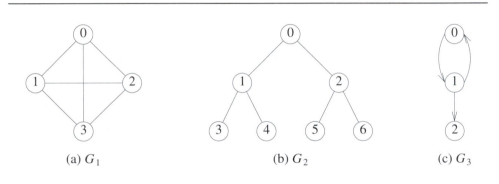

(a) G_1 (b) G_2 (c) G_3

Figure 6.2: Three sample graphs

The set representation of each of these graphs is

$V(G_1) = \{0,1,2,3\}; \quad E(G_1) = \{(0,1),(0,2),(0,3),(1,2),(1,3),(2,3)\}$
$V(G_2) = \{0,1,2,3,4,5,6\}; \quad E(G_2) = \{(0,1),(0,2),(1,3),(1,4),(2,5),(2,6)\}$
$V(G_3) = \{0,1,2\}; \quad E(G_3) = \{<0,1>,<1,0>,<1,2>\}.$

Notice that the edges of a directed graph are drawn with an arrow from the tail to the head. The graph G_2 is a tree; the graphs G_1 and G_3 are not.

Since we define the edges and vertices of a graph as sets, we impose the following restrictions on graphs:

(1)   A graph may not have an edge from a vertex, v, back to itself. That is, edges of the form (v, v) and $<v, v>$ are not legal. Such edges are known as *self edges* or *self loops*. If we permit self edges, we obtain a data object referred to as a *graph with self edges*. An example is shown in Figure 6.3(a).

(2) A graph may not have multiple occurrences of the same edge. If we remove this restriction, we obtain a data object referred to as a *multigraph* (see Figure 6.3(b)).

(a) Graph with a self edge   (b) Multigraph

Figure 6.3: Examples of graphlike structures

The number of distinct unordered pairs (u,v) with $u \neq v$ in a graph with n vertices is $n(n-1)/2$. This is the maximum number of edges in any n-vertex, undirected graph. An n-vertex, undirected graph with exactly $n(n-1)/2$ edges is said to be *complete*. The graph G_1 of Figure 6.2(a) is the complete graph on four vertices, whereas G_2 and G_3 are not complete graphs. In the case of a directed graph on n vertices, the maximum number of edges is $n(n-1)$.

If (u,v) is an edge in $E(G)$, then we shall say the vertices u and v are *adjacent* and that the edge (u,v) is *incident* on vertices u and v. The vertices adjacent to vertex 1 in G_2 are 3, 4, and 0. The edges incident on vertex 2 in G_2 are (0,2), (2,5), and (2,6). If $<u,v>$ is a directed edge, then vertex u is *adjacent to* v, and v is *adjacent from* u. The edge $<u,v>$ is incident to u and v. In G_3, the edges incident to vertex 1 are $<0,1>$, $<1,0>$, and $<1,2>$.

A *subgraph* of G is a graph G' such that $V(G') \subseteq V(G)$ and $E(G') \subseteq E(G)$. Figure 6.4 shows some of the subgraphs of G_1 and G_3.

A *path* from vertex u to vertex v in graph G is a sequence of vertices $u, i_1, i_2, \cdots, i_k, v$ such that $(u, i_1), (i_1, i_2), \cdots, (i_k, v)$ are edges in $E(G)$. If G' is directed, then the path consists of $<u, i_1>, <i_1, i_2>, \cdots, <i_k, v>$ edges in $E(G')$. The *length* of a path is the number of edges on it. A *simple path* is a path in which all vertices except possibly the first and last are distinct. A path such as (0,1), (1,3), (3,2), is also written as 0,1,3,2. Paths 0,1,3,2 and 0,1,3,1 of G_1 are both of length 3. The first is a simple path; the second is not. 0,1,2 is a simple directed path in G_3. 0,1,2,1 is not a path in G_3, as the edge $<2,1>$ is not in $E(G_3)$.

A *cycle* is a simple path in which the first and last vertices are the same. 0,1,2,0 is a cycle in G_1. 0,1,0 is a cycle in G_3. For the case of directed graphs we normally add the prefix "directed" to the terms cycle and path.

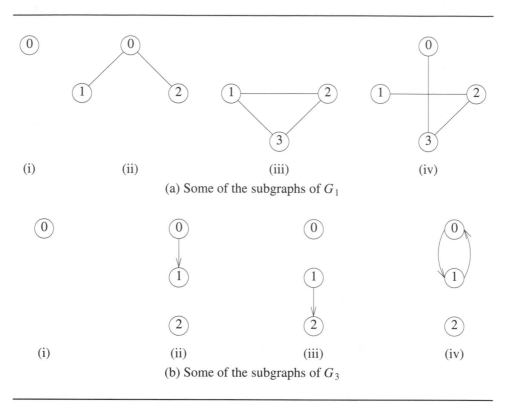

(a) Some of the subgraphs of G_1

(b) Some of the subgraphs of G_3

Figure 6.4: Some subgraphs

In an undirected graph, G, two vertices u and v are said to be *connected* iff there is a path in G from u to v (since G is undirected, this means there must also be a path from v to u). An undirected graph is said to be connected iff for every pair of distinct vertices u and v in $V(G)$ there is a path from u to v in G. Graphs G_1 and G_2 are connected, whereas G_4 of Figure 6.5 is not. A *connected component* (or simply a component), H, of an undirected graph is a *maximal* connected subgraph. By maximal, we mean that G contains no other subgraph that is both connected and properly contains H. G_4 has two components, H_1 and H_2 (see Figure 6.5).

A *tree* is a connected acyclic (i.e., has no cycles) graph.

A directed graph G is said to be *strongly connected* iff for every pair of distinct vertices u and v in $V(G)$, there is a directed path from u to v and also from v to u. The graph G_3 is not strongly connected, as there is no path from vertex 2 to 1. A *strongly connected component* is a maximal subgraph that is strongly connected. G_3 has two strongly connected components (see Figure 6.6).

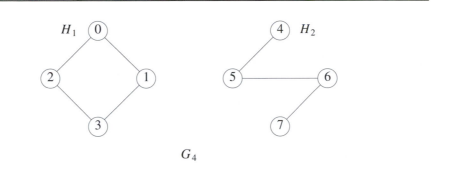

Figure 6.5: A graph with two connected components

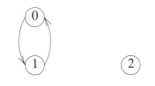

Figure 6.6: Strongly connected components of G_3

The degree of a vertex is the number of edges incident to that vertex. The degree of vertex 0 in G_1 is 3. If G is a directed graph, we define the *in-degree* of a vertex v to be the number of edges for which v is the head. The *out-degree* is defined to be the number of edges for which v is the tail. Vertex 1 of G_3 has in-degree 1, out-degree 2, and degree 3. If d_i is the degree of vertex i in a graph G with n vertices and e edges, then the number of edges is

$$e = (\sum_{i=0}^{n-1} d_i)/2$$

In the remainder of this chapter, we shall refer to a directed graph as a *digraph*. When we use the term *graph*, we assume that it is an undirected graph. Now that we have defined all the terminology we will need, let us consider the graph as an ADT. The resulting specification is given in ADT 6.1.

The operations in ADT 6.1 are a basic set in that they allow us to create any arbitrary graph and do some elementary tests. In later sections of this chapter we will see

---

class *Graph*

{

// **objects**: A nonempty set of vertices and a set of undirected edges,

// where each edge is a pair of vertices.

public:

   Graph (); // Create an empty graph

   void *InsertVertex*(*Vertex v*); // Insert *v* into graph; *v* has no incident edges

   void *InsertEdge*(*Vertex u, Vertex v*);
   // insert edge (*u,v*) into graph

   void *DeleteVertex*(*Vertex v*);
   // Delete *v* and all edges incident to it

   void *DeleteEdge*(*Vertex u, Vertex v*);
   // Delete edge (*u, v*) from the graph

   Boolean IsEmpty ();
   // **if** graph has no vertices return TRUE (1); **else** return FALSE (0)

   List<Vertex> Adjacent(*Vertex v*);
   // return a list of all vertices that are adjacent to *v*

};

ADT 6.1: Abstract data type *Graph*

functions that traverse a graph (depth-first or breadth-first search) and that determine if a graph has special properties (e.g., connected, biconnected, etc.).

6.1.3   Graph Representations

Although several representations for graphs are possible, we shall study only the three most commonly used: adjacency matrices, adjacency lists, and adjacency multilists. Once again, the choice of a particular representation will depend upon the application one has in mind and the functions one expects to perform on the graph.

6.1.3.1 Adjacency Matrix

Let $G = (V, E)$ be a graph with n vertices, $n \geq 1$. The adjacency matrix of G is a two-dimensional $n \times n$ array, say A, with the property that $A[i][j] = 1$ iff the edge (i, j) ($<i, j>$ for a directed graph) is in $E(G)$. $A[i][j] = 0$ if there is no such edge in G. The adjacency matrices for the graphs G_1, G_3, and G_4 are shown in Figure 6.7. The adjacency matrix for an undirected graph is symmetric, as the edge (i, j) is in $E(G)$ iff the edge (j, i) is also in $E(G)$. The adjacency matrix for a directed graph may not be symmetric (as is the case for G_3). The space needed to represent a graph using its adjacency matrix is n^2 bits. About half this space can be saved in the case of undirected graphs by storing only the upper or lower triangle of the matrix.

$$
\begin{array}{c}
\begin{array}{c}
\;0\;1\;2\;3 \\
\begin{array}{c|cccc}
0 & 0 & 1 & 1 & 1 \\
1 & 1 & 0 & 1 & 1 \\
2 & 1 & 1 & 0 & 1 \\
3 & 1 & 1 & 1 & 0 \\
\end{array} \\[4pt]
\text{(a) } G_1
\end{array}
\qquad
\begin{array}{c}
\;0\;1\;2 \\
\begin{array}{c|ccc}
0 & 0 & 1 & 0 \\
1 & 1 & 0 & 1 \\
2 & 0 & 0 & 0 \\
\end{array} \\[4pt]
\text{(b) } G_3
\end{array}
\qquad
\begin{array}{c}
\;0\;1\;2\;3\;4\;5\;6\;7 \\
\begin{array}{c|cccccccc}
0 & 0 & 1 & 1 & 0 & 0 & 0 & 0 & 0 \\
1 & 1 & 0 & 0 & 1 & 0 & 0 & 0 & 0 \\
2 & 1 & 0 & 0 & 1 & 0 & 0 & 0 & 0 \\
3 & 0 & 1 & 1 & 0 & 0 & 0 & 0 & 0 \\
4 & 0 & 0 & 0 & 0 & 0 & 1 & 0 & 0 \\
5 & 0 & 0 & 0 & 0 & 1 & 0 & 1 & 0 \\
6 & 0 & 0 & 0 & 0 & 0 & 1 & 0 & 1 \\
7 & 0 & 0 & 0 & 0 & 0 & 0 & 1 & 0 \\
\end{array} \\[4pt]
\text{(c) } G_4
\end{array}
$$

Figure 6.7: Adjacency matrices

From the adjacency matrix, one may readily determine if there is an edge connecting any two vertices i and j. For an undirected graph the degree of any vertex i is its row sum:

$$\sum_{j=0}^{n-1} A[i][j]$$

For a directed graph the row sum is the out-degree, and the column sum is the in-degree.

Suppose we want to answer a nontrivial question about graphs, such as, How many edges are there in G? or, Is G connected? Adjacency matrices will require at least $O(n^2)$ time, as $n^2 - n$ entries of the matrix (diagonal entries are zero) have to be examined. When graphs are sparse (i.e., most of the terms in the adjacency matrix are zero) one would expect that the former question could be answered in significantly less time, say $O(e + n)$, where e is the number of edges in G, and $e << n^2/2$. Such a speed-up can be made possible through the use of a representation in which only the edges that are in G are explicitly stored. This leads to the next representation for graphs, adjacency lists.

6.1.3.2 Adjacency Lists

In this representation of graphs, the n rows of the adjacency matrix are represented as n linked lists. There is one list for each vertex in G. The nodes in list i represent the vertices that are adjacent from vertex i. Each node has at least two fields: *data* and *link*. The *data* fields contain the indices of the vertices adjacent to vertex i. The adjacency lists for G_1, G_3, and G_4 are shown in Figure 6.8. Notice that the vertices in each list are not required to be ordered. Each list has a head node. The head nodes are sequential, providing easy random access to the adjacency list for any particular vertex. The declaration in C++ for the adjacency list representation uses **class** *List* of Chapter 4.

```
class Graph
{
private:
   List<int> *HeadNodes;
   int n;
public:
   Graph(const int vertices = 0) : n (vertices)
   { HeadNodes = new List<int>[n];};
};
```

For an undirected graph with n vertices and e edges, this representation requires n head nodes and $2e$ list nodes. Each list node has two fields. In terms of the number of bits of storage needed, this count should be multiplied by log n for the head nodes and log n + log e for the list nodes, as it takes O(log m) bits to represent a number of value m. Often, you can sequentially pack the nodes on the adjacency lists, thereby eliminating the use of pointers. In this case, an array *node* $[n + 2e + 1]$ may be used. *node* $[i]$ gives the starting point of the list for vertex i, $0 \le i < n$, and *node* $[n]$ is set to $n + 2e + 1$. The vertices adjacent from vertex i are stored in *node* $[i]$, $\cdots$, *node* $[i + 1] - 1$, $0 \le i < n$. Figure 6.9 shows the representation for the graph G_4 of Figure 6.5.

The degree of any vertex in an undirected graph may be determined by just counting the number of nodes in its adjacency list. So, the number of edges in G may be determined in O($n + e$) time.

For a digraph, the number of list nodes is only e. The out-degree of any vertex may be determined by counting the number of nodes on its adjacency list. Hence, the total number of edges in G can be determined in O($n + e$) time. Determining the in-degree of a vertex is a little more complex. If there is a need to access repeatedly all vertices adjacent to another vertex, then it may be worth the effort to keep another set of lists in addition to the adjacency lists. This set of lists, called *inverse adjacency lists*, will contain one list for each vertex. Each list will contain a node for each vertex adjacent to the vertex it represents (see Figure 6.10).

(a) G_1

(b) G_3

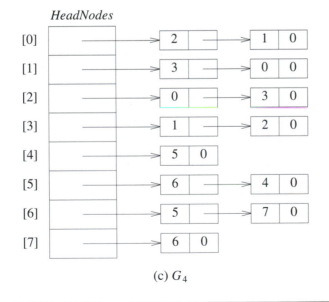

(c) G_4

Figure 6.8: Adjacency lists

int *nodes* [*n* + 2*e + 1];

0	1	2	3	4	5	6	7	8	9	10	11	12	13	14	15	16	17	18	19	20	21	22
9	11	13	15	17	18	20	22	23	2	1	3	0	0	3	1	2	5	6	4	5	7	6

Figure 6.9: Sequential representation of graph G_4

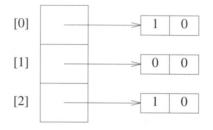

Figure 6.10: Inverse adjacency lists for G_3 (Figure 6.2(c))

Alternatively, one can adopt a simplified version of the list structure used for sparse matrix representation in Chapter 4. Each node now has four fields and represents one edge. The node structure is

tail	head	column link for head	row link for tail			

Figure 6.11 shows the resulting structure for the graph G_3 of Figure 6.2(c). The head nodes are stored sequentially.

6.1.3.3   Adjacency Multilists

In the adjacency-list representation of an undirected graph, each edge (u,v) is represented by two entries, one on the list for u and the other on the list for v. As we shall see, in some situations it is necessary to be able to determine the second entry for a particular edge and mark that edge as having been examined. This can be accomplished easily if the adjacency lists are actually maintained as multilists (i.e., lists in which nodes may be shared among several lists). For each edge there will be exactly one node, but this node

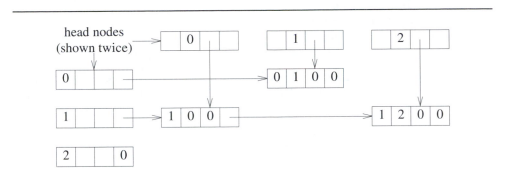

Figure 6.11: Orthogonal list representation for G_3 of Figure 6.2(c)

will be in two lists (i.e., the adjacency lists for each of the two nodes to which it is incident). The new node structure is

m	*vertex*1	*vertex*2	*list*1	*list*2

where *m* is a *Boolean* mark field that may be used to indicate whether or not the edge has been examined. The C++ declarations are

enum *Boolean* {FALSE, TRUE};
class *Graph*; // forward declaration

class *GraphEdge* {
friend *Graph*;
private:
   Boolean m;
   int *vertex*1, *vertex*2;
   GraphEdge **path*1, **path*2;
};

typedef *GraphEdge* *EdgePtr;
class *Graph* {
private:
   EdgePtr *HeadNodes;
   int *n*;
public:
   Graph(**const int**);
};

Graph::Graph(**const int** *vertices* = 0) : *n* (*vertices*)
{ // Set up the array of head nodes
  HeadNodes = **new** *EdgePtr* [*n*];
  for (**int** *i* = 0; *i* < *n*; *i*++) *HeadNodes* [*i*] = 0;
}

The storage requirements are the same as for normal adjacency lists, except for the addition of the mark bit *m*. Figure 6.12 shows the adjacency multilists for G_1 of Figure 6.2(a).

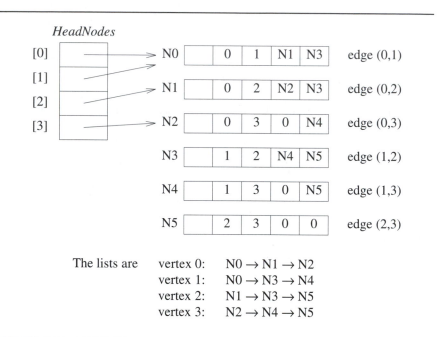

The lists are   vertex 0:   N0 → N1 → N2
                  vertex 1:   N0 → N3 → N4
                  vertex 2:   N1 → N3 → N5
                  vertex 3:   N2 → N4 → N5

Figure 6.12: Adjacency multilists for G_1 of Figure 6.2(a)

6.1.3.4   Weighted Edges

In many applications, the edges of a graph have weights assigned to them. These weights may represent the distance from one vertex to another or the cost of going from one vertex to an adjacent vertex. In these applications, the adjacency matrix entries *A* [*i*][*j*] would keep this information too. When adjacency lists are used, the weight information may be kept in the list nodes by including an additional field, *weight*. A graph with weighted edges is called a *network*.

EXERCISES

1. Does the multigraph of Figure 6.13 have an Eulerian walk? If so, find one.

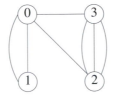

Figure 6.13: A multigraph

2. For the digraph of Figure 6.14 obtain
   (a) the in-degree and out-degree of each vertex
   (b) its adjacency-matrix
   (c) its adjacency-list representation
   (d) its adjacency-multilist representation
   (e) its strongly connected components

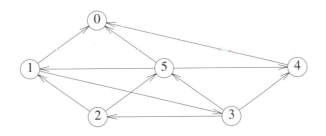

Figure 6.14: A digraph

3. Devise a suitable representation for graphs so that they can be stored on disk. Write an algorithm that reads in such a graph and creates its adjacency matrix. Write another algorithm that creates the adjacency lists from the disk input.

4. Draw the complete undirected graphs on one, two, three, four, and five vertices. Prove that the number of edges in an n-vertex complete graph is $n(n-1)/2$.

5. Is the directed graph of Figure 6.15 strongly connected? List all the simple paths.

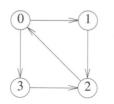

Figure 6.15: A directed graph

6. Obtain the adjacency-matrix, adjacency-list, and adjacency-multilist representations of the graph of Figure 6.15.

7. Show that the sum of the degrees of the vertices of an undirected graph is twice the number of edges.

8. (a) Let G be a connected, undirected graph on n vertices. Show that G must have at least $n-1$ edges and that all connected, undirected graphs with $n-1$ edges are trees.

   (b) What is the minimum number of edges in a strongly connected digraph on n vertices? What form do such digraphs have?

9. For an undirected graph G with n vertices, prove that the following are equivalent:

   (a) G is a tree

   (b) G is connected, but if any edge is removed the resulting graph is not connected

   (c) For any two distinct vertices $u \in V(G)$ and $v \in V(G)$, there is exactly one simple path from u to v

   (d) G contains no cycles and has $n-1$ edges

10. Write a C++ function to input the number of vertices in an undirected graph and its edges one by one and to set up the linked adjacency-list representation of the graph. You may assume that no edge is input twice. What is the run time of your function as a function of the number of vertices and the number of edges?

11. Do the preceding exercise but this time set up the multilist representation.

12. Let G be an undirected, connected graph with at least one vertex of odd degree. Show that G contains no Eulerian walk.

6.2   ELEMENTARY GRAPH OPERATIONS

When we discussed binary trees in Chapter 5, we indicated that tree traversals were among the most frequently used tree operations. Thus, we defined and implemented preorder, inorder, postorder, and level-order tree traversals. An analogous situation occurs in the case of graphs. Given a graph $G = (V, E)$ and a vertex v in $V(G)$, we wish to visit all vertices in G that are reachable from v (i.e., all vertices that are connected to v). We shall look at two ways of doing this: *depth-first search* and *breadth-first search*. Although these methods work on both directed and undirected graphs, the following discussion assumes that the graphs are undirected.

6.2.1   Depth-First Search

We begin by visiting the start vertex v. Next an unvisited vertex w adjacent to v is selected, and a depth-first search from w is initiated. When a vertex u is reached such that all its adjacent vertices have been visited, we back up to the last vertex visited that has an unvisited vertex w adjacent to it and initiate a depth-first search from w. The search terminates when no unvisited vertex can be reached from any of the visited vertices. This function is best described recursively as in Program 6.1.

```
void Graph ::DFS ()  // Driver
{
    visited = new Boolean [n]; // visited is declared as a Boolean* data member of Graph.
    for (int i = 0; i < n; i++) visited [i] = FALSE; // initially, no vertices have been visited
    DFS (0); // start search at vertex 0
    delete [] visited;
}

void Graph::DFS(const int v) // Workhorse
// visit all previously unvisited vertices that are reachable from vertex v
{
    visited [v] = TRUE;
    for ( each vertex w adjacent to v) // actual code depends on graph representation used
        if (! visited [w]) DFS (w);
}
```

Program 6.1: Depth-first search

Example 6.1: Consider the graph G of Figure 6.16(a), which is represented by its adjacency lists as in Figure 6.16(b). If a depth-first search is initiated from vertex 0, then the vertices of *G* are visited in the following order: 0, 1, 3, 7, 4, 5, 2, 6. Since *DFS*(0) visits all vertices that can be reached from 0, the vertices visited, together with all edges in *G* incident to these vertices, form a connected component of *G*. □

(a)

(b)

Figure 6.16: Graph *G* and its adjacency lists

Analysis of *DFS*: When *G* is represented by its adjacency lists, the vertices *w* adjacent to *v* can be determined by following a chain of links. Since *DFS* examines each node in the adjacency lists at most once, and there are 2*e* list nodes, the time to complete the search is O(*e*). If *G* is represented by its adjacency matrix, then the time to determine all vertices adjacent to *v* is O(*n*). Since at most *n* vertices are visited, the total time is O(n^2). □

6.2.2 Breadth-First Search

In a breadth-first search, we begin by visiting the start vertex v. Next, all unvisited vertices adjacent to v are visited. Unvisited vertices adjacent to these newly visited vertices are then visited, and so on. Algorithm *BFS* (Program 6.2) gives the details.

Example 6.2: Consider the graph of Figure 6.16(a). If a breadth-first search is performed beginning at vertex 0, then we first visit vertex 0. Next, vertices 1 and 2 are visited. Then vertices 3, 4, 5, and 6, and finally 7, are visited. □

```
void Graph::BFS(int v)
// A breadth first search of the graph is carried out beginning at vertex v.
// visited [i ] is set to TRUE when v is visited. The algorithm uses a queue
{
    visited = new Boolean [n ]; // visited is declared as a Boolean* data member of Graph.
    for (int i = 0; i < n; i++) visited [i ] = FALSE; // initially, no vertices have been visited
    visited [v ] = TRUE;
    Queue<int> q; // q is a queue
    q.Insert (v ); // add vertex to the queue
    while (!q.IsEmpty ()) {
        v = *q.Delete (v ); // remove vertex v from the queue
        for (all vertices w adjacent to v) // actual code depends on graph representation used
            if (! visited [w ]) {
                q.Insert (w );
                visited [w ] = TRUE;
            }
    } // end of while loop
    delete [] visited;
}
```

Program 6.2: Breadth-first search

Analysis of BFS: Each visited vertex enters the queue exactly once. So, the **while** loop is iterated at most n times. If an adjacency matrix is used, the loop takes $O(n)$ time for each vertex visited. The total time is, therefore, $O(n^2)$. If adjacency lists are used, the loop has a total cost of $d_0 + \cdots + d_{n-1} = O(e)$, where d_i is the degree of vertex i. As in the case of *DFS*, all visited vertices, together with all edges incident to them, form a connected component of G. □

6.2.3 Connected Components

If G is an undirected graph, then one can determine whether or not it is connected by simply making a call to either *DFS* or *BFS* and then determining if there is any unvisited vertex. The connected components of a graph may be obtained by making repeated calls to either *DFS(v)* or *BFS(v)*, where v is a vertex that has not yet been visited. This leads to function *Components* (Program 6.3), which determines the connected components of G. The algorithm uses *DFS* (*BFS* may be used instead if desired). The computing time is not affected. Function *Graph::OutputNewComponent* outputs all vertices visited in the most recent invocation of *DFS*, together with all edges incident on these vertices.

```
void Graph::Components ()
// Determine the connected components of the graph
{
    // visited is assumed to be declared as a Boolean* data member of Graph
    visited = new Boolean [n ];
    for (int i = 0; i < n; i++) visited [i ] = FALSE;
    for (i = 0; i < n; i++)
        if (! visited [i ]) {
            DFS (i); // Find a component
            OutputNewComponent ();
        }
    delete [] visited;
}
```

Program 6.3: Determining connected components

Analysis of *Components*: If G is represented by its adjacency lists, then the total time taken by *DFS* is O(e). The output can be completed in time O(e) if *DFS* keeps a list of all newly visited vertices. Since the **for** loops take O(n) time, the total time to generate all the connected components is O($n + e$). If adjacency matrices are used instead, the time required is O(n^2). □

6.2.4 Spanning Trees

When the graph G is connected, a depth-first or breadth-first search starting at any vertex visits all the vertices in G. In this case the edges of G are partitioned into two sets, T (for tree edges) and N (for nontree edges), where T is the set of edges used or traversed during the search and N the set of remaining edges. The set T may be determined by inserting the statement $T = T \cup \{(v,w)\}$ in the **if** clauses of *DFS* and *BFS*. The edges in T

form a tree that includes all the vertices of G. Any tree consisting solely of edges in G and including all vertices in G is called a *spanning tree*. Figure 6.17 shows a graph and some of its spanning trees.

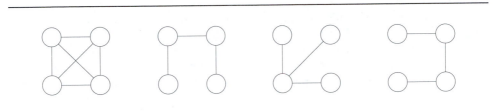

Figure 6.17: A complete graph and three of its spanning trees

As indicated earlier, a spanning tree may be constructed using either a depth-first or a breadth-first search. The spanning tree resulting from a depth-first search is known as a *depth-first spanning tree*. When a breadth-first search is used, the spanning tree is called a *breadth-first spanning tree*. Figure 6.18 shows the spanning trees resulting from a depth-first and breadth-first search starting at vertex 0 of the graph of Figure 6.16.

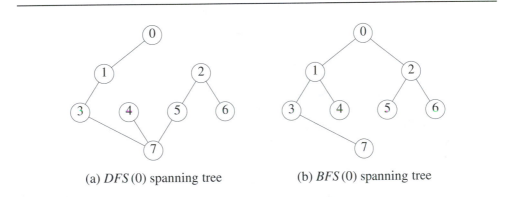

(a) *DFS* (0) spanning tree (b) *BFS* (0) spanning tree

Figure 6.18: Depth-first and breadth-first spanning trees for graph of Figure 6.16

If a nontree edge (v, w) is introduced into any spanning tree T, then a cycle is formed. This cycle consists of the edge (v,w) and all the edges on the path from w to v in T. For example, if the edge $(7,6)$ is introduced into the *DFS* spanning tree of Figure 6.18(a), then the resulting cycle is 7,6,2,5,7. We can use this property of spanning trees to obtain an independent set of circuit equations for an electrical network.

Example 6.3 [*Creation of circuit equations*]: To obtain the circuit equations, we must first obtain a spanning tree for the electrical network. Then we introduce the nontree edges into the spanning tree one at a time. The introduction of each such edge produces a cycle. Next we use Kirchhoff's second law on this cycle to obtain a circuit equation. The cycles obtained in this way are independent (we cannot obtain any of these cycles by taking a linear combination of the remaining cycles), since each contains a nontree edge that is not contained in any other cycle. Thus, the circuit equations are also independent. In fact, we can show that the cycles obtained by introducing the nontree edges one at a time into the spanning tree form a cycle basis. This means that we can construct all other cycles in the graph by taking a linear combination of the cycles in the basis. (For further details, see the Harary text cited in the References and Selected Readings section.) □

Let us examine a second property of spanning trees. A spanning tree is a *minimal subgraph*, G', of G such that $V(G') = V(G)$, and G' is connected. We define a minimal subgraph as one with the fewest number of edges. Any connected graph with n vertices must have at least $n - 1$ edges, and all connected graphs with $n - 1$ edges are trees. Therefore, we conclude that a spanning tree has $n - 1$ edges. (The Exercises explore this property more fully.)

Constructing minimal subgraphs finds frequent application in the design of communication networks. Suppose that the vertices of a graph G represent cities, and the edges represent communication links between cities. The minimum number of links needed to connect n cities is $n - 1$. Constructing the spanning trees of G produces all feasible choices. However, we know that the cost of constructing communication links between cities is rarely the same. Therefore, in practical applications, we assign weights to the edges. These weights might represent the cost of constructing the communication link or the length of the link. Given such a weighted graph, we would like to select the spanning tree that represents either the lowest total cost or the lowest overall length. We assume that the cost of a spanning tree is the sum of the costs of the edges of that tree. Algorithms to obtain minimum-cost spanning trees are studied in Section 6.3.

6.2.5 Biconnected Components

The operations that we have implemented thus far are simple extensions of depth-first and breadth-first searches. The next operation we implement is more complex and requires the introduction of additional terminology. We begin by assuming that G is an undirected, connected graph.

Definition: A vertex v of G is an *articulation point* iff the deletion of v, together with the deletion of all edges incident to v, leaves behind a graph that has at least two connected components. □

Vertices 1, 3, 5, and 7 are the articulation points of the connected graph of Figure 6.19(a).

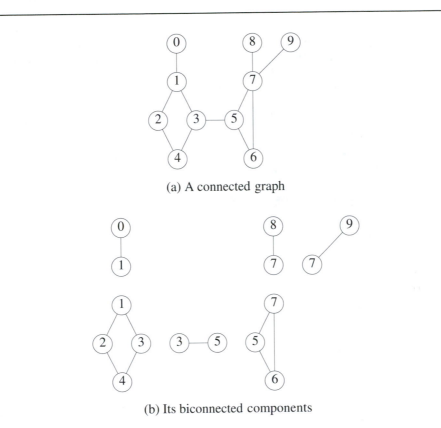

(a) A connected graph

(b) Its biconnected components

Figure 6.19: A connected graph and its biconnected components

Definition: A *biconnected graph* is a connected graph that has no articulation points. □

The graph of Figure 6.19 is not biconnected, and that of Figure 6.16(a) is. Articulation points are undesirable in graphs that represent communication networks. In such graphs the vertices represent communication stations, and the edges represent communication links. The failure of a communication station that is an articulation point results in a loss of communication to stations other than the one that failed. If the communication graph is biconnected, then the failure of a single station results in a loss of communication to and from only that station.

Definition: A *biconnected component* of a connected graph G is a maximal biconnected subgraph H of G. By maximal, we mean that G contains no other subgraph that is both biconnected and properly contains H. □

The graph of Figure 6.19(a) contains six biconnected components. These are shown in Figure 6.19(b). Note that a biconnected graph has just one biconnected component: the whole graph. It is easy to verify that two biconnected components of the same graph can have at most one vertex in common. From this it follows that no edge can be in two or more biconnected components. Hence, the biconnected components of G partition the edges of G.

The biconnected components of a connected, undirected graph G can be found by using any depth-first spanning tree of G. For the graph of Figure 6.19(a) a depth-first spanning tree with root 3 is shown in Figure 6.20(a). This tree is redrawn in Figure 6.20(b) to better reveal the tree structure. This figure also shows the nontree edges of G by broken lines. The numbers outside the vertices give the sequence in which the vertices are visited during the depth-first search. This number is called the *depth-first number*, *dfn*, of the vertex. So, *dfn* $(0) = 5$, and *dfn* $(9) = 9$. Note that if u and v are two vertices such that u is an ancestor of v in the depth-first spanning tree, then *dfn* $(u) <$ *dfn* (v).

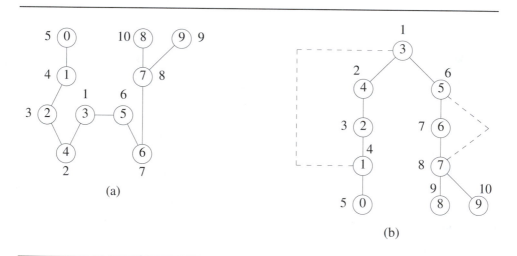

(a)

(b)

Figure 6.20: Depth-first spanning tree of Figure 6.19(a)

The broken lines in Figure 6.20(b) represent nontree edges. A nontree edge (u, v) is a *back edge* with respect to a spanning tree T iff either u is an ancestor of v or v is an ancestor of u. A nontree edge that is not a back edge is called a *cross edge*. The nontree edges $(3, 1)$ and $(5, 7)$ are back edges. From the definition of a depth-first search, one can show that no graph can have cross edges with respect to any of its depth-first spanning trees. From this, it follows that the root of the depth-first spanning tree is an articulation point iff it has at least two children. Further, any other vertex u is an articulation point iff it has at least one child, w, such that it is not possible to reach an ancestor of u using a path composed solely of w, descendants of w, and a single back edge. These observations lead us to define a value low for each vertex of G such that $low(w)$ is the lowest depth-first number that can be reached from w using a path of descendants followed by, at most, one back edge. $low(w)$ is given by the equation

$$low(w) = \min\{dfn(w), \min\{low(x) \mid x \text{ is a child of } w\},$$
$$\min\{dfn(x) \mid (w, x) \text{ is a back edge}\}\}$$

From the preceding discussion it follows that u is an articulation point iff u is either the root of the spanning tree and has two or more children or u is not the root and u has a child w such that $low(w) \geq dfn(u)$. Figure 6.21 gives the dfn and low values for each vertex of the spanning tree of Figure 6.20(b).

vertex	0	1	2	3	4	5	6	7	8	9
dfn	5	4	3	1	2	6	7	8	10	9
low	5	1	1	1	1	6	6	6	10	9

Figure 6.21: *dfn* and *low* values for the spanning tree of Figure 6.20(b)

Function *DFS* is easily modified to compute *dfn* and *low* for each vertex of a connected graph. The result is function *DfnLow* (Program 6.4). This function uses the function *min* 2, which returns the smaller of its two parameters. The function is invoked as *DfnLow* $(x, -1)$, where x is the start vertex for the depth-first search.

The edges of the connected graph may be partitioned into their biconnected components by adding some code to function *DfnLow*. First, note that following the return from *DfnLow* (w, u), $low[w]$ has been computed. If $low[w] \geq dfn[u]$, then a new biconnected component has been identified. By using a stack to save edges when they are first encountered, we can output all edges in a biconnected component, as in function *Biconnected* (Program 6.5).

Establishing the correctness of function *Biconnected* is left as an exercise. Its complexity is $O(n + e)$. Note that function *Biconnected* assumes that the input connected graph has at least two vertices. Connected graphs with just one vertex contain no edges. By convention these graphs are biconnected, and a proper biconnected components function should handle them as a special case, producing a single biconnected component as output.

```
void Graph::DfnLow(const int x) // begin DFS at vertex x
{
    num = 1; // num is an int data member of class Graph
    dfn = new int[n]; // dfn is declared as int* in class Graph
    low = new int[n]; // low is declared as int* in class Graph
    for (int i = 0; i < n; i++) { dfn [i] = low [i] = 0;}
    DfnLow (x,−1); // start at vertex x
    delete [] dfn;
    delete [] low;
}


void Graph::DfnLow (const int u, const int v)
// Compute dfn and low while performing a depth first search beginning at vertex u
// v is the parent (if any) of u in the resulting spanning tree.
{
    dfn [u] = low [u] = num++;
    for ( each vertex w adjacent from u) // actual code depends on graph representation
        if (dfn [w] == 0) { // w is an unvisited vertex
            DfnLow (w,u);
            low [u] = min2(low [u], low [w]);
        }
        else if (w != v) low [u] = min 2(low [u], dfn [w]); // back edge
}
```

Program 6.4: Computing *dfn* and *low*

EXERCISES

1. Apply depth-first and breadth-first searches to the complete graph on four vertices. List the vertices in the order they would be visited.

2. Write a complete C++ function for depth-first search under the assumption that graphs are represented using adjacency matrices. Test the correctness of your function using suitable graphs.

3. Write a complete C++ function for depth-first search under the assumption that graphs are represented using adjacency lists. Test the correctness of your function using suitable graphs.

4. Write a complete C++ function for breadth-first search under the assumption that graphs are represented using adjacency matrices. Test the correctness of your function using suitable graphs.

```
void Graph::Biconnected ()
{
    num = 1; // num is an int data member of class Graph
    dfn = new int[n]; // dfn is declared as int* in Graph
    low = new int[n]; // low is declared as int* in Graph
    for (int i = 0; i < n; i++) { dfn [i] = low [i] = 0;}
    Biconnected (0,-1); // start at vertex 0
    delete [] dfn;
    delete [] low;
}


void Graph::Biconnected (const int u, const int v)
// Compute dfn and low, and output the edges of G by their biconnected components
// v is the parent (if any) of u in the resulting spanning tree.
// S is an initially empty stack declared as a data member of Graph
{
    dfn [u] = low [u] = num++;
    for ( each vertex w adjacent from u) { // actual code depends on graph representation
        if ((v != w) && (dfn [w] < dfn [u])) add (u, w) to stack S;
        if (dfn [w] == 0) { // w is an unvisited vertex
            Biconnected (w,u);
            low [u] = min2(low [u], low [w]);
            if (low [w] >= dfn [u]) {
                cout << "New Biconnected Component: " << endl;
                do {
                    delete an edge from the stack S;
                    let this edge be (x, y);
                    cout << x << ", " << y << endl;
                } while ( (x, y) and (u, w) are not the same edge)
            }
        }
        else if (w != v) low [u] = min2(low [u], dfn [w]); // back edge
}
```

Program 6.5: Outputting biconnected components when $n > 1$

---

5. Write a complete C++ function for breadth-first search under the assumption that graphs are represented using adjacency lists. Test the correctness of your function using suitable graphs.

6. Show how to modify function *DFS* (Program 6.1), as it is used in *Components* (Program 6.3), to produce a list of all newly visited vertices.

7. Prove that when function *DFS* (Program 6.1) is applied to a connected graph, the edges of *T* form a tree.

8. Prove that when function *BFS* (Program 6.2) is applied to a connected graph, the edges of *T* form a tree.

9. Augment the adjacency list representation of a graph, so that a field *data* of type *KeyType* is associated with each *vertex*.

10. Assume the graph representation of the previous exercise. Define an iterator class *BFSVertIter*. A *BFSVertIter* object must be associated with a *Graph* object. Define a function *BFSVertIter::NextVertex*() that returns a pointer to the *data* object associated with a vertex in the graph in *BFS* order starting with vertex 0.

11. Repeat the previous exercise assuming that the graph is to be traversed in *DFS* order.

12. Augment the adjacency list representation of a graph, so that a field *data* of type *KeyType* is associated with each *edge*.

13. Assume the graph representation of the previous exercise. Define an iterator class *BFSEdgeIter*. A *BFSEdgeIter* object must be associated with a *Graph* object. Define a function *BFSEdgeIter::NextEdge* () that returns a pointer to the *data* object associated with an edge in the graph in *BFS* order starting with any edge incident on vertex 0.

14. Repeat the previous exercise assuming that the graph is to be traversed in *DFS* order.

15. Show that if *T* is a spanning tree for the undirected graph *G*, then the addition of an edge e, $e \notin E(T)$ and $e \in E(G)$, to *T* creates a unique cycle.

16. Show that the number of spanning trees in a complete graph with *n* vertices is at least $2^{n-1} - 1$.

17. Let *G* be a connected graph and let *T* be any of its depth-first spanning trees. Show that *G* has no cross edges relative to *T*.

18. Prove that function *Biconnected* (Program 6.5) correctly partitions the edges of a connected graph into the biconnected components of the graph.

19. Let *G* be a connected, undirected graph. Show that no edge of *G* can be in two or more biconnected components of *G*.

6.3 MINIMUM-COST SPANNING TREES

The *cost* of a spanning tree of a weighted, undirected graph is the sum of the costs (weights) of the edges in the spanning tree. A *minimum-cost spanning tree* is a spanning

tree of least cost. Three different algorithms can be used to obtain a minimum-cost spanning tree of a connected, undirected graph. All three use a design strategy called the
greedy method. We shall refer to the three algorithms as Kruskal's, Prim's, and Sollin's
algorithms, respectively.

In the greedy method, we construct an optimal solution in stages. At each stage,
we make the best decision (using some criterion) possible at the time. Since we cannot
change this decision later, we make sure that the decision will result in a feasible solution. The greedy method can be applied to a wide variety of programming problems.
Typically, the selection of an item at each stage is based on either a least-cost or a
highest profit criterion. A feasible solution is one that works within the constraints
specified by the problem.

To construct minimum-cost spanning trees, we use a least-cost criterion. Our solution must satisfy the following constraints:

(1)   We must use only edges within the graph.

(2)   We must use exactly $n - 1$ edges.

(3)   We may not use edges that produce a cycle.

6.3.1   Kruskal's Algorithm

Kruskal's algorithm builds a minimum-cost spanning tree T by adding edges to T one at
a time. The algorithm selects the edges for inclusion in T in nondecreasing order of their
cost. An edge is added to T if it does not form a cycle with the edges that are already in
T. Since G is connected and has $n > 0$ vertices, exactly $n - 1$ edges will be selected for
inclusion in T.

Example 6.4: We will construct a minimum-cost spanning tree of the graph of Figure
6.22(a). We begin with no edges selected. Figure 6.22(b) shows the current graph with
no edges selected. Edge (0,5) is the first edge considered. It is included in the spanning
tree being built. This yields the graph of Figure 6.22(c).

Next, the edge (2,3) is selected and included in the tree (Figure 6.22(d)). The next
edge to be considered is (1,6). Its inclusion in the tree being built does not create a cycle, so we get the graph of Figure 6.22(e). Edge (1,2) is considered next and included in
the tree (Figure 6.22(f)). Of the edges not yet considered, (6,3) has the least cost. It is
considered next. Its inclusion in the tree results in a cycle, so this edge is discarded.
Edge (4,3) is the next edge to be added to the tree being built. This results in the
configuration of Figure 6.22(g). The next edge to be considered is the edge (6,4). It is
discarded, as its inclusion creates a cycle. Finally, edge (5,4) is considered and included
in the tree being built. This completes the spanning tree. The resulting tree (Figure
6.22(h)) has cost 99. ☐

It is somewhat surprising that this straightforward approach should always result
in a minimum-cost spanning tree. We shall soon prove, however, that this is indeed the

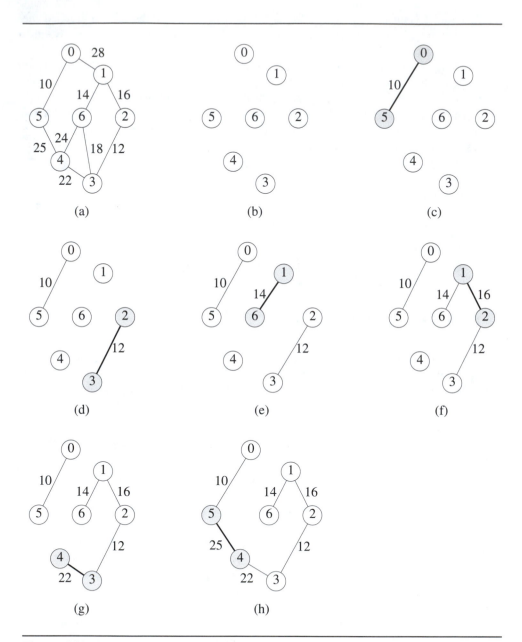

Figure 6.22: Stages in Kruskal's algorithm

case. First, let us look into the details of the algorithm. For clarity, Kruskal's algorithm is written out more formally in Program 6.6. Initially, E is the set of all edges in G. The only functions we wish to perform on this set are

(1) determine an edge with minimum cost (line 3)

(2) delete this edge (line 4)

Both these functions can be performed efficiently if the edges in E are maintained as a sorted sequential list. In Chapter 7 we shall see how to sort these edges into nondecreasing order in time $O(e \log e)$, where e is the number of edges in E. It is not essential to sort all the edges, as long as the next edge for line 3 can be determined easily. This is an instance where a min heap is ideal, as it permits the next edge to be determined and deleted in $O(\log e)$ time. The construction of the heap itself takes $O(e)$ time.

```
1  T = ∅;
2  while ((T contains less than n − 1 edges) && (E not empty)) {
3      choose an edge (v,w) from E of lowest cost;
4      delete (v,w) from E;
5      if ((v,w) does not create a cycle in T) add (v,w) to T;
6      else discard (v,w);
7  }
8  if (T contains fewer than n − 1 edges) cout << "no spanning tree" << endl;
```

Program 6.6: Kruskal's algorithm

To perform line 5 of Program 6.6 efficiently, the vertices in G should be grouped together in such a way that one may easily determine if the vertices v and w are already connected by the earlier selection of edges. If they are, then the edge (v,w) is to be discarded. If they are not, then (v,w) is to be added to T. One possible grouping is to place all vertices in the same connected component of T into a set (all connected components of T will also be trees). Then, two vertices v and w are connected in T iff they are in the same set. For example, when the edge $(3, 6)$ is to be considered, the sets would be $\{0, 5\}, \{1, 2, 3, 6\}$, and $\{4\}$. Vertices 3 and 6 are already in the same set, so the edge $(3, 6)$ is rejected. The next edge to be considered is $(3, 4)$. Since vertices 3 and 4 are in different sets, the edge is accepted. This edge connects the two components $\{1, 2, 3, 6\}$ and $\{4\}$, so these two sets should be unioned to obtain the set representing the new component. Using the set representation scheme of Chapter 5, we can obtain an efficient implementation of line 5. The computing time is, therefore, determined by the time for lines 3 and 4, which in the worst case is $O(e \log e)$. We leave the writing of the resulting algorithm as an exercise. Theorem 6.1 proves that the algorithm resulting from Program 6.6 does yield a minimum-cost spanning tree of G.

Theorem 6.1: Let G be any undirected, connected graph. Kruskal's algorithm generates a minimum-cost spanning tree.

Proof: We shall show the following: (a) Kruskal's method results in a spanning tree whenever a spanning tree exists; and (b) the spanning tree generated is of minimum cost.

For (a), we note that the only edges that get discarded in Kruskal's method are those that result in a cycle. The deletion of a single edge that is on a cycle of a connected graph results in a graph that is also connected. Hence, if G initially is connected, the set of edges in T and E always form a connected graph. Consequently, if G initially is connected, the algorithm cannot terminate with $E = \varnothing$ and $|T| < n - 1$.

Now, let us proceed to establish that the constructed spanning tree, T, is of minimum cost. Since G has a finite number of spanning trees, it must have at least one of minimum cost. Let U be a minimum-cost spanning tree. Both T and U have exactly $n-1$ edges. If $T = U$, then T is of minimum cost, and we have nothing to prove. So, assume that $T \neq U$. Let $k, k > 0$, be the number of edges in T that are not in U. Note that k is also the number of edges in U that are not in T.

We shall show that T and U have the same cost by transforming U into T. This transformation will be done in k steps. At each step, the number of edges in T that are not in U will be reduced by exactly 1. Further, the cost of U will not change as a result of the transformation. As a result, U after k steps of transformation will have the same cost as the initial U and will consist of exactly those edges that are in T. This implies that T is of minimum cost.

Each step of the transformation involves adding to U one edge, e, from T and removing one edge, f, from U. The edges e and f are selected in the following way:

(1)   Let e be the least-cost edge in T that is not in U. Such an edge must exist as $k > 0$.

(2)   When e is added to U, a unique cycle is created. Let f be any edge on this cycle that is not in T. Note that at least one of the edges on this cycle is not in T, as T contains no cycles.

From the way e and f are selected, it follows that $V = U + \{e\} - \{f\}$ is a spanning tree and that T has exactly $k-1$ edges that are not in V. We need to show that the cost of V is the same as that of U. Clearly, the cost of V is the cost of U plus the cost of the edge e minus the cost of the edge f. The cost of e cannot be less than the cost of f, as otherwise the spanning tree V has a smaller cost than the tree U, which is impossible. If e has a higher cost than f, then f is considered before e by Kruskal's algorithm. Since f is not in T, Kruskal's algorithm must have discarded this edge at this time. Hence, f, together with edges in T having a cost less than or equal to the cost of f, must form a cycle. By the choice of e, all these edges are also in U. Hence, U must also contain a cycle. But it does not, as it is a spanning tree. So, the assumption that e is of higher cost than f leads to a contradiction. The only possibility that remains is that e and f have the same cost. Hence, V has the same cost as U. $\square$

6.3.2   Prim's Algorithm

Prim's algorithm, like Kruskal's, constructs the minimum-cost spanning tree edge by edge. However, at all times during the algorithm, the set of selected edges forms a tree. (By contrast, the set of selected edges in Kruskal's algorithm forms a forest at all times.) Prim's algorithm begins with a tree T that contains a single vertex. This vertex can be any of the vertices in the original graph. Then we add a least-cost edge (u, v) to T such that $T \cup \{(u, v)\}$ is also a tree. This edge-addition step is repeated until T contains $n-1$ edges. Notice that edge (u, v) is always such that exactly one of u and v is in T. A high-level description of Prim's algorithm is provided in Program 6.7. This description also provides for the possibility that the input graph may not be connected. In this case there is no spanning tree. Figure 6.23 shows the progress of Prim's algorithm on the graph of Figure 6.22(a).

```
//Assume that G has at least one vertex.
TV = {0}; // start with vertex 0 and no edges
for (T = ∅; T contains fewer than n−1 edges;  add (u, v) to T)
{
    Let (u, v) be a least-cost edge such that u ∈ TV and v ∉ TV;
    if (there is no such edge) break;
    add v to TV;
}
if (T contains fewer than n−1 edges) cout << "no spanning tree" << endl;
```

Program 6.7: Prim's algorithm

Prim's algorithm can be implemented to have a time complexity $O(n^2)$ if we associate with each vertex v not in TV a vertex $near(v)$ such that $near(v) \in TV$ and $cost(near(v), v)$ is the minimum over all such choices for $near(v)$ (we assume that $cost(v, w) = \infty$ if $(v, w) \notin E$). The next edge to add to T is such that $cost(near(v), v)$ is the minimum and $v \notin TV$. Asymptotically faster implementations are also possible. One of these results from the use of Fibonacci heaps, which are studied in Chapter 9. A reference pertaining to the application of Fibonacci heaps to the implementation of Prim's algorithm is provided at the end of Chapter 9. Establishing the correctness of Prim's algorithm is left as an exercise.

6.3.3   Sollin's Algorithm

Sollin's algorithm selects several edges at each stage. At the start of a stage, the selected edges, together with all n graph vertices, form a spanning forest. During a stage we select one edge for each tree in this forest. This edge is a minimum-cost edge that has

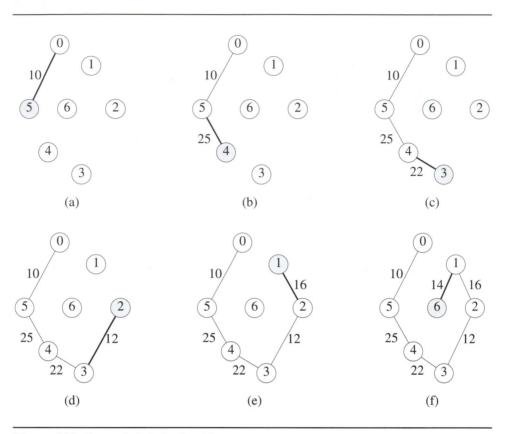

Figure 6.23: Stages in Prim's algorithm

exactly one vertex in the tree. The selected edges are added to the spanning tree being constructed. Note that it is possible for two trees in the forest to select the same edge. So, multiple copies of the same edge are to be eliminated. Also, when the graph has several edges with the same cost, it is possible for two trees to select two different edges that connect them together. These edges will, of course, have the same cost; only one of these should be retained. At the start of the first stage, the set of selected edges is empty. The algorithm terminates when there is only one tree at the end of a stage or when no edges remain to be selected.

Figure 6.24 shows the stages in Sollin's algorithm when it begins with the graph of Figure 6.22(a). The initial configuration of zero selected edges is the same as that shown in Figure 6.22(b). Each tree in this spanning forest is a single vertex. The edges selected by vertices 0, 1, $\cdots$, 6 are, respectively, (0, 5), (1, 6), (2, 3), (3, 2), (4, 3), (5, 0), and (6, 1). The distinct edges in this selection are (0, 5), (1, 6), (2, 3), and (4, 3). Adding these to the set of selected edges results in the configuration of Figure 6.24(a). In the next stage, the tree with vertex set {0, 5} selects the edge (5, 4), and the remaining two trees select the edge (1, 2). Following the addition of these two edges to the set of selected edges, construction of the spanning tree is complete. The resulting spanning tree is shown in Figure 6.24(b). The development of Sollin's algorithm into a C++ function and its correctness proof are left as exercises.

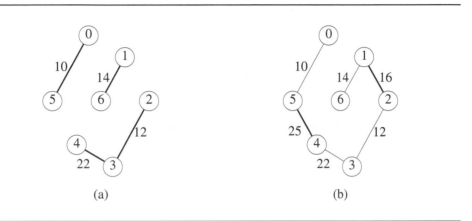

(a)   (b)

Figure 6.24: Stages in Sollin's algorithm

EXERCISES

1. Write out Kruskal's minimum-cost spanning tree algorithm (Program 6.6) as a complete program. You may use as functions the algorithms *WeightedUnion* (Program 5.22) and *CollapsingFind* (Program 5.23). Use algorithm *sort* (Program 1.3) to sort the edges into nondecreasing order by weight.

2. Prove that Prim's algorithm finds a minimum-cost spanning tree for every connected, undirected graph.

3. Refine Program 6.7 into a C++ function to find a minimum-cost spanning tree. The complexity of your function should be $O(n^2)$, where n is the number of vertices in the input graph. Show that this is the case.

4. Prove that Sollin's algorithm finds a minimum-cost spanning tree for every connected, undirected graph.

5. What is the maximum number of stages in Sollin's algorithm? Give this as a function of the number of vertices n in the graph.

6. Obtain a C++ function to find a minimum-cost spanning tree using Sollin's algorithm. What is the complexity of your function?

6.4 SHORTEST PATHS AND TRANSITIVE CLOSURE

Graphs may be used to represent the highway structure of a state or country with vertices representing cities and edges representing sections of highway. The edges may then be assigned weights, which might be the distance between the two cities connected by the edge or the average time to drive along that section of highway. A motorist wishing to drive from city A to city B would be interested in answers to the following questions:

(1)   Is there a path from A to B ?

(2)   If there is more than one path from A to B, which is the shortest path?

The problems defined by (1) and (2) above are special cases of the path problems we shall be studying in this section. An edge weight is also referred to as an edge length or edge cost. We shall use the terms weight, cost, and length interchangeably. The length (cost, weight) of a path is now defined to be the sum of the lengths (costs, weights) of the edges on that path, rather than the number of edges. The starting vertex of the path will be referred to as the *source* and the last vertex the *destination*. The graphs will be di-graphs to allow for one-way streets.

6.4.1   Single Source/All Destinations: Nonnegative Edge Costs

In this problem we are given a directed graph $G = (V,E)$, a length function *length* (i,j), *length* $(i,j) \geq 0$, for the edges of G, and a source vertex v. The problem is to determine a shortest path from v to each of the remaining vertices of G. As an example, consider the directed graph of Figure 6.25(a). The numbers on the edges are the edge lengths. If vertex 0 is the source vertex, then the shortest path from 0 to 1 is 0, 3, 4, 1. The length of this path is $10 + 15 + 20 = 45$. Even though there are three edges on this path, it is shorter than the path 0, 1, which is of length 50. There is no path from 0 to 5. Figure 6.25(b) lists the shortest paths from 0 to 1, 2, 3, and 4. The paths have been listed in nondecreasing order of path length. A greedy algorithm will generate the shortest paths in this order.

Let S denote the set of vertices (including the source v) to which the shortest paths have already been found. For w not in S, let *dist* $[w]$ be the length of the shortest path starting from v, going through only the vertices that are in S, and ending at w. We observe that when paths are generated in nondecreasing order of length,

(1) If the next shortest path is to vertex u, then the path begins at v, ends at u, and goes through only vertices that are in S. To prove this we must show that all of the intermediate vertices on the shortest path to u must be in S. Assume there is a vertex w on this path that is not in S. Then, the v-to-u path also contains a path from v to w that is of length less than that of the v-to-u path. By assumption, the shortest paths are being generated in nondecreasing order of path length, so the shorter path from v to w has been generated already. Hence, there is no intermediate vertex that is not in S.

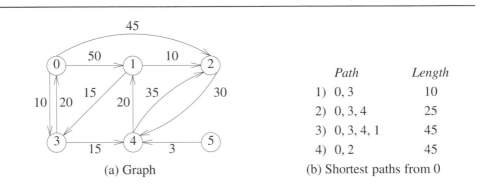

(a) Graph

Path	Length
1) 0, 3	10
2) 0, 3, 4	25
3) 0, 3, 4, 1	45
4) 0, 2	45
(b) Shortest paths from 0	

Figure 6.25: Graph and shortest paths from vertex 0 to all destinations

(2) The destination of the next path generated must be the vertex u that has the minimum distance, $dist[u]$, among all vertices not in S. This follows from the definition of $dist$ and observation (1). If there are several vertices not in S with the same $dist$, then any of these may be selected.

(3) The vertex u selected in (2) becomes a member of S. The shortest v-to-u path is obtained from the selection process of (2). At this point, the length of the shortest paths starting at v, going through vertices only in S, and ending at a vertex w not in S may decrease (i.e., the value of $dist[w]$ may change). If it does change, then the change must be due to a shorter path starting at v going to u and then to w. The intermediate vertices on the v-to-u path and the u to w path must all be in S. Further, the v-to-u path must be the shortest such path; otherwise $dist[w]$ is not defined properly. Also, the u-to-w path can be chosen so that it does not contain any intermediate vertices. Therefore, we may conclude that if $dist[w]$ changes (i.e., decreases), then the change is due to the path from v to u to w, where the path from v to u is the shortest such path and the path from u to w is the edge $<u,w>$. The length of this path is $dist[u]$ + length ($<u,w>$).

The algorithm *ShortestPath*, as first given by Edsger Dijkstra makes use of these observations to determine the length of the shortest paths from v to all other vertices in G. The generation of the paths is a minor extension of the algorithm and is left as an exercise. It is assumed that the n vertices of G are numbered 0 through $n-1$. The set S is maintained as a *Boolean* array with $s[i]$ = FALSE if vertex i is not in S and $s[i]$ = TRUE if it is. It is assumed that the graph itself is represented by its length-adjacency matrix, with $length[i][j]$ being the length of the edge $<i,j>$. If $<i,j>$ is not an edge of the graph and $i \neq j$, $length[i][j]$ may be set to some large number. The choice of this number is arbitrary, although we make two stipulations regarding its value:

(1)   The number must be larger than any of the values in the length matrix.

(2) The number must be chosen so that the statement $dist[u] + length[u][w]$ does not produce an overflow.

Restriction (2) makes MAXINT a poor choice for nonexistent edges. For $i==j$, $length[i][j]$ may be set to any nonnegative number without affecting the outcome of the algorithm. Program 6.8 describes the algorithm. Class *Graph* is defined as follows:

```
class Graph
{
private:
    int length [nmax ][nmax ];
    int dist [nmax ];
    Boolean s [nmax ];
public:
    void ShortestPath(const int, const int);
    int choose(const int);
};
```

```
1 void Graph::ShortestPath(const int n, const int v)
2 // dist [j ], 0 ≤ j <n, is set to the length of the shortest path from vertex v to vertex j
3 // in a digraph G with n vertices and edge lengths given by length [i ][j ].
4 {
5   for (int i = 0; i < n; i++) {s [i ] = FALSE; dist [i ] = length [v ][i ];} // initialize
6   s [v ] = TRUE;
7   dist [v ] = 0;

8   for (i = 0; i < n −2; i++) { // determine n −1 paths from vertex v
9       int u = choose (n);  // choose returns a value u such that:
10                            // dist [u ] = minimum dist [w ], where s [w ] = FALSE
11      s [u ] = TRUE;
12      for (int w = 0; w < n; w++)
13          if (! s [w ])
14              if (dist [u ] + length [u ][w ] < dist [w ])
15                  dist [w ] = dist [u ] + length [u ][w ];
16   } // end of for (i = 0; ...)
17 }
```

Program 6.8: Determining the shortest paths

Analysis of *ShortestPath*: From our earlier discussion, it is easy to see that the algorithm works. The time taken by the algorithm on a graph with n vertices is $O(n^2)$. To see this, note that the **for** loop of line 5 takes $O(n)$ time. The **for** loop of line 8 is executed $n - 2$ times. Each execution of this loop requires $O(n)$ time at line 9 to select the next vertex and again in lines 12 to 15 to update *dist*. So, the total time for this loop is $O(n^2)$. If a list of T vertices currently not in S is maintained, then the number of nodes on this list would at any time be $n - i$. This would speed up lines 9 and 12 to 15, but the asymptotic time would remain $O(n^2)$. This and other variations of the algorithm are explored in the exercises.

Any shortest-path algorithm must examine each edge in the graph at least once, since any of the edges could be in a shortest path. Hence, the minimum possible time for such an algorithm would be $O(e)$. Since length-adjacency matrices were used to represent the graph, it takes $O(n^2)$ time just to determine which edges are in G, so any shortest-path algorithm, that uses this representation must take $O(n^2)$. For this representation, then, algorithm *ShortestPath* is optimal to within a constant factor. Even if a change to adjacency lists is made, only the overall time for the **for** loop of lines 12 to 15 can be brought down to $O(e)$ (since the *dist* can change only for vertices that are adjacent from u). The total time for line 9 remains $O(n^2)$. By using Fibonacci heaps (see Chapter 9) and adjacency lists, the greedy algorithm for the single-source/all-destinations problem can be implemented to have complexity $O(n\log n + e)$. For sparse graphs, this implementation is superior to that of Program 6.8. □

Example 6.5: Consider the eight-vertex digraph of Figure 6.26(a) with length-adjacency matrix as in Figure 6.26(b). Suppose that the source vertex is Boston. The values of *dist* and the vertex u selected in each iteration of the **for** loop of lines 8 to 16 (Program 6.8) are shown in Figure 6.27. Note that the algorithm terminates when only seven of the eight vertices are in S. By the definition of *dist*, the distance of the last vertex, in this case Los Angeles, is correct, as the shortest path from Boston to Los Angeles can go through only the remaining six vertices. □

6.4.2 Single Source/All Destinations: General Weights

We now consider the general case when some or all of the edges of the directed graph G may have negative length. To see that function *ShortestPath* (Program 6.8) does not necessarily give the correct results on such graphs, consider the graph of Figure 6.28. Let $v = 0$ be the source vertex. Since $n = 3$, the loop of lines 8 to 16 is iterated just once; $u = 2$ in line 9, and no changes are made to *dist*. The function terminates with $dist[1] = 7$ and $dist[2] = 5$. The shortest path from 0 to 2 is 0, 1, 2. This path has length 2, which is less than the computed value of $dist[2]$.

When negative edge lengths are permitted, we require that the graph have no cycles of negative length. This is necessary so as to ensure that shortest paths consist of a finite number of edges. For example, consider the graph of Figure 6.29. The length of the shortest path from vertex 0 to vertex 2 is $-\infty$, as the length of the path

$$0, 1, 0, 1, 0, 1, \cdots, 0, 1, 2$$

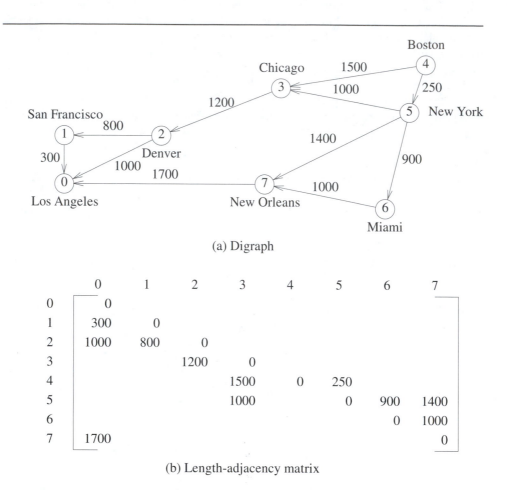

(a) Digraph

(b) Length-adjacency matrix

Figure 6.26: Digraph for Example 6.5

can be made arbitrarily small. This is so because of the presence of the cycle 0, 1, 0, which has a length of -1.

When there are no cycles of negative length, there is a shortest path between any two vertices of an n-vertex graph that has at most $n - 1$ edges on it. To see this, observe that a path that has more than $n - 1$ edges must repeat at least one vertex and hence must contain a cycle. Elimination of the cycles from the path results in another path with the same source and destination. This path is cycle-free and has a length that is no more than that of the original path, as the length of the eliminated cycles was at least zero. We can use this observation on the maximum number of edges on a cycle-free shortest path to obtain an algorithm to determine a shortest path from a source vertex to all remaining

			Distance							
Iteration	S	Vertex selected	LA [0]	SF [1]	DEN [2]	CHI [3]	BOST [4]	NY [5]	MIA [6]	NO [7]
Initial	--	----	$+\infty$	$+\infty$	$+\infty$	1500	0	250	$+\infty$	$+\infty$
1	{4}	5	$+\infty$	$+\infty$	$+\infty$	1250	0	250	1150	1650
2	{4,5}	6	$+\infty$	$+\infty$	$+\infty$	1250	0	250	1150	1650
3	{4,5,6}	3	$+\infty$	$+\infty$	2450	1250	0	250	1150	1650
4	{4,5,6,3}	7	3350	$+\infty$	2450	1250	0	250	1150	1650
5	{4,5,6,3,7}	2	3350	3250	2450	1250	0	250	1150	1650
6	{4,5,6,3,7,2}	1	3350	3250	2450	1250	0	250	1150	1650
	{4,5,6,3,7,2,1}									

Figure 6.27: Action of *ShortestPath* on digraph of Figure 6.26

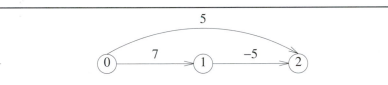

Figure 6.28: Directed graph with a negative-length edge

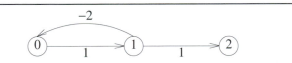

Figure 6.29: Directed graph with a cycle of negative length

vertices in the graph. As in the case of function *ShortestPath* (Program 6.8), we shall compute only the length, $dist[u]$, of the shortest path from the source vertex v to u. An exercise examines the extension needed to construct the shortest paths.

Let $dist^l[u]$ be the length of a shortest path from the source vertex v to vertex u under the constraint that the shortest path contains at most l edges. Then, $dist^1[u] = length[v][u]$, $0 \le u < n$. As noted earlier, when there are no cycles of negative length, we can limit our search for shortest paths to paths with at most $n-1$ edges. Hence, $dist^{n-1}[u]$ is the length of an unrestricted shortest path from v to u.

Our goal then is to compute $dist^{n-1}[u]$ for all u. This can be done using the dynamic programming methodology. First, we make the following observations:

(1)   If the shortest path from v to u with at most k, $k > 1$, edges has no more than $k-1$ edges, then $dist^k[u] = dist^{k-1}[u]$.

(2)   If the shortest path from v to u with at most k, $k > 1$, edges has exactly k edges, then it is comprised of a shortest path from v to some vertex j followed by the edge $<j,u>$. The path from v to j has $k-1$ edges, and its length is $dist^{k-1}[j]$. All vertices i such that the edge $<i,u>$ is in the graph are candidates for j. Since we are interested in a shortest path, the i that minimizes $dist^{k-1}[i] + length[i][u]$ is the correct value for j.

These observations result in the following recurrence for $dist$:

$$dist^k[u] = \min\{dist^{k-1}[u], \min_i\{dist^{k-1}[i] + length[i][u]\}\}$$

This recurrence may be used to compute $dist^k$ from $dist^{k-1}$, for $k = 2, 3, \cdots, n-1$.

Example 6.6: Figure 6.30 gives a seven-vertex graph, together with the arrays $dist^k$, $k = 1, \cdots, 6$. These arrays were computed using the equation just given. □

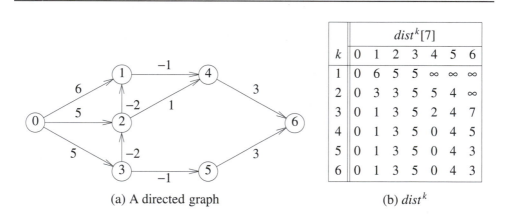

	$dist^k[7]$						
k	0	1	2	3	4	5	6
1	0	6	5	5	∞	∞	∞
2	0	3	3	5	5	4	∞
3	0	1	3	5	2	4	7
4	0	1	3	5	0	4	5
5	0	1	3	5	0	4	3
6	0	1	3	5	0	4	3

(a) A directed graph   (b) $dist^k$

Figure 6.30: Shortest paths with negative edge lengths

An exercise shows that if we use the same memory location $dist[u]$ for $dist^k[u]$, $k = 1, \cdots, n-1$, then the final value of $dist[u]$ is still $dist^{n-1}[u]$. Using this fact and the recurrence for $dist$ shown above, we arrive at the algorithm of Program 6.9 to compute the length of the shortest path from vertex v to each other vertex of the graph. This algorithm is referred to as the Bellman and Ford algorithm.

```
1 void Graph::BellmanFord(const int n, const int v)
2 // Single source all destination shortest paths with negative edge lengths
3 {
4     for (int i = 0; i < n; i++) dist [i] = length [v][i]; // initialize dist
5     for (int k = 2; k <= n−1; k++)
6         for (each u such that u != v and u has at least one incoming edge)
7             for (each <i, u> in the graph)
8                 if (dist [u] > dist [i] + length [i][u]) dist [u] = dist [i] + length [i][u];
9 }
```

Program 6.9: Bellman and Ford algorithm to compute shortest paths

Analysis of *BellmanFord*: Each iteration of the **for** loop of lines 5 to 8 takes $O(n^2)$ time if adjacency matrices are used and $O(e)$ time if adjacency lists are used. The overall complexity is $O(n^3)$ when adjacency matrices are used and $O(ne)$ when adjacency lists are used. The observed complexity of the shortest-path algorithm can be reduced by noting that if none of the *dist* values change on one iteration of the **for** loop of lines 5 to 8, then none will change on successive iterations. So, this loop may be rewritten to terminate either after $n − 1$ iterations or after the first iteration in which no *dist* values are changed, whichever occurs first. Another possibility is to maintain a queue of vertices i whose *dist* value changed on the previous iteration of the **for** loop. These are the only values for i that need to be considered in line 7 during the next iteration. When a queue of these values is maintained, we can rewrite the loop of lines 5 to 8 so that on each iteration, a vertex i is removed from the queue, and the *dist* values of all vertices adjacent from i are updated as in line 8. Vertices whose *dist* value decreases as a result of this are added to the end of the queue unless they are already on it. The loop terminates when the queue becomes empty. These two strategies to improve the performance of function *BellmanFord* are considered in the exercises. Other strategies for improving performance are discussed in the References and Selected Readings section. □

6.4.3   All-Pairs Shortest Paths

In the *all-pairs shortest-path problem,* we are to find the shortest paths between all pairs of vertices u and v, $u \neq v$. This problem can be solved as n independent single-source/all-destinations problems using each of the n vertices of G as a source vertex. If we use this approach on graphs with nonnegative edges, the total time taken would be $O(n^3)$ (or $O(n^2 \log n + ne)$ if Fibonacci heaps are used). On graphs with negative edges the run time will be $O(n^4)$ if adjacency matrices are used and $O(n^2 e)$ if adjacency lists are used.

Using the dynamic programming approach to the design of algorithms, we can obtain a conceptually simpler algorithm that has complexity $O(n^3)$ and works even when G has edges with negative length. Like the Bellman and Ford algorithm, this algorithm requires that G have no cycles with negative length. This algorithm is faster for graphs with negative edges, as long as the graphs have at least $c*n$ edges for some suitable constant c. Its observed run time is also less for dense graphs with nonnegative edge lengths. However, for sparse graphs with nonnegative edge lengths, using the single-source algorithm and Fibonacci heaps results in a faster algorithm for the all-pairs problem.

The graph G is represented by its length-adjacency matrix as described for function *ShortestPath* (Program 6.8). Define $A^k[i][j]$ to be the length of the shortest path from i to j going through no intermediate vertex of index greater than k. Then, $A^{n-1}[i][j]$ will be the length of the shortest i-to-j path in G, since G contains no vertex with index greater than $n-1$. $A^{-1}[i][j]$ is just *length* $[i][j]$, since the only i-to-j paths allowed can have no intermediate vertices on them.

The basic idea in the all-pairs algorithm is to successively generate the matrices $A^{-1}, A^0, A^1, \cdots, A^{n-1}$. If we have already generated A^{k-1}, then we may generate A^k by realizing that for any pair of vertices i and j, one of the following applies:

(1)   The shortest path from i to j going through no vertex with index greater than k does not go through the vertex with index k, so its length is $A^{k-1}[i][j]$.

(2)   The shortest path goes through vertex k. In this case, the path consists of a subpath from i to k and another one from k to j. These subpaths must be the shortest paths from i to k and from k to j going through no vertex with index greater than $k-1$, so their lengths are $A^{k-1}[i][k]$ and $A^{k-1}[k][j]$. Note that this is true only if G has no cycle with negative length containing vertex k. When cycles of negative length are present, the shortest i-to-j path going through no vertices of index greater than k may make several cycles from k to k and thus have a length substantially less than $A^{k-1}[i][k] + A^{k-1}[k][j]$.

The preceding rules yield the following formulas for $A^k[i][j]$:

$$A^k[i][j] = \min\{A^{k-1}[i][j], A^{k-1}[i][k] + A^{k-1}[k][j]\}, \ k \geq 0$$

and

$$A^{-1}[i][j] = length\ [i][j]$$

The algorithm *AllLengths* (Program 6.10) computes $A^{n-1}[i][j]$. The computation is done in place using the array a. The reason this computation can be carried out in place is that $A^k[i][k] = A^{k-1}[i][k]$ and $A^k[k][j] = A^{k-1}[k][j]$, so the in-place computation does not alter the outcome.

```
 1 void Graph::AllLengths(const int n)
 2 // length [n ][n ] is the adjacency matrix of a graph with n vertices.
 3 // a [i ][j] is the length of the shortest path between i and j
 4 {
 5    for (int i = 0; i < n; i++)
 6       for (int j = 0; j < n; j++)
 7          a [i ][j] = length [i ][j];   // copy length into a
 8    for (int k = 0; k < n; k++)   // for a path with highest vertex index k
 9       for (i = 0; i < n; i++)   // for all possible pairs of vertices
10          for (int j = 0; j < n; j++)
11             if ((a [i ][k ] + a [k ][j ]) < a [i ][j ]) a [i ][j ] = a [i ][k ] + a [k ][j ];
12 }
```

Program 6.10: All-pairs shortest paths

Analysis of *AllLengths*: This algorithm is especially easy to analyze because the loop-ing is independent of the data in the matrix a. The total time for function *AllLengths* is $O(n^3)$. An exercise examines the extensions needed to obtain the (i, j) paths with these lengths. Some speed-up can be obtained by noticing that the innermost **for** loop needs be executed only when $a [i][k]$ is not equal to MAXINT. □

Example 6.7: For the digraph of Figure 6.31(a), the initial a matrix, A^{-1}, plus its value after each of three iterations, A^0, A^1, and A^2, is also given in Figure 6.31. □

6.4.4   Transitive Closure

We end this section by studying a problem that is closely related to the all-pairs shortest-path problem. Assume that we have a graph G with unweighted edges. We want to determine if there is a path from i to j for all values of i and j. Two cases are of interest. The first case requires positive path lengths; the second requires only nonnega-tive path lengths. These cases are known as the *transitive closure* and *reflexive transitive closure* of a graph, respectively. We define them as follows:

Definition: The *transitive closure matrix*, denoted A^+, of a graph, G, is a matrix such that $A^+[i][j] = 1$ if there is a path of length > 0 from i to j; otherwise, $A^+[i][j] = 0$. □

Definition: The *reflexive transitive closure matrix*, denoted A^*, of a graph, G, is a matrix such that $A^*[i][j] = 1$ if there is a path of length ≥ 0 from i to j; otherwise, $A^*[i][j] = 0$.
□

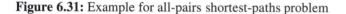

A^{-1}	0	1	2
0	0	4	11
1	6	0	2
2	3	∞	0

A^{0}	0	1	2
0	0	4	11
1	6	0	2
2	3	7	0

(a) Example digraph   (b) A^{-1} (c) A^{0}

A^{1}	0	1	2
0	0	4	6
1	6	0	2
2	3	7	0

A^{2}	0	1	2
0	0	4	6
1	5	0	2
2	3	7	0

(d) A^{1} (e) A^{2}

Figure 6.31: Example for all-pairs shortest-paths problem

Figure 6.32 shows A^{+} and $A*$ for a digraph. Clearly, the only difference between $A*$ and A^{+} is in the terms on the diagonal. $A^{+}[i][i] = 1$ iff there is a cycle of length >1 containing vertex i, whereas $A*[i][i]$ is always one, as there is a path of length 0 from i to i.

We can use function *AllLengths* (Program 6.10) to compute A^{+}. We begin with $length[i][j] = 1$ if $<i,j>$ is an edge in G and $length[i][j] = +\infty$ if $<i,j>$ is not in G. When *AllLengths* terminates, we can obtain A^{+} from the final matrix a by letting $A^{+}[i][j] = 1$ iff $a[i][j] < +\infty$. $A*$ can be obtained from A^{+} by setting all diagonal elements equal to 1. The total time is $O(n^{3})$.

Some simplification is achieved by slightly modifying function *AllLengths*. In this modification, we make *length* and a *Boolean* arrays. Initially, $length[i][j] =$ TRUE iff $<i,j>$ is an edge of G. That is, *length* is the adjacency matrix of the graph. Line 11 of *AllLengths* is replaced by

$a[i][j] = a[i][j] \,||\, (a[i][k] \,\&\&\, a[k][j])$

Upon termination of *AllLengths*, the final matrix a is A^{+}.

The transitive closure of an undirected graph G can be found more easily from its connected components. From the definition of a connected component, it follows that

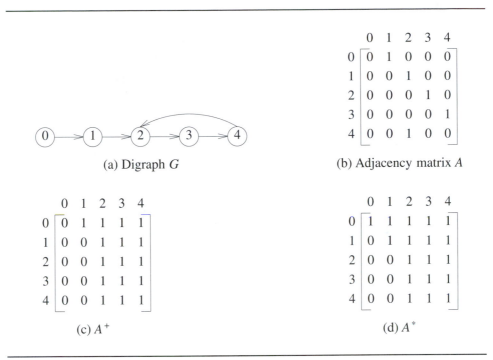

$$
\begin{array}{c|ccccc}
 & 0 & 1 & 2 & 3 & 4 \\
\hline
0 & 0 & 1 & 0 & 0 & 0 \\
1 & 0 & 0 & 1 & 0 & 0 \\
2 & 0 & 0 & 0 & 1 & 0 \\
3 & 0 & 0 & 0 & 0 & 1 \\
4 & 0 & 0 & 1 & 0 & 0 \\
\end{array}
$$

(a) Digraph G (b) Adjacency matrix A

$$
\begin{array}{c|ccccc}
 & 0 & 1 & 2 & 3 & 4 \\
\hline
0 & 0 & 1 & 1 & 1 & 1 \\
1 & 0 & 0 & 1 & 1 & 1 \\
2 & 0 & 0 & 1 & 1 & 1 \\
3 & 0 & 0 & 1 & 1 & 1 \\
4 & 0 & 0 & 1 & 1 & 1 \\
\end{array}
$$

$$
\begin{array}{c|ccccc}
 & 0 & 1 & 2 & 3 & 4 \\
\hline
0 & 1 & 1 & 1 & 1 & 1 \\
1 & 0 & 1 & 1 & 1 & 1 \\
2 & 0 & 0 & 1 & 1 & 1 \\
3 & 0 & 0 & 1 & 1 & 1 \\
4 & 0 & 0 & 1 & 1 & 1 \\
\end{array}
$$

(c) A^{+} (d) A^{*}

Figure 6.32: Graph G and its adjacency matrix A, A^{+}, and $A*$

there is a path between every pair of vertices in the component and there is no path in G between two vertices that are in different components. Hence, if A is the adjacency matrix of an undirected graph (i.e., A is symmetric) then its transitive closure A^{+} may be determined in $O(n^2)$ time by first determining the connected components of the graph. $A^{+}[i][j] = 1$ iff there is a path from vertex i to j. For every pair of distinct vertices in the same component, $A^{+}[i][j] = 1$. On the diagonal, $A^{+}[i][i] = 1$ iff the component containing i has at least two vertices.

EXERCISES

1. Let T be a tree with root v. The edges of T are undirected. Each edge in T has a nonnegative length. Write an algorithm to determine the length of the shortest paths from v to the remaining vertices of T. Your algorithm should have complexity $O(n)$, where n is the number of vertices in T. Show that this is the case.

2. Let G be a directed, acyclic graph with n vertices. Assume that the vertices are numbered 0 through $n-1$ such that all edges are of the form $<i, j>$, where $i < j$. Assume that the graph is available as a set of adjacency lists and that each edge has a length (which may be negative) associated with it. Write an algorithm to

determine the length of the shortest paths from vertex 0 to the remaining vertices. The complexity of your algorithm should be $O(n + e)$, where e is the number of edges in the graph. Show that this is the case.

3. (a) Do the previous exercise, but this time find the length of the longest paths instead of the shortest paths.

   (b) Extend your algorithm of (a) to determine a longest path from vertex 0 to each of the remaining vertices.

4. Using the idea of algorithm *ShortestPath* (Program 6.8), give an algorithm to find a minimum-cost spanning tree whose worst-case time is $O(n^2)$.

5. Use algorithm *ShortestPath* to obtain, in nondecreasing order, the lengths of the shortest paths from vertex 0 to all remaining vertices in the digraph of Figure 6.33.

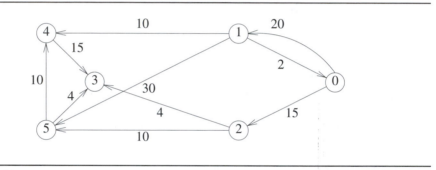

Figure 6.33: A digraph

6. Rewrite algorithm *ShortestPath* under the following assumptions:

   (a) G is represented by its adjacency lists, where each node has three fields: *vertex*, *length*, and *link*. *length* is the length of the corresponding edge and n the number of vertices in G.

   (b) Instead of S (the set of vertices to which the shortest paths have already been found), the set $T = V(G) - S$ is represented using a linked list.

   What can you say about the computing time of your new algorithm relative to that of *ShortestPath*?

7. Modify algorithm *ShortestPath* so that it obtains the shortest paths, in addition to the lengths of these paths. What is the computing time of your algorithm?

8. Using the directed graph of Figure 6.34, explain why *ShortestPath* will not work properly. What is the shortest path between vertices 0 and 6?

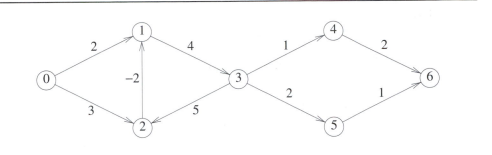

Figure 6.34: Directed graph on which *ShortestPath* does not work properly

9. Prove the correctness of function *BellmanFord* (Program 6.9). Note that this function does not faithfully implement the computation of the recurrence for $dist^k$. In fact, for $k < n - 1$, the *dist* values following iteration k of the **for** loop of lines 5 to 8 may not be $dist^k$.

10. Transform function *BellmanFord* into a C++ function. Assume that graphs are represented using adjacency lists in which each node has an additional field called *length* that gives the length of the edge represented by that node. As a result of this, there is no length-adjacency matrix. Generate some test graphs and test the correctness of your function.

11. Rewrite function *BellmanFord* so that the loop of lines 5 to 8 terminates either after $n - 1$ iterations or after the first iteration in which no *dist* values are changed, whichever occurs first.

12. Rewrite function *BellmanFord* by replacing the loop of lines 5 to 8 with code that uses a queue of vertices that may potentially result in a reduction of other *dist* vertices. This queue initially contains all vertices that are adjacent from the source vertex v. On each successive iteration of the new loop, a vertex i is removed from the queue (unless the queue is empty), and the *dist* values to vertices adjacent from i are updated as in line 8 of Program 6.9. When the *dist* value of a vertex is reduced because of this, it is added to the queue unless it is already on the queue.

    (a) Prove that the new function produces the same results as the original one.

    (b) Show that the complexity of the new function is no more than that of the original one.

13. Compare the run-time performance of the Bellman and Ford functions of the preceding two exercises and that of Program 6.9. For this, generate test graphs that will expose the relative performance of the three functions.

14. Modify function *BellmanFord* so that it obtains the shortest paths, in addition to the lengths of these paths. What is the computing time of your function?

15. Modify function *AllLengths* (Program 6.10) so that it obtains a shortest path for all pairs of vertices. What is the computing time of your new function?

16. Use function *AllLengths* to obtain the lengths of the shortest paths between all pairs of vertices in the graph of Figure 6.33. Does *AllLengths* give the right answers? Why?

17. By considering the complete graph with n vertices, show that the maximum number of simple paths between two vertices is $O((n-1)!)$.

18. Show that $A^+ = A^* \times A$, where matrix multiplication of the two matrices is defined as $a_{ij}^+ = \vee_{k=1}^n a_{ik}^* \wedge a_{kj}$. $\vee$ is the logical **or** operation, and $\wedge$ is the logical **and** operation.

19. Obtain the matrices A^+ and A^* for the digraph of Figure 6.15.

6.5 ACTIVITY NETWORKS

6.5.1 Activity-on-Vertex (AOV) Networks

All but the simplest of projects can be subdivided into several subprojects called activities. The successful completion of these activities results in the completion of the entire project. A student working toward a degree in computer science must complete several courses successfully. The project in this case is to complete the major, and the activities are the individual courses that have to be taken. Figure 6.35 lists the courses needed for a computer science major at a hypothetical university. Some of these courses may be taken independently of others; other courses have prerequisites and can be taken only if all the prerequisites have already been taken. The data structures course cannot be started until certain programming and math courses have been completed. Thus, prerequisites define precedence relations between courses. The relationships defined may be more clearly represented using a directed graph in which the vertices represent courses and the directed edges represent prerequisites.

Definition: A directed graph G in which the vertices represent tasks or activities and the edges represent precedence relations between tasks is an *activity-on-vertex network* or AOV network. □

Figure 6.35(b) is the AOV network corresponding to the courses of Figure 6.35(a). Each edge $<i, j>$ implies that course i is a prerequisite of course j.

Definition: Vertex i in an AOV network G is a *predecessor* of vertex j iff there is a directed path from vertex i to vertex j. i is an *immediate predecessor* of j iff $<i,j>$ is an

Course number	Course name	Prerequisites
C1	Programming I	None
C2	Discrete Mathematics	None
C3	Data Structures	C1, C2
C4	Calculus I	None
C5	Calculus II	C4
C6	Linear Algebra	C5
C7	Analysis of Algorithms	C3, C6
C8	Assembly Language	C3
C9	Operating Systems	C7, C8
C10	Programming Languages	C7
C11	Compiler Design	C10
C12	Artificial Intelligence	C7
C13	Computational Theory	C7
C14	Parallel Algorithms	C13
C15	Numerical Analysis	C5

(a) Courses needed for a computer science degree at a hypothetical university

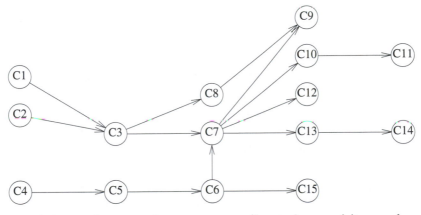

(b) AOV network representing courses as vertices and prerequisites as edges

Figure 6.35: An activity-on-vertex (AOV) network

edge in G. If i is a predecessor of j, then j is a *successor* of i. If i is an immediate predecessor of j, then j is an *immediate successor* of i. □

C3 and C6 are immediate predecessors of C7. C9, C10, C12, and C13 are immediate successors of C7. C14 is a successor, but not an immediate successor, of C3.

Definition: A relation · is *transitive* iff it is the case that for all triples i,j,k, $i·j$ and $j·k \Rightarrow i·k$. A relation · is *irreflexive* on a set S if for no element x in S it is the case that $x·x$. A precedence relation that is both transitive and irreflexive is a *partial order*. □

Notice that the precedence relation defined by course prerequisites is transitive. That is, if course i must be taken before course j (as i is a prerequiste of j), and if j must be taken before k, then i must be taken before k. This fact is not obvious from the AOV network. For example, <C4, C5> and <C5, C6> are edges in the AOV network of Figure 6.35(b). However, <C4, C6> is not. Generally, AOV networks are incompletely specified, and the edges needed to make the precedence relation transitive are implied.

If the precedence relation defined by the edges of an AOV network is not irreflexive, then there is an activity that is a predecessor of itself and so must be completed before it can be started. This is clearly impossible. When there are no inconsistencies of this type, the project is feasible. Given an AOV network, one of our concerns would be to determine whether or not the precedence relation defined by its edges is irreflexive. This is identical to determining whether or not the network contains any directed cycles. A directed graph with no directed cycles is an *acyclic* graph. Our algorithm to test an AOV network for feasibility will also generate a linear ordering, $v_0, v_1, \cdots, v_{n-1}$, of the vertices (activities). This linear ordering will have the property that if vertex i is a predecessor of j in the network, then i precedes j in the linear ordering. A linear ordering with this property is called a *topological order*.

Definition: A *topological order* is a linear ordering of the vertices of a graph such that, for any two vertices i and j, if i is a predecessor of j in the network, then i precedes j in the linear ordering. □

There are several possible topological orders for the network of Figure 6.35(b). Two of these are

> C1, C2, C4, C5, C3, C6, C8, C7, C10, C13, C12, C14, C15, C11, C9

and

> C4, C5, C2, C1, C6, C3, C8, C15, C7, C9, C10, C11, C12, C13, C14

If a student were taking just one course per term, then she or he would have to take them in topological order. If the AOV network represented the different tasks involved in assembling an automobile, then these tasks would be carried out in topological order on an assembly line. The algorithm to sort the tasks into topological order is straightforward and proceeds by listing a vertex in the network that has no predecessor. Then, this vertex together with all edges leading out from it is deleted from the network. These two steps are repeated until all vertices have been listed or all remaining vertices in the network have predecessors, and so none can be removed. In this case there is a cycle in the network, and the project is infeasible. The algorithm is stated more formally in Program 6.11.

Example 6.8: Let us try out our topological sorting algorithm on the network of Figure 6.36(a). The first vertex to be picked in line 5 is 0, as it is the only one with no predeces-

```
1 Input the AOV network.  Let n be the number of vertices.
2 for (int i = 0; i < n; i++) // output the vertices
3 {
4    if (every vertex has a predecessor) return; // network has a cycle and is infeasible.
5    pick a vertex v that has no predecessors;
6    cout << v;
7    delete v and all edges leading out of v from the network;
8 }
```

Program 6.11: Design of a topological sorting algorithm

sors. Vertex 0 and the edges <0, 1>, <0, 2>, and <0, 3> are deleted. In the resulting network (Figure 6.36(b)), vertices 1, 2, and 3 have no predecessor. Any of these can be the next vertex in the topological order. Assume that 3 is picked. Deletion of vertex 3 and the edges <3, 5> and <3, 4> results in the network of Figure 6.36(c). Either 1 or 2 may be picked next. Figure 6.36 shows the progress of the algorithm on the network. □

To obtain a complete algorithm that can be easily translated into a computer program, it is necessary to specify the data representation for the AOV network. The choice of a data representation, as always, depends on the functions you wish to perform. In this problem, the functions are

(1)   decide whether a vertex has any predecessors (line 4)

(2)   delete a vertex together with all its incident edges (line 7)

To perform the first function efficiently, we maintain a count of the number of immediate predecessors each vertex has. The second function is easily implemented if the network is represented by its adjacency lists. Then the deletion of all edges leading out of vertex v can be carried out by decreasing the predecessor count of all vertices on its adjacency list. Whenever the count of a vertex drops to zero, that vertex can be placed onto a list of vertices with a zero count. Then the selection in line 5 just requires removal of a vertex from this list.

As a result of the preceding analysis, we represent the AOV network using adjacency lists. The class definition is as follows:

```
class Graph {
private:
   List<int> *HeadNodes;
   int *count;
   int n;
```

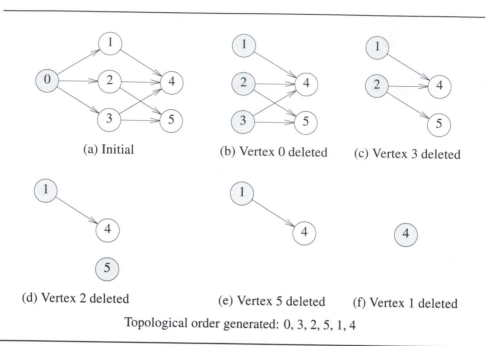

(a) Initial   (b) Vertex 0 deleted   (c) Vertex 3 deleted

(d) Vertex 2 deleted   (e) Vertex 5 deleted   (f) Vertex 1 deleted

Topological order generated: 0, 3, 2, 5, 1, 4

Figure 6.36: Action of Program 6.11 on an AOV network (shaded vertices represent candidates for deletion)

public:
```
  Graph(const int vertices = 0) : n (vertices) {
    HeadNodes = new List<int>[n];
    count = new int[n];
  };
  void TopologicalOrder ();
};
```

$count[i]$, for $0 \le i < n$, contains the in-degree of vertex i, and $HeadNodes[i]$ is a linked list of integers representing edges leaving vertex i. Each list node has two fields: $data$ (which contains the vertex) and $link$. The $count$ array can be set up easily at the time of input. When edge $<i,j>$ is input, the count of vertex j is incremented by 1. Figure 6.37(a) shows the internal representation of the network of Figure 6.36(a).

Inserting these details into the algorithm of Program 6.11, we obtain the C++ program $TopologicalOrder$ (Program 6.12). The list of vertices with zero count is maintained as a stack. A queue could have been used instead, but a stack is slightly simpler. The stack is linked through the $count$ field of the head nodes, since this field is of no use after the count has become zero.

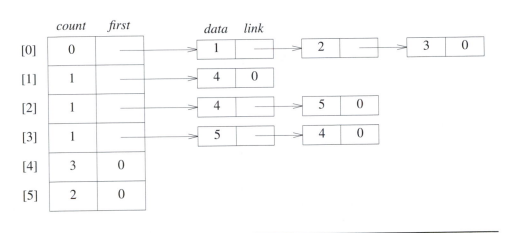

Figure 6.37: Internal representation used by topological sorting algorithm

Analysis of *TopologicalOrder*: As a result of a judicious choice of data structures, the algorithm is very efficient. For a network with n vertices and e edges, the loop of lines 5 and 6 takes $O(n)$ time; lines 8 to 14 take $O(n)$ time over the entire algorithm; and the **while** loop of lines 15 to 20 takes time $O(d_i)$ for each vertex i, where d_i is the out-degree of vertex i. Since this loop is encountered once for each vertex output, the total time for this part of the algorithm is $O((\Sigma_{i=0}^{n-1} d_i)+n) = O(e + n)$. Hence, the asymptotic computing time of the algorithm is $O(e+n)$. It is linear in the size of the problem! □

6.5.2 Activity-on-Edge (AOE) Networks

An activity network closely related to the AOV network is the *activity-on-edge*, or *AOE*, *network*. The tasks to be performed on a project are represented by directed edges. Vertices in the network represent events. Events signal the completion of certain activities. Activities represented by edges leaving a vertex cannot be started until the event at that vertex has occurred. An event occurs only when all activities entering it have been completed. Figure 6.38(a) is an AOE network for a hypothetical project with 11 tasks or activities: $a_1, \cdots, a_{11}$. There are nine events: 0, 1, $\cdots$, 8. The events 0 and 8 may be interpreted as ''start project'' and ''finish project,'' respectively. Figure 6.38(b) gives interpretations for some of the nine events. The number associated with each activity is the time needed to perform that activity. Thus, activity a_1 requires 6 days, whereas a_{11} requires 4 days. Usually, these times are only estimates. Activities a_1, a_2, and a_3 may be carried out concurrently after the start of the project. Activities a_4, a_5, and a_6 cannot

```
1 void Graph::TopologicalOrder ()
2 // The n vertices of a network are listed in topological order
3 {
4     int top = −1;
5     for (int i = 0; i < n; i++) // create a linked stack of vertices with
6         if (count [i ] == 0) { count [i ] = top; top = i;} // no predecessors

7     for (i = 0; i < n; i++)
8         if (top == −1) { cout << " network has a cycle" << endl; return;}
9         else {
10            int j = top; top = count [top ]; // unstack a vertex
11            cout << j << endl;
12            ListIterator<int> li (HeadNodes [j ]);
13            if (! li.NotNull ()) continue;
14            int k = *li.First ();
15            while (1) { // decrease the count of the successor vertices of j
16                count [k ]−−;
17                if (count [k ] == 0) { count [k ] = top; top = k;} // add vertex k to stack
18                if (li.NextNotNull ()) k = *li.Next (); // k is a successor of j
19                else break;
20            }
21        } // end of else
22 }
```

Program 6.12: Topological order

be started until events 1, 2, and 3, respectively, occur. Activities a_7 and a_8 can be carried out concurrently after the occurrence of event 4 (i.e., after a_4 and a_5 have been completed). If additional ordering constraints are to be put on the activities, dummy activities whose time is zero may be introduced. Thus, if we desire that activities a_7 and a_8 not start until both events 4 and 5 have occurred, a dummy activity a_{12} represented by an edge <5,4> may be introduced.

Activity networks of the AOE type have proved very useful in the performance evaluation of several types of projects. This evaluation includes determining such facts about the project as what is the least amount of time in which the project may be completed (assuming there are no cycles in the network), which activities should be speeded to reduce project length, and so on.

Since the activities in an AOE network can be carried out in parallel, the minimum time to complete the project is the length of the longest path from the start vertex to the finish vertex (the length of a path is the sum of the times of activities on this path). A path of longest length is a *critical path*. The path 0, 1, 4, 6, 8 is a critical path in the net-

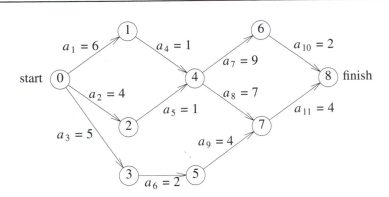

(a) Activity network of a hypothetical project

event	interpretation
0	start of project
1	completion of activity a_1
4	completion of activities a_4 and a_5
7	completion of activities a_8 and a_9
8	completion of project

(b) Interpretation of some of the events in the network of (a)

Figure 6.38: An AOE network

work of Figure 6.38(a). The length of this critical path is 18. A network may have more than one critical path (the path 0, 1, 4, 7, 8 is also critical).

The *earliest time* that an event i can occur is the length of the longest path from the start vertex 0 to the vertex i. The earliest time that event v_4 can occur is 7. The earliest time an event can occur determines the *earliest start time* for all activities represented by edges leaving that vertex. Denote this time by $e(i)$ for activity a_i. For example, $e(7)=e(8)=7$.

For every activity a_i, we may also define the *latest time*, $l(i)$, that an activity may start without increasing the project duration (i.e., length of the longest path from start to finish). In Figure 6.38(a) we have $e(6)=5$ and $l(6)=8$, $e(8)=7$ and $l(8)=7$.

All activities for which $e(i)=l(i)$ are called *critical activities*. The difference $l(i)-e(i)$ is a measure of the criticality of an activity. It gives the time by which an activity may be delayed or slowed without increasing the total time needed to finish the project. If activity a_6 is slowed down to take 2 extra days, this will not affect the project finish time. Clearly, all activities on a critical path are strategic, and speeding up non-critical activities will not reduce the project duration.

The purpose of critical-path analysis is to identify critical activities so that resources may be concentrated on these activities in an attempt to reduce project finish time. Speeding a critical activity will not result in a reduced project length unless that activity is on all critical paths. In Figure 6.38(a) the activity a_{11} is critical, but speeding it up so that it takes only 3 days instead of 4 does not reduce the finish time to 17 days. This is so because there is another critical path (0, 1, 4, 6, 8) that does not contain this activity. The activities a_1 and a_4 are on all critical paths. Speeding a_1 by 2 days reduces the critical path length to 16 days. Critical-path methods have proved very valuable in evaluating project performance and identifying bottlenecks.

Critical-path analysis can also be carried out with AOV networks. The length of a path would now be the sum of the activity times of the vertices on that path. By analogy, for each activity or vertex we could define the quantities $e(i)$ and $l(i)$. Since the activity times are only estimates, it is necessary to reevaluate the project during several stages of its completion as more accurate estimates of activity times become available. These changes in activity times could make previously noncritical activities critical, and vice versa.

Before ending our discussion on activity networks, let us design an algorithm to calculate $e(i)$ and $l(i)$ for all activities in an AOE network. Once these quantities are known, then the critical activities may easily be identified. Deleting all noncritical activities from the AOE network, all critical paths may be found by just generating all paths from the start-to-finish vertex (all such paths will include only critical activities and so must be critical, and since no noncritical activity can be on a critical path, the network with noncritical activities removed contains all critical paths present in the original network).

6.5.2.1   Calculation of Early Activity Times

When computing the early and late activity times, it is easiest first to obtain the earliest event time, $ee[j]$, and latest event time, $le[j]$, for all events, j, in the network. Thus if activity a_i is represented by edge $<k,l>$, we can compute $e(i)$ and $l(i)$ from the following formulas:

$$e(i)=ee[k]$$

and $\qquad\qquad\qquad\qquad\qquad\qquad\qquad\qquad\qquad\qquad\qquad\qquad\qquad$ (6.1)

$$l(i)=le[l]-\text{duration of activity } a_i$$

The times $ee[j]$ and $le[j]$ are computed in two stages: a forward stage and a backward stage. During the forward stage we start with $ee[0]=0$ and compute the remaining early start times, using the formula

$$ee[j]=\max_{i\in P(j)}\{ee[i]+\text{duration of}<i,j>\} \qquad\qquad (6.2)$$

where $P(j)$ is the set of all vertices adjacent to vertex j. If this computation is carried out in topological order, the early start times of all predecessors of j would have been computed prior to the computation of $ee[j]$. The algorithm to do this is obtained easily from algorithm *TopologicalOrder* (Program 6.12) by doing the following:

(1)   Define a **struct** *Pair* with two **public int** data members *vertex* and *dur*. It is assumed that *dur* contains the activity duration.

(2)   Define *HeadNodes* to be an array of *List<Pair>*s. Replace *List<int>* with *List<Pair>* in function *Graph::Graph()*. Replace *ListIterator<int>* with *ListIterator<Pair>* in line 12 of *TopologicalOrder*.

(3)   Replace line 14 with: *Pair p = *li.First ()*;
and line 18 with: **if** *(li.NextNotNull ()) p = *li.Next ()*;

(4)   Insert the lines
int $k = p.vertex$;
if $(ee[k] < ee[j] + p.dur) \ ee[k] = ee[j] + p.dur$;
between lines 15 and 16.

It is assumed that the array *ee* is initialized to zero. This modification results in the evaluation of Eq. (6.2) in parallel with the generation of a topological order. $ee(j)$ is updated each time the $ee(i)$ of one of its predecessors is known (i.e., when i is ready for output). The step **cout** $<< j <<$ **endl**; of line 11 may be omitted.

To illustrate the working of the modified *TopologicalOrder* algorithm, let us try it out on the network of Figure 6.38(a). The adjacency lists for the network are shown in Figure 6.39(a). The order of nodes on these lists determines the order in which vertices will be considered by the algorithm. At the outset, the early start time for all vertices is 0, and the start vertex is the only one in the stack. When the adjacency list for this vertex is processed, the early start time of all vertices adjacent from 0 is updated. Since vertices 1, 2, and 3 are now in the stack, all their predecessors have been processed, and Eq. (6.2) has been evaluated for these three vertices. $ee[5]$ is the next one determined. When vertex 5 is being processed, $ee[7]$ is updated to 11. This, however, is not the true value for $ee[7]$, since Eq. (6.2) has not been evaluated over all predecessors of 7 (v_4 has not yet been considered). This does not matter, as 7 cannot get stacked until all its predecessors have been processed. $ee[4]$ is next updated to 5 and finally to 7. At this point $ee[4]$ has been determined, as all the predecessors of 4 have been examined. The values of $ee[6]$ and $ee[7]$ are next obtained. $ee[8]$ is ultimately determined to be 18, the length of a critical path. You may readily verify that when a vertex is put into the stack, its early time has been correctly computed. The insertion of the new statement does not change the asymptotic computing time; it remains $O(e+n)$.

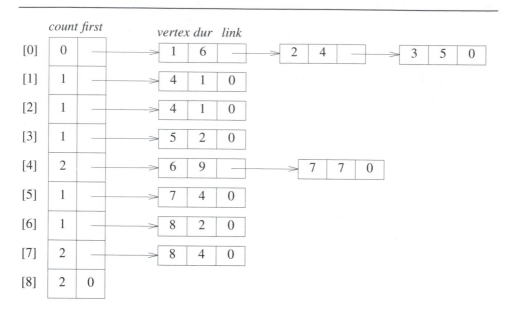

(a) Adjacency lists for Figure 6.38(a)

ee	[0]	[1]	[2]	[3]	[4]	[5]	[6]	[7]	[8]	Stack
initial	0	0	0	0	0	0	0	0	0	[0]
output 0	0	6	4	5	0	0	0	0	0	[3, 2, 1]
output 3	0	6	4	5	0	7	0	0	0	[5, 2, 1]
output 5	0	6	4	5	0	7	0	11	0	[2, 1]
output 2	0	6	4	5	5	7	0	11	0	[1]
output 1	0	6	4	5	7	7	0	11	0	[4]
output 4	0	6	4	5	7	7	16	14	0	[7, 6]
output 7	0	6	4	5	7	7	16	14	18	[6]
output 6	0	6	4	5	7	7	16	14	18	[8]
output 8										

(b) Computation of *ee*

Figure 6.39: Computing *ee* using modified *TopologicalOrder* (Program 6.12)

6.5.2.2 Calculation of Late Activity Times

In the backward stage the values of *le* [*i*] are computed using a function analogous to that used in the forward stage. We start with *le* [*n*−1]=*ee* [*n*−1] and use the equation

$$le [j] = \min_{i \in S(j)} \{le [i] - \text{duration of} <j,i>\} \qquad (6.3)$$

where $S(j)$ is the set of vertices adjacent from vertex j. The initial values for $le [i]$ may be set to $ee [n-1]$. Basically, Eq. (6.3) says that if $<j,i>$ is an activity and the latest start time for event i is $le [i]$, then event j must occur no later than $le [i] - $ duration of $<j,i>$. Before $le [j]$ can be computed for some event j, the latest event time for all successor events (i.e., events adjacent from j) must be computed. These times can be obtained in a manner identical to the computation of the early times by using inverse adjacency lists and making similar modifications to algorithm *TopologicalOrder* (Program 6.12). The *count* field of a head node initially is the out-degree of the vertex.

Figure 6.40 describes the process on the network of Figure 6.38(a). If the forward stage has already been carried out and a topological ordering of the vertices obtained, then the values of $le [i]$ can be computed directly, using Eq. (6.3), by performing the computations in the reverse topological order. The topological order generated in Figure 6.39(b) is 0, 3, 5, 2, 1, 4, 7, 6, 8. We may compute the values of $le [i]$ in the order 8, 6, 7, 4, 1, 2, 5, 3, 0, as all successors of an event precede that event in this order. This is done in Figure 6.40(c). In practice, one would usually compute both ee and le. The procedure would then be to compute ee first, using algorithm *TopologicalOrder*, modified as discussed for the forward stage, and then to compute le directly from Eq. (6.3) in reverse topological order.

Using the values of ee (Figure 6.39) and of le (Figure 6.40), and Eq. (6.1), we may compute the early and late times $e(i)$ and $l(i)$ and the degree of criticality (also called slack) of each task. Figure 6.41 gives the values. The critical activities are $a_1, a_4, a_7, a_8, a_{10}$, and a_{11}. Deleting all noncritical activities from the network, we get the directed graph or critical network of Figure 6.42. All paths from 0 to 8 in this graph are critical paths, and there are no critical paths in the original network that are not paths in this graph.

As a final remark on activity networks, we note that the algorithm *Topological Order* detects only directed cycles in the network. There may be other flaws, such as vertices not reachable from the start vertex (Figure 6.43). When a critical-path analysis is carried out on such networks, there will be several vertices with $ee [i] = 0$. Since all activity times are assumed > 0, only the start vertex can have $ee [i] = 0$. Hence, critical-path analysis can also be used to detect this kind of fault in project planning.

EXERCISES

1. Does the following set of precedence relations ($<$) define a partial order on the elements 0 thru 4? Why?

$$0 < 1; \ 1 < 3; \ 1 < 2; \ 2 < 3; \ 2 < 4; \ 4 < 0$$

2. (a) For the AOE network of Figure 6.44 obtain the early, $e()$, and late, $l()$, start times for each activity. Use the forward-backward approach.

   (b) What is the earliest time the project can finish?

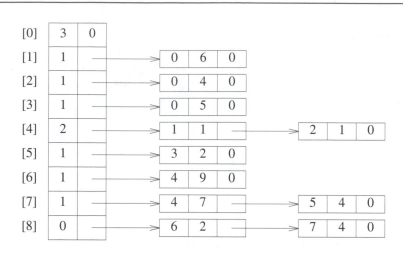

(a) Inverse adjacency lists for Figure 6.38(a)

le	[0]	[1]	[2]	[3]	[4]	[5]	[6]	[7]	[8]	Stack
initial	18	18	18	18	18	18	18	18	18	[8]
output 8	18	18	18	18	18	18	16	14	18	[7,6]
output 7	18	18	18	18	7	10	16	14	18	[5,6]
output 5	18	18	18	8	7	10	16	14	18	[3,6]
output 3	3	18	18	8	7	10	16	14	18	[6]
output 6	3	18	18	8	7	10	16	14	18	[4]
output 4	3	6	6	8	7	10	16	14	18	[2,1]
output 2	2	6	6	8	7	10	16	14	18	[1]
output 1	0	6	6	8	7	10	16	14	18	[0]

(b) Computation of *le*

Figure 6.40: Computing *le* for the AOE network of Figure 6.38(a) (continued on next page)

(c) Which activities are critical?

(d) Is there any single activity whose speed-up would result in a reduction of the project length?

3. Define a critical AOE network to be an AOE network in which all activities are critical. Let G be the undirected graph obtained by removing the directions and weights from the edges of the network.

(a) Show that the project length can be decreased by speeding up exactly one

$le\,[8] = ee\,[8] = 18$
$le\,[6] = \min\{le\,[8] - 2\} = 16$
$le\,[7] = \min\{le\,[8] - 4\} = 14$
$le\,[4] = \min\{le\,[6] - 9,\ le\,[7] - 7\} = 7$
$le\,[1] = \min\{le\,[4] - 1\} = 6$
$le\,[2] = \min\{le\,[4] - 1\} = 6$
$le\,[5] = \min\{le\,[7] - 4\} = 10$
$le\,[3] = \min\{le\,[5] - 2\} = 8$
$le\,[0] = \min\{le\,[1] - 6,\ le\,[2] - 4,\ le\,[3] - 5\} = 0$

(c) Computation of le using a reverse topological order

Figure 6.40: Computing le for the AOE network of Figure 6.38(a)

activity	early time e	late time l	slack $l - e$	critical $l - e = 0$
a_1	0	0	0	Yes
a_2	0	2	2	No
a_3	0	3	3	No
a_4	6	6	0	Yes
a_5	4	6	2	No
a_6	5	8	3	No
a_7	7	7	0	Yes
a_8	7	7	0	Yes
a_9	7	10	3	No
a_{10}	16	16	0	Yes
a_{11}	14	14	0	Yes

Figure 6.41: Early, late, and criticality values

activity if there is an edge in G that lies on every path from the start vertex to the finish vertex. Such an edge is called a bridge. Deletion of a bridge from a connected graph separates the graph into two connected components.

(b) Write an $O(n + e)$ algorithm using adjacency lists to determine whether the connected graph G has a bridge. If G has a bridge, your algorithm should output one such bridge.

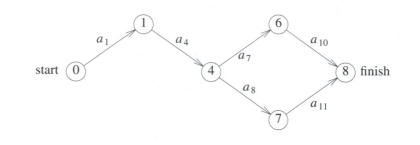

Figure 6.42: Graph obtained after deleting all noncritical activities

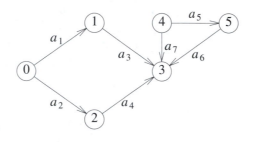

Figure 6.43: AOE network with some nonreachable activities

4. Write a C++ program that inputs an AOE network and outputs the following:
   (a) A table of all events together with their earliest and latest times.
   (b) A table of all activities together with their early and late times. This table should also list the slack for each activity and identify all critical activities (see Figure 6.41).
   (c) The critical network.
   (d) Whether or not the project length can be reduced by speeding a single activity. If so, then by how much?

5. Define an iterator class *TopoIterator* for iterating through the vertices of a directed acyclic graph in topological order.

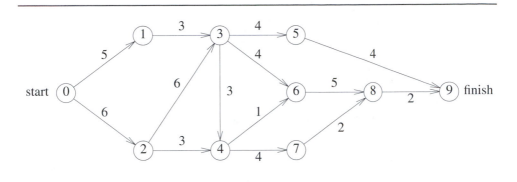

Figure 6.44: An AOE network

6.6   REFERENCES AND SELECTED READINGS

Euler's original paper on the Königsberg bridge problem makes interesting reading. This paper has been reprinted in: "Leonhard Euler and the Königsberg bridges," *Scientific American*, 189:1, 1953, pp. 66-70.

The biconnected-component algorithm is due to Robert Tarjan. This, together with a linear-time algorithm to find the strongly connected components of a directed graph, appears in the paper "Depth-first search and linear graph algorithms," by R. Tarjan, *SIAM Journal on Computing*, 1:2, 1972, pp. 146-159.

Prim's minimum-cost spanning tree algorithm was actually first proposed by Jarnik in 1930 and rediscovered by Prim in 1957. Since virtually all references to this algorithm give credit to Prim, we continue to refer to it as Prim's algorithm. Similarly, the algorithm we refer to as Sollin's algorithm was first proposed by Boruvka in 1926 and rediscovered by Sollin several years later. For an interesting discussion of the history of the minimum spanning tree problem, see "On the history of the minimum spanning tree problem," by R. Graham and P. Hell, *Annals of the History of Computing*, 7:1, 1985, pp. 43-57.

Further algorithms on graphs may be found in *The Design and Analysis of Computer Algorithms*, by A. Aho, J. Hopcroft, and J. Ullman, Addison-Wesley, Reading, MA, 1974; *Graph Theory with Applications to Engineering and Computer Science*, by N. Deo, Prentice-Hall, Englewood Cliffs, NJ, 1974; *Combinatorial Optimization*, by E. Lawler, Holt, Reinhart and Winston, New York, 1976; *Flows in Networks*, by L. Ford and D. Fulkerson, Princeton University Press, Princeton, NJ, 1962; and *Integer Programming and Network Flows*, by T. C. Hu, Addison-Wesley, Reading, MA, 1970.

6.7   ADDITIONAL EXERCISES

1. Program 6.13 was obtained by Stephen Barnard to find an Eulerian walk in a connected, undirected graph that has no vertices with odd degree.

Path Graph::euler (vertex v)
```
1 {
2    Path path = { };
3    for ((all vertices w  adjacent to v) && (edge (v,w) not yet used)) {
4       mark edge (v,w) as used;
5       path = {(v,w)} ∪ euler (w) ∪ path;
6    }
7    return path;
8 }
```

Program 6.13: Finding an Eulerian walk

    (a)   Show that if G is represented by its adjacency multilists and *path* by a linked list, then function *euler* works in time $O(n + e)$.

    (b)   Prove by induction on the number of edges in G that this algorithm does obtain an Eulerian walk for all graphs G having such a walk. The initial call to *euler* can be made with any vertex v.

    (c)   At termination, what has to be done to determine whether or not G has an Eulerian walk?

2. A *bipartite graph* $G = (V, E)$ is an undirected graph whose vertices can be partitioned into two disjoint sets, A and $B = V - A$, with the following properties: (1) No two vertices in A are adjacent in G, and (2) no two vertices in B are adjacent in G. The graph G_4 of Figure 6.5 is bipartite. A possible partitioning of V is $A = \{0,3,4,6\}$ and $B = \{1,2,5,7\}$. Write an algorithm to determine whether a graph G is bipartite. If G is bipartite your algorithm should obtain a partitioning of the vertices into two disjoint sets, A and B, satisfying properties (1) and (2) above. Show that if G is represented by its adjacency lists, then this algorithm can be made to work in time $O(n + e)$, where $n = |V|$ and $e = |E|$.

3. Show that every tree is a bipartite graph.

4. Prove that a graph G is bipartite iff it contains no cycles of odd length.

5. The *radius* of a tree is the maximum distance from the root to a leaf. Given a connected, undirected graph, write a function to find a spanning tree of minimum radius. (Hint: Use breadth-first search.) Prove that your algorithm is correct.

6. The *diameter* of a tree is the maximum distance between any two vertices. Given a connected, undirected graph, write an algorithm for finding a spanning tree of minimum diameter. Prove the correctness of your algorithm.

7. Let $G[n][n]$ be a wiring grid. $G[i][j] > 0$ represents a grid position that is blocked; $G[i][j] = 0$ represents an unblocked position. Assume that positions $[a][b]$ and $[c][d]$ are blocked positions. A path from $[a][b]$ to $[b][c]$ is a sequence of grid positions such that

    (a) $[a][b]$ and $[c][d]$ are, respectively, the first and last positions on the path

    (b) successive positions of the sequence are vertically or horizontally adjacent in the grid

    (c) all positions of the sequence other than the first and last are unblocked positions

    The length of a path is the number of grid positions on the path. We wish to connect positions $[a][b]$ and $[c][d]$ by a wire of shortest length. The wire path is a shortest grid path between these two vertices. Lee's algorithm for this works in the following steps:

    (a) [Forward step] Start a breadth-first search from position $[a][b]$, labeling unblocked positions by their shortest distance from $[a][b]$. To avoid conflicts with existing labels, use negative labels. The labeling stops when the position $[c][d]$ is reached.

    (b) [Backtrace] Use the labels of (a) to label the shortest path between $[a][b]$ and $[c][d]$, using the unique label $w > 0$ for the wire. For this, start at position $[c][d]$.

    (c) [Clean-up] Change the remaining negative labels to 0.

    Write algorithms for each of the three steps of Lee's algorithm. What is the complexity of each step?

8. Another way to represent a graph is by its incidence matrix, INC. There is one row for each vertex and one column for each edge. Then INC[i][j] = 1 if edge j is incident to vertex i. The incidence matrix for the graph of Figure 6.16(a) is given in Figure 6.45. The edges of Figure 6.16(a) have been numbered from left to right and top to bottom. Rewrite function *DFS* (Program 6.1) so that it works on a graph represented by its incidence matrix.

9. If ADJ is the adjacency matrix of a graph $G = (V,E)$, and INC is the incidence matrix, under what conditions will ADJ = INC $\times$ INC^T $-$ I, where INC^T is the transpose of matrix INC? I is the identity matrix, and the matrix product $C = A \times B$, where all matrices are $n \times n$, is defined as $c_{ij} = \vee_{k=0}^{n-1} a_{ik} \wedge b_{kj}$. $\vee$ is the || operation, and $\wedge$ is the && operation.

10. An edge (u, v) of a connected, undirected graph G is a *bridge* iff its deletion from G results in a graph that is not connected. In the graph of Figure 6.19, the edges $(0, 1)$, $(3, 5)$, $(7, 8)$, and $(7, 9)$ are bridges. Write an algorithm that runs in $O(n + e)$

$$
\begin{array}{c}
\quad\; 0\; 1\; 2\; 3\; 4\; 5\; 6\; 7\; 8\; 9 \\
\begin{array}{c}
0 \\ 1 \\ 2 \\ 3 \\ 4 \\ 5 \\ 6 \\ 7
\end{array}
\left[
\begin{array}{cccccccccc}
1 & 1 & 0 & 0 & 0 & 0 & 0 & 0 & 0 & 0 \\
1 & 0 & 1 & 1 & 0 & 0 & 0 & 0 & 0 & 0 \\
0 & 1 & 0 & 0 & 1 & 1 & 0 & 0 & 0 & 0 \\
0 & 0 & 1 & 0 & 0 & 0 & 1 & 0 & 0 & 0 \\
0 & 0 & 0 & 1 & 0 & 0 & 0 & 1 & 0 & 0 \\
0 & 0 & 0 & 0 & 1 & 0 & 0 & 0 & 1 & 0 \\
0 & 0 & 0 & 0 & 0 & 1 & 0 & 0 & 0 & 1 \\
0 & 0 & 0 & 0 & 0 & 0 & 1 & 1 & 1 & 1
\end{array}
\right]
\end{array}
$$

Figure 6.45: Incidence matrix of graph of Figure 6.16(a)

time to find the bridges of G. n and e are, respectively, the number of vertices and edges of G. (Hint: Use the ideas in function *Biconnected* (Program 6.5).)

11. Write a set of computer programs for manipulating graphs. Such a collection should allow input and output of arbitrary graphs, determining connected components, spanning trees, minimum-cost spanning trees, biconnected components, shortest paths, and so on. The capability of attaching weights to the edges should also be provided. Test the correctness of your program suite using suitable test data.

CHAPTER 7

SORTING

7.1 MOTIVATION

In this chapter, we use the term *list* to mean a collection of records, each record having one or more fields. The fields used to distinguish among the records are known as *keys*. Since the same list may be used for several different applications, the key fields for record identification depend on the particular application. For instance, we may regard a telephone directory as a list, each record having three fields: name, address, and phone number. The key is usually the person's name. However, we may wish to locate the record corresponding to a given number, in which case the phone number field would be the key. In yet another application we may desire the phone number at a particular address, so the address field could also be the key.

Once we have a collection of records, there are at least two ways in which to store them: sequentially or nonsequentially. For the time being let us assume we have a sequential list f, and we wish to retrieve a record with a certain key value k. If f has n records with $f[i].key$ the key value for record i, $1 \leq i \leq n$, then we may carry out the retrieval by examining the key values $f[n].key, \cdots, f[1].key$, in that order, until the correct record is located. Such a search is known as a sequential search, since the records are examined sequentially. Program 7.1 gives a sequential search function that uses the following data type:

```
class Element
{
public
    int getKey() const { return key ;};
    void setKey(int k) { key = k;}};
private:
    int key;
    // other fields
      .
      .
};
```

We use functions *getKey* () and *setKey* () to get and set data member *key*. Note that the declaration of function *getKey* () is followed by the **const** keyword. This makes *getKey* () a **const** member function, which means that it must not modify any of the data members of **class** *Element*. A member function that is to be invoked by a **const** class object must be declared as a **const** member function. Since we will occasionally be using function *getKey*() on objects of type **const** *Element*, we declare it as a **const** member function.

Finally, note that even though the expression *e . key* is invalid in a C++ program because an attempt is made to access a private data member, we use it in our descriptions of the algorithms for simplicity.

```
int SeqSearch (Element *f, const int n, const int k)
// Search a list f with key values f[1]. key,  ··· ,f[n]. key. Return i
// such that f [i]. key = = k.  If there is no such record, return 0.
{
    int i = n;
    f [0]. setKey(k);
    while (f [i]. getKey () != k) i−−;
    return i;
}
```

Program 7.1: Sequential search

Note that the introduction of the dummy record 0 with $f[0]. key = k$ simplifies the search by eliminating the need for an end-of-list test ($i < 1$) in the **while** loop. Although this might appear to be a minor improvement, it actually reduces the run time considerably for large n. If no record in the list has key value k, then $i = 0$, and the above function requires $n + 1$ comparisons. The number of key comparisons made in the case of a successful search depends on the position of the key in the list. If all keys are distinct and key $f[i]. key$ is being searched for, then $n − i + 1$ key comparisons are made. The average number of comparisons for a successful search is, therefore,

$$\sum_{1 \leq i \leq n} (n − i + 1)/n = (n + 1)/2.$$

It is possible to do much better when looking up phone numbers. The fact that the entries in the list (i.e., the telephone directory) are in lexicographic order (on the name key) enables one to look up a number while examining only a very few entries in the list. Binary search (see Chapter 1) is one of the better-known methods for searching an ordered, sequential list. A binary search takes only O($\log n$) time to search a list with n records. This is considerably better than the O(n) time required by a sequential search. We note that when a sequential search is performed on an ordered list, the conditional of the **while** loop of *SeqSearch* can be changed to $f[i].getKey() > k$. This improves the performance for the case of unsuccessful searches.

Getting back to our example of the telephone directory, we notice that neither a sequential nor a binary search strategy corresponds to the search method actually employed by humans. If we are looking for a name that begins with the letter W, we start the search toward the end of the directory rather than at the middle. A search method based on this interpolation scheme would begin by comparing k with $f[i].key$, where $i = ((k - f[l].key)/(f[u].key - f[l].key)) * n$, and $f[l].key$ and $f[u].key$ are the values of the smallest and largest keys in the list. An interpolation search can be used only when the list is ordered. The behavior of such a search depends on the distribution of the keys in the list.

We have seen that as far as the searching problem is concerned, something is to be gained by maintaining the list in an ordered manner if the list is to be searched repeatedly. Let us now look at another example in which the use of ordered lists greatly reduces the computational effort. The problem we are now concerned with is that of comparing two lists of records containing data that are essentially the same but have been obtained from two different sources. Such a problem could arise, for instance, in the case of the United States Internal Revenue Service (IRS), which might receive millions of forms from various employers stating how much they paid their employees and then another set of forms from individual employees stating how much they received. So we have two lists of records, and we wish to verify that there is no discrepancy between the two sets of information. Since the forms arrive at the IRS in a random order, we may assume a random arrangement of the records in the lists. The keys here are the social security numbers of the employees.

Let the two lists be $F1$ and $F2$ with keys $F1[i].key$ and $F2[i].key$. We make the following assumptions about the required verification:

(1) If there is no record in the employee list corresponding to a key $F1[i].key$ in the employer list, a message is to be sent to the employee.

(2) If the reverse is true, then a message is to be sent to the employer.

(3) If there is a discrepancy between two records with the same key, a message to this effect is to be output.

Function *Verify1* (Program 7.2) solves the verification problem by directly comparing the two unsorted lists. Its complexity is O(mn). On the other hand, if we first sort the two lists and then do the comparison, we can carry out the verification task in time

---

```
void Verify1(Element* F1, Element* F2, const int n, const int m)
// Compare two unordered lists F1 and F2 of size n and m, respectively.
{
    Boolean *marked = new Boolean [m ];
    for (int i = 1; i <= m; i++) marked [i ] = FALSE;

    for (i = 1; i <= n; i++)
    {
        int j = SeqSearch(F2, m, F1[i ]. getKey ()) ;
        if (j == 0) cout << F1[i ]. getKey () << " not in F2 " << endl; // satisfies (1)
        else
        {
            if (F1[i ]. other != F2[j ]. other) // satisfies (3)
                cout << "Discrepancy in " << F1[i ]. getKey () << ": "
                        << F1[i ]. other << " and " << F2[j ]. other << endl;
            marked [j ] = TRUE; // mark the record in F2[j ] as being seen
        }
    }
    for (i = 1; i <= m; i + +)
        if (! marked [i ]) cout << F2[i ]. getKey () << " not in F1. " << endl; // satisfies (2)
    delete [ ] marked ;
}
```

Program 7.2: Verifying two lists using a sequential search

$O(t_{sort}(n)+t_{sort}(m) + n + m)$, where $t_{sort}(n)$ is the time needed to sort a list of n records. As we shall see, it is possible to sort n records in $O(n\log n)$ time, so the computing time becomes $O(\max\{n\log n, m\log m\})$. Function *Verify2* (Program 7.3) achieves this time.

We have seen two important uses of sorting: (1) as an aid in searching and (2) as a means for matching entries in lists. Sorting also finds application in the solution of many other more complex problems, e.g., from operations research and job scheduling. In fact, it is estimated that over 25 percent of all computing time is spent on sorting, with some installations spending more than 50 percent of their computing time sorting lists. Consequently, the problem of sorting has great relevance in the study of computing. Unfortunately, no one method is the best for all initial orderings of the list being sorted. We shall therefore study several methods, indicating when one is superior to the others.

First let us formally state the problem we are about to consider. We are given a list of records $(R_1, R_2, \cdots, R_n)$. Each record, R_i, has key value K_i. In addition, we assume an ordering relation ($<$) on the keys so that for any two key values x and y, $x = y$ or $x < y$ or $y < x$. The ordering relation ($<$) is assumed to be transitive (i.e., for any three values x, y, and z, $x < y$ and $y < z$ implies $x < z$). The sorting problem then is that of

---

```
void Verify2(Element* F1, Element* F2, const int n, const int m)
// Same task as Verify1. However this time sort F1 and F2 so that the keys are in
// increasing order in each list. We assume that the keys in each list are identical
{
    sort(F1, n);
    sort(F2, m);
    int i = 1; int j = 1;
    while (( i <= n) && (j <= m))
        switch (compare (F1[i]. getKey (), F2[j]. getKey ()))
        {
            case '<': cout << F1[i]. getKey () << " not in F2" << endl;
                      i++;
                      break;
            case '=': if (F1[i]. other != F2[j]. other)
                          cout << "Discrepancy in " << F1[i]. getKey () << ": " << F1[i]. other
                               << " and " << F2[j]. other << endl;
                      i ++; j ++;
                      break;
            case '>': cout << F2[j]. getKey () << " not in F1" << endl;
                      j ++;
        }
    if (i <= n) PrintRest(F1, i, n, 1); // print records i through n of F1
    else if (j <= m) PrintRest(F2, j, m, 2); // print records j through m of F2
}
```

Program 7.3: Fast verification of two lists

finding a permutation, σ, such that $K_{\sigma(i)} \leq K_{\sigma(i+1)}$, $1 \leq i \leq n - 1$. The desired ordering is $(R_{\sigma(1)}, R_{\sigma(2)}, \cdots, R_{\sigma(n)})$.

Note that when the list has several key values that are identical, the permutation, σ, is not unique. We shall distinguish one permutation, σ_s, from the others that also order the list. Let σ_s be the permutation with the following properties:

(1) $K_{\sigma_s(i)} \leq K_{\sigma_s(i+1)}$, $1 \leq i \leq n - 1$.

(2) If $i < j$ and $K_i == K_j$ in the input list, then R_i precedes R_j in the sorted list.

A sorting method that generates the permutation σ_s is *stable*.

We characterize sorting methods into two broad categories: (1) internal methods (i.e., methods to be used when the list to be sorted is small enough so that the entire sort can be carried out in main memory) and (2) external methods (i.e., methods to be used on larger lists). The following internal sorting methods will be developed: insertion sort, quick sort, merge sort, heap sort, and radix sort. This development will be followed by a discussion of external sorting.

7.2 INSERTION SORT

The basic step in this method is to insert a record R into a sequence of ordered records, $R_1, R_2, \cdots, R_i$ ($K_1 \leq K_2, \cdots, \leq K_i$) in such a way that the resulting sequence of size $i + 1$ is also ordered. Function *insert* (Program 7.4) accomplishes this insertion. It assumes the existence of an artificial record R_0 with key $K_0 = $ MININT (i.e, all keys are $\geq K_0$).

```
void insert(const Element e, Element *list, int i)
// Insert element e with key e . key into the ordered sequence list [0], · · · , list [i ]
// such that the resulting sequence is also ordered. Assume that e . key ≥ list [0]. key.
// The array list must have space allocated for at least i + 2 elements
{
    while (e . getKey () < list [i ]. getKey ())
    {
        list [i +1] = list [i ];
        i − −;
    }
    list [i +1] = e;
}
```

Program 7.4: Insertion into a sorted list

The use of R_0 enables us to simplify the **while** loop, avoiding a test for end of list (i.e., $j < 1$). In insertion sort, we begin with the ordered sequence R_0, R_1 and successively insert the records $R_2, R_3, \cdots, R_n$. Since each insertion leaves the resultant sequence ordered, the list with n records can be ordered making $n - 1$ insertions. The details are given in function *InsertionSort* (Program 7.5).

Analysis of *InsertionSort*: In the worst case *insert* $(e, list, i)$ makes $i + 1$ comparisons before making the insertion. Hence its complexity is $O(i)$. *InsertionSort* invokes *insert* for $i = j - 1 = 1, 2, \cdots, n - 1$. So, the worst-case time is

$$O(\sum_{i=1}^{n-1} (i +1)) = O(n^2).$$

We can also obtain an estimate of the computing time of this method based on the relative disorder in the input list. Record R_i is *left out of order* (LOO) iff $R_i < \max_{1 \leq j < i}\{R_j\}$.

```
void InsertionSort(Element *list, const int n)
// Sort list in nondecreasing order of key
{
    list [0] . setKey(MININT) ;
    for (int j = 2; j <= n; j++)
        insert(list [j], list, j−1);
}
```

Program 7.5: Insertion sort

The insertion step has to be carried out only for those records that are LOO. If k is the number of LOO records, the computing time is $O((k + 1)n)$. The worst-case time is still $O(n^2)$. We can also show that the average time is $O(n^2)$. □

Example 7.1: Assume that $n = 5$ and the input key sequence is 5, 4, 3, 2, 1. After each insertion we have

j	[1]	[2]	[3]	[4]	[5]
−	**5**	4	3	2	1
2	**4**	**5**	3	2	1
3	**3**	**4**	**5**	2	1
4	**2**	**3**	**4**	**5**	1
5	**1**	**2**	**3**	**4**	**5**

For convenience, only the key field of each record is displayed, and the sorted part of the list is shown in bold. Since the input list is in reverse order, as each new record R_i is inserted into the ordered sublist $R_1, \cdots, R_{i-1}$, the entire sublist is shifted right by one position. Thus, this input sequence exhibits the worst-case behavior of insertion sort. □

Example 7.2: Assume that $n = 5$ and the input key sequence is 2, 3, 4, 5, 1. After each iteration we have

j	[1]	[2]	[3]	[4]	[5]
–	2	3	4	5	1
2	2	3	4	5	1
3	2	3	4	5	1
4	2	3	4	5	1
5	1	2	3	4	5

In this example, only R_5 is LOO, and the time for each $j = 2, 3$, and 4 is O(1), whereas for $j = 5$ it is O(n). □

It should be fairly obvious that *InsertionSort* is stable. The fact that the computing time is O($(k + 1)n$) = O(kn) makes this method very desirable in sorting sequences in which only a very few records are LOO (i.e., $k<<n$). The simplicity of this scheme makes it about the fastest sorting method for $n \leq 20$ (for example).

Variations

1. ***Binary insertion sort:*** We can reduce the number of comparisons made in an insertion sort by replacing the sequential searching technique used in *insert* (Program 7.4) with binary search. The number of record moves remains unchanged.

2. ***List insertion sort:*** The elements of the list are represented as a linked list rather than as an array. The number of record moves becomes zero because only the link fields require adjustment. However, we must retain the sequential search used in *insert*.

EXERCISES

1. Write the status of the list $F = (12, 2, 16, 30, 8, 28, 4, 10, 20, 6, 18)$ at the end of each phase of *InsertionSort* (Program 7.5).

2. Write a C++ function that implements binary insertion sort. What is the worst-case number of comparisons made by your sort function? What is the worst-case number of record moves made? How do these compare with the corresponding numbers for Program 7.5?

3. Write a C++ function that implements linked insertion sort. What is the worst-case number of comparisons made by your sort function? What is the worst-case number of record moves made? How do these compare with the corresponding numbers for Program 7.5?

7.3   QUICK SORT

We now turn our attention to a sorting scheme with very good average behavior. The quick-sort scheme developed by C. A. R. Hoare has the best average behavior among the sorting methods we shall be studying. In insertion sort the pivot key K_i currently controlling the insertion is placed into the correct spot with respect to the sorted sublist $(R_1, \cdots, R_{i-1})$. Quick sort differs from insertion sort in that the pivot key K_i is placed at the correct spot with respect to the whole list. Thus, if key K_i is placed in position $s(i)$, then $K_j \le K_{s(i)}$ for $j < s(i)$, and $K_j \ge K_{s(i)}$ for $j > s(i)$. Hence, after this positioning has been done, the original list is partitioned into two sublists, one consisting of records $R_1, \cdots, R_{s(i)-1}$ and the other of records $R_{s(i)}+1, \cdots, R_n$. Since in the sorted sequence all records in the first sublist must appear to the left of $s(i)$ and all in the second sublist to the right of $s(i)$, these two sublists may be sorted independently.

Function *QuickSort* (Program 7.6) is the resulting function. Function *InterChange(list, a, b)* performs $t = list[a]$; $list[a] = list[b]$; $list[b] = t$; . To sort elements 1 through n of a list *list*, the function invocation is *QuickSort (list, 1, n)*. Function *QuickSort* assumes that $list[n + 1]$ has been set to have a key at least as large as the remaining keys.

Example 7.3: The input list has 10 records with keys (26, 5, 37, 1, 61, 11, 59, 15, 48, 19). Figure 7.1 gives the status of the list at each call of *QuickSort*. Square brackets indicate sublists yet to be sorted. ☐

Analysis of *QuickSort*: The worst-case behavior of *QuickSort* is examined in Exercise 2 and shown to be $O(n^2)$. However, if we are lucky, then each time a record is correctly positioned, the sublist to its left will be of the same size as that to its right. This would leave us with the sorting of two sublists, each of size roughly $n/2$. The time required to position a record in a list of size n is $O(n)$. If $T(n)$ is the time taken to sort a list of n records, then when the list splits roughly into two equal parts each time a record is positioned correctly, we have

$$T(n) \le cn + 2T(n/2), \text{ for some constant } c$$

$$\le cn + 2(cn/2 + 2T(n/4))$$

$$\le 2cn + 4T(n/4)$$

$$.$$

$$.$$

$$.$$

$$\le cn \log_2 n + nT(1) = O(n \log n)$$

```
void QuickSort(Element *list, const int left, const int right)
// Sort records list [left], · · · , list [right] into nondecreasing order on field key.
// Key pivot = list [left]. key is arbitrarily chosen as the pivot key. Pointers i and j
// are used to partition the sublist so that at any time list [m]. key ≤ pivot, m < i,
// and list [m]. key ≥ pivot, m > j.  It is assumed that list [left]. key ≤ list [right + 1]. key.
{
  if (left < right) {
    int i = left,
        j = right + 1,
        pivot = list [left]. getKey ();
    do {
      do i + +; while (list [i]. getKey () < pivot);
      do j − −; while (list [j]. getKey () > pivot);
      if (i < j) InterChange(list, i, j);
    } while (i < j);
    InterChange(list, left, j);

    QuickSort(list, left, j−1);
    QuickSort(list, j +1, right);
  }
}
```

Program 7.6: Quick sort

R_1	R_2	R_3	R_4	R_5	R_6	R_7	R_8	R_9	R_{10}	left	right
[26	5	37	1	61	11	59	15	48	19]	1	10
[11	5	19	1	15]	26	[59	61	48	37]	1	5
[1	5]	11	[19	15]	26	[59	61	48	37	1	2
1	5	11	[19	15]	26	[59	61	48	37]	4	5
1	5	11	15	19	26	[59	61	48	37]	7	10
1	5	11	15	19	26	[48	37]	59	[61]	7	8
1	5	11	15	19	26	37	48	59	[61]	10	10
1	5	11	15	19	26	37	48	59	61		

Figure 7.1: Quick-sort example

Lemma 7.1 shows that the average computing time for function *QuickSort* is $O(n \log n)$. Moreover, experimental results show that as far as average computing time is concerned, quick sort is the best of the internal sorting methods we shall be studying.

Lemma 7.1: Let $T_{avg}(n)$ be the expected time for function *QuickSort* to sort a list with n records. Then there exists a constant k such that $T_{avg}(n) \le kn \log_e n$ for $n \ge 2$.

Proof: In the call to *QuickSort* (*list*, 1, n), K_1 gets placed at position j. This leaves us with the problem of sorting two sublists of size $j - 1$ and $n - j$. The expected time for this is $T_{avg}(j - 1) + T_{avg}(n - j)$. The remainder of the algorithm clearly takes at most cn time for some constant c. Since j may take on any of the values 1 to n with equal probability, we have

$$T_{avg}(n) \le cn + \frac{1}{n} \sum_{j=1}^{n} (T_{avg}(j - 1) + T_{avg}(n - j)) = cn + \frac{2}{n} \sum_{j=0}^{n-1} T_{avg}(j), \; n \ge 2 \quad (7.1)$$

We may assume $T_{avg}(0) \le b$ and $T_{avg}(1) \le b$ for some constant b. We shall now show $T_{avg}(n) \le kn \log_e n$ for $n \ge 2$ and $k = 2(b + c)$. The proof is by induction on n.

Induction base: For $n = 2$, Eq. (7.1) yields $T_{avg}(2) \le 2c + 2b \le kn \log_e 2$.

Induction hypothesis: Assume $T_{avg}(n) \le kn \log_e n$ for $1 \le n < m$.

Induction step: From Eq. (7.1) and the induction hypothesis we have

$$T_{avg}(m) \le cm + \frac{4b}{m} + \frac{2}{m} \sum_{j=2}^{m-1} T_{avg}(j) \le cm + \frac{4b}{m} + \frac{2k}{m} \sum_{j=2}^{m-1} j \log_e j \quad (7.2)$$

Since $j \log_e j$ is an increasing function of j, Eq. (7.2) yields

$$T_{avg}(m) \le cm + \frac{4b}{m} + \frac{2k}{m} \int_2^m x \log_e x \, dx = cm + \frac{4b}{m} + \frac{2k}{m} \left[\frac{m^2 \log_e m}{2} - \frac{m^2}{4} \right]$$

$$= cm + \frac{4b}{m} + km \log_e m - \frac{km}{2} \le km \log_e m, \; \text{for } m \ge 2 \quad \square$$

Unlike insertion sort, where the only additional space needed was for one record, quick sort needs stack space to implement the recursion. If the lists split evenly, as in the above analysis, the maximum recursion depth would be $\log n$, requiring a stack space of $O(\log n)$. The worst case occurs when the list is split into a left sublist of size $n - 1$ and a right sublist of size 0 at each level of recursion. In this case, the depth of recursion becomes n, requiring stack space of $O(n)$. The worst-case stack space can be reduced by a factor of 4 by realizing that right sublists of size less than 2 need not be stacked. An asymptotic reduction in stack space can be achieved by sorting smaller sublists first. In this case the additional stack space is at most $O(\log n)$.

Variation

Quick sort using a median of three: Our version of quick sort always picked the key of the first record in the current sublist as the pivot. A better choice for this pivot is the median of the first, middle, and last keys in the current sublist. Thus, *pivot* = *median* $\{K_l, K_{(l+r)/2}, K_r\}$. For example, *median*$\{10, 5, 7\} = 7$ and *median*$\{10, 7, 7\} = 7$.

EXERCISES

1. Write the status of the list $F = (12, 2, 16, 30, 8, 28, 4, 10, 20, 6, 18)$ at the end of each phase of *QuickSort* (Program 7.6).

2. (a) Show that *QuickSort* takes $O(n^2)$ time when the input list is already in sorted order.

   (b) Show that the worst-case time complexity of *QuickSort* is $O(n^2)$.

   (c) Why is *list* [*left*] . *key* ≤ *list* [*right* + 1] . *key* required in *QuickSort*?

3. (a) Write a nonrecursive version of *QuickSort* incorporating the median-of-three rule to determine the pivot key.

   (b) Show that this function takes $O(n \log n)$ time on an already sorted list.

4. Show that if smaller sublists are sorted first, then the recursion in *QuickSort* can be simulated by a stack of depth $O(\log n)$.

5. Quick sort is an unstable sorting method. Give an example of an input list in which the order of records with equal keys is not preserved.

7.4   HOW FAST CAN WE SORT?

Both of the sorting methods we have seen so far have a worst-case behavior of $O(n^2)$. It is natural at this point to ask the question, What is the best computing time for sorting that we can hope for? The theorem we shall prove shows that if we restrict our question to sorting algorithms in which the only operations permitted on keys are comparisons and interchanges, then $O(n \log n)$ is the best possible time.

The method we use is to consider a tree that describes the sorting process. Each vertex of the tree represents a key comparison, and the branches indicate the result. Such a tree is called a *decision tree*. A path through a decision tree represents a sequence of computations that an algorithm could produce.

Example 7.4: Let us look at the decision tree obtained for insertion sort working on a list with three records (Figure 7.2). The input sequence is R_1, R_2, and R_3, so the root of the tree is labeled [1, 2, 3]. Depending on the outcome of the comparison between keys K_1 and K_2, this sequence may or may not change. If $K_2 < K_1$, then the sequence becomes [2, 1, 3]; otherwise it stays [1, 2, 3]. The full tree resulting from these comparisons is given in Figure 7.2.

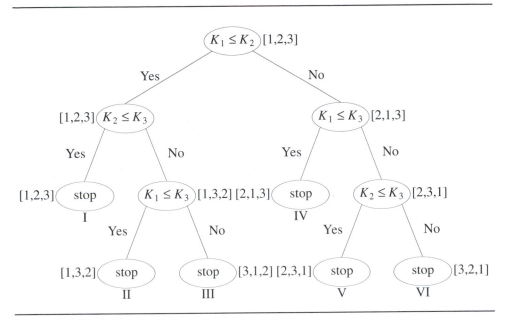

Figure 7.2: Decision tree for insertion sort

The leaf nodes are labeled I to VI. These are the only points at which the algorithm may terminate. Hence, only six permutations of the input sequence are obtainable from this algorithm. Since all six of these are different, and $3! = 6$, it follows that this algorithm has enough leaves to constitute a valid sorting algorithm for three records. The maximum depth of this tree is 3. Figure 7.3 gives six different orderings of the key values 7, 9, and 10, which show that all six permutations are possible. □

Theorem 7.1: Any decision tree that sorts n distinct elements has a height of at least $\log_2(n!) + 1$.

Proof: When sorting n elements, there are $n!$ different possible results. Thus, every decision tree for sorting must have at least $n!$ leaves. But a decision tree is also a binary tree, which can have at most 2^{k-1} leaves if its height is k. Therefore, the height must be at least $\log_2 n! + 1$. □

Corollary: Any algorithm that sorts only by comparisons must have a worst-case computing time of $\Omega(n \log n)$.

Proof: We must show that for every decision tree with $n!$ leaves, there is a path of length $cn\log_2 n$, where c is a constant. By the theorem, there is a path of length $\log_2 n!$.

leaf	permutation	sample input key values that give the permutation
I	1 2 3	[7, 9, 10]
II	1 3 2	[7, 10, 9]
III	3 1 2	[9, 10, 7]
IV	2 1 3	[9, 7, 10]
V	2 3 1	[10, 7, 9]
VI	3 2 1	[10, 9, 7]

Figure 7.3: Sample input permutations

Now

$$n! = n(n-1)(n-2) \cdots (3)(2)(1) \geq (n/2)^{n/2}$$

So, $\log_2 n! \geq (n/2)\log_2(n/2) = \Omega(n\log n)$. □

Using a similar argument and the fact that binary trees with 2^n leaves must have an average root-to-leaf path length of $\Omega(n \log n)$, we can show that the average complexity of comparison-based sorting methods is $\Omega(n \log n)$.

7.5 MERGE SORT

7.5.1 Merging

Before looking at the merge-sort method to sort n records, let us see how one may merge two sorted lists to get a single sorted list. We shall examine two different algorithms. The first one, Program 7.7, is very simple and uses O(n) additional space. The two lists to be merged are ($initList_1$, $\cdots$, $initList_m$) and ($initList_{m+1}$, $\cdots$, $initList_n$). The resulting merged list is ($mergedList_1$, $\cdots$, $mergedList_n$).

Analysis of *merge*: At each iteration of the **for** loop, *iResult* increases by 1. The total increment in *iResult* is $n - l + 1$. Hence, the **for** loop is iterated at most $n - l + 1$ times. The **if** statement moves at most one record per iteration. The total time is therefore O($n - l + 1$).

If each record has a size s, then the time is O($s(n - l + 1)$). When s is greater than 1, we can use linked lists for ($initList_1$, $\cdots$, $initList_m$) and ($initList_{m+1}$, $\cdots$, $initList_n$) and obtain a new sorted linked list containing these $n - l + 1$ records. Now, we will not

```
void merge(Element *initList, Element *mergedList, const int l, const int m, const int n)
// (initList [l ], · · · , initList [m ]) and (initList [m + 1], · · · , initList [n ]) are
// sorted lists with keys initList [l ]. key ≤ · · · ≤ initList [m ]. key and
// initList [m + 1]. key ≤ · · · ≤ initList [n ]. key. These lists are merged to obtain
// the sorted list (mergedList [l ], · · · , mergedList [n ]),
// where mergedList [l ]. key ≤ · · · ≤ mergedList [n ]. key.
{
    for (int i1 = l, iResult = l, i2 = m +1;  // i1, i2, and iResult are positions in the three lists
        i1 <= m && i2 <= n; // both input lists not yet exhausted
        iResult++)
      if (initList [i1]. getKey () <= initList [i2]. getKey ())
      {
        mergedList [iResult ] = initList [i1];
        i1++;
      }
      else
      {
        mergedList [iResult ] = initList [i2];
        i2++;
      }
    if (i1 > m)
      // (mergedList_{iResult}, · · · , mergedList_n) = (initList_{i2}, · · · , initList_n)
      for (int t = i2; t <= n; t++)
        mergedList [iResult +t −i2] = initList [t ];
    else
      // (mergedList_{iResult}, · · · , mergedList_m) = (initList_{i1}, · · · , initList_m)
      for (int t = i1; t <= m; t++)
        mergedList [iResult +t −i1] = initList [t ];
}
```

Program 7.7: Merging two sorted lists

need the additional space for $n − l + 1$ records as needed in *merge* for the array *mergedList*. Instead, space for $n − l + 1$ links is needed. The merge time becomes $O(n − l + 1)$ and is independent of s. Note that $n − l + 1$ is the number of records being merged. □

The second merging algorithm we shall consider is more complex. However, it requires only $O(1)$ additional space. We assume that $l = 1$. With this assumption the total number of records in the two lists being merged is n. Our discussion will make the further simplifying assumptions that n is a perfect square and that the number of records in each of the two lists to be merged is a multiple of $\sqrt{n}$. The development of the full algorithm with these assumptions removed is left as an exercise.

Suppose that $n = 36$ and that each of the two lists to be merged has 18 records. The first line of Figure 7.4 gives an example. Only the record keys are shown. We assume that the sorted key sequence is 0, 1, . . ., a, b, . . ., z. The vertical bar separates the two sorted lists of size 18 each. Each list can be thought of as consisting of sorted blocks of size $\sqrt{n} = 6$. The first step in the O(1) merge is to create a block that consists of the $\sqrt{n}$ records with the largest keys. This is done by scanning the two sorted lists from the right end to the left end. From this scan we discover that the $\sqrt{n}$ largest keys are those that are boxed in line 2 of Figure 7.4.

Figure 7.4: First eight lines for O(1) space merge example

Next, the records from the second list that are in the set of $\sqrt{n}$ records with largest keys are exchanged with the same number of records just to the left of those in the first list that are in this set. This exchange results in the configuration of line 3 of the figure. The vertical bars partition the n records into blocks of $\sqrt{n}$ consecutive records. Notice that the $\sqrt{n}$ records with largest keys form a single block. This block is now swapped with the leftmost block, and the rightmost block is sorted to get line 4. The $\sqrt{n} - 1$ blocks, excluding the one with the largest keys, are sorted by their rightmost records to get line 5. This completes the preprocessing needed to commence the merge.

The merge consists of several merge substeps, in each of which two segments of records are merged together. The first segment is the longest sorted sequence of records beginning at block two. Observe that this will always end at a block boundary. The second sequence consists solely of the next block. In the case of line 5, both of these sequences consist of exactly one block. A merge substep uses three place markers, which are depicted in line 5 by the symbol •. The leftmost marker indicates the position where the next merged record is to go. The second marker points to the next unmerged record of the first segment, and the third marker points to the next unmerged record of the second segment. Initially these are, respectively, positioned at the first records of the leftmost block, segment one, and segment two. The two segments are merged by comparing the two keys indicated by the second and third markers and exchanging the record with smaller key (in case of a tie, the record in the first segment is used) with the record indicated by the first marker. Following the first such exchange, we get line 6. Lines 7 and 8 show the configuration following each of the next two exchanges. This merge exchanging continues until all of the first segment has been merged. In our example, eight more records are merged before the current merge substep terminates. Line 1 of Figure 7.5 shows the configuration after the records with keys 3, 4, and 5 have been merged; line 2 shows the configuration following the merging of the records with keys 6, 7, and 8; and line 3 shows the status after segment one has been fully merged.

The following observations allow us to conclude that the merge of a merge substep can always be done as just described without using extra space beyond that needed to exchange two records:

(1)   There are $\sqrt{n}$ records from the initial position of the first marker to that of the second marker.

(2)   The second segment has $\sqrt{n}$ records.

(3)   Because of the tie breaker rule and the initial ordering of blocks by their last records, the first segment will be fully merged before the second.

When a merge substep is complete, the $\sqrt{n}$ records with largest keys are contiguous, and the first marker points to the first of these records. The third marker points to the first unmerged record in the second segment. The first segment for the next merge substep is the longest sorted segment that begins at the third marker. This segment always ends at a block boundary. The next block forms the second segment. In the case of

0 1 2 3 4 5 u x w 6 8 a|v y z 7 9 b|c e g i j k|d f h o p q|l m n r s t

0 1 2 3 4 5 6 7 8 u w a|v y z x 9 b|c e g i j k|d f h o p q|l m n r s t

0 1 2 3 4 5 6 7 8 9 a w|v y z x u b|c e g i j k|d f h o p q|l m n r s t

0 1 2 3 4 5 6 7 8 9 a w v y z x u b c e g i j k|d f h o p q|l m n r s t

0 1 2 3 4 5 6 7 8 9 a b c d e f g h i j k v z u|y x w o p q|l m n r s t

0 1 2 3 4 5 6 7 8 9 a b c d e f g h i j k v z u y x w o p q|l m n r s t

0 1 2 3 4 5 6 7 8 9 a b c d e f g h i j k l m n o p q y x w|v z u r s t

0 1 2 3 4 5 6 7 8 9 a b c d e f g h i j k l m n o p q r s t|v z u y x w

Figure 7.5: Last eight lines for O(1) space merge example

our example, the first segment begins at the record with key b and the second begins at the record with key d. Line 4 of Figure 7.5 shows the initial positions of the three markers. Line 5 shows the configuration after the first segment has been fully merged.

The first segment for the next merge substep begins at the record pointed at by the third marker. We find a longest sorted sequence that begins here. This consists of just three records. The next block forms the second sequence. The initial positions of the three markers for the third sort substep are shown in line 6 of the figure. Line 7 shows the status after this substep is complete. Now the longest sorted sequence that begins at the third marker consists of the records with keys r, s, and t. Since there is no next block, the second segment is empty. The last merge substep results in the configuration of line 8. Since the second segment is empty to begin with, the last merge substep can be performed using just two markers that move to the right one position at a time. We simply exchange the records indicated by these two markers.

Once the merge substeps have been performed, the block of records with largest keys is at the right end and may be sorted using an O(1) space sorting algorithm such as insertion sort. The steps involved in the O(1) space merge algorithm just described are summarized in Program 7.8.

// Steps in an O(1) space merge when the total number of records, n, is a perfect square,
// and the number of records in each of the lists to be merged is a multiple of $\sqrt{n}$.

Step 1: Identify the $\sqrt{n}$ records with largest keys. This is done by following right to left along the two lists to be merged.

Step 2: Exchange the records of the second list that were identified in Step 1 with those just to the left of those identified from the first list so that the $\sqrt{n}$ records with largest keys are contiguous.

Step 3: Swap the block of $\sqrt{n}$ largest records with the leftmost block (unless it is already the leftmost block). Sort the rightmost block.

Step 4: Reorder the blocks, excluding the block of largest records, into nondecreasing order of the last key in the blocks.

Step 5: Perform as many merge substeps as needed to merge the $\sqrt{n} - 1$ blocks, other than the block with the largest keys.

Step 6: Sort the block with the largest keys.

Program 7.8: O(1) space merge

Analysis of O(1) space merge: For the complexity analysis, we see that Steps 1 and 2 and the swapping of Step 3 each take $O(\sqrt{n})$ time and O(1) space. The sort of Step 3 can be done in $O(n)$ time and O(1) space using insertion sort. Step 4 can be done in $O(n)$ time and O(1) space using a selection sort (see Chapter 1). Note that selection sort sorts m records using $O(m^2)$ key comparisons and $O(m)$ record moves. When selection sort is used to implement Step 4 of Program 7.8, each block of $\sqrt{n}$ records is regarded as a single record with key equal to that of the last record in the block. So, each record move of selection sort actually moves a block of size $\sqrt{n}$. The number of key comparisons is $O(n)$, and although the number of block moves is $O(\sqrt{n})$, the time needed for these moves is $O(n)$. Note that if insertion sort is used in place of selection sort, the time becomes $O(n^{1.5})$, as insertion sort makes $O(m^2)$ record moves when sorting m records. So, in this application insertion sort is inferior to selection sort. The total number of merge substeps is at most $\sqrt{n} - 1$. The end point of the first segment for each merge substep can be found in time proportional to the number of blocks in the segment, as we need merely find the first block whose last key is greater than the first key of the next block. The time for each substep is therefore linear in the number of records merged. Hence, the total time for Step 5 is O(n). The sort of Step 6 can be done in O(n) time using either a selection or an insertion sort. When the steps of Program 7.8 are implemented as described here, the total time is O(n), and the additional space used is O(1). □

7.5.2 Iterative Merge Sort

This version begins by interpreting the input as n sorted lists, each of length 1. These lists are merged by pairs to obtain $n/2$ lists, each of size 2 (if n is odd, then one list is of size 1). These $n/2$ lists are then merged by pairs, and so on until we are left with only one list. The example below illustrates the process.

Example 7.5: The input list is (26, 5, 77, 1, 61, 11, 59, 15, 48, 19). The tree of Figure 7.6 illustrates the sublists being merged at each pass. □

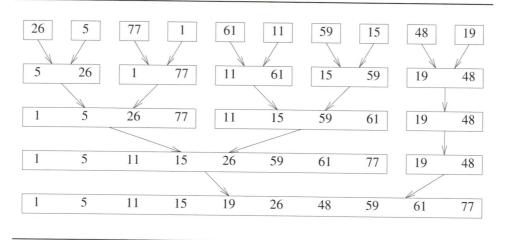

Figure 7.6: Merge tree

Since a merge sort consists of several merge passes, it is convenient first to write a function (Program 7.9) for this. Now the sort can be done by repeatedly invoking this function as in Program 7.10.

Analysis of *MergeSort*: Function *MergeSort* makes several passes over the records being sorted. In the first pass, lists of size 1 are merged. In the second, the size of the lists being merged is 2. On the ith pass the lists being merged are of size 2^{i-1}. Consequently, a total of $\lceil \log_2 n \rceil$ passes are made over the data. Since two lists can be merged in linear

```
void MergePass(Element *initList, Element *resultList, const int n, const int l)
// One pass of merge sort. Adjacent pairs of sublists of length l are
// merged from list initList to list resultList. n is the number of records in initList
{
    for (int i = 1; // i is the first position in the first of the two sublists being merged
         i <= n - 2*l + 1; // Are enough elements remaining to form two sublists of length l?
         i += 2*l)
        merge(initList, resultList, i, i + l - 1, i + 2 * l - 1);

    // merge remaining list of length < 2 * l
    if ((i + l - 1) < n) merge(initList, resultList, i, i + l - 1, n);
    else for (int t = i; t <= n; t++) resultList [t] = initList [t];
}
```

Program 7.9: Merge pass

```
void MergeSort(Element *list, const int n)
// Sort list list into nondecreasing order of the keys list [1]. key, ..., list [n]. key.
{
    Element *tempList = new Element[n +1];
    // l is the length of the sublist currently being merged
    for (int l = 1; l < n; l *= 2)
    {
        MergePass(list, tempList, n, l);
        l *= 2;
        MergePass(tempList, list, n, l); // interchange role of list and tempList
    }
    delete [ ] tempList;
}
```

Program 7.10: Merge sort

time (function *merge*), each pass of merge sort takes O(n)time. The total computing time is O(nlogn). □

It is easy to verify that *MergeSort* results in a stable sorting function.

7.5.3   Recursive Merge Sort

In the recursive formulation we divide the list to be sorted into two roughly equal parts called the left and the right sublists. These sublists are sorted recursively, and the sorted sublists are merged.

Example 7.6: The input list (26, 5, 77, 1, 61, 11, 59, 15, 49, 19) is to be sorted using the recursive formulation of merge sort. If the sublist from *left* to *right* is currently to be sorted, then its two sublists are indexed from *left* to $\lfloor (left + right)/2 \rfloor$ and from $\lfloor (left + right)/2 \rfloor + 1$ to *right*. The sublist partitioning that takes place is described by the binary tree of Figure 7.7. Note that the sublists being merged are different from those being merged in *MergeSort*. □

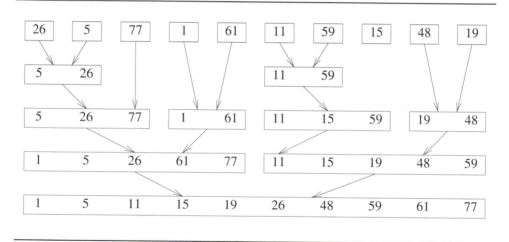

Figure 7.7: Sublist partitioning for recursive merge sort

From the preceding example, we see that if function *merge* (Program 7.7) is used to merge sorted sublists from one array into another, then it is necessary to copy sublists. For example to merge [5, 26] and [77], we would have to copy [77] into the same array as [5, 26]. To avoid this unnecessary copying of sublists, we look to a linked list representation for sublists. This results in an efficient recursive version of merge sort.

Each element is assumed to have three fields: *link*, *key*, and *other*. The structure is defined as

```
class Element
{
private:
   int key;
   Field other;
   int link;
public:
   Element() { link = 0 ;};
};
```

For simplicity, we assume that all functions that require access to the private members of *Element* are declared as **friend**s of *Element*. *list* [*i*] . *link* and *list* [*i*] . *key* are the link and key value fields in record *i*, $1 \le i \le n$. Note that for this application, the *link* fields are integers and not pointers. We assume that initially *list*[*i*] . *link* = 0, $1 \le i \le n$. Thus, each record is initially in a chain containing only itself. Let *start*1 and *start*2 be pointers to two chains of records. The records on each chain are assumed linked in nondecreasing order of the key field. Let **int** *ListMerge* (*list*, *start*1, *start*2) be a function that merges two chains *start*1 and *start*2 in array *list* and returns the first position of the resulting chain that is linked in nondecreasing order of key values. The recursive version of merge sort is given by function *rMergeSort* (Program 7.11). To sort the list $x_1, \cdots, x_n$ this function is invoked as *rMergeSort* (*x*, 1, *n*). The start of the chain ordered as described earlier is returned. If the list is to be physically rearranged into this order, one of the schemes discussed in Section 7.8 may be used. Function *ListMerge* is given in Program 7.12.

---

int *rMergeSort*(*Element* ∗ *list*, **const int** *left*, **const int** *right*)
// List *list* = (*list* [*left*], $\cdots$, *list* [*right*]) is to be sorted on the field *key*.
// *link* is a link field in each record that is initially 0.
// *rMergeSort* returns the index of the first element in the sorted chain.
// *list* [0] is a record for intermediate results used only in *ListMerge*.
```
{
   if (left >= right) return left;
   int mid = (left + right)/2;
   return ListMerge(list,
                 rMergeSort(list, left, mid), // sort left half
                 rMergeSort(list, mid + 1, right)); // sort right half
}
```

Program 7.11: Recursive merge sort

```
int ListMerge(Element *list, const int start1, const int start2)
// The sorted linked lists whose first elements are indexed by start1 and start2,
// respectively, are merged to obtain the sorted linked list. The index of the first element of the
// sorted list is returned. Integer links are used.
{
    int iResult = 0;
    for (int i1 = start1, i2 = start2; i1 && i2; )
        if (list [i1]. key <= list [i2]. key) {
            list [iResult ]. link = i1;
            iResult = i1; i1 = list [i1]. link;
        }
        else {
            list [iResult ]. link = i2;
            iResult = i2; i2 = list [i2]. link;
        }

    // move remainder
    if (i1 == 0) list [iResult ]. link = i2;
    else list [iResult ]. link = i1;
    return list [0]. link;
}
```

Program 7.12: Merging linked lists

Analysis of *rMergeSort:* It is easy to see that the recursive merge sort is stable, and its computing time is O(n log n). □

Variation

Natural merge sort: We can modify *MergeSort* to take into account the prevailing order within the input list. In this implementation we make an initial pass over the data to determine the sublists of records that are in order. The merge sort then uses these initially ordered sublists for the remainder of the passes. Figure 7.8 shows natural merge sort using the input sequence of Example 7.6.

EXERCISES

1. Write a function to shift the records (x_1, $\cdots$, x_n) circularly to the right by p, $0 \le p \le n$, positions. Your function should have time complexity O(n) and space complexity O(1). (Hint: Use three calls to a segment reversal function.)

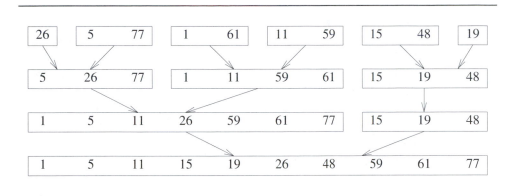

Figure 7.8: Natural merge sort

2. The two sorted lists $(x_1, \cdots, x_m)$ and $(x_{m+1}, \cdots, x_n)$ are to be merged to get the sorted list $(x_l, \cdots, x_n)$. Let $s = \lfloor \sqrt{n} \rfloor$.

(a) Assume that one of these lists has fewer than s records. Write a function to merge the two sorted lists in $O(n)$ time while using only $O(1)$ additional space. Show that your function actually has these complexities. (Hint: If the first list has fewer than s elements, then find the position, q, in the merged list of the first element of the first list; perform a circular shift of $q-1$ as in the preceding exercise. This circular shift involves only the records of the first list and the first $q-1$ records of the second. Following the circular shift, the first q records are in their final merged positions. Repeat this process for the second, third, and remaining elements of the initial first list.)

(b) Assume that both lists have at least s elements. Write a merge function with the same asymptotic complexity as that for (a). Show that your function actually has this complexity. (Hint: Partition the first list such that the first block has $s_1, 0 \le s_1 < s$, records and the remainder have s records. Partition the second list so that the last block has $s_2, 0 \le s_2 < s$ records. If $s_1 \ne 0$, then compare the first blocks of the two lists to identify the s_1 records with smallest key. Perform a swap as in Step 2 of Program 7.8 so that these s_1 records are in the leftmost block of the first list. If $s_2 \ne 0$, then using a similar process, we can get the s_2 records with largest keys into the rightmost block of the second list. Now, the leftmost block of size s_1 and the rightmost block of size s_2 are sorted. Following this, we may forget about them. The remaining blocks of the first and second lists may be arranged in sorted order using the merge function of part (a). Next, Program 7.8 may be used to merge them.)

(c) Use the functions for (a) and (b) to obtain an $O(n)$ time and $O(1)$ space function to merge two lists of arbitrary size.

(d) Compare the run time of the merge function of (c) with that of Program 7.7. Use $m = n/2$ and the values $n = 100, 250, 500, 1000, 2000, 5000,$ and 10,000. For each value of n use ten randomly generated pairs of sorted lists and compute the average merge time. Plot these for the two merge functions. What conclusions can you draw?

(e) Modify your function for part (b) so that it does not use the function of (a) to rearrange records in the first and second lists into sorted order. Rather, the last and first blocks of the first and second lists, respectively, are sorted. To find the largest s records we need to look at the last two blocks of the first list and the last block of the second list. Program this function and obtain run times using the data of (d). Add these to your plot of (d).

(f) Program the $O(1)$ space merge procedure as described by Huang and Langston in their paper cited in the References and Selected Readings section. This procedure begins by partitioning the first list as in (b). The second list is partitioned into blocks of size s, except for the last block whose size s_2 is such that $s \le s_2 < 2*s$. The largest s records are found and placed in the rightmost block of the first list. This is called the merge buffer. The rightmost block of the second list (i.e., the one with size s_2) is sorted. If $s_1 > 0$, the leftmost block of the first list is merged with the leftmost block of the second list using the last s_1 positions of the merge buffer. A swap of the leftmost s_1 records and those in the rightmost s_1 positions of the merge buffer results in moving the s_1 smallest records to their final place and also restores the merge buffer to contain the largest s records. Now we can forget about the first s_1 records and proceed to move the merge buffer to the leftmost block of size s and sort the remaining blocks by their last records. One of these blocks is of size s_2, and the sort should take this into account. Obtain the run times for this function using the data of (d). Add these results to your plot of (d). What conclusions can you draw?

3. Write the status of the list $F = (12, 2, 16, 30, 8, 28, 4, 10, 20, 6, 18)$ at the end of each phase of *MergeSort* (Program 7.10).

4. Suppose we use Program 7.8 to obtain a merge sort function. Is the resulting function a stable sort?

5. Prove that *MergeSort* is stable.

6. Write an iterative natural merge sort function using arrays as in function *MergeSort*. How much time does this function take on an initially sorted list? Note that *MergeSort* takes $O(n \log n)$ on such an input list. What is the worst-case computing time of the new function? How much additional space is needed?

7. Do the previous exercise using linked lists.

7.6 HEAP SORT

Although the merge sort scheme discussed in the previous section has a computing time of O(n log n), both in the worst case and as average behavior, it requires additional storage proportional to the number of records in the file being sorted. By using the O(1) space merge algorithm, the space requirements can be reduced to O(1). The resulting sort algorithm is significantly slower than the original one. The sorting method we are about to study, heap sort, requires only a fixed amount of additional storage and at the same time has as its worst-case and average computing time O(n log n). Although heap sort is slightly slower than merge sort using O(n) additional space, it is faster than merge sort using O(1) additional space.

In heap sort, we utilize the max-heap structure introduced in Chapter 5. The deletion and insertion functions associated with max heaps directly yield an O(n log n) sorting method. The n records are first inserted into an initially empty heap. Next, the records are extracted from the heap one at a time. It is possible to create the heap of n records faster by using the function *adjust* (Program 7.13). This function takes a binary tree T, whose left and right subtrees satisfy the heap property but whose root may not, and adjusts T so that the entire binary tree satisfies the heap property. If the depth of the tree with root *root* is d, then the **for** loop is executed at most d times. Hence the computing time of *adjust* is O(d).

```
void adjust(Element *tree, const int root, const int n)
// Adjust the binary tree with root root to satisfy the heap property. The left and right
// subtrees of root already satisfy the heap property.  No node has index greater than n.
{
    Element e = tree [root ];
    int k = e . getKey ();
    for (int j = 2*root; j <= n; j *= 2)
    { // first find max of left and right child
        if (j < n)
            if (tree [j ]. getKey () < tree [j +1]. getKey ()) j++;
        // compare max child with k. If k is max, then done
        if (k >= tree [j ]. getKey ()) break;
        tree [j /2] = tree [j ]; // move jth record up the tree
    }
    tree [j /2] = e;
}
```

Program 7.13: Adjusting a max heap

To sort the list, first we create a max heap by using *adjust* repeatedly, as in the first **for** loop of function *HeapSort* (Program 7.14). Next, we make $n - 1$ passes over the list. On each pass, we exchange the first record in the heap with the last record. Since the first record always contains the highest key, this record is now in its sorted position. We then decrement the heap size and readjust the heap. For example, on the first pass, we place the record with the highest key in the *n*th position; on the second pass, we place the record with the second highest key in position $n - 1$; and on the *i*th pass, we place the record with the *i*th highest key in position $n - i + 1$. The invocation is *HeapSort(list, n)*.

---

void *HeapSort*(*Element* **list*, **const int** *n*)
// The list *list* = (*list* [1], $\cdots$, *list* [*n*]) is sorted into nondecreasing order of the field *key*.
{
    for (**int** $i = n/2$; $i >= 1$; $i--$) // convert *list* into a heap
      adjust(*list*, *i*, *n*);

    for ($i = n-1$; $i >= 1$; $i--$) // sort *list*
    {
      Element $t = list [i +1]$; // interchange $list_1$ and $list_{i+1}$
      $list [i +1] = list [1]$;
      $list [1] = t$;
      adjust(*list*, 1, *i*); // recreate heap
    }
}

Program 7.14: Heap sort

Example 7.7: The input list is (26, 5, 77, 1, 61, 11, 59, 15, 48, 19). If we interpret this list as a binary tree, we get the tree of Figure 7.9(a). Figure 7.9(b) depicts the max heap after the first **for** loop of *HeapSort*. Figure 7.10 shows the array of records following each of the first seven iterations of the second **for** loop. The portion of the array that still represents a max heap is shown as a binary tree; the sorted part of the array is shown as an array. $\square$

Analysis of *HeapSort*: Suppose $2^{k-1} \leq n < 2^k$, so the tree has k levels and the number of nodes on level i is $\leq 2^{i-1}$. In the first **for** loop, *adjust* (Program 7.13) is called once for each node that has a child. Hence, the time required for this loop is the sum, over each level, of the number of nodes on a level multiplied by the maximum distance the node can move. This is no more than

$$\sum_{1 \leq i \leq k} 2^{i-1}(k-i) = \sum_{1 \leq i \leq k-1} 2^{k-i-1} i \leq n \sum_{1 \leq i \leq k-1} i/2^i < 2n = O(n)$$

In the next **for** loop, $n - 1$ applications of *adjust* are made with maximum depth $k = \lceil \log_2 (n + 1) \rceil$. Hence, the computing time for this loop is $O(n \log n)$. Consequent-

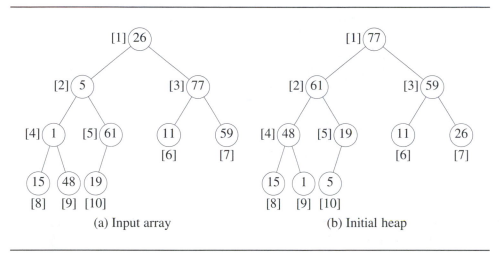

(a) Input array (b) Initial heap

Figure 7.9: Array interpreted as a binary tree

ly, the total computing time is O(*n* log *n*). Note that apart from some simple variables, the only additional space needed is space for one record to carry out the interchange in the second **for** loop. □

EXERCISES

1. Write the status of the list $F = (12, 2, 16, 30, 8, 28, 4, 10, 20, 6, 18)$ at the end of each phase of *HeapSort* (Program 7.14).

2. Heap sort is unstable. Give an example of an input list in which the order of records with equal keys is not preserved.

7.7   SORTING ON SEVERAL KEYS

We now look at the problem of sorting records on several keys, $K^1, K^2, \cdots, K^r$ (K^1 is the most significant key and K^r the least). A list of records $R_1, \cdots, R_n$ is said to be sorted with respect to the keys $K^1, K^2, \cdots, K^r$ iff for every pair of records i and j, $i < j$ and $(K_i^1, \cdots, K_i^r) \le (K_j^1, \cdots, K_j^r)$. The r-tuple $(x_1, \cdots, x_r)$ is less than or equal to the r-tuple $(y_1, \cdots, y_r)$ iff either $x_i = y_i$, $1 \le i \le j$, and $x_{j+1} < y_{j+1}$ for some $j < r$, or $x_i = y_i$, $1 \le i \le r$.

For example, the problem of sorting a deck of cards may be regarded as a sort on two keys, the suit and face values, with the following ordering relations:

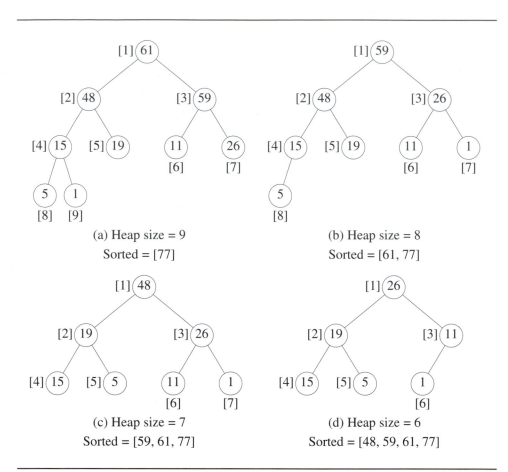

(a) Heap size = 9
Sorted = [77]

(b) Heap size = 8
Sorted = [61, 77]

(c) Heap size = 7
Sorted = [59, 61, 77]

(d) Heap size = 6
Sorted = [48, 59, 61, 77]

Figure 7.10: Heap sort example (continued on next page)

K^1 [Suits]:   ♣ < ♦ < ♥ < ♠

K^2 [Face values]:   2 < 3 < 4 ⋯ < 10 < J < Q < K < A

A sorted deck of cards therefore has the following ordering:

$$2♣, \ldots, A♣, \ldots, 2♠, \ldots, A♠$$

There are two popular ways to sort on multiple keys. In the first, we begin by sorting on the most significant key K^1, obtaining several ''piles'' of records, each having the same value for K^1. Then each of these piles is independently sorted on the key K^2 into ''subpiles'' such that all the records in the same subpile have the same values for K^1 and K^2. The subpiles are then sorted on K^3, and so on, and the piles are combined. Using

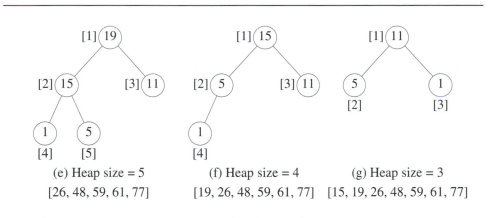

(e) Heap size = 5
[26, 48, 59, 61, 77]

(f) Heap size = 4
[19, 26, 48, 59, 61, 77]

(g) Heap size = 3
[15, 19, 26, 48, 59, 61, 77]

Figure 7.10: Heap sort example

this method on our card deck example, we would first sort the 52 cards into four piles, one for each of the suit values, then sort each pile on the face value. Then we would place the piles on top of each other to obtain the desired ordering.

A sort proceeding in this fashion is referred to as a most-significant-digit-first (MSD) sort. The second way, quite naturally, is to sort on the least significant digit first (LSD). An LSD sort would mean sorting the cards first into 13 piles corresponding to their face values (key K^2). Then, we would place the 3's on top of the 2's, $\cdots$, the kings on top of the queens, the aces on top of the kings; we would turn the deck upside down and sort on the suit (K^1) using a stable sorting method to obtain four piles, each orderd on K^2; and we would combine the piles to obtain the required ordering on the cards.

Comparing the two functions outlined here (MSD and LSD), we see that LSD is simpler, as the piles and subpiles obtained do not have to be sorted independently (provided the sorting scheme used for sorting on the keys K^i, $1 \le i < r$, is stable). This in turn implies less overhead.

The terms LSD and MSD specify only the order in which the keys are to be sorted. They do not specify how each key is to be sorted. When sorting a card deck manually, we generally use an MSD sort. The sorting on suit is done by a *bin sort* (i.e., four ''bins'' are set up, one for each suit value and the cards are placed into their corresponding bins). Next, the cards in each bin are sorted using an algorithm similar to insertion sort. However, there is another way to do this. First use a bin sort on the face value. To do this we need 13 bins, one for each distinct face value. Then collect all the cards together as described above and perform a bin sort on the suits using four bins. Note that a bin sort requires only O(n) time if the spread in key values is O(n).

LSD or MSD sorting can be used to sort even when the records have only one key. For this, we interpret the key as being composed of several subkeys. For example, if the keys are numeric, then each decimal digit may be regarded as a subkey. So, if the keys are in the range $0 \leq K \leq 999$, we can use either the LSD or MSD sorts for three keys (K^1, K^2, K^3), where K^1 is the digit in the hundredths place, K^2 the digit in the tens place, and K^3 the digit in the units place. Since $0 \leq K^i \leq 9$ for each key K^i, the sort on each key can be carried out using a bin sort with 10 bins.

In a *radix sort*, we decompose the sort key using some radix r. When r is 10, we get the decimal decomposition described above. When $r = 2$, we get binary decomposition of the keys. In a radix-r sort, the number of bins required is r.

Assume that the records to be sorted are $R_1, \cdots, R_n$. The record keys are decomposed using a radix of r. This results in each key having d digits in the range 0 through $r - 1$. Thus, we shall need r bins. The records are assumed to have a *link* field. The records in each bin will be linked together into a chain with $f[i]$, $0 \leq i \leq r$, a pointer to the first record in bin i and $e[i]$, a pointer to the last record in bin i. These chains will operate as queues. Function *RadixSort* (Program 7.15) formally presents the LSD radix-r method. Also, it is assumed that the key field of each record is an array $key[d]$ with $0 \leq key[i] < r$ for $0 \leq i < d$. Once again, for simplicity, we assume that function *Radix-Sort* has direct access to the fields of *Element*.

Analysis of RadixSort: *RadixSort* makes d passes over the data, each pass taking $O(n + r)$ time. Hence, the total computing time is $O(d(n + r))$. In the sorting of numeric data, the value of d will depend on the choice of the radix r and also on the largest key. Different choices of r will yield different computing times. $\Box$

Example 7.8: Suppose we are to sort 10 numbers in the range $[0, 999]$. Each decimal digit in the key will be regarded as a subkey. So, the value of d is 3, and that of r is 10. The input list is linked and has the form given in Figure 7.11(a). The nodes are labeled $R_1, \cdots, R_{10}$. Figure 7.11 shows the queues formed when sorting on each of the digits, as well as the lists after the queues have been collected from the 10 bins. $\Box$

EXERCISES

1. Write the status of the list $F = (12, 2, 16, 30, 8, 28, 4, 10, 20, 6, 18)$ at the end of each phase of *RadixSort* (Program 7.15). Use $r = 10$.

2. Under what conditions would an MSD radix sort be more efficient than an LSD radix sort?

3. Does *RadixSort* result in a stable sort when used to sort numbers as in Example 7.8?

4. Write a sort function to sort records $R_1, \cdots, R_n$ lexically on keys $(K^1, \cdots, K^r)$ for the case when the range of each key is much larger than n. In this case, the bin-sort scheme used in *RadixSort* to sort within each key becomes inefficient (why?). What scheme would you use to sort within a key if we desired a function with (a) good worst-case behavior, (b) good average behavior, (c) small n, say <15?

```
void RadixSort(Element *list, const int d, const int n)
// Records list = (list [1], · · · , list [n ]) are sorted on the keys key [0], · · · , key [d−1].
// The range of each key is 0 ≤ key [i ] < radix.  radix is a constant.
// Sorting within a key is done using a bin sort.
{
    int e [radix ], f [radix ]; // queue pointers
    for (int i = 1; i <= n; i++) list [i ] . link = i + 1; // link into a chain starting at current
    list [n ] . link = 0; int current = 1;
    for (i = d − 1; i >= 0; i −−) // sort on key key [i ]
    {
        for (int j = 0; j < radix; j ++) f [j ] = 0; // initialize bins to empty queues
        for ( ; current; current = list [current ] . link) { // put records into queues
            int k = list [current ] . key [i ];
            if (f [k ] == 0) f [k ] = current;
            else list [e [k ]] . link = current;
            e [k ] = current;
        }
        for (j = 0; f [j ] == 0; j ++); // find first nonempty queue
        current = f [j ]; int last = e [j ];
        for (int k = j + 1; k < radix; k ++) // concatenate remaining queues
            if (f [k ]) {
                list [last ] . link = f [k ];
                last = e [k ];
            }
        list [last ] . link = 0;
    } // end of for (i = d − 1; i >= 0; i −−)
}
```

Program 7.15: LSD radix sort

5. If we have n records with integer keys in the range $[0, n^2)$, then they may be sorted in $O(n \log n)$ time using heap or merge sort. Radix sort on a single key (i.e., $d = 1$ and $r = n^2$) takes $O(n^2)$ time. Show how to interpret the keys as two subkeys so that radix sort will take only $O(n)$ time to sort n records. (Hint: Each key, K_i, may be written as $K_i = K_i^1 n + K_i^2$ with K_i^1 and K_i^2 integers in the range $[0, n)$.)

6. Generalize the method of the previous exercise to the case of integer keys in the range $(0, n^p)$ obtaining an $O(pn)$ sorting method.

7. Experiment with *RadixSort* to see how it performs relative to the comparison-based sort methods discussed in earlier sections.

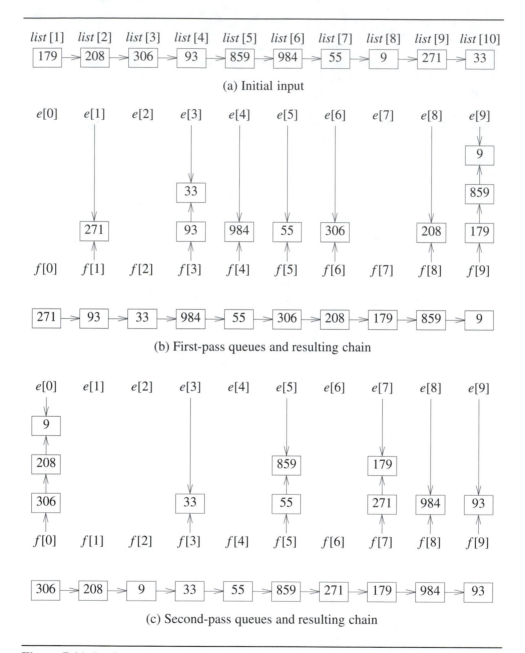

Figure 7.11: Radix sort example (continued on next page)

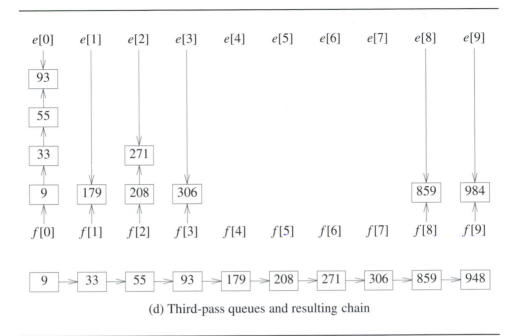

(d) Third-pass queues and resulting chain

Figure 7.11: Radix sort example

7.8   LIST AND TABLE SORTS

Apart from radix sort and recursive merge sort, all the sorting methods we have looked at require excessive data movement. That is, as the result of a comparison, records may be physically moved. This tends to slow down the sorting process when records are large. When sorting lists with large records, it is necessary to modify the sorting methods so as to minimize data movement. Methods such as insertion sort and merge sort can be easily modified to work with a linked list rather than a sequential list. In this case each record will require an additional link field. Instead of physically moving the record, we change its link field to reflect the change in the position of the record in the list. At the end of the sorting process, the records are linked together in the required order. In many applications (e.g., when we just want to sort lists and then output them record by record on some external media in the sorted order), this is sufficient. However, in some applications it is necessary to physically rearrange the records *in place* so that they are in the required order. Even in such cases, considerable savings can be achieved by first performing a linked-list sort and then physically rearranging the records according to the order specified in the list. This rearranging can be accomplished in linear time using some additional space.

   If the list, *F*, has been sorted so that at the end of the sort, *first* is a pointer to the first record in a linked list of records, then each record in this list will have a key that is greater than or equal to the key of the previous record (if there is a previous record). To physically rearrange these records into the order specified by the list, we begin by interchanging records R_1 and R_{first}. Now, the record in the position R_1 has the smallest key. If $first \neq 1$, then there is some record in the list whose link field is 1. If we could change this link field to indicate the new position of the record previously as position 1, then we would be left with records $R_2, \cdots, R_n$ linked together in nondecreasing order. Repeating the above process will, after $n - 1$ iterations, result in the desired rearrangement. The snag, however, is that in a singly linked list we do not know the predecessor of a node. To overcome this difficulty, our first rearrangement function, $list1$ (Program 7.16), begins by converting the singly linked list $first$ into a doubly linked list and then proceeds to move records into their correct places.

```
void list1(Element *list, const int n, int first)
// Rearrange the sorted chain first so that the records list [1], · · · , list [n]
// are in sorted order. Each record has an additional link field linkb.
{
   int prev = 0;
   for (int current = first; current; current = list [current ]. link)
   // convert chain into a doubly linked list
   {
      list [current ]. linkb = prev;
      prev = current;
   }

   for (int i = 1; i < n ; i ++) // move list first to position i while
   {                            // maintaining the list
      if (first != i) {
         if (list [i ]. link) list [list [i ]. link ]. linkb = first;
         list [list [i ]. linkb ]. link = first;
         Element a = list [first]; list [first] = list [i ]; list [i ] = a;
      }
      first = list [i ]. link;
   }
}
```

Program 7.16: Rearranging records using a doubly linked list

Example 7.9: After a list sort on the input list (26, 5, 77, 1, 61, 11, 59, 15, 48, 19) has been made, the list is linked as in Figure 7.12(a) (only the key and link fields of each record are shown). Following the links starting at R_{first}, we obtain the logical sequence of records $R_4, R_2, R_6, R_8, R_{10}, R_1, R_9, R_7, R_5,$ and R_3. This sequence corresponds to the key sequence 1, 5, 11, 15, 19, 26, 48, 59, 61, 33. Filling in the backward links, we

i	R_1	R_2	R_3	R_4	R_5	R_6	R_7	R_8	R_9	R_{10}
key	26	5	77	1	61	11	59	15	48	19
link	9	6	0	2	3	8	5	10	7	1

(a) Linked list following a list sort, *first* = 4

i	R_1	R_2	R_3	R_4	R_5	R_6	R_7	R_8	R_9	R_{10}
key	26	5	77	1	61	11	59	15	48	19
link	9	6	0	2	3	8	5	10	7	1
linkb	10	4	5	0	7	2	9	6	1	8

(b) Corresponding doubly linked list, *first* = 4

Figure 7.12: Sorted linked lists

get the doubly linked list of Figure 7.12(b). Figure 7.13 shows the list following the first four iterations of the second **for** loop of *list*1. The changes made in each iteration are shown in boldface. □

Analysis of *list1*: If there are n records in the list, then the time required to convert the chain *first* into a doubly linked list is O(n). The second **for** loop is iterated $n - 1$ times. In each iteration, at most two records are interchanged. This requires three record moves. If each record is m words long, then the cost per interchange is $3m$. The total time is therefore O(nm).

The worst case of $3(n - 1)$ record moves is achievable. For example, consider the input key sequence $R_1, R_2, \cdots, R_n$, with $R_2 < R_3 < \cdots < R_n$ and $R_1 > R_n$. □

Although several modifications to *list*1 are possible, one of particular interest was given by M. D. MacLaren. This modification results in a rearrangement function, *list*2, in which no additional link fields are necessary. In this function (Program 7.17), after the record R_p is exchanged with R_i, the link field of the new R_i is set to p to indicate that the original record was moved. This, together with the observation that *first* must always be $\geq i$, permits a correct reordering of the records.

Example 7.10: The data is the same as in Example 7.9. After the list sort we have the configuration of Figure 7.12(a). The configuration after each of the first five iterations of the **for** loop of *list*2 is shown in Figure 7.14. □

Analysis of *list2*: The sequence of record moves for *list*2 is identical to that for *list*1. Hence, in the worst case $3(n - 1)$ record moves for a total cost of O(nm) are made. No

i	R_1	R_2	R_3	R_4	R_5	R_6	R_7	R_8	R_9	R_{10}
key	1	5	77	26	61	11	59	15	48	19
link	2	6	0	9	3	8	5	10	7	4
linkb	0	4	5	10	7	2	9	6	4	8

(a) Configuration after first iteration of the **for** loop of *list*1, *first* = 2

i	R_1	R_2	R_3	R_4	R_5	R_6	R_7	R_9	R_9	R_{10}
key	1	5	77	26	61	11	59	15	48	19
link	2	6	0	9	3	8	5	10	7	4
linkb	0	4	5	10	7	2	9	6	4	8

(b) Configuration after second iteration, *first* = 6

i	R_1	R_2	R_3	R_4	R_5	R_6	R_7	R_8	R_9	R_{10}
key	1	5	11	26	61	77	59	15	48	19
link	2	6	8	9	6	0	5	10	7	4
linkb	0	4	2	10	7	5	9	6	4	8

(c) Configuration after third iteration, *first* = 8

i	R_1	R_2	R_3	R_4	R_5	R_6	R_7	R_8	R_9	R_{10}
key	1	5	11	15	61	77	59	26	48	19
link	2	6	8	10	6	0	5	9	7	8
linkb	0	4	2	6	7	5	9	10	8	8

(d) Configuration after fourth iteration, *first* = 10

Figure 7.13: Example for *list*1 (Program 7.16)

node is examined more than once in the **while** loop. So, the total time for the **while** loop is O(n). □

Although the asymptotic computing time for both *list*1 and *list*2 is the same, and the same number of record moves is made in either case, we would expect *list*2 to be slightly faster than *list*1 because each time two records are interchanged, *list*1 does more work than *list*2 does. *list*1 is inferior to *list*2 in both space and time considerations.

```
void list2(Element *list, const int n, int first)
// Same function as list1 except that a second link field linkb is not required
{
    for (int i = 1; i < n; i++)
    // Find correct record to place into ith position.The index of this record must
    // be ≥ i, as records in positions 1, 2, · · · , i − 1 are already correctly positioned.
    {
        while (first < i) first = list [first].link;
        int q = list [first].link; // list_q is next record in nondecreasing order
        if (first != i)
        // interchange list_i and list_first moving list_first to its correct spot as
        // list_first has ith smallest key. Also set link from old position of list_i to new one
        {
            Element t = list [i ];
            list [i ] = list [first]; list [first] = t; list [i ].link = first;
        }
        first = q;
    }
}
```

Program 7.17: Rearranging records using only one link field

The list-sort technique is not well suited for quick sort and heap sort. The sequential representation of the heap is essential to heap sort. For these sort methods, as well as for methods suited to list sort, one can maintain an auxiliary table, t, with one entry per record. The entries in this table serve as an indirect reference to the records.

At the start of the sort, $t[i] = i$, $1 \leq i \leq n$. If the sorting function requires an interchange of R_i and R_j, then only the table entries (i.e., $t[i]$ and $t[j]$) need to be interchanged. At the end of the sort, the record with the smallest key is $R_{t[1]}$ and that with the largest $R_{t[n]}$. The required permutation on the records is $R_{t[1]}, R_{t[2]}, \cdots, R_{t[n]}$ (see Figure 7.15). This table is adequate even in situations such as binary search, where a sequentially ordered list is needed. In other situations, it may be necessary to physically rearrange the records according to the permutation specified by t.

The function to rearrange records corresponding to the permutation $t[1]$, $t[2]$, $\cdots$, $t[n]$ is a rather interesting application of a theorem from mathematics: Every permutation is made up of disjoint cycles. The cycle for any element i is made up of i, $t[i]$, $t^2[i]$, $\cdots$, $t^k[i]$, where $t^j[i] = t[t^{j-1}[i]]$, $t^0[i] = i$, and $t^k[i] = i$. Thus, the permutation t of Figure 7.15 has two cycles, the first involving R_1 and R_5 and the second involving R_4, R_3, and R_2. Function $table$ (Program 7.18) utilizes this cyclic decomposition of a permutation. First, the cycle containing R_1 is followed, and all records are moved to their correct positions. The cycle containing R_2 is the next one examined un-

i	R_1	R_2	R_3	R_4	R_5	R_6	R_7	R_8	R_9	R_{10}
key	**1**	5	77	**26**	61	11	59	15	48	19
link	**4**	6	0	**9**	3	8	5	10	7	1

(a) Configuration after first iteration of the **for** loop of *list2*, *first* = 2

i	R_1	R_2	R_3	R_4	R_5	R_6	R_7	R_8	R_9	R_{10}
key	1	5	77	26	61	11	59	15	48	19
link	4	6	0	9	3	8	5	10	7	1

(b) Configuration after second iteration, *first* = 6

i	R_1	R_2	$\mathbf{R_3}$	R_4	R_5	$\mathbf{R_6}$	R_7	R_8	R_9	R_{10}
key	1	5	**11**	26	61	**77**	59	15	48	19
link	4	6	**6**	9	3	**0**	5	10	7	1

(c) Configuration after third iteration, *first* = 8

i	R_1	R_2	R_3	$\mathbf{R_4}$	R_5	R_6	R_7	$\mathbf{R_8}$	R_9	R_{10}
key	1	5	11	**15**	61	77	59	**26**	48	19
link	4	6	6	**8**	3	0	5	**9**	7	1

(d) Configuration after fourth iteration, *first* = 10

i	R_1	R_2	R_3	R_4	$\mathbf{R_5}$	R_6	R_7	R_8	R_9	$\mathbf{R_{10}}$
key	1	5	11	15	**19**	77	59	26	48	**61**
link	4	6	6	8	**10**	0	5	9	7	**3**

(e) Configuration after fifth iteration, *first* = 1

Figure 7.14: Example for *list2* (Program 7.17)

less this cycle has already been examined. The cycles for R_3, R_4, $\cdots$, R_{n-1} are followed in this order. The result is a physically sorted list.

When processing a trivial cycle for R_i (i.e., $t[i] = i$), no rearrangement involving record R_i is required, since the condition $t[i] = i$ means that the record with the ith smallest key is R_i. In processing a nontrivial cycle for record R_i (i.e., $t[i] \neq i$), R_i is moved to a temporary position p, then the record at $t[i]$ is moved to i; next the record at $t[t[i]]$ is moved to $t[i]$, and so on until the end of the cycle $t^k[i]$ is reached and the record at p is moved to $t^{k-1}[i]$.

Auxiliary table t before sorting

Table t after sorting

Figure 7.15: Table sort

```
void table(Element *list, const int n, int *t)
// Rearrange list [1], · · · , list [n ] to correspond to the sequence
// list [t [1]], · · · , list [t [n ]], n ≥ 1.
{
   for (int i = 1; i < n; i ++)
      if (t [i ] != i)  { // there is a non-trivial cycle starting at i
         Element p = list [i ]; int j = i;
         do {
            int k = t [j ]; list [j ] = list [k ]; t [j ] = j;
            j = k;
         } while (t [j ] != i);
         list [j ] = p; // j is position for record p
         t [j ] = j;
      } // end of if statement
}
```

Program 7.18: Table sort

Example 7.11: Suppose we start with the table t of Figure 7.16(a). This figure also shows the record keys. The table configuration is that following a table sort. There are two nontrivial cycles in the permutation specified by t. The first is R_1, R_3, R_8, R_6, R_1. The second is R_4, R_5, R_7, R_4. During the first iteration ($i = 1$) of the **for** loop of *table* (Program 7.18), the cycle $R_1, R_{t[1]}, R_{t^2[1]}, R_{t^3[1]}, R_1$ is followed. Record R_1 is moved to a temporary spot P; $R_{t[1]}$ (i.e., R_3) is moved to the position R_1; $R_{t^2[1]}$ (i.e., R_8) is moved to R_3; R_6 is moved to R_8; and finally P is moved to R_6. Thus, at the end of the first iteration we have the table configuration of Figure 7.16(b).

	R_1	R_2	R_3	R_4	R_5	R_6	R_7	R_8
key	35	14	12	42	26	50	31	18
t	3	2	8	5	7	1	4	6

(a) Initial configuration

key	12	14	18	42	26	35	31	50
t	1	2	3	5	7	6	4	8

(b) Configuration after rearrangement of first cycle

key	12	14	18	26	31	35	42	50
t	1	2	3	4	5	6	7	8

(c) Configuration after rearrangement of second cycle

Figure 7.16: Table sort example

For $i = 2$ or 3, $t[i] = i$, indicating that these records are already in their correct positions. When $i = 4$, the next nontrivial cycle is discovered, and the records on this cycle (R_4, R_5, R_7, R_4) are moved to their correct positions. Following this we have the table configuration of Figure 7.16(c).

For the remaining values of i ($i = 5, 6,$ and 7), $t[i] = i$, and no more nontrivial cycles are found. $\square$

Analysis of *table*: If each record uses m words of storage, then the additional space needed is m words for p plus a few more for variables such as $i, j,$ and k. To obtain an estimate of the computing time, we observe that the **for** loop is executed $n - 1$ times. If for some value of i, $t[i] \neq i$, then there is a nontrivial cycle including $k > 1$ distinct records $R_i, R_{t[i]}, \cdots, R_{t^{k-1}[i]}$. Rearranging these records requires $k + 1$ record moves. Following this, the records involved in this cycle are not moved again at any time in the algorithm, as $t[j] = j$ for all such records R_j. Hence, no record can be in two different nontrivial cycles. Let k_l be the number of records on a nontrivial cycle starting at R_l when $i = l$ in the **for** loop. Let $k_l = 0$ for a trivial cycle. The total number of record moves is

$$\sum_{l=0,\,k_l\neq0}^{n-1} (k_l+1)$$

Since the records on nontrivial cycles must be different, $\sum k_l \leq n$. The total number of record moves is maximum when $\sum k_l = n$ and there are $\lfloor n/2 \rfloor$ cycles. When n is even, each cycle contains two records. Otherwise, one cycle contains three and the others two each. In either case the number of record moves is $\lfloor 3n/2 \rfloor$. One record move costs $O(m)$ time. The total computing time is therefore $O(mn)$. $\square$

Comparing *list2* (Program 7.17) and *table*, we see that in the worst case, *list2* makes $3(n-1)$ record moves, whereas *table* makes only $\lfloor 3n/2 \rfloor$ record moves. For larger values of m it is worthwhile to make one pass over the sorted list of records, creating a table t corresponding to a table sort. This would take $O(n)$ time. Then *table* could be used to rearrange the records in the order specified by t.

EXERCISES

1. Complete Example 7.9.

2. Complete Example 7.10.

3. Write a version of selection sort (see Chapter 1) that works on a linked chain of records.

4. Write a table sort version of quick sort. Now during the sort, records are not physically moved. Instead, $t[i]$ is the index of the record that would have been in position i if records were physically moved around as in *QuickSort* (Program 7.6). Begin with $t[i] = i$, $1 \leq i \leq n$. At the end of the sort, $t[i]$ is the index of the record that should be in the ith position in the sorted list. So now function *table* may be used to rearrange the records into the sorted order specified by t. Note that this reduces the amount of data movement taking place when compared to *QuickSort* for the case of large records.

5. Do Exercise 4 for the case of insertion sort.

6. Do Exercise 4 for the case of merge sort.

7. Do Exercise 4 for the case of heap sort.

7.9   SUMMARY OF INTERNAL SORTING

Of the several sorting methods we have studied, no one method is best. Some methods are good for small n, others for large n. Insertion sort is good when the list is already partially ordered. Because of the low overhead of the method, it is also the best sorting method for "small" n. Merge sort has the best worst-case behavior but requires more storage than heap sort. Quick sort has the best average behavior, but its worst-case behavior is $O(n^2)$. The behavior of radix sort depends on the size of the keys and the choice of r.

Figure 7.17 gives the average running times for *InsertionSort* (Program 7.5), *QuickSort* (Program 7.6, using the median-of-three rule), *MergeSort* (Program 7.10), and *HeapSort* (Program 7.14). These were obtained on an IBM-PC. Figure 7.18 is a plot of these times. As can be seen for n up to about 20, *InsertionSort* is the fastest. *QuickSort* is the fastest for larger values of n. In practice, therefore, it would be worthwhile to combine *InsertionSort* and *QuickSort*. *QuickSort* uses *InsertionSort* when the sublist size is below about 20.

n	quick	merge	heap	insert
0	0.041	0.027	0.034	0.032
10	1.064	1.524	1.482	0.775
20	2.343	3.700	3.680	2.253
30	3.700	5.587	6.153	4.430
40	5.085	7.800	8.815	7.275
50	6.542	9.892	11.583	10.892
60	7.987	11.947	14.427	15.013
70	9.587	15.893	17.427	20.000
80	11.167	18.217	20.517	25.450
90	12.633	20.417	23.717	31.767
100	14.275	22.950	26.775	38.325
200	30.775	48.475	60.550	148.300
300	48.171	81.600	96.657	319.657
400	65.914	109.829	134.971	567.629
500	84.400	138.033	174.100	874.600
600	102.900	171.167	214.400	
700	122.400	199.240	255.760	
800	142.160	230.480	297.480	
900	160.400	260.100	340.000	
1000	181.000	289.450	382.250	

Times in hundredths of a second

Figure 7.17: Average times for sort methods

EXERCISES

1. [***Count Sort***] The simplest known sorting method arises from the observation that the position of a record in a sorted list depends on the number of records with smaller keys. Associated with each record there is a *count* field used to determine

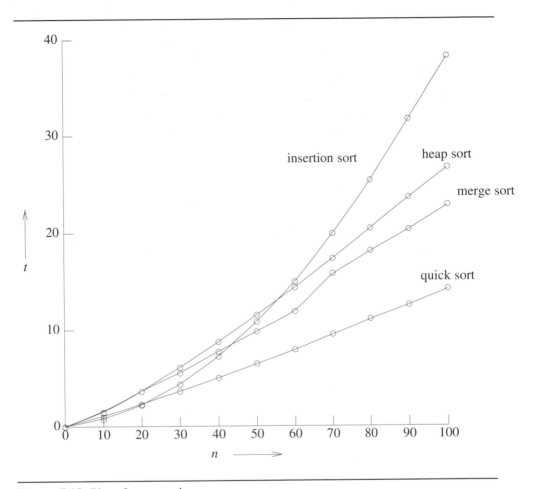

Figure 7.18: Plot of average times

the number of records that must precede this one in the sorted list. Write a function to determine the count of each record in an unordered list. Show that if the list has n records, then all the counts can be determined by making at most $n(n-1)/2$ key comparisons.

2. Write a function similar to *table* (Program 7.18) to rearrange the records of a list if, with each record, we have a count of the number of records preceding it in the sorted list (see Exercise 1).

3. Obtain Figures 7.17 and 7.18 for the worst-case run time.

4. [*Programming Project*] The objective of this assignment is to come up with a composite sorting function that is good on the worst-time criterion. The candidate sort methods are (a) insertion sort, (b) quick sort, (c) merge sort, (d) heap sort.

   To begin with, program these sort methods in C++. In each case, assume that n integers are to be sorted. In the case of quick sort, use the median-of-three method. In the case of merge sort, use the iterative method (as a separate exercise, you might wish to compare the run times of the iterative and recursive versions of merge sort and determine what the recursion penalty is in your favorite language using your favorite compiler). Check out the correctness of the programs using some test data. Since quite detailed and working functions are given in the book, this part of the assignment should take little effort. In any case, no points are earned until after this step.

   To obtain reasonably accurate run times, you need to know the accuracy of the clock or timer you are using. Determine this by reading the appropriate manual. Let the clock accuracy be δ. Now, run a pilot test to determine ballpark times for your four sorting functions for $n = 5, 10, 20, 30, 40, 50$, and 100. You will notice times of 0 for many of these values of n. The other times may not be much larger than the clock accuracy.

   To time an event that is smaller than or near the clock accuracy, repeat it many times and divide the overall time by the number of repetitions. You should obtain times that are accurate to within 1%.

   We need worst-case data for each of the four sort methods. The worst-case data for insertion sort are easy to generate. Just use the sequence n, $n-1$, $n-2$, $\cdots$, 1. Worst-case data for merge sort can be obtained by working backward. Begin with the last merge your function will perform and make this work hardest. Then look at the second-to-last merge, and so on. Use this logic to obtain a program that will generate worst-case data for merge sort for each of the above values of n.

   Generating worst-case data for heap sort is the hardest, so, here we shall use a random permutation generator (one is provided in Program 7.19). We shall generate random permutations of the desired size, clock heap sort on each of these, and use the max of these times to approximate to the worst-case time. You will be able to use more random permutations for smaller values of n than for larger. For no value of n should you use fewer than 10 permutations. Use the same technique to obtain worst-case times for quick sort.

   Having settled on the test data, we are ready to perform our experiment. Obtain the worst-case times. From these times you will get a rough idea when one function performs better than the other. Now, narrow the scope of your experiments and determine the exact value of n when one sort method outperforms another. For some methods, this value may be 0. For instance, each of the other three methods may be faster than quick sort for all values of n.

   Plot your findings on a single sheet of graph paper. Do you see the n^2 behavior of insertion sort and quick sort and the $n\log n$ behavior of the other two

```
void permute(Element *a, int n)
// Random permutation generator.
{
    for (int i = n; i >= 2; i−−)
    {
        int j = rand () % i + 1; // j = random integer in the range [1, i]
        Element k = a [j]; a [j] = a [i]; a [i] = k;
    }
}
```

Program 7.19: Random permutation generator

methods for suitably large n (about n > 20)? If not, there is something wrong with your test or your clock or with both. For each value of n determine the sort function that is fastest (simply look at your graph). Write a composite function with the best possible performance for all n. Clock this function and plot the times on the same graph sheet you used earlier.

A word of **CAUTION**: If you are using a multiprocess computer, make all your final runs at about the same time. On these computers, the clocked time will vary significantly with the amount of computer work load. Comparing the run times of an insertion sort run made at 2:00 p.m. with the run times of a merge sort run made at 2:00 a.m. will not be very meaningful.

WHAT TO TURN IN
You are required to submit a report that states the clock accuracy, the number of random permutations tried for heap sort, the worst-case data for merge sort and how you generated it, a table of times for the above values of n, the times for the narrowed ranges, the graph, and a table of times for the composite function. In addition, your report must be accompanied by a complete listing of the program used by you (this includes the sorting functions and the main program for timing and test-data generation).

5. Repeat the previous exercise for the case of average run times. Average-case data are usually very difficult to create, so use random permutations. This time, however, do not repeat a permutation many times to overcome clock inaccuracies. Instead, use each permutation once and clock the overall time (for a fixed n).

6. Assume you are given a list of five-letter English words and are faced with the problem of listing these words in sequences such that the words in each sequence are anagrams (i.e., if x and y are in the same sequence, then word x is a permutation of word y). You are required to list out the fewest such sequences. With this restriction, show that no word can appear in more than one sequence. How would you go about solving this problem?

7.   Assume you are working in the census department of a small town where the number of records, about 3000, is small enough to fit into the internal memory of a computer. All the people currently living in this town were born in the United States. There is one record for each person in this town. Each record contains (a) the state in which the person was born, (b) county of birth, and (c) name of person. How would you produce a list of all persons living in this town? The list is to be ordered by state. Within each state the persons are to be listed by their counties, the counties being arranged in alphabetical order. Within each county, the names are also listed in alphabetical order. Justify any assumptions you make.

8.   [**Bubble Sort**] In a bubble sort several left-to-right passes are made over the array of records to be sorted. In each pass, pairs of adjacent records are compared and exchanged if necessary. The sort terminates following a pass in which no records are exchanged.

   (a)   Write a C++ function for bubble sort.

   (b)   What is the worst-case complexity of your function?

   (c)   How much time does your function take on a sorted array of records?

   (d)   How much time does your function take on an array of records that are in the reverse of sorted order?

9.   Redo the preceding exercise beginning with an unsorted chain of records and ending with a sorted chain.

10.   [**Programming Project**] The objective of this exercise is to study the effect of the size of an array element on the computational time of various sorting algorithms.

   (a)   Use templates to implement insertion sort, quick sort, iterative merge sort, and heap sort functions.

   (b)   Use these functions to sort arrays of (*i*) characters (**char**), (*ii*) integers (**int**), (*iii*) floating point numbers (**float**), and (*iv*) rectangles (Assume that a rectangle is represented by the coordinates of its bottom left point and its height and width, all of which are of type **float**. Assume, also, that rectangles are to be sorted in non-decreasing order of their areas.)

   (c)   Obtain a set of run times for each algorithm-data type pair specified above. (There should be sixteen such pairs.) To obtain a set of run times of an algorithm-data type pair, you should run the algorithm on at least four arrays of different sizes containing elements of the appropriate data type. The elements in an array should be generated using a random number generator

   (d)   Draw tables and graphs displaying your experimental results. What do you conclude from the experiments?

7.10 EXTERNAL SORTING

7.10.1 Introduction

In this section, we assume that the lists to be sorted are so large that the whole list cannot be contained in the internal memory of a computer, making an internal sort impossible. We shall assume that the list (or file) to be sorted resides on a disk. Most of the concepts developed for a disk sort also apply when the file resides on a tape. The term *block* refers to the unit of data that is read from or written to a disk at one time. A block generally consists of several records. For a disk, there are three factors contributing to the read/write time:

(1)   *Seek time:* time taken to position the read/write heads to the correct cylinder. This will depend on the number of cylinders across which the heads have to move.

(2)   *Latency time:* time until the right sector of the track is under the read/write head.

(3)   *Transmission time:* time to transmit the block of data to/from the disk.

The most popular method for sorting on external storage devices is merge sort. This method consists of two distinct phases. First, segments of the input list are sorted using a good internal sort method. These sorted segments, known as *runs*, are written onto external storage as they are generated. Second, the runs generated in phase one are merged together following the merge-tree pattern of Figure 7.6, until only one run is left. Because the simple merge function *merge* (Program 7.7) requires only the leading records of the two runs being merged to be present in memory at one time, it is possible to merge large runs together. It is more difficult to adapt the other internal sort methods considered in this chapter to external sorting.

Example 7.12: A list containing 4500 records is to be sorted using a computer with an internal memory capable of sorting at most 750 records. The input list is maintained on disk and has a block length of 250 records. We have available another disk that may be used as a scratch pad. The input disk is not to be written on. One way to accomplish the sort using the general function outlined above is to

(1) Internally sort three blocks at a time (i.e., 750 records) to obtain six runs R_1 to R_6. A method such as heap sort, merge sort, or quick sort could be used. These six runs are written onto the scratch disk (Figure 7.19).

(2) Set aside three blocks of internal memory, each capable of holding 250 records. Two of these blocks will be used as input buffers and the third as an output buffer. Merge runs R_1 and R_2. This merge is carried out by first reading one block of each of these runs into input buffers. Blocks of runs are merged from the input buffers into the output buffer. When the output buffer gets full, it is written onto the disk. If an input buffer gets empty, it is refilled with another block from the same run. After runs R_1 and R_2 are merged, R_3 and R_4 and finally R_5 and R_6 are merged. The result of this pass is three runs, each containing 1500 sorted records or six blocks. Two of these runs are now merged using the input/output buffers set up as above to obtain a run of size

Figure 7.19: Blocked runs obtained after internal sorting

3000. Finally, this run is merged with the remaining run of size 1500 to obtain the desired sorted list (Figure 7.20). □

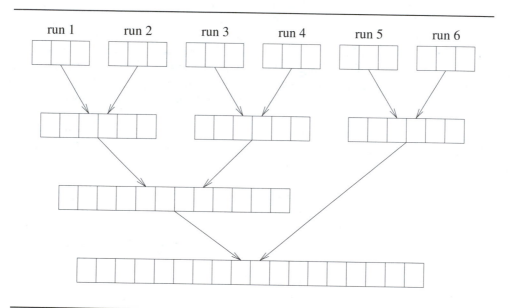

Figure 7.20: Merging the six runs

To analyze the complexity of external sort, we use the following notation:

t_s = maximum seek time

t_l = maximum latency time

t_{rw} = time to read or write one block of 250 records

$t_{IO}=$ time to input or output one block

$\quad = t_s + t_l + t_{rw}$

$t_{IS}=$ time to internally sort 750 records

$nt_m=$ time to merge n records from input buffers to the output buffer

We shall assume that each time a block is read from or written onto the disk, the maximum seek and latency times are experienced. Although this is not true in general, it will simplify the analysis. The computing times for the various operations in our 4500-record example are given in Figure 7.21.

operation	time
(1) read 18 blocks of input, $18t_{IO}$, internally sort, $6t_{IS}$, write 18 blocks, $18t_{IO}$	$36t_{IO} + 6t_{IS}$
(2) merge runs 1 to 6 in pairs	$36t_{IO} + 4500t_m$
(3) merge two runs of 1500 records each, 12 blocks	$24t_{IO} + 3000t_m$
(4) merge one run of 3000 records with one run of 1500 records	$36t_{IO} + 4500t_m$
total time	$132t_{IO} + 12{,}000t_m + 6t_{IS}$

Figure 7.21: Computing times for disk sort example

The contribution of seek time can be reduced by writing blocks on the same cylinder or on adjacent cylinders. A close look at the final computing time indicates that it depends chiefly on the number of passes made over the data. In addition to the initial input pass made over the data for the internal sort, the merging of the runs requires 2-2/3 passes over the data (one pass to merge 6 runs of length 750 records, two-thirds of a pass to merge two runs of length 1500, and one pass to merge one run of length 3000 and one of length 1500). Since one full pass covers 18 blocks, the input and output time is $2 \times (2\text{-}2/3 + 1) \times 18\, t_{IO} = 132t_{IO}$. The leading factor of 2 appears because each record that is read is also written out again. The merge time is $2\text{-}2/3 \times 4500t_m = 12{,}000t_m$. Because of this close relationship between the overall computing time and the number of passes made over the data, future analysis will be concerned mainly with counting the number of passes being made. Another point to note regarding the above sort is that no attempt was made to use the computer's ability to carry out input/output and CPU operation in parallel and thus overlap some of the time. In the ideal situation we would overlap almost all the input/output time with CPU processing so that the real time would be approximately $132 \, t_{IO} \approx 12,000 \, t_m + 6t_{IS}$.

If we have two disks, we can write on one, read from the other, and merge buffer loads already in memory in parallel. A proper choice of buffer lengths and buffer handling schemes will result in a time of almost $66t_{IO}$. This parallelism is an important consideration when sorting is being carried out in a nonmultiprogramming environment. In this situation, unless input/output and CPU processing is going on in parallel, the CPU is idle during input/output. In a multiprogramming environment, however, the need for the sorting program to carry out input/output and CPU processing in parallel may not be so critical, since the CPU can be busy working on another program (if there are other programs in the system at the time) while the sort program waits for the completion of its input/output. Indeed, in many multiprogramming environments it may not even be possible to achieve parallel input, output, and internal computing because of the structure of the operation system.

The number of merge passes over the runs can be reduced by using a higher-order merge than two-way merge. To provide for parallel input, output, and merging, we need an appropriate buffer-handling scheme. Further improvement in run time can be obtained by generating fewer (or equivalently longer) runs than are generated by the strategy described above. This can be done using a loser tree. The loser-tree strategy to be discussed in Section 7.10.4 results in runs that are on the average almost twice as long as those obtained by the above strategy. However, the generated runs are of varying size. As a result, the order in which the runs are merged affects the time required to merge all runs into one. We consider these factors now.

7.10.2 k-Way Merging

The two-way merge function *merge* (Program 7.7) is almost identical to the merge function just described (Figure 7.20). In general, if we start with m runs, the merge tree corresponding to Figure 7.20 will have $\lceil \log_2 m \rceil + 1$ levels, for a total of $\lceil \log_2 m \rceil$ passes over the data list. The number of passes over the data can be reduced by using a higher-order merge (i.e., k-way merge for $k \geq 2$). In this case, we would simultaneously merge k runs together. Figure 7.22 illustrates a four-way merge of 16 runs. The number of passes over the data is now two, versus four passes in the case of a two-way merge. In general, a k-way merge on m runs requires $\lceil \log_k m \rceil$ passes over the data. Thus, the input/output time may be reduced by using a higher-order merge.

The use of a higher-order merge, however, has some other effects on the sort. To begin with, k runs of size $S_1, S_2, S_3, \cdots, S_k$ can no longer be merged internally in $O(\Sigma_1^k \, S_i)$ time. In a k-way merge, as in a two-way merge, the next record to be output is the one with the smallest key. The smallest has now to be found from k possibilities and it could be the leading record in any of the k runs. The most direct way to merge k runs is to make $k - 1$ comparisons to determine the next record to output. The computing time for this is $O((k - 1) \, \Sigma_1^k \, S_i)$. Since $\log_k m$ passes are being made, the total number of

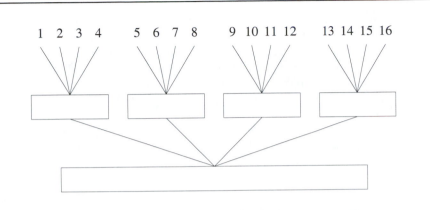

Figure 7.22: A four-way merge on 16 runs

key comparisons is $n(k-1)\log_k m = n(k-1)\log_2 m/\log_2 k$, where n is the number of records in the list. Hence, $(k-1)/\log_2 k$ is the factor by which the number of key comparisons increases. As k increases, the reduction in input/output time will be outweighed by the resulting increase in CPU time needed to perform the k-way merge.

For large k (say, $k \geq 6$) we can achieve a significant reduction in the number of comparisons needed to find the next smallest element by using a loser tree with k leaves (see Chapter 5). In this case, the total time needed per level of the merge tree is $O(n \log_2 k)$. Since the number of levels in this tree is $O(\log_k m)$, the asymptotic internal processing time becomes $O(n \log_2 k \log_k m) = O(n \log_2 m)$. This is independent of k.

In going to a higher-order merge, we save on the amount of input/output being carried out. There is no significant loss in internal processing speed. Even though the internal processing time is relatively insensitive to the order of the merge, the decrease in input/output time is not as much as indicated by the reduction to $\log_k m$ passes. This is so because the number of input buffers needed to carry out a k-way merge increases with k. Although $k+1$ buffers are sufficient, in the next section we shall see that the use of $2k+2$ buffers is more desirable. Since the internal memory available is fixed and independent of k, the buffer size must be reduced as k increases. This in turn implies a reduction in the block size on disk. With the reduced block size, each pass over the data results in a greater number of blocks being written or read. This represents a potential increase in input/output time from the increased contribution of seek and latency times involved in reading a block of data. Hence, beyond a certain k value the input/output time will increase despite the decrease in the number of passes being made. The optimal value for k depends on disk parameters and the amount of internal memory available for buffers.

7.10.3   Buffer Handling for Parallel Operation

If k runs are being merged together by a k-way merge, then we clearly need at least k input buffers and one output buffer to carry out the merge. This, however, is not enough if
input, output, and internal merging are to be carried out in parallel. For instance, while
the output buffer is being written out, internal merging has to be halted, since there is no
place to collect the merged records. This can be overcome through the use of two output
buffers. While one is being written out, records are merged into the second. If buffer
sizes are chosen correctly, then the time to output one buffer will be the same as the CPU
time needed to fill the second buffer. With only k input buffers, internal merging will
have to be held up whenever one of these input buffers becomes empty and another block
from the corresponding run is being read in. This input delay can also be avoided if we
have $2k$ input buffers. These $2k$ input buffers have to be used cleverly to avoid reaching
a situation in which processing has to be held up because of a lack of input records from
any one run. Simply assigning two buffers per run does not solve the problem.

Example 7.13: Assume that a two-way merge is carried out using four input buffers,
$in[i]$, $0 \leq i \leq 3$, and two output buffers, $ou[0]$ and $ou[1]$. Each buffer is capable of holding two records. The first few records of run 0 have key value 1, 3, 5, 7, 8, 9. The first
few records of run 1 have key value 2, 4, 6, 15, 20, 25. Buffers $in[0]$ and $in[2]$ are assigned to run 0. The remaining two input buffers are assigned to run 1. We start the
merge by reading in one buffer load from each of the two runs. At this time the buffers
have the configuration of Figure 7.23(a). Now runs 0 and 1 are merged using records
from $in[0]$ and $in[1]$. In parallel with this, the next buffer load from run 0 is input. If we
assume that buffer lengths have been chosen such that the times to input, output, and
generate an output buffer are all the same, then when $ou[0]$ is full, we have the situation
of Figure 7.23(b). Next, we simultaneously output $ou[0]$, input into $in[3]$ from run 1,
and merge into $ou[1]$. When $ou[1]$ is full, we have the situation of Figure 7.23(c). Continuing in this way, we reach the configuration of Figure 7.23(e). We now begin to output $ou[1]$, input from run 0 into $in[2]$, and merge into $ou[0]$. During the merge, all
records from run 0 get used before $ou[0]$ gets full. Merging must now be delayed until
the inputting of another buffer load from run 0 is completed. $\square$

Example 7.13 makes it clear that if $2k$ input buffers are to suffice, then we cannot
assign two buffers per run. Instead, the buffer must be floating in the sense that an individual buffer may be assigned to any run depending upon need. In the buffer assignment
strategy we shall describe, there will at any time be at least one input buffer containing
records from each run. The remaining buffers will be filled on a priority basis (i.e., the
run for which the k-way merging algorithm will run out of records first is the one from
which the next buffer will be filled). One may easily predict which run's records will be
exhausted first by simply comparing the keys of the last record read from each of the k
runs. The smallest such key determines this run. We shall assume that in the case of
equal keys, the merge process first merges the record from the run with least index. This
means that if the key of the last record read from run i is equal to the key of the last

Figure 7.23: Example showing that two fixed buffers per run are not enough for continued parallel operation

record read from run j, and $i < j$, then the records read from i will be exhausted before those from j. So, it is possible to have more than two bufferloads from a given run and only one partially full buffer from another run. All bufferloads from the same run are queued together. Before formally presenting the algorithm for buffer utilization, we make the following assumptions about the parallel processing capabilities of the computer system available:

(1) We have two disk drives and the input/output channel is such that we can simultaneously read from one disk and write onto the other.

(2) While data transmission is taking place between an input/output device and a block of memory, the CPU cannot make references to that same block of memory. Thus, it is not possible to start filling the front of an output buffer while it is being written out. If this were possible, then by coordinating the transmission and merging rate, only one output buffer would be needed. By the time the first record for the new output block is determined, the first record of the previous output block has been written out.

(3) To simplify the discussion we assume that input and output buffers are of the same size.

Keeping these assumptions in mind, we provide a high-level description of the algorithm obtained using the strategy outlined earlier and then illustrate how it works through an example. Our algorithm, Program 7.20, merges k-runs, $k \geq 2$, using a k-way merge. $2k$ input buffers and two output buffers are used. Each buffer is a continuous block of memory. Input buffers are queued in k queues, one queue for each run. It is assumed that each input/output buffer is long enough to hold one block of records. Empty buffers are placed on a linked stack. The algorithm also assumes that the end of each run has a sentinel record with a very large key, say $+\infty$. It is assumed that all other records have key value less than that of the sentinel record. If block lengths, and hence buffer lengths, are chosen such that the time to merge one output buffer load equals the time to read a block, then almost all input, output, and computation will be carried out in parallel. It is also assumed that in the case of equal keys, the k-way merge algorithm first outputs the record from the run with the smallest index.

We make the following observations about Program 7.20:

(1) For large k, determination of the queue that will be exhausted first can be found in $\log_2 k$ comparisons by setting up a loser tree for $last[i]$, $0 \leq i < k$, rather than making $k - 1$ comparisons each time a buffer load is to be read in. The change in computing time will not be significant, since this queue selection represents only a very small fraction of the total time taken by the algorithm.

(2) For large k, function $kwaymerge$ uses a tree of losers (see Chapter 5).

(3) All input and output except for the input of the initial k blocks and the output of the last block is done concurrently with computing. Since, after k runs have been

---

{Steps in buffering algorithm}

Step 1: Input the first block of each of the k runs, setting up k linked queues, each having one block of data. Put the remaining k input blocks into a linked stack of free input blocks. Set *ou* to 0.

Step 2: Let *LastKey* [i] be the last key input from run i. Let *NextRun* be the run for which *LastKey* is minimum. If *LastKey* [*NextRun*] $\neq +\infty$, then initiate the input of the next block from run *NextRun*.

Step 3: Use a function *kwaymerge* to merge records from the k input queues into the output buffer *ou*. Merging continues until either the output buffer gets full or a record with key $+\infty$ is merged into *ou*. If, during this merge, an input buffer becomes empty before the output buffer gets full or before $+\infty$ is merged into *ou*, the *kwaymerge* advances to the next buffer on the same queue and returns the empty buffer to the stack of empty buffers. However, if an input buffer becomes empty at the same time as the output buffer gets full or $+\infty$ is merged into *ou*, the empty buffer is left on the queue, and *kwaymerge* does not advance to the next buffer on the queue. Rather, the merge terminates.

Step 4: Wait for any ongoing disk input/output to complete.

Step 5: If an input buffer has been read, add it to the queue for the appropriate run. Determine the next run to read from by determining *NextRun* such that *LastKey* [*NextRun*] is minimum.

Step 6: If *LastKey* [*NextRun*] $\neq +\infty$, then initiate reading the next block from run *NextRun* into a free input buffer.

Step 7: Initiate the writing of output buffer *ou*. Set *ou* to $1 - ou$.

Step 8: If a record with key $+\infty$ has been not been merged into the output buffer, go back to Step 3. Otherwise, wait for the ongoing write to complete and then terminate.

Program 7.20: k-way merge with floating buffers

merged, we would probably begin to merge another set of k runs, the input for the next set can commence during the final merge stages of the present set of runs. That is, when *LastKey* [*NextRun*] $= +\infty$ in Step 6, we begin reading one by one the first blocks from each of the next set of k runs to be merged. So, over the entire sorting of a file the only time that is not overlapped with the internal merging time is the time to input the first k blocks and that to output the last block.

(4)   The algorithm assumes that all blocks are of the same length. Ensuring this may require inserting a few dummy records into the last block of each run following the sentinel record with key $+\infty$.

Example 7.14: To illustrate the algorithm of Program 7.20, let us trace through it while it performs a three-way merge on the three runs of Figure 7.24. Each run consists of four blocks of two records each; the last key in the fourth block of each of these three runs is $+\infty$. We have six input buffers and two output buffers. Figure 7.25 shows the status of the input buffer queues, the run from which the next block is being read, and the output buffer being output at the beginning of each iteration of the loop of Steps 3 through 8 of the buffering algorithm.

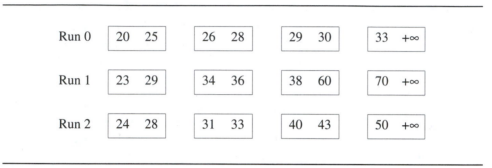

Figure 7.24: Three runs

From line 5 of Figure 7.25 it is evident that during the k-way merge, the test for "output buffer full?" should be carried out before the test "input buffer empty?", as the next input buffer for that run may not have been read in yet, so there would be no next buffer in that queue. In lines 3 and 4 all six input buffers are in use, and the stack of free buffers is empty. □

We end our discussion of buffer handling by proving that Program 7.20 is correct.

Theorem 7.2: The following are true for Program 7.20:

(1)   In Step 6, there is always a buffer available in which to begin reading the next block.

(2)   During the k-way merge of Step 3, the next block in the queue has been read in by the time it is needed.

Proof: (1) Each time we get to Step 6 of the algorithm, there are at most $k + 1$ buffer loads in memory, one of these being in an output buffer. For each queue there can be at most one buffer that is partially full. If no buffer is available for the next read, then the remaining k buffers must be full. This means that all the k partially full buffers are empty (as otherwise there will be more than $k+1$ buffer loads in memory). From the way the merge is set up, only one buffer can be both unavailable and empty. This may happen only if the output buffer gets full exactly when one input buffer becomes empty. But

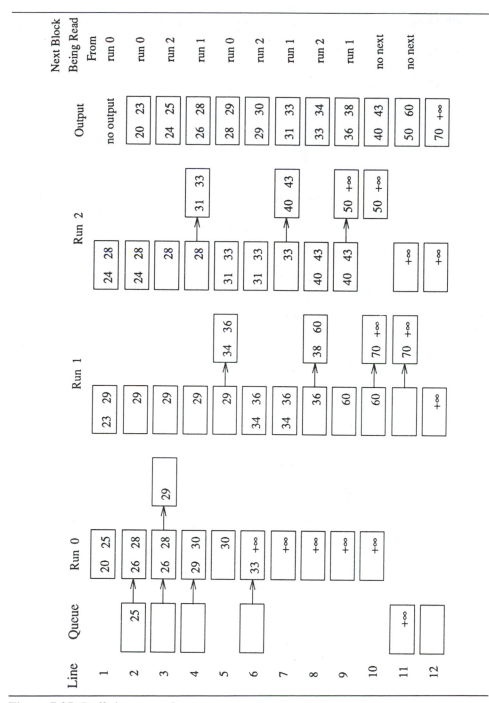

Figure 7.25: Buffering example

$k > 1$ contradicts this. So, there is always at least one buffer available when Step 6 is being executed.

(2) Assume this is false. Let run R_i be the one whose queue becomes empty during *kwaymerge*. We may assume that the last key merged was not $+\infty$, since otherwise *kwaymerge* would terminate the merge rather than get another buffer for R_i. This means that there are more blocks of records for run R_i on the input file, and $LastKey[i] \neq +\infty$. Consequently, up to this time whenever a block was output, another was simultaneously read in. Input and output therefore proceeded at the same rate, and the number of available blocks of data was always k. An additional block is being read in, but it does not get queued until Step 5. Since the queue for R_i has become empty first, the selection rule for choosing the next run to read from ensures that there is at most one block of records for each of the remaining $k - 1$ runs. Furthermore, the output buffer cannot be full at this time, as this condition is tested for before the input-buffer-empty condition. Thus, fewer than k blocks of data are in memory. This contradicts our earlier assertion that there must be exactly k such blocks of data. $\square$

7.10.4   Run Generation

Using conventional internal sorting methods such as those discussed earlier in this chapter, it is possible to generate runs that are only as large as the number of records that can be held in internal memory at one time. Using a tree of losers, it is possible to do better than this. In fact, the algorithm we shall present will, on the average, generate runs that are twice as long as obtainable by conventional methods. This algorithm was devised by Walters, Painter, and Zalk. In addition to being capable of generating longer runs, this algorithm will allow for parallel input, output, and internal processing.

We assume that input/output buffers have been set up appropriately for maximum overlapping of input, output, and internal processing. Wherever there is an input/output instruction in the run-generation algorithm, it is assumed that the operation takes place through the input/output buffers. The run generation algorithm uses a tree of losers. We assume that there is enough space to construct such a tree for k records, $r[i]$, $0 \leq i < k$. Each node, i, in this tree has one field $l[i]$. $l[i]$, $1 \leq i < k$, represents the loser of the tournament played at node i. Each of the k record positions $r[i]$ has a run number $rn[i]$, $0 \leq i < k$. This field enables us to determine whether or not $r[i]$ can be output as part of the run currently being generated. Whenever the tournament winner is output, a new record (if there is one) is input, and the tournament is replayed as discussed in Chapter 5.

Function *runs* (Program 7.21) is an implementation of the loser tree strategy just discussed. The variables used in this function have the following significance:

```
1  void runs(Element *r)
2  {
3    r = new Element[k];
4    int *key = new int[k ]; int *rn = new int[k ]; int *l = new int[k ];
5    for (int i = 0; i < k; i++) {  // input records
6      InputRecord (r [i ]); rn [i ] = 1;
7    }
8    InitializeLoserTree ();
9    q = l [0]; // tournament winner
10   int rq = 1; int rc = 1; int rmax = 1; int LastKey = MAXINT;
11   while(1) { // output runs
12     if (rq != rc) { // end of run
13       output end of run marker;
14       if (rq > rmax) return;
15       else rc = rq;
16     }
17     WriteRecord (r [q ]); LastKey = key [q ]; // output record r[q]
18     // input new record into tree
19     if (end of input) rn [q ] = rmax + 1;
20     else {
21       ReadRecord (r [q ]);
22       if (key [q ] < LastKey)  // new record belongs to next run
23         rn [q ] = rmax = rq + 1;
24       else rn [q ] = rc;
25     }
26     rq = rn [q ];
27     // adjust losers
28     for (t = (k +q)/2; t; t /= 2;) // t is initialized to be parent of q
29       if ((rn [l [t ]] < rq) || ((rn [l [t ]] == rq) && (key [l [t ]] < key [q ])))
30       { // t is the winner
31         int temp = q; q = l [t ]; l [t ] = temp;
32         rq = rn [q ];
33       }
34   }
35   delete [ ] r ; delete [ ] key;
36   delete [ ] rn ; delete [ ] l;
37 }
```

Program 7.21: Run generation using a loser tree

$$r[i], 0 \le i < k \quad \dots \quad \text{the } k \text{ records in the tournament tree}$$
$$key[i], 0 \le i < k \quad \dots \quad \text{key value of record } r[i]$$
$$l[i], 1 \le i < k \quad \dots \quad \text{loser of the tournament played at node } i$$
$$l[0] \quad \dots \quad \text{winner of the tournament}$$
$$rn[i], 0 \le i < k \quad \dots \quad \text{the run number to which } r[i] \text{ belongs}$$
$$rc \quad \dots \quad \text{run number of current run}$$
$$q \quad \dots \quad \text{overall tournament winner}$$
$$rq \quad \dots \quad \text{run number for } r[q]$$
$$rmax \quad \dots \quad \text{number of runs that will be generated}$$
$$LastKey \quad \dots \quad \text{key value of last record output}$$

The loop of lines 11 to 34 repeatedly plays the tournament outputting records. The variable *LastKey* is made use of in line 22 to determine whether or not the new record input, $r[q]$, can be output as part of the current run. If $key[q] < LastKey$ then $r[q]$ cannot be output as part of the current run rc, as a record with larger key value has already been output in this run. When the tree is being readjusted (lines 27 to 33), a record with lower run number wins over one with a higher run number. When run numbers are equal, the record with lower key value wins. This ensures that records come out of the tree in nondecreasing order of their run numbers. Within the same run, records come out of the tree in nondecreasing order of their key values. *rmax* is used to terminate the function. In line 19, when we run out of input, a record with run number $rmax + 1$ is introduced. When this record is ready for output, the function terminates from line 14.

Analysis of *runs*: When the input list is already sorted, only one run is generated. On the average, the run size is almost $2k$. The time required to generate all the runs for an n run list is O($n \log k$), as it takes O($\log k$) time to adjust the loser tree each time a record is output. □

7.10.5 Optimal Merging of Runs

The runs generated by function *runs* may not be of the same size. When runs are of different size, the run merging strategy employed so far (i.e., make complete passes over the collection of runs) does not yield minimum run times. For example, suppose we have four runs of length 2, 4, 5, and 15, respectively. Figure 7.26 shows two ways to merge these using a series of two-way merges. The circular nodes represent a two-way merge using as input the data of the children nodes. The square nodes represent the initial runs. We shall refer to the circular nodes as *internal nodes* and the square ones as *external nodes*. Each figure is a *merge tree*.

In the first merge tree, we begin by merging the runs of size 2 and 4 to get one of size 6; next this is merged with the run of size 5 to get a run of size 11; finally this run of size 11 is merged with the run of size 15 to get the desired sorted run of size 26. When merging is done using the first merge tree, some records are involved in only one merge, and others are involved in up to three merges. In the second merge tree, each record is

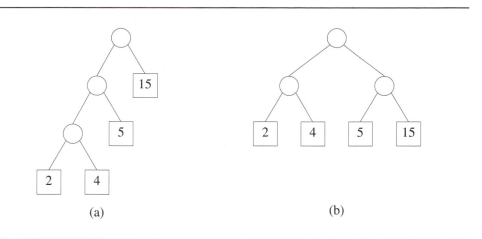

(a)   (b)

Figure 7.26: Possible two-way merges

involved in exactly two merges. This corresponds to the strategy in which complete merge passes are repeatedly made over the data.

The number of merges that an individual record is involved in is given by the distance of the corresponding external node from the root. So, the records of the run with 15 records are involved in one merge when the first merge tree of Figure 7.26 is used and in two merges when the second tree is used. Since the time for a merge is linear in the number of records being merged, the total merge time is obtained by summing the products of the run lengths and the distance from the root of the corresponding external nodes. This sum is called the *weighted external path length*. For the two trees of Figure 7.26, the respective weighted external path lengths are

$$2 \cdot 3 + 4 \cdot 3 + 5 \cdot 2 + 15 \cdot 1 = 43$$

and

$$2 \cdot 2 + 4 \cdot 2 + 2 + 5 \cdot 2 + 15 \cdot 2 = 52$$

The cost of a k-way merge of n runs of length q_i, $1 \le i \le n$, is minimized by using a merge tree of degree k that has minimum weighted external path length. We shall consider the case $k = 2$ only. The discussion is easily generalized to the case $k > 2$ (see the exercises).

We briefly describe another application for binary trees with minimum weighted external path length. Suppose we wish to obtain an optimal set of codes for messages $M_1, \cdots, M_{n+1}$. Each code is a binary string that will be used for transmission of the corresponding message. At the receiving end the code will be decoded using a *decode tree*. A decode tree is a binary tree in which external nodes represent messages. The binary bits in the code word for a message determine the branching needed at each level of the decode tree to reach the correct external node. For example, if we interpret a zero as a left branch and a one as a right branch, then the decode tree of Figure 7.27 corresponds to codes 000, 001, 01, and 1 for messages M_1, M_2, M_3, and M_4, respectively. These codes are called Huffman codes. The cost of decoding a code word is proportional to the number of bits in the code. This number is equal to the distance of the corresponding external node from the root node. If q_i is the relative frequency with which message M_i will be transmitted, then the expected decoding time is

$$\sum_{1 \leq i \leq n+1} q_i d_i$$

where d_i is the distance of the external node for message M_i from the root node. The expected decoding time is minimized by choosing code words resulting in a decode tree with minimal weighted external path length.

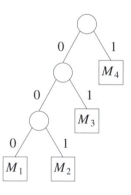

Figure 7.27: A decode tree

A very nice solution to the problem of finding a binary tree with minimum weighted external path length has been given by D. Huffman. The following class definition is assumed:

```
class BinaryTree {
public:
    BinaryTree(BinaryTree bt1, BinaryTree bt2) {
        root →LeftChild = bt1.root;
        root →RightChild = bt2.root;
        root →weight = bt1.root →weight + bt2.root →weight;
    }
private:
    BinaryTreeNode *root;
}
```

Function *huffman* (Program 7.22) makes use of a list *l* of extended binary trees. Each node in a tree has three fields: *weight*, *LeftChild*, and *RightChild*. Initially, all trees in *l* have only one node. For each tree this node is an external node, and its weight is one of the provided q_i's. During the course of the function, for any tree *t* in *l* with depth greater than one, $t.root \rightarrow weight$ is the sum of weights of all external nodes in *t*. Function *huffman* uses the functions *List::Size()*, *List::DeleteMinWeight()* and *list::Insert()*. *l.Size()* returns the number of elements in *l*. *l.DeleteMinWeight()* returns a tree in *l* with minimum *weight* and removes it from *l*; *l.Insert(bt)* adds the new tree *bt* to the list *l*.

```
void huffman(List<BinaryTree> l)
// l is a list of single node binary trees as described above
{
    int n = l. Size (); // number of binary trees in l
    for (int i = 0; i < n−1; i ++) { // loop n−1 times
        BinaryTree first = l. DeleteMinWeight ();
        BinaryTree second = l. DeleteMinWeight ();
        BinaryTree *bt = new BinaryTree(first, second);
        l. Insert (bt);
    }
}
```

Program 7.22: Finding a binary tree with minimum weighted external path length

Example 7.15: Suppose we have the weights $q_1 = 2$, $q_2 = 3$, $q_3 = 5$, $q_4 = 7$, $q_5 = 9$, and $q_6 = 13$. Then the sequence of trees we would get is given in Figure 7.28 (the number in a circular node represents the sum of the weights of external nodes in that subtree).

The weighted external path length of this tree is

$$2 \cdot 4 + 3 \cdot 4 + 5 \cdot 3 + 13 \cdot 2 + 7 \cdot 2 + 9 \cdot 2 = 93$$

By comparison, the best complete binary tree has weighted path length 95. □

Analysis of *huffman*: The main loop is executed $n - 1$ times. If *l* is maintained as a heap (see Section 5.6), then each call to *DeleteMinWeight* and *Insert* requires only O(log$n$) time. Hence, the asymptotic computing time is O($n$log$n$). The correctness proof is left as an exercise. □

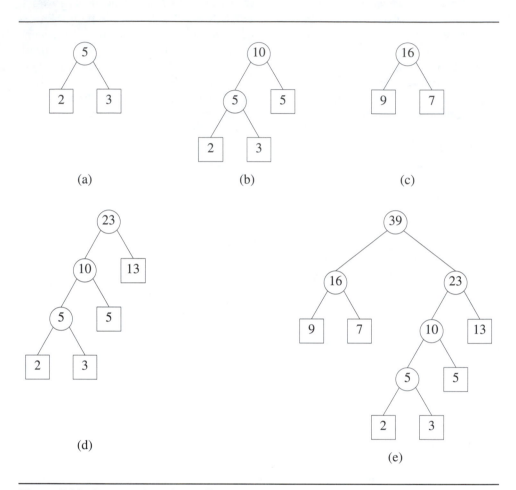

Figure 7.28: Construction of a Huffman tree

EXERCISES

1. (a) *n* records are to be sorted on a computer with a memory capacity of S records ($S << n$). Assume that the entire S-record capacity may be used for input/output buffers. The input is on disk and consists of m runs. Assume that each time a disk access is made, the seek time is t_s and the latency time is t_l. The transmission time is t_t per record transmitted. What is the total input time for phase two of external sorting if a k-way merge is used with internal memory partitioned into input/output buffers to permit overlap of input, output, and CPU processing as in *buffering* (Program 7.20)?

(b) Let the CPU time needed to merge all the runs together be t_{CPU} (we may assume it is independent of k and hence constant). Let $t_s = 80\ ms$, $t_l = 20ms$, $n = 200,000$, $m = 64$, $t_t = 10^{-3}$ sec/record, and $S = 2000$. Obtain a rough plot of the total input time, t_{input}, versus k. Will there always be a value of k for which $t_{CPU} \approx t_{input}$?

2. (a) Show that function *huffman* (Program 7.22) correctly generates a binary tree of minimal weighted external path length.

(b) When n runs are to be merged together using an m-way merge, Huffman's method can be generalized to the following rule: "First add $(1 - n) \bmod (m - 1)$ runs of length zero to the set of runs. Then, repeatedly merge the m shortest remaining runs until only one run is left." Show that this rule yields an optimal merge pattern for m-way merging.

7.11   REFERENCES AND SELECTED READINGS

A comprehensive discussion of sorting and searching may be found in *The Art of Computer Programming: Sorting and Searching*, by D. Knuth, vol. 3, Addison-Wesley, Reading, MA, 1973.

Two other useful references on sorting are *Sorting and Sort Systems*, by H. Lorin, Addison-Wesley, Reading, MA, 1975, and *Internal Sorting Methods Illustrated with PL/1 Programs*, by R. Rich, Prentice-Hall, Englewood Cliffs, NJ, 1972.

Two references on quick sort are "Quicksort," by C. A. R. Hoare, *The Computer Journal*, 5, 1962, pp. 10-15, and "The analysis of quicksort programs," by R. Sedgewick, *Acta Informatica*, 7, 1976/77, pp. 327-355.

Figures 7.17 and 7.18 are taken from *Software Development in Pascal*, Third Edition, by S. Sahni, Camelot Publishing Co., MN, 1993.

The O(1)-space, linear-time merge algorithm is from the paper: "Practical in-place merging," by B. Huang and M. Langston, *CACM*, 31:3, 1988, pp. 348-352.

For more on Huffman codes see "An optimum encoding with minimum longest code and total number of digits," by E. Schwartz, *Information and Control*, 7, 1964, pp. 37-44.

CHAPTER **8**

HASHING

8.1 THE SYMBOL TABLE ABSTRACT DATA TYPE

We have all used a *dictionary*, and many of us have a word processor equipped with a limited dictionary, that is, a spelling checker. In this chapter, we consider the dictionary, as an ADT. Examples of dictionaries are found in many applications, including the spelling checker, the thesaurus, the data dictionary found in database management applications, and the symbol tables generated by loaders, assemblers, and compilers.

In computer science, we generally use the term *symbol table* rather than dictionary, when referring to the ADT. Viewed from this perspective, we define a symbol table as a set of name-attribute pairs. The characteristics of the name and attribute vary according to the application. For example, in a thesaurus, the name is a word, and the attribute is a list of synonyms for the word; in a symbol table for a compiler, the name is an identifier, and the attributes might include an initial value and a list of lines that use the identifier.

Generally we want to perform the following operations on a symbol table:

(1)   determine if a particular name is in the table

(2)   retrieve the attributes of that name

(3)   modify the attributes of that name

(4)   insert a new name and its attributes

(5)   delete a name and its attributes

ADT 8.1 provides the complete specification of the symbol table ADT.

---

template <**class** *Name*, *Attribute*>
class *SymbolTable*
// **objects**: a set of name-attribute pairs, where the names are unique
{
public:
   SymbolTable(**int** *size* = *defaultsize*);
   // Create an empty symbol table with capacity *size*

   Boolean IsIn(*Name name*);
   // if *name* is in symbol table, return TRUE (1); else return FALSE (0)

   Attribute ∗Find(*Name name*);
   // if *name* is in symbol table, return a pointer to the corresponding attribute; else return 0.

   void *Insert*(*Name name*, *Attribute attr*);
   // if *name* is in symbol table, then replace its existing attribute with *attr*;
   // else, insert the pair (*name*, *attr*) into the symbol table

   void *Delete*(*Name name*);
   // if *name* is in symbol table, delete (*name*, *attr*) from symbol table
};

ADT 8.1: Abstract data type *SymbolTable*

Although ADT 8.1 lists several operations, there are only three basic operations on symbol tables: searching, inserting, and deleting. Therefore, when choosing a symbol table representation, we must make sure that we can implement these operations efficiently. For example, we could use the binary search tree introduced in Chapter 5 to represent a symbol table. If our search tree contained n identifiers, the worst-case complexity for these operations would be $O(n)$. In Chapter 10 we introduce several refinements of the binary search tree data structure that reduce the time per operation to $O(\log n)$. In this chapter we examine a technique for search, insert, and delete operations that has very good expected performance. The technique is referred to as *hashing*. Unlike search tree methods which rely on identifier comparisons to perform a search, hashing relies on a formula called the *hash function*. We divide our discussion of hashing into two parts: *static hashing* and *dynamic hashing*.

8.2 STATIC HASHING

8.2.1 Hash Tables

In *static hashing* the identifiers are stored in a fixed-size table called the *hash table*. The address or location of an identifier, x, is obtained by computing some arithmetic function, h, of x. $h(x)$ gives the address of x in the table. This address will be referred to as the hash or home address of x. The memory available to maintain the symbol table is assumed to be sequential. This memory is referred to as the hash table, ht. The hash table is partitioned into b buckets, $ht[0]$, $\cdots$, $ht[b-1]$. Each bucket is capable of holding s records. Thus, a bucket is said to consist of s slots, each slot being large enough to hold one record. Usually $s = 1$, and each bucket can hold exactly one record. A hash function, $h(x)$, is used to perform an identifier transformation on x. $h(x)$ maps the set of possible identifiers onto the integers 0 through $b-1$. If we limit the identifiers to be at most six characters long, with the first one being a letter and the remaining either letters or decimal digits, then there are $T = \sum_{0 \le i \le 5} 26 \times 36^i > 1.6 \times 10^9$ distinct possible values for x. Any reasonable application, however, uses only a very small fraction of these.

Definition: The *identifier density* of a hash table is the ratio n/T, where n is the number of identifiers in the table and T is the total number of possible identifiers. The *loading density* or *loading factor* of a hash table is $\alpha = n/(sb)$. $\square$

Since the number of identifiers, n, in use is usually several orders of magnitude less than the total number of possible identifiers, T, the number of buckets, b, in the hash table is also much less than T. Therefore, the hash function h must map several different identifiers into the same bucket. Two identifiers, I_1, and I_2, are said to be *synonyms* with respect to h if $h(I_1) = h(I_2)$. Distinct synonyms are entered into the same bucket as long as all the s slots in that bucket have not been used. An *overflow* is said to occur when a new identifier I is mapped or hashed by h into a full bucket. A *collision* occurs when two nonidentical identifiers are hashed into the same bucket. When the bucket size s is 1, collisions and overflows occur simultaneously.

Example 8.1: Consider the hash table ht with $b = 26$ buckets and $s = 2$. Assume that there are $n = 10$ distinct identifiers and that each identifier begins with a letter. The loading factor, α, for this table is $10/52 = 0.19$. The hash function h must map each of the possible identifiers into one of the numbers 0 to 25. If the internal binary representation for the letters A to Z corresponds to the numbers 0 to 25, respectively, then the function h defined by $h(x) =$ the first character of x will hash all identifiers x into the hash table. The identifiers GA, D, A, G, L, A2, A1, A3, A4, and E will be hashed into buckets 6, 3, 0, 6, 11, 0, 0, 0, 0, and 4, respectively, by this function. The identifiers A, A1, A2, A3, and A4 are synonyms. So also are G and GA. Figure 8.1 shows the identifiers GA, D, A, G, and A2 entered into the hash table.

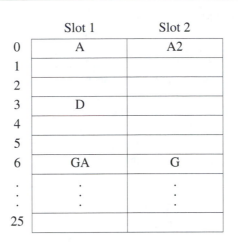

	Slot 1	Slot 2
0	A	A2
1		
2		
3	D	
4		
5		
6	GA	G
.	.	.
.	.	.
.	.	.
25		

Figure 8.1: Hash table with 26 buckets and two slots per bucket

Note that GA and G are in the same bucket and each bucket has two slots. Similarly, the synonyms A and A2 are in the same bucket. The next identifier, A1, hashes into the bucket ht [0]. This bucket is full and a search of the bucket indicates that A1 is not in the bucket. An overflow has now occurred. Where in the table should A1 be entered so that it may be retrieved when needed? ☐

When no overflows occur, the time required to enter or search for identifiers using hashing depends only on the time required to compute the hash function h and the time to search one bucket. Since the bucket size, s, is usually small (for internal tables s is usually 1) the search for an identifier within a bucket is carried out using a sequential search. The time is independent of n.

The hash function of Example 8.1 is not well suited for the application we have in mind because of the very large number of collisions and resulting overflows that occur. This is so because it is not unusual to find programs in which many of the variables begin with the same letter. Ideally, we would like to choose a function h that is both easy to compute and results in very few collisions. Since the ratio b/T is usually very small, it is impossible to avoid collisions altogether.

In summary, hashing schemes perform an identifier transformation through the use of a hash function h. It is desirable to choose a function h that is easy to compute and also minimizes the number of collisions. Since the size of the identifier space, T, is usually several orders of magnitude larger than the number of buckets, b, and s is small, overflows necessarily occur. Hence, a mechanism to handle overflows is also needed.

8.2.2   Hash Functions

A hash function, h, transforms an identifier, x, into a bucket address in the hash table. As mentioned earlier, the desired properties of such a function are that it be easy to compute and that it minimize the number of collisions. A function such as the one discussed earlier is not a very good choice for a hash function for symbol tables, even though it is easy to compute. The reason for this is that the function depends only on the first character in the identifier. Since many programs use several identifiers with the same first letter, we expect several collisions to occur. In general, then, we would like the function to depend upon all the characters in the identifiers. In addition, we would like the hash function to be such that it does not result in a biased use of the hash table for random inputs; i.e., if x is an identifier chosen at random from the identifier space, then we want the probability that $h(x) = i$ to be $1/b$ for all buckets i. Then a random x has an equal chance of hashing into any of the b buckets. A hash function satisfying this property will be called a *uniform hash function*.

Several kinds of uniform hash functions are in use. We shall describe four of these.

8.2.2.1   Mid-Square

The mid-square function has found much use in symbol table applications. This function, h_m, is computed by squaring the identifier and then using an appropriate number of bits from the middle of the square to obtain the bucket address; the identifier is assumed to fit into one computer word. Since the middle bits of the square usually depend on all the characters in the identifier, different identifiers are expected to result in different hash addresses with high probability, even when some of the characters are the same. Figure 8.2 shows the bit configurations resulting from squaring some sample identifiers. The number of bits to be used to obtain the bucket address depends on the table size. If r bits are used, the range of values is 2^r, so the size of hash tables is chosen to be a power of two when this kind of scheme is used.

8.2.2.2   Division

Another simple choice for a hash function is obtained by using the modulo (%) operator. The identifier x is divided by some number M, and the remainder is used as the hash address for x. The hash function is

$$f_D(x) = x \% M$$

This function gives bucket addresses in the range 0 through $(M - 1)$, so the hash table is at least of size $b = M$. The choice of M is critical. If M is a power of 2, then $h_D(x)$ depends only on the least significant bits of x. For instance, if each character is

Identifier	Internal Representation	
x	x	x^2
A	1	1
A1	134	20420
A2	135	20711
A3	136	21204
A4	137	21501
A9	144	23420
B	2	4
C	3	11
G	7	61
DMAX	4150130	21526443617100
DMAX1	415013034	5264473522151420
AMAX	1150130	135423617100
AMAX1	115013034	3454246522151420

Figure 8.2: Internal representations of x and x^2 in octal notation (x is input right-justified, zero-filled, six bits or two octal digits per character)

represented by six bits, and identifiers are stored right-justified in a 60-bit word with leading bits filled with zeros (Figure 8.3), then with $M = 2^i$, $i \le 6$, the identifiers A1, B1, C1, X41, DNTXY1, etc., all have the same bucket address. With $M = 2^i$, $i \le 12$, the identifiers AXY, BXY, WTXY, etc., have the same bucket address.

	48 bits									48 bits						
0	0	0	0	0	0	A	1		A	1	0	0	0	0	0	0

right-justified zero-filled   left-justified

Figure 8.3: Identifier A1 right- and left-justified and zero-filled (six bits per character)

Since programmers have a tendency to use many variables with the same suffix, the choice of M as a power of two would result in many collisions. This choice of M would have even more disastrous results if the identifier x were stored left-justified and zero-filled. Then, all one-character identifiers would map to the same bucket, 0, for $M = 2^i$, $i \le 54$; all two-character identifiers would map to the bucket 0 for $M = 2^i$, $i \le 48$, and so on. As a result of this observation, we see that when the division function h_D is used as a hash function, the table size should not be a power of two, whereas when the mid-square function h_m is used, the table size is a power of two.

If M is divisible by two, then odd keys are mapped to odd buckets (as the remainder is odd), and even keys are mapped to even buckets. The use of the hash table is thus biased.

Let $x = x_1 x_2$ and $y = x_2 x_1$ be two identifiers, each consisting of the characters x_1 and x_2. If the internal binary representation of x_1 has value $C(x_1)$, and that for x_2 has value $C(x_2)$, then if each character is represented by six bits, the numeric value of x is $2^6 C(x_1) + C(x_2)$, and that for y is $2^6 C(x_2) + C(x_1)$. If p is a prime number that divides M, then:

$$(f_D(x) - f_D(y)) \% p = (2^6 C(x_1) \% p + C(x_2) \% p \\ - 2^6 C(x_2) \% p - C(x_1) \% p) \% p$$

If $p = 3$, then

$$(f_D(x) - f_D(y)) \% p = (64 \% 3\ C(x_1) \% 3 + C(x_2) \% 3 \\ - 64 \% 3\ C(x_2) \% 3 - C(x_1) \% 3) \% 3 \\ = C(x_1) \% 3 + C(x_2) \% 3 - C(x_2) \% 3 - C(x_1) \% 3 \\ = 0 \% 3$$

That is, permutations of the same set of characters are hashed at a distance a multiple of three apart. Programs in which many variables are permutations of each other would again result in a biased use of the table and hence result in many collisions. This happens because $64 \% 3 = 1$. The same behavior can be expected when 7 divides M, as $64 \% 7 = 1$.

These difficulties can be avoided by making M a prime number. Then, the only factors of M are M and 1. Donald Knuth has shown that when M divides $r^k \pm a$, where k and a are small numbers and r is the radix of the character set (in the example above $r = 64$), then $x \% M$ tends to be a simple superposition of the characters in x. Thus, a prime number such that M does not divide $r^k \pm a$ for small k and a would be a good choice for M. In Section 8.2.3 we shall see other reasons for choosing M as a prime number. In practice it has been observed that it is sufficient to choose M such that it has no prime divisors less than 20.

8.2.2.3   Folding

In this method the identifier x is partitioned into several parts, all but possibly the last being of the same length. These partitions are then added together to obtain the hash address for x. There are two ways of carrying out this addition. In the first, all but the last partition are shifted so that the least significant bit of each lines up with the corresponding bit of the last partition. The different partitions are now added together to get $h(x)$. This method is known as *shift folding*. In the second method, *folding at the boundaries*, the identifier is folded at the partition boundaries, and digits falling into the same position are added together to obtain $h(x)$. This is equivalent to reversing every other partition and then adding.

Example 8.2: Suppose that $x = 12320324111220$, and we partition it into parts that are three decimal digits long. The partitions are $P_1 = 123$, $P_2 = 203$, $P_3 = 241$, $P_4 = 112$, and $P_5 = 20$. Using shift folding, we obtain

$$h(x) = \sum_{1=1}^{5} P_i = 123 + 203 + 241 + 112 + 20 = 699$$

When folding at the boundaries is used, we first reverse P_2 and P_4 to obtain 302 and 211, respectively. Next, the five partitions are added to obtain $h(x) = 123 + 302 + 241 + 211 + 20 = 897$. □

8.2.2.4 Digit Analysis

This method is particularly useful in the case of a static file where all the identifiers in the table are known in advance. Each identifier x is interpreted as a number using some radix r. The same radix is used for all the identifiers in the table. Using this radix, the digits of each identifier are examined. Digits having the most skewed distributions are deleted. Enough digits are deleted so that the number of remaining digits is small enough to give an address in the range of the hash table.

   In Section 8.2.4, we compare the various methods used to generate a hash address. Of these methods, the one most suitable for general-purpose applications is the division method with a divisor, M, such that M has no prime factors less than 20.

8.2.3 Overflow Handling

8.2.3.1 Open Addressing

There are two ways to handle overflows: *open addressing* and *chaining*. In open addressing, we assume the hash table is an array. For simplicity, we assume that $s = 1$. The class definitions used are in Program 8.1.

   To detect collisions and overflows, the hash table, *ht*, is initialized so that each slot contains the null identifier. When a new identifier is hashed into a full bucket, we need to find another bucket for this identifier. The simplest solution is to find the closest unfilled bucket. This is called *linear probing* or *linear open addressing*.

Example 8.3: Assume we have a 26-bucket table with one slot per bucket and the following identifiers: GA, D, A, G, L, A2, A1, A3, A4, Z, ZA, E. For simplicity we choose the hash function $h(x) = $ first character of x. Initially, all entries in the table are null.

```
struct identifier {
   char *id;
   int n;
};

// assume that operators == and != are defined for identifier
int operator==(identifier&, identifier&);
int operator!=(identifier&, identifier&);

class SymbolTable {
public:
   SymbolTable(int size = defaultsize) {
      buckets = size;
      ht = new identifier [buckets ];
   };
private:
   int buckets;
   identifier *ht;
};
```

Program 8.1: Symbol table class definition

Since $h(GA) = 6$, and $ht[6]$ is empty, GA and any other information making up the record are entered into $ht[6]$. D and A get entered into the buckets $ht[3]$ and $ht[0]$, respectively. The next identifier G has $h(G) = 6$. This bucket is already used by GA. The next vacant slot is $ht[7]$, so G is entered there. L enters $ht[11]$. A2 collides with A at $ht[0]$, the bucket overflows, and A2 is entered at the next vacant slot, $ht[1]$. A1, A3, and A4 are entered at $ht[2]$, $ht[4]$, and $ht[5]$, respectively. Z is entered at $ht[25]$, ZA at $ht[8]$ (the hash table is used circularly), and E collides with A3 at $ht[4]$ and is eventually entered at $ht[9]$. Figure 8.4 shows the resulting table. □

When linear open addressing is used to handle overflows, a hash table search for identifier x proceeds as follows:

(1)   compute $h(x)$

(2)   examine identifiers at positions $ht[h(x)]$, $ht[h(x) + 1]$, $\cdots$, $ht[h(x) + j]$, in this order, until one of the following happens:

   (a) $ht[h(x) + j] = x$; in this case x is found.

   (b) $ht[h(x) + j]$ is null; x is not in the table.

   (c)   We return to the starting position $h(x)$; the table is full and x is not in the table.

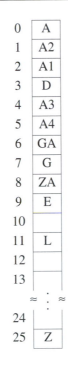

0	A
1	A2
2	A1
3	D
4	A3
5	A4
6	GA
7	G
8	ZA
9	E
10	
11	L
12	
13	
24	
25	Z

Figure 8.4: Hash table with linear probing (26 buckets, one slot per bucket)

LinearSearch (Program 8.2) is the resulting search function.

In Example 8.3 we saw that when linear probing is used to resolve overflows, identifiers tend to cluster together, and moreover, adjacent clusters tend to coalesce, thus increasing the search time. To locate the identifier ZA in the table of Figure 8.4, it is necessary to examine $ht[25]$, $ht[0]$, $\cdots$, $ht[8]$ — a total of 10 comparisons. This is far worse than the worst-case behavior for the tree tables we shall see in Chapter 10. If each of the identifiers in the table of Figure 8.4 is retrieved exactly once, then the number of buckets examined is 1 for A, 2 for A2, 3 for A1, 1 for D, 5 for A3, 6 for A4, 1 for GA, 2 for G, 10 for ZA, 6 for E, 1 for L, and 1 for Z — for a total of 39 buckets examined. The average number examined is 3.25 buckets per identifier.

An analysis of linear probing shows that the expected average number of identifier comparisons, P, to look up an identifier is approximately $(2 - \alpha)/(2 - 2\alpha)$, where α is the loading density. This is the average over all possible sets of identifiers yielding the given loading density and using a uniform function h. In Example 8.3, $\alpha = 12/26 = .47$ and $P = 1.5$. Even though the average number of probes is small, the worst case can be quite large.

```
int SymbolTable::LinearSearch(const identifier& x, int (*hashfunc) (identifier))
// Search the hash table ht (each bucket has exactly one slot) for x using linear probing.
// Return j such that if x is already in the table, then ht [ j ] = x.  If x is not in the table,
// return −1. The hash function hashfunc is passed as an argument to LinearSearch.
{
    int i = hashfunc (x);
    for (int j = i; ht [ j ].id && ht [ j ] != x; ) {
        j = (j+1) % buckets;  // treat the table as circular
        if (j == i) return −1; // back to start point
    }
    if (ht [ j ] == x) return j; else return −1;
}
```

Program 8.2: Linear search

One of the problems with linear open addressing is that it tends to create clusters of identifiers. Moreover, these clusters tend to merge as more identifiers are entered, leading to bigger clusters. Some improvement in the growth of clusters and hence in the average number of probes needed for searching can be obtained by *quadratic probing*. Linear probing was characterized by searching the buckets $(h(x) + i) \% b$, $0 \le i \le b - 1$, where b is the number of buckets in the table. In quadratic probing, a quadratic function of i is used as the increment. In particular, the search is carried out by examining buckets $h(x)$, $(h(x) + i^2) \% b$, and $(h(x) - i^2) \% b$ for $1 \le i \le (b - 1)/2$. When b is a prime number of the form $4j + 3$, for j an integer, the quadratic search described above examines every bucket in the table. (For the proof, refer to the article by Radke cited in the References and Selected Readings section). Figure 8.5 lists some primes of the form $4j + 3$.

Prime	j	Prime	j
3	0	43	10
7	1	59	14
11	2	127	31
19	4	251	62
23	5	503	125
31	7	1019	254

Figure 8.5: Some primes of the form $4j + 3$

An alternative method to retard the growth of clusters is to use a series of hash functions $h_1, h_2, \cdots, h_m$. This method is known as *rehashing*. Buckets $h_i(x), 1 \leq i \leq m$ are examined in that order. Yet another alternative, random probing, is explored in the exercises.

8.2.3.2 Chaining

Linear probing and its variations perform poorly because the search for an identifier involves comparison with identifiers that have different hash values. In the hash table of Figure 8.4, for instance, searching for the identifier ZA involves comparisons with the buckets $ht[0]$ to $ht[7]$, even though none of the identifiers in these buckets had a collision with $ht[25]$ and so cannot possibly be ZA. Many of the comparisons can be saved if we maintain lists of identifiers, one list per bucket, each list containing all the synonyms for that bucket. If this is done, a search involves computing the hash address $h(x)$ and examining only those identifiers in the list for $h(x)$. Since the sizes of these lists are not known in advance, the best way to maintain them is as linked chains. Additional space for a link is required in each slot. Each chain has a head node. The head node, however, usually is much smaller than the other nodes, since it has to retain only a link. Since the lists are to be accessed at random, the head nodes should be sequential. We assume that they are numbered 0 to $b-1$ if the hash function h has range 0 to $b-1$.

When chaining is used on the data of Example 8.3, the hash chains of Figure 8.6 are obtained. To insert a new identifier, x, into a chain, we must first verify that it is not currently on the chain. Following this, x may be inserted at any position of the chain. In the example of Figure 8.6, new identifiers were inserted at the front of the chains. The number of probes needed to search for any of the identifiers is one for each of A4, D, E, G, L, and ZA; two for each of A3, GA, and Z; three for A1; four for A2; and five for A, for a total of 24. The average is now two, which is considerably less than the average for linear probing.

The class definitions in Program 8.3 assume the existence of **struct** *identifier* as in Program 8.1. The search algorithm for hash tables with chaining is given in Program 8.4.

The expected number of identifier comparisons can be shown to be $\approx 1 + \alpha/2$, where α is the loading density n/b (b = number of head nodes). For $\alpha = 0.5$ this figure is 1.25, and for $\alpha = 1$ it is about 1.5. This scheme has the additional advantage that only the b head nodes must be sequential and reserved at the beginning. Each head node, however, will be at most one-half to one word long. The other nodes will be much bigger and are allocated only as needed. This could represent an overall reduction in space required for certain loading densities, despite the links. If each record in the table is five words long, $n = 100$, and $\alpha = 0.5$, then the hash table will be of size $200 \times 5 = 1000$ words. Only 500 of these are used, as $\alpha = 0.5$. On the other hand, if chaining is used with one full word per link, then 200 words are needed for the head nodes ($b = 200$). Each head node is one word long. One hundred nodes of six words each are needed for the records. The total space needed is thus 800 words, or 20% less than when no chaining was being used. When α is close to 1, the average number of probes using

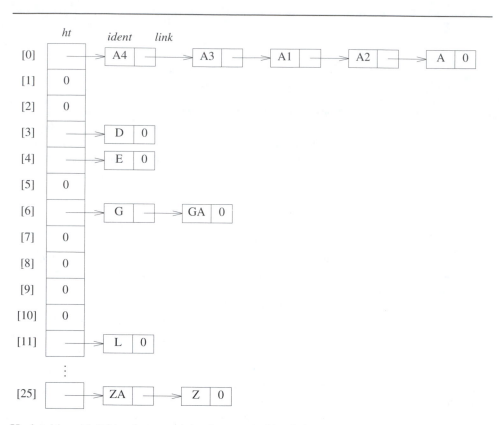

Hash table with 26 buckets; each bucket can hold a link.

Figure 8.6: Hash chains corresponding to Figure 8.4

linear probing or its variations becomes quite large, and the additional space used for chaining can be justified by the reduction in the expected number of probes needed for retrieval. Deletion can be done by removing a node from its chain. The problem of deleting entries when open addressing is used is explored in the exercises.

The results of this section tend to imply that the performance of a hash table depends only on the method used to handle overflows and is independent of the hash function as long as a uniform hash function is used. Although this is true when the identifiers are selected at random from the identifier space, it is not true in practice. In practice, there is a tendency to make a biased use of identifiers. Many identifiers in use have a common suffix or prefix or are simple permutations of other identifiers. Hence, in practice we would expect different hash functions to result in different hash table performance. The table of Figure 8.7 presents the results of an empirical study conducted by

```
class ListNode {
friend SymbolTable;
private:
    identifier ident;
    ListNode *link;
};

typedef ListNode* ListPtr;

class SymbolTable {
public:
    SymbolTable(int size = defaultsize) {
        buckets = size;
        ht = new ListPtr [buckets ];
    };
private:
    int buckets;
    ListPtr *ht;
};
```

Program 8.3: Class definitions for chain search

```
identifier* SymbolTable::ChainSearch(const identifier& x, int (*hashfunc) (identifier) )
// Search the chained hash table ht for x. On termination, return a pointer
// to the identifier in the hashtable.  If the identifier does not exist, return 0
{
    int j = hashfunc (x) // compute headnode address
    // search the chain starting at ht [j ]
    for (ListPtr l = ht [j ]; l; l = l →link)
        if (l →ident == x) return &l →ident;
    return 0;
}
```

Program 8.4: Chain search

Lum, Yuen, and Dodd. The values in each column give the average number of bucket accesses made in searching eight different tables with 33,575, 24,050, 4909, 3072, 2241, 930, 762, and 500 identifiers each. As expected, chaining outperforms linear open addressing as a method for overflow handling. In looking over the figures for the various hash functions, we see that division is generally superior to the other types of hash functions. For a general application it is therefore recommended that the division method be used. The divisor should be a prime number, although choosing a divisor that has no prime factors less than 20 is sufficient. The table also gives the theoretical expected number of bucket accesses based on random keys.

$\alpha = \dfrac{n}{b}$	0.50		0.75		0.90		0.95	
Hash Function	Chain	Open	Chain	Open	Chain	Open	Chain	Open
mid square	1.26	1.73	1.40	9.75	1.45	37.14	1.47	37.53
division	1.19	4.52	1.31	7.20	1.38	22.42	1.41	25.79
shift fold	1.33	21.75	1.48	65.10	1.40	77.01	1.51	118.57
bound fold	1.39	22.97	1.57	48.70	1.55	69.63	1.51	97.56
digit analysis	1.35	4.55	1.49	30.62	1.52	89.20	1.52	125.59
theoretical	1.25	1.50	1.37	2.50	1.45	5.50	1.48	10.50

(Adapted from V. Lum, P. Yuen, and M. Dodd, *CACM*, 14:4, 1971)

Figure 8.7: Average number of bucket accesses per identifier retrieved

8.2.4 Theoretical Evaluation of Overflow Techniques

The experimental evaluation of hashing techniques indicates a very good performance over conventional techniques such as balanced trees. The worst-case performance for hashing can, however, be very bad. In the worst case, an insertion or a search in a hash table with n identifiers may take $O(n)$ time. In this section, we present a probabilistic analysis for the expected performance of the chaining method and state without proof the results of similar analyses for the other overflow handling methods. First, we formalize what we mean by expected performance.

Let $ht[0..b-1]$ be a hash table with b buckets, each bucket having one slot. Let h be a uniform hash function with range $[0, b-1]$. If n identifiers $x_1, x_2, \cdots, x_n$ are entered into the hash table, then there are b^n distinct hash sequences $h(x_1), h(x_2), \cdots, h(x_n)$. Assume that each of these is equally likely to occur. Let S_n denote the expected number of identifier comparisons needed to locate a randomly chosen x_i, $1 \le i \le n$. Then, S_n is the average number of comparisons needed to find the jth key x_j, averaged over $1 \le j \le n$, with each j equally likely, and averaged over all b^n hash sequences, assuming each of these also to be equally likely. Let U_n be the expected number of identifier comparisons when a search is made for an identifier not in the hash table. This hash table contains n identifiers. The quantity U_n may be defined in a manner analogous to that used for S_n.

Theorem 8.1: Let $\alpha = n/b$ be the loading density of a hash table using a uniform hashing function h. Then

(1) for linear open addressing

$$U_n \approx \frac{1}{2}\left[1 + \frac{1}{(1-\alpha)^2}\right]$$

$$S_n \approx \frac{1}{2}\left[1 + \frac{1}{1-\alpha}\right]$$

(2) for rehashing, random probing, and quadratic probing

$$U_n \approx 1/(1-\alpha)$$

$$S_n \approx -\left[\frac{1}{\alpha}\right]\log_e(1-\alpha)$$

(3) for chaining

$$U_n \approx \alpha$$

$$S_n \approx 1 + \alpha/2$$

Proof: Exact derivations of U_n and S_n are fairly involved and can be found in Knuth's book *The Art of Computer Programming: Sorting and Searching* (see the References and Selected Readings section). Here we present a derivation of the approximate formulas for chaining. First, we must make clear our count for U_n and S_n. If the identifier x being sought has $h(x) = i$, and chain i has k nodes on it (not including the head node), then k comparisons are needed if x is not on the chain. If x is j nodes away from the head node, $1 \le j \le k$, then j comparisons are needed.

When the n identifiers are distributed uniformly over the b possible chains, the expected number in each chain is $n/b = \alpha$. Since U_n equals the expected number of identifiers on a chain, we get $U_n = \alpha$.

When the ith identifier, x_i, is being entered into the table, the expected number of identifiers on any chain is $(i - 1)/b$. Hence, the expected number of comparisons needed to search for x_i after all n identifiers have been entered is $1 + (i - 1)/b$ (this assumes that new entries will be made at the end of the chain). Thus,

$$S_n = \frac{1}{n}\sum_{i=1}^{n}\{1 + (i - 1)/b\} = 1 + \frac{n - 1}{2b} \approx 1 + \frac{\alpha}{2} \quad \square$$

EXERCISES

1. Write an algorithm to delete identifier x from a hash table that uses hash function h and linear open addressing to resolve collisions. Show that simply setting the slot previously occupied by x to null does not solve the problem. How must algorithm *LinearSearch* (Program 8.2) be modified so that a correct search is made in the situation when deletions are permitted? Where can a new identifier be inserted?

2. (a) Show that if quadratic searching is carried out in the sequence $(h(x) + q^2)$, $(h(x) + (q-1)^2)$, $\cdots$, $(h(x) + 1)$, $h(x)$, $(h(x) - 1)$, $\cdots$, $(h(x) - q^2)$ with $q = (b-1)/2$, then the address difference $\% \ b$ between successive buckets being examined is

$$b - 2, b - 4, b - 6, \ldots, 5, 3, 1, 1, 3, 5, \ldots, b - 6, b - 4, b - 2$$

   (b) Write an algorithm to search a hash table ht of size b for the identifier x. Use h as the hash function and the quadratic probe scheme discussed in the text to resolve overflows. If x is not in the table, it is to be entered. Use the results of part (a) to reduce the computations.

3. [*Morris 1968*] In random probing, the search for an identifier, x, in a hash table with b buckets is carried out by examining the buckets in the order $h(x)$, $(h(x) + S(i)) \% b$, $1 \le i \le b - 1$ where $S(i)$ is a pseudo random number. The random number generator must satisfy the property that every number from 1 to $b - 1$ must be generated exactly once as i ranges from 1 to $b - 1$.

   (a) Show that for a table of size 2^r, the following sequence of computations generates numbers with this property:

   Initialize R to 1 each time the search routine is called.
   On successive calls for a random number do the following:
   $R \mathrel{*}= 5$
   $R =$ low order $r + 2$ bits of R
   $S(i) = R/4$

   (b) Write search and insert algorithms for a hash table using random probing and the mid-square hash function. Use the random number generator of (a).

   It can be shown that for this method, the expected value for the average number of comparisons needed to search for x is $-(1/\alpha)\log(1 - \alpha)$ for large tables (α is the loading factor).

4. Write an algorithm to list all the identifiers in a hash table in lexicographic order. Assume the hash function h is $h(x) =$ first character of x, and linear probing is used. How much time does your algorithm take?

5. Let the binary representation of identifier x be $x_1 x_2$. Let $|x|$ denote the number of bits in x and let the first bit of x_1 be 1. Let $|x_1| = \lceil |x|/2 \rceil$ and $|x_2| = \lfloor |x|/2 \rfloor$. Consider the following hash function

$$h(x) = \text{middle } k \text{ bits of } (x_1 \text{ XOR } x_2)$$

where XOR is the exclusive-or operator. Is this a uniform hash function if identifiers are drawn at random from the space of allowable C++ identifiers? What can you say about the behavior of this hash function in actual symbol table usage?

6. [*T. Gonzalez*] Design a symbol table representation that allows you to search, insert, and delete an identifier x in $O(1)$ time. Assume that $0 \le x < m$ and that $m + n$ units of space are available, where n is the number of insertions to be made. (Hint: Use two arrays, $a[n]$ and $b[m]$, where $a[i]$ will be the $(i+1)$th identifier inserted into the table. If x is the ith identifier inserted, then $b[x] = i$.) Write algorithms to search, insert, and delete identifiers. Note that you cannot initialize either a or b to zero as this would take $O(n + m)$ time. Note that x is an integer.

7. [*T. Gonzalez*] Let $S = \{x_1, x_2, \cdots, x_n\}$ and $T = \{y_1, y_2, \cdots, y_r\}$ be two sets. Assume $1 \le x_i \le m$, $1 \le i \le n$, and $1 \le y_i \le m$, $1 \le i \le r$. Using the idea of Exercise 6, write an algorithm to determine if $S \subseteq T$. Your algorithm should work in $O(r + n)$ time. Since $S \equiv T$ iff $S \subseteq T$ and $T \subseteq S$, one can determine in linear time whether two sets are equivalent. How much space is needed by your algorithm?

8. [*T. Gonzalez*] Using the idea of Exercise 6, write an $O(n + m)$ time algorithm to carry out the function of algorithm *Verify2* (Program 7.3). How much space does your algorithm need?

9. Using the notation of Section 8.2.4, show that when linear open addressing is used

$$S_n = \frac{1}{n} \sum_{i=0}^{n-1} U_i$$

Using this equation and the approximate equality

$$U_n \approx \frac{1}{2} \left[1 + \frac{1}{(1 - \alpha)^2} \right] \quad \text{where } \alpha = \frac{n}{b}$$

show that

$$S_n \approx \frac{1}{2} \left[1 + \frac{1}{(1 - \alpha)} \right]$$

10. [*Guttag*] The following set of operations defines a symbol table that handles a language with block structure. Write a specification for this data type in the style of ADT 8.1.

INIT	creates an empty table
ENTERB	indicates a new block has been entered
ADD	places an identifier and its attributes in the table
LEAVEB	deletes all identifiers that are defined in the innermost block
RETRIEVE	returns the attributes of the most recently defined identifier
ISINB	returns true if the identifier is defined in the innermost block, else false

8.3   DYNAMIC HASHING

8.3.1   Motivation for Dynamic Hashing

One of the most important classes of software is the database management system, or DBMS. In a DBMS the user enters a query, and the system translates it and retrieves the resulting data. Fast access time is essential, as a DBMS typically holds large sets of information. Another key characteristic of a DBMS is that the amount of information can vary a great deal with time. Various data structures have been suggested for storing the data in a DBMS. In this section, we examine an extension of hashing that permits the technique to be used by a DBMS.

Traditional hashing schemes as described in the previous section are not ideal. This follows from the fact that one must statically allocate a portion of memory to hold the hash table. This hash table is used to point to the pages used to hold identifiers, or it may actually hold the identifiers themselves. In either case, if the table is allocated to be as large as possible, then space can be wasted. If it is allocated to be too small, then when the data exceed the capacity of the hash table, the entire file must be restructured, a time-consuming process. The purpose of *dynamic hashing* (also referred to as *extendible hashing*) is to retain the fast retrieval time of conventional hashing while extending the technique so that it can accommodate dynamically increasing and decreasing file size without penalty.

We assume that a file F is a collection of records R. Each record has a key field K by which it is identified. Records are stored in pages or buckets whose capacity is p. We will try to develop algorithms that minimize access to pages, since they are typically stored on disk and their retrieval into memory dominates any operation. The measure of space utilization is the ratio of the number of records, n, divided by the total space, mp, where m is the number of pages.

8.3.2   Dynamic Hashing Using Directories

Consider an example in which an identifier consists of two characters, and each character is represented by three bits. Figure 8.8 gives a list of some of these identifiers.

identifiers	binary represenation
A0	100 000
A1	100 001
B0	101 000
B1	101 001
C0	110 000
C1	110 001
C2	110 010
C3	110 011

Figure 8.8: Some identifiers that require three bits per character

Consider placing these identifiers into a table that has four pages. Each page can hold at most two identifiers, and each page is indexed by the two-bit sequence 00, 01, 10, and 11, respectively. We use the two low-order bits of each identifier to determine in which page of the table to place it. The result of placing A0, B0, C2, A1, B1, and C3 is shown in Figure 8.9. Note that we select the bits from least significant to most significant.

Branching at the root is determined by the least significant bit. If this bit is zero, the upper branch is taken; otherwise, the lower branch is taken. Branching at the next level is determined by the second least significant bit, and so on. A0 and B0 are in the first page since their two low-order bits are 0 and 0. The second page contains only C2. To reach this page, we first branch on the least significant bit of C2 (i.e., 0) and then on the next bit (i.e., 1). The third page contains A1 and B1. To reach this page, we first branch on the least significant bit of A1 or B1. This bit is one for both A1 and B1. Next, we branch on the next bit, which is zero for both. The last page contains C3, with a bit pattern of 11. We use the term *trie* to denote a binary tree in which we locate an identifier by following its bit sequence. (We shall describe tries in greater detail in Chapter 10.) Notice that the nodes of this trie always branch in two directions corresponding to 0 or 1. Only the leaf nodes of the trie contain a pointer to a page.

Now suppose we try to insert a new identifier, say C5, into Figure 8.9(a). Since the two low-order bits of C5 are 1 and 0, we must place it in the third page. However, this page is full, and an overflow occurs. A new page is added, and the depth of the trie increases by one level. This is shown in Figure 8.9(b). If we now try to insert the new identifier C1, an overflow of the page containing A1 and B1 occurs. A new page is ob-

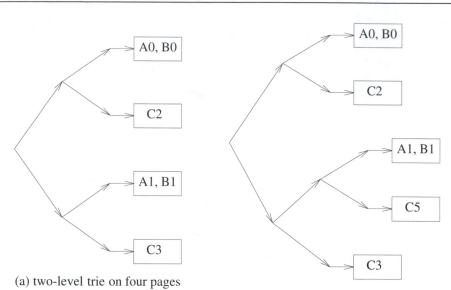

(a) two-level trie on four pages

(b) inserting C5 with overflow

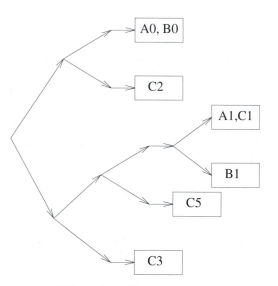

(c) inserting C1 with overflow

Figure 8.9: A trie to hold identifiers

tained, and the three identifiers are divided between the two pages according to their four low-order bits.

From this example one can see that two major problems exist. First, the access time for a page depends on the number of bits needed to distinguish the identifiers. Second, if the identifiers have a skewed distribution, the tree is also skewed. Both of these factors increase the retrieval time. Fagin et al. (1979) present a method, which they call *extendible hashing*, for solving these problems. To avoid the skewed distribution of identifiers, a hash function is used. This function takes the key and produces a random set of binary digits. To avoid the long search down the trie, the trie is mapped to a directory.

A *directory* is a table of page pointers. If k bits are needed to distinguish the identifiers, the directory has 2^k entries indexed $0, \cdots, 2^k-1$. To find the page for an identifier, we use the integer with binary representation equal to the last k bits of the identifier. The page pointed at by this directory entry is searched. Figure 8.10 shows the directories corresponding to the three tries in Figure 8.9. The first directory contains four entries indexed from 0 to 3 (the binary representation of each index is shown in Figure 8.10). Each entry contains a pointer to a page. This pointer is shown as an arrow in the figure. The letter above each pointer is a page label. The page labels were obtained by labeling the pages of Figure 8.9(a) top to bottom, beginning with the label a. The page contents are shown immediately after the page pointer. To see the correspondence between the directory and the trie, notice that if the bits in the directory index are used to follow a path in the trie (beginning with the least significant bit), we will reach the page pointed at by the corresponding directory entry.

The second directory contains eight entries indexed from 0 to 7, and the third has 16 entries indexed from 0 to 15. Page a of the second directory (Figure 8.10(b)) has two directory entries (000 and 100) pointing to it. The page contents are shown only once. Page b has two pointers to it, page c has one pointer, page d has one pointer, and page e has two pointers. In Figure 8.10(c) there are six pages with the following number of pointers, respectively: 4, 4, 1, 1, 2, and 4.

Using a directory to represent a trie allows the table of identifiers to grow and shrink dynamically. This, of course, assumes that the operating system can give us more pages or return pages to available storage with little or no difficulty. In addition, accessing any page requires only two steps. In the first step, we use the hash function to find the address of the directory entry, and in the second, we retrieve the page associated with the address.

Unfortunately, if the keys are not uniformly divided among the pages, the directory can grow quite large. However, most of the entries point to the same pages. To prevent this from happening, we cannot use the bit sequence of the keys themselves. Instead we translate the bits into a random sequence using a *uniform hash function* as discussed in the previous section. In contrast to the previous section, however, we need a *family* of hash functions, because, at any point, we may require a different number of bits to distinguish the new key. One solution is the family

$$hash_i: key \rightarrow \{0 \ldots 2^{i-1}\}, \, 1 \leq i \leq d$$

00 $\xrightarrow{a}$ A0, B0	000 $\xrightarrow{a}$ A0, B0	0000 $\xrightarrow{a}$ A0, B0
01 $\xrightarrow{c}$ A1, B1	001 $\xrightarrow{c}$ A1, B1	0001 $\xrightarrow{c}$ A1, C1
10 $\xrightarrow{b}$ C2	010 $\xrightarrow{b}$ C2	0010 $\xrightarrow{b}$ C2
11 $\xrightarrow{d}$ C3	011 $\xrightarrow{e}$ C3	0011 $\xrightarrow{f}$ C3
	100 $\xrightarrow{a}$	0100 $\xrightarrow{a}$
	101 $\xrightarrow{d}$ C5	0101 $\xrightarrow{e}$ C5
	110 $\xrightarrow{b}$	0110 $\xrightarrow{b}$
	111 $\xrightarrow{e}$	0111 $\xrightarrow{f}$
		1000 $\xrightarrow{a}$
		1001 $\xrightarrow{d}$ B1
		1010 $\xrightarrow{b}$
		1011 $\xrightarrow{f}$
		1100 $\xrightarrow{a}$
		1101 $\xrightarrow{e}$
		1110 $\xrightarrow{b}$
		1111 $\xrightarrow{f}$
(a) 2 bits	(b) 3 bits	(c) 4 bits

Figure 8.10: Tries collapsed into directories

where $hash_i$ is simply $hash_{i-1}$ with either a zero or one appended as the new leading bit of the result. Thus, $hash(key, i)$ might be a function that produces a random number of i bits from the identifier key.

Some important twists are associated with this approach. For example, suppose a page identified by i bits overflows. We allocate a new page and rehash the identifiers into those two pages. The identifiers in both pages have their low-order i bits in common. We refer to these pages as *buddies*. When the number of identifiers in two buddy pages is no more than the capacity of a single page, then we coalesce the two pages into one.

Suppose a page that can hold only p records now contains p records, and a new record is to be added. The operating system allocates a new page. All $p + 1$ keys are rehashed, using one more bit and divided between the two pages. If the number of bits used is greater than the depth (the number of bits or $\log_2$ of the directory size) of the directory, the whole directory doubles in size and its depth increases by 1. If all $p + 1$ records are hashed to one of the two pages, the split operation has to be repeated. Fortunately, this is a fairly rare occurrence. When this happens, the depth of the directory can be reduced using a compressed trie as discussed in Chapter 10.

Program 8.5 contains a set of pseudo-C++ programs that provide many of the details for implementing directory-based dynamic hashing.

```
const int WordSize = 5;  // maximum number of directory bits
const int PageSize = 10; // maximum size of a page
const int MaxDir = 32; // maximum size of a directory
struct TwoChars { char str[2];};
struct page {
    int LocalDepth; // number of bits to distinguish ids
    TwoChars names[PageSize]; // the actual identifiers
    int NumIdents; // number of identifiers in this page
};
typedef page* paddr;
struct record { // a sample record
    TwoChars KeyField;
    int IntData;
    char CharData;
};
paddr rdirectory[MaxDir]; // will contain pointers to pages
int gdepth; // not to exceed WordSize

paddr hash(const TwoChars& key, const int precision);
// key is hashed using a uniform hash function, and the low order precision bits
// are returned as the page address.

paddr buddy(const paddr index);
// Take an address of a page and return the page's buddy; i.e., the leading bit is
// complemented.

int size(const paddr ptr);
// Return the number of identifiers in the page

paddr coalesce(const paddr ptr, const paddr buddy);
// Combine page ptr and its buddy, buddy into a single page.

Boolean PageSearch(const TwoChars& key, const paddr index);
// Search page index for key key. If found, return TRUE; otherwise return FALSE
```

int *convert*(**const** *paddr p*);
// Convert a pointer to a page to an equivalent integer.

void *enter*(**const** *record r*, **const** *paddr p*);
// Insert the new record *r* into the page pointed at by *p*

void *PageDelete*(**const** *TwoChar& key*, **const** *paddr p*);
// Remove the record with key *key* from the page pointed at by *p*

paddr find(**const** *TwoChars& key*)
// Search for a record with key *key* in the file. If found, return the address of the page in
// which it was found. If not found, return 0;
{
   paddr index = hash (*key,gdepth*);
   int *IntIndex = convert* (*index*);
   paddr ptr = rdirectory [*IntIndex*];
   if (*PageSearch*(*key, ptr*) **return** *ptr*;
   else return 0;
}

void *insert*(**const** *record& r*, **const** *TwoChars& key*)
// Insert a new record into the file pointed at by the directory
{
   paddr p = find (*key*); // check if key is present
   if (*p*) **return;** // key already in
   if (*p →NumIdents* != *PageSize*) { // page not full
     enter (*r,p*); *p →NumIdents* ++;
   }
   else {
     Split the page into two, insert the new key, and
     update *gdepth* if necessary; if this causes *gdepth*
     to exceed *WordSize*, print an error and terminate.
   }
}

void *Delete*(**const** *TwoChars& key*)
// Find and delete the record with key *key*
{
   paddr p = find (*key*);
   if (*p*) {
     PageDelete(*key, p*);
     if (*size* (*p*) + *size* (*buddy* (*p*)) <= *PageSize*) *coalesce*(*p, buddy* (*p*));
   }
}

void *main* () {} // main program

Program 8.5: Extendible hashing

8.3.3   Analysis of Directory-based Dynamic Hashing

The most important feature of the directory version of extendible hashing is the guarantee that retrieving any page requires only two disk accesses. Thus, its performance is very good. However, we pay for this performance in space. Recall that adding identifiers that are not uniformly distributed can double the directory size. Since many of the pointers could point to the same page, we have a lot of wasted storage.

A second criterion for judging hashing schemes is the space utilization. This is defined as the ratio of the number of records stored in the table divided by the total amount of space allocated. Several researchers (Fagin, Larson, and Mendelson) have analyzed this measure for different variations of dynamic hashing. They have all reached similar conclusions, namely, that without any special strategies for handling overflows, the space utilization is approximately 69%. Each of their derivations is complex and relies on assumptions about the distribution of the identifiers. Here we will follow the derivation given by Mendelson.

Let $L(k)$ stand for the expected number of leaf nodes needed to hold k records. When all the records fit in a single page, $L(k) = 1$. The interesting case is when k exceeds the page size. In this case, the number of records in the two subtrees of the root have a symmetric binomial distribution. From this it follows that there will be j keys in the left subtree and $k - j$ in the right, each with a given probability, which is

$$\binom{k}{j} (1/2)^k$$

This implies that the number of leaf pages in the left subtree is $L(j)$ and the number in the right subtree is $L(k - j)$. Thus, one can express $L(k)$ by the following formula:

$$L(k) = \frac{1}{2^k} \sum_{j=0}^{k} \binom{k}{j} \{L(j) + L(k-j)\} = 2^{1-k} \sum_{j=0}^{k} \binom{k}{j} L(j)$$

Mendelson goes on to show that

$$L(k) \approx \frac{k}{p\ln2}$$

It follows that the storage utilization is the number of records k divided by the product of the page size p and the number of leaf nodes $L(k)$, or that

$$utilization = \frac{k}{pL(k)} \approx \ln2 \approx 0.69$$

To see that Mendelson's estimate is reasonable, suppose there is no overflow strategy other than doubling the directory size. We have a full page with p records and attempt to insert a $p+1$'st record, which causes an overflow. With a uniform hash function we now have two pages, each containing about $p/2$ identifiers, or a space utilization of 50%. After the process of inserting and deleting continued for a while, we expect that a recently split page would be at least half full. Thus, space utilization should be at least 50% but certainly less than 100%.

When a page overflows, it may double the directory size. To avoid this, we introduce the concept of overflow pages. Instead of increasing the directory, an overflow causes the allocation of a new page. The pointer to this page is stored in the main page. Rather than storing new identifiers in the main page, we place them in the overflow page. As we shall see, this increases storage utilization, but at the expense of increased retrieval time.

Assume that an overflow page is the same size as a regular page and that both pages are full with p records, making a total of $2p$ records. Suppose an overflow now occurs. We obtain a new page and distribute the keys among the three pages. The utilization is $2p/3p$, or 66%. On the other hand, suppose that the overflow page has a capacity of $p/2$ rather than p. If we redistribute the keys as before, then a total of $3p/2$ records is divided over a capacity of $2p$. This produces a utilization of 3/4, or 75%. Thus, we see that although overflow pages increase utilization, they also increase retrieval time.

Determining the ideal size for the overflow page has been investigated by Larson and others. Larson concludes that if a space utilization below 80% is sufficient, then the size of the overflow pages can vary widely, say from p to $p/2$. However, higher space utilizations require an increasingly narrow range of overflow page sizes, because utilization begins to oscillate, and access time increases significantly. To cope with this problem, we could monitor the space utilization of the file so that when it achieves some predetermined amount, say the 80 percent ratio, the algorithm resumes splitting.

We can also analyze the size of the directory in terms of the number of records, n, that are stored in the file. Fagin estimates this as

$$2 \left\lceil \log \frac{n}{p \ln 2} \right\rceil$$

Figure 8.11 contains a table given by Flajolet that shows the expected directory size for various numbers of records, n, and page size, p. For example, we would need a directory of size 62,500 to store one million records using a page size of 50. This is substantial and indicates that the directory may have to be stored using auxiliary storage.

In the event that the hash function does not evenly distribute the identifiers across the pages, more sophisticated techniques are required. Lomet suggests that, in the directory scheme, we do not view pages as of a fixed size but allow them to grow. Thus, any given page may be composed of several subpages. As more identifiers map to this page, its storage is expanded. This leads to different strategies for maintaining the identifiers within the page. The simplest strategy is to keep the identifiers in the order they were entered into the table. However, sequential searching is time-consuming, especially as the identifier list gets long. An alternate strategy is to treat each subpage as a dynamically hashed directoryless structure. We describe its maintenance in Section 8.3.3.

n	5	10	p 20	50	100	200
10^3	1.5K	0.3K	0.1K	0.0K	0.0K	0.0K
10^4	25.6K	4.8K	1.7K	0.5K	0.2K	0.00K
10^5	424.1K	68.2K	16.8K	4.1K	2.0K	1.0K
10^6	6.9M	1.02M	0.26M	62.5K	16.8K	8.1K
10^7	111.11M	11.64M	2.25M	0.52M	0.26M	0.13M

Figure 8.11: Directory size given n records and p page size

Simulation

One important way to measure the performance of any new data structure is to carry out a series of experiments. Each experiment makes use of the algorithms that implement the data structure. Various distributions of identifiers are given to the algorithms with the resultant behavior tabulated. In the case of dynamic hashing, three factors are especially important to monitor. These are (1) access time, (2) insertion time, and (3) total space. The dependent parameters are (1) the number of records, (2) the page size, (3) the directory size, (4) the size of main memory for holding the directory and identifiers, and (5) the time to process page faults.

Fagin et al. have done such a series of experiments. They found that in all cases, extendible hashing performed at least as well or better than B-trees, a popular competitor. In the case of access time and insertion time, extendible hashing was clearly superior. For space utilization the two methods were about equal.

8.3.4   Directoryless Dynamic Hashing

The previous section assumed the existence of a directory that points to pages. One criticism of this approach is that it always requires at least one level of indirection. If we assume that we have a continuous address space large enough to hold all the records, we can eliminate the directory. In effect, this leaves it to the operating system to break the address space into pages and to manage moving them into and out of memory. This scheme is referred to as *directoryless hashing* or *linear hashing*.

Consider the trie of Figure 8.9(a), which has two levels and indexes four pages. In the new method, the two-bit addresses are the actual addresses of these pages (actually they are an offset of some base address). Thus, the hash function delivers the actual address of a page containing the key. Moreover, every value produced by the hash function must point to an actual page. In contrast to the directory scheme, in which a single page might be pointed at by several directory entries, in the directoryless scheme there must exist a unique page for every possible address. Figure 8.12 shows a simple trie and its mapping to contiguous memory without a directory.

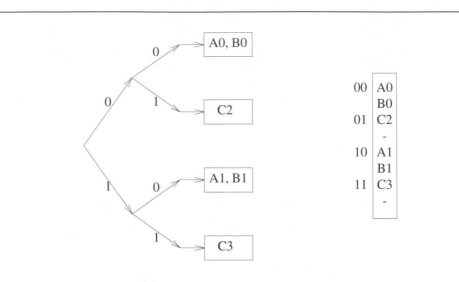

Figure 8.12: A trie mapped to directoryless, continuous storage

What happens when a page overflows? We could double the size of the address space, but this is wasteful. Instead, whenever an overflow occurs, we add a new page to the end of the file and divide the identifiers in one of the pages between its original page and the new page. This complicates the handling of the family of hash functions somewhat. However, if we had simply added one bit to the result of the hash function, the table size would have to be doubled. By adding only one page, the hash function must distinguish between pages addressed by r bits and those addressed by $r+1$ bits. We will show how this is done in a moment.

Figure 8.13 provides an example of directoryless hashing after two insertions. Initially, there are four pages, each addressed by two bits (Figure 8.13(a)). Two of the pages are full, and two have one identifier each. When C5 is inserted, it hashes to the page whose address is 10 (Figure 8.13(b)). Since that page is full, an overflow node is allocated to hold C5. At the same time, we add a new page at the end of the storage, rehash the identifiers in the first page, and split them between the first and new page. Unfortunately, none of the new identifiers go into the new page. The first page and the new page are now addressed by three bits, not two as shown in Figure 8.13(b). In the next step, we insert the identifier C1. Since it hashes to the same page as C5, we use another overflow node to store it. We add another new page to the end of the file and rehash the identifiers in the second page. Once again none go into the new page. (Note that this is largely a result of not using a uniform hash function.) Now the first two pages and the two new pages are all addressed using three bits. Eventually the number of pages will double, thereby completing one phase. A new phase then begins.

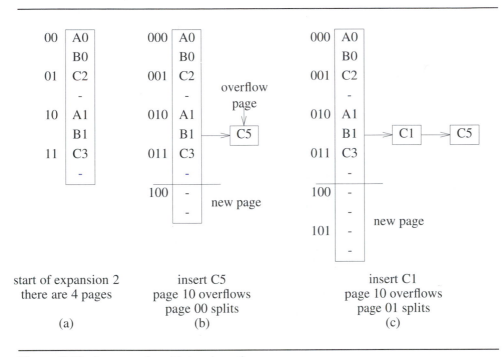

Figure 8.13: An example with two insertions

Consider Figure 8.14, which shows the state of file expansion during the rth phase at some time q. At the beginning of the rth phase, there are 2^r pages, all addressed by r bits. In the figure, q new pages have been added. To the left of the q line are the pages that have already been split. To the right of the q line are the pages remaining to be split up to the line labeled r. To the right of the r line are the pages that have been added during this phase of the process. Each page in this section of the file is addressed by $r + 1$ bits. Note that the q line is an indicator of which page gets split next. The modified hash function is given in Program 8.6. All pages less than q require $r + 1$ bits. The function $hash(key, r)$ is in the range $[0, 2^{r-1}]$, so if the result is less than q, we rehash using $r + 1$ bits. This gives us either the page to the left of q or the one above $2^r - 1$. The directory-less method always requires overflows.

One sees that for many retrievals the time will be one access, namely, for those identifiers that are in the page directly addressed by the hash function. However, for others, substantially more than two accesses might be required as one moves along the

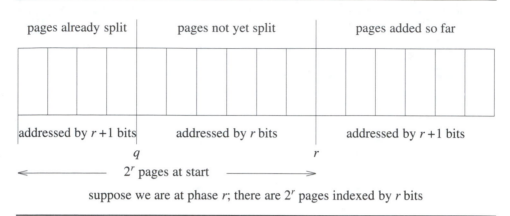

suppose we are at phase r; there are 2^r pages indexed by r bits

Figure 8.14: The *r*th phase of expansion of directoryless method

if $(hash\,(key,r) < q)$ $page = hash\,(key,r+1)$;
else $page = hash\,(key,r)$;
If neccessary, then follow overflow pointers.

Program 8.6: Modified hash function

overflow chain. When a new page is added and the identifiers split across the two pages, all identifiers including the overflows are rehashed.

Another fact about this method is that space utilization is not good. As can be seen from Figure 8.13, some extra pages are empty, and yet overflow pages are being used. Litwin has shown that space utilization is approximately 60%. He offers an alternate strategy pursued in the exercises. The term *controlled splitting* refers to splitting the ''next page'' only when storage utilization exceeds a predefined amount. Litwin suggests that until 80% utilization is reached, other pages continue to overflow.

A natural way to handle overflows is to use one of the traditional hashing schemes discussed earlier, such as open addressing. Recall that open addressing searches the file linearly from the home bucket, looking either for the identifier or for an open spot.

From the example, one sees that the longest overflow chains will occur for those pages that are near the end of the expansion phase, as they are the last to be split. By contrast, those pages that are split early are generally not full.

EXERCISES

1. The text points out that nonuniform distributions of keys cause a skewed directory and a waste of directory space. One way to avoid this problem in the directory scheme is to store the directory not as a table but as a forest of tries. A new key is hashed to one of the tries, and then its nodes are traversed to a leaf node that points to a page containing the desired record. Splitting is still required. The tries grow and contract with respect to the file. Write out the algorithms for maintaining a trie as a directory.

2. In extendible hashing, given a directory of size d, suppose two pointers point to the same page. All identifiers will share a number of low-order bits in common. How many? If four pointers point to the same page, how many bits do the identifiers have in common?

3. Another way of handling overflows in directory-based dynamic hashing is to permit a page to be divided into as many multiple pages as necessary to hold all identifiers that hash to that page. Then you assign a limit on the size of the directory you are willing to accept, and once that size has been reached, a page just continues to grow. Modify the algorithms in Program 8.5 to implement this strategy.

4. Prove that in directory-based dynamic hashing, a page can be pointed at by a number of pointers that is a power of two.

5. We have not talked much about how to organize the identifiers within a page for fast retrieval. Consider an unordered list, an ordered list, and hashing and compare their merits.

6. Function *insert* (Program 8.5) is a complete C++ program except for a few lines of pseudocode. Replace the pseudocode by actual C++ code that places all identifiers in page p into the *temp* area and then rehashes those identifiers back into either page p or q.

7. Program 8.5 contains a reference to a function *coalesce* that combines the identifiers in two pages into a single page. Using the types and functions already defined, write a C++ version of this function.

8. Take the formula given by Mendelson for the number of leaf pages required to store k records in a directory-based dynamic hashing scheme and formally derive the approximation that $L(k)$ is about equal to $k/(p\ln 2)$, where p is the page size.

9. Larson has suggested using open addressing in a directoryless dynamic hashing method to handle overflows. The problem is that pages that have yet to be split will have the most overflows, but these pages are stored contiguously. Instead, he suggests that pages be split alternately, so that next to an unsplit page is a split page. Show how the hashing function must be rewritten to handle this scheme.

8.4   REFERENCES AND SELECTED READINGS

Several interesting and enlightening works on hash tables exist. Some of these are "Scatter storage techniques," by R. Morris, *CACM*, 11:1, 1968, pp. 38-44; "Key to address transform techniques: A fundamental performance study on large existing formatted files," by V. Lum, P. Yuen, and M. Dodd, *CACM*, 14:4, 1971, pp. 228-239; "The quadratic quotient method: A hash code eliminating secondary clustering," by J. Bell, *CACM*, 13:2, 1970, pp. 107-109; "Full table quadratic searching for scatter storage," by A. Day, *CACM*, 13:8, 1970, pp. 481-482; "Identifier search mechanisms: A survey and generalized model," by D. Severence, *ACM Computing Surveys*, 6:3, 1974, pp. 175-194; "Hash table methods," by W. Mauer and T. Lewis, *ACM Computing Surveys*, 7:1, 1975, pp. 5-20; *The Art of Computer Programming: Sorting and Searching*, vol. 3, by D. Knuth, Addison-Wesley, Reading, MA, 1973; "Reducing the retrieval time of scatter storage techniques," by R. Brent, *CACM*, 16:2, 1973, pp. 105-109; "General performance analysis of key-to-address transformation methods using an abstract file concept," by V. Lum, *CACM*, 16:10, 1973, pp. 603-612; and "The use of quadratic residue research," by C. Radke, *CACM*, 13:2, 1970, pp. 103-105.

In the literature, Larson was the first to introduce a method he called dynamic hashing. Litwin followed. Fagin et al. called their method extendible hashing. Fagin uses a directory scheme that doubles in size on expansion. Larson used a linked tree structure as the representation of the directory with pointers to pages in the leaves. The references are "Dynamic hashing," by P. Larson, *BIT*, 18, 1978, pp. 184-201; "Virtual hashing: A dynamically changing hashing," by W. Litwin, *Proc. Int. Conf. on Very Large Databases*, Berlin, 1978, pp. 517-523; and "Extendible hashing - A fast access method for dynamic files," by R. Fagin, J. Nievergelt, N. Pippenger, and H. Strong, *ACM Trans. on Database Systems*, 4:3, 1979, pp. 315-344.

An excellent overview of dynamic hashing techniques and variations can be found in: "Dynamic hashing schemes," by R. Enbody and H. Du, *ACM Computing Surveys*, 20:2, 1988, pp. 85-113.

Some other papers on dynamic hashing are: "On the performance evaluation of extendible hashing and trie searching," by P. Flajolet, *Acta Informatica*, 20, 1983, pp. 345-369; "Bounded index exponential hashing," by D. Lomet, *ACM Trans. on Database Systems*, 8:1, 1983, pp. 136-165; "Analysis of extendible hashing," by H. Mendelson, *IEEE Trans. on Software Engineering*, se-8, 6, 1982, pp. 611-619; and "Dynamic hashing schemes," by K. Ramamohanarao and J. Lloyd, *The Computer Journal*, 25:4, 1982, pp. 478-485.

Scholl introduces two methods to improve storage utilization by deferring the splitting of pages and handling overflows internally. This gives a tradeoff between storage utilization and access time. See "New file organizations based on dynamic hashing," by M. Scholl, *ACM Trans. Database Systems*, 6:1, 1981, pp. 194-211.

CHAPTER 9

HEAP STRUCTURES

9.1 MIN-MAX HEAPS

9.1.1 Definitions

A *double-ended priority queue* is a data structure that supports the following operations:

(1)   inserting an element with an arbitrary key

(2)   deleting an element with the largest key

(3)   deleting an element with the smallest key

When only insertion and one of the two deletion operations are to be supported, a min heap or a max heap may be used (see Chapter 5). A min-max heap supports all of the above operations.

Program 9.1 defines an abstract base class *DEPQ* consisting of a pure virtual member function for each double-ended priority queue operation. Functions *DeleteMin* and *DeleteMax* return the deleted *Element*, where the class *Element* is assumed to have a data member *key* of type *KeyType*. The min-max heap is then implemented as a derived class of *DEPQ* thus ensuring that all three *DEPQ* operations are implemented.

Definition: A *min-max heap* is a complete binary tree such that if it is not empty, each element has a data member called *key*. Alternating levels of this tree are min levels and

```
template <class KeyType>
class DEPQ {
public:
    virtual void Insert(const Element<KeyType>&) = 0 ;
    virtual Element<KeyType>* DeleteMax(Element<KeyType>&) = 0 ;
    virtual Element<KeyType>* DeleteMin(Element<KeyType>&) = 0 ;
};
```

Program 9.1: Class definition of a double-ended priority queue

max levels, respectively. The root is on a min level. Let x be any node in a min-max heap. If x is on a min (max) level then the element in x has the minimum (maximum) key from among all elements in the subtree with root x. A node on a min (max) level is called a *min (max)* node. □

An example of a min-max heap with 12 elements is shown in Figure 9.1. The value in each node is the key of the element in that node. We use shaded circles for max nodes and unshaded circles for min nodes.

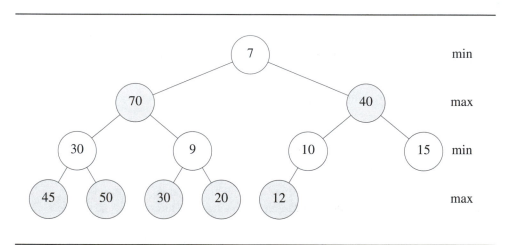

Figure 9.1: A 12-element min-max heap

Program 9.2 defines the *MinMaxHeap* class. The min-max heap is stored in a one-dimensional array h using the standard array representation of a complete binary tree (see Section 5.2.3.1). The data member n represents the number of elements currently in the min-max heap, while *MaxSize* represents the maximum number of elements allowed in it. The constructor *MinMaxHeap*::*MinMaxHeap* initializes *MaxSize* and *n* and allocates memory for *h*.

---

template <class *KeyType***>**
class *MinMaxHeap* **: public** *DEPQ<KeyType>* {
public:
   MinMaxHeap(**const int**); // constructor
   ~*MinMaxHeap*( ); // destructor
   void *Insert*(**const** *Element<KeyType>*&);
   Element<KeyType>∗ *DeleteMax*(*Element<KeyType>*&);
   Element<KeyType>∗ *DeleteMin*(*Element<KeyType>*&);
private:
  Element<KeyType> ∗*h* ;
  int *n* ;   // Current size of the min-max heap
  int *MaxSize* ; // Maximum allowable size of the min-max heap

// Other private members used for implementing *MinMaxHeap* operations

  .
  .
  .

};

template <class *KeyType***>** // constructor definition
MinMaxHeap<KeyType>::*MinMaxHeap* (**const int** *sz* = DefaultHeapSize)
: *MaxSize*(*sz*), *n*(0)
{
  h = **new** *Element<KeyType>* [*MaxSize* + 1]; // *h*[0] is not used
}

Program 9.2: Class definition and constructor of a minmax heap

9.1.2 Insertion into a Min-Max Heap

Suppose we wish to insert the element with key 5 into this min-max heap. Following the insertion, we will have a 13-element min-max heap with the shape shown in Figure 9.2.

As in the case of heaps, the insertion algorithm for min-max heaps follows the path from the new node *j* to the root. Comparing the new key 5 with the key 10 that is in the parent of *j*, we see that since the node with key 10 is on a min level, and $5 < 10$, 5 is guaranteed to be smaller than all keys in nodes that are both on max levels and on the path from *j* to the root. Hence, the min-max heap property is to be verified only with respect to min nodes on the path from *j* to the root. First, the element with key 10 is

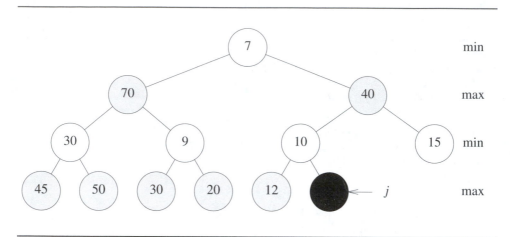

Figure 9.2: Min-max heap of Figure 9.1 with new node *j*

moved to node *j*. Then the element with key 7 is moved to the former position of 10. Finally, the new element with key 5 is inserted into the root. The min-max heap following the insertion is shown in Figure 9.3(a). Thick circles denote nodes whose contents were modified by the insertion.

Next, suppose we wish to insert an element with key 80 into the min-max heap of Figure 9.1. The resulting min-max heap has 13 elements and has the shape shown in Figure 9.2. Since $80 > 10$, and 10 is on a min level, we are assured that 80 is larger than all keys in nodes that are both on min levels and on the path from *j* to the root. Hence, the min-max heap property is to be verified only with respect to max nodes on the path from *j* to the root. There is only one such node in the min-max heap of Figure 9.1. This node has key 40. The element with key 40 is moved to *j*, and the new element is inserted into the node formerly occupied by this element. The resulting min-max heap is shown in Figure 9.3(b).

The preceding insertion examples lead to function *MinMaxHeap::Insert* (Program 9.3).

Function *MinMaxHeap::Insert* uses the functions *MinMaxHeap::VerifyMax*, *MinMaxHeap::VerifyMin*, and *MinMaxHeap::level*. The function *MinMaxHeap::level* determines whether a node is on a min or a max level of a min-max heap. The function *MinMaxHeap::VerifyMax* (Program 9.4) begins at a max node *i* and follows the path of max nodes from *i* to the root of the min-max heap *h*. It searches for the correct node to insert the element *x*. This node has the property that all max nodes above it and on the path to the root have key values at least as large as *x.key*. Further, all max nodes below it and on the path from *i* have key values smaller than *x.key*. During the search, max nodes with keys smaller than *x.key* are moved down one max level.

Function *MinMaxHeap::VerifyMin* is similar to *MinMaxHeap::VerifyMax* except that it begins at a min node *i* and follows the path of min nodes from *i* to the root. *x* is

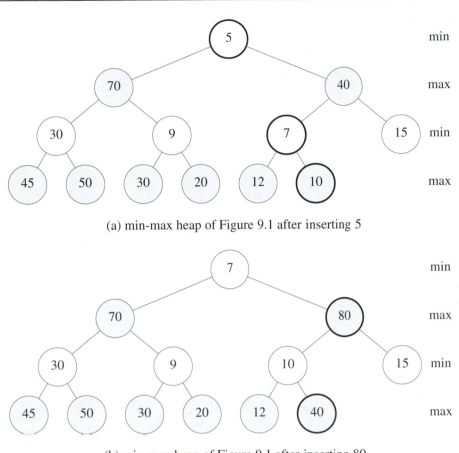

(a) min-max heap of Figure 9.1 after inserting 5

(b) min-max heap of Figure 9.1 after inserting 80

Figure 9.3: Insertion into a min-max heap

inserted into one of the encountered min nodes to preserve the min-max heap property. The formal development of *MinMaxHeap*::*VerifyMin* and *MinMaxHeap*::*level* is left as an exercise.

Analysis of *MinMaxHeap*::*Insert*: The correctness of *MinMaxHeap*::*Insert* is easily established. Further, since a min-max heap with *n* elements has O(log *n*) levels, the complexity of function *MinMaxHeap*::*Insert* is O(log *n*). □

```
template <class KeyType>
void MinMaxHeap<KeyType>::Insert(const Element<KeyType>& x)
// Insert x into the min-max heap h.
{
    if (n == MaxSize) { MinMaxFull() ; return;}
    n ++;
    int p = n /2; // p is the parent of the new node
    if (!p) { h[1] = x; return;} // insertion into an initially empty heap
    switch (level(p)) {
        case MIN:
            if (x . key < h [p ]. key)
            {               // follow min levels
                h [n ] = h [p ] ;
                VerifyMin(p, x);
            }
            else
                VerifyMax(n, x);   // follow max levels
            break;
        case MAX:
            if (x . key > h [p ]. key)
            {               // follow max levels
                h[n] = h[p] ;
                VerifyMax(p, x) ;
            }
            else
                VerifyMin(n, x);   // follow min levels
    } // end of switch
} // end of Insert
```

Program 9.3: Insertion into a min-max heap

9.1.3 Deletion of the Min Element

If we wish to delete the element with the smallest key, then this element is in the root. In the case of the min-max heap of Figure 9.1, we are to delete the element with key 7. Following the deletion, we will be left with a min-max heap that has 11 elements. Its shape is that shown in Figure 9.4. The node with key 12 is deleted from the heap, and the element with key 12 is reinserted into the heap. As in the case of deletion from a min or max heap, the reinsertion is done by examining the nodes of Figure 9.4 from the root down toward the leaves.

```
template <class KeyType>
void MinMaxHeap<KeyType>::VerifyMax(int i, const Element<KeyType>& x)
// Follow max nodes from the max node i to the root and insert x at proper place.
{
    for (int gp = i/4;      // grandparent of i
            gp && (x . key > h [gp ]. key);
            gp /= 4)
    {  // move h[gp] to h[i]
        h[i] = h[gp];
        i = gp;
    }
    h[i] = x ; // x is to be inserted into node i
}
```

Program 9.4: Searching for the correct max node for insertion

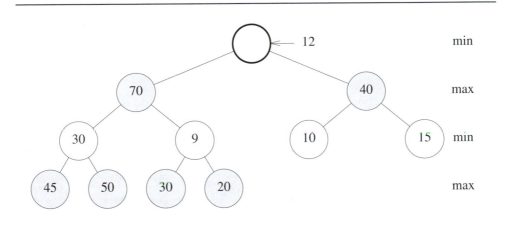

Figure 9.4: Shape of Figure 9.1 following deletion of the min item

In a general situation, we are to reinsert an element x into a min-max heap, h, whose root is empty. We consider the two cases:

(1)   *The root has no children.* In this case x is to be inserted into the root.

(2)   *The root has at least one child.* Now the smallest key in the min-max heap is in one of the children or grandchildren of the root. We determine which of these

nodes has the smallest key. Let this be node k. The following possibilities need to be considered:

(a) $x.key \leq h[k].key$. x may be inserted into the root, as there is no element in h with key smaller than $x.key$.

(b) $x.key > h[k].key$ and k is a child of the root. Since k is a max node, it has no descendants with key larger than $h[k].key$. Hence, node k has no descendants with key larger than $x.key$. So, the element $h[k]$ may be moved to the root, and x can be inserted into node k.

(c) $x.key > h[k].key$, and k is a grandchild of the root. In this case, too, $h[k]$ may be moved to the root. Let p be the parent of k. If $x.key > h[p].key$, then $h[p]$ and x are to be interchanged. This ensures that the max node p contains the largest key in the subheap with root p. At this point we are faced with the problem of inserting x into the subheap with root k. The root of this sub-min-max heap is presently empty. This is quite similar to our initial situation, in which we were to insert x into the min-max heap h with root 1, and node 1 was initially empty.

In our example, $x.key = 12$, and the smallest key in the children and grandchildren of the root node is 9. Let k denote the node that contains this key, and let p be its parent. Since $9 < 12$ and k is a grandchild of the root, we are in case 2(c). The element with key 9 (i.e., $h[k]$) is moved to the root. Since $x.key = 12 < 70 = h[p].key$, we do not interchange x and $h[p]$. The present configuration is shown in Figure 9.5. We must now reinsert x into the sub-min-max heap with root k. The smallest key from among the children and grandchildren of node k is 20. Since $12 < 20$, we are in case 2(a), and the element x is inserted into $h[k]$.

The preceding discussion results in the function *MinMaxHeap::DeleteMin* (Program 9.5). This function uses a function, *MinMaxHeap::MinChildGrandChild(i)*, that determines the child or grandchild of the node i that has the smallest key. If both a child and a grandchild of i have the smallest key, it is preferable that *MinChildGrandChild* return the address of the child, as this prevents further iterations of the **while** statement of *DeleteMin*. Notice that even though *DeleteMin* does not explicitly check for the case when $n = 1$ initially, this is handled correctly, and an empty min-max heap results from the deletion.

Analysis of *MinMaxHeap::DeleteMin*: In each iteration of the **while** statement of *DeleteMin*, a constant amount of work is done. Also, in each iteration (except possibly the last), i moves down two levels. Since a min-max heap is a complete binary tree, h has O(log n) levels. Hence, the complexity of *DeleteMin* is O(log n). □

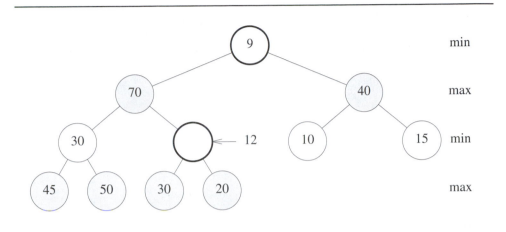

Figure 9.5: Figure 9.4 following the move of the element with key 9

EXERCISES

1. Write the function *MinMaxHeap<KeyType>::VerifyMin* defined in connection with insertion into a min-max heap.

2. Write the function *MinMaxHeap<KeyType>::level(i)*, which determines whether node *i* of a min-max heap is on a min or a max level.

3. Write the function *MinMaxHeap<KeyType>::MinChildGrandChild(i)*, which returns the child or grandchild of node *i* of a min-max heap that has the smallest key. You may assume that *i* has at least one child.

4. Write the function *MinMaxHeap<KeyType>::DeleteMax* to delete the element with maximum key in a min-max heap. Your algorithm should run in O(log *n*) time for a min-max heap with *n* elements.

5. Write a function to initialize a min-max heap with *n* elements. Do this using a series of adjust steps as used in the initialization of a max heap (see Chapter 5). Show that your function takes O(*n*) time rather than the O(*n* log *n*) time that would be taken if initialization were done by performing *n* insertions into an initially empty heap.

```
template <class KeyType>
Element<KeyType>* MinMaxHeap<KeyType>::DeleteMin(Element<KeyType>& y)
// Delete and return an element with minimum key from the min-max heap
{
    if (!n) {MinMaxEmpty(); return 0;}
    // Save root and last element; update heap size
    y = h[1];
    Element<KeyType> x = h [n − −];

    // Initialize for reinsertion of x
    int i = 1, j = n/2;

    // Find place to insert x
    while (i<=j)
    {  // i has a child, case (2)
            int k = MinChildGrandChild(i) ;
            if (x . key <= h [k ] . key)
                    break;  // case 2(a), x is to be inserted into h[i]
            else {  // case 2(b) or (c)
                    h[i] = h[k] ;
                    if (k <= 2*i + 1)
                            break;  // k is a child of i, case 2(b)
                    else {  // k is a grandchild of i, case 2(c)
                            int p = k/2 ;  // parent of k
                            if (x . key > h [p ] . key) {
                                Element<KeyType> t = h [p ] ; h [p ] = x ; x = t ;
                            }
                    } // end of if (k <= 2*i + 1)
                    i = k ;
            } // end of if (x.key <= h[k].key)
    } // end of while
    h[i] = x ;
    return &y ;
} // end of DeleteMin
```

Program 9.5: Deleting the element with minimum key

9.2   DEAPS

9.2.1   Definition

A deap is a double-ended heap that supports the double-ended priority-queue operations of insert, delete-min, and delete-max. As in the case of the min-max heap, these operations take logarithmic time on a deap. However, the deap is faster by a constant factor, and the algorithms are simpler.

Definition: A *deap* is a complete binary tree that is either empty or satisfies the following properties:

(1)   The root contains no element.

(2)   The left subtree is a min heap.

(3)   The right subtree is a max heap.

(4)   If the right subtree is not empty, then let i be any node in the left subtree. Let j be the corresponding node in the right subtree. If such a j does not exist, then let j be the node in the right subtree that corresponds to the parent of i. The key in node i is less than or equal to that in j. □

An example 11-element deap is shown in Figure 9.6. The nodes in the max heap are shaded, while those of the min heap are unshaded. The root of the min heap contains 5, and the root of the max heap contains 45. The min heap node with 10 corresponds to the max heap node with 25, whereas the min heap node with 15 corresponds to the max heap node with 20. For the node containing 9, the node j defined in property (4) of the deap definition is the max heap node that contains 40.

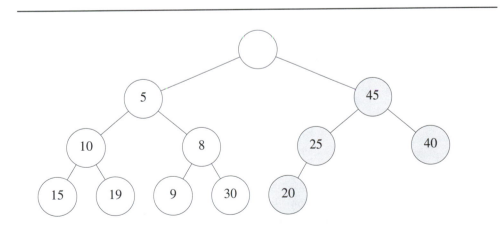

Figure 9.6: An 11-element deap

From the definition of a deap, it is evident that in an n-element deap, $n > 1$, the min element is in the root of the min heap, and the max element is in the root of the max heap. If $n = 1$, then the min and max elements are the same and are in the root of the min heap. Since a deap is a complete binary tree, it may be stored as an implicit data structure in a one-dimensional array in much the same way as min, max, and min-max heaps are stored. In the case of a deap, position 1 of the array is not utilized. Since the number of elements in the deap is n, the last occupied position in this array is $n + 1$. If i is a node in the min heap, then its corresponding node in the max heap is $i + 2^{\lfloor \log_2 i \rfloor - 1}$. Hence, the j defined in property (4) of the definition is given by

$$j = i + 2^{\lfloor \log_2 i \rfloor - 1};$$
$$\textbf{if } (j > n + 1) \; j \mathbin{/}= 2 ;$$

Notice that if property (4) of the deap definition is satisfied by all leaf nodes of the min heap, then it is also satisfied by all remaining nodes of the min heap.

Program 9.6 defines the *Deap* class. The deap is stored in a one-dimensional array d. The data member n represents the number of elements currently in the deap, while *MaxSize* represents the maximum number of elements allowed in it. The constructor *Deap*::*Deap* initializes *MaxSize* and n and allocates memory for d.

9.2.2 Insertion into a Deap

Suppose we wish to insert an element with key 4 into the deap of Figure 9.6. Following this insertion, the deap will have 12 elements in it and will thus have the shape shown in Figure 9.7. j points to the new node in the deap.

The insertion process begins by comparing the key 4 to the key in j's corresponding node, i, in the min heap. This node contains 19. To satisfy property (4), we move the 19 to node j. Now, if we use the min heap insertion algorithm (see Chapter 5) to insert 4 into position i, we get the deap of Figure 9.8.

If instead of inserting a 4, we were to insert a 30 into the deap of Figure 9.6, then the resulting deap would have the same shape as in Figure 9.7. Comparing 30 with the key 19 in the corresponding node i, we see that property (4) may be satisfied by using the max heap insertion algorithm to insert 30 into position j. This results in the deap of Figure 9.9.

The case in which the new node, j, is a node of the min heap is symmetric to the case just discussed. The function to insert into a deap is given in Program 9.7.

The functions used by *Deap*::*Insert* are specified as follows:

(1) *Deap* ::*DeapFull* (). This signals an error. The insertion cannot proceed, as there is no space in the deap to accommodate the additional element.

(2) *Deap* ::*MaxHeap*(**int** p). This is a boolean function that returns the value TRUE iff p is a position in the max heap of the deap.

(3) *Deap* ::*MinPartner*(**int** p). This function computes the min heap node that corresponds to the max heap position p. This is given by $p - 2^{\lfloor \log_2 p \rfloor - 1}$.

```
template <class KeyType>
class Deap : public DEPQ<KeyType> {
public:
    Deap (const int);
    ~Deap();
    void Insert(const Element<KeyType>&);
    Element<KeyType>* DeleteMin(Element<KeyType>&);
    Element<KeyType>* DeleteMax(Element<KeyType>&);
private:
    Element<KeyType> *d ;
    int n;                  // current size of Deap
    int MaxSize;            // Maximum allowable size of Deap

// Other private member functions of Deap follow

    .
    .
    .

};

template <class KeyType>
Deap<KeyType>::Deap (const int sz = DefaultHeapSize)
: MaxSize (sz), n(0)
{
    d = new Element<KeyType> [MaxSize + 2];     // d[0] and d[1] are not used
}
```

Program 9.6: Class definition and constructor of a deap

(4) $Deap::MaxPartner(\textbf{int } p)$. This function computes the max heap node that corresponds to the parent of the min heap position p. This is given by $(p + 2^{\lfloor \log_2 p \rfloor - 1}) / 2$.

(5)   The functions $Deap::MinInsert$ and $Deap::MaxInsert$ insert an element into a specified position of a min and max heap, respectively, by following the path from this position toward the root of the respective heap. Elements are moved down as necessary until the correct place to insert the new element is found. This process differs from that used in Chapter 5 to insert into a min or max heap only in that the root is now at position 2 or 3 rather than at 1.

Analysis of $Deap::Insert$:   The correctness of function $Deap::Insert$ is easily established. Its complexity is O(log n), as the time taken is linear in the height of the deap, which is O(log n). $\square$

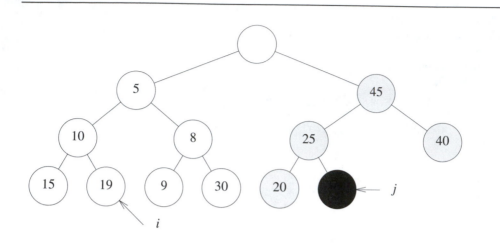

Figure 9.7: Shape of a 12-element deap

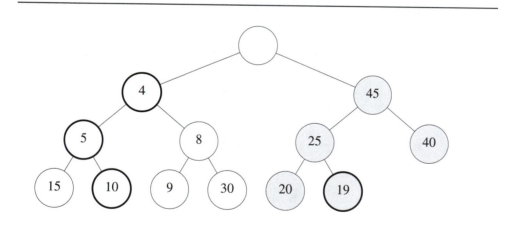

Figure 9.8: Deap of Figure 9.6 following the insertion of 4

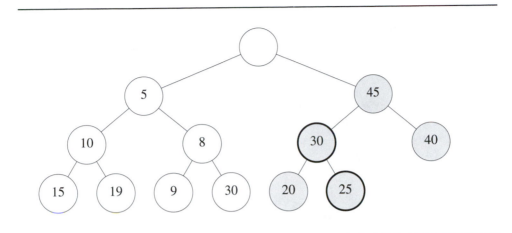

Figure 9.9: Deap of Figure 9.6 following the insertion of 30

9.2.3 Deletion of the Min Element

A high-level description of the deletion process is given in Program 9.8. The strategy is first to transform the deletion of the element from the root of the min heap to the deletion of an element from a leaf position in the min heap. This is done by following a root-to-leaf path in the min heap, ensuring that the min heap properties are satisfied on the preceding levels of the heap. This process has the effect of shifting the empty position initially at the min heap root to a leaf node p. This leaf node is then filled by the element, t, initially in the last position of the deap. The insertion of t into position p of the min heap is done as in $Deap::Insert$ (Program 9.7) except that the specification of $Deap::MaxPartner(i)$ is changed to

$$j = i + 2^{\lfloor \log_2 i \rfloor - 1};$$
$$\textbf{if } (j > n + 1) \, j \, /= 2;$$

and the insertion does not increase the size of the deap.

Suppose we wish to remove the minimum element from the deap of Figure 9.6. We first place the last element (i.e., the one with key 20) into a temporary element t. Next, the vacancy created in position 2 by the deletion of the min element is filled by moving from position 2 to a leaf. Each move is preceded by a step that moves the smaller of the elements in the children of the current node up. Then, we move to the position previously occupied by the moved element. First, the 8 is moved up to position 2. Then the 9 is moved to position 5, which was formerly occupied by the 8. Now we have an empty leaf (position 10). To do a deap insertion here, we compare 20 with the key 40 in its max partner. Since 20 < 40, no exchange is needed, and we proceed to insert the 20 into the min heap beginning at the empty leaf 10. This results in the deap of Figure 9.10.

```
template <class KeyType>
void Deap<KeyType>::Insert(const Element<KeyType>& x) {
// Insert x into the deap
  int i;
  if (n == MaxSize) {DeapFull(); return;}
  n++ ;
  if (n == 1) { d[2] = x; return;} // insertion into an empty deap
  int p = n + 1; // p is the new last position of the deap
  switch (MaxHeap(p)) {
          case TRUE: // p is a position in the max heap
                    i = MinPartner(p);
                    if (x . key < d [i] . key) {
                              d[p] = d[i] ;
                              MinInsert(i, x);
                    }
                    else MaxInsert(p, x);
                    break;
          case FALSE: // p is a position in the min heap
                    i = MaxPartner(p);
                    if (x . key > d [i] . key) {
                              d[p] = d[i];
                              MaxInsert(i, x);
                    }
                    else MinInsert(p, x);
  } // end of the switch statement
} // end of Insert
```

Program 9.7: Inserting into a deap

Nodes whose contents were modified as a result of the insertion are represented by thick circles.

Analysis of Deap::DeleteMin: One may verify that *Deap* ::*DeleteMin* works correctly regardless of whether the last position in the deap is in the min or max heap. The complexity is $O(\log n)$, as the height of a deap is $O(\log n)$. □

EXERCISES

1. Complete function *Deap* ::*Insert* (Program 9.7) by writing all the functions it uses. Test the insertion function by running it on a computer. Generate your own test data.

template <class *KeyType***>**
Element <KeyType>* Deap<KeyType>::DeleteMin(Element<KeyType>& x)
//Delete and return the min element from the deap.
{

   if (!*n*) {*DeapEmpty*(); **return** 0;}
   x = d [2];
   p = n + 1;
   Element<KeyType> *t = d* [*p*] ; *n* − − ;
   for (int *i* = 2; *i* has a child; *i = j*)
   {
      Let *j* be the child with smaller key;
      d [*i*] = *d* [*j*];
   }
   Do a deap insertion of *t* at position *i*;
   return &*x*;
} // end of *DeleteMin*

Program 9.8: Deleting the min element

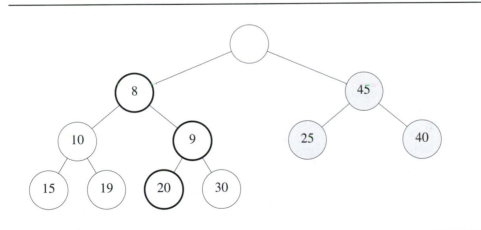

Figure 9.10: Deap of Figure 9.6 following deletion of the min element

2. Refine function *Deap*::*DeleteMin* (Program 9.8) into a C++ function. Test the correctness of your function running it on a computer using test data of your choice.

3. Write a function to initialize a deap with n elements. Your function must run in $O(n)$ time. Show that your function actually has this running time. (Hint: Proceed as in the initialization of a min heap or max heap.)

4. Write the functions to perform all double-ended priority-queue operations, both for a min-max heap and for a deap.

   (a) Use suitable test data to test the correctness of your functions.

   (b) Create a random list of n elements and a random sequence of insert, delete-min, and delete-max operations of length m. This latter sequence is created such that the probability of an insert is approximately 0.5, whereas that of each type of delete is approximately 0.25. Initialize a min-max heap and a deap to contain the n elements in the first random list. Now, measure the time to perform the m operations using the min-max heap as well as the deap. Divide this time by m to get the average time per operation. Do this for $n = 100, 500, 1000, 2000, \cdots, 5000$. Let m be 5000. Tabulate your computing times.

   (c) Based on your experiments, what can you say about the relative merits of the two double-ended priority-queue schemes?

5. Use a two-array representation for a deap. One of these arrays, say A, represents the min heap, and the other, say B, represents the max heap. Let n_A be the number of elements in A and n_B the number of elements in B. The number of elements, n, in the deap is $n_A + n_B$.

   (a) Obtain an upper and lower bound for n_A as a function of n_B (i.e., determine $g(n_B)$ and $h(n_B)$ such that $g(n_B) \leq n_A \leq h(n_B)$).

   (b) Which node of max heap B corresponds to min heap node $A[i]$, $1 \leq i \leq n_A$?

   (c) Write deap-insert, delete-min, and delete-max functions using this two-array representation.

   (d) Use suitable test data to test the correctness of your functions.

   (e) Compare the performance of the two-array representation and that of the single array representation. For this comparison, design an experiment similar to that described in part (b) of the previous exercise.

6. Obtain an exact count of the worst-case number of key comparisons that can be made during each of the double-ended priority-queue operations when a min-max heap is used. Do this also for the case when a deap is used. What can you say about the expected worst-case performance of these two methods? Can you think of a way to reduce the worst-case number of comparisons using a binary search (without affecting the number of element moves)?

9.3   LEFTIST TREES

In the preceding section we extended the definition of a priority queue by requiring that both delete-max and delete-min operations be permissible. In this section, we consider a different extension. Suppose that in addition to the normal priority-queue operations, we are also required to support the operation of *combine*. This requires us to combine two priority queues into a single priority queue. One application for this is when the server for one priority queue shuts down. At this time, it is necessary to combine its priority queue with that of a functioning server.

Let n be the total number of elements in the two priority queues that are to be combined. If heaps are used to represent priority queues, then the combine operation takes $O(n)$ time. Using a leftist tree, the combine operation as well as the normal priority-queue operations take logarithmic time.

Leftist trees are defined using the concept of an extended binary tree. An *extended binary tree* is a binary tree in which all empty binary subtrees have been replaced by a square node. Figure 9.11 shows two examples of binary trees. Their corresponding extended binary trees are shown in Figure 9.12. The square nodes in an extended binary tree are called *external nodes*. The original (circular) nodes of the binary tree are called *internal nodes*.

Figure 9.11: Two binary trees

Let x be a node in an extended binary tree. Let *LeftChild* (x) and *RightChild* (x), respectively, denote the left and right children of the internal node x. Define *shortest* (x) to be the length of a shortest path from x to an external node. It is easy to see that *shortest* (x) satisfies the following recurrence:

$$shortest\,(x) = \begin{cases} 0 & \text{if } x \text{ is an external node} \\ 1 + \min\,\{shortest\,(LeftChild\,(x)),\ shortest\,(RightChild\,(x))\} & \text{otherwise} \end{cases}$$

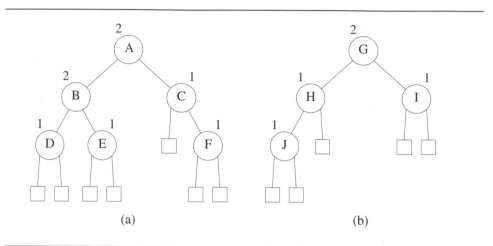

(a)	(b)

Figure 9.12: Extended binary trees corresponding to Figure 9.11

The number outside each internal node x of Figure 9.12 is the value of *shortest* (x).

Definition: A *leftist tree* is a binary tree such that if it is not empty, then

$$shortest\ (LeftChild\ (x)) \geq shortest\ (RightChild\ (x))$$

for every internal node x. □

The binary tree of Figure 9.11(a), which corresponds to the extended binary tree of Figure 9.12(a), is not a leftist tree, as *shortest* $(LeftChild\ (C)) = 0$, whereas *shortest* $(RightChild(C)) = 1$. The binary tree of Figure 9.11(b) is a leftist tree.

Lemma 9.1: Let x be the root of a leftist tree that has n (internal) nodes.

(a) $n \geq 2^{shortest(x)} - 1$

(b) The rightmost root to external node path is the shortest root to external node path. Its length is *shortest* (x).

Proof: (a) From the definition of *shortest* (x) it follows that there are no external nodes on the first *shortest* (x) levels of the leftist tree. Hence, the leftist tree has at least

$$\sum_{i=1}^{shortest(x)} 2^{i-1} = 2^{shortest(x)} - 1$$

internal nodes. (b) This follows directly from the definition of a leftist tree. □

Leftist trees are represented using nodes that have the following data members: *LeftChild*, *RightChild*, *shortest*, and *data*. We assume that *data* is an *Element* with at least the member *key* of type *KeyType*. We note that the concept of an external node is introduced merely to arrive at clean definitions. The external nodes are never physically present in the representation of a leftist tree. Rather the appropriate child data member (*LeftChild* or *RightChild*) of the parent of an external node is set to 0. Program 9.9 contains the class definitions of *LeftistNode* and *MinLeftistTree*.

---

template <class *KeyType***> class** *MinLeftistTree***;** // forward declaration

template <class *KeyType***>**
class *LeftistNode* {
friend class *MinLeftistTree<KeyType>***;**
private:
        *Element<KeyType> data***;**
        LeftistNode *LeftChild, *RightChild***;**
        int *shortest***;**
};

template <class *KeyType***>**
class *MinLeftistTree* **: public** *MinPQ<KeyType>* {
public:
        // constructor
        *MinLeftistTree(LeftistNode<KeyType> *init = 0) root(init)* { };

        // the three min-leftist tree operations
        void *Insert*(**const** *Element<KeyType>*&);
        Element<KeyType> DeleteMin(Element<KeyType>*&);
        void *MinCombine(MinLeftistTree<KeyType>*);
private:
        LeftistNode<KeyType> MinUnion(LeftistNode<KeyType>*,
                               LeftistNode<KeyType>);

        LeftistNode<KeyType> *root***;**
};

Program 9.9: Class definition of a leftist tree

Definition: A *min leftist tree* (*max leftist tree*) is a leftist tree in which the key value in each node is no larger (smaller) than the key values in its children (if any). In other words, a min (max) leftist tree is a leftist tree that is also a min (max) tree. □

Two min leftist trees are shown in Figure 9.13. The number inside a node x is the key of the element in x, and the number outside x is *shortest* (x). The operations insert, delete-min (delete-max), and combine can be performed in logarithmic time using a min (max) leftist tree. We shall continue our discussion using min leftist trees.

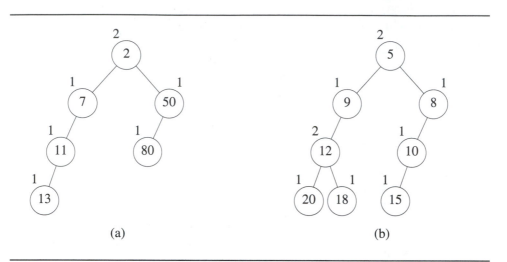

(a)   (b)

Figure 9.13: Examples of min leftist trees

The insert and delete-min operations can both be performed by using the combine operation. To insert an element x into a min leftist tree, we first create a min leftist tree that contains the single element x. Then we combine the two min leftist trees. To delete the min element from a nonempty min leftist tree, we combine the min leftist trees *root →LeftChild* and *root →RightChild* and delete the node *root*.

The combine operation itself is quite simple. Suppose that two min leftist trees are to be combined. First, a new binary tree containing all elements in both trees is obtained by following the rightmost paths in one or both trees. This binary tree has the property that the key in each node is no larger than the keys in its children (if any). Next, the left and right subtrees of nodes are interchanged as necessary to convert this binary tree into a leftist tree.

As an example, consider combining the two min leftist trees of Figure 9.13. To obtain a binary tree that contains all the elements in each tree and that satisfies the required relationship between parent and child keys, we first compare the root keys 2 and 5. Since $2 < 5$, the new binary tree should have 2 in its root. We shall leave the left subtree of 2 unchanged and combine 2's right subtree with the entire binary tree rooted at 5. The resulting binary tree will become the new right subtree of 2. When combining the right subtree of 2 and the binary tree rooted at 5, we notice that $5 < 50$. So, 5 should be in the root of the combined tree. Now, we proceed to combine the subtrees with root 8 and 50. Since $8 < 50$ and 8 has no right subtree, we can make the subtree with root 50 the right subtree of 8. This gives us the binary tree of Figure 9.14(a). Hence, the result of combining the right subtree of 2 and the tree rooted at 5 is the tree of Figure 9.14(b). When this is made the right subtree of 2, we get the binary tree of Figure 9.14(c). The leftist tree that is made a subtree is represented by shading its nodes, in each case. To convert this into a leftist tree, we begin at the last modified root (i.e., 8) and trace back to the overall root, ensuring that *shortest* (*LeftChild* ( )) ≥ *shortest* (*RightChild* ( )). This inequality holds at 8 but not at 5 and 2. Simply interchanging the left and right subtrees at these nodes causes the inequality to hold. The result is the leftist tree of Figure 9.14(d). The pointers that were interchanged are represented by dotted lines in the figure.

The function to combine two leftist trees is given in Program 9.10. This function makes use of the recursive function *LeftistTree* ::*MinUnion* which combines two nonempty leftist trees. Function *Leftist* ::*MinUnion* intertwines the following two steps:

(1)   create a binary tree that contains all the elements, the root of each subtree has the smallest key in that subtree

(2)   ensure that each node has a left subtree whose *shortest* value is greater than or equal to that of its right subtree

Analysis of *Leftist::MinCombine:* Since *MinUnion* moves down the rightmost paths in the two leftist trees being combined, and since the lengths of these paths are at most logarithmic in the number of elements in each tree, the combining of two leftist trees with a total of n elements is done in time O(log n). □

EXERCISES

1. Let t be an arbitrary binary tree represented using the node structure for a leftist tree.

    (a)   Write a function to initialize the *shortest* data member of each node in t.

    (b)   Write a function to convert t into a leftist tree.

    (c)   What is the complexity of each of these two functions?

2. Compare the performance of leftist trees and min heaps under the assumption that the only operations to be performed are insert and delete-min. For this, do the following:

    (a)   Create a random list of n elements and a random sequence of insert and delete-min operations of length m. The latter sequence is created such that the probability of an insert or delete-min operation is approximately 0.5. Initialize a min leftist tree and a min heap to contain the n elements in the first random list. Now, measure the time to perform the m operations using the min leftist tree as well as the min heap. Divide this time by m to get the average time per operation. Do this for n = 100, 500, 1000, 2000, $\cdots$, 5000. Let m be 5000. Tabulate your computing times.

    (b)   Based on your experiments, make some statements about the relative merits of the two priority-queue schemes.

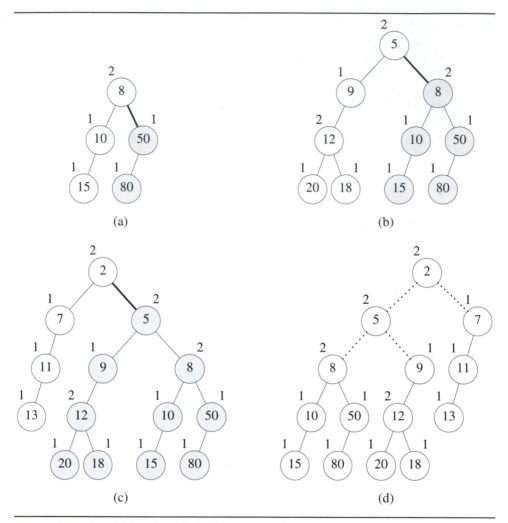

Figure 9.14: Combining the min leftist trees of Figure 9.13

3. Write a function to initialize a min leftist tree with n elements. Assume that the node structure is the same as that used in the text. Your function must run in $\Theta(n)$ time. Show that this is the case. Can you think of a way to do this initialization in $\Theta(n)$ time such that the resulting min leftist tree is also a complete binary tree?

4. Write a function to delete the element in node x of a min leftist tree. Assume that each node has the data members *LeftChild*, *RightChild*, *parent*, *shortest*, and *data*. The *parent* data member of a node points to its parent in the leftist tree. What is the complexity of your algorithm?

```
template <class KeyType>
void MinLeftistTree<KeyType>::MinCombine(MinLeftistTree<KeyType> *b)
// Combine the min leftist tree b with the given min leftist tree.
// b is set to the empty min leftist tree.
{
    if (!root) root = b→root;
    else if (b→root) root = MinUnion(root, b→root);
    b→root = 0 ;
}
```

```
template<class KeyType>
LeftistNode<KeyType>* MinLeftistTree<KeyType>::MinUnion(LeftistNode<KeyType> *a
                                                        LeftistNode<KeyType> *b)
// Recursive function to combine two nonempty min leftist trees rooted
// at a and b. The root of the resulting min leftist tree is returned.
{
    // Set a to be min leftist tree with smaller root.
    if (a →data . key > b →data . key)
            {LeftistNode<KeyType> *t = a; a = b; b = t;}
    // Create binary tree such that the smallest key in each subtree is in the root
    if (!a→RightChild) a→RightChild = b;
    else a→RightChild = MinUnion(a→RightChild, b);
    // Leftist Tree property
    if (!a→LeftChild) {
            // interchange subtrees
            a→LeftChild = a→RightChild; a→RightChild = 0;
    }
    else if (a→LeftChild→shortest < a→RightChild→shortest)
    { // interchange subtrees
                    LeftistNode<KeyType> *t = a→LeftChild;
                    a→LeftChild = a→RightChild; a→RightChild = t;
    }
    // Set shortest data member
    if (!a→RightChild) a→shortest = 1;
    else a→shortest = a→RightChild→shortest + 1;
    return a ;
}
```

Program 9.10: Combining two min leftist trees

5. [*Lazy deletion*] Another way to handle the deletion of arbitrary elements from a min leftist heap is to use a Boolean data member, *deleted*, in place of the *parent* data member of the previous exercise. When an element is deleted, its *deleted* data member is set to TRUE. However, the node is not physically deleted. When a delete-min operation is performed, we first search for the minimum element not deleted by performing a limited preorder search. This preorder search traverses only the upper part of the tree as needed to identify the min element. All deleted elements encountered are physically deleted, and their subtrees are combined to obtain the new min leftist tree.

   (a) Write a function to delete the element in node *x* of a min leftist tree.

   (b) Write another function to delete the min element from a min leftist tree from which several elements have been deleted using the former function.

   (c) What is the complexity of the latter as a function of the number of deleted elements encountered and the number of elements in the entire tree?

6. [*Skewed heaps*] A *skewed heap* is a min tree that supports the min leftist tree operations: insert, delete-min, and combine in amortized time (see Section 9.4 for a definition of amortized time) $O(\log n)$ per operation. As in the case of min leftist trees, insertions and deletions are performed using the combine operation, which is carried out by following the rightmost paths in the two heaps being combined. However, unlike min leftist trees, the left and right subtrees of all nodes (except the last) on the rightmost path in the resulting heap are interchanged.

   (a) Write insert, delete-min, and combine functions for skewed heaps.

   (b) Compare the running times of these with those for the same operations on a min leftist tree. Use random sequences of insert, delete-min, and combine operations.

9.4 BINOMIAL HEAPS

9.4.1 Cost Amortization

A *binomial heap* is a data structure that supports the same functions (i.e., insert, delete-min (or delete-max), and combine) as those supported by leftist trees. Unlike leftist trees, where an individual operation can be performed in $O(\log n)$ time, it is possible that certain individual operations performed on a binomial heap may take $O(n)$ time. However, if we amortize (spread out) part of the cost of expensive operations over the inexpensive ones, then the amortized complexity of an individual operation is either $O(1)$ or $O(\log n)$ depending on the type of operation.

Let us examine more closely the concept of cost amortization (we shall use the terms *cost* and *complexity* interchangeably). Suppose that a sequence I1, I2, D1, I3, I4, I5, I6, D2, I7 of insert and delete-min operations is performed. Assume that the *actual cost* of each of the seven inserts is one. By this, we mean that each insert takes one unit of time. Further, suppose that the delete-min operations D1 and D2 have an actual cost of eight and ten, respectively. So, the total cost of the sequence of operations is 25.

In an amortization scheme we charge some of the actual cost of an operation to other operations. This reduces the charged cost of some operations and increases that of others. The *amortized cost* of an operation is the total cost charged to it. The cost transferring (amortization) scheme is required to be such that the sum of the amortized costs of the operations is greater than or equal to the sum of their actual costs. If we charge one unit of the cost of a delete-min operation to each of the inserts since the last delete-min operation (if any), then two units of the cost of D1 get transferred to I1 and I2 (the charged cost of each increases by one), and four units of the cost of D2 get transferred to I3 to I6. The amortized cost of each of I1 to I6 becomes two, that of I7 is equal to its actual cost (i.e., one), and that of each of D1 and D2 becomes 6. The sum of the amortized costs is 25, which is the same as the sum of the actual costs.

Now suppose we can prove that no matter what sequence of insert and delete-min operations is performed, we can charge costs in such a way that the amortized cost of each insertion is no more than two and that of each deletion is no more than six. This will enable us to make the claim that the actual cost of any insert / delete-min sequence is no more than $2 * i + 6 * d$ where i and d are, respectively, the number of insert and delete-min operations in the sequence. Suppose that the actual cost of a deletion is no more than ten, and that of an insertion is one. Using actual costs, we can conclude that the sequence cost is no more than $i + 10 * d$. Combining these two bounds, we obtain $\min\{2 * i + 6 * d, i + 10 * d\}$ as a bound on the sequence cost. Hence, using the notion of cost amortization, we can obtain tighter bounds on the complexity of a sequence of operations. We shall use the notion of cost amortization to show that although individual delete operations on a binomial heap may be expensive, the cost of any sequence of binomial heap operations is actually quite small.

9.4.2 Definition of Binomial Heaps

As in the case of heaps and leftist trees, there are two varieties of binomial heaps, min and max. A *min binomial heap* is a collection of min trees; a *max binomial heap* is a collection of max trees. We shall explicitly consider min binomial heaps only. These will be referred to as *B-heaps*. Figure 9.15 shows an example of a B-heap that is made up of three min trees.

Using B-heaps, we can perform an insert and a combine in O(1) actual and amortized time and a delete-min in O(log *n*) amortized time. B-heaps are represented using nodes that have the following data members: *degree*, *child*, *link*, and *data*. The *degree* of a node is the number of children it has; the *child* data member is used to point to any one of its children (if any); the *link* data member is used to maintain singly linked circular lists of siblings. All the children of a node form a singly linked circular list, and the node points to one of these children. Additionally, the roots of the min trees that comprise a B-heap are linked to form a singly linked circular list. The B-heap is then

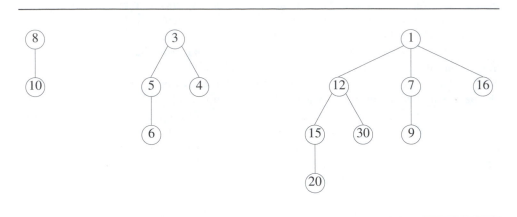

Figure 9.15: A B-heap with three min trees

pointed at by a single pointer *min* to the min tree root with smallest key. Program 9.11 contains the class definitions for *BinomialNode* and *BinomialTree*.

Figure 9.16 shows the representation for the example of Figure 9.15. To enhance the readability of this figure, we have used bidirectional arrows to join together nodes that are in the same circular list. When such a list contains only one node, no such arrows are drawn. Each of the key sets {10}, {6}, {5,4}, {20}, {15, 30}, {9}, {12, 7, 16}, and {8, 3, 1} denotes the keys in one of the circular lists of Figure 9.16. *min* is the pointer to the B-heap. Note that an empty B-heap has a 0 pointer.

9.4.3 Insertion into a Binomial Heap

An element *x* may be inserted into a B-heap by first putting *x* into a new node and then inserting this node into the circular list pointed at by *min*. The pointer *min* is reset to this new node only if *min* is 0 or the key of *x* is smaller than the key in the node pointed at by *min*. It is evident that these insertion steps can be performed in O(1) time.

9.4.4 Combining Two Binomial Heaps

To combine two nonempty B-heaps, we combine the top circular lists of each into a single circular list. The new B-heap pointer is the *min* pointer of one of the two trees, depending on which has the smaller key. This can be determined with a single comparison. Since two circular lists can be combined into a single one in O(1) time, a combine takes only O(1) time.

---

template <class *KeyType*> **class** *BinomialTree*; // forward declaration

template <class *KeyType*>
class *BinomialNode* {
friend class *BinomialTree<KeyType>*;
private:
        Element<KeyType> data;
        BinomialNode<KeyType> *child, *link;
        int *degree*;
};

template <class *KeyType*>
class *BinomialTree* : **public** *MinHeap<KeyType>* {
public:
        BinomialTree(BinomialNode<KeyType> *init = 0) min(init) { };

        // the three binomial tree operations
        void *Insert*(**const** *Element<KeyType>&*);
        Element<KeyType>* DeleteMin(Element<KeyType>&);
        void *MinCombine(BinomialTree<KeyType>*)*;

private:
        BinomialNode<KeyType> *min;
};

Program 9.11: Class definition of a binomial tree

9.4.5 Deletion of Min Element

If *min* is 0, then the B-heap is empty, and a deletion cannot be performed. Assume that *min* is not 0. *min* points to the node that contains the min element. This node is deleted from its circular list. The new B-heap consists of the remaining min trees and the sub-min trees of the deleted root. Figure 9.17 shows the situation for the example of Figure 9.15.

     Before forming the circular list of min tree roots, we repeatedly join together pairs of min trees that have the same degree (the degree of a nonempty min tree is the degree of its root). *This min tree joining is done by making the min tree whose root has a larger key a subtree of the other (ties are broken arbitrarily).* When two min trees are joined, the degree of the resulting min tree is one larger than the original degree of each min tree, and the number of min trees decreases by one. For our example, we may first join either the min trees with roots 8 and 7 or those with roots 3 and 12. If the first pair is

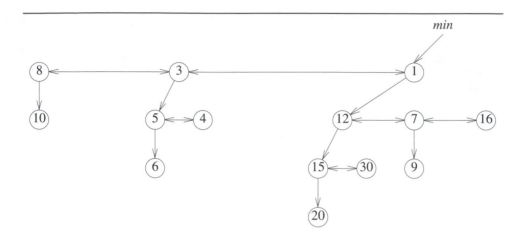

Figure 9.16: B-heap of Figure 9.15 showing child pointers and sibling lists

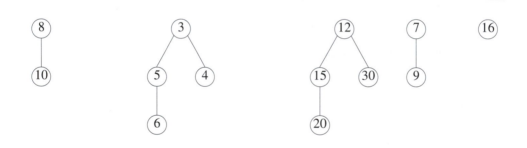

Figure 9.17: The B-heap of Figure 9.15 following the deletion of the min element

joined, the min tree with root 8 is made a subtree of the min tree with root 7. We now have the min tree collection of Figure 9.18. There are three min trees of degree two in this collection. If the pair with roots 7 and 3 is picked for joining, the resulting min tree collection is that of Figure 9.19. Shaded nodes in Figure 9.18 and Figure 9.19 denote the min tree that was made a subtree in the previous step. Since the min trees in this collection have different degrees, the min tree joining process terminates.

The min tree joining step is followed by a step in which the min tree roots are linked together to form a circular list and the B-heap pointer is reset to point to the min tree root with smallest key. The steps involved in a delete-min operation are summarized in Program 9.12.

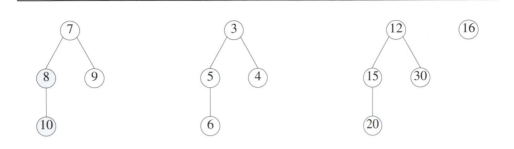

Figure 9.18: The B-heap of Figure 9.17 following the joining of the two degree-one min trees

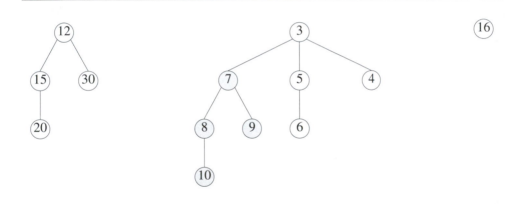

Figure 9.19: The B-heap of Figure 9.18 following the joining of two degree-two min trees

Step 1 takes $O(1)$ time. Step 2 can be done in $O(1)$ time by copying over the data from the next node (if any) in the circular list and physically deleting that node instead. However, since Step 3 requires us to visit all nodes in the circular list of roots, it is not necessary to delete *min* and leave behind a circular list. In Step 3, we can simply examine all nodes other than *min* in the root-level circular list.

Step 3 may be implemented by using an array, *tree*, that is indexed from 0 to the maximum possible degree, *MaxDegree*, of a min tree. Initially all entries in this array are 0. Let s be the number of min trees in *min* and y. The lists *min* and y created in Step 2 are scanned. For each min tree p in the lists *min* and y created in Step 2, the code of Program 9.13 is executed. The function *JoinMinTrees* makes the input tree with larger

---

template<class *KeyType*>
Element<KeyType>* Binomial<KeyType>::DeleteMin(Element<KeyType>& x)

// Delete the min element from the B-heap. This element is returned in *x*.

Step 1: [Handle empty B-heap] **if** (!*min*) { *DeletionError*(); **return** 0;}

Step 2: [Deletion from nonempty B-heap] $x = min \rightarrow data$; $y = min \rightarrow child$; delete *min* from its circular list; following this deletion, *min* points to any remaining node in the resulting list; if there is no such node, then $min = 0$;

Step 3: [Min-tree joining] Consider the min trees in the lists *min* and *y*; join together pairs of min trees of the same degree until all remaining min trees have different degrees;

Step 4: [Form min tree root list] Link the roots of the remaining min trees (if any) together to form a circular list; set *min* to point to the root (if any) with minimum key; **return** &*x*;

Program 9.12: Steps in a delete-min operation

root a subtree of the other tree. The resulting tree is returned in the first parameter. In the end, the array *tree* contains pointers to the min trees that are to be linked together in Step 4. Since each time a pair of min trees is joined the total number of min trees decreases by one, the number of joins is at most $s - 1$. Hence, the complexity of Step 3 is $O(MaxDegree + s)$.

```
for (d = p →degree;tree[d]; d ++)
{
    JoinMinTrees (p, tree [d ]) ;
    tree [d ] = 0 ;
}
tree [d ] = p ;
```

Program 9.13: Code to handle min tree *p* encountered during a scan of lists *min* and *y*

Step 4 is accomplished by scanning *tree* [0] , . . . , *tree* [*MaxDegree*] and linking together the min trees found. During this scan, the min tree with minimum key may also be determined. The complexity of Step 4 is $O(MaxDegree)$.

9.4.6   Analysis

Definition: The *binomial tree,* B_k, *of degree k* is a tree such that if $k = 0$, then the tree has exactly one node, and if $k > 0$, then the tree consists of a root whose degree is k and whose subtrees are $B_0, B_1, \cdots, B_{k-1}$. $\square$

   The min trees of Figure 9.15 are B_1, B_2, and B_3, respectively. One may verify that B_k has exactly 2^k nodes. Further, if we start with a collection of empty B-heaps and perform inserts, combines, and delete-mins only, then the min trees in each B-heap are binomial trees. These observations enable us to prove that when only inserts, combines, and delete-mins are performed, we can amortize costs such that the amortized cost of each insert and combine is O(1), and that of each delete-min is O(log n).

Lemma 9.2: Let a be a B-heap with n elements that results from a sequence of insert, combine, and delete-min operations performed on a collection of initially empty B-heaps. Each min tree in a has degree $\leq \log_2 n$. Consequently, *MaxDegree* $\leq \lfloor \log_2 n \rfloor$, and the actual cost of a delete-min operation is O(log $n + s$).

Proof: Since each of the min trees in a is a binomial tree with at most n nodes, none can have degree greater than $\lfloor \log_2 n \rfloor$. $\square$

Theorem 9.1: If a sequence of n insert, combine, and delete-min operations is performed on initially empty B-heaps, then we can amortize costs such that the amortized time complexity of each insert and combine is O(1), and that of each delete-min operation is O(log n).

Proof: For each B-heap, define the quantities *#insert* and *LastSize* in the following way: When an initially empty B-heap is created or when a delete-min operation is performed on a B-heap, its *#insert* value is set to zero. Each time an insert is done on a B-heap, its *#insert* value is increased by one. When two B-heaps are combined, the *#insert* value of the resulting B-heap is the sum of the *#insert* values of the B-heaps combined. Hence, *#insert* counts the number of inserts performed on a B-heap or its constituent B-heaps since the last delete-min operation performed in each. When an initially empty B-heap is created, its *LastSize* value is zero. When a delete-min operation is performed on a B-heap, its *LastSize* is set to the number of min trees it contains following this delete. When two B-heaps are combined, the *LastSize* value for the resulting B-heap is the sum of the *LastSize* values in the two B-heaps that were combined. One may verify that the number of min trees in a B-heap is always equal to *#insert + LastSize*.

   Consider any individual delete-min operation in the operation sequence. Assume this is from the B-heap a. Observe that the total number of elements in all the B-heaps is at most n, as only inserts add elements, and at most n inserts can be present in a sequence of n operations. Let $u = a. \, min \rightarrow degree \leq \log_2 n$.

   From Lemma 9.2, the actual cost of this delete-min operation is O(log $n + s$). The log n term is due to *MaxDegree* and represents the time needed to initialize the array *tree* and to complete Step 4. The s term represents the time to scan the lists *min* and y and to perform the $s-1$ (at most) min tree joins. We see that $s = \#insert + LastSize + u - 1$. If we charge $\#insert$ units of cost to the insert operations that contribute to the count $\#insert$ and $LastSize$ units to the delete-mins that contribute to the count $LastSize$ (each such delete-min operation is charged a number of cost units equal to the number of min trees it left behind), then only $u - 1$ of the s cost units remain. Since $u \leq \log_2 n$, and since the number of min trees in a B-heap immediately following a delete-min operation is $\leq \log_2 n$, the amortized cost of a delete-min operation becomes $O(\log_2 n)$.

Since this charging scheme adds at most one unit to the cost of any insert, the amortized cost of an insert becomes $O(1)$. The amortization scheme used does not charge anything extra to a combine. So, the actual and amortized costs of a combine are also $O(1)$. $\square$

From the preceding theorem and the definition of cost amortization, it follows that the actual cost of any sequence of i inserts, c combines, and dm delete-min operations is $O(i + c + dm \log i)$.

EXERCISES

1. Let S be an initially empty stack. We wish to perform two operations on S: $add(x)$ and $DeleteUntil(x)$. These are defined as follows:

    (a) $add(x)$: Add the element x to the top of the stack S. This operation takes $O(1)$ time per invocation.

    (b) $DeleteUntil(x)$: Delete elements from the top of the stack up to and including the first x encountered. If p elements are deleted, the time taken is $O(p)$.

    Consider any sequence of n stack operations (*add*s and *DeleteUntil*s). Show how to amortize the cost of the *add* and *DeleteUntil* operations so that the amortized cost of each is $O(1)$. From this, conclude that the time needed to perform any such sequence of operations is $O(n)$.

2. Let x be an unsorted array of n elements. The function $x::search(n,i,y)$ searches x for y by examining $x[i]$, $[i+1]$, and so on, in that order, for the least j such that $x[j] = y$. If no such j is found, j is set to $n + 1$. On termination, function *search* sets i to j. Assume that the time required to examine a single element of x is $O(1)$.

    (a) What is the worst-case complexity of *search*?

    (b) Suppose that a sequence of m searches is performed beginning with $i = 1$. Use a cost amortization scheme that assigns costs both to elements and to search operations. Show that it is always possible to amortize costs so that the amortized cost of each element is $O(1)$ and that of each search is also $O(1)$. From this, conclude that the cost of the sequence of m searches is $O(m + n)$.

3. Prove that the binomial tree B_k has 2^k nodes, $k \geq 0$.

4. Compare the performance of leftist trees and B-heaps under the assumption that the only permissible operations are insert and delete-min. For this, do the following:

   (a) Create a random list of n elements and a random sequence of insert and delete-min operations of length m. The number of delete-mins and inserts should be approximately equal. Initialize a min leftist tree and a B-heap to contain the n elements in the first random list. Now, measure the time to perform the m operations using the min leftist tree as well as the B-heap. Divide this time by m to get the average time per operation. Do this for $n = 100, 500, 1000, 2000, \cdots, 5000$. Let m be 5000. Tabulate your computing times.

   (b) Based on your experiments, make some statements about the relative merits of the two data structures.

5. Why do you think Binomial Heaps are so named?

9.5 FIBONACCI HEAPS

9.5.1 Definition

A *Fibonacci heap* is a data structure that supports the three binomial heap operations: insert, delete-min (or delete-max), and combine, as well as the following additional operations:

(1) *decrease key*: Decrease the key of a specified node by a given positive amount.

(2) *delete*: Delete the element in a specified node.

The first of these can be done in $O(1)$ amortized time and the second in $O(\log n)$ amortized time. The binomial heap operations can be performed in the same asymptotic times using a Fibonacci heap as they can be using a binomial heap.

There are two varieties of Fibonacci heaps: min and max. A *min Fibonacci heap* is a collection of min trees; a *max Fibonacci heap* is a collection of max trees. We shall explicitly consider min Fibonacci heaps only. These will be referred to as F-heaps. B-heaps are a special case of F-heaps. Thus, all the examples of B-heaps in the preceding section are also examples of F-heaps. As a consequence, in this section, we shall refer to these examples as F-heaps. To represent an F-heap, the B-heap representation is augmented by adding two data members, *parent* and *ChildCut*, to each node. The *parent* data member is used to point to the node's parent (if any). The significance of the *ChildCut* data member will be described later. In addition, the singly linked circular lists are replaced by doubly linked circular lists. This requires us to replace the data member *link* by the data members *LeftLink* and *RightLink*.

The basic operations insert, delete-min, and combine are performed exactly as for the case of B-heaps. We examine the remaining two operations: (1) delete an arbitrary node b from an F-heap, and (2) decrease the key in the arbitrary node b by a positive amount.

9.5.2   Deletion from an F-Heap

To delete an arbitrary node b from a F-heap, we do the following:

(1)   If $min = b$, then do a delete-min; otherwise do Steps 2, 3, and 4 below.

(2)   Delete b from its doubly linked list.

(3)   Combine the doubly linked list of b's children with the doubly linked list pointed at by min into a single doubly linked list. Trees of equal degree are not joined as in a delete-min operation.

(4)   Dispose of node b.

For example, if we delete the node containing 12 from the F-heap of Figure 9.15, we get the F-heap of Figure 9.20. The actual cost of an arbitrary delete is $O(1)$ unless the min element is being deleted. In this case the deletion time is the time for a delete-min operation.

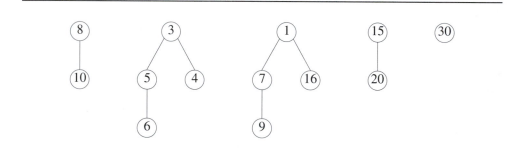

Figure 9.20: F-heap of Figure 9.15 following the deletion of 12

9.5.3   Decrease Key

To decrease the key in node b we do the following:

(1)   Reduce the key in b.

(2)   If b is not a min tree root and its key is smaller than that in its parent, then delete b from its doubly linked list and insert it into the doubly linked list of min tree roots.

(3)   Change *min* to point to *b* if the key in *b* is smaller than that in *min*.

Suppose we decrease the key 15 in the F-heap of Figure 9.15 by 4. The resulting F-heap is shown in Figure 9.21. The cost of performing a decrease-key operation is O(1).

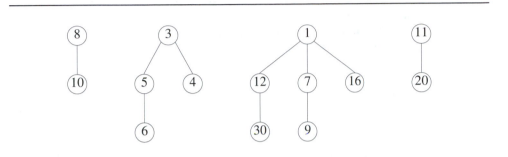

Figure 9.21: F-heap of Figure 9.15 following the reduction of 15 by 4

9.5.4   Cascading Cut

With the addition of the delete and decrease-key operations, the min trees in an F-heap need not be binomial trees. In fact, it is possible to have degree-*k* min trees with as few as $k+1$ nodes. As a result, the analysis of Theorem 9.1 is no longer valid. The analysis of Theorem 9.1 requires that each min tree of degree *k* have an exponential (in *k*) number of nodes. When decrease-key and delete operations are performed as described above, this is no longer true. To ensure that each min tree of degree *k* has at least c^k nodes for some *c*, $c > 1$, each delete and decrease-key operation must be followed by a *cascading-cut* step. For this, we add the Boolean data member *ChildCut* to each node. The value of this data member is useful only for nodes that are not the root of a min tree. In this case, the *ChildCut* data member of node *x* has the value TRUE iff one of the children of *x* was cut off (i.e., removed) after the most recent time *x* was made the child of its current parent. This means that each time two min trees are joined in a delete-min operation, the *ChildCut* data member of the root with larger key should be set to FALSE. Further, whenever a delete or decrease-key operation deletes a node *q* that is not a min tree root from its doubly linked list (Step 2 of delete and decrease key), then the cascading-cut step is invoked. During this step, we examine the nodes on the path from the parent *p* of the deleted node *q* up to the nearest ancestor of the deleted node with *ChildCut* = FALSE. If there is no such ancestor, then the path goes from *p* to the root of the min tree containing *p*. All nonroot nodes on this path with *ChildCut* data member TRUE are deleted from their respective doubly linked lists and added to the doubly linked list of min tree root nodes of the F-heap. If the path has a node with *ChildCut* data member FALSE, this data member is changed to TRUE.

Figure 9.22 gives an example of a cascading cut. Figure 9.22(a) is the min tree containing 14 before a decrease-key operation that reduces this key by 4. The *ChildCut* data members are shown only for the nodes on the path from the parent of 14 to its nearest ancestor with *ChildCut* = FALSE. Nodes with *ChildCut* = TRUE are shaded in the figure. All unshaded nodes have *ChildCut* = FALSE. During the decrease-key operation, the min tree with root 14 is deleted from the min tree of Figure 9.22(a) and becomes a min tree of the F-heap. Its root now has key 10. This is the first min tree of Figure 9.22(b). During the cascading cut, the min trees with roots 12, 10, 8, and 6 are cut off from the min tree with root 2. Thus, the single min tree of Figure 9.22(a) becomes six min trees of the resulting F-heap. The *ChildCut* value of 4 becomes TRUE. All other *ChildCut* values are unchanged.

9.5.5 Analysis

Lemma 9.3: Let a be an F-heap with n elements that results from a sequence of insert, combine, delete-min, delete, and decrease-key operations performed on initially empty F-heaps.

(a) Let b be any node in any of the min trees of a. The degree of b is at most $\log_\phi m$, where $\phi = (1+\sqrt{5})/2$, and m is the number of elements in the subtree with root b.

(b) *MaxDegree* $\leq \lfloor \log_\phi n \rfloor$, and the actual cost of a delete-min operation is $O(\log n + s)$.

Proof: We shall prove (a) by induction on the degree of b. Let N_i be the minimum number of elements in the subtree with root b when b has degree i. We see that $N_0 = 1$ and $N_1 = 2$. So, the inequality of (a) holds for degrees 0 and 1. For $i > 1$, let $c_1, \cdots, c_i$ be the i children of b. Assume that c_j was made a child of b before $c_{j+1}, j < i$. Hence, when $c_k, k \leq i$, was made a child of b, the degree of b was at least $k - 1$. The only F-heap operation that makes one node a child of another is delete-min. Here, during a join min tree step, one min tree is made a subtree of another min tree of equal degree. Hence, at the time of joining, the degree of c_k must have been equal to that of b. Subsequent to joining, its degree can decrease as a result of a delete or decrease-key operation. However, following such a join, the degree of c_k can decrease by at most one, as an attempt to cut off a second child of c_k results in a cascading cut at c_k. Such a cut causes c_k to become the root of a min tree of the F-heap. Hence, the degree, d_k, of c_k is at least $\max\{0, k - 2\}$. So, the number of elements in c_k is at least N_{d_k}. This implies that

$$N_i = N_0 + \sum_{k=0}^{i-2} N_k + 1 = \sum_{k=0}^{i-2} N_k + 2$$

One may show (see the exercises) that the Fibonacci numbers satisfy the equality

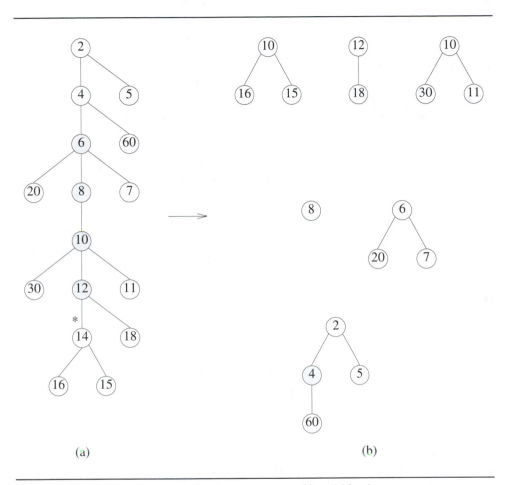

(a)   (b)

Figure 9.22: A cascading cut following a decrease of key 14 by 4

$$F_h = \sum_{k=0}^{h-2} F_k + 1, h > 1, F_0 = 0, \text{ and } F_1 = 1$$

From this we may obtain the equality $N_i = F_{i+2}$, $i \geq 0$. Further, since $F_{i+2} \geq \phi^i$, $N_i \geq \phi^i$. Hence, $i \leq \log_\phi m$. (b) is a direct consequence of (a). $\square$

Theorem 9.2: If a sequence of n insert, combine, delete-min, delete, and decrease-key operations is performed on an initially empty F-heap, then we can amortize costs such that the amortized time complexity of each insert, combine, and decrease-key operation is O(1) and that of each delete-min and delete operation is O($\log n$). The total time complexity of the entire sequence is the sum of the amortized complexities of the individual operations in the sequence.

Proof: The proof is similar to that of Theorem 9.1. The definition of *#insert* is unchanged. However, that of *LastSize* is augmented by requiring that following each delete and decrease-key operation, *LastSize* be changed by the net change in the number of min trees in the F-heap (in the example of Figure 9.22 *LastSize* is increased by 5). With this modification, we see that at the time of a delete-min operation $s = $ *#insert* + *LastSize* + $u - 1$. *#insert* units of cost may be charged, one each, to the *#insert* insert operations that contribute to this count, and *LastSize* units may be charged to the delete-min, delete, and decrease-key operations that contribute to this count. This results in an additional charge of at most $\log_\phi n$ to each contributing delete-min and delete operation and of one to each contributing decrease-key operation. As a result, the amortized cost of a delete-min operation is $O(\log n)$.

Since the total number of cascading cuts is limited by the total number of deletes and decrease-key operations (as these are the only operations that can set *ChildCut* to TRUE), the cost of these cuts may be amortized over the delete and decrease-key operations by adding one to their amortized costs. The amortized cost of deleting an element other than the min element becomes $O(\log n)$, as its actual cost is $O(1)$ (excluding the cost of the cascading-cut sequence that may be performed); at most one unit is charged to it from the amortization of all the cascading cuts; and at most $\log_\phi n$ units are charged to it from a delete-min operation.

The amortized cost of a decrease-key operation is $O(1)$, as its actual cost is $O(1)$ (excluding the cost of the ensuing cascading cut); at most one unit is charged to it from the amortization of all cascading cuts; and at most one unit is charged from a delete-min operation.

The amortized cost of an insert is $O(1)$, as its actual cost is one, and at most one cost unit is charged to it from a delete-min operation. Since the amortization scheme transfers no charge to a combine operation, its actual and amortized costs are the same. This cost is $O(1)$. □

From the preceding theorem, it follows that the complexity of any sequence of F-heap operations is $O(i + c + dk + (dm + d) \log i)$ where i, c, dk, dm, and d are, respectively, the number of insert, combine, decrease-key, delete-min, and delete operations in the sequence.

9.5.6   Application to the Shortest-Paths Problem

We conclude this section on F-heaps by considering their application to the single-source/all-destinations algorithm of Chapter 6. Let S be the set of vertices to which a shortest path has been found and let $dist(i)$ be the length of a shortest path from the source vertex to vertex i, $i \in S$, that goes through only vertices in S. On each iteration of the shortest-path algorithm, we need to determine an i, $i \in \bar{S}$, such that $dist(i)$ is minimum and add this i to S. This corresponds to a delete-min operation on $\bar{S}$. Further, the $dist$ values of the remaining vertices in $\bar{S}$ may decrease. This corresponds to a decrease-key operation on each of the affected vertices. The total number of decrease-key operations is bounded by the number of edges in the graph, and the number of delete-min operations is $n - 2$. S begins with $n - 1$ vertices. If we implement S as an F-heap using *dist* as the key, then $n - 1$ inserts are needed to initialize the F-heap. Additionally, $n - 2$ delete-min operations and at most e decrease-key operations are needed. The total time for all these operations is the sum of the amortized costs for each. This is $O(n \log n + e)$. The remainder of the algorithm takes $O(n)$ time. Hence if an F-heap is used to represent S, the complexity of the shortest-path algorithm becomes $O(n \log n + e)$. This is an asymptotic improvement over the implementation discussed in Chapter 6 if the graph does not have $\Omega(n^2)$ edges. If this single-source algorithm is used n times, once with each of the n vertices in the graph as the source, then we can find a shortest path between every pair of vertices in $O(n^2 \log n + ne)$ time. Once again, this represents an asymptotic improvement over the $O(n^3)$ dynamic programming algorithm of Chapter 6 for graphs that do not have $\Omega(n^2)$ edges. It is interesting to note that $O(n \log n + e)$ is the best possible implementation of the single-source algorithm of Chapter 6, as the algorithm must examine each edge and may be used to sort n numbers (which takes $O(n \log n)$ time).

EXERCISES

1. Prove that if we start with empty F-heaps and perform only the operations insert, combine, and delete-min, then all min trees in the F-heaps are binomial trees.

2. Can all the functions on an F-heap be performed in the same amount of time using singly linked circular lists rather than doubly linked circular lists? (Note that we can delete from an arbitrary node x of a singly linked circular list by copying over the data in the next node and then deleting the next node rather than the node x.)

3. Show that if we start with empty F-heaps and do not perform cascading cuts, then it is possible for a sequence of F-heap operations to result in degree-k min trees that have only $k + 1$ nodes, $k \geq 1$.

4. Suppose we change the rule for a cascading cut so that such a cut is performed only when a node loses a third child rather than when it loses a second child. For this, the *ChildCut* data member is changed so that it can have the values 0, 1, and 2. When a node acquires a new parent, its *ChildCut* data member is set to 1. Each time a node has a child cut off (during a delete or decrease-key operation), its *ChildCut* data member is increased by one (unless this data member is already two). If the *ChildCut* data member is already two, a cascading cut is performed.

    (a) Obtain a recurrence equation for N_i, the minimum number of nodes in a min tree with degree i. Assume that we start with an empty F-heap and that all operations (except cascading cut) are performed as described in the text. Cascading cuts are performed as described above.

    (b) Solve the recurrence of part (a) to obtain a lower bound on N_i.

(c) Does the modified rule for cascading cuts ensure that the minimum number of nodes in any min tree of degree i is exponential in i?

(d) For the new cascading-cut rule, can you establish the same amortized complexities as for the original rule? Prove the correctness of your answer.

(e) Answer parts (c) and (d) under the assumption that cascading cuts are performed only after k children of a node have been cut off. Here, k is a fixed constant ($k = 2$ for the rule used in the text, and $k = 3$ for the rule used earlier in this exercise).

(f) How do you expect the performance of F-heaps to change as larger values of k (see part (e)) are used?

5. Write C++ template class definitions for *FibonacciNode* and *FibonacciHeap*.

6. Write C++ member functions to implement the following *FibonacciHeap* operations:

(a) Create an empty F-heap.

(b) Insert element x into an F-heap.

(c) Perform a delete-min operation on an F-heap and return the deleted element.

(d) Delete and return the element in node b of an F-heap.

(e) Decrease the key in the node b of an F-heap by some positive amount c.

Note that all operations must leave behind properly structured F-heaps. Your functions for (d) and (e) must perform cascading cuts. Test the correctness of your functions by running them on a computer using suitable test data.

7. For the Fibonacci numbers F_k and the numbers N_i of Lemma 9.3, prove the following:

(a) $F_h = \sum_{k=0}^{h-2} F_k + 1, h > 1.$

(b) Use (a) to show that $N_i = F_{i+2}, i \geq 0$.

(c) Use the equality

$$F_k = \frac{1}{\sqrt{5}}(\frac{1+\sqrt{5}}{2})^k - \frac{1}{\sqrt{5}}(\frac{1-\sqrt{5}}{2})^k, k \geq 0$$

to show that $F_{k+2} \geq \phi^k, k \geq 0$, where $\phi = (1+\sqrt{5})/2$.

8. Implement the single-source shortest-path algorithm of Chapter 6 using the data structures recommended there as well as F-heaps. However, use adjacency lists rather than an adjacency matrix. Generate 10 connected undirected graphs with different edge densities (say 10%, 20%, $\cdots$, 100% of maximum) for each of the cases $n = 100, 200, \cdots, 500$. Assign random costs to the edges (use a uniform random number generator in the range [1, 1000]). Measure the run times of the

two implementations of the shortest-path algorithms. Plot the average times for each n.

9.6   REFERENCES AND SELECTED READINGS

Min-max heaps were developed in "Min-max heaps and generalized priority queues," by M. Atkinson, J. Sack, N. Santoro, and T. Strothotte, *Communications of the ACM*, 29:10, 1986, pp. 996-1000. This paper also contains extensions of min-max heaps.

The deap data structure was invented by Svante Carlsson. The reference is "The deap: A double-ended heap to implement double-ended priority queues," *Information Processing Letters*, 26, 1987, pp. 33-36.

Leftist trees were invented by C. Crane. See, *Linear Lists and Priority Queues as Balanced Binary Trees*, Technical report CS-72-259, Computer Science Dept., Stanford University, Palo Alto, CA, 1972.

Further discussion of leftist trees may be found in *Data Structures and Network Algorithms*, by R. Tarjan, SIAM, Philadelphia, PA, 1983.

The exercise on lazy deletion is from "Finding minimum spanning trees," by D. Cheriton and R. Tarjan, *SIAM Journal on Computing*, 5, 1976, pp. 724-742.

B-heaps and F-heaps were invented by M. Fredman and R. Tarjan. Their work is reported in the paper "Fibonacci heaps and their uses in improved network optimization algorithms," *JACM*, 34:3, 1987, pp. 596-615. This paper also describes several variants of the basic F-heap as discussed here, as well as the application of F-heaps to the assignment problem and to the problem of finding a minimum-cost spanning tree. Their result is that using F-heaps, minimum-cost spanning trees can be found in $O(e\beta(e,n))$ time, where $\beta(e,n) \leq \log^* n$ when $e \geq n$. $\log^* n = \min\{i \mid \log^{(i)} n \leq 1\}$, $\log^{(0)} n = n$, and $\log^{(i)} n = \log(\log^{(i-1)} n)$. The complexity of finding minimum-cost spanning trees has been further reduced to $O(e\log\beta(e,n))$. The reference for this is "Efficient algorithms for finding minimum spanning trees in undirected and directed graphs," by H. Gabow, Z. Galil, T. Spencer, and R. Tarjan, *Combinatorica*, 6:2, 1986, pp. 109-122.

9.7   ADDITIONAL EXERCISE

1. [**Programming Project:**] Implement the inheritance hierarchy of Figure 9.23 consisting of data structures described in Chapters 5 and 9. Dashed boxes represent abstract base classes. The abstract base class *MergeableMinPQ* represents an ADT which, in addition to being a min priority queue, contains an operation that merges two min priority queues. The dotted box represents all corresponding max ADTs not shown in the figure.

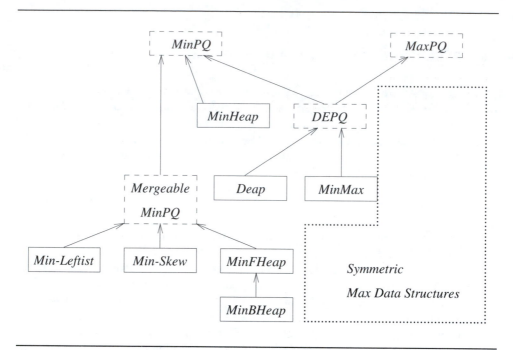

Figure 9.23: Inheritance hierarchy for additional exercise

CHAPTER 10

SEARCH STRUCTURES

10.1   OPTIMAL BINARY SEARCH TREES

Binary search trees were introduced in Chapter 5. In this section, we consider the construction of binary search trees for a static set of identifiers. That is, we make no additions to or deletions from the set. Only searches are performed.

A sorted file can be searched using a binary search. For this search, we can construct a binary search tree with the property that searching this tree using the function *search* (Program 5.21) is equivalent to performing a binary search on the sorted file. For instance, a binary search on the file (**do, if, while**) corresponds to using algorithm *search* on the binary search tree of Figure 10.1. Although this tree is a full binary tree, it may not be the optimal binary search tree to use when the probabilities with which different identifiers are sought are different.

To find an optimal binary search tree for a given static file, we must first decide on a cost measure for search trees. When searching for an identifier at level k, function *search* makes k iterations of the **for** loop. Since this **for** loop determines the cost of the search, it is reasonable to use the level number of a node as its cost.

Consider the two search trees of Figure 10.2. The second of these requires at most three comparisons to decide whether the identifier being sought is in the tree. The first binary tree may require four comparisons, since any identifier that alphabetically follows **for** but precedes **if** will test four nodes. Thus, as far as worst-case search time is concerned, the second binary tree is more desirable than the first. To search for an identifier

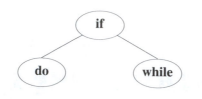

Figure 10.1: Binary search tree corresponding to a binary search on the file (**do, if, while**)

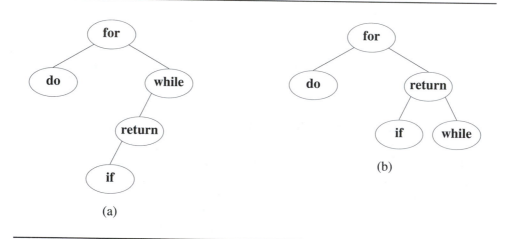

(a)

(b)

Figure 10.2: Two binary search trees

in the first tree takes one comparison for the **for**, two for each of **do** and **while**, three for **return**, and four for **if**. Assuming that each identifier is sought with equal probability, the average number of comparisons for a successful search is 2.4. For the second binary search tree this amount is 2.2. Thus, the second tree has a better average behavior, too.

In evaluating binary search trees, it is useful to add a special "square" node at every null link. Doing this to the trees of Figure 10.2 yields the trees of Figure 10.3. Remember that every binary tree with n nodes has $n + 1$ null links and therefore will have $n + 1$ square nodes. We shall call these nodes *external* nodes because they are not part of the original tree. The remaining nodes will be called *internal* nodes. Each time a binary search tree is examined for an identifier that is not in the tree, the search terminates at an external node. Since all such searches are unsuccessful searches, external nodes will also be referred to as *failure nodes*. A binary tree with external nodes added is an *extended binary tree*. The concept of an extended binary tree as just defined is the same as that defined in connection with leftist trees in Chapter 9. Figure 10.3 shows the extended binary trees corresponding to the search trees of Figure 10.2.

(a)

(b)

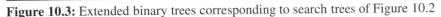

Figure 10.3: Extended binary trees corresponding to search trees of Figure 10.2

We define the *external path length* of a binary tree to be the sum over all external nodes of the lengths of the paths from the root to those nodes. Analogously, the *internal path length* is the sum over all internal nodes of the lengths of the paths from the root to those nodes. The internal path length, I, for the tree of Figure 10.3(a) is

$$I = 0 + 1 + 1 + 2 + 3 = 7$$

Its external path length, E, is

$$E = 2 + 2 + 4 + 4 + 3 + 2 = 17$$

Exercise 1 of this section shows that the internal and external path lengths of a binary tree with n internal nodes are related by the formula $E = I + 2n$. Hence, binary trees with the maximum E also have maximum I. Over all binary trees with n internal nodes, what are the maximum and minimum possible values for I? The worst case, clearly, is when the tree is skewed (i.e., when the tree has a depth of n). In this case,

$$I = \sum_{i=0}^{n-1} i = n(n-1)/2$$

To obtain trees with minimal I, we must have as many internal nodes as close to the root as possible. We can have at most 2 nodes at distance 1, 4 at distance 2, and in general, the smallest value for I is

$$0 + 2 * 1 + 4 * 2 + 8 * 3 + \cdots +$$

One tree with minimal internal path length is the complete binary tree defined in Section 5.2. If we number the nodes in a complete binary tree as in Section 5.3, then we see that the distance of node i from the root is $\lfloor \log_2 i \rfloor$. Hence, the smallest value for I is

$$\sum_{1 \le i \le n} \lfloor \log_2 i \rfloor = O(n \log_2 n)$$

Let us now return to our original problem of representing a symbol table as a binary search tree. If the binary search tree contains the identifiers $a_1, a_2, \cdots, a_n$ with $a_1 < a_2 < \cdots < a_n$, and the probability of searching for each a_i is p_i, then the total cost of any binary search tree is

$$\sum_{1 \le i \le n} p_i \cdot \text{level}(a_i)$$

when only successful searches are made. Since unsuccessful searches (i.e., searches for identifiers not in the table) will also be made, we should include the cost of these searches in our cost measure, too. Unsuccessful searches terminate with algorithm *search* returning a 0 pointer (Program 5.17). Every node with a null subtree defines a point at which such a termination can take place. Let us replace every null subtree by a failure node. The identifiers not in the binary search tree may be partitioned into $n + 1$ classes E_i, $0 \le i \le n$. E_0 contains all identifiers X such that $X < a_1$. E_i contains all identifiers X such that $a_i < X < a_{i+1}$, $1 \le i < n$, and E_n contains all identifiers X, $X > a_n$. It is easy to see that for all identifiers in a particular class E_i, the search terminates at the same failure node, and it terminates at different failure nodes for identifiers in different classes. The failure nodes may be numbered 0 to n, with i being the failure node for class E_i, $0 \le i \le n$. If q_i is the probability that the identifier being sought is in E_i, then the cost of the failure nodes is

$$\sum_{0 \le i \le n} q_i \cdot (\text{level(failure node } i) - 1)$$

Therefore, the total cost of a binary search tree is

$$\sum_{1 \le i \le n} p_i \cdot \text{level}(a_i) + \sum_{0 \le i \le n} q_i \cdot (\text{level (failure node } i) - 1) \qquad (10.1)$$

An *optimal binary search tree* for the identifier set $a_1, \cdots, a_n$ is one that minimizes Eq. (10.1) over all possible binary search trees for this identifier set. Note that since all searches must terminate either successfully or unsuccessfully, we have

$$\sum_{1 \le i \le n} p_i + \sum_{0 \le i \le n} q_i = 1$$

Example 10.1: Figure 10.4 shows the possible binary search trees for the identifier set $(a_1, a_2, a_3) = $ (**do, if, while**).

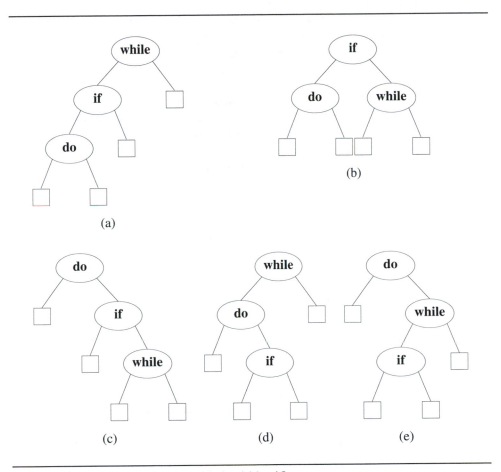

Figure 10.4: Binary search trees with three identifiers

With equal probabilities, $p_i = q_j = 1/7$ for all i and j, we have

$$\text{cost (tree } a) = 15/7; \text{ cost (tree } b) = 13/7$$
$$\text{cost (tree } c) = 15/7; \text{ cost (tree } d) = 15/7$$
$$\text{cost (tree } e) = 15/7$$

As expected, tree b is optimal. With $p_1 = 0.5$, $p_2 = 0.1$, $p_3 = 0.05$, $q_0 = 0.15$, $q_1 = 0.1$, $q_2 = 0.05$, and $q_3 = 0.05$ we have

$$\text{cost (tree } a) = 2.65; \text{ cost (tree } b) = 1.9$$
$$\text{cost (tree } c) = 1.5; \text{ cost (tree } d) = 2.05$$
$$\text{cost (tree } e) = 1.6$$

Tree c is optimal with this assignment of p's and q's. $\square$

How does one determine the optimal binary search tree? We could proceed as in Example 10.1 and explicitly generate all possible binary search trees, then compute the cost of each tree, and determine the tree with minimum cost. Since the cost of an n-node binary search tree can be determined in $O(n)$ time, the complexity of the optimal binary search tree algorithm is $O(n \, N(n))$, where $N(n)$ is the number of distinct binary search trees with n identifiers. From Section 5.12 we know that $N(n) = O(4^n / n^{3/2})$. Hence, this brute-force algorithm is impractical for large n. We can find a fairly efficient algorithm by making some observations about the properties of optimal binary search trees.

Let $a_1 < a_2 < \cdots < a_n$ be the n identifiers to be represented in a binary search tree. Let T_{ij} denote an optimal binary search tree for $a_{i+1}, \cdots, a_j, i < j$. By convention T_{ii} is an empty tree for $0 \le i \le n$, and T_{ij} is not defined for $i > j$. Let c_{ij} be the cost of the search tree T_{ij}. By definition c_{ii} will be 0. Let r_{ij} be the root of T_{ij}, and let

$$w_{ij} = q_i + \sum_{k=i+1}^{j} (q_k + p_k)$$

be the weight of T_{ij}. By definition $r_{ii} = 0$, and $w_{ii} = q_i$, $0 \le i \le n$. Therefore, T_{0n} is an optimal binary search tree for $a_1, \cdots, a_n$. Its cost is c_{0n}, its weight is w_{0n}, and its root is r_{0n}.

If T_{ij} is an optimal binary search tree for $a_{i+1}, \cdots, a_j$, and $r_{ij} = k$, then k satisfies the inequality $i < k \le j$. T_{ij} has two subtrees L and R. L is the left subtree and contains the identifiers $a_{i+1}, \cdots, a_{k-1}$, and R is the right subtree and contains the identifiers $a_{k+1}, \cdots, a_j$ (Figure 10.5). The cost c_{ij} of T_{ij} is

$$c_{ij} = p_k + \text{cost } (L) + \text{cost } (R) + \text{weight } (L) + \text{weight } (R) \tag{10.2}$$

where weight $(L) = \text{weight } (T_{i,k-1}) = w_{i,k-1}$, and weight $(R) = \text{weight } (T_{kj}) = w_{kj}$.

From Eq. (10.2) it is clear that if c_{ij} is to be minimal, then $\text{cost}(L) = c_{i,k-1}$ and $\text{cost}(R) = c_{kj}$, as otherwise we could replace either L or R by a subtree with a lower cost, thus getting a binary search tree for $a_{i+1}, \cdots, a_j$ with a lower cost than c_{ij}. This violates the assumption that T_{ij} is optimal. Hence, Eq. (10.2) becomes

$$c_{ij} = p_k + c_{i,k-1} + c_{kj} + w_{i,k-1} + w_{kj}$$

$$= w_{ij} + c_{i,k-1} + c_{kj} \tag{10.3}$$

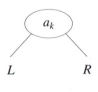

Figure 10.5: An optimal binary search tree T_{ij}

Since T_{ij} is optimal, it follows from Eq. (10.3) that $r_{ij} = k$ is such that

$$w_{ij} + c_{i,k-1} + c_{kj} = \min_{i < l \leq j}\{w_{ij} + c_{i,l-1} + c_{lj}\}$$

or

$$c_{i,k-1} + c_{kj} = \min_{i < l \leq j}\{c_{i,l-1} + c_{lj}\} \tag{10.4}$$

Equation (10.4) gives us a means of obtaining T_{0n} and c_{0n}, starting from the knowledge that $T_{ii} = \phi$ and $c_{ii} = 0$.

Example 10.2: Let $n = 4$ and $(a_1, a_2, a_3, a_4) = (\textbf{do, if, return, while})$. Let $(p_1, p_2, p_3, p_4) = (3, 3, 1, 1)$ and $(q_0, q_1, q_2, q_3, q_4) = (2, 3, 1, 1, 1)$. The p's and q's have been multiplied by 16 for convenience. Initially, $w_{ii} = q_i$, $c_{ii} = 0$, and $r_{ii} = 0$, $0 \leq i \leq 4$. Using Eqs. (10.3) and (10.4), we get

$$
\begin{aligned}
w_{01} &= p_1 + w_{00} + w_{11} = p_1 + q_1 + w_{00} = 8 \\
c_{01} &= w_{01} + \min\{c_{00} + c_{11}\} = 8 \\
r_{01} &= 1 \\
w_{12} &= p_2 + w_{11} + w_{22} = p_2 + q_2 + w_{11} = 7 \\
c_{12} &= w_{12} + \min\{c_{11} + c_{22}\} = 7 \\
r_{12} &= 2 \\
w_{23} &= p_3 + w_{22} + w_{33} = p_3 + q_3 + w_{22} = 3 \\
c_{23} &= w_{23} + \min\{c_{22} + c_{33}\} = 3
\end{aligned}
$$

$$r_{23} = 3$$
$$w_{34} = p_4 + w_{33} + w_{44} = p_4 + q_4 + w_{33} = 3$$
$$c_{34} = w_{34} + \min\{c_{33} + c_{44}\} = 3$$
$$r_{34} = 4$$

Knowing $w_{i,i+1}$ and $c_{i,i+1}$, $0 \le i < 4$, we can use Eqs. (10.3) and (10.4) again to compute $w_{i,i+2}$, $c_{i,i+2}$, $r_{i,i+2}$, $0 \le i < 3$. This process may be repeated until w_{04}, c_{04}, and r_{04} are obtained. The table of Figure 10.6 shows the results of this computation. From the table, we see that $c_{04} = 32$ is the minimal cost of a binary search tree for a_1 to a_4. The root of tree T_{04} is a_2. Hence, the left subtree is T_{01} and the right subtree T_{24}. T_{01} has root a_1 and subtrees T_{00} and T_{11}. T_{24} has root a_3; its left subtree is therefore T_{22} and right subtree T_{34}. Thus, with the data in the table it is possible to reconstruct T_{04}. Figure 10.7 shows T_{04}. □

	0	1	2	3	4
0	$w_{00} = 2$ $c_{00} = 0$ $r_{00} = 0$	$w_{11} = 3$ $c_{11} = 0$ $r_{11} = 0$	$w_{22} = 1$ $c_{22} = 0$ $r_{22} = 0$	$w_{33} = 1$ $c_{33} = 0$ $r_{33} = 0$	$w_{44} = 1$ $c_{44} = 0$ $r_{44} = 0$
1	$w_{01} = 8$ $c_{01} = 8$ $r_{01} = 1$	$w_{12} = 7$ $c_{12} = 7$ $r_{12} = 2$	$w_{23} = 3$ $c_{23} = 3$ $r_{23} = 3$	$w_{34} = 3$ $c_{34} = 3$ $r_{34} = 4$	
2	$w_{02} = 12$ $c_{02} = 19$ $r_{02} = 1$	$w_{13} = 9$ $c_{13} = 12$ $r_{13} = 2$	$w_{24} = 5$ $c_{24} = 8$ $r_{24} = 3$		
3	$w_{03} = 14$ $c_{03} = 25$ $r_{03} = 2$	$w_{14} = 11$ $c_{14} = 19$ $r_{14} = 2$			
4	$w_{04} = 16$ $c_{04} = 32$ $r_{04} = 2$				

Figure 10.6: Computation of c_{04} and r_{04}. The computation is carried out by row from row 0 to row 4

Example 10.2 illustrates how Eq. (10.4) may be used to determine the c's and r's, as well as how to reconstruct T_{0n} knowing the r's. Let us examine the complexity of this function to evaluate the c's and r's. The evaluation function described in Example 10.2

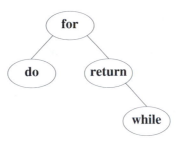

Figure 10.7: Optimal binary search tree for Example 10.2

requires us to compute c_{ij} for $(j - i) = 1, 2, \cdots, n$ in that order. When $j - i = m$, there are $n - m + 1$ c_{ij}'s to compute. The computation of each of these c_{ij}'s requires us to find the minimum of m quantities (see Eq. (10.4)). Hence, each such c_{ij} can be computed in time $O(m)$. The total time for all c_{ij}'s with $j - i = m$ is therefore $O(nm - m^2)$. The total time to evaluate all the c_{ij}'s and r_{ij}'s is

$$\sum_{1 \leq m \leq n} (nm - m^2) = O(n^3)$$

Actually we can do better than this using a result due to D. E. Knuth that states that the optimal l in Eq. (10.4) may be found by limiting the search to the range $r_{i,j-1} \leq l \leq r_{i+1,j}$. In this case, the computing time becomes $O(n^2)$ (see Exercise 3). Algorithm *obst* (Program 10.1) uses this result to obtain in $O(n^2)$ time the values of w_{ij}, r_{ij}, and c_{ij}, $0 \leq i \leq j \leq n$. The actual tree T_{0n} may be constructed from the values of r_{ij} in $O(n)$ time. The algorithm for this is left as an exercise.

Class *BST* of Chapter 5 is augmented to include *obst* as a private member function. Function *obst* is called by a BST constructor function that constructs an optimal binary search tree, given the success and failure probability arrays, $p[\ ]$ and $q[\ ]$, the array of identifiers $a[\ ]$, and the number of identifiers n. The array elements $p[0]$ and $a[0]$ are not used. Class *BST* also includes the private data members r, c, and w; these are declared as two-dimensional arrays of integers.

EXERCISES

1. (a) Prove by induction that if T is a binary tree with n internal nodes, I its internal path length, and E its external path length, then $E = I + 2n, n \geq 0$.

   (b) Using the result of (a), show that the average number of comparisons s in a successful search is related to the average number of comparisons, u, in an unsuccessful search by the formula

---

```
template <class KeyType>
BST<KeyType>::obst(int *p, int *q, Element<KeyType> *a, int n )
// Given n distinct identifiers a₁ < a₂ < ··· < aₙ, and probabilities pⱼ, 1 ≤ j ≤ n, and
// qᵢ, 0 ≤ i ≤ n this algorithm computes the cost cᵢⱼ of optimal binary search trees Tᵢⱼ
// for identifiers aᵢ₊₁, ··· , aⱼ. It also computes rᵢⱼ, the root of Tᵢⱼ. wᵢⱼ is the weight of Tᵢⱼ.
{
    for (int i = 0; i < n; i++) {
        w[i][i] = q[i]; r[i][i] = c[i][i] = 0;  // initialize
        w[i][i+1] = q[i] + q[i+1] + p[i+1];  // optimal trees with one node
        r[i][i+1] = i + 1;
        c[i][i+1] = w[i][i+1];
    }
    w[n][n] = q[n]; r[n][n] = c[n][n] = 0;
    for (int m = 2; m <= n; m++)  // find optimal trees with m nodes
        for (i = 0; i <= n − m; i++)
        {
            int j = i + m;
            w[i][j] = w[i][j − 1] + p[j] + q[j];
            int k = KnuthMin(i,j);
            // KnuthMin returns a value k in the range [r[i, j − 1], r[i + 1, j]]
            // minimizing c[i, k − 1] + c[k,j]
            c[i][j] = w[i][j] + c[i][k − 1] + c[k][j]; // Eq. (10.3)
            r[i][j] = k;
        }
} // end of obst
```

Program 10.1: Finding an optimal binary search tree

$$s = (1 + 1/n)u − 1, n \geq 1$$

2. Using algorithm *obst* (Program 10.1), compute w_{ij}, r_{ij}, and c_{ij}, $0 \leq i < j \leq 4$, for the identifier set (a_1, a_2, a_3, a_4) = (**else**, **private**, **return**, **template**), with $p_1 = 1/20$, $p_2 = 1/5$, $p_3 = 1/10$, $p_4 = 1/20$, $q_0 = 1/5$, $q_1 = 1/10$, $q_2 = 1/5$, $q_3 = 1/20$, and $q_4 = 1/20$. Using the r_{ij}'s, construct the optimal binary search tree.

3. (a) Complete function *obst* by providing the code for function *KnuthMin*.

   (b) Show that the computing time of algorithm *obst* is $O(n^2)$.

   (c) Write a C++ function *BST::construct* to construct the optimal binary search tree T_{0n} given the roots r_{ij}, $0 \leq i < j \leq n$. Show that this can be done in time $O(n)$.

4. Implement in C++ a BST constructor that constructs an optimal binary search tree, given the success and failure probability arrays $p[\ ]$ and $q[\ ]$, the array of identifiers $a[\ ]$, and the number of identifiers n. This constructor must utilize the helping member functions *obst* and *construct* of the previous exercise.

5. Since, often, only the approximate values of the p's and q's are known, it is perhaps just as meaningful to find a binary search tree that is nearly optimal (i.e., its cost, Eq. (10.1), is almost minimal for the given p's and q's). This exercise explores an $O(n \log n)$ algorithm that results in nearly optimal binary search trees. The search tree heuristic we shall study is

   Choose the root a_k such that $|w_{0,k-1} - w_{k,n}|$ is as small as possible. Repeat this procedure to find the left and right subtrees of a_k.

   (a) Using this heuristic obtain the resulting binary search tree for the data of Exercise 2. What is its cost?

   (b) Write a C++ algorithm implementing the above heuristic. The time complexity of your algorithm should be $O(n \log n)$.

   An analysis of the performance of this heuristic may be found in the paper by Melhorn (see the References and Selected Readings section).

10.2 AVL TREES

Dynamic tables may also be maintained as binary search trees. In Chapter 5, we saw how insertions and deletions can be performed on binary search trees. Figure 10.8 shows the binary search tree obtained by entering the months JANUARY to DECEMBER in that order into an initially empty binary search tree by using function *insert* (Program 5.19).

The maximum number of comparisons needed to search for any identifier in the tree of Figure 10.8 is six for NOVEMBER. The average number of comparisons is (1 for JANUARY + 2 each for FEBRUARY and MARCH + 3 each for APRIL, JUNE and MAY + $\cdots$ + 6 for NOVEMBER)/12 = 42/12 = 3.5. If the months are entered in the order JULY, FEBRUARY, MAY, AUGUST, DECEMBER, MARCH, OCTOBER, APRIL, JANUARY, JUNE, SEPTEMBER, NOVEMBER, then the tree of Figure 10.9 is obtained.

The tree of Figure 10.9 is well balanced and does not have any paths to a leaf node that are much longer than others. This is not true of the tree of Figure 10.8, which has six nodes on the path from the root to NOVEMBER and only two nodes on the path to APRIL. Moreover, during the construction of the tree of Figure 10.9, all intermediate trees obtained are also well balanced. The maximum number of identifier comparisons needed to find any identifier is now 4, and the average is $37/12 \approx 3.1$. If the months are entered in lexicographic order, instead, the tree degenerates to a chain as in Figure 10.10.

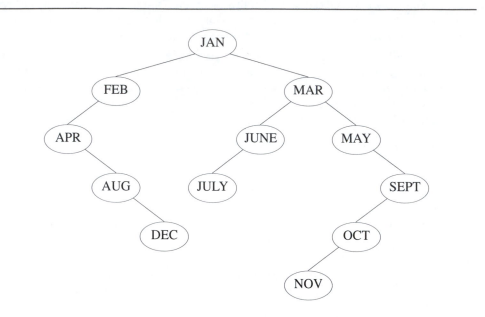

Figure 10.8: Binary search tree obtained for the months of the year

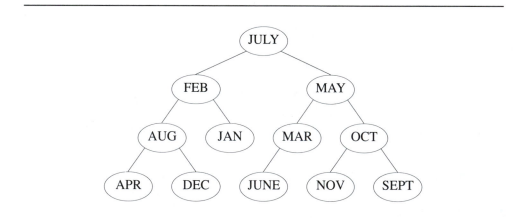

Figure 10.9: A balanced tree for the months of the year

The maximum search time is now 12 identifier comparisons, and the average is 6.5. Thus, in the worst case, binary search trees correspond to sequential searching in an ordered file. When the identifiers are entered in a random order, the tree tends to be balanced as in Figure 10.9. If all permutations are equally probable, then the average search and insertion time is O(log n) for an n-node binary search tree.

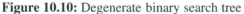

Figure 10.10: Degenerate binary search tree

From our earlier study of binary trees, we know that both the average and maximum search time will be minimized if the binary search tree is maintained as a complete binary tree at all times. However, since we are dealing with a dynamic situation, it is difficult to achieve this ideal without making the time required to insert an identifier very high. This is so because in some cases it would be necessary to restructure the whole tree to accommodate the new entry and at the same time have a complete binary search tree. It is, however, possible to keep the trees balanced to ensure both an average and worst-case retrieval time of O(log n) for a tree with n nodes. In this section, we study one method of growing balanced binary trees. These balanced trees will have satisfactory search and insertion time properties. Other ways to maintain balanced search trees are studied in later sections.

In 1962, Adelson-Velskii and Landis introduced a binary tree structure that is balanced with respect to the heights of subtrees. As a result of the balanced nature of this type of tree, dynamic retrievals can be performed in O(log n) time if the tree has n nodes in it. At the same time, a new identifier can be entered or deleted from such a tree in time O(log n). The resulting tree remains height-balanced. This tree structure is called an AVL tree. As with binary trees, it is natural to define AVL trees recursively.

Definition: An empty tree is height-balanced. If T is a nonempty binary tree with T_L and T_R as its left and right subtrees respectively, then T is *height-balanced* iff (1) T_L and T_R are height-balanced and (2) $| h_L - h_R | \leq 1$ where h_L and h_R are the heights of T_L and T_R, respectively. $\square$

The definition of a height-balanced binary tree requires that every subtree also be height-balanced. The binary tree of Figure 10.8 is not height-balanced, since the height of the left subtree of the tree with root APRIL is 0 and that of the right subtree is 2. The tree of Figure 10.9 is height-balanced while that of Figure 10.10 is not. To illustrate the processes involved in maintaining a height-balanced binary search tree, let us try to construct such a tree for the months of the year. This time let us assume that the insertions are made in the following order: MARCH, MAY, NOVEMBER, AUGUST, APRIL, JANUARY, DECEMBER, JULY, FEBRUARY, JUNE, OCTOBER, SEPTEMBER. Figure 10.11 shows the tree as it grows and the restructuring involved in keeping the tree balanced. The numbers above each node represent the difference in heights between the left and right subtrees of that node. This number is referred to as the balance factor of the node.

Definition: The *balance factor*, $BF(T)$, of a node T in a binary tree is defined to be $h_L - h_R$, where h_L and h_R, respectively, are the heights of the left and right subtrees of T. For any node T in an AVL tree, $BF(T) = -1, 0,$ or 1. $\square$

Inserting MARCH and MAY results in the binary search trees (a) and (b) of Figure 10.11. When NOVEMBER is inserted into the tree, the height of the right subtree of MARCH becomes 2, whereas that of the left subtree is 0. The tree has become unbalanced. To rebalance the tree, a rotation is performed. MARCH is made the left child of MAY, and MAY becomes the root (Figure 10.11(c)). The introduction of AUGUST leaves the tree balanced (Figure 10.11(d)).

The next insertion, APRIL, causes the tree to become unbalanced again. To rebalance the tree, another rotation is performed. This time, it is a clockwise rotation. MARCH is made the right child of AUGUST, and AUGUST becomes the root of the subtree (Figure 10.11(e)). Note that both of the previous rotations were carried out with respect to the closest parent of the new node that had a balance factor of ±2. The inser-

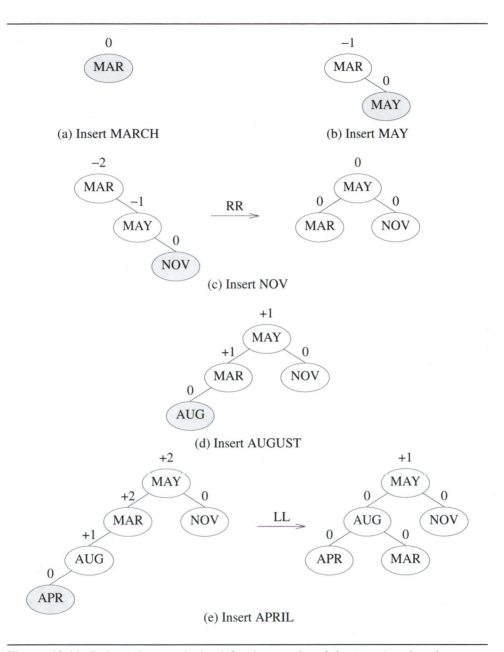

Figure 10.11: Balanced trees obtained for the months of the year (continued on next page)

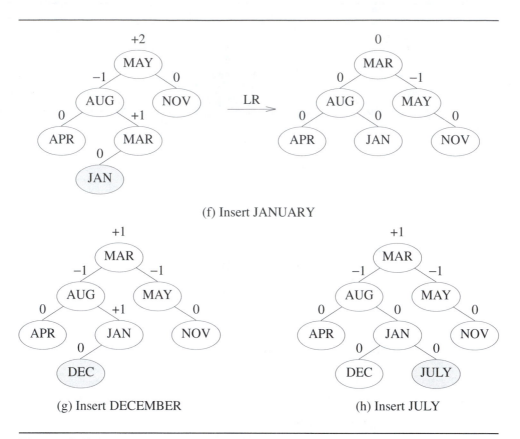

(f) Insert JANUARY

(g) Insert DECEMBER   (h) Insert JULY

Figure 10.11: Balanced trees obtained for the months of the year (continued on next page)

tion of JANUARY results in an unbalanced tree. This time, however, the rotation involved is somewhat more complex than in the earlier situations. The common point, however, is that the rotation is still carried out with respect to the nearest parent of JANUARY with a balance factor ± 2. MARCH becomes the new root. AUGUST, together with its left subtree, becomes the left subtree of MARCH. The left subtree of MARCH becomes the right subtree of AUGUST. MAY and its right subtree, which have identifiers greater than MARCH, become the right subtree of MARCH. (If MARCH had had a nonempty right subtree, this could have become the left subtree of MAY, since all identifiers would have been less than MAY.)

Inserting DECEMBER and JULY necessitates no rebalancing. When FEBRUARY is inserted, the tree becomes unbalanced again. The rebalancing process is very similar to that used when JANUARY was inserted. The nearest parent with balance fac-

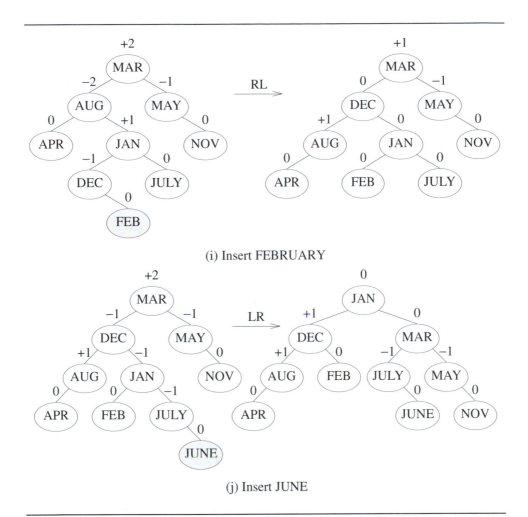

(i) Insert FEBRUARY

(j) Insert JUNE

Figure 10.11: Balanced trees obtained for the months of the year (continued on next page)

tor ±2 is AUGUST. DECEMBER becomes the new root of that subtree. AUGUST, with its left subtree, becomes the left subtree. JANUARY, with its right subtree, becomes the right subtree of DECEMBER; FEBRUARY becomes the left subtree of JANUARY. (If DECEMBER had had a left subtree, it would have become the right subtree of AUGUST.) The insertion of JUNE requires the same rebalancing as in Figure 10.11(f). The rebalancing following the insertion of OCTOBER is identical to that following the insertion of NOVEMBER. Inserting SEPTEMBER leaves the tree balanced.

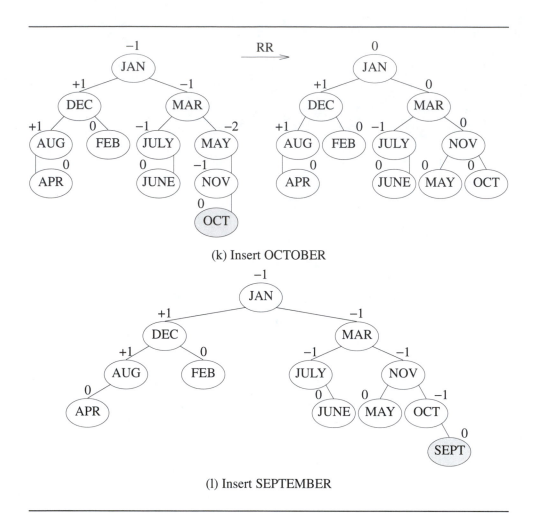

(k) Insert OCTOBER

(l) Insert SEPTEMBER

Figure 10.11: Balanced trees obtained for the months of the year

In the preceding example we saw that the addition of a node to a balanced binary search tree could unbalance it. The rebalancing was carried out using four different kinds of rotations: LL, RR, LR, and RL (Figure 10.11 (e), (c), (f), and (i), respectively). LL and RR are symmetric, as are LR and RL. These rotations are characterized by the nearest ancestor, A, of the inserted node, Y, whose balance factor becomes ±2. The following characterization of rotation types is obtained:

LL: new node Y is inserted in the left subtree of the left subtree of A

LR: Y is inserted in the right subtree of the left subtree of A

RR: Y is inserted in the right subtree of the right subtree of A

RL: Y is inserted in the left subtree of the right subtree of A

Figure 10.12 shows the LL, LR, and RR rotations in terms of abstract binary trees. The RL rotations are similar to the LR rotations. The root node in each of the trees of the figures represents the nearest ancestor whose balance factor has become ± 2 as a result of the insertion. A moment's reflection will show that if a height-balanced binary tree becomes unbalanced as a result of an insertion, then these are the only four cases possible for rebalancing. In the example of Figure 10.11 and in the rotations of Figure 10.12, notice that the height of the subtree involved in the rotation is the same after rebalancing as it was before the insertion. This means that once the rebalancing has been carried out on the subtree in question, examining the remaining tree is unneccessary. The only nodes whose balance factors can change are those in the subtree that is rotated.

To carry out the rotations of Figure 10.12, it is necessary to locate the node A around which the rotation is to be performed. As remarked earlier, this is the nearest ancestor of the newly inserted node whose balance factor becomes ± 2. For a node's balance factor to become ± 2, its balance factor must have been ± 1 before the insertion. Therefore, before the insertion, the balance factors of all nodes on the path from A to the new insertion point must have been 0. With this information, the node A is readily determined to be the nearest ancestor of the new node having a balance factor ± 1 before insertion. To complete the rotations, the address of F, the parent of A, is also needed. The changes in the balance factors of the relevant nodes are shown in Figure 10.12. Knowing F and A, these changes can be carried out easily.

What happens when the insertion of a node does not result in an unbalanced tree (see Figure 10.11 (a), (b), (d), (g), (h), and (l))? Although no restructuring of the tree is needed, the balance factors of several nodes change. Let A be the nearest ancestor of the new node with balance factor ± 1 before insertion. If, as a result of the insertion, the tree did not get unbalanced, even though some path length increased by 1, it must be that the new balance factor of A is 0. If there is no ancestor A with a balance factor ± 1 (as in Figure 10.11 (a), (b), (d), (g), and (l)), let A be the root. The balance factors of nodes from A to the parent of the new node will change to ± 1 (see Figure 10.11 (h); $A =$ JANUARY). Note that in both cases, the procedure to determine A is the same as when rebalancing is needed. The remaining details of the insertion-rebalancing process are spelled out in algorithm $Avl::Insert$ (Program 10.2). The class definitions in use are

template <class *KeyType***> class** *AVL***;**

template <class *KeyType***>**
class *AvlNode* **{**
friend class *AVL<KeyType>***;**
private:
    *Element<KeyType> data***;**
    *AvlNode *LeftChild, *RightChild***;**
    int *bf***;**
};

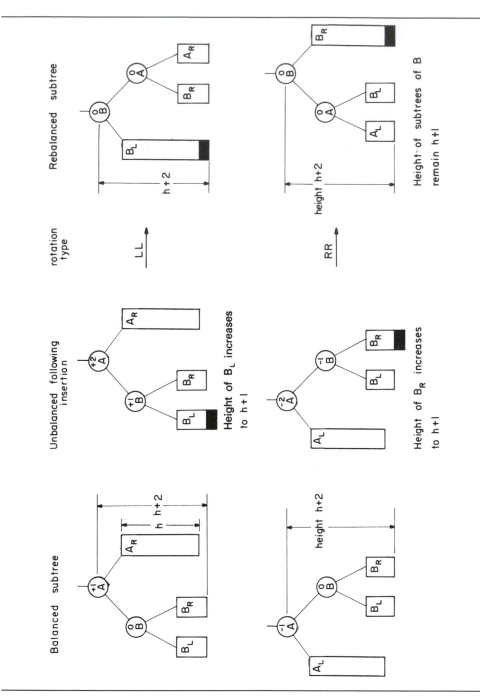

Figure 10.12: Rebalancing rotations (continued on next page)

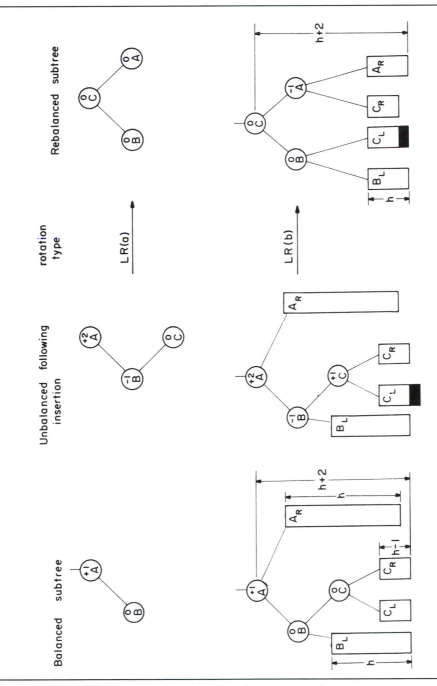

Figure 10.12: Rebalancing rotations (continued on next page)

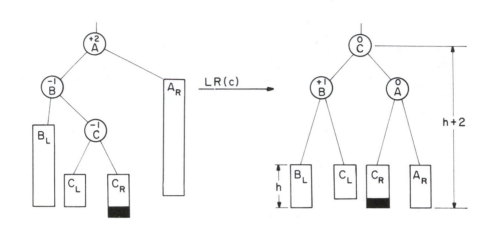

Figure 10.12: Rebalancing rotations

template <class *KeyType***>**
class AVL {
public:
    AVL(AvlNode<KeyType> *init = 0) : root (init) {};
    *Boolean Insert(**const** Element<KeyType>&);*
    *Boolean Delete(**const** Element<KeyType>&);*
    AvlNode<KeyType> Search(**const** Element<KeyType>&);*

private:
    AvlNode<KeyType> *root;
};

---

template <class *KeyType***>**
*Boolean AVL<KeyType>::Insert(**const** Element<KeyType>& x)*
// The identifier *x* is inserted into the AVL tree.
AvlNode<KeyType> *a, *b, *c, *f, *p, *q, *y, *clchild, *crchild;
Boolean Found, Unbalanced;
int *d;*
{
  if (!*root*) { *//* special case: empty tree
    y = **new** *AvlNode<KeyType>; y→data = x; root = y; root→bf* = 0;
    root→LeftChild = root→RightChild = 0; **return** TRUE;
  }

```
// phase 1: Locate insertion point for x. a keeps track of the most recent node with
// balance factor ±1, and f is the parent of a. q follows p through the tree.
f = 0; a = p = root; q = 0; Found = FALSE;
while(p && !Found) { // search for insertion point for x
    if (p→bf) { a = p; f = q;}
    if (x.key < p→data.key) { q = p; p = p→LeftChild;} // take left branch
    else if (x.key > p→data.key) { q = p; p = p→RightChild;}
        else {y = p; Found = TRUE;}
} // end of while
if (!Found) {
    //phase 2: Insert and rebalance. x is not in the tree and
    // may be inserted as the appropriate child of q.
    y = new AvlNode<KeyType>; y→data = x;
    y→LeftChild = y→RightChild = 0; y→bf = 0;
    if (x.key < q→data.key) q→LeftChild = y; // insert as left child
    else q→RightChild = y; // insert as right child
    //Adjust balance factors of nodes on path from a to q. Note that by the definition
    // of a, all nodes on this path must have balance factors of 0 and so will change to
    // ±1.  d = +1 implies that x is inserted in the left subtree of a. d = −1 implies
    // that x is inserted in the right subtree of a.
    if (x.key > a→data.key) {
        p = a→RightChild; b = p; d = −1;
    }
    else {
        p = a→LeftChild; b = p; d = 1;
    }
    while (p!= y)
        if (x.key > p→data.key) { // height of right increases by 1
            p→bf = −1; p = p→RightChild;
        }
        else { // height of left increases by 1
            p→bf = 1; p = p→LeftChild;
        }
    //Is tree unbalanced?
    Unbalanced = TRUE;
    if ( !(a→bf) || !(a→bf + d) ) { // tree still balanced
        a→bf += d; Unbalanced = FALSE;
    }
    if (Unbalanced) { // tree unbalanced, determine rotation type
        if (d == 1) { // left imbalance
            if (b→bf == 1) { // rotation type LL
                a→LeftChild = b→RightChild;
                b→RightChild = a; a→bf = 0; b→bf = 0;
            }
```

```
        else { // rotation type LR
            c = b→RightChild;
            b→RightChild = c→LeftChild;
            a→LeftChild = c→RightChild;
            c→LeftChild = b;
            c→RightChild = a;
            switch (c→bf) {
                case 1: // LR(b)
                    a→bf = −1; b→bf = 0;
                    break;
                case −1: // LR(c)
                    b→bf = 1; a→bf = 0;
                    break;
                case 0:  // LR(a)
                    b→bf = 0; a→bf = 0;
                    break;
            }
            c→bf = 0; b = c; // b is the new root
        } // end of LR
    } // end of left imbalance
    else { // right imbalance: this is symmetric to left imbalance
    }
    // Subtree with root b has been rebalanced and is the new subtree.
    if (!f) root = b;
    else if (a == f→LeftChild) f→LeftChild = b;
        else if (a == f→RightChild) f→RightChild = b;
    } // end of if Unbalanced
    return TRUE;
  } // end of if(!found)
  return FALSE;
}// end of AVL::Insert
```

Program 10.2: Insertion into an AVL tree

To really understand the insertion algorithm, you should try it out on the example of Figure 10.11. An analysis of the algorithm reveals that if h is the height of the tree before insertion, then the time to insert a new identifier is $O(h)$. This is the same as for unbalanced binary search trees, although the overhead is significantly greater now. In the case of binary search trees, however, if there were n nodes in the tree, then h could, in the worst case, be n (Figure 10.10), and the worst case insertion time would be $O(n)$. In the case of AVL trees, however, h can be at most $O(\log n)$, so the worst-case insertion time is $O(\log n)$. To see this, let N_h be the minimum number of nodes in a height-balanced tree of height h. In the worst case, the height of one of the subtrees will be $h - 1$ and that of the other $h - 2$. Both of these subtrees are also height balanced.

Hence, $N_h = N_{h-1} + N_{h-2} + 1$, and $N_0 = 0$, $N_1 = 1$ and $N_2 = 2$. Note the similarity between this recursive definition for N_h and that for the Fibonacci numbers $F_n = F_{n-1} + F_{n-2}$, $F_0 = 0$, and $F_1 = 1$. In fact, we can show that $N_h = F_{h+2} - 1$ for $h \geq 0$ (see Exercise 2). From Fibonacci number theory it is known that $F_h \approx \phi^h / \sqrt{5}$, where $\phi = (1 + \sqrt{5})/2$. Hence, $N_h \approx \phi^{h+2} / \sqrt{5} - 1$. This means that if there are n nodes in the tree, then its height, h, is at most $\log_\phi (\sqrt{5}(n + 1)) - 2$. The worst-case insertion time for a height-balanced tree with n nodes is, therefore, O(log n).

The exercises show that it is possible to find and delete a node with identifier X and to find and delete the kth node from a height-balanced tree in O(log n) time. Results of an empirical study of deletion in height-balanced trees may be found in the paper by Karlton et al. (see the References and Selected Readings section). Their study indicates that a random insertion requires no rebalancing, a rebalancing rotation of type LL or RR, and a rebalancing rotation of type LR and RL, with probabilities 0.5349, 0.2327, and 0.2324, respectively. Figure 10.13 compares the worst-case times of certain operations on sorted sequential lists, sorted linked lists, and AVL trees.

Operation	Sequential list	Linked list	AVL tree
Search for x	O(log n)	O(n)	O(log n)
Search for kth item	O(1)	O(k)	O(log n)
Delete x	O(n)	O(1)[1]	O(log n)
Delete kth item	O($n - k$)	O(k)	O(log n)
Insert x	O(n)	O(1)[2]	O(log n)
Output in order	O(n)	O(n)	O(n)

1. Doubly linked list and position of x known
2. Position for insertion known

Figure 10.13: Comparison of various structures

EXERCISES

1. (a) Convince yourself that Figure 10.12 takes care of all the possible situations that may arise when a height-balanced binary tree becomes unbalanced as a result of an insertion. Alternately, come up with an example that is not covered by any of the cases in this figure.

   (b) Complete Figure 10.12 by drawing the tree configurations for the rotations RL (a), (b), and (c).

2. Prove by induction that the minimum number of nodes in an AVL tree of height h is $N_h = F_{h+2} - 1$, $h \geq 0$.

3. Complete algorithm *Avl::Insert* (Program 10.2) by filling in the steps needed to re-balance the tree if the imbalance is of type RL.

4. Obtain the height-balanced trees corresponding to those of Figure 10.11 using algorithm *Avl::Insert*, starting with an empty tree, on the following sequence of insertions: DECEMBER, JANUARY, APRIL, MARCH, JULY, AUGUST, OCTOBER, FEBRUARY, NOVEMBER, MAY, JUNE. Label the rotations according to type.

5. Assume that each node in an AVL tree has the data member *lsize*. For any node, a, $a \rightarrow lsize$ is the number of nodes in its left subtree plus one. Write an algorithm *Avl::Find(k)* to locate the *k*th smallest identifier in the tree. Show that this can be done in O(log *n*) time if there are *n* nodes in the tree.

6. Rewrite algorithm *Avl::Insert* with the added assumption that each node has an *lsize* data member as in Exercise 5. Show that the insertion time remains O(log *n*).

7. Write an algorithm to list the nodes of an AVL tree in ascending order of *data.key* data members. Show that this can be done in O(*n*) time if the tree has *n* nodes.

8. Write an algorithm to delete the node with key *x* from an AVL tree. The resulting tree should be restructured if necessary. Show that the time required for this is O(log *n*) when there are *n* nodes in the tree. [Hint: If *x* is not in a leaf, then replace *x* by the largest value in its left subtree or the smallest value in its right subtree. Continue until the deletion propagates to a leaf. Deletion from a leaf can be handled using the reverse of the transformations used for insertion.]

9. Do Exercise 8 for the case when each node has an *lsize* data member and the *k*th smallest key is to be deleted.

10. Write an algorithm to merge the nodes of the two AVL trees to obtain a new AVL tree. What is the computing time of your algorithm?

11. Write an algorithm to split an AVL tree into two AVL trees such that all identifiers in one tree are $\leq x$, and all those in the other are $> x$.

12. Complete Figure 10.13 by adding a column for hashing.

13. For a fixed k, $k \geq 1$, we define a height-balanced tree $HB(k)$ as below:

    Definition: An empty binary tree is an $HB(k)$ tree. If T is a nonempty binary tree with T_L and T_R as its left and right subtrees, then T is $HB(k)$ iff (a) T_L and T_R are $HB(k)$ and (b) $|h_L - h_R| \leq k$, where h_L and h_R are the heights of T_L and T_R, respectively. □

    (a) Obtain the rebalancing transformations for $HB(2)$.

    (b) Write an insertion algorithm for $HB(2)$ trees.

10.3   2-3 TREES

10.3.1   Definition and Properties

By considering search trees of degree greater than 2, we can arrive at tree structures for which the insertion and deletion algorithms are simpler than those for AVL trees. Yet these algorithms have O(log n) complexity. In this section, we shall look at a special case of B-trees. General B-trees are studied in a later section. The special case we shall consider here is called a 2-3 tree. This name reflects the fact that each internal node in a 2-3 tree has degree two or three. A degree-two node is called a 2-*node*; a degree-three node is called a 3-*node*.

Definition: A *2-3 tree* is a search tree that either is empty or satisfies the following properties:

(1)   Each internal node is a 2-node or a 3-node. A 2-node has one element; a 3-node has two elements.

(2)   Let *LeftChild* and *MiddleChild* denote the children of a 2-node. Let *dataL* be the element in this node, and let *dataL.key* be its key. All elements in the 2-3 subtree with root *LeftChild* have key less than *dataL.key*, whereas all elements in the 2-3 subtree with root *MiddleChild* have key greater than *dataL.key*.

(3)   Let *LeftChild*, *MiddleChild*, and *RightChild* denote the children of a 3-node. Let *dataL* and *dataR* be the two elements in this node. Then, *dataL.key* < *dataR.key*; all keys in the 2-3 subtree with root *LeftChild* are less than *dataL.key*; all keys in the 2-3 subtree with root *MiddleChild* are less than *dataR.key* and greater than *dataL.key*; and all keys in the 2-3 subtree with root *RightChild* are greater than *dataR.key*.

(4)   All external nodes are at the same level. □

An example of a 2-3 tree is given in Figure 10.14. As in the case of leftist trees, external nodes are introduced only to make it easier to define and talk about 2-3 trees. External nodes are not physically represented inside a computer. Rather, the corresponding child data member of the parent of each external node is set to 0.

The number of elements in a 2-3 tree with height h (i.e., the external nodes are at level $h+1$) is between $2^h - 1$ and $3^h - 1$. To see this, note that the first bound applies when each internal node is a 2-node, and the second bound applies when each internal node is a 3-node. These two cases represent the two extremes. A 2-3 tree with some 2-nodes and some 3-nodes will have a number of elements somewhere between these two bounds. Hence, the height of a 2-3 tree with n elements is between $\lceil \log_3(n+1) \rceil$ and $\lceil \log_2(n+1) \rceil$.

A 2-3 tree may be represented using the following class definitions:

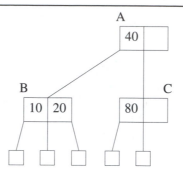

Figure 10.14: Example of a 2-3 tree

template <class *KeyType*> **class** *Two3*; // forward declaration

template <class *KeyType*>
class *Two3Node* {
friend class *Two3<KeyType>*;
private:
     Element<KeyType> dataL, dataR;
     *Two3Node *LeftChild, *MiddleChild, *RightChild* ;
};

template <class *KeyType*>
class *Two3* {
public:
     *Two3(KeyType max, Two3Node<KeyType> *init = 0)*
      : **MAXKEY***(max), root(init)* {}; // constructor
     *Boolean Insert***(const** *Element<KeyType>&*);
     *Boolean Delete***(const** *Element<KeyType>&*);
     Two3Node<KeyType> Search***(const** *Element<KeyType>&*);

private:
     *Two3Node<KeyType> *root*;
     KeyType MAXKEY;
};

We shall assume that no element has key MAXKEY and adopt the convention that a 2-node has *dataR. key* = MAXKEY. Its single element is kept in *dataL*, and *LeftChild* and *MiddleChild* point to its two children. Its *RightChild* data member may be assigned any arbitrary value.

10.3.2 Searching a 2-3 Tree

The search algorithm for binary search trees is easily extended to obtain the search function *Two3::Search* (Program 10.3), which searches a 2-3 tree for a node that contains an element with key x. The search function uses a function *compare* that compares a key x with the keys in a given node p. It returns the value 1, 2, 3, or 4, respectively, depending upon whether x is less than the first key, between the first and second keys, greater than the second key, or equal to one of the keys in node p. The number of iterations of the **for** loop is bounded by the height of the 2-3 tree. Hence, if the tree has n nodes, the complexity of *Two3::Search* is O(log n).

```
template <class KeyType>
Two3Node<KeyType>* Two3<KeyType>::Search(const Element<KeyType>& x)
//Search the 2-3 tree for an element x.  If the element is not in the tree, then
// return 0.  Otherwise, return a pointer to the node that contains this element.
{
    for (Two3Node<KeyType> *p = root; p;)
        switch(p→compare(x)) {
            case 1: p = p→LeftChild; break;
            case 2: p = p→MiddleChild; break;
            case 3: p = p→RightChild; break;
            case 4: return p;// x is one of the keys in p
        } // end of switch and for
} // end of Search
```

Program 10.3: Searching a 2-3 tree

10.3.3 Insertion into a 2-3 Tree

Insertion into a 2-3 tree is fairly simple. Consider inserting an element with key 70 into the 2-3 tree of Figure 10.14. First we search for this key. If the key is already in the tree, then the insertion fails, as all keys in a 2-3 tree are distinct. Since 70 is not in our example 2-3 tree, it may be inserted. For this, we need to know the leaf node encountered during the search for 70. Note that whenever we search for a key that is not in the 2-3 tree, the search encounters a unique leaf node. The leaf node encountered during the search for 70 is the node C, with key 80. Since this node has only one element, the new element may be inserted here. The resulting 2-3 tree is shown in Figure 10.15(a).

Next, consider inserting an element x with key 30. This time the search encounters the leaf node B. Since B is a 3-node, it is necessary to create a new node, D. D will contain the element that has the larger key of the two elements currently in B and x.

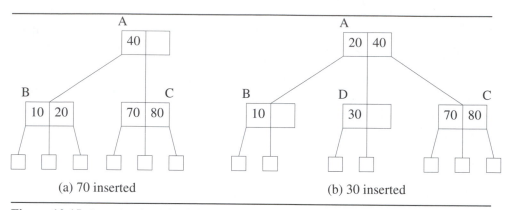

(a) 70 inserted   (b) 30 inserted

Figure 10.15: Insertion into the 2-3 tree of Figure 10.14

The element with the smallest key will be in B, and the element with the median key, together with a pointer to D, will be inserted into the parent A of B. The resulting 2-3 tree is shown in Figure 10.15(b).

As a final example, consider the insertion of an element x with key 60 into the 2-3 tree of Figure 10.15(b). The leaf node encountered during the search for 60 is node C. Since C is a 3-node, a new node, E, is created. Node E contains the element with the largest key (80). Node C contains the element with the smallest key (60). The element with the median key (70), together with a pointer to the new node, E, is to be inserted into the parent A of C. Again, since A is a 3-node, a new node, F, containing the element with the largest key among {20, 40, 70} is created. As before, A contains the element with the smallest key. B and D remain the left and middle children of A, respectively, and C and E become these children of F. If A had a parent, then the element with the median key 40 and a pointer to the new node, F, would be inserted into this parent node. Since A does not have a parent, we create a new root, G, for the 2-3 tree. Node G contains the element with key 40, together with a left-child pointer to A and a middle-child pointer to F. The new 2-3 tree is as shown in Figure 10.16.

Each time an attempt is made to add an element into a 3-node p, a new node q is created. This is referred to as a node *split*. We say that node p is split into p, q, and the median element. Putting the ideas in the preceding discussion together, we get the insertion function of Program 10.4.

This function makes use of several functions whose development is left as an exercise. We specify the task performed by each below (The template parameter *<KeyType>* is omitted for simplicity):

(1)   **void** *Two3::NewRoot*(**const** *Element& x, Two3Node *a*): This is invoked when the root of the 2-3 tree is to change. The single element x is inserted into the new root, while a is made its *MiddleChild*. The old root becomes the *LeftChild* of the new root.

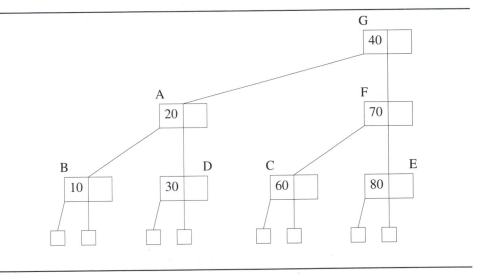

Figure 10.16: Insertion of 60 into the 2-3 tree of Figure 10.15(b)

(2) *Two3Node* Two3::FindNode*(**const** *Element& x*): This is a modified version of *Two3::Search* (Program 10.3). It searches a nonempty 2-3 tree for the presence of an element with key *x.key*. If this key is present, then it returns 0. Otherwise, it returns a pointer to the leaf node encountered in the search. Function *Two3::Insert* uses the variable *p* to store the pointer returned by *FindNode*. *FindNode* also creates a data structure that enables us to return from *p* to *root*. This data structure could be a list of the nodes on the path from *root* to *p*. Such a data structure is needed, as following a node split, it is necessary to access the parent of the node that was split.

(3) **void** *InsertionError*(): When an attempt to insert an element whose key corresponds to that of an element already in the 2-3 tree is made, an insertion error occurs. This function signals an error.

(4) **void** *Two3Node::PutIn*(**const** *Element& x, Two3Node *a*): This function is used to insert an element *x* into a node (**this**) that has exactly one element in it. The subtree *a* is to be placed immediately to the right of *x*. So, if *x* becomes *dataL*, then *a* becomes *MiddleChild*, and the previous values of *dataL* and *MiddleChild* move to *dataR* and *RightChild*, respectively. If *x* becomes *dataR*, then *a* becomes *RightChild*.

(5) *Element& Two3::Split*(*Two3Node* p, Element& x, Two3Node *olda, Two3Node *a*): This operates on a *Two3Node* (*p*) that initially contains two elements as follows: The newly created, empty node pointed at by *a* will contain the element with the largest key from among the two elements initially in *p* and the element *x*.

```
template <class KeyType>
Boolean Two3<KeyType>::Insert(const Element<KeyType>& y)
// Insert the element y into the 2-3 tree only if it does not already contain an element
// with the same key.
{
    Two3Node<KeyType> *p;
    Element<KeyType> x = y;
    if (x.key >= MAXKEY) return FALSE; // invalid key
    if (!root) { NewRoot(x, 0); return TRUE;} // empty 2-3 tree
    if (!(p = FindNode(x))) {InsertionError(); return FALSE;}// key already in 2-3 tree
    for (Two3Node<KeyType> *a = 0 ; ;)
        if (p→dataR.key == MAXKEY) {// p is a 2-node
            p→PutIn(x, a);
            return TRUE ;
        }
        else { //p is a 3-node
            Two3Node<KeyType> *olda = a;
            a = new(Two3Node<KeyType>);
            x = Split( p, x, olda, a);
            if (root == p) {// root has been split
                NewRoot(x, a);
                return TRUE;
            }
            else p = p→parent();
        } // end of p is a 3-node and for loop
}// end of Insert
```

Program 10.4: Insertion into a 2-3 tree

The element with the smallest key will be the only element left in p. The three original children pointers of p and the pointer *olda* will occupy the four children data members that need to be defined in p and a. The function returns the element with the median key.

In *Insert*, x denotes the element to be inserted into node p, and a denotes the node that was newly created at the last iteration of the **for** loop. As for the complexity analysis, we see that the total time taken is proportional to the height of the 2-3 tree. Hence, insertion into a 2-3 tree with n elements takes O($\log n$) time.

10.3.4   Deletion from a 2-3 Tree

Deletion from a 2-3 tree is conceptually no harder than insertion. If we are deleting an element that is not in a leaf node, then we transform this into a deletion from a leaf node by replacing the deleted element with a suitable element that is in a leaf. For example, if we are to delete the element with key 50 that is in the root of Figure 10.17(a), then this element may be replaced by either the element with key 20 or the element with key 60. Both are in leaf nodes. In a general situation, we may use either the element with the largest key in the subtree on the left or the element with the smallest key in the subtree on the right of the element being deleted.

Henceforth, we shall consider only the case of deletion from a leaf node. Let us begin with the tree of Figure 10.17(a). To delete the element with key 70, we must merely set $dataR.key$ = MAXKEY in node C. The result is shown in Figure 10.17(b). To delete the element with key 90 from the 2-3 tree of Figure 10.17(b), we need to shift $dataR$ to $dataL$ and set $dataR.key$ = MAXKEY in node D. This results in the 2-3 tree of Figure 10.17(c).

Next consider the deletion of the element with key 60. This leaves node C empty. Since the left sibling, B, of C is a 3-node, we can move the element with key 20 into the $dataL$ position of the parent node A and move the element with key 50 from the parent to node C. After setting $dataR.key$ = MAXKEY in B, the 2-3 tree takes the form shown in Figure 10.17(d). This data movement operation is called a *rotation*. When the element with key 95 is deleted, node D becomes empty. The rotation performed when the 60 was deleted is not possible now, as the left sibling, C, is a 2-node. This time we move the 80 into the left sibling, C, and delete node D. We shall refer to this operation as a *combine*. In a combine, one node is deleted, whereas in a rotation, no nodes are deleted. The deletion of 95 results in the 2-3 tree of Figure 10.17(e). Deleting the element with key 50 from this tree results in the 2-3 tree of Figure 10.17(f). Now consider deleting the element with key 10 from this tree. Node B becomes empty. At this time, we examine B's right sibling, C, to see if it is a 2-node or a 3-node. If it is a 3-node, we can perform a rotation similar to that done during the deletion of 60. If it is a 2-node, then a combine is performed. Since C is a 2-node, we proceed in a manner similar to the deletion of 95. This time the elements with keys 20 and 80 are moved into B, and node C is deleted. This, however, causes the parent node A to have no elements. If the parent had not been a root, we would examine its left or right sibling, as we did when nodes C (deletion of 60) and D (deletion of 95) became empty. Since A is the root, it is simply deleted, and B becomes the new root (Figure 10.17(g)).

The steps involved in deletion from a leaf node p of a 2-3 tree are summarized in Program 10.5.

For a rotation, there are three cases, depending on whether p is the left, middle, or right child of its parent, r. If p is the left child of r, then let q be the right sibling of p. Otherwise, let q be the left sibling of p. Note that regardless of whether r is a 2-node or a 3-node, q is well defined. The three rotation cases are shown pictorially in Figure 10.18.

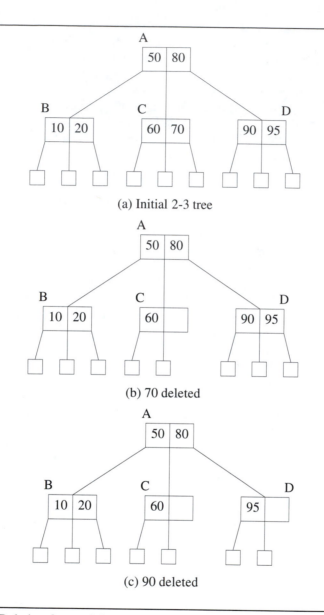

(a) Initial 2-3 tree

(b) 70 deleted

(c) 90 deleted

Figure 10.17: Deletion from a 2-3 tree (continued on next page)

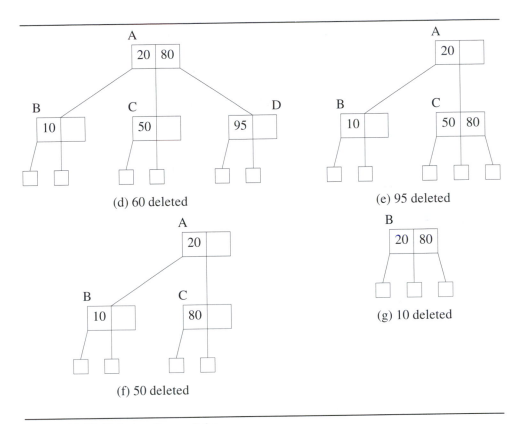

Figure 10.17: Deletion from a 2-3 tree

A "?" denotes a situation in which the content of the data member is irrelevant. a, b, c, and d denote the children (i.e., roots of subtrees) of nodes.

Figure 10.19 shows the two cases for a combine when p is the left child of r. We leave it as an exercise to obtain the figures for the cases when p is a middle child and when p is a right child.

The refinement of Step 1 of Program 10.5 into C++ code is shown in Program 10.6. The codes for rotation and combine for the case when p is the left child of r are given in Programs 10.7 and 10.8, respectively. We leave the development of the complete deletion function as an exercise.

Analysis of 2-3 tree deletion: It should be evident that an individual rotation or combine takes $O(1)$ time. If a rotation is performed, deletion is completed. If a combine is performed, p moves up one level in the 2-3 tree. Hence, the number of combines that can be performed during a deletion cannot exceed the height of the 2-3 tree. Consequently, deletion from a 2-3 tree with n elements takes $O(\log n)$ time. $\square$

Step 1: Modify node p as necessary to reflect its status after the desired element has been deleted.

Step 2: **for** (; p has zero elements && $p \mathrel{!=} root$; $p = r$)
       {
            let r be the parent of p, and let q be the left or right sibling of p (as appropriate);
            if (q is a 3-node) perform a rotation
            else perform a combine;
       }

Step 3: If p has zero elements, then p must be the root. The left child of p becomes the new root, and node p is deleted.

Program 10.5: Steps in deletion from a leaf of a 2-3 tree

EXERCISES

1. Write the function *compare* used in Program 10.3.

2. (a) Develop the functions *FindNode*, *NewRoot*, *PutIn*, and *split* used by function *Two3::Insert* (Program 10.4). Put these together and test the correctness of function *Two3::Insert*.

   (b) Use random insertions and measure the height of the resulting 2-3 trees with $n = 100$, 1000, and 10,000 elements.

3. Complete Figure 10.19 by providing the figures for the case in which p is a middle child and p is a right child.

4. Develop a complete C++ function to delete the element with key x from a 2-3 tree. Test this function using at least five different 2-3 trees of your choice. For each of these perform at least six successive deletions.

5. Write a function to perform the *ThreeWayJoin* operation defined in Section 5.7.5 for binary search trees. This time, assume that A and B are 2-3 trees and that the result of the join is also a 2-3 tree. You may assume that the heights of the two input 2-3 trees are known. You should be able to perform the join in $O(\mid height\,(A) - height\,(B)\mid)$ time. (Hint: If $height\,(A) > height\,(B)$, follow the rightmost path from A to a node Y such that $height\,(Y) = height\,(B) + 1$; now attempt to insert x, together with a pointer to B, into node Y.)

6. Do the previous exercise for the case of a *TwoWayJoin* (see Section 5.7.5).

7. Write a function to perform the *Split* operation defined in Section 5.7.5 for binary search trees. This time, assume that A is a 2-3 tree and that the resulting trees B and C are also 2-3 trees. Can you do this operation in $O(height\,(A))$ time?

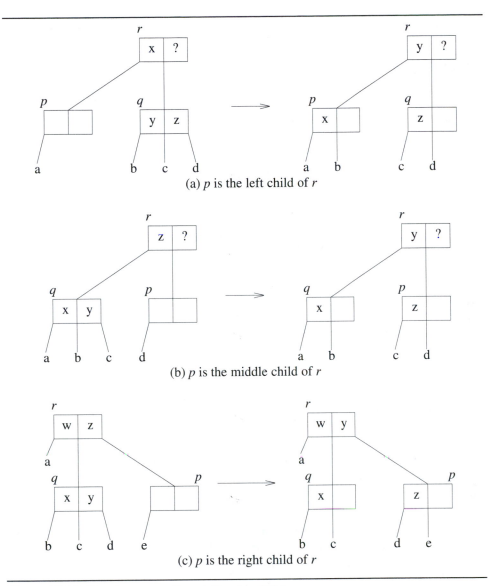

(a) p is the left child of r

(b) p is the middle child of r

(c) p is the right child of r

Figure 10.18: The three cases for rotation in a 2-3 tree

8. Any algorithm that merges two sorted lists of size n and m, respectively, must make at least $n + m - 1$ comparisons in the worst case. What implications does this result have on the time complexity of a comparison-based algorithm that combines two 2-3 trees that have n and m elements, respectively?

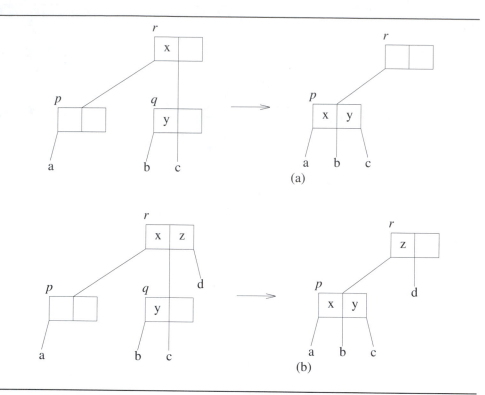

Figure 10.19: Combining in a 2-3 tree when *p* is the left child of *r*

9. In Chapter 7, we showed that every comparison-based algorithm to sort *n* elements must make O(*n* log *n*) comparisons in the worst case. What implications does this result have on the complexity of initializing a 2-3 tree with *n* elements?

10. Consider a variation of a 2-3 tree in which elements are kept only in leaf nodes. Each leaf has exactly one element. The remaining nodes are 2-nodes or 3-nodes. Each such node keeps only the values *largeA* = largest key in any leaf in its left subtree and *largeB* = largest key in any leaf in its middle subtree. As before, all external nodes are at the same level.

    (a)   Define two node structures such that one is suitable to represent a leaf node and the other to represent a nonleaf node.

    (b)   Write a function to search a 2-3 tree represented in this way.

    (c)   Write a function to insert an element *x* into this tree.

    (d)   Write a deletion function for such a 2-3 tree.

    (e)   Show that each of the above operations can be performed in O(log *n*) time, where *n* is the number of elements (i.e., leaf nodes) in the tree.

```
template<class KeyType>
Two3<KeyType>::DeleteKey (Two3Node<KeyType>* p, const Element<KeyType>& x)
//Key x.key is to be deleted from the leaf node p.
{
   if ( x.key == p→dataL.key) // delete first element
      if (p →dataR.key != MAXKEY )
      { // p is a 3-node
         p →dataL = p →dataR; p →dataR.key =  MAXKEY;
      }
      else p →dataL.key = MAXKEY; // p is a 2-node
   else p →dataR.key =  MAXKEY; // delete second element
}
```

Program 10.6: Refinement of Step 1 of Program 10.5

```
//Rotation when p is the left child of r.  q is the middle child of r.
p →dataL = r →dataL;
p →MiddleChild = q →LeftChild;
r →dataL = q →dataL;

q →dataL = q →dataR;
q →LeftChild = q →MiddleChild;
q →MiddleChild = q →RightChild;
q →dataR.key = MAXKEY;
```

Program 10.7: C++ code for a rotation when p is the left child of r

11. Let T and U be two 2-3 trees in which keys are kept in the leaves only (see preceding exercise). Let V be a similar tree thet contains all key values in T and U. Write an algorithm to construct V from T and U. What is the complexity of your algorithm?

12. Write insertion and deletion algorithms for 2-3 trees assuming that an additional data member, f, is associated with each key value. $f = 1$ iff the corresponding key value has not been deleted. Deletions should be accomplished by setting the corresponding $f = 0$, and insertions should make use of deleted space whenever possible without restructuring the tree.

13. Write algorithms to search and delete keys from a 2-3 tree by position; that is, *Search* (k) finds the kth smallest key, and *Delete* (k) deletes the kth smallest key in the tree. (Hint: To do this efficiently, additional information must be kept in each node. With each pair (K_i, A_i) keep $N_i = \Sigma_{j=0}^{i-1}$ (number of key values in the subtree $A_j + 1$).) What are the worst-case computing times of your algorithms?

```
//Combine when p is the left child of r. q is the right sibling of p.
p →dataL = r →dataL;
p →dataR = q →dataL;
p →MiddleChild = q →LeftChild;
p →RightChild = q →MiddleChild;

if ( r →dataR.key) = MAXKEY) // r was a 2-node
    r →dataL.key = MAXKEY;
else {
    r →dataL = r →dataR;
    r →dataR.key = MAXKEY;
    r →MiddleChild = r →RightChild;
}
```

Program 10.8: Code to perform a combine when *p* is the left child of *r*

14. Modify the 2-3 insertion (Program 10.4) algorithm so that we first check to see if either the nearest left sibling or the nearest right sibling of *p* has fewer than two keys. If so, no node` is split. Instead, a rotation is performed, moving either the smallest or largest key in *p* to its parent. The corresponding key in the parent, together with a subtree, is moved to the sibling of *p*, which has space for another key value.

10.4   2-3-4 TREES

10.4.1   Definition and Properties

A 2-3-4 tree is an extension of a 2-3 tree to the case in which 4-nodes (i.e., nodes with four children) are also permitted.

Definition: A *2-3-4 tree* is a search tree that either is empty or satisfies the following properties:

(1)   Each internal node is a 2-, 3-, or 4-node. A 2-node has one element, a 3-node has two elements, and a 4-node has three elements.

(2)   Let *LeftChild* and *LeftMidChild* denote the children of a 2-node. Let *dataL* be the element in this node, and let *dataL.key* be its key. All elements in the 2-3-4 subtree with root *LeftChild* have key less than *dataL.key*, and all elements in the 2-3-4 subtree with root *LeftMidChild* have key greater than *dataL.key*.

(3)   Let *LeftChild*, *LeftMidChild*, and *RightMidChild* denote the children of a 3-node. Let *dataL* and *dataM* be the two elements in this node. Then, *dataL.key* <

dataM. key; all keys in the 2-3-4 subtree with root *LeftChild* are less than *dataL. key*; all keys in the 2-3-4 subtree with root *LeftMidChild* are less than *dataM. key* and greater than *dataL. key*; and all keys in the 2-3-4 subtree with root *RightMidChild* are greater than *dataM. key*.

(4) Let *LeftChild*, *LeftMidChild*, *RightMidChild* and *RightChild* denote the children of a 4-node. Let *dataL*, *dataM*, and *dataR* be the three elements in this node. Then, *dataL. key* < *dataM. key* < *dataR. key*; all keys in the 2-3-4 subtree with root *LeftChild* are less than *dataL. key*; all keys in the 2-3-4 subtree with root *LeftMid-Child* are less than *dataM. key* and greater than *dataL. key*; all keys in the 2-3-4 subtree with root *RightMidChild* are greater than *dataM. key* but less than *dataR. key*; and all keys in the 2-3-4 subtree with root *RightChild* are greater than *dataR. key*.

(5) All external nodes are at the same level. □

A 2-3-4 tree may be represented using nodes defined as

template <class *KeyType*> **class** *Two34*; // forward declaration

template <class *KeyType*>
class *Two34Node* {
friend class *Two34<KeyType>*;
private:
   Element<KeyType> dataL, dataM, dataR ;
   Two34Node *LeftChild, *LeftMidChild, *RightMidChild, *RightChild**;
};

As in the case of 2-3 trees, we shall assume that no element has key MAXKEY. We shall adopt the convention that a 2-node will have *dataM. key* = MAXKEY. The single element is kept in *dataL*, and *LeftChild* and *LeftMidChild* point to its two children. A 3-node has *dataR. key* = MAXKEY and the *LeftChild*, *LeftMidChild*, and *RightMidChild* data members point to its three subtrees. An example of a 2-3-4 tree using these conventions and nodes defined by class *Two* 34 is shown in Figure 10.20.

If a 2-3-4 tree of height h has only 2-nodes, then it contains $2^h - 1$ elements. If it contains only 4-nodes, then the number of elements is $4^h - 1$. A 2-3-4 tree of height h with a mixture of 2-, 3-, and 4-nodes, has between $2^h - 1$ and $4^h - 1$ elements. In other words, the height of a 2-3-4 tree with n elements is between $\lceil \log_4(n+1) \rceil$ and $\lceil \log_2(n+1) \rceil$.

2-3-4 trees have an advantage over 2-3 trees in that insertion and deletion can be performed by a single root-to-leaf pass rather than by a root-to-leaf pass followed by a leaf-to-root pass. As a result, the corresponding algorithms are simpler. More interestingly, a 2-3-4 tree can be represented efficiently as a binary tree (called a red-black tree). This results in a more efficient utilization of space than does the use of nodes of type *Two3* in the case of 2-3 trees and of type *Two34* in the case of 2-3-4 trees. Note that

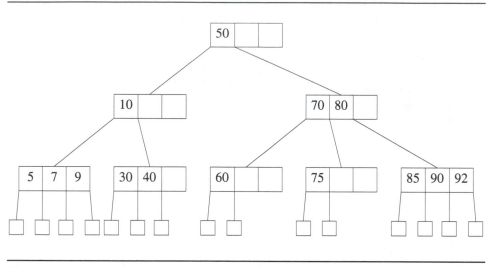

Figure 10.20: Example of a 2-3-4 tree

modifying the definitions of the classes *Two*3 and *Two*34 to use a **union** class that has only as many data members as necessary for the node in use does not improve the efficiency of space utilization, as enough space to accommodate the largest node is allocated whenever a **union** class is created. Using the strategy of Chapter 4 to represent heterogeneous lists to implement *Two*3 and *Two*34 trees results in improved space utilization. This approach is studied in the exercises.

We shall examine the representation of 2-3-4 trees as binary trees in the next section. In this section, we shall see how insertions and deletions can be performed by making a single top-down, root-to-leaf pass over the 2-3-4 tree.

10.4.2 Top-down Insertion

If the leaf node into which the element is to be inserted is a 4-node, then this node splits and a backward (leaf-to-root) pass is initiated. This backward pass terminates when either a 2- or 3-node is encountered, or when the root is split. To avoid the backward pass, we split 4-nodes on the way down the tree. As a result, the leaf node into which the insertion is to be made is guaranteed to be a 2- or 3-node. The element to be inserted may be added to this node without any further node-splitting.

There are three different situations to consider for a 4-node:

(1)   It is the root of the 2-3-4 tree.

(2)   Its parent is a 2-node.

(3)   Its parent is a 3-node.

The splitting transformations for cases (1) and (2) are shown in Figures 10.21 and 10.22, respectively. For case (3), Figure 10.23 shows the transformation when the 4-node is the left child of the 3-node, and Figure 10.24 shows it for the case when the 4-node is the left middle child. The remaining case, when the 4-node is the right middle child of the 3-node, is symmetric to the case when it is the left child and is left as an exercise. It is easy to see that if the transformations of Figures 10.21, 10.22, and 10.23 are used to split 4-nodes on the way down the 2-3-4 tree, then whenever a nonroot 4-node is encountered, its parent cannot be a 4-node. Notice that the transformation for a root 4-node increases the height of the 2-3-4 tree by one, whereas the remaining transformations do not affect its height.

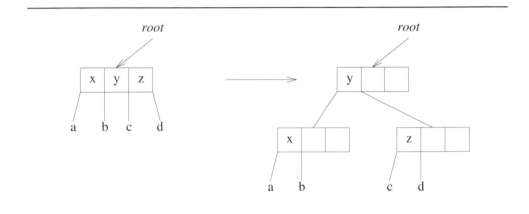

Figure 10.21: Transformation when the 4-node is the root

The function to insert element *y* into a 2-3-4 tree represented with nodes of class *Two34* takes the form given in Program 10.9. The functions used by this program are specified below.:

(1) **void** *Two34<KeyType>::NewRoot*(**const** *Element<KeyType>& y*): This creates a single-node 2-3-4 tree with only the element *y* in it.

(2) *Boolean Two34<KeyType>::FourNode(Two34Node<KeyType> * p)*: This is a Boolean-valued function that returns the value TRUE iff *p* is a 4-node.

(3) **void** *Two34<KeyType>::SplitRoot*(): This uses the transformation of Figure 10.21 to split a root that is a 4-node.

(4) *Node234 Two34<KeyType>::NodeType(Two34Node<KeyType> * p)*: This returns the value TwoNode if *p* is a 2-node and the value ThreeNode otherwise.

(5) **void** *Two34<KeyType>::SplitChildOf2(Two34Node <KeyType> *p, Two34Node <KeyType> *q)*: This uses the transformations of Figure 10.22 to split the 4-node *q* that is a child of a given 2-node *p*.

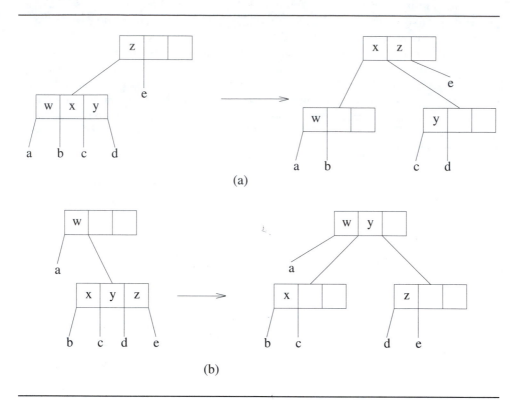

(a)

(b)

Figure 10.22: Transformation when the 4-node is the child of a 2-node

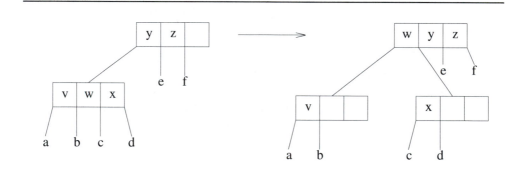

Figure 10.23: Transformation when the 4-node is the left child of a 3-node

Figure 10.24: Transformation when the 4-node is the left middle child of a 3-node

(6)   **void** *Two34<KeyType>::SplitChildOf3(Two34Node <KeyType> *p, Two34Node <KeyType> *q)*: This uses the transformations of Figures 10.23 and 10.24 to split the 4-node *q* that is a child of a given 3-node *p*.

(7)   *result Two34Node<KeyType>::compare(***const** *Element<KeyType>& y)*: This compares the key of the element *y* with the keys in the given node (**this**). The possible outputs from this function and the corresponding conditions are

  (a)   equal: *y. key* equals the key of one of the elements in **this**

  (b)   leaf: **this** is a leaf node

  (c)   lChild: *y. key* < **this**→*dataL. key*

  (d)   lmChild: **this**→*dataL. key* < *y. key* < **this**→*dataM. key*

  (e)   rmChild: **this**→*dataM. key* < *y. key* < **this**→*dataR. key*

  (f)   rChild: *y. key* > **this**→*dataR. key*

  If y and **this** *satisfy more than one of these conditions (e.g., conditions (b) and (d)), then the first is used.*

(8)   **void** *Two34<KeyType>::InsertionError()*: This handles the case when the element *y* to be inserted has a key equal to that of an element already in the 2-3-4 tree.

(9)   **void** *Two34Node<KeyType>::PutIn(***const** *Element<KeyType>& y)*: This adds the element to be inserted (*y*) to the given leaf node. This leaf node is either a 2-node or a 3-node.

  The complexity of *Two34::Insert* is readily seen to be O(log *n*), where *n* is the number of elements in the 2-3-4 tree.

```
template <class KeyType>
Boolean Two34<KeyType>::Insert(const Element<KeyType>& y)
// Insert element y into the 2-3-4 tree.
{
    if (y.key >= MAXKEY) return FALSE;
    if (!root) {NewRoot(y); return TRUE;} // insertion into an empty 2-3-4 tree
    if (FourNode(root)) SplitRoot();
    for (Two34Node<KeyType> *p = root, *q = 0 ; ;)
        //q is parent of p
        if (FourNode(p)) {
            if (NodeType(q) == TwoNode) SplitChildOf2(p, q);
            else SplitChildOf3(p, q);
            p = q; // back up to parent for next comparison
        }
        q = p;
        switch (p→compare(y)) {
            case equal:  InsertionError(); return FALSE; // key is duplicated
            case leaf: p->PutIn(y); return TRUE;
            case lChild: p = p→LeftChild; break;
            case lmChild: p = p→LeftMidChild; break;
            case rmChild: p = p→RightMidChild; break;
            case rChild: p = p→RightChild; break;
        } // end of switch
    } // end of for
} // end of Insert
```

Program 10.9: Insertion into a 2-3-4 tree

10.4.3 Top-down Deletion

As in the case of 2-3 trees, the deletion of an arbitrary element from a 2-3-4 tree may be reduced to that of a deletion of an element that is in a leaf node. If the element to be deleted is in a leaf that is a 3-node or a 4-node, then its deletion leaves behind a 2-node or a 3-node. In this case, no restructuring work is required. Hence, to avoid a backward (leaf-to-root) restructuring path (as performed in the case of 2-3 trees), it is necessary to ensure that at the time of deletion, the element to be deleted is in a 3-node or a 4-node. This is accomplished by restructuring the 2-3-4 tree during the downward (root-to-leaf) pass.

The restructuring strategy requires that whenever the search moves to a node on the next level, this node must be a 3-node or a 4-node. Suppose the search is presently at node p and will move next to node q. Note that q is a child of p and is determined by the relationship between the key of the element to be deleted and the keys of the elements in *p*. The following cases are to be considered:

(1) *p* is a leaf. In this case, the element to be deleted is either in *p* or not in the tree. If the element to be deleted is not in *p*, then the deletion is unsuccessful. Assume that this is not the case. By the nature of the restructuring process, *p* can be a 2-node only if it is also the root. The deletion results in an empty tree.

(2) *q* is not a 2-node. In this case, the search moves to *q*, and no restructuring is needed.

(3) *q* is a 2-node, and its nearest sibling, *r*, is also a 2-node (if *q* is the left child of *p*, then its nearest sibling is the left middle child of *p*; otherwise, the nearest sibling is its left sibling). Now, if *p* is a 2-node, it must be the root, and we perform the transformation of Figure 10.21 in reverse. That is, *p*, *q*, and *r* are combined to form a 4-node, and the height of the tree decreases by 1. If *p* is a 3-node or a 4-node, then we perform, in reverse, the 4-node splitting transformation for the corresponding case (Figures 10.22 through 10.24).

(4) *q* is a 2-node, and its nearest sibling, *r*, is a 3-node. In this case, we perform the transformation of Figure 10.25. This figure shows only the transformations for the case when *q* is the left child of a 3-node *p*. The cases when *q* is the left middle child, right middle child, or right child, and when *p* is a 2-node (in this case *p* is the root) or a 4-node are similar.

(5) *q* is a 2-node and its nearest sibling, *r*, is a 4-node. This is similar to the case when *r* is a 3-node.

These transformations guarantee that a backward restructuring pass is not needed following the deletion from a leaf node. We leave the development of the deletion function as an exercise.

EXERCISES

1. Complete Figure 10.23 by drawing the splitting transformations for the case when the 4-node is the right middle child of a 3-node.

2. Complete function *Two34::Insert* (Program 10.9) by writing the code for all the functions used. Test your function using randomly generated keys.

3. Use the deletion transformations described in the text to obtain a function to delete an element *y* from a 2-3-4 tree represented using nodes of class *Two34*. The deletion should be performed in a top-down manner. To handle deletion from an interior node, you may need to make two top-down passes. Show that the complexity of your algorithm is $O(\log n)$, where *n* is the number of elements initially in the tree.

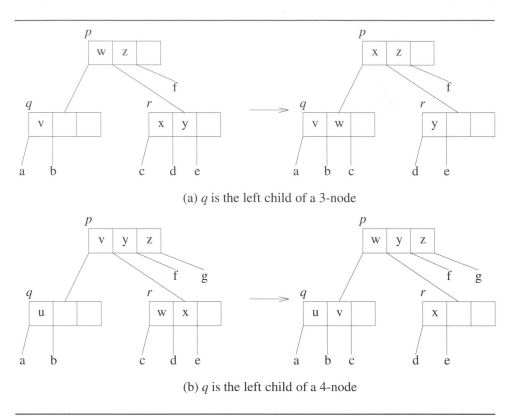

(a) q is the left child of a 3-node

(b) q is the left child of a 4-node

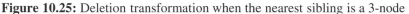

Figure 10.25: Deletion transformation when the nearest sibling is a 3-node

4. Write a function to perform the *ThreeWayJoin* operation defined in Section 5.7.5 for binary search trees. This time, assume that A and B are 2-3-4 trees and that the result of the join is also a 2-3-4 tree. You may assume that the heights of the two input 2-3-4 trees are known. You should be able to perform the join in $O(|\ height\ (A) - height\ (B)\ |)$ time. (Hint: If $height\ (A) > height\ (B)$, follow the rightmost path from A to a node Y such that $height\ (Y) = height\ (B) + 1$; now attempt to insert x, together with a pointer to B, into node Y.)

5. Do the previous exercise for the case of a *TwoWayJoin* (see Section 5.7.5).

6. Write a function to perform the *Split* operation (see Section 5.7.5) for binary search trees. This time, assume that A is a 2-3-4 tree and that the resulting trees, B and C, are also 2-3-4 trees. Can you do this operation in $O(height\ (A))$ time?

7. **[Programming Project]**: Implement top-down *Search*, *Insert*, and *Delete* operations on the 2-3-4 tree using three different node classes *TwoNode*, *ThreeNode*, and *FourNode*. (**Hint**: use the strategy of Section 4.12.)

10.5   RED-BLACK TREES

10.5.1   Definition and Properties

A *red-black tree* is a binary tree representation of a 2-3-4 tree. The child pointers of a node in a red-black tree are of two types: red and black. If the child pointer was present in the original 2-3-4 tree, it is a black pointer. Otherwise, it is a red pointer. The *RedBlackNode* class is defined as

enum *Color* { red, black };

template <class *KeyType*> **class** *RedBlackTree*;

template <class *KeyType*>
class *RedBlackNode* {
friend class *RedBlackTree<KeyType>*;
private:
   Element<KeyType> data;
   *RedBlackNode<KeyType> *LeftChild, *RightChild*;
   Color LeftColor, RightColor;
};

An alternate node structure in which each node has a single color data member may be used instead. The value of this data member is the color of the pointer from the node's parent. Thus, a red node has a red pointer from its parent, and a black node has a black pointer from its parent. The root node is, by definition, a black node. We examine this structure in the exercises. The former structure is better suited for top-down insertion and deletion; the latter is better suited for algorithms that make a bottom-to-top restructuring pass. When drawing a red-black tree, we shall use a solid line to represent a black pointer and a broken one to represent a red pointer. A 2-3-4 tree represented using nodes of type *Two 34Node* is transformed into its red-black representation as follows:

(1)   A 2-node *p* is represented by the *RedBlackNode* *q* with both its color data members black, and *data = dataL*; *q →LeftChild = p →LeftChild*, and *q →RightChild = p →LeftMidChild*.

(2)   A 3-node *p* is represented by two *RedBlackNodes* connected by a red pointer. There are two ways in which this may be done (see Figure 10.26; color data members are not shown).

(3)   A 4-node is represented by three *RedBlackNodes*, one of which is connected to the remaining two by red pointers (see Figure 10.27; color data members are not shown).

The red-black tree representation of the 2-3-4 tree of Figure 10.20 is given in Figure 10.28. External nodes and color data members are not shown. One may verify that a red-black tree satisfies the following properties:

Figure 10.26: Transforming a 3-node into two *RedBlackNodes*

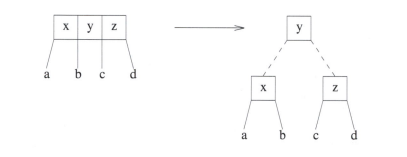

Figure 10.27: Transforming a 4-node into three *RedBlackNodes*

(P1) It is a binary search tree.

(P2) Every root-to-external-node path has the same number of black links (this follows from the fact that all external nodes of the original 2-3-4 tree are on the same level, and black pointers represent original pointers).

(P3) No root-to-external-node path has two or more consecutive red pointers (this follows from the nature of the transformations of Figures 10.26 and 10.27).

An alternate definition of red-black trees is possible. In this definition, we associate a rank with each node x in the tree. This value is not explicitly stored in each node. Rather, if the rank of the root (also called the rank of the tree) is known, then the rank of every other node can be computed by traversing the binary tree and using the color information of the nodes/pointers. A binary tree is a red-black tree iff it satisfies the following properties:

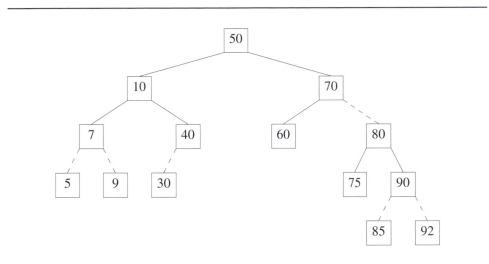

Figure 10.28: Red-black representation of the 2-3-4 tree of Figure 10.20

(Q1) It is a binary search tree.

(Q2) The rank of each external node is 0.

(Q3) Every internal node that is the parent of an external node has rank 1.

(Q4) For every node x that has a parent $p(x)$, $rank(x) \leq rank(p(x)) \leq rank(x) + 1$.

(Q5) For every node x that has a grandparent $gp(x)$, $rank(x) < rank(gp(x))$.

     Intuitively, we see that each node x of a 2-3-4 tree T is represented by a collection of nodes in its corresponding red-black tree. All nodes in this collection have a rank equal to $height(T) - level(x) + 1$. So, each time there is a rank change in a path from the root of the red-black tree, there is a level change in the corresponding 2-3-4 tree. Black pointers go from a node of a certain rank to one whose rank is one less; red pointers connect two nodes of the same rank. Lemma 10.1 is an immediate consequence of the properties of a 2-3-4 tree.

Lemma 10.1: Every red-black tree RB with n (internal) nodes satisifies the following:

(1) $height(RB) \leq 2\lceil \log_2(n + 1)\rceil$

(2) $height(RB) \leq 2 rank(RB)$

(3) $rank(RB) \leq \lceil \log_2(n + 1)\rceil$ □

10.5.2 Searching a Red-Black Tree

Since every red-black tree is a binary search tree, it can be searched using exactly the same algorithm used to search an ordinary binary search tree. The pointer colors are not used during this search.

10.5.3 Top-down Insertion

An insertion can be carried out in one of two ways: top-down or bottom-up. In a top-down insertion, a single root-to-leaf pass is made over the red-black tree. A bottom-up insertion makes both a root-to-leaf and a leaf-to-root pass. To make a top-down insertion, we use the 4-node splitting transformations described in Figures 10.21 through 10.24. In terms of red-black trees, these transformations take the form given in Figures 10.29 through 10.32. The case when a 4-node is the right middle child of a 3-node is symmetric to the case when it is the left child (Figure 10.31).

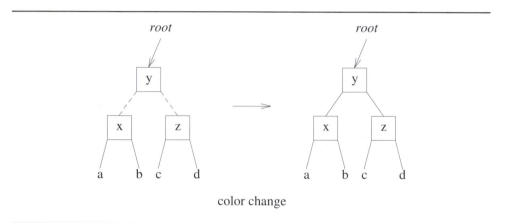

color change

Figure 10.29: Transformation for a root 4-node

We can detect a 4-node simply by looking for nodes q for which both color data members are red. Such nodes, together with their two children, form a 4-node. When such a q is detected, the transformations of Figures 10.29 through 10.32 are accomplished as follows:

(1) Change both of the colors of q to black.

(2) If q is the left (right) child of its parent, then change the left (right) color of its parent to red.

(3) If we now have two consecutive red pointers, then one is from the grandparent, gp, of q to the parent, p, of q and the other from p to q. Let the direction of the first of

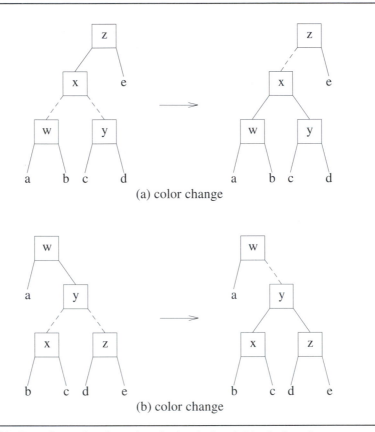

(a) color change

(b) color change

Figure 10.30: Transformation for a 4-node that is the child of a 2-node

these be X and that of the second be Y. We shall use L (R) to denote a left (right) direction. XY = LL, LR, and RL in Figures 10.31(a), 10.32(a), and 10.32(b), respectively. For the case symmetric to Figure 10.31(a) that arises when the 4-node is a right middle child of a 3-node, XY = RR. A rotation similar to that performed in AVL trees is needed. We describe the rotation for the case XY = LL. Now, node p takes the place previously occupied by gp; the right child of p becomes the left child of gp, and gp becomes the right child of p.

Note that when the 4-node to be split is a root or the child of a 2-node or that of a ''nicely'' oriented 3-node (as in Figure 10.31(b)), color changes suffice. Pointers need to be changed only when the 4-node is the child of a 3-node that is not ''nicely'' oriented (as in Figures 10.31(a) and 10.32). We leave the development of the formal insertion function as an exercise.

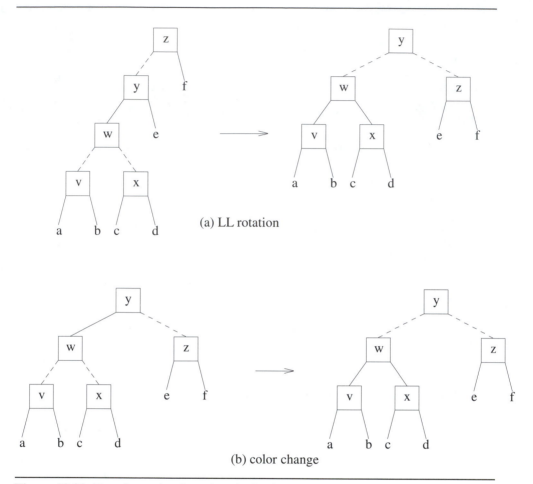

(a) LL rotation

(b) color change

Figure 10.31: Transformation for a 4-node that is the left child of a 3-node

10.5.4 Bottom-up Insertion

In a bottom-up insertion, we search the red-black tree for the key to be inserted. This search is unsuccessful. No transformations are made during this downward pass. The element to be inserted is added as the appropriate child of the node last encountered. A red pointer is used to join the new node to its parent. Following this, all root-to-external-node paths have the same number of black pointers. However, it is possible for one such path to have two consecutive red pointers. This violates the red-black property P3 that no root-to-external-node path has two consecutive red pointers. Let these two pointers be $<p, q>$ and $<q, r>$. The first is from node p to node q, and the second is from node q to node r. Let s be the sibling (if any) of node q. $s = 0$, if q has no sibling.

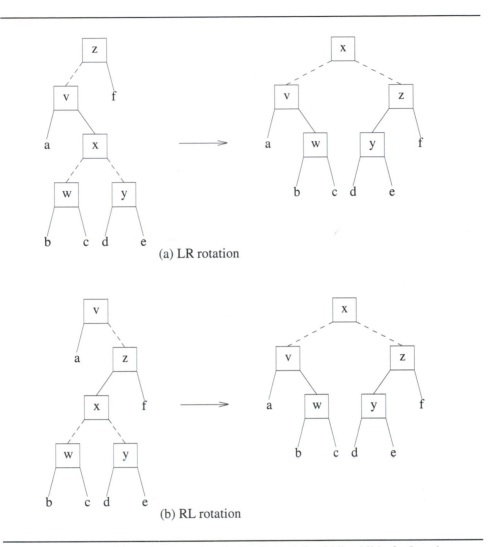

(a) LR rotation

(b) RL rotation

Figure 10.32: Transformation for a 4-node that is the left middle child of a 3-node

The violation is classified as an XYZ violation, where X = L if $<p, q>$ is a left pointer, and X = R otherwise; Y = L if $<q, r>$ is a left pointer, and Y = R otherwise; and Z = r if $s \neq 0$ and $<p, s>$ is a red pointer, and Z = b otherwise.

The color change transformations of Figure 10.33 handle the violation cases LLr and LRr. Similar transformations handle the cases RRr and RLr. In these figures, the subtrees a, b, c, d, and e may be empty and the pointer from the parent of y nonexistent (if y is the root). These color changes potentially propagate the violation up the tree and may need to be reapplied several times. Note that the color change does not affect the

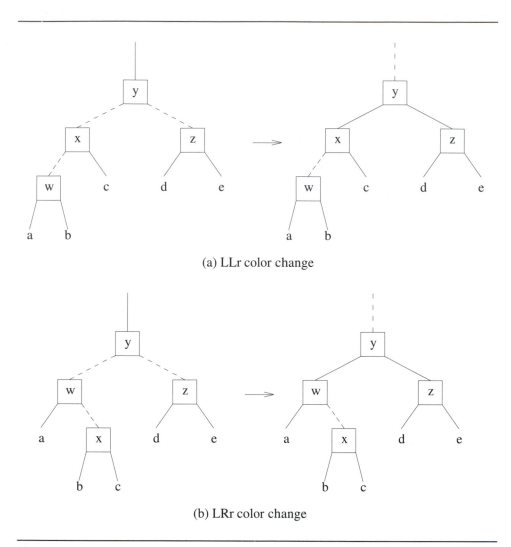

(a) LLr color change

(b) LRr color change

Figure 10.33: LLr and LRr color changes for bottom-up insertion

number of black pointers on a root-to-external-node path. Figure 10.34 shows the rotations needed for the cases LLb and LRb. The cases RRb and RLb are symmetric to LLb and LRb, respectively. The rotations of this figure do not propagate the violation. Hence, at most one rotation can be performed. Once again, we observe that these rotations do not affect the number of black pointers on any root-to-external-node path.

In comparing the top-down and the bottom-up insertion methods, we note that in the top-down method, O(log n) rotations can be performed, whereas only one rotation is

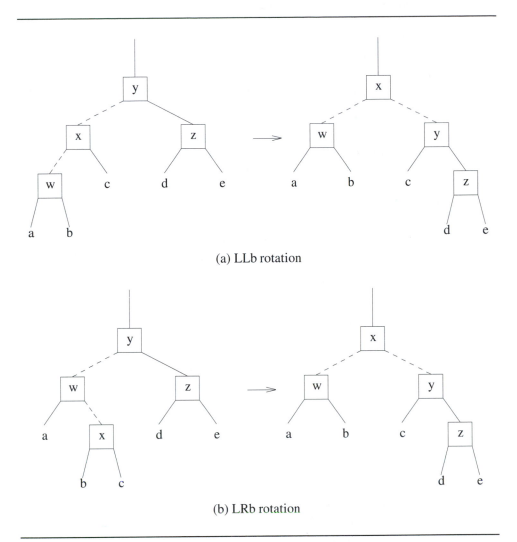

(a) LLb rotation

(b) LRb rotation

Figure 10.34: LLb and LRb rotations for bottom-up insertion

possible in the bottom-up method. Both methods may perform O(log *n*) color changes. However, the top-down method can be used in pipeline mode to perform several insertions in sequence. The bottom-up method cannot be used in this way.

10.5.5 Deletion from a Red-Black Tree

For top-down deletion from a leaf, we note that if the leaf from which the deletion is to occur is the root, then the result is an empty red-black tree. If the leaf is connected to its parent by a red pointer, then it is part of a 3-node or a 4-node, and the leaf may be deleted from the tree. If the pointer from the parent to the leaf is a black pointer, then the leaf is a 2-node. Deletion from a 2-node requires a backward restructuring pass. To avoid this, we ensure that the deletion leaf has a red pointer from its parent. This is accomplished by using the insertion transformations in the reverse direction, together with red-black transformations corresponding to the 2-3-4 deletion transformations (3) and (4) (q is a 2-node whose nearest sibling is a 3- or 4-node), and a 3-node transformation that switches from one 3-node representation to the other as necessary to ensure that the search for the element to be deleted moves down a red pointer.

Since most of the insertion and deletion transformations can be accomplished by color changes and require no pointer changes or data shifts, these operations take less time using red-black trees than when a 2-3-4 tree is represented using nodes of type *Two34Node*.

The development of the bottom-up deletion transformations is left as an exercise.

10.5.6 Joining and Splitting Red-Black Trees

In Section 5.7.5, we defined the following operations on binary search trees: *ThreeWay-Join*, *TwoWayJoin*, and *Split*. Each of these can be performed in logarithmic time on red-black trees. The operation *C.ThreeWayJoin* (A, x, B) can be performed as follows:

Case 1: If A and B have the same rank (see properties Q1 to Q5), then let C be constructed by creating a new root with *data* data member x; color data members black; *LeftChild* data member A; and *RightChild* data member B. The rank of C is one more than the ranks of A and B.

Case 2: If $rank(A) > rank(B)$, then follow *RightChild* pointers from A to the first node Y that has rank equal to $rank(B)$. Properties Q1 to Q5 guarantee the existence of such a node. Let $p(Y)$ be the parent of Y. From the definition of Y, it follows that $rank(p(Y)) = rank(Y) + 1$. Hence, the pointer from $p(Y)$ to Y is a black pointer. Create a new node, Z, with *data* data member x; color data members black; *LeftChild* Y (i.e., node Y and its subtrees become the left subtree of Z); and *RightChild* B. Z is made the right child of $p(Y)$, and the link from $p(Y)$ to Z has color red. Note that this transformation does not change the number of black pointers on any root-to-external-node path. However, it may cause the path from the root to Z to contain two consecutive red pointers. If this happens, then the transformations used to handle this in a bottom-up insertion are performed. These transformations may increase the rank of the tree by one.

Case 3: The case $rank(A) < rank(B)$ is similar to Case 2.

Analysis of join: The correctness of the function just described is easily established. Case 1 takes O(1) time; each of the remaining two cases takes O(| *rank* (*A*) − *rank* (*B*) |) time under the assumption that the rank of each red-black tree is known prior to computing the join. Hence, a three-way join can be done in O(log *n*) time, where *n* is the number of nodes in the two trees being joined. A two-way join can be performed in a similar manner. Note that there is no need to add parent data members to the nodes to perform a join, as the needed parents can be saved on a stack as we move from the root to the node *Y*. □

We now turn our attention to the split operation. Assume for simplicity that the splitting key, *i*, is actually present in the red-black tree *A*. Under this assumption, the split operation *A . Split* (*i*, *B*, , *x*, *C*) can be performed as in Program 10.10.

Step 1: Search *A* for the node *P* that contains the record with key *i*. Copy the record to the reference parameter *x*. Initialize *B* and *C* to be the left and right subtrees of *P*, respectively.

Step 2:

```
for (Q = parent(P);Q;P = Q, Q = parent(Q))
    if( P == Q→LeftChild) C.ThreeWayJoin(C, Q→data, Q→RightChild)
    else B.ThreeWayJoin(Q→LeftChild, Q→data, B);
}
```

Program 10.10: Splitting a red-black tree

We first locate the splitting element, *x*, in the red-black tree. Let *P* be the node that contains this element. The left subtree of *P* contains elements with key less than *i*. *B* is initialized to be this subtree. All elements in the right subtree of *P* have a key larger than *i*, and *C* is initialized to be this subtree. In Step 2, we trace the path from *P* to the root of the red-black tree *A*. During this traceback, two kinds of subtrees are encountered. One of these contains elements with keys that are larger than *i* as well as all keys in *C*. This happens when the traceback moves from a left child of a node to its parent. The other kind of subtree contains elements with keys that are smaller than *i*, as well as smaller than all keys in *B*. This happens when we move from a right child to its parent. In the former case a three-way join with *C* is performed, and in the latter a three-way join with *B* is performed. One may verify that the two-step procedure outlined here does indeed implement the split operation for the case when *i* is the key of a record in the tree *A*. It is easily extended to handle the case when the tree *A* contains no record with key *i*.

Analysis of split: Call a node red if the pointer to it from its parent is red. The root and all nodes that have a black pointer from their parent are black. Let *r*(*X*) be the rank of node *X* in the unsplit tree. First, we shall show that during a split, if *P* is a black node in the unsplit tree, and $Q \neq 0$, then

$$r(Q) \geq \max\{r(B), r(C)\}$$

where $P, Q, B,$ and C are as defined at the start of an iteration of the **for** loop in Step 2.

From the definition of rank, the inequality holds at the start of the first iteration of the **for** loop regardless of the color of P. If P is red initially, then its parent, Q, exists and is black. Let q' be the parent of Q. If $q' = 0$, then there is no Q at which the inequality is violated. So, assume $q' \neq 0$. From the definition of rank and the fact that Q is black, it follows that $r(q') = r(Q) + 1$. Let B' and C' be the trees B and C following the three-way join of Step 2. Since $r(B') \leq r(B) + 1$ and $r(C') \leq r(C) + 1$, $r(q') = r(Q) + 1 \geq \max\{r(B), r(C)\} + 1 \geq \max\{r(B'), r(C')\}$. So, the inequality holds the first time Q points to a node with a black child P (i.e., at the start of the second iteration of the **for** loop, when $Q = q'$).

Having established the induction base, we can proceed to show that the inequality holds at all subsequent iterations when Q points to a node with a black child P. Suppose Q is currently pointing to a node q with a black child $P = p$. Assume that the inequality holds. We shall show that it will hold again the next time Q is at a node with a black P. For there to be such a next time, the parent q' of q must exist. If q is black, the proof is similar to that provided for a black Q and a red P in the induction base.

If q is red, then q' is black. Further, for there to be a next time when Q is at a node with a black P, q must have a grandparent q'', as when Q moves to q' and P to q, $Q = q'$ has a red child $P = q$. Let B' and C' represent the B and C trees following the iteration that begins with $P = p$ and $Q = q$. Similarly, let B'' and C'' represent these trees following the iteration that begins with $P = q$ and $Q = q'$.

Suppose that C is joined with q and its right subtree R to create C'. If $r(C) = r(R)$, then $r(C') = r(C) + 1$, and C' has two black children (recall that when the rank increases by one, the root has two black children). If $C'' = C'$, then $B = B'$ is combined with q' and its left subtree L' to form B''. Since $r(L') \leq r(q')$, $r(B'') \leq \max\{r(B), r(L')\} + 1$, and $r(q'') = r(q') + 1 = r(q) + 1$, $r(B'') \leq r(q'')$. Also, $r(C'') = r(C') = r(C) + 1 \leq r(q) + 1 \leq r(q'')$. So, the inequality holds when $Q = q''$. If $C'' \neq C'$, then C' is combined with q' and its right subtree R' to form C''. If $r(R') \geq r(C')$, then $r(C'') \leq r(R') + 1 \leq r(q') + 1 = r(q'')$. If $r(R') < r(C')$, then $r(C'') = r(C')$, as C' has two black children, and the join of $C', q',$ and R' does not increase the rank. Once again, $r(C'') \leq r(q'')$, and the inequality holds when $Q = q''$.

If $r(C) > r(R)$ and $r(C') = r(C)$, then $r(q'') = r(q) + 1 \geq \max\{r(B), r(C)\} + 1 \geq \max\{r(B''), r(C'')\}$. If $r(C') = r(C) + 1$, then C' has two black children, and $r(C'') \leq r(q) + 1 = r(q'')$. Also, $r(B'') \leq r(q'')$. So, the inequality holds when $Q = q''$. The case $r(C) < r(R)$ is similar.

The case when B is joined with q and its left subtree L is symmetric.

Using the rank inequality just established, we can show that whenever Q points to a node with a black child, the total work done in Step 2 of the splitting algorithm from initiation to the time Q reaches this node is $O(r(B) + r(C) + r(Q))$. Here, B and C are, respectively, the current red-black trees with values smaller and larger than the splitting value. Since $r(Q) \geq \max\{r(B), r(C)\}$, the total work done in Step 2 is $O(r(Q))$. From this, it follows that the time required to perform a split is O(log n), where n is the number of nodes in the tree to be split. □

EXERCISES

1. (a) Show that every binary tree obtained by transforming a 2-3-4 tree as described in the text satisfies properties Q1 to Q5.

    (b) Show that every binary tree that satisfies properties Q1 to Q5 represents a 2-3-4 tree and can be obtained from this 2-3-4 tree using the transformations of the text.

2. Write a function to convert a 2-3-4 tree into its red-black representation. What is the time complexity of your function?

3. Write a function to convert a red-black tree into its 2-3-4 representation. What is the time complexity of your function?

4. Let T be a red-black tree with rank r. Write a function to compute the rank of each node in the tree. The time complexity of your function should be linear in the number of nodes in the tree. Show that this is the case.

5. Compare the worst-case height of a red-black tree with n nodes and that of an AVL tree with the same number of nodes.

6. Rewrite function *Two* 34::*Insert* (Program 10.9) so that it inserts an element into a 2-3-4 tree represented as a red-black tree.

7. Obtain the symmetric transformations for Figures 10.33 and 10.34.

8. Obtain a function to delete an element y from a 2-3-4 tree represented as a red-black tree. Use the top-down method. Test the correctness of this function by running it on a computer. Generate your own test data.

9. Do the previous exercise using the bottom-up method.

10. The number of color data members in a node of a red-black tree may be reduced to one. In this case the color of a node represents the color of the pointer (if any) from the node's parent to that node. Write the corresponding insert and delete functions using the top-down approach. How would this change in the node structure affect the efficiency of the insert and delete functions?

11. Do the previous exercise using the bottom-up approach.

12. (a) Use the strategy described in this section to obtain a C++ function to compute a three-way join. Assume the existence of a function *rebalance* (X) that performs the necessary transformations if the tree pointer to node X is the second of two consecutive red pointers. The complexity of this function may be assumed to be O(*level* (X)).

    (b) Prove the correctness of your function.

    (c) What is the time complexity of your function?

13. Obtain a function to perform a two-way join on red-black trees. You may assume the existence of functions to search, insert, delete, and perform a three-way join. What is the time complexity of your two-way join function?

14. Use the strategy suggested in Program 10.10 to obtain a C++ function to perform the split operation in a red-black tree T. The complexity of your algorithm must be O($height\,(T)$). Your function must work when the splitting key i is present in T and when it is not present in T.

15. Complete the complexity proof for the split operation by showing that whenever Q has a black child, the total work done in Step 2 of the splitting algorithm from initiation to the time that Q reaches the current node is O($r\,(Q)$).

16. Program the search, insert, and delete operations for AVL trees, 2-3 trees, 2-3-4 trees, and red-black trees.

 (a) Test the correctness of your functions.

 (b) Generate a random sequence of n inserts of distinct values. Use this sequence to initialize each of the data structures. Next, generate a random sequence of searches, inserts, and deletes. In this sequence, the probability of a search should be 0.5, that of an insert 0.25, and that of a delete 0.25. The sequence length is m. Measure the time needed to perform the m operations in the sequence using each of the above data structures.

 (c) Do part (b) for $n = 100$, 1000, 10,000, and 100,000 and $m = n$, 2n, and 4n.

 (d) What can you say about the relative performance of these data structures?

10.6   B-TREES

10.6.1   Definition of m-Way Search Trees

The balanced search trees that we have studied so far (AVL trees, 2-3 trees, 2-3-4 trees, and red-black trees) allow us to search, insert, and delete entries from a table in O(log n) time, where n is the number of entries in the table. These structures are well suited to applications in which the table is small enough to be accommodated in internal memory. However, when the table is too large for this, these structures do not have good performance. This is because we must now retrieve the nodes of the search tree structure from a disk (for example). These nodes are retrieved one at a time as needed. So, for example, when searching a 2-3 tree for an element with key x, we would retrieve only those nodes that are on the search path from the root to the node that contains the desired element. As a result, the number of disk accesses for a search is O(h), where h is the height of the 2-3 tree. When $n = 1000$, h can be as high as 10. So, searching a 2-3 tree that is stored on a disk and that has 1000 elements could require up to 10 disk accesses. Since the time required for a disk access is significantly more than that for an internal memory access, we seek structures that would reduce the number of disk accesses.

We shall use the term *index* to refer to a symbol table that resides on a disk. The symbol table may be assumed to be too large to be accommodated in the internal memory of the target computer. To obtain better performance, we shall use search trees whose degree is quite large.

Definition: An *m-way search tree*, either is empty or satisfies the following properties:

(1)   The root has at most m subtrees and has the following structure:

$$n, A_0, (K_1, A_1), (K_2, A_2), \cdots, (K_n, A_n)$$

where the A_i, $0 \le i \le n < m$, are pointers to subtrees, and the K_i, $1 \le i \le n < m$, are key values.

(2) $K_i < K_{i+1}$, $1 \le i < n$.

(3)   All key values in the subtree A_i are less than K_{i+1} and greater than K_i, $0 < i < n$.

(4)   All key values in the subtree A_n are greater than K_n, and those in A_0 are less than K_1.

(5)   The subtrees A_i, $0 \le i \le n$, are also m-way search trees. □

An m-way search tree may be represented as

```
template <class KeyType>
class Mtree {
public:
    Triple<KeyType> Search(const KeyType& );
protected:
    Mnode<KeyType> root;
    int m;
};
```

The return type of function *Search*, *Triple*, is defined later. We may verify that AVL trees are two-way search trees, 2-3 trees are three-way search trees, and 2-3-4 trees are four-way search trees. Of course, there are two-way search trees that are not AVL trees, three-way search trees that are not 2-3 trees, and four-way search trees that are not 2-3-4 trees. A three-way search tree that is not a 2-3 tree is shown in Figure 10.35.

10.6.2   Searching an *m*-Way Search Tree

Suppose we wish to search the m-way search tree T for the key value x. Assume that T resides on a disk. We begin by retrieving the root node from the disk. Assume that this node has the structure given in the definition of an m-way search tree. For convenience, assume that $K_0 = -\infty$ and $K_{n+1} = +\infty$. By searching the keys of the root, we determine i

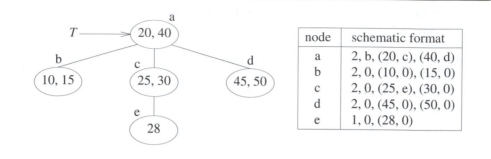

node	schematic format
a	2, b, (20, c), (40, d)
b	2, 0, (10, 0), (15, 0)
c	2, 0, (25, e), (30, 0)
d	2, 0, (45, 0), (50, 0)
e	1, 0, (28, 0)

Figure 10.35: Example of a three-way search tree that is not a 2-3 tree

such that $K_i \leq x < K_{i+1}$. If $x = K_i$, then the search is complete. If $x \neq K_i$, then from the definition of an m-way search tree, it follows that if x is in the tree, it must be in subtree A_i. So, we retrieve the root of this subtree from the disk and proceed to search it. This process continues until either we find x or we have determined that x is not in the tree (the search leads us to an empty subtree). When the number of keys in the node being searched is small, a sequential search (as in the case of 2-3 and 2-3-4 trees) is used. When this number is large, a binary search may be used. A high-level description of the algorithm to search an m-way search tree is given in Program 10.11.

In a tree of degree m and height h, the maximum number of nodes is

$$\sum_{0 \leq i \leq h-1} m^i = (m^h - 1)/(m - 1)$$

Since each node has at most $m - 1$ keys, the maximum number of keys in an m-way tree index of height h is $m^h - 1$. For a binary tree with $h = 3$ this figure is 7. For a 200-way tree with $h = 3$ we have $m^h - 1 = 8 * 10^6 - 1$.

Clearly, the potentials of high-order search trees are much greater than those of low-order search trees. To achieve a performance close to that of the best m-way search trees for a given number of keys n, the search tree must be balanced. The particular variety of balanced m-way search trees we shall consider here is known as a B-tree. In defining a B-tree, it is convenient to reintroduce the concept of failure nodes. Recall that a failure node represents a node that can be reached during a search only if the value x being sought is not in the tree.

10.6.3   Definition and Properties of a B-Tree

Definition: A *B-tree of order m* is an m-way search tree that either is empty or satisfies the following properties:

```
template <class KeyType>
 Triple<KeyType> Mtree<KeyType>::Search(const KeyType& x)
// Search the m-way search tree residing on disk for the key value x. Individual node
// format is n, A₀, (K₁,A₁),  ···, (Kₙ,Aₙ), n < m. An object of type Triple (r,i,j) is
// returned.  j = 1 implies that x is found at node location r with key Kᵢ. Otherwise, j = 0,
// and r is the location of the node into which x can be inserted.
{
    K₀ = - MAXKEY;
    for (Mnode<KeyType> *p = root, *q = 0; p; q = p, p = Aᵢ)
    {
        get node located at p from disk;
        let this node define n, A₀, (K₁, A₁),  ···, (Kₙ, Aₙ);
        Kₙ₊₁ = MAXKEY;
        obtain i such that Kᵢ <= x < Kᵢ₊₁;
        if ( x == Kᵢ) return (p, i, 1); // x has been found
    }
    // x is not in the tree; return location of node into which insertion can take place
    return (q, i, 0);
} // end of Search
```

Program 10.11: Searching an *m*-way search tree

(1)   The root node has at least two children.

(2)   All nodes other than the root node and failure nodes have at least $\lceil m/2 \rceil$ children.

(3)   All failure nodes are at the same level. □

A B-tree may be implemented as a derived class of *Mtree* as follows.

```
template <class KeyType>
class Btree: public Mtree<KeyType>
{
public:
    // Search is inherited from Mtree
    Boolean Insert(const KeyType& x);
    Boolean Delete(const KeyType& x);
};
```

Observe that a 2-3 tree is a B-tree of order 3, and a 2-3-4 tree is a B-tree of order 4. Also, notice that all B-trees of order 2 are full binary trees. Hence, B-trees of order 2 exist only when the number of key values is $2^k - 1$ for some k. However, for any $n \geq 0$ and any $m > 2$, there is a B-tree of order m that contains n keys.

10.6.3.1 Number of Key Values in a B-Tree

A B-tree of order m in which all failure nodes are at level $l+1$ has at most $m^l - 1$ keys. What is the minumum number, N, of keys in such a B-tree? From the definition of a B-tree we know that if $l > 1$, the root node has at least two children. Hence, there are at least two nodes at level 2. Each of these nodes must have at least $\lceil m/2 \rceil$ children. Thus, there are at least $2 \lceil m/2 \rceil$ nodes at level 3. At level 4 there must be at least $2 \lceil m/2 \rceil^2$ nodes, and continuing this argument, we see that there are at least $2 \lceil m/2 \rceil^{l-2}$ nodes at level l when $l > 1$. All of these nodes are nonfailure nodes. If the key values in the tree are $K_1, K_2, \cdots, K_N$ and $K_i < K_{i+1}$, $1 \le i < N$, then the number of failure nodes is $N + 1$. This is so because failures occur for $K_i < x < K_{i+1}$, $0 \le i \le N$, where $K_0 = -\infty$ and $K_{N+1} = +\infty$. This results in $N + 1$ different nodes that one could reach while searching for a key value x that is not in the B-tree. Therefore, we have

$$
\begin{aligned}
N + 1 &= \text{number of failure nodes} \\
&= \text{number of nodes at level } l + 1 \\
&\ge 2 \lceil m/2 \rceil^{l-1}
\end{aligned}
$$

so $N \ge 2 \lceil m/2 \rceil^{l-1} - 1$, $l \ge 1$.

This in turn implies that if there are N key values in a B-tree of order m, then all nonfailure nodes are at levels less than or equal to l, $l \le \log_{\lceil m/2 \rceil}\{(N + 1)/2\} + 1$. The maximum number of accesses that have to be made for a search is l. Using a B-tree of order $m = 200$, an index with $N \le 2 \times 10^6 - 2$ will have $l \le \log_{100}\{(N + 1)/2\} + 1$. Since l is an integer, we obtain $l \le 3$. For $n \le 2 \times 10^8 - 2$ we get $l \le 4$. Thus, the use of a high-order B-tree results in a tree index that can be searched making a very small number of disk accesses, even when the number of entries is very large.

10.6.3.2 Choice of m

B-trees of high order are desirable, since they result in a reduction in the number of disk accesses needed to search an index. If the index has N entries, then a B-tree of order $m = N + 1$ has only one level. This choice of m clearly is not reasonable, since by assumption the index is too large to fit in internal memory. Consequently, the single node representing the index cannot be read into memory and processed. In arriving at a reasonable choice for m, we must keep in mind that we are really interested in minimizing the total amount of time needed to search the B-tree for a value x. This time has two components: (1) the time for reading in the node from the disk and (2) the time needed to search this node for x. Let us assume that each node of a B-tree of order m is of a fixed size and is large enough to accommodate n, A_0, and $m-1$ triples (K_i, A_i, B_i), $1 \le j < m$. Notice that although in the definition of an m-way search tree we had pairs (K_i, A_i), in practice, these will be triples (K_i, A_i, B_i), where B_i gives the address, on disk, of the record with key K_i (as before, A_i points to a subtree of the B-tree). If the K_i are at most α

characters long and the A_i and B_i each β characters long, then the size of a node is approximately $m(\alpha + 2\beta)$ characters. The time required to read in a node is therefore

$$t_s + t_l + m(\alpha + 2\beta) t_c = a + bm$$

where

$$a = t_s + t_l = \text{seek time} + \text{latency time}$$
$$b = (\alpha + 2\beta)t_c, \text{ and } t_c = \text{transmission time per character}$$

If binary search is used to search each node of the B-tree, then the internal processing time per node is $c \log_2 m + d$ for some constants c and d. The total processing time per node is thus

$$\tau = a + bm + c \log_2 m + d$$

For an index with N entries, the number of levels, l, is bounded by

$$l \le \log_{\lceil m/2 \rceil}\{(N+1)/2\} + 1 \le f \frac{\log_2\{(N+1)/2\}}{\log_2 m} \text{ for some constant } f$$

The maximum search time is therefore

$$g\left\{ \frac{a + d}{\log_2 m} + \frac{bm}{\log_2 m} + c \right\} \text{ seconds}$$

where $g = f * \log_2\{(N + 1)/2\}$.

We therefore desire a value of m that minimizes the maximum search time. If the disk drive available has $t_s = 1/100$ sec and $t_l = 1/40$ sec, then $a = 0.035$ sec. Since d is typically a few microseconds, we may ignore it in comparison with a. Hence, $a + d \approx a = 0.035$ sec. If each key value is at most six characters long, and each A_i and B_i is three characters long, $\alpha = 6$ and $\beta = 3$. If the transmission rate t_c is 5×10^{-6} sec/charac (corresponding to a track capacity of 5000 characters), then $b = (\alpha + 2\beta)t_c = 6 \times 10^{-5}$ sec. The formula for the maximum search time now becomes

$$g\left\{ \frac{35}{\log_2 m} + \frac{0.06m}{\log_2 m} + 1000c \right\} \text{ milliseconds}$$

This function is tabulated in Figure 10.36 and plotted in Figure 10.37. It is evident that there is a wide range of values of m for which nearly optimal performance is achieved. This corresponds to the almost flat region $m \in [50, 400]$. If the lowest value of m in this region results in a node size greater than the allowable capacity of an input buffer, the value of m will be determined by the buffer size.

m	Search time (sec)
2	35.12
4	17.62
8	11.83
16	8.99
32	7.38
64	6.47
128	6.10
256	6.30
512	7.30
1024	9.64
2048	14.35
4096	23.40
8192	40.50

Figure 10.36: Values of $(35 + .06m)/\log_2 m$

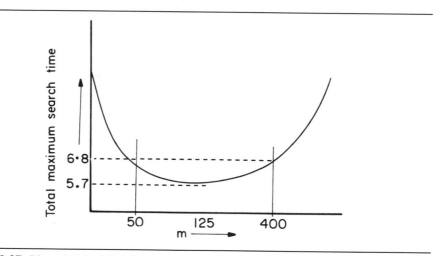

Figure 10.37: Plot of $(35+.06m)/\log_2 m$

10.6.4   Insertion into a B-Tree

The algorithm to insert a new key into a B-tree is a generalization of the two-pass insertion algorithm for 2-3 trees. Although for $m > 3$ we could also generalize the top-down insertion algorithm described for 2-3-4 trees, this is not desirable, as this algorithm splits many nodes, and each time we change a node, it has to be written to disk. This increases the number of disk accesses.

The insertion algorithm for B-trees of order m first performs a search to determine the leaf node, p, into which the new key is to be inserted. If the insertion of the new key into p results in p having m keys, the node p is split. Otherwise, the new p is written to the disk, and the insertion is complete. To split the node, assume that following the insertion of the new key, p has the format

$$m, A_0, (K_1, A_1), \cdots, (K_m, A_m), \quad \text{and} \quad K_i < K_{i+1}, 1 \le i < m$$

The node is split into two nodes, p and q, with the following formats:

$$\text{node } p: \lceil m/2 \rceil - 1, A_0, (K_1 A_1), \cdots, (K_{\lceil m/2 \rceil - 1}, A_{\lceil m/2 \rceil - 1}) \tag{10.5}$$

$$\text{node } q: m - \lceil m/2 \rceil, A_{\lceil m/2 \rceil}, (K_{\lceil m/2 \rceil + 1}, A_{\lceil m/2 \rceil + 1}), \cdots, (K_m, A_m)$$

The remaining key, $K_{\lceil m/2 \rceil}$, and a pointer to the new node, q, form a tuple $(K_{\lceil m/2 \rceil}, q)$. This is to be inserted into the parent of p. Before attempting this, the nodes p and q are written to disk.

As in the case of 2-3 trees, inserting into the parent may require us to split the parent, and this splitting process can propagate all the way up to the root. When the root splits, a new root with a single key is created, and the height of the B-tree increases by one. A high-level description of the insertion algorithm is given in Program 10.12. **Analysis of *Btree::Insert*:** If h is the height of the B-tree, then h disk accesses are made during the top-down search. In the worst case, all h of the accessed nodes may split during the bottom-up splitting pass. When a node other than the root splits, we need to write out two nodes. When the root splits, three nodes are written out. If we assume that the h nodes read in during the top-down pass can be saved in memory so that they are not to be retrieved from disk during the bottom-up pass, then the number of disk accesses for an insertion is at most h (downward pass) + $2(h - 1)$ (nonroot splits) + 3 (root split) = $3h + 1$.

The average number of disk accesses is, however, approximately $h + 1$ for large m. To see this, suppose we start with an empty B-tree and insert N values into it. The total number of nodes split is at most $p - 2$, where p is the number of nonfailure nodes in the final B-tree with N entries. This upper bound of $p - 2$ follows from the observation that each time a node splits, at least one additional node is created. When the root splits, two additional nodes are created. The first node created results from no splitting, and if a B-tree has more than one node, then the root must have split at least once. Figure 10.38 shows that $p - 2$ is the best possible upper bound on the number of nodes split in the creation of a p-node B-tree when $p > 2$ (note that there is no B-tree with $p = 2$). A B-

---

template <class *KeyType* >
Boolean Btree<KeyType>::Insert(**const** *KeyType& x*)
//Key value *x* is inserted into a B-tree of order *m* which resides on a disk.
{
   Triple< KeyType> $(p, i, j) = Search(x)$; // *p* is location of node for insertion
   if (*j*) **return** FALSE; // *x* is already in the B-Tree
   Mnode<KeyType> *$*A = 0$;
   for (*KeyType* $K = x$; *p*; $K = K_{\lceil m/2 \rceil}, A = q, p = p \rightarrow parent\,()$)
   //(K, A) is the tuple to be inserted
   {
      insert (K,A) into appropriate position in node at location *p*;
      let the resulting node have the form: $n, A_0, (K_1, A_1), \cdots, (K_n, A_n)$;
      if ($n <= m - 1$) { // resulting node is not too big
         output node located at *p* onto disk; **return** TRUE;
      }
      // node located at *p* has to be split
      let node *p* and node *q* be defined as in Eq. (10.5);
      output nodes *p* and *q* onto the disk;
   }
   // a new root is to be created
   Create a new node *r* with format 1, *root*, (K, A);
   root =*r*; **output** *root* onto disk;
} // end of *Btree::Insert*

Program 10.12: Insertion into a B-tree

tree of order *m* with *p* nodes has at least $1 + (\lceil m/2 \rceil - 1)(p - 1)$ keys, as the root has at least one key and remaining nodes have at least $\lceil m/2 \rceil - 1$ keys each. The average number of splits, s_{avg}, may now be determined as follows:

$$s_{avg} = (\text{total number of splits})/N$$
$$\leq (p - 2)/\{1 + (\lceil m/2 \rceil - 1)(p - 1)\}$$
$$< 1/(\lceil m/2 \rceil - 1)$$

For $m = 200$ this means that the average number of node splits is less than $1/99$ per key inserted. The number of disk accesses in an insertion is $h + 2s - 1$, where *s* is the number of nodes that are split during the insertion. So, the average number of disk accesses is $h + 2s_{avg} + 1 < h + 101/99 \approx h + 1$. □

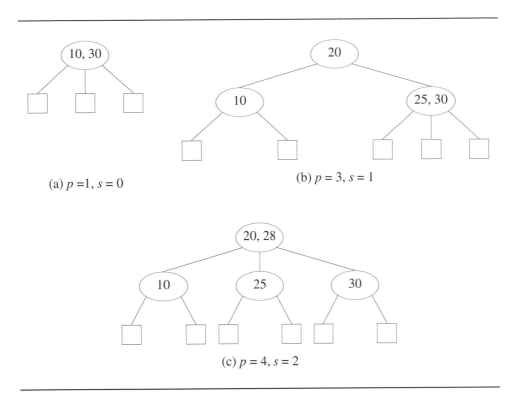

(a) $p = 1$, $s = 0$

(b) $p = 3$, $s = 1$

(c) $p = 4$, $s = 2$

Figure 10.38: B-trees of order 3

10.6.5 Deletion from a B-Tree

The deletion algorithm for B-trees is also a generalization of the deletion algorithm for 2-3 trees. First, we search for the key x that is to be deleted. If x is found in a node, z, that is not a leaf, then the position occupied by x in z is filled by a key from a leaf node of the B-tree. Suppose that x is the ith key in z (i.e., $x = K_i$). Then x may be replaced by either the smallest key in the subtree A_i or the largest in the subtree A_{i-1}. Both of these keys are in leaf nodes. In this way the deletion of x from a nonleaf node is transformed into a deletion from a leaf.

There are four possible cases when deleting from a leaf node p. In the first, p is also the root. If the root is left with at least one key, the changed root is written to disk and we are done. Otherwise, the B-tree is empty following the deletion. In the remaining cases, p is not the root. In the second case, following the deletion, p has at least $\lceil m/2 \rceil - 1$ keys. The modified leaf is written to disk, and we are done.

In the third case, p has $\lceil m/2 \rceil - 2$ keys, and its nearest sibling, q, has at least $\lceil m/2 \rceil$ keys. To determine this, we examine only one of the two (at most) nearest siblings that p may have. p is deficient, as it has one less than the minimum number of keys required. q has more keys than the minimum required. As in the case of a 2-3 tree, a rotation is performed. In this rotation, the number of keys in q decreases by one, and the number in p increases by one. As a result, neither p nor q is deficient following the rotation. The rotation leaves behind a valid B-tree. Let r be the parent of p and q. If q is the nearest right sibling of p, then let i be such that K_i is the ith key in r, all keys in p are less than K_i, and all those in q are greater than K_i. For the rotation, K_i is replaced by the first (i.e., smallest) key in q, K_i becomes the rightmost key in p, and the leftmost subtree of q becomes the rightmost subtree of p. The changed nodes p, q, and r are written to disk, and the deletion is complete. The case when q is the nearest left sibling of p is similar.

In the fourth case for deletion, p has $\lceil m/2 \rceil - 2$ keys, and q has $\lceil m/2 \rceil - 1$ keys. So, p is deficient, and q has the minimum number of keys permissible for a nonroot node. Now, nodes p and q and the key K_i are combined to form a single node. The combined node has $(\lceil m/2 \rceil - 2) + (\lceil m/2 \rceil - 1) + 1 = 2\lceil m/2 \rceil - 2 \le m - 1$ keys, which will, at most, fill the node. The combined node is written to disk. The combining operation reduces the number of keys in the parent node, r, by one. If the parent does not become deficient (i.e., it has at least one key if it is the root and at least $\lceil m/2 \rceil - 1$ keys if it is not the root), the changed parent is written to disk, and we are done. Otherwise, if the deficient parent is the root, it is discarded, as it has no keys. If the deficient parent is not the root, it has exactly $\lceil m/2 \rceil - 2$ keys. To remove this deficiency, we first attempt a rotation with one of r's nearest siblings. If this is not possible, a combine is done. This process of combining can continue up the B-tree only until the children of the root are combined.

The details are provided in algorithm *Btree::Delete* (Program 10.13). To reduce the worst-case performance of the algorithm, only the nearest left or nearest right sibling of a node is examined.

```
template <class KeyType>
Boolean Btree<KeyType>::Delete (const KeyType& x)
// Delete x from a B-tree of order m that resides on a disk.
{
    Triple<KeyType> (p, i, j) = Search(x);
    if (!j) return FALSE; //x is not in the tree
    let p be of the form n, A₀, (K₁,A₁), · · · , (Kₙ,Aₙ) and Kᵢ = x;
    if (A₀) { //deletion from a nonleaf; find key to move up
        //move to right subtree
        for ( q = Aᵢ;  q is not a leaf node; q = A₀�q);
        // assume that q is of the form  n_q, A₀�q, (K₁�q, A₁ᵠ), · · · , (Kₙᵠ, Aₙᵠ);
        replace Kᵢ in node p by K₁ᵠ and write the altered node p onto disk;

        p = q; i = 1;
        let n, A₀, (K₁,A₁), · · · , (Kₙ,Aₙ) be as defined by the new node p;
    } // end of if (A₀)
```

// delete K_i from node p, a leaf
delete (K_i, A_i) from $p = [n, A_0, (K_1, A_1), \cdots, (K_n, A_n)]$; replace n by $n - 1$;
while $((n < \lceil m/2 \rceil - 1) \ \&\&\ p \ != root)$ {
    if p has a nearest right sibling y {
        let $y : n_y, A_0^y, (K_1^y, A_1^y), \cdots, (K_n^y, A_n^y)$;
        let $z : n_z, A_0^z, (K_1^z, A_1^z), \cdots, (K_n^z, A_n^z)$ be the parent of p and y;
        let $A_j^z = y$ and $A_{j-1}^z = p$;
        if $(n_y >= \lceil m/2 \rceil)$ { // redistribute key values
            $(K_{n+1}, A_{n+1}) = (K_j^z, A_0^y)$; $n = n + 1$; //update node p
            $K_j^z = K_1^y$; //update node z
            $(n_y, A_0^y, (K_1^y, A_1^y), \cdots) = (n_y - 1, A_1^y, (K_2^y, A_2^y), \cdots)$; //update node y
            output nodes p, y, z onto disk;
            return TRUE;
        } // end of **if** $(n_y >= \lceil m/2 \rceil)$
        //combine nodes p, K_j^z, and y
        $r = 2 * \lceil m/2 \rceil - 2$;
        output $r, A_0, (K_1, A_1), \cdots, (K_n, A_n), (K_j^z, A_0^y), (K_1^y, A_1^y), \cdots, (K_n^y, A_n^y)$
        onto disk at location p;
        //update
        $(n, A_0 \cdots) = (n_z - 1, A_0^z, \cdots, (K_{j-1}^z, A_{j-1}^z), (K_{j+1}^z, A_{j+1}^z) \cdots)$
        $p = z$;
    } // end of **if** p has a nearest right sibling
    else { //node p must have a left sibling
        // this is symmetric to the case where p has a right sibling, and is left as an exercise
    } // end of **if-else** and **while**
  if (n) **output** p: $(n, A_0, \cdots, (K_n, A_n))$
  else $root = A_0$; //change root
} // end of *Btree* ::*Delete*

Program 10.13: Deletion from a B-tree

Analysis of *Btree::Delete*: Once again, we assume that disk nodes accessed during the downward search pass may be saved in a stack, so they do not need to be reaccessed from the disk during the upward restructuring pass. For a B-tree of height h, h disk accesses are made to find the node from which the key is to be deleted and to transform the deletion to a deletion from a leaf. In the worst case, a combine takes place at each of the last $h - 2$ nodes on the root-to-leaf path, and a rotation takes place at the second node on this path. The $h - 2$ combines require this many disk accesses to retrieve a nearest sibling for each node and another $h - 2$ accesses to write out the combined nodes. The rotation requires one access to read a nearest sibling and three to write out the three nodes that are changed. The total number of disk accesses is $3h$.

    The deletion time can be reduced at the expense of disk space and a slight increase in node size by including a delete bit, F_i, for each key value, K_i, in a node. Then we can set $F_i = 1$ if K_i has not been deleted and $F_i = 0$ if it has. No physical deletion takes place. In this case a delete requires a maximum of $h + 1$ accesses (h to locate the node containing x and 1 to write out this node with the appropriate delete bit set to 0). With this strategy, the number of nodes in the tree never decreases. However, the space used by deleted entries can be reused during further insertions (see Exercises). As a result, this strategy has little effect on search and insert times (the number of levels increases very slowly when m is large). The time taken to insert an item may even decrease slightly because of the ability to reuse deleted entry space. Such reuses would not require us to split any nodes. □

Some variations of B-trees are examined in the Exercises.

10.6.6   Variable-Size Key Values

With a node format of the form n, A_0, (K_1, A_1), $\cdots$, (K_n, A_n), the first problem created by the use of variable-size key values, K_i, is that a binary search can no longer be carried out, since, given the location of the first tuple (K_1, A_1), and n, we cannot easily determine K_n or even the location of $K_{(1+n)/2}$. When the range of key value size is small, it is best to allocate enough space for the largest key value. When the range in sizes is large, storage may be wasted, and another node format may be better (i.e., the format n, A_0, α_1, α_2, $\cdots$, α_n, (K_1, A_1), $\cdots$, (K_n, A_n), where α_i is the address of K_i in internal memory, i.e., K_i = memory (α_i)). In this case, a binary search of the node can still be made. The use of variable-size nodes is not recommended, since this would require a more complex storage management system. More importantly, the use of variable-size nodes would result in degraded performance during insertion, as insertion into a node requires requesting a larger node to accommodate the new value being inserted. Consequently, nodes of a fixed size should be used. The size should allow for at least $m - 1$ key values of the largest size. During insertions, however, we can relax the requirement that each node have $\leq m - 1$ key values. Instead, a node will be allowed to hold as many values as can fit into it and will contain at least $\lceil m/2 \rceil - 1$ values. The resulting performance will be at least as good as that of a B-tree of order m. Another possibility is to use some kind of key sampling scheme to reduce the key value size so as not to exceed some predetermined size d. Some possibilities are truncating prefixes and suffixes, removing vowels, etc. Whatever scheme is used, some provision will have to be made for handling synonyms (i.e., distinct key values that have the same sampled value).

EXERCISES

1. Show that all B-trees of order 2 are full binary trees.

2. (a)   Insert the keys 62, 5, 85, and 75 one at a time into the order-5 B-tree of Figure 10.39. Show the new tree after each key is added. Do the insertion using the insertion process described in the text.

    (b)   Assuming that the tree is kept on a disk and one node may be retrieved at a time, how many disk accesses are needed to make each insertion? State any assumptions you make.

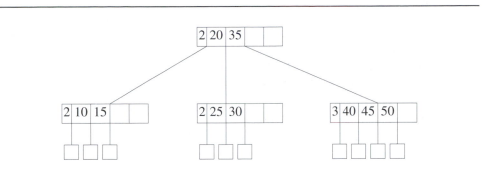

Figure 10.39: B-tree of order 5

    (c)   Delete the keys 45, 40, 10, and 25 from the order-5 B-tree of Figure 10.39. Show the tree following each deletion. The deletions are to be performed using the deletion process described in the text.

    (d)   How many disk accesses are made for each of the deletions?

3.   Complete the symmetric case of algorithm *Btree::Delete* (Program 10.13).

4.   Write insertion and deletion algorithms for B-trees assuming that with each key value is associated an additional data member, f, such that $f = 1$ iff the corresponding key value has not been deleted. Deletions should be accomplished by setting the corresponding $f = 0$, and insertions should make use of deleted space whenever possible without restructuring the tree.

5.   Write algorithms to search and delete keys from a B-tree by position; that is, *Search* (k) finds the kth smallest key, and *Delete* (k) deletes the kth smallest key in the tree. (Hint: To do this efficiently, additional information must be kept in each node. With each pair (K_i, A_i) keep $N_i = \Sigma_{j=0}^{i-1}$ (number of key values in the subtree A_j + 1).) What are the worst-case computing times of your algorithms?

6.   The text assumed a node structure that was sequential. However, we need to perform the following functions on a B-tree node: search, insert, delete, join, and split.

    (a)   Explain why each of these functions is important during a search, insert, and delete operation in the B-tree.

    (b)   Explain how a red-black tree could be used to represent each node. You will need to use integer pointers and regard each red-black tree as embedded in an array.

    (c)   What kind of performance gain/loss do you expect using red-black trees for each node instead of a sequential organization? Try to quantify your answer.

7. Modify algorithm *Btree::Insert* (Program 10.12) so that when node p has m keys, we first check to see if either the nearest left sibling or the nearest right sibling of p has fewer than $m - 1$ key values. If so, p is not split. Instead, a rotation is performed moving either the smallest or largest key in p to its parent. The corresponding key in the parent, together with a subtree, is moved to the sibling of p that has space for another key value.

8. [***Bayer and McCreight***] The idea of the preceding exercise can be extended to obtain improved B-tree performance. If the nearest sibling, p, of p already has $m - 1$ key values, then we can split both p and q to obtain three nodes p, q, and r with each node containing $\lfloor (2m - 2)/3 \rfloor, \lfloor (2m - 1)/3 \rfloor$, and $\lfloor 2m/3 \rfloor$ key values. Figure 10.40 describes the splitting procedure when q is p's nearest right sibling.

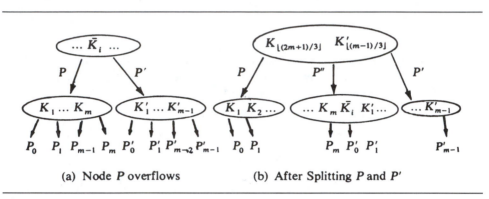

(a) Node P overflows   (b) After Splitting P and P'

Figure 10.40: Splitting P and its nearest right sibling, P'

Rewrite algorithm *Btree::Insert* so that node splittings occur only as described here.

9. A *B*-tree* of order m is a search tree that either is empty or satisfies the following properties:

    (a) The root node has at least two and at most $2\lfloor (2m - 2)/3 \rfloor + 1$ children.

    (b) The remaining nonfailure nodes have at most m and at least $\lceil (2m - 1)/3 \rceil$ children each.

    (c) All failure nodes are on the same level.
    For a B*-tree of order m that contains N key values, show that if $x = \lceil (2m - 1)/3 \rceil$, then

    (a) the height, h, of the B*-tree satisfies $h \le 1 + \log_x \{(N + 1)/2\}$

    (b) the number of nodes p in the B*-tree satisifies $p \le 1 + (N - 1)/(x - 1)$
    What is the average number of splits per insert if a B*-tree is built up starting from an empty B*-tree?

10. Using the splitting technique of Exercise 8, write an algorithm to insert a new key value, x, into a B*-tree of order m. How many disk accesses are made in the worst case and on the average? Assume that the B-tree was initially of depth l and that it is maintained on a disk. Each access retrieves or writes one node.

11. Write an algorithm to delete the identifier x from a B*-tree of order m. What is the maximum number of accesses needed to delete x from a B*-tree of depth l? Make the same assumptions as in Exercise 10.

12. The basic idea of a B-tree may be modified to obtain a B'-tree. A B'-tree of order m is similar to a B-tree of order m except that in a B'-tree all identifiers are placed in leaf nodes. If P is a nonleaf node in a B'-tree and is of degree j, then the node format for P is $j, L(1), L(2), \cdots, L(j-1)$, where $L(i)$, $1 \le i < j$, is the value of the largest key in the ith subtree of P. Figure 10.41 shows a B'-tree of order 5. Notice that in a B'-tree, the key values in the leaf nodes increase from left to right. Only the leaf nodes contain such information as the address of records having that key value. If there are n key values in the tree, then there are n leaf nodes. Write an algorithm to search for x in a B'-tree of order m. How many disk accesses are needed?

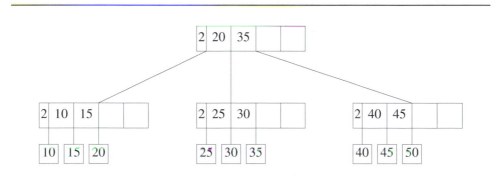

Figure 10.41: Example of a B'-tree

13. For a B'-tree of order m write an algorithm to insert x. How many disk accesses are needed?

14. Write an algorithm to delete x from a B'-tree of order m. Since all key values are in leaf nodes, this deletion always corresponds to a deletion from a leaf. What is the number of disk accesses?

15. Let T and U be two B'-trees of order m. Let V be a B'-tree of order m containing all key values in T and U. Write an algorithm to construct V from T and U. How many disk accesses are made?

16.   Obtain search, insert, and delete algorithms for B'-trees of order m. If the tree re-
      sides on disk, how many disk accesses are needed in the worst case for each of the
      three operations? Assume the tree has n leaf nodes.

17.   [*Programming Project*] Evaluate the relative performance of B-trees, B*-trees,
      and B'-trees for search, insert, and delete operations.

10.7   SPLAY TREES

We have studied balanced search trees that allow one to perform operations such as
search, insert, delete, join, and split in O(log n) worst-case time per operation. In the
case of priority queues, we saw that if we are interested in amortized complexity rather
than worst-case complexity, simpler structures can be used. This is also true for search
trees. Using a splay tree, we can perform the operations in O(log n) amortized time per
operation.

A *splay tree* is a binary search tree in which each search, insert, delete, and join
operation is performed in the same way as in an ordinary binary search tree (see Chapter
5) except that each of these operations is followed by a *splay*. In a split, however, we
first perform a splay. This makes the split very easy to perform. A splay consists of a sequence of rotations. For simplicity, we assume that each of the operations is always successful. A failure can be modeled as a different successful operation. For example, an
unsuccesful search may be modeled as a search for the element in the last node encountered in the unsuccessful search, and an unsuccessful insert may be modeled as a successful search. With this assumption, the start node for a splay is obtained as follows:

(1)   *search*: The splay starts at the node containing the element being sought.

(2)   *insert*: The start node for the splay is the newly inserted node.

(3)   *delete*: The parent of the physically deleted node is used as the start node for the
      splay. If this node is the root, then no splay is done.

(4)   *ThreeWayJoin*: No splay is done.

(5)   *split*: Suppose that we are splitting with respect to the key i and that key i is actu-
      ally present in the tree. We first perform a splay at the node that contains i and
      then split the tree. As we shall see, splitting following a splay is very simple.

Splay rotations are performed along the path from the start node to the root of the
binary search tree. These rotations are similar to those performed for AVL trees and
red-black trees. Let q be the node at which the splay is being performed. Initially, q is
the node at which the splay starts. The following steps define a splay:

(1)   If q either is 0 or the root, then the splay terminates.

(2)   If q has a parent, p, but no grandparent, then the rotation of Figure 10.42 is per-
      formed, and the splay terminates.

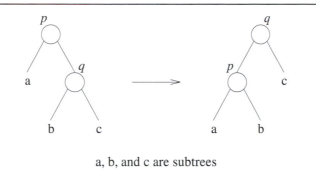

a, b, and c are subtrees

Figure 10.42: Rotation when q is a right child and has no grandparent

(3)   If q has a parent, p, and a grandparent, gp, then the rotation is classified as LL (p is the left child of gp, and q is the left child of p), LR (p is the left child of gp, and q is the right child of p), RR, or RL. The RR and RL rotations are shown in Figure 10.43. LL and LR rotations are symmetric to these. The splay is repeated at the new location of q.

Notice that all rotations move q up the tree and that following a splay, q becomes the new root of the search tree. As a result, splitting the tree with respect to a key, i, is done simply by performing a splay at i and then splitting at the root. Figure 10.44 shows a binary search tree before, during, and after a splay at the shaded node.

In the case of Fibonacci heaps, we obtained the amortized complexity of an operation by using an explicit cross-charging scheme. The analysis for splay trees will use a *potential* technique. Let P_0 be the initial potential of the search tree, and let P_i be its potential following the ith operation in a sequence of m operations. The amortized time for the ith operation is defined to be

$$\text{(actual time for the } i\text{th operation)} + P_i - P_{i-1}$$

That is, the amortized time is the actual time plus the change in the potential. Rearranging terms, we see that the actual time for the ith operation is

$$\text{(amortized time for the } i\text{th operation)} + P_{i-1} - P_i$$

Hence, the actual time needed to perform the m operations in the sequence is

$$\sum_i \text{(amortized time for the } i\text{th operation)} + P_0 - P_m$$

Since each operation other than a join involves a splay whose actual complexity is of the same order as that of the whole operation, and since each join takes $O(1)$ time, it is sufficient to consider only the time spent performing splays.

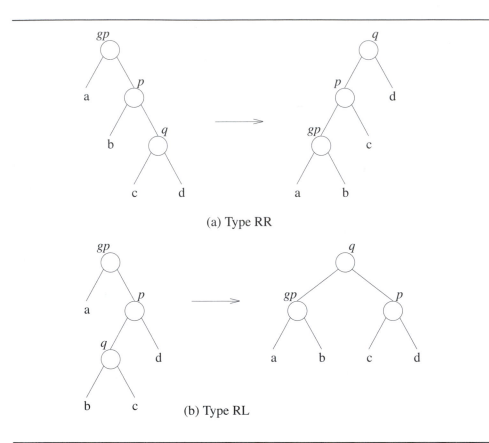

(a) Type RR

(b) Type RL

Figure 10.43: RR and RL rotations

Each splay consists of several rotations. We shall assign to each rotation a fixed cost of one unit. The choice of a potential function is rather arbitrary. The objective is to use one that results in as small a bound on the time complexity as is possible. We now define the potential function we shall use. Let the size, $s(i)$, of the subtree with root i be the total number of nodes in it. The rank, $r(i)$, of node i is equal to $\lfloor \log_2 s(i) \rfloor$. The potential of the tree is $\sum_i r(i)$. The potential of an empty tree is defined to be zero.

Suppose that in the tree of Figure 10.44(a), the subtrees a, b, $\cdots$, j are all empty. Then $(s(1), \cdots, s(9)) = (9, 6, 3, 2, 1, 4, 5, 7, 8)$; $r(3) = r(4) = 1$; $r(5) = 0$; and $r(9) = 3$. In Lemma 10.2 we use r and r', respectively, to denote the rank of a node before and after a rotation.

Lemma 10.2: Consider a binary search tree that has n elements/nodes. The amortized cost of a splay operation that begins at node q is at most $3(\lfloor \log_2 n \rfloor - r(q)) + 1$.

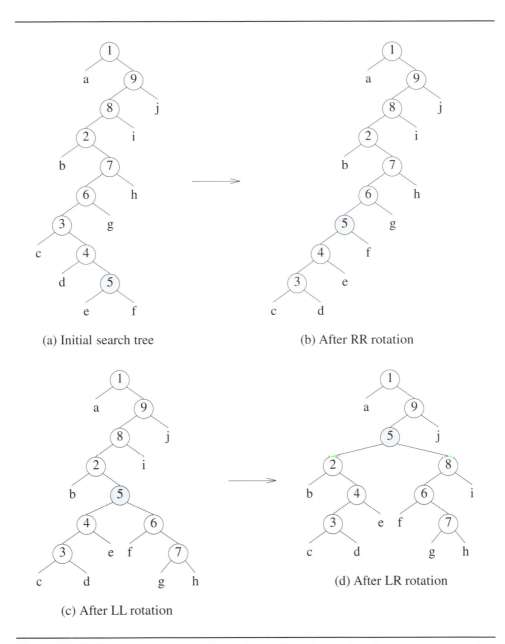

(a) Initial search tree

(b) After RR rotation

(c) After LL rotation

(d) After LR rotation

Figure 10.44: Rotations in a splay beginning at shaded node (continued on next page)

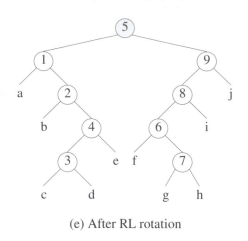

a   j

b   i

c   d   e   f   g   h

(e) After RL rotation

Figure 10.44: Rotations in a splay beginning at the shaded node

Proof: Consider the three steps in the definition of a splay:

(1)   In this case, q either is 0 or the root. This step does not alter the potential of the tree, so its amortized and actual costs are the same. This cost is 1.

(2)   In this step, the rotation of Figure 10.42 (or the symmetric rotation for the case when q is the left child of p) is performed. Since only the ranks of p and q are affected, the potential change, ΔP, is $r'(p) + r'(q) - r(p) - r(q)$. Further, since $r'(p) \leq r(p)$, $\Delta P \leq r'(q) - r(q)$. The amortized cost of this step (actual cost plus potential change) is, therefore, no more than $r'(q) - r(q) + 1$.

(3)   In this step only the ranks of q, p, and gp change. So, $\Delta P = r'(q) + r'(p) + r'(gp) - r(q) - r(p) - r(gp)$. Since, $r(gp) = r'(q)$,

$$\Delta P = r'(p) + r'(gp) - r(q) - r(p) \quad \text{-- (1)}$$

Consider an RR rotation. From Figure 10.43(a), we see that $r'(p) \leq r'(q)$, $r'(gp) \leq r'(q)$, and $r(q) \leq r(p)$. So, $\Delta P \leq 2(r'(q) - r(q))$. If $r'(q) > r(q)$, $\Delta P \leq 3(r'(q) - r(q)) - 1$. If $r'(q) = r(q)$, then $r'(q) = r(q) = r(p) = r(gp)$. Also, $s'(q) > s(q) + s'(gp)$. Consequently, $r'(gp) < r'(q)$. To see this, note that if $r'(gp) = r'(q)$, then $s'(q) > 2^{r(q)} + 2^{r'(gp)} = 2^{r(q)+1}$, which violates the definition of rank. Hence, from (1), $\Delta P \leq 2(r'(q) - r(q)) - 1 = 3(r'(q) - r(q)) - 1$. So, the amortized cost of an RR rotation is at most $1 + 3(r'(q) - r(q)) - 1 = 3(r'(q) - r(q))$.

This bound may be obtained for LL, LR, and RL rotations in a similar way.

The lemma now follows by observing that Steps 1 and 2 are mutually exclusive and can occur at most once. Step 3 occurs zero or more times. Summing up over the amortized cost of a single occurrence of Steps 1 or 2 and all occurrences of Step 3, we obtain the bound of the lemma. $\square$

Theorem 10.1: The total time needed for a sequence of m search, insert, delete, join, and split operations performed on a collection of initially empty splay trees is $O(m \log n)$, where $n, n > 0$, is the number of inserts in the sequence.

Proof: Since none of the splay trees has more than n nodes, no node has rank more than $\lfloor \log_2 n \rfloor$. A search (excluding the splay) does not change the rank of any node and hence does not affect the potential of the splay tree involved. An insert (excluding the splay) increases, by one, the size of every node on the path from the root to the newly inserted node. This causes the ranks of the nodes with size $2^k - 1$ to change. There are at most $\lfloor \log_2 n \rfloor + 1$ such nodes on any insert path. So, each insert (excluding the splay) increases the potential by at most this much. Each join increases the total potential of all the splay trees by at most $\lfloor \log_2 n \rfloor$. Deletions do not increase the potential of the involved splay tree except for any increase that results from the splay step. The split operation (excluding the splay step) reduces the overall potential by an amount equal to the rank of the tree just before the split (but after the splay that precedes it). So, the potential increase, PI, attributable to the m operations (exclusive of that attributable to the splay steps of the operations) is $O(m \log n)$.

From our definition of the amortized cost of a splay operation, it follows that the time for the sequence of operations is the sum of the amortized costs of the splays, the potential change $P_0 - P_m$, and PI. From Lemma 10.2, it follows that the sum of the amortized costs is $O(m \log n)$. The initial potential, P_0, is 0, and the final potential, P_m, is ≥ 0. So, the total time is $O(m \log n)$. $\square$

EXERCISES

1. Obtain figures corresponding to Figures 10.42 and 10.43 for the symmetric splay rotations.

2. What is the maximum height of a splay tree that is created as the result of n insertions made into an initially empty splay tree? Give an example of a sequence of inserts that results in a splay tree of this height.

3. Complete the proof of Lemma 10.2 by providing the proof for the case of an RL rotation. Note that the proofs for LL and LR rotations are similar to those for RR and RL rotations, respectively, as the rotations are symmetric.

4. Explain how a two-way join should be performed in a splay tree so that the amortized cost of each splay tree operation remains $O(\log n)$.

5. Explain how a split with respect to key i is to be performed when key i is not present in the splay tree. The amortized cost of each splay tree operation should be $O(\log n)$.

6. Implement the splay tree data structure as a derived class of a Binary Search Tree.

7. [**Sleator and Tarjan**] Suppose we modify the definition of $s(i)$ used in connection with the complexity analysis of splay trees. Let each node i have a positive weight $p(i)$. Let $s(i)$ be the sum of the weights of all nodes in the subtree with root i. The rank of this subtree is $\log_2 s(i)$.

(a) Let t be the root of a splay tree. Show that the amortized cost of a splay that begins at node q is at most $3(r(t) - r(q)) + 1$, where r is the rank just before the splay.

(b) Let S be a sequence of n inserts and m searches. Assume that each of the n inserts adds a new element to the splay tree and that all searches are successful. Let $p(i), p(i) > 0$, be the number of times element i is sought. The $p(i)$'s satisfy the following equality:

$$\sum_{i=1}^{n} p(i) = m$$

Show that the total time spent on the m searches is

$$O\left(m + \sum_{i=1}^{n} p(i) \log(m/p(i))\right)$$

Note that since $\Omega\left(m + \sum_{i=1}^{n} p(i) \log(m/p(i))\right)$ is an information theoretic bound on the search time in a static search tree (the optimal binary search tree of Section 10.1 is an example of such a tree), splay trees are optimal to within a constant factor for the representation of a static set of elements.

10.8 DIGITAL SEARCH TREES

10.8.1 Definition

A *digital search tree* is a binary tree in which each node contains one element. The element-to-node assignment is determined by the binary representation of the element keys. Suppose that we number the bits in the binary representation of a key from left to right beginning at one. Then bit one of 1000 is 1, and bits two, three, and four are 0. All keys in the left subtree of a node at level i have bit i equal to zero whereas those in the right subtree of nodes at this level have bit $i = 1$. Figure 10.45(a) shows a digital search tree. This tree contains the keys 1000, 0010, 1001, 0001, 1100, and 0000.

Suppose we are to search for the key $k = 0011$ in the tree of Figure 10.45(a). k is first compared with the key in the root. Since k is different from the key in the root, and since bit one of k is 0, we move to the left child, b, of the root. Now, since k is different from the key in node b, and bit two of k is 0, we move to the left child, d, of b. Since k is different from the key in node d and since bit three of k is one, we move to the right child

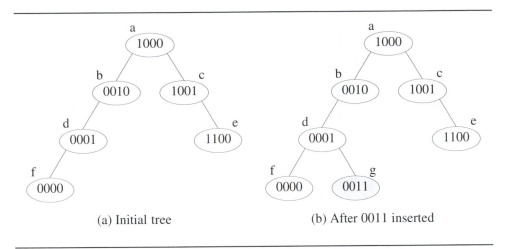

(a) Initial tree   (b) After 0011 inserted

Figure 10.45: Digital search trees

of d. Node d has no right child to move to. From this we conclude that $k = 0011$ is not in the search tree. If we wish to insert k into the tree, then it is to be added as the right child of d. When this is done, we get the digital search tree of Figure 10.45(b).

The digital search tree functions to search and insert are quite similar to the corresponding functions for binary search trees. The essential difference is that the subtree to move to is determined by a bit in the search key rather than by the result of the comparison of the search key and the key in the current node. The deletion of an item in a leaf is done by removing the leaf node. To delete from any other node, the deleted item must be replaced by a value from any leaf in its subtree and that leaf removed.

Each of these operations can be performed in $O(h)$ time, where h is the height of the digital search tree. If each key in a digital search tree has $KeySize$ bits, then the height of the digital search tree is at most $KeySize + 1$.

10.8.2 Binary Tries

When we are dealing with very long keys, the cost of a key comparison is high. We can reduce the number of key comparisons to one by using a related structure called *Patricia* (*P*ractical *a*lgorithm *t*o *r*etrieve *i*nformation *c*oded *i*n *a*lphanumeric). We shall develop this structure in three steps. First, we introduce a structure called a binary trie. Then we transform binary tries into compressed binary tries. Finally, from compressed binary tries we obtain Patricia. Since binary tries and compressed binary tries are introduced only as a means of arriving at Patricia, we do not dwell much on how to manipulate these structures. A more general version of binary tries (called a trie) is considered later.

A *binary trie* is a binary tree that has two kinds of nodes: *branch nodes* and *element nodes*. A branch node has the two data members *LeftChild* and *RightChild*. It has no *data* data member. An element node has the single data member *data*. Branch nodes are used to build a binary tree search structure similar to that of a digital search tree. This search structure leads to element nodes.

Figure 10.46 shows a six-element binary trie. To search for an element with key k, we use a branching pattern determined by the bits of k. The ith bit of k is used at level i. If it is zero, the search moves to the left subtree. Otherwise, it moves to the right subtree. To search for 0010 we first follow the left child, then again the left child, and finally the right child.

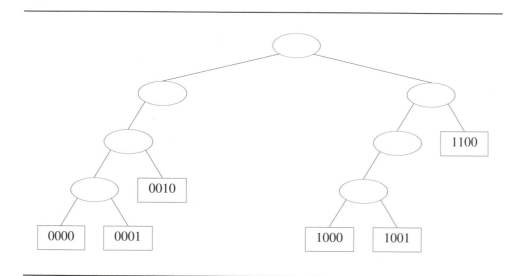

Figure 10.46: Example of a binary trie

Observe that a successful search in a binary trie always ends at an element node. Once this element node is reached, the key in this node is compared with the key we are searching for. This is the only key comparison that takes place. An unsuccessful search may terminate either at an element node or at a 0 pointer.

The binary trie of Figure 10.46 contains branch nodes whose degree is one. By adding another data member, *BitNumber*, to each branch node, we can eliminate all degree-one branch nodes from the trie. The *BitNumber* data member of a branch node gives the bit number of the key that is to be used at this node. Figure 10.47 gives the binary trie that results from the elimination of degree-one branch nodes from the binary trie of Figure 10.46. The number outside a node is its *BitNumber*. A binary trie that has been modified in this way to contain no branch nodes of degree one is called a *compressed binary trie*.

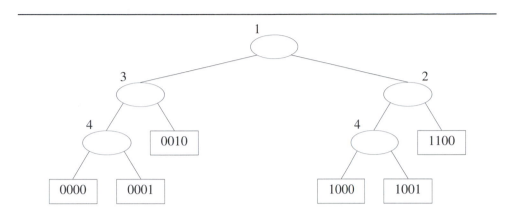

Figure 10.47: Binary trie of Figure 10.46 with degree-one nodes eliminated

10.8.3   Patricia

Compressed binary tries may be represented using nodes of a single type. The new nodes, called *augmented branch nodes*, are the original branch nodes augmented by the data member *data*. The resulting structure is called *Patricia* and is obtained from a compressed binary trie in the following way:

(1)   Replace each branch node by an augmented branch node.

(2)   Eliminate the element nodes.

(3)   Store the data previously in the element nodes in the *data* data members of the augmented branch nodes. Since every nonempty compressed binary trie has one less branch node than it has element nodes, it is necessary to add one augmented branch node. This node is called the *head node*. The remaining structure is the left subtree of the head node. The head node has *BitNumber* equal to zero. Its right-child data member is not used. The assignment of data to augmented branch nodes is done in such a way that the *BitNumber* in the augmented branch node is less than or equal to that in the parent of the element node that contained this data.

(4)   Replace the original pointers to element nodes by pointers to the respective augmented branch nodes.

When these transformations are performed on the compressed trie of Figure 10.47, we get the structure of Figure 10.48. Let *root* be the root of Patricia. *root* is 0 iff the Patricia is empty. A Patricia with one element is represented by a head node whose left-child data member points to itself (Figure 10.49(a)). We can distinguish between pointers that pointed originally to branch nodes and those that pointed to element nodes

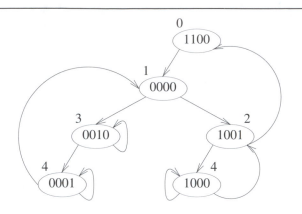

Figure 10.48: An example of Patricia

by noting that, in Patricia, the former pointers are directed to nodes with a greater *BitNumber* value, whereas pointers of the latter type are directed to nodes whose *BitNumber* value either is equal to or less than that in the node where the pointer originates.

10.8.3.1 Search

To search for an element with key k, we begin at the head node and follow a path determined by the bits in k. When an element pointer is followed, the key in the node reached is compared with k. This is the only key comparison made. No comparisons are made on the way down. Suppose we wish to search for $k = 0000$ in the Patricia instance of Figure 10.48. We begin at the head node and follow the left-child pointer to the node with 0000. The bit-number data member of this node is 1. Since bit one of k is 0, we follow the left child pointer to the node with 0010. Now bit three of k is used. Since this is 0, the search moves to the node with 0001. The bit-number data member of this node is 4. The fourth bit of k is zero, so we follow the left-child pointer. This brings us to a node with bit-number data member less than that of the node we moved from. Hence, an element pointer was used. Comparing the key in this node with k, we find a match, and the search is successful.

Next, suppose that we are to search for $k = 1011$. We begin at the head node. The search moves successively to the nodes with 0000, 1001, 1000, and 1001. k is compared with 1001. Since k is not equal to 1001, we conclude that there is no element with this key. The function to search a Patricia is given in Program 10.14. This function returns a pointer to the last node encountered in the search. If the key in this node is k, the search is successful. Otherwise, the Patricia contains no element with key k. The function $bit(i,j)$ returns the jth bit (the leftmost bit is bit one) of i.

```
template <class KeyType>
PatNode<KeyType>* Patricia<KeyType>::Search(const Element<KeyType>& x)
// Search the Patricia for the key x.key.  y is set to point to the last node encountered.
{
    if (!root) return 0; // Patricia is empty
    PatNode<KeyType> *y = root→LeftChild; // move to left child of head node
    for (PatNode<KeyType> *p = root; y→BitNumber > p→BitNumber;) {
    // follow a branch pointer
        p = y;
        if (!bit(x.key, y→BitNumber))  y = y→LeftChild;
        else y = y→RightChild;
    }
    return y;
}
```

Program 10.14: Searching Patricia

10.8.3.2   Insertion

Let us now examine how we can insert new elements. Suppose we begin with an empty instance and wish to insert an element with key 1000. The result is an instance that has only a head node (Figure 10.49(a)). Next, consider inserting an element with key $k = 0010$. First, we search for this key using function *Patricia::Search* (Program 10.14). The search terminates at the head node. Since 0010 is not equal to the key $q = 1000$ in this node, we know that 0010 is not currently in the Patricia instance, so the element may be inserted. For this, the keys k and q are compared to determine the first (i.e., leftmost) bit at which they differ. This is bit one. A new node containing the element with key k is added as the left-child of the head node. Since bit one of k is zero, the left child data member of this new node points to itself, and its right-child data member points to the head node. The bit-number data member is set to 1. The resulting Patricia instance is shown in Figure 10.49(b).

Suppose that the next element to be inserted has $k = 1001$. The search for this key ends at the node with $q = 1000$. The first bit at which k and q differ is bit $j = 4$. Now we search the instance of Figure 10.49(b) using only the first $j - 1 = 3$ bits of k. The last move is from the node with 0010 to that with 1000. Since this is a right-child move, a new node containing the element with key k is to be inserted as the right child of 0010. The bit-number data member of this node is set to $j = 4$. As bit four of k is 1, the rightchild data member of the new node points to itself and its left-child data member points to the node with q. Figure 10.49(c) shows the resulting structure.

To insert $k = 1100$ into Figure 10.49(c), we first search for this key. Once again, $q = 1000$. The first bit at which k and q differ is $j = 2$. The search using only the first $j - 1$ bits ends at the node with 1001. The last move is a right child move from 0010. A new node containing the element with key k and bit-number data member $j = 2$ is added as the right child of 0010. Since bit j of k is one, the right-child data member of the new node points to itself. Its left-child data member points to the node with 1001 (this was previously the right child of 0010). The new Patricia instance is shown in Figure 10.49(d). Figure 10.49(e) shows the result of inserting an element with key 0000, and Figure 10.49(f) shows the Patricia instance following the insertion of 0001.

The preceding discussion leads to the insertion function *Patricia::Insert* (Program 10.15). Its complexity is O(h), where h is the height of the Patricia. h can be as large as min$\{KeySize + 1, n\}$, where *KeySize* is the number of bits in a key and n is the number of elements. When the keys are uniformly distributed, the height is O(log n). We leave the development of the deletion function as an exercise.

EXERCISES

1. Write the digital search tree functions for the search, insert, and delete operations. Assume that each key has *KeySize* bits and that the function *bit* (k, i) returns the ith (from the left) bit of the key k. Show that each of your functions has complexity O(h), where h is the height of the digital search tree.

2. Write the binary trie functions for the search, insert, and delete operations. Assume that each key has *KeySize* bits and that the function *bit* (k, i) returns the ith (from the left) bit of the key k. Show that each of your functions has complexity O(h), where h is the height of the binary trie.

3. Write the compressed binary trie functions for the search, insert, and delete operations. Assume that each key has *KeySize* bits and that the function *bit* (k, i) returns the ith (from the left) bit of the key k. Show that each of your functions has complexity O(h), where h is the height of the compressed binary trie.

4. Write a function to delete the element with key k from a Patricia. The complexity of your function should be O(h), where h is the height of the Patricia. Show that this is the case.

10.9 TRIES

10.9.1 Definition

A trie is an index structure that is particulary useful when key values are of varying size. This data structure is a generalization of the binary trie that was developed in the preceding section.

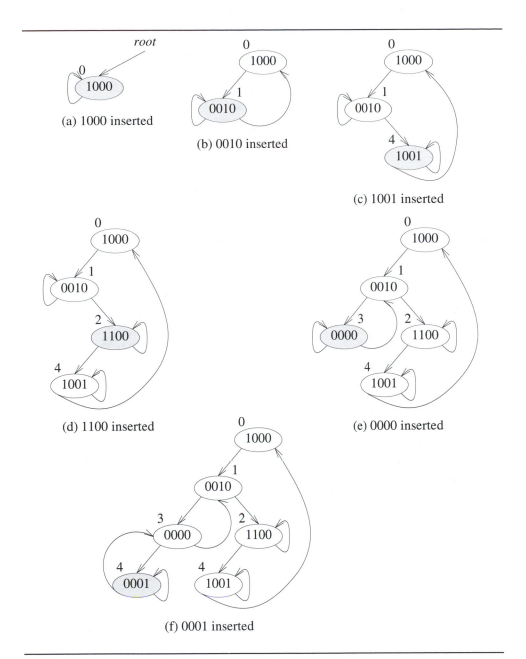

Figure 10.49: Insertion into Patricia

---

template <**class** *KeyType*>
Boolean Patricia<KeyType>::Insert(**const** *Element<KeyType>*& *x*)
// Insert *x* into the Patricia
{
   if (!*root*) { // Patricia is empty
      root = **new** *PatNode<KeyType>*; *root*→*BitNumber* = 0; *root*→*data* = *x*;
      root→*LeftChild* = *root*; **return** TRUE;
   }
   int *k* = *x.key*;
   PatNode<KeyType> **y* = *Search*(*x*);
   if (*y*→*data.key* == *k*){ InsertionError(); **return** FALSE;}

   // find first bit where *k* and *y* →*data. key* differ
   for (**int** *j* = 1; *bit(k, j)* == *bit(y*→*data.key, j)*; *j*++) ;

   // Search Patricia using first *j* − 1 bits of *k*
   PatNode<KeyType> **s* = *root*→*LeftChild*, **p* = *root*;
   while ((*s*→*BitNumber* > *p*→*BitNumber*) && (*s*→*BitNumber* < *j*)) {
      p = *s*;
      if (!(*bit(k, s*→*BitNumber)*)) *s* = *s*→*LeftChild*;
      else *s* = *s*→*RightChild*;
   }

   // Insert *x* as a child of *p*
   PatNode<KeyType> **z*;
   z = **new** *PatNode<KeyType>*;
   z→*data* = *x*; *z*→*BitNumber* = *j*;
   if (!*Bit(k,j)*) {
      z→*LeftChild* = *z*; *z*→*RightChild* = *s*;
   }
   else {
      z→*LeftChild* = *s*; *z*→*RightChild* = *z*;
   }

   if (*s* == *p*→*LeftChild*) *p*→*LeftChild* = *z*;
   else *p*→*RightChild* = *z*;
   return TRUE;
} // end of Patricia::Insert

Program 10.15: Insertion into Patricia

A *trie* is a tree of degree $m \geq 2$ in which the branching at any level is determined not by the entire key value, but by only a portion of it. As an example, consider the trie of Figure 10.50. The trie contains two types of nodes: *element node*, and *branch node*. An element node has only a *data* data member; a branch node contains pointers to subtrees. Since we assume that each character is one of the 26 letters of the alphabet, a branch node has 27 pointer data members. The extra pointer data member is used for the blank character (denoted *b̵*). This character is used to terminate all keys, as a trie requires that no key be a prefix of another (see Figure 10.51).

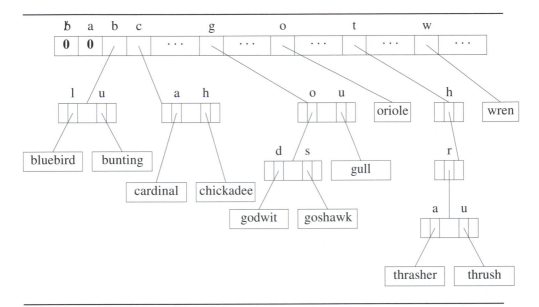

Figure 10.50: Trie created using characters of key value from left to right, one at a time

At the first level all key values are partitioned into disjoint classes depending on their first character. Thus, *root →link* [*i*] points to a subtrie containing all key values beginning with the *i*th letter. On the *j*th level the branching is determined by the *j*th character. When a subtrie contains only one key value, it is replaced by a node of type element. This node contains the key value, together with other relevant information, such as the address of the record with this key value.

10.9.2 Searching a Trie

Searching a trie for a key value x requires breaking up x into its constituent characters and following the branches determined by these characters. The function *Trie::Search* (Program 10.16) assumes that $p = 0$ is not a branch node and that $p \to key$ is the key value represented in p if p is an element node.

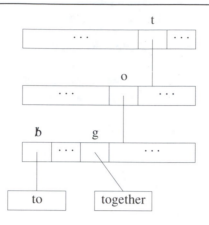

Figure 10.51: Trie showing need for a terminal character (in this case a blank)

```
 template <class KeyType>
TrieNode<KeyType>* Trie<KeyType>::Search (const Element<KeyType>& x)
// Search a trie for key value x.key.  It is assumed that branching on
// the ith level is determined by the ith character of the key value.
{
// Assume we can always concatenate at least one trailing blank to x . key.
    k = x^.^key; concatenate (k, ' ');
    TrieNode<KeyType> *p = root;
    for(int i = 1; p is a branch node; p = p →link [c ], i++)
        c = ith character of k;
    if (p == 0 ‖ p →key != x)  return 0;
    else return p;
} // end of Trie::Search
```

Program 10.16: Searching a trie

Analysis of *Trie::Search:* The search algorithm for tries is very straightforward, and one may readily verify that the worst-case search time is $O(l)$, where l is the number of levels in the trie (including both branch and element nodes).

   In the case of an index, all trie nodes will reside on disk, so at most l disk accesses will be made during search. When the nodes reside on disk, the C++ pointer type cannot be used, as C++ does not allow input/output of pointers. The link data member will now be implemented as an integer. □

10.9.3   Sampling Strategies

Given a set of key values to be represented in an index, the number of levels in the trie will depend on the strategy or key sampling technique used to determine the branching at each level. This can be defined by a sampling function, *sample* (x,i), which appropriately samples x for branching at the ith level. In the trie of Figure 10.50 and in the search algorithm *Trie*::*Search* (Program 10.16) this function is *sample* $(x,i) = i$th character of x. Some other choices for this function are

(1)   *sample* $(x,i) = x_{n-i+1}$

(2)   *sample* $(x,i) = x_{r(x,i)}$ for $r(x,i)$ a randomization function

(3)   *sample* $(x,i) = \begin{cases} x_{i/2} & \text{if } i \text{ is even} \\ x_{n-(i-1)/2} & \text{if } i \text{ is odd} \end{cases}$

where $x = x_1 x_2 \cdots x_n$.

For each of these functions, one may easily construct key value sets for which the particular function is best (i.e., it results in a trie with the fewest number of levels). The trie of Figure 10.50 has five levels. Using function (1) on the same key values yields the trie of Figure 10.52, which has only three levels. An optimal sampling function for this data set will yield a trie that has only two levels (Figure 10.53). Choosing the optimal sampling function for any particular set of values is very difficult. In a dynamic situation, with insertion and deletion, we wish to optimize average performance. In the absence of any further information on key values, probably the best choice would be function (2).

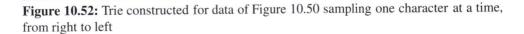

Figure 10.52: Trie constructed for data of Figure 10.50 sampling one character at a time, from right to left

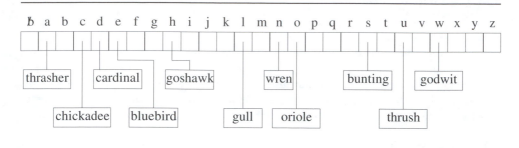

Figure 10.53: An optimal trie for the data of Figure 10.50 sampling on the first level done by using the fourth character of the key values

Although all our examples of sampling have involved single-character sampling we need not restrict ourselves to this. The key value may be interpreted as consisting of digits using any radix we desire. Using a radix of 27^2 would result in two-character sampling. Other radixes would give different samplings.

The maximum number of levels in a trie can be kept low by adopting a different strategy for element nodes. These nodes can be designed to hold more than one key value. If the maximum number of levels allowed is l, then all key values that are synonyms up to level $l - 1$ are entered into the same element node. If the sampling function is chosen correctly, there will be only a few synonyms in each element node. The element node will therefore be small and can be processed in internal memory. Figure 10.54 shows the use of this strategy on the trie of Figure 10.50 with $l = 3$. In further discussion we shall, for simplicity, assume that the sampling function in use is *sample* (x,i) = ith character of x and that no restriction is placed on the number of levels in the trie.

10.9.4 Insertion into a Trie

Insertion into a trie is straightforward. We shall illustrate the procedure by two examples and leave the formal writing of the algorithm as an exercise. Let us consider the trie of Figure 10.50 and insert into it the keys bobwhite and bluejay. First, we have x = bobwhite and we attempt to search for bobwhite. This leads us to node σ, where we discover that $\sigma.link['o'] = 0$. Hence, x is not in the trie and may be inserted here (see Figure 10.55). Next, x = bluejay, and a search of the trie leads us to the element node that contains bluebird. The keys bluebird and bluejay are sampled until the sampling results in two different values. This happens at the fifth letter. Figure 10.55 shows the trie after both insertions.

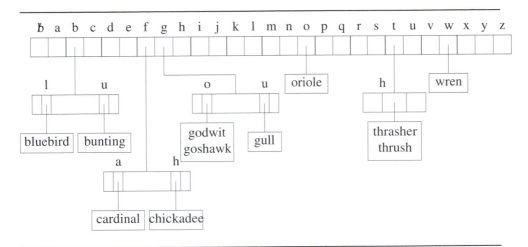

Figure 10.54: Trie obtained for data of Figure 10.50 when number of levels is limited to 3; keys have been sampled from left to right, one character at a time

10.9.5 Deletion from a Trie

Once again, we shall not present the deletion algorithm formally but will look at two examples to illustrate some of the ideas involved in deleting entries from a trie. From the trie of Figure 10.55, let us first delete bobwhite. To do this we set $\sigma.link[\text{'o'}]$ equal to 0. No other changes need to be made. Next, let us delete bluejay. This deletion leaves us with only one key value in the subtrie, δ_3. This means that the node δ_3 may be deleted, and ρ can be moved up one level. The same can be done for nodes δ_1 and δ_2. Finally, the node σ is reached. The subtrie with root σ has more than one key value. Therefore, ρ cannot be moved up any more levels, and we set $\sigma.link[\text{'l'}]$ equal to ρ. To facilitate deletions from tries, it is useful to add a *count* data member in each branch node. This data member contains the number of children the node has.

As in the case of binary tries, we can define compressed tries in which each branch node has at least two children. In this case, each branch node is augmented to have an additional data member, *skip*, that indicates the number of levels of branching that have been eliminated (alternately, we can have a data member, *sample*, that indicates the sampling level to use).

10.9.6 Node Structure

So far, we have assumed that each branch node has a number of pointer data members equal to the number of distinct values for *sample* (x,i). This permits an access time of

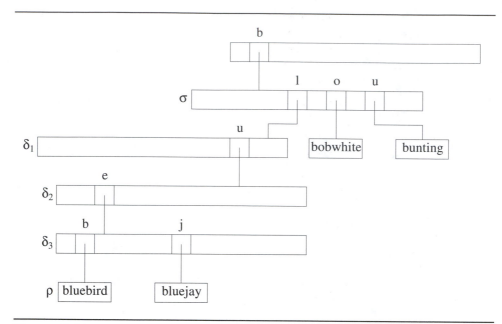

Figure 10.55: Section of trie of Figure 10.50 showing changes resulting from inserting bobwhite and bluejay

O(1) for any pointer in the node. However, many of the pointer data members in a branch node can be expected to be 0. We can improve the space requirements of tries at the expense of increased pointer access time. One possibility is to set up each node as a hash table of pointers. In this case, C++ pointers cannot be used. Rather, we must simulate pointers using integers. The use of hash tables results in an expected access time of O(1) per (simulated) pointer. Another possibility is to represent each branch node as a linked list (chain) in which each node represents one of the non-0 pointers of the branch node. The access time for a pointer is now linear in the number of nodes on the chain.

EXERCISES

1. (a) Draw the trie obtained for the following data:

    AMIOT, AVENGER, AVRO, HEINKEL, HELLDIVER, MACCHI,
    MARAUDER, MUSTANG, SPITFIRE, SYKHOI

    Sample the keys from left to right one character at a time.

    (b) Using single-character sampling, obtain a trie with the fewest number of levels.

2. Explain how a trie could be used to implement a spelling checker.

3. Explain how a trie could be used to implement an auto-command completion program. Such a program would maintain a library of valid commands. It would then accept a user command, character by character, from a keyboard. When a sufficient number of characters had been input to uniquely identify the command, it would display the complete command on the computer monitor.

4. Write an algorithm to insert a key value x into a trie in which the keys are sampled from left to right, one character at a time.

5. Do Exercise 4 with the added assumption that the trie is to have no more than six levels. Synonyms are to be packed into the same element node.

6. Write an algorithm to delete x from a trie under the assumptions of Exercise 4. Assume that each branch node has a *count* data member equal to the number of element nodes in the subtrie for which it is the root.

7. Do Exercise 6 for the trie of Exercise 5.

8. In the trie of Figure 10.55 the nodes δ_1 and δ_2 each have only one child. Branch nodes with only one child may be eliminated from tries by maintaining a *skip* data member with each node. The value of this data member equals the number of characters to be skipped before obtaining the next character to be sampled. Thus, we can have *skip* $[\delta_3] = 2$ and delete the nodes δ_1 and δ_2. Write algorithms to search, insert, and delete from tries in which each branch node has a *skip* data member.

9. Assume that the branch nodes of a compressed trie are represented using a hash table (one for each node). Each such hash table is augmented with a count and skip value as described above. Describe how this change to the node structure affects the time and space complexity of the trie data structure.

10. Do the previous exercise for the case when each branch node is represented by a chain in which each node has two data members: *pointer* and *link*, where *pointer* points to a subtrie and *link* points to the next node in the chain. The number of nodes in the chain for any branch node equals the number of non-0 pointers in that node. Each chain is augmented by a skip value. Draw the chain representation of the compressed version of the trie of Figure 10.50.

10.10 DIFFERENTIAL FILES

10.10.1 The Concept

Consider an application where we are maintaining an indexed file. For simplicity, assume that there is only one index and hence just a single key. Further assume that this is a dense index (i.e., one that has an entry for each record in the file) and that updates to the file (inserts, deletes, and changes to an existing record) are permitted. It is necessary to keep a backup copy of the index and file so that we can recover from accidental loss or failure of the working copy. This loss or failure may occur for a variety of reasons, which include corruption of the working copy due to a malfunction of the hardware or software. We shall refer to the working copies of the index and file as the *master index* and *master file*, respectively.

Since updates to the file and index are permitted, the backup copies of these generally differ from the working copies at the time of failure. So, it is possible to recover from the failure only if, in addition to the backup copies, we have a log of all updates made since the backup copies were created. We shall call this log the *transaction log*. To recover from the failure, it is necessary to process the backup copies and the transaction log to reproduce an index and file that correspond to the working copies at the time of failure. The time needed to recover is therefore a function of the sizes of the backup index and file and the size of the transaction log. The recovery time can be reduced by making more frequent backups. This results in a smaller transaction log. Making sufficiently frequent backups of the master index and file is not practical when these are very large and when the update rate is very high.

When only the file (but not the index) is very large, a reduction in the recovery time may be obtained by keeping updated records in a separate file called the *differential file*. The master file is unchanged. The master index is, however, changed to reflect the position of the most current version of the record with a given key. We assume that the addresses for differential-file records and master-file records are different. As a result, by examining the address obtained from a search of the master index, we can tell whether the most current version of the record we are seeking is in the master file or in the differential file. The steps to follow when accessing a record with a given key are given in Program 10.17(b). Program 10.17(a) gives the steps when a differential file is not used.

Notice that when a differential file is used, the backup file is an exact replica of the master file. Hence, it is necessary to backup only the master index and differential file frequently. Since these are relatively small, it is feasible to do this. To recover from a failure of the master index or differential file, the transactions in the transaction log need to be processed using the backup copies of the master file, index, and differential file. The transaction log can be expected to be relatively small, as backups are done more frequently. To recover from a failure of the master file, we need merely make a new copy of its backup. When the differential file becomes too large, it is necessary to create a new version of the master file by merging the old master file and the differential file. This also results in a new index and an empty differential file. It is interesting to note that using a differential file as suggested does not affect the number of disk accesses needed to perform a file operation (see Program 10.17).

Suppose that both the index and the file are very large. In this case the differential-file scheme discussed above does not work as well, as it is not feasible to backup the master index as frequently as is necessary to keep the transaction log sufficiently small. We can get around this difficulty by using a differential file and a differential index. The master index and master file remain unchanged as updates are performed. The differential file contains all newly inserted records and the current ver-

Step 1:   Search master index for record address.

Step 2:   Access record from this master file address.

Step 3:   If this is an update, then update master index, master file, and transaction log.

(a) No differential file

Step 1:   Search master index for record address.

Step 2:   Access record from either the master file or the differential file, depending on the address obtained in Step 1.

Step 3:   If this is an update, then update master index, differential file, and transaction log.

(b) Differential file in use

Step 1:   Search differential index for record address. If the search is unsuccessful, then search the master index.

Step 2:   Access record from either the master file or the differential file, depending on the address obtained in Step 1.

Step 3:   If this is an update, then update differential index, differential file, and transaction log.

(c) Differential index and file in use

Step 1:   Query the Bloom filter. If the answer is "maybe," then search differential index for record address. If the answer is "no" or if the differential index search is unsuccessful, then search the master index.

Step 2:   Access record from either the master file or the differential file, depending on the address obtained in Step 1.

Step 3:   If this is an update, then update Bloom filter, differential index, differential file, and transaction log.

(d) Differential index and file and Bloom filter in use

Program 10.17: Access steps

sions of all changed records. The differential index is an index to the differential file. This also has null address entries for deleted records. The steps needed to perform a file operation when both a differential index and file are used are given in Program 10.17(c). Comparing with Program 10.17(a), we see that additional disk accesses are frequently needed, as we will often first query the differential index and then the master index. Observe that the differential file is much smaller than the master file, so most requests are satisfied from the master file.

When a differential index and file are used, we must backup both of these with high frequency. This is possible, as both are relatively small. To recover from a loss of the differential index or file, we need to process the transactions in the transaction log using the available backup copies. To recover from a loss of the master index or master file, a copy of the appropriate backup needs to be made. When the differential index and/or file becomes too large, the master index and/or file is reorganized so that the differential index and/or file becomes empty.

10.10.2 Bloom Filters

The performance degradation that results from the use of a differential index can be considerably reduced by the use of a *Bloom filter*. This is a device that resides in internal memory and accepts queries of the following type: Is key k in the differential index? If queries of this type can be answered accurately, then there will never be a need to search both the differential and master indexes for a record address. Clearly, the only way to answer queries of this type accurately is to have a list of all keys in the differential index. This is not possible for differential indexes of reasonable size.

A Bloom filter does not answer queries of the above type accurately. Instead of returning one of "yes" and "no" as its answer, it returns one of "maybe" and "no". When the answer is "no," then we are assured that the key k is not in the differential index. In this case, only the master index is to be searched, and the number of disk accesses is the same as when a differential index is not used. If the answer is "maybe," then the differential index is searched. The master index needs to be searched only if k is not found in the differential index. Program 10.17(d) gives the steps to follow when a Bloom filter is used in conjunction with a differential index.

A *filter error* occurs whenever the answer to the Bloom filter query is "maybe" and the key is not in the differential index. Both the differential and master indexes are searched only when a filter error occurs. To obtain a performance close to that when a differential index is not in use, we must ensure that the probability of a filter error is close to zero.

Let us take a look at a Bloom filter. Typically, it consists of m bits of memory and h uniform and independent hash functions $f_1, \cdots, f_h$. Initially all m filter bits are zero, and the differential index and file are empty. When key k is added to the differential index, bits $f_1(k), \cdots, f_h(k)$ of the filter are set to 1. When a query of the type "Is key k in the differential index?" is made, bits $f_1(k), \cdots, f_h(k)$ are examined. The query answer is "maybe" if all these bits are 1. Otherwise, the answer is "no." One may verify that whenever the answer is "no," the key cannot be in the differential index and that when the answer is "maybe," the key may or may not be in the differential index.

We can compute the probability of a filter error in the following way. Assume that initially there are n records and that u updates are made. Assume that none of these is an insert or a delete. Hence, the number of records remains unchanged. Further, assume that the record keys are uniformly distributed over the key (or identifier) space and that the probability that an update request is for record i is $1/n$, $1 \le i \le n$. From these assumptions, it follows that the probability that a particular update does not modify record i is $1 - 1/n$. So, the probability that none of the u updates modifies record i is $(1 - 1/n)^u$. Hence, the expected number of unmodified records is $n(1 - 1/n)^u$, and the probability that the $(u+1)$'st update is for an unmodified record is $(1 - 1/n)^u$.

Next, consider bit i of the Bloom filter and the hash function f_j, $1 \le j \le h$. Let k be the key corresponding to one of the u updates. Since f_j is a uniform hash function, the probability that $f_j(k) \ne i$ is $1 - 1/m$. As the h hash functions are independent, the probability that $f_j(k) \ne i$ for all h hash functions is $(1 - 1/m)^h$. If this is the only update, the probability that bit i of the filter is zero is $(1 - 1/m)^h$. From the assumption on update requests, it follows that the probability that bit i is zero following the u updates is $(1 - 1/m)^{uh}$. From this, we conclude that if after u updates we make a query for an unmodified record, the probability of a filter error is $(1 - (1 - 1/m)^{uh})^h$. The probability, $P(u)$, that an arbitrary query made after u updates results in a filter error is this quantity times the probability that the query is for an unmodified record. Hence,

$$P(u) = (1 - 1/n)^u (1 - (1 - 1/m)^{uh})^h$$

Using the approximation

$$(1 - 1/x)^q \sim e^{-q/x}$$

for large x, we obtain

$$P(u) \sim e^{-u/n} (1 - e^{-uh/m})^h$$

when n and m are large.

Suppose we wish to design a Bloom filter that minimizes the probability of a filter error. This probability is highest just before the master index is reorganized and the differential index becomes empty. Let u denote the number of updates done up to this time. In most applications, m is determined by the amount of memory available, and n is fixed. So, the only variable in design is h. Differentiating $P(u)$ with respect to h and setting the result to zero yields

$$h = (\log_e 2)m/u \sim 0.693m/u$$

We may verify that this h yields a minimum for $P(u)$. Actually, since h has to be an integer, the number of hash functions to use either is $\lceil 0.693m/u \rceil$ or $\lfloor 0.693m/u \rfloor$, depending on which one results in a smaller $P(u)$.

EXERCISES

1. By differentiating $P(u)$ with respect to h, show that $P(u)$ is minimized when $h = (\log_e 2)m/u$.

2. Suppose that you are to design a Bloom filter with minimum $P(u)$ and that $n = 100{,}000$, $m = 5000$, and $u = 1000$.

(a)   Using any of the results obtained in the text, compute the number, h, of hash functions to use. Show your computations.

(b)   What is the probability, $P(u)$, of a filter error when h has this value?

10.11   REFERENCES AND SELECTED READINGS

The $O(n^2)$ optimum binary search tree algorithm is from "Optimum binary search trees," by D. Knuth, *Acta Informatica*, 1:1, 1971, pp. 14-25.

For a discussion of heuristics that obtain in $O(n \log n)$ time nearly optimal binary search trees, see "Nearly optimal binary search trees," by K. Melhorn, *Acta Informatica*, 5, 1975, pp. 287-295; and "Binary search trees and file organization," by J. Nievergelt, *ACM Computing Surveys*, 6:3, 1974, pp. 195-207.

The original paper on AVL trees by G. M. Adelson-Velskii and E. M. Landis appears in *Dokl. Acad. Nauk.*, SSR (Soviet Math), 3, 1962, pp. 1259-1263. Additional algorithms to manipulate AVL trees may be found in "Linear lists and priority queues as balanced binary trees," by C. Crane, Technical Report STAN-CS-72-259, Computer Science Dept., Stanford University, Palo Alto, CA, 1972; and *The Art of Computer Programming: Sorting and Searching* by D. Knuth, Addison-Wesley, Reading, MA, 1973 (Section 6.2.3).

Results of an empirical study of height-balanced trees appear in "Performance of height-balanced trees," by P. L. Karlton, S. H. Fuller, R. E. Scroggs, and E. B. Koehler, *CACM*, 19:1, 1976, pp. 23-28.

2-3 trees and 2-3-4 trees are a special case of B-trees. A good reference is *The Art of Computer Programming: Sorting and Searching*, by D. Knuth, Addison-Wesley, Reading, MA, 1973. The variations of 2-3 trees referred to in the exercises are from *The Design and Analysis of Computer Algorithms*, by A. Aho, J. Hopcroft, and J. Ullman, Addison-Wesley, Reading, MA, 1974; and *Data Structures and Algorithms*, by A. Aho, J. Hopcroft, and J. Ullman, Addison-Wesley, Reading, MA, 1983.

Red-black trees were invented by R. Bayer. The reference is "Symmetric binary B-trees: Data structure and maintenance," *Acta Informatica*, 1:4, 1972, pp. 290-306.

Our treatment of red-black trees is taken from Guibas and Sedgewick. The top-down single-pass insertion and deletion algorithms for 2-3-4 trees are also from them. The reference is "A dichromatic framework for balanced trees," by L. Guibas and R. Sedgewick, *Proceedings of the 19th IEEE Symposium on Foundations of Computer Science*, 1978, pp. 8-21.

Bottom-up insertion and deletion algorithms for red-black trees were proposed by R. Tarjan in the paper "Updating a balanced search tree in $O(1)$ rotations," *Information Processing Letters*, 16:5, 1983, pp. 253-257.

The paper "Planar point location using persistent search trees," by N. Sarnak and R. Tarjan, *CACM*, 27:7, 1986, pp. 669-679, develops a persistent variety of red-black trees. A persistent data structure is one in which all previous versions plus the current version of the data structure can be accessed efficiently. This paper also applies persistent red-black trees to the planar point location problem.

Splay trees were invented by D. Sleator and R. Tarjan. Their paper "Self-adjusting binary search trees," *JACM*, 32:3, 1985, pp. 652-686, provides several other analyses of splay trees, as well as variants of the basic splaying technique discussed in the text. Our analysis is modeled after that in *Data Structures and Network Algorithms*, by R. Tarjan, SIAM Publications, Philadelphia, PA, 1983.

Several other data structures provide good amortized performance for priority-queue and search-tree operations. The exercises examine some of these. The references for these additional structures are "Self-adjusting heaps," by D. Sleator and R. Tarjan, *SIAM Journal on Computing*, 15:1, 1986, pp. 52-69; and "Biased search trees," by S. Bent, D. Sleator, and R. Tarjan, *SIAM Journal on Computing*, 14:3, 1985, pp. 545-568.

Digital search trees were first proposed by E. Coffman and J. Eve in *CACM*, 13, 1970, pp. 427-432.

The structure Patricia was developed by D. Morrison. Digital search trees, tries, and Patricia are analyzed in the book *The Art of Computer Programming: Sorting and Searching* by D. Knuth, Addison-Wesley, Reading, MA, 1973.

The linear time suffix tree construction algorithm is from E. McCreight. It is described in "A space-economical suffix tree construction algorithm," by E. McCreight, *JACM*, 23:2, 1978, pp. 262-272.

Our development of differential files parallels that of Severence and Lohman in the paper "Differential files: Their application to the maintenance of large databases," by D. Severence and G. Lohman, *ACM Transactions on Database Systems*, 1:3, 1976, pp. 256-267. This paper also provides several advantages of using differential files. The assumptions of uniformity made in the filter error analysis are unrealistic, as, in practice, future accesses are more likely to be for records previously accessed. Several authors have attempted to take this into account. Two references are "A practical guide to the design of differential file architectures," by H. Aghili and D. Severance, *ACM Transactions on Database Systems*, 7:2, 1982, pp. 540-565; and "A regression approach to performance analysis for the differential file architecture," by T. Hill and A. Srinivasan, *Proceedings of the Third IEEE International Conference on Data Engineering*, 1987, pp. 157-164.

INDEX